Schapero — work ignored by economists

M T W T F SS
C L CL
Q M M WS

7 8 11

Exam

show how the item contributes to

1) Heather's purpose

2) Be detailed

CITIES AND URBAN LIFE

THIRD EDITION

CITIES AND URBAN LIFE

JOHN J. MACIONIS
KENYON COLLEGE

VINCENT N. PARRILLO
WILLIAM PATERSON UNIVERSITY

PEARSON

Prentice
Hall

Upper Saddle River, New Jersey 07458

Library of Congress Cataloging-in-Publication Data
Macionis, John J.
    Cities and urban life/John J. Macionis, Vincent N. Parrillo.—3rd ed.
    p. cm.
Includes bibliographical references and index.
ISBN 0-13-111395-X (case)
    1. Cities and towns.   2. Cities and towns—History.   3. Sociology, Urban.
4. City and town life.   I. Parrillo, Vincent N.   II. Title.

HT151.M335 2004
307.76—dc21

2003040593

AVP/Publisher: Nancy Roberts
Managing Editor: Sharon Chambliss
Production Editor: Cheryl A. Keenan
Copyeditor: Virginia Rubens
Proofreader: Alison Lorber
Editorial Assistant: Lee Peterson
Prepress and Manufacturing Buyer:
    Mary Ann Gloriande
Director of Marketing: Beth Mejia
Marketing Assistant: Adam Laitman
Cover Design: Kiwi Design

Cover Art Director: Jayne Conte
Line Art Illustrations: Maria Piper
Director, Image Resource Center: Melinda Reo
Manager, Rights and Permissions: Zina Arabia
Interior Image Specialist: Beth Brenzel
Image Permissions Coordinator: Debbie Hewitson
Photo Researcher: Kathy Ringrose
Cover and Chapter Art: Barton Stabler/
    Stock Illustration Source, Inc.
Box Art: Teofilo Olivieri/
    Stock Illustration Source, Inc.

T.S. Eliot poems on pages 2 and 412 courtesy of Faber and Faber Ltd. Extracts on pages 118-121 from *Edge City* by Joel Garreau. Copyright 1991 by Joel Garreau. Used by permission of Doubleday, a division of Random House, Inc.

This book was set in 10/11 Baskerville by Lithokraft
and was printed and bound by RR Donnelley & Sons Company.
The cover was printed by Phoenix Color Corp.

© 2004, 2001, 1998 by Pearson Education Inc.
Upper Saddle River, New Jersey 07458

Printed in the United States of America
10 9 8 7 6 5 4 3

ISBN: 0-13-111395-X

Pearson Education LTD., London
Pearson Education Australia PTY, Limited, Sydney
Pearson Education Singapore, Pte. Ltd
Pearson Education North Asia Ltd, Hong Kong
Pearson Education Canada, Ltd., Toronto
Pearson Educación de Mexico, S. A. de C.V.
Pearson Education—Japan, Tokyo
Pearson Education Malaysia, Pte. Ltd
Pearson Education, Upper Saddle River, New Jersey

To the memory of E. Digby Baltzell
mentor, friend,
and maverick sociologist
—John J. Macionis

To Donald L. Halsted
mentor, friend,
and inspiration
—Vincent N. Parrillo

CONTENTS

PART   V   GLOBAL URBANIZATION

Chapter 13   Cities in the Developing World   **368**

PART   VI   THE PLANNING AND EVALUATION OF CITIES

Chapter 14   Planning the Urban Environment   **411**

SPECIAL FEATURES

CITYSCAPE

CRITICAL THINKING

LOOKING BACK

THE CITY IN LITERATURE

PREFACE

Now that we have entered a new century—indeed, a new millennium—the world stands on the brink of a historic landmark: In a few years, a majority of the planet's people will live in cities. Urban living is rapidly becoming the *norm* for members of our species. Surely, there is no more compelling reason to undertake the study of cities and urban life.

THE BASIC APPROACH

The approach of this text is multidisciplinary but fundamentally sociological. Readers will find here the enduring contributions of the classical European social thinkers, including Max Weber, Karl Marx, Ferdinand Tönnies, Georg Simmel, and Emile Durkheim, as well as those of early pioneers in North America, including Robert Park and Louis Wirth. Of course, many men and women have stood on the shoulders of these giants and extended our understanding. Thus, this text also considers the ideas of a host of contemporary urbanists, including Henri Lefebvre, Jane Jacobs, Manuel Castells, John Logan, Harvey Molotch, Kevin Lynch, Lyn Lofland, Carol Stack, Herbert Gans, Michael Sorkin, and Michael Dear.

Yet, as this string of well-known names suggests, urban studies rests on research and theory developed within many disciplines. *Cities and Urban Life*, therefore, is truly a multidisciplinary text that draws together the work of historians (Chapter 2: "The Origins and Development of the World's Cities," and Chapter 3: "The Development of North American Cities"); sociologists (Chapter 4: "Cities and Suburbs of the Twenty-First Century," Chapter 5:

"Urban Sociology: The Classic Statements," Chapter 10: "Social Class: Urban and Suburban Lifestyles," Chapter 11: "Race, Ethnicity, and Gender: Urban Diversity," and Chapter 12: "Housing, Education, Crime: Confronting Urban Problems"); social psychologists (Chapter 6: "Social Psychology: The Urban Experience"); geographers and urban ecologists (Chapter 7: "Geography and Spatial Perspectives: Making Sense of Space"); political economists working within various disciplines (Chapter 9: "The New Urban Sociology: The City and Capitalism"); anthropologists (Chapter 8: "Comparative Urbanism: The City and Culture," and Chapter 13: "Cities in the Developing World"); and architects as well as city planners (Chapter 14: "Planning the Urban Environment").

THE ORGANIZATION OF THIS TEXT

Part I of the text, "Understanding the City," introduces the main questions and themes that resonate throughout the book (Chapter 1). Part II, "History of Cities and New Trends," surveys the historical development of cities, noting how urban life has often differed in striking ways from contemporary patterns we take for granted (Chapters 2 and 3), and the current trends of sprawl, edge cities, and gated communities that are shaping the cities and suburbs of the new century (Chapter 4). Part III, "Disciplinary Perspectives," highlights the various disciplinary orientations that, together, have so advanced our understanding of cities (Chapters 5 through 9). Part IV, "The Anatomy of the City," focuses on the social organization of today's cities in

North America, highlighting how urban living reflects the importance of social class (Chapter 10), race, ethnicity, and gender (Chapter 11), as well as forcing us to confront vexing problems such as housing, education, and crime (Chapter 12). Part V, "Global Urbanization," offers a look at the history and current urbanization in four major world regions: Latin America, Africa, the Middle East, and Asia (Chapter 13). It is in these areas of the world that urbanization is now most rapid, with cities reaching unprecedented size. Finally, Part VI, "The Planning and Evaluation of Cities," examines the architectural, social, and political dimensions of urban planning, as well as points out the problems that prevent cities from living up to their promise of improving everyone's lives (Chapter 14).

FOUR KEY THEMES

This attempt to tell the urban story will lead us to consider a wide range of issues and to confront countless questions. Yet four main themes guide this exploration, and it is useful to make these explicit. To put it another way, whatever else a student entering the field of urban studies might learn, he or she must pay attention to these themes:

1. *Cities and urban life vary according to time and place.* Since the idea of the city came to our ancestors some 10,000 years ago, the urban scene has been re-created time and again, all around the world, in countless ways. The authors—informed by their own travels to some 60 of the world's nations—have labored to portray this remarkable diversity throughout this text.
2. *Cities reflect and intensify society and culture.* Although cities vary in striking ways, everywhere they stand as physical symbols of human civilization. For example, nowhere do we perceive the inward-looking world of the Middle Ages better than in the walled medieval cities of that era. Similarly, modern U.S. cities are powerful statements about the contemporary forces of industrial capitalism.
3. *Cities reveal the best and the worst about the human condition.* Another way to "read" cities is as

testimony to the achievements and failings of a way of life. Thus, while New York boasts some spectacular architecture, exciting public parks, vital art galleries, and vibrant concert halls, it also forces us to confront chronic prejudice, wrenching poverty, and sometimes explosive violence.

4. *Cities offer the promise—but not always the reality —of a better life.* At least since the time of the ancient Greeks, people have recognized that the city holds the promise of living "the good life." Yet all urban places fall short of this ideal in some ways, and in a number of today's cities, people are struggling valiantly simply to survive. The great promise of urban living, coupled with the daunting problems of actual cities, provokes us to ask how (or, indeed, if) we can intentionally and thoughtfully make urban places better. Although we are realistic about the problems, we remain optimistic about the possibilities.

SPECIAL FEATURES OF THE TEXT

Two special features warrant the attention of readers.

Boxes First, each chapter contains several boxed inserts. These boxes are of five kinds. *Critical Thinking* boxes ask readers to grapple with a particular problem or question, assess some evidence, and reach a reasoned conclusion. *Urban Living* boxes provide a picture of the city "at street level"—that is, a close-up look at how people really live. *Looking Back* boxes amplify the historical content of the text, reminding us that our cities are built on the past, culturally and, indeed, literally. *The City in Literature* boxes are testimony to our belief that writers and poets (from Charles Dickens, Walt Whitman, and T. S. Eliot to Paul Theroux, John Steinbeck, Tom Wolfe, James Baldwin, Elijah Anderson, and Francine Garcia-Hallcom) have special abilities to capture the sights and sounds—and sometimes even the soul —of cities. Finally, *Cityscape boxes* present an extended literary account or scholarly analysis of some significant dimension of urban life.

Case Studies   The text includes eight case studies that offer a broad sociohistorical look at major cities in various regions of the world as they illustrate a chapter's key points. The cities profiled in these case studies are London (Chapter 2), New York (Chapter 3), Portland, Oregon (Chapter 4), Ming Peking (Chapter 8), Hellenic Athens (Chapter 8), Communist Beijing (Chapter 8), Chicago (Chapter 11), and Toronto (Chapter 14).

WHAT'S NEW IN THE THIRD EDITION

This new edition reflects a number of changes.

First, the chapters contain new, detailed data from the 2000 census that offer valuable insights into the growing diversity of U.S. society and the resulting changes to our cities and suburbs.

Second, in these post 9-11 days, we all understand the especial vulnerability of cities to acts of terrorism. Several sections of this book discuss that concern, and Chapter 3 discusses the efforts of New York City to move beyond the devastation.

Third, Chapter 7 contains a new section on the Los Angeles School and the postmodernist view of the linkages among global capitalism, social differentiation, and local political fragmentation.

Fourth, Chapter 9 offers expanded discussion of cities and the world economy, and adds a new section evaluating the transformation of public space into packaged, thematic environments.

Fifth, Chapter 14 acquaints readers with the goals of Toronto's new master plan, one that could easily serve as a plan for all cities.

In addition, the entire text has been rewritten and updated, with new statistical data, the results of research published in the last four years, a number of new boxes and other features, and a new photo program.

ACKNOWLEDGMENTS

First, and most important, the authors wish to acknowledge the role played by James L. Spates, of Hobart and William Smith Colleges, in an earlier version of this book, titled *The Sociology of Cities,* coauthored by Jim Spates and John Macionis. Although Vince Parrillo and John Macionis have significantly revised that effort at many levels, Jim's ideas and enthusiasm for cities are still evident here.

Parrillo and Macionis wish to thank the editorial team at Prentice Hall for their efforts in making this text a reality. Particular thanks go to Nancy Roberts, publisher-sociology, for originally signing the project and helping to get the work under way, and to Sharon Chambliss, managing editor for sociology, for handling the review and production of this manuscript. Cheryl Keenan did a masterful job in guiding the book through technical production and an ontime delivery date. We are grateful to Virginia Rubens for copyediting and to Melanie Belkin for preparing the index. Finally, we wish to thank Kathy Ringrose for selecting the striking photographs that appear in the book.

For their efforts reviewing part or all of the manuscript and generously sharing their ideas with us, we gratefully acknowledge for this edition: Mark Abrahamson, University of Connecticut, Robert L. Boyd, Mississippi State University and Jerome Krase, Brooklyn College. For the second edition: Leo Pinard, California Polytechnic State University-San Luis Obispo; David Prok, Baldwin Wallace College; and James D. Tasa, Eric Community College-North. For the first edition: Ronald S. Edari, University of Wisconsin; and Daniel J. Monti, Boston University.

John J. Macionis
Kenyon College
Gambier, Ohio 43022
E-mail: macionis@kenyon.edu
http://www.TheSociologyPage.com

Vincent N. Parrillo
William Paterson University
Wayne, New Jersey 07470
E-mail: parrillov@wpunj.edu
http://www.wpunj.edu/cohss/sociology/parrillo

EXPLORING THE CITY

"This music crept by me upon the waters"
And along the Strand, up Queen Victoria
  Street.
O City city, I can sometimes hear
Beside a public bar in Lower Thames Street,
The pleasant whining of a mandolin
And a clatter and a chatter from within
Where fishmen lounge at noon: where the
  walls
Of Magnus Martyr hold
Inexplicable splendour of Ionian white and
  gold.

T. S. Eliot, "The Waste Land"

Let us go then, you and I,
When the evening is spread out against the sky
Like a patient etherised upon a table;
Let us go, through certain half-deserted streets,
The muttering retreats
Of restless nights in one-night cheap hotels
And sawdust restaurants with oyster-shells:
Streets that follow like a tedious argument
Of insidious intent
To lead you to an overwhelming question . . .
Oh, do not ask, "What is it?"
Let us go and make our visit.

T. S. Eliot, "The Love Song
of J. Alfred Prufrock"

WHY STUDY THE CITY?

Cities! Most of us share poet T. S. Eliot's fascination with urban places—settings of intense
excitement, great mystery, and striking
human diversity. With the poet, most of us
probably agree that cities (London was the object of Eliot's interest) are places we would
love to visit—but, of course, we wouldn't want
to live there! On the one hand, little compares
with the excitement of visiting a major city
such as New York, Toronto, Chicago, or San
Francisco. Arriving at the airport (there may
be several), we make our way through crowds
of people in search of the baggage claim area
(checking the monitor to see which carousel is
the correct one), then grab a cab for downtown and watch for the skyline coming up. We
pull up in front of a downtown hotel and
check in, staying just long enough to drop off
our bags. Then, out on the streets, we find

block after block of shops selling all kinds of
things we never find at home, and pass by
every imaginable sort of person—the old and
the young, the rich and the poor, the up and
coming as well as the down and out. People
say that virtually anything can and does happen in big cities—and it doesn't take long to
realize that they're right!

Across North America, more than three out
of four of us live in urban places, and even
more of us build our lives around cities. We
are born in cities (or near them), grow up in
or near one (probably in a suburb), go to a
college in or near a city (maybe one some distance away from our hometowns), and eventually settle down in or near a city that
becomes "home." Across the continent, much
of our favorite entertainment—including
sports contests, films, and musical events—is
city based. We might as well admit it: We are a
nation of city slickers, and the urban way of
life, or urbanism, has become the norm in
both Canada and the United States. To study
the city, therefore, is to study ourselves.

Yet the city is more than what our personal
experiences reveal. It is a dynamic entity unto
itself, the most powerful drawing card in
human history. In 1900, cities were home to
just 9 percent of the world's population. Now,
a century later, almost half the world's people
live in them. If present trends continue, by
2025 cities will be home to two-thirds of humanity (Brockerhoff, 1996:4).

The city is thus the setting for all aspects of
the human drama: the highest learning collid-
ing with the grossest ignorance, unimaginable
wealth juxtaposed with the most abject poverty.
Historically, most people drawn to the city have
been able to realize their hopes of a higher
standard of living—but will this continue to be
true in the new megacities such as Mexico City,
Rio de Janeiro, Cairo, New Delhi, and Tokyo?
(See the world map preceding this chapter to
locate these and other prominent cities.) Such
places are adding to their millions of residents
so rapidly that they cannot provide basic services (water, housing, electricity) to many of
their people. If such growth is not checked
soon, poverty and suffering for billions may be
inescapable, not to mention ecological disasters

unparalleled in history. To study the city, therefore, is also to study a uniquely powerful form of human settlement: a physical and social environment with the potential for both satisfying and frustrating the entire spectrum of human needs.

An important theme of this book is the fact that cities do not exist entirely by themselves. They are inextricably bound up with the larger societies of which they are a part. For centuries, the city has been the heart, the lifeblood, of various civilizations—the center of economic, political, and artistic events. In cities we find both the triumphs and the tragedies of the human story. For example, we associate Hellenic Athens, Renaissance Florence, and Elizabethan London with great achievements of the human spirit, while we link classical Rome and Nazi Berlin with savage human degradation. In each case, a cultural setting helped shape the city's character: During the fourth century B.C.E.,[1] the Greeks raised Athens to a pinnacle of human accomplishment, while the rise of Nazism in Germany in the post–World War I era led to Berlin's infamous decadence.

The connection between the city and a broader culture is no less evident today. In its cities exists much of what is great about the United States: intellectual excellence, political freedom, and artistic vitality. Of course, these same cities exhibit this country's greatest failings, including grinding poverty and sometimes-savage racial prejudice. To study the city, then, is also to examine the society in which it exists.

Understanding the city, therefore, is crucial in order to comprehend modern existence. But how we choose to study the city is also important. The city is a complex reality that yields few easy answers. Our approach here is to study the city much as we would a poem. In encountering a new poem, most people wonder, "What does it mean?" We may ask, "What is the poem's topic?" "What meter does it use?" "What is its place in the poet's works?" For example, someone might ask what T. S. Eliot means by "the walls of Magnus Martyr" in the lines that opened this chapter—a reference to a particularly beautiful London church, Saint Magnus Martyr, built by Sir Christopher Wren in the seventeenth century. Or we might examine the phrase "inexplicable splendour of Ionian white and gold"—a reference to the startling white and gold interior of Magnus Martyr, which reminded Eliot of the glories of the Ionian period of classical Greece.

Central as these "what" questions are, U.S. poet John Ciardi (1959, chap. 1) believed that we also need to consider the mood the poem creates in us, its readers, as well as the deeper subtleties conveyed in how the poem's words play together. Our concern, wrote Ciardi, should not be "to arrive at a definition and close the book, but to arrive at an experience" (1959:666). In other words, Ciardi maintains, only by asking *how* a poem transmits its meaning—by experiencing how all its complex elements fit together—will we fully comprehend the poem. The same is true of cities.

If we look only at the facts of urban life, we will surely miss its dynamic soul. The city will appear dull and lifeless, a collection only of concrete buildings, bureaucracies, unemployment rates. But if we also ask the "how" questions, which link these factual elements to human lives, the city springs to life as a set of vital, dynamic forces.

In studying the city, then, we must not ask merely "What is it?" We must, as Eliot suggests in his poem, "go and make our visit." We must probe beyond the descriptions and the statistics to the broader and deeper reality of urban life. This book will help you do just that, and the remainder of this chapter offers an overview of the steps we will follow.

THE COMPLEXITY OF THE CITY: VARIOUS PERSPECTIVES

The city may well be the most complex of all human creations. As a result, it cannot be understood using any single point of view. While

---

[1]The designation B.C.E. ("before the common era") is used in place of B.C. ("before Christ") in recognition of the religious pluralism of North American society. Similarly, we use C.E. ("common era") in place of A.D. (*Anno Domini*, "in the year of our lord").

The congested, bustling activity captured in this woodcut drawing of London in the 1870s helps us visualize the sights and sounds, the grandeur and squalor, that attracted millions of people to live, work, play, or visit within its boundaries.

this book is fundamentally sociological in its orientation, it draws together insights, theories, and statistics from a wide variety of related disciplines, among them history, archaeology, psychology, geography, economics, and political science. As we now explain, all these perspectives are vital for grasping the living entity that is the contemporary city.

The City in History

Today, cities are so much a part of our lives that they seem both natural and inevitable. You may be surprised to learn, then, that in the larger picture of human history, cities are a very new idea, indeed. Although the human species has existed on the earth for at least 100,000 years, cities began to appear a scant 10,000 years ago. Moreover, it wasn't until the last 3,000 years that cities became relatively numerous and inhabited by significant numbers of people. And only today are we reaching the point at which most of the world's people will be urbanites.

Then, too, urban life itself has changed dramatically over time. As an example, consider the massive changes undergone by San Francisco. Today San Francisco is a thoroughly modern U.S. city, famed for its hills, cable cars, fog, and natural beauty. It also has a particularly easygoing lifestyle, about which Geoffrey Moorhouse once wrote:

> No one who visits San Francisco for the first time can fail to be aware of the pleasantly relaxed atmosphere. You are not perpetually admonished by well-wishers about the dangers of getting mugged, as visitors usually are in New York. It seems true that shop assistants here are more amiable than elsewhere, less bent on treating their customers as components of the cash register; when they say "Have a nice day," they sound as though they mean it and not as if it were a ritual phrase learned to help trade. Watch people move about the streets if you want to appreciate what San Francisco has done to them. Except at rush hour, they tend to stroll. There is nothing comparable here to downtown New York or the heart of London, where the word "perambulation" may now be considered redundant except at weekends, having long since been banished by the general push and shove. (1979:24)

But such was not always the case. Changes to San Francisco through its brief century and a half of existence have been profound, as historic documents attest. One such document is Richard Henry Dana's *Two Years Before the Mast* (1947, originally published in 1862), one of the greatest of nineteenth-century seagoing journals, a part of which you can read in the next Looking Back box.[2]

What happened to San Francisco between Dana's two visits was gold, discovered in 1849. Almost overnight the sleepy little village of Yerba Buena, the nearest port for outfitting the Sierra Nevada mines, was transformed into a feverish city. Not for another 70 years would Moorhouse's sophisticated, "laid-back" San Francisco begin to appear. Thus, we can see the importance of studying the city historically. Without benefit of hindsight, we might easily fool ourselves into thinking that cities, although perhaps smaller in the past, were always more or less like those we know today.

Luckily, our understanding of past cities doesn't rely only on historical documents such as Dana's account of early San Francisco. In recent years urban archaeologists have made major strides in the study of urban settings about which little or no written material is available.

Abandoned cities, or cities rebuilt on earlier foundations, still contain traces of their earlier existence, providing clues for archaeologists trained in the careful excavation and analysis of artifacts. From such clues, they can piece together a picture of how a city's people lived: how they built their houses and organized their families, what they thought important enough to portray in paintings, what level of technology they employed, what they commonly drank or ate. By unearthing many such clues, archaeologists allow long-dead cities to spring back to life.

[2]Various kinds of boxes are included in each chapter to illustrate key points and themes. When you encounter a reference to a particular box, take a minute or two to read it before going on with the chapter.

LOOKING BACK

San Francisco's Massive Changes

Shipping from New York, Richard Henry Dana first visited San Francisco, then called Yerba Buena ("good herbs"), in 1835. Here is what he saw:

[Near the] mouth of the bay . . . is a high point on which the [Presidio Mexican military outpost] is built. Behind this point is the little harbor, or bight, called Yerba Buena, in which trading vessels anchor, and, near it, the Mission of Delores. There was no other habitation on this side of the Bay, except a shanty of rough boards put up by a man named Richardson, who was doing a little trading between the vessels and the Indians. . . . We came to anchor near the mouth of the bay, under a high and beautifully sloping hill, upon which herds of hundreds and hundreds of red deer, and the stag, with his high branching of antlers, were bounding about, looking at us for a moment, and then starting off, affrighted at the noises we made at seeing the variety of their beautiful attitudes and motion. . . .

That was hardly the San Francisco of Geoffrey Moorhouse; nor does it much resemble this description of Dana's, written in 1859 after a second visit:

We bore round the point toward the old anchoring ground of hide ships, and there, covering the sand hills and the valleys, stretching from the water's edge to the base of the great hills, and from the old Presidio to the Mission, flickering all over with lamps of its streets and houses, lay a city of one hundred thousand inhabitants. . . . The dock into which we drew, and the streets about it, were densely crowded with express wagons and hand-carts to take luggage, coaches and cabs for passengers, and with men. . . . Through this crowd I made my way, along the well-built and well-lighted streets, as alive as by day, where boys in high keyed voices were already crying the latest New York papers; and between one and two o'clock in the morning found myself comfortably abed in a commodious room, in the Oriental Hotel, which stood, as well as I could learn, on the filled-up cove, and not far from the spot where we used to beach our boats from the Alert.

When I awoke in the morning, and looked from my windows over the city of San Francisco, with its townhouses, towers, and steeples; its courthouses, theaters, and hospitals; its daily journals; its well-filled learned professions; its fortresses and light houses; its wharves and harbor, with their thousand-ton clipper ships, more in number than London or Liverpool sheltered that day . . . ; when I looked across the bay to the eastward, and beheld a beautiful town on the fertile wooded Shores of the Contra Costa [the area of today's Oakland and Berkeley] and steamers, large and small, the ferryboats of the Contra Costa, and capacious freighters and passenger-carriers to all parts of the great bay and its horizon—when I saw all these things, and reflected on what I once was and saw here, and what now surrounded me, I could scarcely keep my hold on reality at all, or the genuineness of anything, and seemed to myself like one who had moved in "worlds not realized."

Source: Richard Henry Dana, *Two Years Before the Mast* (New York: Heritage, 1947), pp. 196, 203, 320–22.

One of the most important finds in recent years was the 1965 discovery of the pre-Incan site of Gran Pajaten, a legendary lost city of Peru, located 360 miles north of Lima, the capital. Imagine trekking through the high jungles of South America and finding the ruins of a vast system of jungles of South America and finding the ruins of a vast system of walls and terraces, buildings and tombs and statuary, all perched on the steep, cloud-shrouded eastern slope of the Andes [Mountains] overlooking a nameless river, [ruins] of an early, resourceful and mysterious people whose civilization flourished long before the glory days of the Incas. (Wilford, 1985:A1)

Lost for centuries, Gran Pajaten appears to be only one of the region's lost urban sites (another was found nearby in 1997). Archaeologists regard the Gran Pajaten site as one of the most important pre-Columbian ruins discovered since the 1911 finding of Machu Picchu, also in Peru, hundreds of miles to the south. The citadel of Gran Pajaten dates back to 2000 B.C.E., and was occupied until the Incas conquered it in the early sixteenth century. What astonishes the scholars is how the city, clearly part of a highly developed civilization, thrived in such an inhospitable environment—within a dense jungle, surrounded by almost perpetual clouds and rain, some 8,600 feet above sea level. Only five authorized expeditions have gone to study the city thus far, although 21 others went to loot (Salzar, 1997).

Archaeology also plays a role in contemporary cities. Most cities exist on the rubble of their own past. Take London, for example. Over the course of its 2,000-year history, this city has risen some 30 feet, building on its own refuse. In 1997, ten excavation sites in and around London Bridge unearthing Roman London—established in the first century C.E.—brought new discoveries. Archaeologists found two different types of Roman building, one type made with timber frames and clay walls and floors, and later, more substantial masonry buildings, some with mortar floors and plaster walls, both of which served as the homes of artisans, with shops or workshops in front and living quarters behind. Also uncovered were many artifacts of everyday life, including oil lamps for lighting homes and vessels used for cooking and drinking (Jubilee, 1997). Closer to home, archaeologists completed an excavation on New York's Wall Street a decade ago, uncovering artifacts from the original Dutch settlement of 1625.

Two chapters of this text survey cities in human history. Chapter 2 reviews major urban developments from the beginnings of cities some ten millennia ago right up to the urban events of this century. We will see that the urban story is one of continuous and striking change. Chapter 3 highlights how cities have developed in the United States and Canada. Here, too, we will find astonishing changes—changes hinted at in Dana's account of San Francisco. We will see the alterations of North American urban life as cities grew from the small, isolated colonial centers of the seventeenth century to sprawling environments with populations often reaching into multimillions. Next, in Chapter 4, we examine recent urban trends that will shape urban and suburban lifestyles for at least part of the twenty-first century: sprawl, edge cities, gated communities, and common-interest developments (CIDs).

The Emergence of Urban Sociology

One key goal of this text is understanding how sociologists have studied the city. Although historians have been looking at cities for centuries, sociologists are more recent arrivals on the scene. As Chapter 5 explains, early sociologists in the late nineteenth century lived during a period of dramatic urban upheaval and, naturally, they turned their attention to cities. They tried to understand just how the Industrial Revolution transformed the small villages of both Europe and North America into huge, chaotic metropolises. In the City in Literature box, novelist Charles Dickens provides a remarkable description of the seemingly perpetual growth of nineteenth-century London.

Many early sociologists shared Dickens's pessimistic vision of the city. Their works portray the city as a dangerous place where the traditional values of social life—a sense of community, a caring for other people—were systematically torn apart. However, recent sociological research shows that many of these concerns about the destructiveness of urban living were based on faulty evidence. In the light of contemporary research, the city emerges as a

THE CITY IN LITERATURE

London, the Devouring City

[Harriet Carker] often looked with compassion . . . upon the stragglers who came wandering into London by the great highway hard by, and who, footsore and weary, and gazing fearfully at the huge town before them, as if foreboding that their misery there would be but as a drop of water in the sea, or as a grain of sea-sand on the shore, went shrinking on, cowering before the angry weather, and looking as if the very elements rejected them. Day after day, such travellers crept past, but always, as she thought, in one direction—always towards the town. Swallowed up in one phase or other of its immensity, towards which they seemed impelled by a desperate fascination, they never returned. Food for the hospitals, the churchyards, the prisons, the river, fever, madness, vice, and death—they passed on to the monster, roaring in the distance, and were lost.

Source: Charles Dickens, *Dombey and Son* (London: Chapman and Hall, 1848), chap. 33.

more neutral phenomenon. Neither good nor bad in and of themselves, cities have been pushed in one direction or the other by the cultural forces at work in a particular time and place. Thus, the horrors of nineteenth-century London appear to be primarily a product of the massive industrialization taking place within a capitalist society, and not a result of something inherently urban.

Social Psychology: The Urban Experience

With more than three-fourths of North Americans living in cities, any student of cities needs to explore the urban experience. How and why do cities stimulate us so much? Do cities change people in one way or another?

We know that the city trips our emotions—a point clearly illustrated in the Cityscape box on pages 10–11, as one sociologist recalls his visit to "the Big Apple": New York. Although these reactions are certainly personal, they are also *social* in two senses. First, it is the social environment of the city itself that generates them. Second, they are social in that they are common; they resonate with most of us as well.

These social dimensions of the urban experience also figure in our analysis. Urbanism —a concept referring to those social–psychological aspects of life, personality patterns, and behavioral adaptations influenced by the city—is the focal point of Chapter 6.

Urban Geography and Ecology

Why did people cluster together to form cities in the first place? In the fourth century B.C.E., the Greek philosopher Aristotle provided a timeless answer: People come together in cities for security; they remain there in order to live the good life. For the ancient Greeks, cities satisfied a need for security. In an age of few laws and fewer treaties, groups frequently preyed on one another. For protection, people came together in a single location, often a natural fortification such as the Acropolis in Aristotle's Athens. Where natural defenses were not available, people built walls. But a site could become a city only with other geographical assets: water, access to transportation routes, and the ability to produce or import enough goods to meet the population's needs.

Aristotle said People come together for security it the "good life"

But once cities began, people made a remarkable discovery. Mixing together in large numbers not only afforded protection; it generated more profitable trade and stimulated intellectual life as well. People began to hail the city as offering the potential for what Aristotle termed "the good life."

The importance of a city's physical location, and of how people come to arrange themselves within the urban area, has led urbanists to develop two related areas of study: (1) *urban geography,* which focuses on the significance of the city's location and natural resources; and (2) *urban ecology,* which analyzes how people spread out within an urban area. Let us illustrate each of these areas of study.

A city's geographical location has a great deal to do with how life in that city is lived. Take the two largest U.S. cities, New York and Los Angeles. Centered on Manhattan Island, surrounded by rivers, New York City has a land base of bedrock physically able to support tall buildings. By contrast, Los Angeles stretches out across a semiarid basin that, geologically speaking, makes the building of skyscrapers a shaky business indeed. These different settings translate into very different daily routines, as Joseph Giovannini, a part-time resident of both cities, notes:

New York and Los Angeles have fundamentally different spatial premises. Space in New York collects people; in Los Angeles it separates them. New Yorkers occupy a community; Angelenos occupy their own privacy. New York is an environment of people; Los Angeles is an environment of vehicular movement. New York is a vertical city, and Los Angeles, despite its hills and mountains, is horizontally organized. . . .

The urban patterns that shape attitudes in the two cities are as simple as the daily commute. In Los Angeles, I coasted downhill in my '59 Studebaker Lark, accompanied by FM music. If I timed the freeways correctly to avoid bottlenecks, the drive to work from my office in Venice was a rumination. . . .

In New York, the half-hour commute is a very different half hour. It starts in the elevator, where I might encounter another tenant: We chat. Then, a brief conversation with the doorman; perhaps a passing greeting to a neighbor on the street, and then another chat at the corner newsstand. [After my subway ride, when] I arrive at Times Square, I sometimes head for my morning coffee and pastry at the Lucky Star Delicatessen, where I talk to Mervat, an Egyptian waitress; then, on the elevator in The Times building, I meet more people before sitting down at my desk. (1983:147)

Geography is only one cause of the differing social dynamics that distinguish cities. Various categories of people stake out particular areas within the city, particular activities come to dominate certain districts—and both of these change over time. Such shifts interest urban ecologists, who seek to understand how people choose to locate and rearrange themselves in urban space. One well-documented ecological process is *invasion and succession,* by which whole sections of a city change. A new "high-tech" area in an adjacent suburb may rather suddenly upstage an old industrial district. Almost overnight, the older district starts to look tawdry. Secondhand stores, "gentlemen's clubs," and pornographic bookstores replace the older, more respectable businesses. Before long, income levels in the area drop and the few remaining original businesses close their doors. Where once executives and working people trod the city sidewalks, now one finds only prostitutes, drug dealers, and petty criminals. With this succession, the process of change is complete.

The same process of invasion and succession may occur in residential areas as new categories of people enter an established neighborhood. An example is contained in The City in Literature box on page 12, in which novelist Paul Theroux describes the reaction of Mr. Gawber, a traditional British civil servant and long-term London resident, to ethnic changes in his neighborhood. The very presence of these new people offends Mr. Gawber, who refuses to see any good in his new neighbors—a hard attitude not likely to foster good relations.

Mr. Gawber has seen a lot of change in London; understanding some of these changes offers some insight into this man's rancor. Gawber is a member of London's old middle class.

CITYSCAPE

New York, New York!

As a child, I lived in a suburb of Springfield, Massachusetts. I must've been about eleven years old the first time I ever went to New York City. I remember I was so excited that I could hardly sleep for a week before.

New York? It seemed absolutely incomprehensible. To my mind, Springfield and Boston weren't even cities compared to New York. They were outposts, back country. New York was in a class by itself—gargantuan, mysterious, the city of cities, the place where everything important (other than the Red Sox) happened. I had read about it; I had seen it in the movies; I knew about people who lived there. I was going.

We took the train from Springfield. Four hours! Imagine being eleven years old and waiting four hours on a train to get to New York! I counted the cities (hardly looked at them, couldn't care less) as we went by— Hartford, New Haven, Stamford, whatever. Finally: the outskirts!

Our approach was through the Bronx and Harlem, tenement areas. I had never seen so many buildings. They went on for miles and all seemed huge and alike. I saw the back alleys, the clothes strung from windows, and pigeon cages on the roofs. I knew tremendously exciting things were happening here. This was where the boxer Rocky Graziano grew up (I had read his autobiography,

Somebody Up There Likes Me, a dozen times), where *West Side Story* gang wars took place, where the people who worked *On the Waterfront* lived. (In retrospect, it seems crass, even cruel, this attitude about the poor. I had no comprehension of the suffering, the degradation that more often than not accompanied such existences. I was a suburban kid, hyped up by all the media I had been exposed to.)

After what seemed an eternity, during which the train repeatedly slowed, stopped, and went slowly forward again, we finally stopped for good. All the people on the train except my mother and myself (bumpkins both!) got up, put their coats on, grabbed their briefcases, and started out. We piled onto the platform; I pulled myself, our three suitcases, and my mother after the crowd. Inside the main lobby of Grand Central, I was awestruck. I knew it was going to be big, this was *cavernous! I mean, you could hardly see the roof!* And there were the haze, the incredible echoes, the indecipherable voices of the train announcers, and no fewer than five hundred thousand people going every which way. We were in New York!

Somehow we got to the street—I have no recollection how—and once again I was stupefied, this time by the traffic, the hurrying people, the huge buildings. My mother suggested we take a cab to the hotel. Although excited by this prospect, I argued against it: "Let's not," I said, "It's only 14 blocks to our hotel. It's just around the corner. Nobody can get lost in New York. Everything's numbered,

His father, impoverished, had come to the city early in the twentieth century to work for the huge civil service that had evolved to control London's growth. Over the years, the Gawbers, proud of their accomplishments, enjoyed solid, well-ordered lives in a "good" neighborhood.

After World War II, however, London changed radically. The soldiers came home, followed closely by thousands upon thousands of the British Empire's far-flung subjects: Africans; Asians; people from the islands of the West Indies such as Jamaica, Trinidad, and the streets go one way, the avenues another (I wasn't sure which). Let's walk." A bit skeptical, my mother agreed. Carrying our not inconsiderable baggage, we headed over to Fifth Avenue.

What do I remember? The lions on the steps of the New York Public Library. They were larger than any statues I had ever seen. The library itself was huge: The library in Springfield was about a third the size, and the library in my suburb wasn't even as large as one of the lions. People: in suits, in dresses, in uniforms and clothing that I hardly imagined existed. Orthodox Jews in their traditional raiment; Blacks and Asians; young kids in motorcycle jackets with their hair slicked back (delinquents); bums lying in the street or panhandling.

And, I remember the street—the newsstands, with more papers and magazines than I could believe. I took mental notes on one block: a department store, a book store, a record store, a fashion shop, a Florsheim shoe store. Then another: a department store, a Kelly Girls office, a restaurant . . . , and another Florsheim shoe store! Springfield had three shoe stores within its entire city limits, all different companies. Two Florsheim shoe stores in two blocks? I could hardly believe it. How could they stay in business?

The next thing I remember is my mother grabbing my shoulder and yelling at me to be careful. I was three steps into the street on a "Don't Walk" signal. Yellow cabs and Cadillacs were coming at me, honking like crazy. They weren't about to stop. In my daze I had just kept walking, looking at everything and astonished by a third Florsheim shoe store

across the street. As I leaped back onto the curb, the horns were honking and the cabbies were glaring and shaking their fists.

At this point, my mother said we were taking a cab the rest of the way to the hotel, no matter how close it was. I didn't argue. I was exhausted. I hailed a cab like a native (I'd seen them do it in hundreds of movies). We got in. The cabbie looked around and said, "Where to, Mack?" A bit ruffled by his demeanor, I said in a confident, firm voice: "The Hotel——" (I've forgotten the name). The cabbie looked at me, frowned, looked impatient, and then asked gruffly, "Where's that, Mack?"

What? In every story I'd ever read, in every film I'd ever seen about New York, you just got into the cab, said the name of the hotel, and the cab took off. Cabbies knew all the hotels in New York. I suddenly realized New York was so big they didn't know all the hotels. And this cabbie couldn't care less. I fumbled about for the address, my suave facade completely blown. My mother finally found it. The cabbie grabbed it, snorted, and turned around. We roared off.

I smashed back into the seat, sliding through a piece of fresh gum thoughtfully left by a prior passenger. All I remember about the ride is that we almost got in twelve accidents, that the cabbie yelled at other drivers a lot, that the meter went up awfully fast, and that we passed eight more Florsheim shoe stores on the way.

Source: James L. Spates, Hobart and William Smith Colleges.

Tobago; and immigrants from India. Postwar conditions prompted the immigration, for the war had devastated many colonies' economies. To make matters more complicated, many colonies were in the midst of political turmoil. In such a climate, many of the empire's colonial

subjects decided to seek a better life in England. Many who arrived in London had little money and few skills to support themselves.

Some settled in Gawber's neighborhood partly because the massive wartime bombing of London had decreased property values in

Mr. Gawber's dad came to the city, London, for a better life, which did happen. After WWII, London was a mess full of poor people, and many races.

THE CITY IN LITERATURE

Mr. Gawber's London—A Neighborhood in Transition

Once, this road had the preserved well-tended look of . . . [houses with] painted trim, owned by families for their cozy size and kept in repair. But the houses on Volta—with servants' bells in every room and names like The Sycamores—had fallen into the hands of speculators and building firms and enterprising landlords, who partitioned them with thin walls, sealing off serving hatches and doors, building kitchens in back bedrooms, installing toilets in broom cupboards, bolting a sink or a cooker on a landing so the stacked dishes were in full view of the street. . . .

Mr. Gawber had been born in number twelve and he had grown up in it. . . . He had attended the boys' school, Saint Dunstan's, at the top of the road and the Anglican church at the bottom. Now the church was Baptist and mostly black. . . . He stayed away. He had seen the street's residents grow old and die or retire to the country, and after the war the houses had moved into a phase of decline that was, even now, unchecked. The new occupants were numerous, they were every human color, and the street was made nearly impassable by their parked cars. . . . The window boxes were empty, the hedges torn out, the gardens paved for cars and motorbikes. . . . It was not a bad road—there were many worse—but it would never improve. Eventually it would be . . . pulled down and tan apartment blocks built on it. That was the pattern. . . .

Mr. Gawber thought: I am a relic from that other age. Lately, he had studied the new families. They were . . . Negroes and Irishmen who wore bicycle clips; dog-faced boys in mangy fur coats and surly mothers with red babies and children with broken teeth and very old men who inched down the sidewalk tapping canes. . . .

In the warm weather . . . the life in those houses spilled into Volta Road—babies were wheeled out for approval, youths met and tinkered with motorbikes and taunted girls; arguments turned into fights, shameless courtships into loud weddings. . . . This evening they were out: Wangoosa mending his bicycle, Churchill dandling his baby, the Indian tuning his Land Rover, each one claiming his portion of the road. He wished these families away.

Mr. Gawber destroyed it with his eyes. He policed the ruins and found the idlers guilty of causing a nuisance and a breach of the peace, of unlawful assembly, uttering menaces, outraging the public modesty, and tax evasion. He blew a shrill whistle and had them carted off, then leveled the road, reducing the houses to a field of broken bricks and lumbers, and he let the grass reassert itself and cover the rubble with its green hair. It would serve them right.

Source: Paul Theroux, *The Family Arsenal* (Boston: Houghton Mifflin, 1976), pp. 34–37.

that area. Speculating real-estate agents bought up the available housing and rented it to the newcomers at affordable prices. The poverty and colonial lifestyles of the newcomers offended and threatened traditionalists, many of whom packed up and left. Gawber was among the few who remained to fume at the newcomers, who symbolized the demise of his "orderly and decent life."

Such study of ecological changes over time helps our understanding of the social dynamics of city life, just as geography provides insight into the physical arrangements. These interrelated elements provide the subject matter of Chapter 7.

Comparative Urbanism: The City and Culture

As we have already suggested, the city does not exist in a vacuum. It is "powered" by its people, who represent a particular way of life, or culture. By the term *culture,* we mean the basic beliefs, values, and technology that characterize a city in a particular historical era. Any society's culture is reproduced and intensified in the city.

Technology provides a good example. If we were to visit the London of a century and a half ago, we likely would be shocked to see how different it was from the cities of today. Yes, we would find a bustling business district and lots of people—but there the similarity would end. Rather than a sprawling metropolitan area with extensive suburbs and shopping centers, crisscrossed by superhighways and adorned with skyscrapers, we would find a relatively compact city, with all its hustle going on in narrow, winding streets of astonishing filth. Once again, Charles Dickens, who lived there, provides us with an illustration:

> LONDON. . . . Implaccable November weather. As much mud in the streets as if the waters had but newly retreated from the face of the earth. . . . Smoke lowering down from chimney pots, making a soft black drizzle, with flakes of soot in it as big as full-grown snow-flakes—gone into mourning, one might imagine, for the death of the sun. Dogs, undistinguishable in mire. Horses, scarcely better; splashed to their very blinkers. Foot passengers, jostling one another's umbrellas, in a general infection of ill-temper, and losing their foothold at street-corners, where tens of thousands of other foot passengers have been slipping and sliding since the day broke (if this day ever broke), adding new deposits to the crust upon crust of mud . . . and accumulating at compound interest. (*Bleak House,* 1853, p. 1)

Inevitable as they seem to us, clean, paved streets, clean air, the skyscraper, the superhighway, and the large, sprawling suburb are very recent urban phenomena, all products of a certain level of technological development. The skyscraper only became feasible in the latter part of the nineteenth century, when steel-frame buildings and electrically powered elevators were developed. Similarly, sprawling suburbs are unthinkable without superhighways or mass public transportation linking cities and suburbs; these, in turn, are dependent on technological innovations such as steel, railroads, electricity, and the private automobile. Finally, paved streets became common in cities only in the twentieth century, and it wasn't until the 1950s and 1960s that clean air acts were passed in the United States to curtail exhaust excesses like those Dickens described. A given level of technology, then, has much to do with the urban experience.

In the same way, cultural beliefs play a major role in shaping city life. Americans, for instance, live out distinctly American beliefs and values in an urban setting. Consider that well-known urban institution, the cab-driver, who earns a living performing essentially a public service: transporting people from one location to another. Because of differing cultural orientations, an examination of London cabbies would turn up rather striking differences from, say, New York cabbies.

First, the relationship between drivers and fleet owners is less adversarial in London. Although there are some "gypsy cabs"—taxis privately owned or leased by their drivers—large companies control most of the cabs in New York and other U.S. cities (Moreno, 1997; Vidich, 1976). The central U.S. value of maximizing private profit no doubt plays a role in fleet owners trying to pay drivers the smallest portion of the fare possible and drivers either cheating the fleet owner (and sometimes the public) or learning to skillfully maximize tips. In London, however, little conflict exists between drivers and fleet owners, mainly because more than 40 percent of London's drivers (compared with a mere handful in New York) own their own cabs and are beholden to no one. Because of the threat that any driver may "go independent," fleet owners in London must be more solicitous of drivers

The Church of Our Lady before Tyn, with its magnificent Gothic steeples, dominates the cityscape of Prague in the Czech Republic. The Old Town retains many medieval qualities: visual domination by the cathedral, no central business district, narrow streets, buildings with commercial enterprises at street level and residences on the floors above.

and more competitive in terms of benefits offered (Buckland, 1968).

Second, the British maintain far more government control of the cab industry than is the case in the United States, and there are stringent requirements concerning the character and ability of drivers and strict enforcement of the regulations on the upkeep of cabs (Buckland, 1968; Georgano, 1973). This control reinforces a traditional value that competes with profit making in the minds of London's drivers and owners: pride. With cabs in good repair and personnel "up to a certain mark," London's taxi people have the *esprit de corps* of an elite group. Although restricted from cutting corners to maximize profit, most British drivers and fleet owners would not do so even if they could. Similarly, although many of London's cabbies struggle to make ends meet, they find it undignified to manipulate passengers for tips, as often happens in U.S. cities (Buckland, 1968, chap. 7).

In comparison, government control is anathema to many Americans. New York fleet owners have lobbied long, hard, and successfully to keep government regulation to a minimum. With fewer restrictions and a powerful profit motive, they have been able to hire less-experienced drivers and let cabs deteriorate tremendously (Vidich, 1976, chaps. 6–7). The result is more profit but also a lower quality of service and noticeably less pride.

It would be impossible to understand the differences between English and American cabdrivers without a careful study of the role that cultural beliefs play in the urban setting. So central is this issue to the study of cities that we devote all of Chapter 8 to it.

Unlike the medieval Old Town section of Prague with its central cathedral and lower surrounding buildings, North American cities typically include a central business district with few residences, expressways, wider streets for cars, and a skyline dominated by tall commercial buildings, as illustrated in this view of Atlanta, Georgia.

The New Urban Sociology: The City and Capitalism

Just as important as a city's geographical setting and its cultural framework is its ability to generate trade—to be economically prosperous. Aristotle said that initially people came to cities for security. True enough, particularly at the time he was writing. But throughout history, people have flocked to the city for many reasons, chief among them the belief that, in the city, they would significantly improve their material standard of living. An excellent case in point is Hsiang Tzu, a Chinese peasant who went to Peking, China's capital city, in the 1930s:

When he saw the bustle of people and horses, heard the ear-piercing racket, smelled the dry stink of the road, and trod the powdery, churned-up gray dirt, Hsiang Tzu wanted to kiss it, kiss that gray stinking dirt, adorable dirt, dirt that grew silver dollars! He had no father or mother, brother or sister, and no relatives. The only friend he had was this ancient city. This city gave him everything. Even starving here was better than starving in the country. There were things to look at, sounds to listen to, color and voices everywhere. All you needed was to be willing to sell your strength. There was so much money it couldn't be counted. There were ten thousand kinds of grand things here that would never be eaten up or worn out. Here, if you begged for food, you could even get things like meat and vegetable soup. All they had in the village was cornmeal cakes. (Lao, 1979:31)

Although Hsiang Tzu's experience occurred half a world away from North America, it might have taken place anywhere. His hope that life in the city would fulfill his dreams is the same as the hopes of the millions upon millions of immigrants who came to Canada and the United States from rural and poor backgrounds around the turn of this century. These people, including many of our grandparents and great-grandparents, settled in cities across both nations in an attempt to make their fortunes.

Comparisons of medieval and contemporary cities reveal the growing importance of the economic function of cities over the centuries. In the Middle Ages, although cities were already important centers of trade, other areas of life also were thriving. All one has to do is look at the physical layout of cities built in the Middle Ages—with their central cathedral as the tallest building—to see the importance of religion in the lives of the people. With the coming of the Industrial Revolution, however, all that began to change. Cities became ever more important as centers of wealth. Skyscrapers, large factories, and office buildings sprang up to meet the economic demands of millions. The churches that had previously dominated the skyline were dwarfed by the new "central business district."

Study of the economics of land use was, until the 1960s, dependent on an ecological model (see Chapter 7). Since then, many social scientists from a variety of disciplines have embraced a new perspective called *urban political economy*. Looking at the decline of manufacturing in cities, the migration to the suburbs and the Sunbelt, mushrooming cities in poor nations, and a growing world economy, the new breed of urban researchers concluded that natural processes could not explain these changes and their economic impact on cities. Instead, they argue, decision-making within political and economic institutions, often thousands of miles away, affects a city economically, politically, socially, and even physically. Some, but not all, advocates of this perspective are neo-Marxists. Regardless of their philosophical orientation, their theoretical emphasis focuses on investment decisions and economic trends that determine a city's fortunes. We will look at the structural imperatives of urban political economy, and their ramifications on urban poverty, in Chapter 9.

THE ANATOMY OF MODERN NORTH AMERICAN CITIES

Chapters 2 through 9 provide the basic framework for a detailed analysis of the cities of the contemporary world. Then our attention returns to North America for a detailed analysis of the cities most of us know best. Even though urban population growth has slowed in Canada and the United States, this by no means suggests that the situation of our cities today is stagnant and unchanging. Far from it. Recent decades have been a period of enormous change for North American cities.

In the United States, the much-publicized movement to Sunbelt (southern and western) cities is one such change. As Table 1–1 indicates, with a few exceptions, Sunbelt cities have gained markedly in population in the last decade, while midwestern and northeastern cities have generally declined. Growing significantly were the cities of Austin, Phoenix, San Diego, San Jose, and San Antonio, all in the South and West. Declining substantially were Detroit, Cleveland, Washington, D.C., Baltimore, and Philadelphia, all in the Midwest or Northeast. Moving against the trend were New York City, which increased in population, and New Orleans and Birmingham, which lost people.

A second recent development is a nationwide trend toward living in smaller cities or in areas farther away from the central cities. For instance, the census shows that the areas surrounding the suburbs are growing most rapidly. Thus, just as people moved from central cities to suburbs a generation ago, now they are moving still farther from the urban core.

What accounts for these marked changes? Demographers suggest that, although many older Americans prefer to remain in the community where they spent most of their adult lives ("aging in place"), retirement magnet areas attract many affluent seniors. A retirement home in Dade County, Florida (Miami's home county), Austin, Texas, or Sun City, Arizona (near Phoenix) has become an attraction that millions have no desire to resist.

MANY Retirement people are moving to the "sun."
others "aging in place"

people like having their own "living space" instead of living in the city

Second, the last two decades have seen an increasing exodus of business and industry from center cities, occasioned by a desire to escape high taxation, congestion, outmoded plants, high union wages, and excessive heating costs (the latter two factors primarily in the North). In many cases, firms have moved south or west. In other instances, they have moved to areas on the periphery of the center city. In either case, they have pulled their employees with them. The employees' choice to live in smaller cities, towns, and rural areas results partly from their desire to be near relocated businesses or industries and partly from the long-standing desire to be free of congestion and to have "living space" in affordable housing. Earlier suburbs, built primarily in the 1950s and 1960s, were the first manifestation of this cultural value. The decentralization indicated by recent census data confirms that this trend is continuing.

Whatever the final explanations for these demographic changes, their effects are profound. Those cities with declining population

TABLE 1–1 Populations of the Thirty Largest U.S. Cities, 2000

2000 Ranking	City	2000 Population	1990 Population	1990 Ranking	Percent Change
1	New York	8,008,000	7,323,000	1	+ 10.7
2	Los Angeles	3,695,000	3,486,000	2	+ 6.0
3	Chicago	2,896,000	2,783,000	3	+ 4.0
4	Houston	1,954,000	1,698,000	4	+ 15.1
5	Philadelphia	1,518,000	1,586,000	5	− 4.3
6	Phoenix	1,321.000	989,000	10	+ 33.6
7	San Diego	1,223,000	1,111,000	6	+ 10.1
8	Dallas	1,189,000	1,007,000	8	+ 18.1
9	San Antonio	1,145,000	997,000	9	+ 26.9
10	Detroit	951,000	1,028,000	7	− 7.5
11	San Jose, CA	895,000	783,000	11	+ 14.2
12	Indianapolis	782,000	732,000	13	+ 6.9
13	San Francisco	777,000	724,000	14	+ 7.3
14	Jacksonville, FL	737,000	635,000	16	+ 15.8
15	Columbus, OH	711,000	636,000	15	+ 11.8
16	Austin	657,000	494,000	25	+ 32.8
17	Baltimore	651,000	736,000	12	− 11.5
18	Memphis	650,000	619,000	18	+ 5.0
19	Milwaukee	597,000	628,000	17	− 6.0
20	Boston	589,000	574,000	20	+ 2.6
21	Washington, DC	572,000	607,000	19	− 5.7
22	El Paso	564,000	516,000	22	+ 9.3
23	Seattle	563,000	516,000	21	+ 9.1
24	Denver	555,000	468,000	28	+ 18.6
25	Nashville-Davidson	546,000	488,000	20	+ 11.7
26	Charlotte, NC	541,000	427,000	33	+ 26.7
27	Fort Worth	535,000	448,000	29	+ 20.2
28	Portland, OR	529,000	486,000	27	+ 8.9
29	Oklahoma City	506,000	445,000	30	+ 13.8
30	Tucson	487,000	417,000	34	+ 16.7

Source: U.S. Bureau of the Census.

lose federal funding and political representation. As a result, such cities must cut budgets, services, and aid to the poor and elderly, decreasing further their attractiveness as places to live. Because of lost revenues, inner suburbs also begin to deteriorate as people move away. On the other hand, the small cities and towns gaining population are likely to "get rich quick." This growth is a mixed blessing, however—many long-time residents of outlying areas, accustomed to traditional rural lifestyles, now find themselves assailed by an invasion of "city slickers."

What is life like in these cities of ours? Who lives in them? Why do they live there? What are the problems these cities face? Such questions will be answered in three chapters (Chapters 10, 11, and 12) that look at North American urban social structure. By _social structure, we mean the recurrent patterns of city life that are shaped significantly by the unequal distribution of important urban resources, including wealth, power, and prestige._

One aspect of social structure concerns the wide variety of lifestyles within our cities. Often, these lifestyles coincide with different geographical districts of the city. In downtown areas, for example, we are likely to see well-dressed businesspeople—many of whom live in apartments. Older residential neighborhoods may provide the sights, sounds, and even smells of exotic cultural diversity. Still other neighborhoods contain the city's poor, who struggle every day to survive. In many suburban areas, single-family homes dominate—replete with children and the ever-present automobile.

Lifestyles are, of course, much more than matters of individual choice. They reflect dimensions of social difference, often taking the form of social inequality—the focus of Chapters 10 and 11. Like virtually all other societies, the United States and Canada contain marked _social stratification,_ the hierarchical ranking of people in terms of valued resources. Wealth is certainly one important dimension of social stratification; U.S. cities, especially, provide striking contrasts between well-heeled urbanites who live lives of material comfort and others who must persevere just to survive.

Very often, this difference is closely related to other dimensions of social difference: race, ethnicity, and gender. Once ignored in the urban public sphere, women are now more likely to hold public office, at least in cities with populations of 25,000 or more (MacManus and Bullock, 1995:162). From both historical and contemporary viewpoints, however, women's lives and city experiences have reflected the realities of gender, interwoven with those of social class, race, and ethnicity. In a still-continuing historic pattern, North American cities attract immigrants of different races and ethnic origin; on arrival many find themselves at or near the bottom of the urban hierarchy. With time, many improve their situation, but others continue to suffer from a wide range of problems associated with poverty. Consider, for example, in the City in Literature box, African American novelist James Baldwin's assertion that racial difference is a fundamental element of U.S. urban life.

Social power—the ability to achieve one's ends and to shape events—is yet another important dimension of inequality. For those with considerable wealth, urban living is often the experience of shaping their own lives (and, indeed, the lives of others); by contrast, for poorer urbanites, many of whom are members of racial and ethnic minorities, life in the city is a grim matter of trying to cope with forces that seem overwhelming.

Of course, none of these structural patterns exists exclusively in cities. Social stratification is as important in small towns in New Hampshire as it is in Concord, the capital; people perceive racial distinctions as keenly in rural Ohio as they do in Columbus; and "power politics" is the name of the game in rural Wyoming, just as it is in Cheyenne. Nevertheless, because these structural patterns have shaped our cities so strongly, we can hardly ignore them.

On another level, however, because cities concentrate everything human in a small space, they intensify the effects of class, race, ethnicity, gender, and power. If we care to look, we can be buffeted by visions of wealth and poverty, of power and powerlessness of such extremity as to be nearly incomprehensible. The Looking Back box gives such contrasting

THE CITY IN LITERATURE

Race and the City

The life of the city is hard for everybody. But, baby, try it if you're black. We began to move across the river [from Harlem] to the Bronx and . . . all those [white people] fled in terror. One of the results is the present disaster called the South Bronx where nobody can live. The movement of white people in this country has been—and it is terrifying to say this, but time to face it, a furious attempt to get away from the niggers.

Source: James Baldwin in "Symposium: Literature and the Urban Experience," *Humanities* 1:4 (July/August 1980), p. 3.

visions. It depicts the staggering wealth and power of J. Pierpont Morgan, the late-nineteenth-century industrialist, and contrasts his life with the shattering poverty and powerlessness of Jurgis and Ona Rudkis, new arrivals from Lithuania living in the immigrant camps of Chicago in the same period. Both Morgan and the Rudkises worked extremely hard. Yet, in part because of his early advantages, Morgan gained fabulous wealth and power, while the Rudkises, despite all their efforts, were doomed to failure. The structural organization of wealth and power in the city was against them from the start.

The kind of numbing poverty experienced by the Rudkises has by no means disappeared, as a walk through the poor neighborhoods of almost any major North American city will reveal. Indeed, poverty for millions continues as only one of the significant problems that beset the urban environment. Three other closely related, significant urban issues are problems related to housing, education, and crime. An analysis of these problems and their implications is the focus of Chapter 12.

THE CITY IN WORLD PERSPECTIVE

If any one thing should astound us, it is how popular cities have become the world over. As a human invention, cities are scarcely 10,000 years old; but, as the centuries have passed, they have become both much larger and far more numerous. To put it slightly differently, once people become aware of the advantages of cities—protection, increased material standard of living, a more stimulating mental and social life—they don't want to live anywhere else. The process of *urbanization—the concentration of people in cities and other densely populated areas*—continues as strongly today as ever before. Demographers measure this process by the growing proportion of a population living in urban locales.

For example, in 1800 only one city, Beijing, had 1 million residents; now the world contains 130 cities where a million or more people reside. Table 1–2 on page 22 makes the point even more powerfully. Reporting the percentage of urban people living in the world's seven major geographical areas between the years 1920 and 2000, the table shows that urbanization is an unmistakable trend everywhere. In fact, the world's cities are growing by 1 million people each week. By 2025, more than two-thirds of the planet's people will be urban dwellers (Brockerhoff, 1996:4).

But there are distinct regional patterns in urban growth. If we examine the table for the percentages of growth between 1960 and 2000, we see that all regions gained urban population. Yet in the more industrialized

LOOKING BACK

Wealth and Power—and the Lack of It—in the City

J. Pierpont Morgan

The offices of the J. P. Morgan Company were at 23 Wall Street. The great financier came to work one morning dressed in a dark blue suit, a black overcoat with a collar of lamb's wool and a top hat. He affected fashions slightly out of date. When he stepped out of his limousine, the car robe fell around his feet. One of the several bank officers who had rushed out to meet him disentangled the robe and hung it over the robe rail on the inside of the door. The chauffeur thanked him profusely. Somehow the speaking tube had come off its hook and another officer of the bank replaced it. In the meantime Morgan had marched into the building, assistants, aides and even some of the firm's customers circling him like birds. Morgan carried a gold-headed cane. . . . Accepting the obeisances of his employees, he strode to his office, a modest glass-paneled room where he was visible to everyone and everyone was visible to him. He was helped with his hat and coat. He was wearing a wing collar and an ascot. . . . Pierpont Morgan was that classic American hero, a man born to extreme wealth who by dint of hard work and ruthlessness multiplies the family fortune until it is out of sight. He controlled 741 directorships in 112 corporations. He had once arranged a loan to the United States Government that had saved it from bankruptcy. . . . Moving about in private railroad cars or yachts he crossed all borders and was at home everywhere in the world. He was a monarch of the invisible, transnational kingdom of capital whose sovereignty was everywhere granted.

Jurgis and Ona Rudkis

[That] afternoon [Jurgis] and Ona went out to take a walk and look about them, to see more of this district which was to be their home. In back of the yards the dreary two-story frame houses were scattered farther apart, and there were great spaces bare—that seemingly had been overlooked by the great sore of a city as it spread itself over the surface of the prairie. These bare places were grown up with dingy, yellow weeds hiding innumerable tomato cans; innumerable children played upon them, chasing one another here and there, screaming and fighting. . . .

[The streets] through which Jurgis and Ona were walking resembled streets less than they did a miniature topographical map. The roadway was commonly several feet lower than the level of the houses, which were sometimes joined by high boardwalks; there were no pavements—there were mountains and valleys and rivers, gullies and ditches, and great hollows full of stinking green water. In these pools the children played, and rolled about in the mud of the streets; here and there one noticed them digging in it, after trophies which they had stumbled on. One wondered about this, and also about the swarms of flies which hung about the scene, literally blackening the air, and the strange, fetid odor which assailed one's nostrils, a ghastly

areas of the world—North America and Europe—urban growth has slowed considerably in recent years. For instance, the urban population of the United States in 1960 was 69.9 percent; by 2000 it had inched upward to just 77 percent.

odor, of all the dead things of the universe. It impelled the visitor to questions—and then the residents would explain, quietly, that all this was "made" land, and that it had been "made" by using it as a dumping ground for the city garbage. After a few years the unpleasant effect of this would pass away, it was said; but meantime, in hot weather—and especially when it rained— the flies were apt to be annoying. Was it not unhealthful? The stranger would ask, and the residents would answer, "Perhaps; but there is no telling."

Three years later, Jurgis got a job in the stockyards, and, after much scrimping, he, Ona, and the family bought a house. Or so they thought. In actuality, the house they had "bought" had been rented to them by land speculators taking unscrupulous advantage of the Rudkises' ignorance of the fine print in the contract. When another family came along who could pay more, the Rudkises were unceremoniously turned out into the cold. What follows is Jurgis's realization of what has happened and his powerlessness to do anything about it.

The whole long agony came back to him. Their sacrifices in the beginning, their three hundred dollars that they had scraped together, all they owned in the world, all that stood between them and starvation! . . . Why, they had put their very souls into their payments on that house, they had paid for it with their sweat and tears—yes, more, with their very life blood. Dede Antanas had died of the struggle to earn that money—he would have been alive and strong today if he had not had to work in Durham's dark cellars to earn his share. And Ona, too, had given her health and strength to pay for it—she was wrecked and ruined because of it; and so was he, who

had been a big, strong man three years ago, and now sat there shivering, broken, cowed, weeping like a hysterical child. . . .

Jurgis could see all the truth now. . . . Ah, God, the horror of it, the monstrous, hideous, demoniacal wickedness of it! He and his family, helpless women and children, struggling to live, ignorant and defenseless and forlorn as they were—and the enemies that had been lurking for them, crouching upon their trail and thirsting for their blood! That first lying circular, that smooth tongued slippery [real estate] agent! That trap of the extra payments, the interest, and all the other charges that they had not the means to pay, and would never have attempted to pay! And then all the tricks of the packers, their masters, the tyrants who ruled them—the shutdowns and the scarcity of work, the irregular hours and the cruel speeding up, the lowering of wages, the raising of prices! The mercilessness of nature about them, of heat and cold, rain and snow; the mercilessness of the city, of the country in which they lived, of its laws and customs that they did not understand! All of these things had worked together for the company that had marked them for its prey and was waiting for its chance. And now, with this last hideous injustice, its time had come, and it had turned them out bag and baggage, and taken their house and sold it again! And they could do nothing, they were tied hand and foot—the law was against them, the whole machinery of society was at their oppressors' command!

Sources: Morgan extract: E. L. Doctorow, *Ragtime* (New York: Bantam, 1975), pp. 157–59; Rudkis extract: from *The Jungle*, pp. 28–29, 176–77, by Upton Sinclair. Used by permission of Viking Penguin, a division of Penguin Group (USA).

The area of greatest urban growth is now in the developing world—in Latin America, Africa, the Middle East, and Asia (see Figure

1–1). In fact, when we consult the figures on urban growth rates by country, we find that the ten countries with the highest urban growth

TABLE 1–2   Percentage of Urban Population in Major Areas of the World, 1920–2000

Area	1920	1940	1960	2000
Europe	32	37	41	75
North America	38	45	57	77
Latin America (Central and South America)	14	19	32	75
Africa	5	7	13	38
Asia	7	11	17	37
Oceania	34	38	50	70
The World	14	19	25	47

Source: "Growth of the World's Urban and Rural Population: 1920–2000," *International Social Development Review* 1(1969), p. 52; People & the Planet at *http://www.peopleandplanet.net*, accessed July 20, 2002.

rates are all in these four regions; those with the lowest rates, with one exception (Uruguay, in South America), are all in Europe, North America, and Japan. Moreover, when we scan a list of all the world's nations ranked in order of their urban growth rates, we must look down through 150 countries before we encounter an industrial nation (Canada) (UN, 2000).

Why should this concern us? Aren't growing cities generally a good thing? After all, cities produce jobs, generate better health care, and stimulate improvements in technology and the arts. The answer to this question is double-edged: Sometimes they do these things, but not always; and often, when they do them, they do them for only some of the city's people.

In fact, throughout most of the developing world, the urban situation is desperate and, in some places, is even getting worse. Recent decades have witnessed hundreds of millions of people, enticed by the promise of a better life, moving into the cities of Latin America, Africa, the Middle East, and Asia. Most of these cities cannot keep up with the incoming tide. The results are poverty, malnutrition, and disease for many people. The Urban Living box on page 24 provides a poignant example of this in the Dominican Republic in the West Indies. Fortunately, the kind of disaster that prompted this story does not happen

often, but the conditions reported still exist in many shantytowns throughout the world.

The grave situation in the Dominican Republic is common throughout the world's poor nations. Chapter 13 examines the cities of Latin America, Africa, the Middle East, and Asia, and offers analysis highlighting their urban problems and successes.

URBAN SOCIOLOGY AND THE QUALITY OF CITY LIFE

The city is a living, dynamic entity. Its capacity to concentrate human efforts means that urban places contain the greatest potential for improving the quality of human life.

From its beginnings millennia ago, people have come to the city with hopes and dreams of living "the good life." But when all is said and done, has the city lived up to its billing? True, many cities boast material living standards that are higher than they ever have been in history; but this is not the case for everyone. Further, in many cities of the developing world, material living standards are appallingly low—destitution in many cities is not the exception but the rule. Then, too, focusing on material standards alone may be a mistake. What about security, which was Aristotle's first concern? Despite a steadily declining urban crime rate in recent years, many areas in U.S. cities are so dangerous that

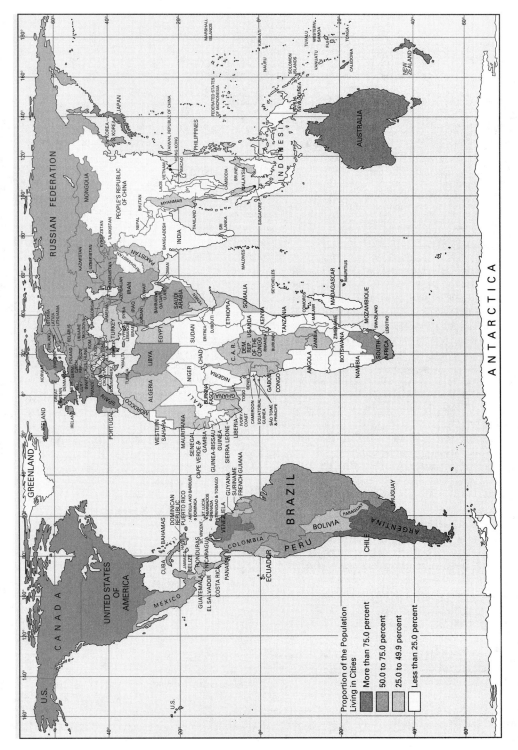

FIGURE 1–1 Urbanization in Global Perspective

Source: Peters Atlas of the World (1990).

Proportion of the Population Living in Cities

- More than 75.0 percent
- 50.0 to 75.0 percent
- 25.0 to 49.9 percent
- Less than 25.0 percent

23

URBAN LIVING

The Shantytowns of San Juan de la Maguana

West of Santo Domingo, the Dominican Republic capital, lies the banana-producing region of San Juan de la Maguana. In September 1998, Hurricane Georges, with winds up to 130 miles an hour, lashed this area for 16 hours. The storm entombed five entire shantytowns there, including a basin area called Mesopotamia, in several feet of mud and rock, burying about 200 people. While the hurricane caused over 200 deaths and mass destruction throughout the Caribbean and Florida, this region of the impoverished Caribbean nation was the hardest hit, with 20,000 people devastated by wind and flooding. Of the 49,000 homes destroyed, about 2,500 have been replaced through the U.S. Agency for International Development (USAID), including the provision of water, sanitation, and electricity. This relief effort has not been enough for the displaced, ever-growing population. So the shantytowns exist again, the squatters living in houses stacked so close to one another that the edges often overlap.

Most of these dwellings are without indoor plumbing and there is no plan for the drainage of latrines.

San Juan de la Maguana is but one of the shantytown areas. The communities of squatters, so poor that they cannot pay any amount of rent, sprouted on the outskirts of the island's main cities, as they have in Puerto Rico and in other Latin American, African, and Asian countries. Millions of people throughout the developing world live in comparably unhealthy and dangerously situated shantytowns. Built from castoff scraps of lumber and tin by people who often have not even heard of building codes, they sprawl across river flood plains and low-lying coastal strips where tidal flooding is common, or else on hillsides where deadly mudslides take their toll.

People who abandoned the countryside in search of better jobs and were unable to find affordable housing occupy these Dominican shantytowns, like others throughout the developing world. Until the economic problems in these countries are solved, better housing will not be the answer, because people still won't be able to pay even a minimal amount for housing.

people cannot go out alone, especially at night, without fear of being mugged, raped, or murdered. What about strong, community-oriented neighborhoods? Once a primary element of U.S. cities, these, too, have weakened in recent decades—and, in some areas, have disappeared altogether.

We need to understand the whole range of conditions that contribute to a more stimulating, fulfilling urban life. In bits and pieces throughout this book, evidence regarding the positive and negative elements of the city will

emerge. We will comment on some of this evidence as we proceed and, in the final chapter, we will pull together these ideas as we examine urban planning and offer some thoughtful speculation about the future of cities.

Because of the ever-increasing importance of the city to the future of human civilization, sizing up the potential of urban places for meeting human needs is clearly essential. Are we necessarily heirs to the city of rage, racial prejudice, and exploitation that Mr. Gawber, James Baldwin, and Jurgis and Ona Rudkis

As this scene of New Year's revelers in Times Square shows, a city is a dynamic, living entity, but not just on such special occasions. A city's night life—with its excitement, bright neon lights, variety of activities, crowds of people, and sense of adventure—lures people of all ages and backgrounds to come and be part of one of its many simultaneous happenings.

encountered? Or can the city become the ideal suggested by historian Lewis Mumford in the following passage?

city magnifies
life's dimensions

The mission of the city is to further [the human being's] conscious participation in the cosmic and historic process. Through its own complex and enduring structure, the city vastly augments [human beings'] ability to interpret these processes and take an active, formative part in them, so that every phase of the drama it stages shall have, to the highest degree possible, the illumination of consciousness, the stamp of purpose, the color of love. That magnification of all the dimensions of life, through emotional communion, rational communication, technological mastery, and above all, dramatic representation, has been the supreme office of the city in history. And it remains the chief reason for the city's continued existence. (1961:576)

To answer, we must "go and make our visit."

CHAPTER 2

THE ORIGINS AND DEVELOPMENT OF THE WORLD'S CITIES

Can you imagine the United States without great cities such as New York, Chicago, or San Francisco? It would be like thinking about Egypt without Cairo, Japan without Tokyo, France without Paris, or England without London. Why are entire countries so closely bound up with cities? The answer, as this chapter will explain, is that much of the story of human history is centered in cities. In fact, the words *city* and *civilization* are both derived from a single Latin root—*civitas*; indeed, to be civilized is to live in or near a city.

This was not always the case, however. Most knowledgeable people today recognize the importance of cities because we live in an era in which the city is the dominant form of human association and is becoming more so every day. In the larger picture of human history, however, the city is a "wide-eyed infant"—a very recent arrival on the human scene.

URBAN ORIGINS

When and where did the first cities develop? What were they like? How did they change over time? Here we shall offer brief answers to these crucial questions. Before we can do so, however, we must look far back in time to see just how recently we human beings began making history on this earth.

To get a better perspective on where we are in relation to human history, let us utilize astronomer Carl Sagan's concept of a cosmic calendar. Sagan (1977) suggested that we imagine the entire history of our planet compressed into a single calendar year. What does such a vision suggest? To begin with, for almost the entire history of the universe (beginning with the "Big Bang"—corresponding to January 1), the human species did not exist. In fact, our species, *Homo sapiens*, appeared on earth roughly 100,000 years ago (December 31 in Sagan's year). Another 90,000 years passed before permanent settlements—even in the form of small villages—existed. The emergence of the first cities, then, and with them of the way of life we commonly call "civilization," occurred only about

10,000 years ago (8000 B.C.E.)—in the last minute of Sagan's year! It would be several thousand years more, around 3000 B.C.E., before cities became common. Even then they contained only a small proportion of the world's population.

It is only in the last several centuries (the last second in Sagan's year) that the world has acquired a sizable urban population. As recently as 1940 the proportion of the world's population living in cities was only 19 percent. In 2000, this figure had grown to 47 percent. The existence of the city and of the urban way of life that we so readily take for granted, in other words, is a very recent and momentous change in the history of the world.

Archaeology: Digging the Early City

Learning about the first cities has been a gradual process filled with difficulties. Urban scholars have relied heavily on the work of archaeologists to gain an understanding of early settlements. Through excavation and techniques for determining the age of artifacts, we have learned much about the social life of people who left little formal record of their existence. Often, however, simply finding the sites of early cities—frequently buried beneath the surface, hidden by dense plant growth, or even covered by a current metropolis—is a matter of hard work and a bit of luck. Once an ancient city is found, excavation must proceed carefully to avoid damaging the remains. Finally, even when a city has been excavated successfully, archaeologists do not always offer the same interpretations of findings at a given site.

Moreover, our understanding of early urban settlements is subject to continuous revision. Ongoing investigations at old sites, and the discovery of new locations (such as the recent excavation at Gran Pajaten in Peru), provide a steady stream of new data. In addition, techniques of analysis continually improve, often leading to a reformulation of beliefs urbanists held with certainty only a few years before.

We still have much to learn; nevertheless, there is much that we do know about early cities, and this chapter summarizes a great deal of that knowledge. First, we examine cities as they took form in the ancient world, and then we consider how, as the centuries passed, cities reflected the changing character of human civilization.

The First Permanent Settlements

Human beings like us first appeared on the earth about 100,000 years ago. All the evidence now at hand suggests that, for the next 90,000 years, our ancestors lived as hunters and gatherers—hunting game and gathering vegetation over large areas. Most followed the animals and moved with the seasons, without permanent settlements, in small groups ranging in size from 25 to 50 individuals. Frequently these family bands would camp in a place for a few weeks because the hunting was good or the vegetation was plentiful. When the game left the area or the vegetation went out of season, the people moved on.

Then, around 10,000 years ago, near the end of the last Ice Age, a change occurred. It happened slowly and without any evident drama. Nonetheless it was to be one of the most momentous changes in human history: People began to settle down in one place and to evolve more complex social structures. Civilization as we know it was beginning. Why did it happen?

Many archaeologists now think the link between civilization and permanent settlements had something to do with population density (Cohen, 1977). As time passed, the number of hunter-gatherer tribes grew. Gradually, they began to deplete the natural resources that had formed the mainstay of their existence for millennia. Game became scarce and vegetation was depleted.

How could these nomads solve the food shortage problem? They could wander over larger areas, but that was difficult and threatened to place them in direct competition with other groups. They could carry extra food from areas of abundance, but this would be burdensome without the use of animals— which had not yet been domesticated. A better possibility was to settle in the most fertile areas and raise their own food. This option was the one that won out. Many experts view the domestication of plants, sometimes called the agricultural revolution, as the single most important event in human history (Mumford, 1961:55). For the first time, people could stay in one place and—once a food surplus could be produced—could allow some members of the group to pursue interests other than seeking food, such as crafts and science.

Over a period of some 5,000 years, villages began and multiplied. Humans created permanent settlements where they raised crops and learned to domesticate animals for use in the fields or as a food supply. Permanent settlements also transformed patterns of social structure. Most important, these settlements were all characterized by *a more complex division of labor.* For the first time people began doing many different, specialized tasks to "earn a living." This was a radical shift from the social structure that prevailed in hunter-gatherer tribes. In nomadic groups everyone knew a bit about everything. No one was a full-time doctor, lawyer, priest, or trader. Only permanent settlements afforded people the opportunity to specialize, not just in food production, but also in religion, military affairs, trade, and a host of other occupations.

Specialization benefited everyone: The farmer gained the protection of the military and the value of the priest's greater insight into matters religious, while the priest and the soldier received the fruits of the farmer's labors. In short, these early settlements provided the possibility of living a life based more on choice than on tradition. As Dora Jane Hamblin (1973:9) has suggested, "No longer was every man forced to be a hunter or a farmer, every woman a mother and a housekeeper." Such a tantalizing variety, "offering the possibility of following a personal bent rather than a parent's footsteps, must have been as powerful a lure in 8000 B.C.E. as in the twentieth century."

Linked to the more complex division of labor was a second major element in the social structure of these early settlements: *a hierarchical power structure.* Hunting and gathering societies tend to be egalitarian. That is, while people perform a few different tasks in daily life, all work is deemed equally important to the welfare of the group. For example, hunting (typically done by men) is no more important than gathering food or caring for children (usually women's tasks). Furthermore, with the limited productive technology possessed by hunter-gatherers, there are few resources beyond those needed for daily life; no one is able to amass much more wealth than anyone else.

All that changed as permanent settlements developed. Moreover, the use of power—the ability to demand the compliance of others—increased as settlements became more complex (Fried, 1967). There is a good reason for this. A more complex division of labor requires the unequal distribution of power in order for activity to be efficient. For instance, if farmers are to support a large number of people who are doing other things, someone has to oversee the collection and distribution of the food surplus. Some form of administrative leadership—a king, a council of elders—therefore becomes necessary. This leadership can oversee other important tasks as well, such as the construction of buildings, walls for defense, or irrigation systems; the collection of taxes; and long-range planning (Sjoberg, 1973).

Of course, there is another advantage of a hierarchical power structure, at least for those nearer the top: Higher-ups are rewarded for their efforts (or by their very control over others) with greater wealth and prestige. There is ample historical (as well as modern) evidence that positions of power are not always used for the good of all.

Given a more complex division of labor and the development of a hierarchical power structure, a third element was necessary for cities to emerge: *the development of a productive surplus.* Earlier we noted that many archaeologists believe that the rise of agriculture was the main reason people traded hunting and gathering for permanent settlements. A similar process was at work in the gradual transition from village to town to city. Specifically, a growing population could not be supported without an increasing surplus of food. This notion of "agricultural primacy"—food surplus supporting permanent settlements—has been reinforced by the discovery of the remains of domesticated plants and animals at early urban sites around the world.

To sum up, around 8000 B.C.E., hunting and gathering societies began to increase in size. As a response to population increase, people began to settle down and take up agriculture as a way of life. These permanent settlements were characterized by increasingly complex social structures organized around a division of labor and a hierarchical power structure. Such settlements depended on a productive surplus. As these elements coalesced, they fed on each other: The division of labor led to more efficient use of human and natural resources, which in turn led to a greater division of labor and a more intricate power structure, and so on. As this happened, villages turned into towns, and then towns became the first cities.

The City Emerges

What do we know of these earliest cities? We begin with what is thought to be the first city: Jericho. The modern city of Jericho and its ancient ruins lie just to the north of the Dead Sea, in present-day Israel (see Figure 2–1 on pages 34–35).

Jericho

When it is approached by air, Jericho stands out as a tiny green oasis set in a glittering expanse of desert. The modern city is a cluster of lush parks, palm trees and attractive homes. . . . Just north of the modern city is a bulging mound, which is of far greater significance to archaeologists than the present Jericho. They have carved up the mound into a network of trenches to study the layers of civilization below the surface; for beneath this now welted and pock-marked ground lies the evidence of a much earlier Jericho, and in fact the oldest city yet to be discovered anywhere in the world. (Hamblin, 1973:29)

The partial excavation of the Neolithic city of Catal Hüyük has already provided archaeologists with many clues about the social life of its inhabitants. Discovered in the late 1950s,
the site rapidly became internationally famous due to the large size and dense occupation
of the settlement, as well as the spectacular wall paintings and other art uncovered inside
the houses.

With the excavation of Jericho, the history of cities has been largely rewritten. Previously, it was believed that the first cities arose in the Fertile Crescent region of Mesopotamia (present- day Iraq) about 3500 B.C.E. The work of archaeologists at Jericho, notably Kathleen Kenyon, has established the fact that Jericho was a "developing city" as early as ten millennia ago; it was a city that had become "ancient when the pyramids were new" (Hamblin, 1973:29).

Research at Jericho, however, has sparked a debate: At what point may one speak of a permanent settlement as being a "city"? Kenyon (1957, 1970) argues that a population of about 600 people and substantial buildings allow Jericho to be considered a city about 8000 B.C.E. Others disagree, citing Jericho's small size by today's standards. Size, however, is not the only important factor. Density and the complexity of social life—involving a broad range of activities and a hierarchy of power relations—add to Jericho's claim to city status.

What made Jericho different from other settlements of its time was the presence of houses made of sun-dried brick, a surrounding wall, a tower, and a large trench, all suggesting an advanced division of labor and a hierarchical social order that could oversee large-scale public works. The wall further points to a recognition of the need for defense and for protection from the elements. Even after 10,000 years of erosion, its ruins are some 12 feet high and 6 feet thick at the base. The trench, cut into solid rock, is about 27 feet across and 9 feet deep. Although archaeologists are not sure what it was used for (to hold water?), certainly a complex, cooperative effort was necessary to create it.

A short account of the later history of Jericho holds an interesting lesson in the history of urban settlements. It would seem that the original settlers of Jericho did not remain after about 7000 B.C.E., when a second group took up residence. This second group was more technologically advanced than the original settlers, constructing rectangular houses of bricks and mortar with plaster walls and floors. Around this time, trade with outsiders appears to have developed, adding to Jericho's cosmopolitan character. Then, about 1,000 years later—close to 6000 B.C.E.—the site was inexplicably abandoned, and remained so for a millennium.

Resettlement began about 5000 B.C.E., providing yet another twist to Jericho's story. The later settlers were markedly less advanced in their technology, digging only primitive shelters, and no public works are traceable to this period. Then, with the coming of the Bronze Age about 3000 B.C.E., a far more advanced culture prevailed. Artwork is evident, possibly linked to the civilization in Mesopotamia to the east or Egypt to the southwest. By the time settlement of ancient Jericho came to an end about 1500 B.C.E., many other groups had lived within the city.

The story of Jericho teaches us that the history of cities must not be oversimplified. Cities do not always grow in population and gain technical capacity. Discontinuity and unexpected events change developmental patterns again and again, as we shall see in the remainder of this chapter.

Catal Hüyük — 6000 B.C.E

Evidence produced by excavation at Jericho places the beginning of city life between 8000 and 7000 B.C.E. By 6000 B.C.E., other sites, such as Catal Hüyük (pronounced Sha-tal Hoo-yook) in present-day Turkey, had become well developed. Originally settled on a 32-acre site (three times larger than Jericho), Catal Hüyük eventually supported a population of some 6,000. This strange, streetless city was composed of mud-brick dwellings clustered together like the cells of a beehive, with windowless walls facing outward. Small windows built high in the inner walls provided light, and the only entrances were on the roofs, reachable by ladders. This construction design was so secure

that no trace has been found of any plunder or massacre during the city's nearly 1,000 years of existence. The Cityscape box on page 32 offers a portrait of life in this early city.

THE FIRST URBAN REVOLUTION: CITY-STATES AND URBAN EMPIRES

Although scattered cities such as Jericho and Catal Hüyük thrived in the period between 7000 and 4000 B.C.E., it was not until about 3500 B.C.E. that urban development accelerated to a point where large numbers of cities flourished.

The earliest cities, like Jericho, clearly demonstrated their ability to generate security and wealth for fairly large numbers of people. Thus, more and more people came to the city to share in these benefits. The *idea* of the city was taking hold. No longer were many people content to live the relatively backward life of the tribe, the village, or the town. They wanted the benefits of the city: more choice, unprecedented material wealth, and ongoing excitement.

So cities grew in number and in population. But growth also brought problems: A rising population demanded more and more goods and services. And the needs of the city's inhabitants had to be managed in some way. Some cities responded to this challenge by making their social structure even more complex: They created the state.

The central feature of the state is its ability to wield power over many people—essentially to dictate everyone's rights and responsibilities: who has to live where, who has to serve in the military, and so on. With such power the city's leaders can do pretty much what they like in order to solve (or create) the city's problems —they can reorganize production, determine who will be educated, and, perhaps most important, make alliances and wage war to capture land, population, and resources.

With the emergence of the state as a form of social organization came the first city-states—cities that controlled surrounding regions, including a number of other towns,

CITYSCAPE

MUD BRICK WALL

Daily Life in Catal Hüyük, 6000 B.C.E.

When the first light of dawn struck . . . on a spring morning in the year 6000 B.C.E., it brushed lightly across the flat roofs of tightly built mud-brick houses. . . . The houses turned blank, doorless walls to the world. The household entrance was by way of the roof through either a wooden doorway or a thatch opening onto a ladder. Doors at ground level could have let in anything from floodwaters to wild animals: the roof holes and ladders provided security. . . .

Inside one of the houses the father stirred. . . . From his leather pouch he grasped a lump of yellowish, crystalline sulfur collected on his last trip to the hills, and a flint tool that he had fashioned to his needs. . . . With this prehistoric Boy Scout knife the man could make wood shavings, strike a spark, feed the spark with sulfur and produce a fire within minutes. . . . The man made a fire on the hearth while his wife went through a small doorless opening in the mud-brick wall to the family food-storage niche. In it was a bin about a yard high, made of clay and very clean. She drew some grain from a small hole at the bin's bottom: it was always filled from the top and emptied from the bottom so that the oldest grain, or that most exposed to damp, would be used first. The wife moved slowly. She was heavy with another child, and she was getting old: almost 28.

On that mythical morning the family ate a gruel of grain and milk, supplemented by bits of meat left over from a previous meal. The mother nursed the baby while she fed the next-oldest with a spoon made from a cow's rib bone. . . .

Then there was work to do. . . .

The man and the woman might have tended fields or flocks, but not many towns-folk could have been farmers—no compact community of 6,000 people could have grown enough food to support itself while doing all the other things that Catal Hüyük residents did. The city must have traded goods and services for supplies from the surrounding region. The woman of the house might conceivably have made baskets for such trade. Or the man might have spent his days as a craftsman, for although no specialized tools were found in his home, there is ample evidence in the city of skillfully woven textiles, good pottery and beautiful art work.

Source: Dora Jane Hamblin, *The First Cities* (New York: Time–Life, 1973), pp. 43–46, excerpts.

1st   URBAN   REVOLUTION 4000 BCE to 500 CE

villages, and rural lands. As time passed, some of these city-states conquered or made alliances with others to form the world's first urban empires—much larger regions, usually dominated by a single central city. These early urban empires emerged around the world—in Mesopotamia, Egypt, the Indus River Valley, China, Central America, and South America—and they "pushed" the city as a form of human settlement to ever-greater complexity and population size.

This, then, was the period of the first urban revolution (Childe, 1950). From approximately 4000 B.C.E. to 500 C.E., urban sites multiplied and their populations grew to sizes previously unknown in human history (Rome at its apex surpassed a million people).

In retrospect, the first urban revolution appears to have been something of a mixed blessing. The city's greatest positive attributes are its ability to improve people's standard of living, provide choice in the conduct of life, and stimulate the human imagination. On the other hand, these first cities also had rigid social class divisions that extended the city's benefits to only a small minority of the urban population. With the emergence of city-states and urban empires, human warfare and bloodshed rose to unparalleled levels.

With all this in mind, then, we now turn to brief descriptions of some of the first urban empires.

The Near East: Mesopotamia and Egypt

Iraq

The first urban empire was in the Fertile Crescent region of the Tigris and Euphrates Rivers in the southern portion of present-day Iraq. This region, known in ancient times as Mesopotamia or Sumer, began evolving significant cities as early as 4000 B.C.E. Cities such as Uruk, Eridu, and Ur (see Figure 2–1) represent a significant extension of world urbanization not only because they were larger than their earlier counterparts but also because of their more complex social structures. Wheat and barley were important domesticated crops, and city dwellers enjoyed the advantages of major technological advances such as oxen-pulled plows and the wheel (Sjoberg, 1965; Stavrianos, 1983).

Rise of Mesopotamian Cities

The cities of the region reached their greatest development about 2800 B.C.E. Uruk, it is estimated, covered an area of about 1,100 acres (Adams, 1966:69) and supported a population as high as 50,000 (Hamblin, 1973:89). All the Mesopotamian (Sumerian) cities were theocracies, ruled by a priest-king. A ruling elite that controlled and protected the area around the city, including its agricultural land, exacted a portion of the agricultural surplus as tribute and stored it in the major temple (Sjoberg, 1965).

Uruk and other Mesopotamian cities had highly complex social structures, including a power hierarchy and a pronounced division of labor. Excavations have established the existence of monumental public buildings, including ziggurats (religious shrines); extensive trade arrangements; a system of writing (cuneiform); mathematics; and a code of law. Sumerian texts noting the concerns of everyday life still survive. In these accounts, sheep, goats, and cattle are tabulated, taxed, and exchanged; children are shepherded to school—as today, often against their will—by concerned parents; a council of elders meets to consider grievances against the inhabitants of an adjoining city-state; and a politician attempts to win the favor of the populace with tax reductions (Wenke, 1999). Clearly these cities had advanced to a point at which parallels may easily be drawn with cities of our own experience.

Early Mesopotamian urban life was centered, however, on the temple and on religious beliefs. The populace recognized thousands of gods, and the temples, like the palaces, were large and opulently decorated. People of less favorable social position lived in irregularly organized houses along the narrow, unpaved, winding streets (Sjoberg, 1965). The complex social structure also resulted in a strong military elite and made possible an increasing capacity to wage war. Frequently under attack, Mesopotamian cities were walled defensively (Hamblin, 1973).

After about 3500 B.C.E., the cities began to be organized as politically distinct city-states, each exerting its influence over a broad region. Although these city-states were independent of one another and were often at war, they did represent a common civilization. They shared a common cultural heritage and, as far as the outside world was concerned, saw themselves as possessors of a unique, even superior, culture (Wenke, 1999).

About 2350 B.C.E., the city-states were forcibly united into one of the first urban empires. Sargon, a general from the city of Akkad, fought battle after battle with rival city-states, vanquishing all. According to an Akkadian document, as each southern city fell to his marching armies, Sargon captured "many kings, smashed many city walls," and finally "cleansed his weapons in the sea"—the Persian Gulf (Wenke, 1999:419). With the Gulf region under control, Sargon turned his

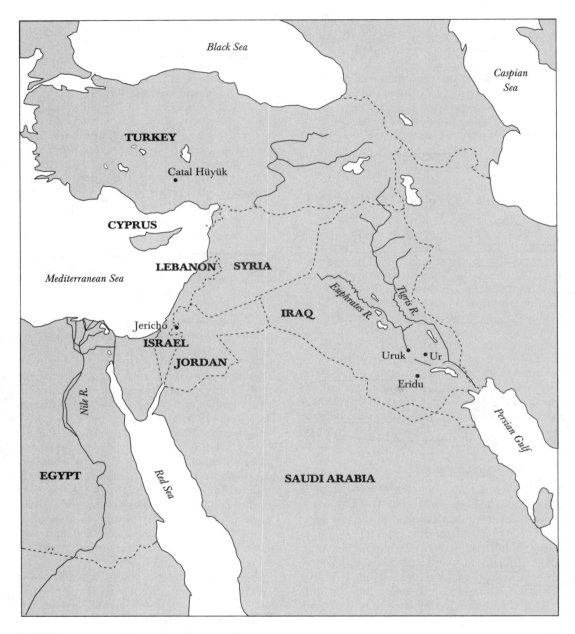

FIGURE 2–1   Asia Minor: The Earliest Cities

FIGURE 2–1 *(continued)*

eyes to cities in what are now Syria, Lebanon, and Iran, attempting to spread his empire westward.

Control of the conquered cities was apparently tenuous, as Sargon's successors had to refight his battles again and again to maintain Akkadian dominance. Even with this effort, their control was short-lived. Around 2200 B.C.E., the empire crumbled under attack from semi-nomadic peoples. It reasserted itself once more around 2100 B.C.E., when the invaders were cast out and an empire based at Ur—the Ur III Dynasty—was established. One ruler, Ur-Nammu, like Sargon before him, set his sights on faraway borders, and he reconquered much of the territory previously occupied by the Akkadian leader. He rebuilt the cities, constructed irrigation systems and roads, and reestablished the rule of law in many of these urban areas. But time was to take the measure of his dynasty as well; in 2004 B.C.E., the Elamites invaded from the north and led the then king of Ur away in captivity, shattering the empire.

This pattern of conflict persisted throughout the region until the birth of Christ. The Assyrian Empire dominated the region around 700 B.C.E., and the Persian Empire followed around 500 B.C.E.

The importance of this continual trading of urban dominance was that it spurred the development of cities and their influence throughout the Near East. In an effort to maintain control of their empires, each set of rulers tried to develop their cities as much as their culture and technology would permit. The cities of the region were continually renewed with inventions, innovations, and new ideas supplied by trade and people of different backgrounds.

Although it would be too much to say that these cities contained all of the civilization that existed in their era, they were key centers. They were "containers" in a double sense: They literally encircled their population and their valued goods with walls, and, more figuratively, they served as the place where all the themes of Mesopotamian culture could be found.

Egyptian Cities

The Great Pyramids of Giza are modern reminders of another empire that flourished shortly after the rise of cities in Mesopotamia. The archaeological record of Egyptian cities is less detailed than that of their Mesopotamian counterparts, but it appears that by 3100 B.C.E., the cities of Memphis and Hierakonopolis were established under the control of Menes, the first pharaoh of a united Egypt.

There are a number of reasons why the record of the earliest Egyptian cities is less clear. First, their buildings were made of unbaked brick and other materials that have not stood the test of time. Second, the early Egyptians apparently built and abandoned their cities frequently. As a result, although the cities were crucial centers of Egyptian civilization, none maintained its dominance long enough to reach a very large size (Sjoberg, 1965; Kemp, 1977–78). The sites of many of these cities are mapped in Figure 2–2 on page 37.

Although the cities that emerged in Egypt went through what we now think is the normal process of early development—from village to town and, finally, to city—they were rather distinct from those in Mesopotamia. Egyptian civilization was focused on the ruling pharaoh, and each had his city—a religious and political center built to reflect his power, which, by 2500 B.C.E., was virtually absolute. More than a secular leader or priest, the pharaoh was believed to be a god, and his singular dominance of the Nile region created a relatively peaceful history.

Thus we find little evidence in early Egypt of city walls. Each capital city became a pharaoh's administrative center, and much of the activity of urban artisans was directed toward construction of a palace for his pleasure in this life and an opulent tomb to provide for his needs in the life to come. Although not as large as those of Mesopotamia, these Egyptian cities were characterized by distinctive urban traits, including a clear power structure and division of labor, social inequality, and an administrative organization (utilizing hieroglyphic writing, papyrus paper, and ink) to oversee public needs and maintain the pharaoh's control.

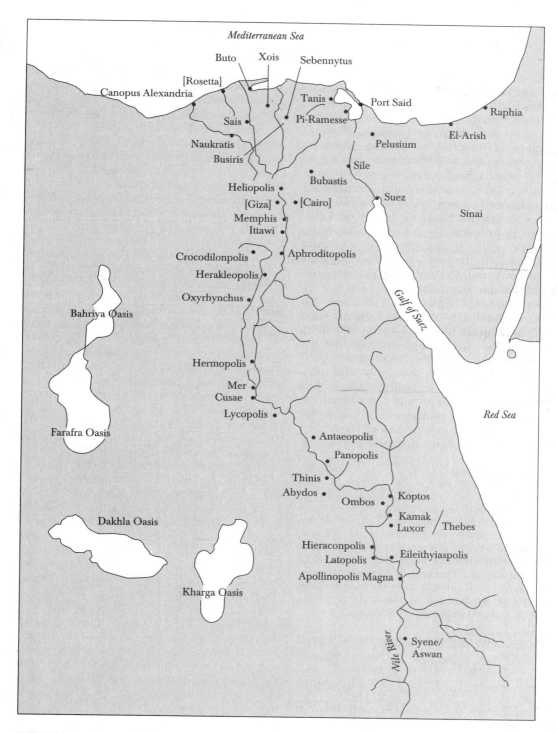

FIGURE 2–2 Egypt and the Nile: The Pharaonic Cities (modern cities are bracketed)

Source: Adapted from Jacquetta Hawkes, *The First Great Civilizations* (New York: Knopf, 1973), p. 287.

But if the early Egyptian cities were peaceful, those that followed were not. Egypt's later history, like that of Mesopotamia, is riddled with conflict within the empire and with other empires. During the period known as the Old Kingdom (2700–2180 B.C.E.), the pharaohs made forays into neighboring territories to procure goods. Successful in many of these adventures, they used their plundered wealth and captured slaves to build cities and palaces. It was two pharaohs of this period—Cheops and his son, Cephren—who built the Great Pyramids of Giza between 2600 and 2500 B.C.E., still the most colossal monuments ever constructed. Cephren was also responsible for the Sphinx at Giza.

Then, around 2180 B.C.E., the Old Kingdom collapsed, famine spread, and rioting in the cities was rampant. One document of the time, written by the sage Ipuwer, suggests that the general populace, rising in anger against their condition, deposed the politically weak pharaoh, entered the hall of justice, ransacked its offices, carried off its archives, destroyed the official census, and murdered the hall's officials. This ushered in a period of terror and redistribution of wealth. Wrote Ipuwer:

> The wrong doer is everywhere. . . . A man takes his shield when he goes to plough. A man smites his brother, his mother's son. Men sit in the bushes until the benighted traveller comes, in order to plunder his load. The robber has riches. . . . He who possessed no property is now a man of wealth. The poor man is full of joy. Every town says: Let us subdue the powerful among us. . . . The owners of robes are now in rags. . . . Gold and lapis lazuli, silver and turquoise are fastened on the necks of female slaves. (quoted in Hawkes, 1973:298)

The First Intermediate Period, characterized by the rule of kings whose tenure was very short-lived, lasted less than 200 years, the end marked by Menthuhotep I reuniting Egypt and proclaiming his capital at Thebes. The general pattern then repeated itself. For 200 years—the Middle Kingdom—Egypt regained its power and rebuilt its cities. One pharaoh, Amenemhet III, undertook a massive soil reclamation project, constructing canals to divert the Nile into previously uncultivable areas and increasing productive capacity immensely. After his death, things once again fell into disarray. A Second Intermediate Period lasted about 200 years (1800–1570 B.C.E.), during which no fewer than 217 kings ruled in Egypt, a figure probably explained by multiple dynasties rising and falling and by frequent coups.

Urban greatness once again reappeared in the New Kingdom era (1500–1100 B.C.E.). This was the period of the minor pharaoh Tutankhamun—the only pharaoh whose grave site in the Valley of the Kings was undisturbed by pillaging robbers—and of Ramses II, the pharaoh who conquered much of the Near East for Egypt and may have been Moses' adversary in his attempts to free the Jews from Egyptian servitude. Ramses rebuilt many of Egypt's cities, created a new capital, Pi-Ramesse, on the Mediterranean; and constructed self-glorifying yet magnificent temples at Karnak, Luxor, and Abu Simbel. The Asian territories were lost around 1100 B.C.E., and the next 300 years saw the last decline of pharaonic Egypt. From 800 to 671 B.C.E., the African rulers of Kush—a former Egyptian outpost to the south—controlled Egypt.

Near Eastern empires inflicted the final indignities. The Assyrians conquered Egypt in 671 B.C.E. and, though expelled less than 20 years later, were followed by the Persians in 525 B.C.E. The Persians more or less dominated the region until 332 B.C.E., the year Alexander the Great arrived, was accepted as pharaoh, and built his city, Alexandria, at the head of the Nile. From then on, Egypt was at the mercy of foreign overlords.

The development of cities in the Nile region raises an interesting question as to the possible diffusion of urban influence from Mesopotamia. History records frequent contact between the two regions. Were the Egyptian cities created independently, or was the city idea imported? Debate continues, but the currently dominant belief is that some urban influences were carried by traders or nomads from early cities in Mesopotamia toward both Egypt in the west and the Indus Valley in the east (Stavrianos,

1983). In all three regions, however, city life emerged in its own special fashion and included clearly distinct and unique aspects that revealed the stamp of the local civilization (Sjoberg, 1965:49).

The Indus Region

To the east of Mesopotamia, along the Indus River of present-day India and Pakistan, was a third ecologically favorable area where early cities emerged. Excavations have yielded the remains of two highly developed cities that were centers of a regional civilization beginning about 2500 B.C.E. Both were prominent in urban history until about 1500 B.C.E. Moenjo-Daro was situated on the Indus River about 175 miles from the Arabian Sea; Harappa was about 350 miles further north on one of the river's tributaries. Each had a population as high as 40,000 and represented an urban civilization distinct in many ways from those we have considered thus far.

Research by C. C. Lamberg-Karlovsky and Martha Lamberg-Karlovsky (1973) suggests that the Indus cities probably were linked by trade routes with Mesopotamian cities through other outposts such as Tepe Yahya, midway between the two areas (Figure 2–1). It is also likely that trading in such products as jade linked this area eastward with central Asia.

Moenjo-Daro would have seemed familiar to a modern visitor. A thriving seaport, the city was constructed with the same gridiron pattern common to most Western cities today. Hamblin writes:

> As long ago as 2500 b.c., [Moenjo-Daro] and the half dozen cities of the Indus Valley had already put to use the crisscross gridiron system of street layout—an urban convention long thought to have been invented by the Greeks of a later era. Moenjo-Daro was planned with a broad boulevard 30 feet wide, running north and south, and crossed at right angles every 200 yards or so by somewhat smaller east-west streets. Along these impressive avenues were shops and food stands. The blocks between were served by narrow curving lanes five to ten feet wide. (1973:123)

Perhaps the most remarkable discovery about this city was the uncovering of a well-established city sanitation system. Along the streets were brick-lined open sewers that carried away house drainage. Bathrooms—including several sit-down toilets—have been discovered by archaeologists, indicating the presence in 2500 B.C.E. of an urban luxury not commonly found in European cities until the nineteenth century.

Within the city numerous craft specialists were in operation, including potters, weavers, brick makers, and copper and bronze metalworkers (Sjoberg, 1965). A citadel, the city's administrative center, may have included a granary for storage of food surplus.

Unlike either Mesopotamia or Egypt, however, Moenjo-Daro does not show evidence of a single, all-powerful leader or a preoccupation with temples and god-monuments. Rather, Moenjo-Daro shows evidence of extensive "good living." Hamblin suggests that the city

> must have been among the first places to provide its citizens with a broadly based, comparatively high standard of living. Most of its people seem to have lived in considerable comfort, in near identical mud-brick houses, along near identical streets that were served by near identical drainage systems. The ruins of residential areas struck one archaeologist as "miles of monotony." But that monotony suggests, in its uniformity, an even distribution of the population, and thus the well-being that goes with a large, prosperous middle class. (1973:144)

Until 20 or 30 years ago it was commonly thought that Mesopotamia, Egypt, and the Indus River Valley contained the cities from which all later cities took their pattern. Recent archaeological research now makes this claim doubtful. Apparently, cities emerged in many places around the world independently of one another. Two other regions where this occurred were China and the Americas.

A Glance Eastward: China

Cities in China go back to at least 2000 B.C.E. Present knowledge suggests that the earliest was Po, the first capital of the Shang Dynasty.

Cheng-cho
1st
2nd
Shang capital

The excavated site of ancient Moenjo-Daro in the Indus River Valley reveals a surprisingly modern grid pattern of housing (left) and a sanitation system of brick-lined open sewers (trench, bottom and right). What the photo does not reveal is the uniformity of its north–south boulevard, 30 feet wide, and east–west cross streets about every 200 yards.

Very little is known about this city because excavations are incomplete.

Fortunately, the second and third Shang capitals have been studied in more detail. The second capital, Cheng-chou, was at its height about 1600 B.C.E. A rectangular wall 4.5 miles in length and over 30 feet high enclosed an area of about 1.5 square miles, which contained the city's administrative and ceremonial centers. In this fortified area the political and religious elite lived apart from the common people. Outside the enclosure lived artisans—bronze workers and craftspeople.

An-yang was the third Shang capital. Archaeological excavation has uncovered remnants of its larger pattern, by which the central city was linked to the surrounding area. As in Cheng-chou, the residences of artisans and craft workers were just outside a walled area. In the region immediately beyond, numerous villages formed a network of trade, supplying agricultural and other specialized products to the city (Chang, 1977).

What existed in China, then, was a type of urban settlement somewhat more diffused than in the areas already considered. Rather than concentrating all their political, religious, and craft activities in a single, center-city area, the Chinese set priests and rulers apart from the remainder of the urban population. At some distance from their protected, walled enclosure, residents of satellite villages participated in the life of the urban area as a whole.

A Glance Westward: The Americas

The last major region in which early cities developed was nearer home—in Mesoamerica, specifically the area of present-day central Mexico, the Yucatan Peninsula, and Guatemala; and western

in South America, particularly the western part of that continent. The history of these areas reveals, once again, several familiar patterns: A more productive agricultural technology and the formation of a complex social structure accompanied the rise of cities. But the case of Mesoamerica is also of interest because it represents several significant areas of contrast to urban development elsewhere.

The area was inhabited at least as early as 20,000 B.C.E. Cultivation of plants had been achieved by 7000 B.C.E., but, in contrast to other areas of the world where cities arose, the area was not well suited to the production of large surpluses, partly because of its rocky, mountainous terrain and partly because the people lacked domestic animals and a solid source of agricultural protein. The traditional digging stick rather than the plow remained the primary tool of cultivation for millennia, and Mesoamerica never embraced farming in the sense that other regions did. Rather, its groups developed a mixed economy in which hunting and other undomesticated resources continued to play a very important part. Nevertheless, one cultivated crop, maize (corn), contributed to a sturdy and nutritious diet.

By 1500 B.C.E. early villages of mud-walled houses had been established. Because hunting continued to play a major role in the economy, these village sites moved with some frequency. In some villages, Olmec and Maya tribes built elaborate ceremonial centers that served large populations, employing many craftspeople in their design and construction. Serving as a place of permanent residence for only a small number of priests at the outset, these ceremonial centers slowly grew in size and complexity. Before the birth of Christ they had become full-fledged cities.

The same process occurred later on the western coast of South America in present-day Peru and Bolivia. Perhaps the most famous urban empire of this region was that of the Incas, with its capital in the city of Cuzco. Less well known, but as important, was the urban empire of Chimor on the north coast of Peru (Mosley, 1975). Its capital, Chan Chan, began as a city around the same time that the Inca

urban centers evolved—about 800 C.E. At its height (approximately 1450 C.E.), Chan Chan ruled over a large hinterland as a major challenger to the Inca empire.

Note that this was a *regal/ritual* city—an important urban center with a population of no more than 30,000. As the term suggests, a regal/ritual city is used primarily by the ruling class: Chan Chan's rulers lived there year round and used most of the city's buildings for their own pleasure and for the rituals of Chimor culture. Only a small group of artisans, servants, and peasants were allowed to share in that part of the urban environment. All the rest of the empire's people were forced to live in the surrounding towns or rural areas and do the ruling class's bidding, including paying taxes and laboring on city projects.

In 1470 Chan Chan's challenge provoked the Incas to conquer the Chimor empire and subjugate its inhabitants. However, even this dominance was not to last. By the end of the century, Columbus was to land in the New World. Not long after that, the Spanish, and later the Portuguese, would arrive in Mesoamerica and South America in force. Under the European onslaught these proud urban empires would fall like dominoes and a new type of city would arise—a process described in Chapter 13.

Despite conditions that were unique to the hemisphere, cities arose indigenously in the Americas as they had in other regions of the world. These cities, from a historical standpoint, were highly sophisticated and equal in complexity to those found elsewhere. For example, a thousand years before the Aztecs, Teotihuacan was the religious capital of Mexico. An urban center of massive structures that was at its peak around 600 C.E., it supported a population of perhaps 200,000 in a city physically larger than imperial Rome itself (Millon, 1970; Kornberg, 1975). Its 8 square miles were laid out in a specific grid plan, with its north–south avenues containing palaces and pyramid temples with impressive sculptures. The city's housing complexes were large and contained a number of rooms, all opening out onto patios. Some were built, like the pyramid temples, of a red volcanic rock that was mined locally. Towering over the city was the Pyramid of the Sun, rising at a sharp angle from its 720-by-760-foot base to a height of 216 feet. Probably constructed in the first century C.E., it would have taken thousands of laborers 50 years to build, according to expert estimates (Matos, 1990).

Summary: Traits of Early Cities

Human beings first devised cities about 10,000 years ago. As shown graphically in Figure 2–3, they had become quite common in the Near East by 4000 B.C.E., in the Indus River Valley by 2500 B.C.E., and in China by 2000 B.C.E. Their appearance in the Americas came somewhat later, around 500 B.C.E.

All early cities were characterized by some combination of favorable ecological conditions, some sort of trade or food surplus, and a complex social structure (a fairly sophisticated division of labor and a power hierarchy). Beyond these important characteristics, some other similarities and a few differences may be mentioned.

First, early cities do not show any smooth progression of growth. On the one hand, the transition from the first permanent settlements to full-fledged cities took a long time— from about 8000 B.C.E. to 3000 B.C.E. On the other hand, city histories the world over are marked by discontinuity and change, rise and fall. Sometimes, as in Teotihuacan, one group occupied a city for its entire duration; sometimes, as in Jericho, many groups came and went.

Second, as population centers, early cities were small. Most were mere towns by today's standards. A population of about 10,000 was usual, and even the largest settlements never went much beyond the quarter-million mark.

Third, regarding the power structure, many early cities had a theocratic character—a fused religious and political elite in which kings were also priests and, not infrequently, "gods." This fusion allowed a type of double control over the city's population and its problems. Royalty could, in the name of heaven, impose taxes and even servitude. Of course, the character of this elite structure varied. It was sharply evident in Egypt, China, and Teotihuacan, while it was more subdued in the Indus city of Moenjo-Daro. But, everywhere, the first cities were characterized by inequalities in power and benefits: Usually the few prospered and the many got by as best they could.

Finally, what of the quality of life in early cities? In comparison with modern Western cities, it was probably not very high—life was usually hard, relatively short, and subject to considerable uncertainty. Yet there is substantial variation here as well. Moenjo-Daro appears to have afforded a higher standard of living to more residents than was the case in more sharply class-divided cities elsewhere. Other factors, such as war and slavery, also must have had a powerful effect on the quality of life experienced by many early city dwellers.

The city, particularly after it reached the state and empire stage, was more often than not an instrument of death and destruction as one urban center tried to conquer another. To some extent this increase in bloodshed cannot be blamed on the city as such. Rather, the use of systematic warfare seems more coincident with primitive agriculture and the coming of the first permanent settlements around 8000 B.C.E. Apparently, agricultural techniques produced a productive surplus for the first time. This surplus, in turn, attracted people to settlements and induced some of them to conquer other groups in an effort to procure even more surplus. When urban areas became common around 4000 B.C.E., these human appetites were magnified to a level unknown before in history.

In short, the development of the city was a most decisive event in human history. The early city magnified human activity in all its dimensions. People knew more, did more, and found more possibilities open to them. Such has always been the city's promise: to provide a better life. As we turn to the development of Western cities in the next section,

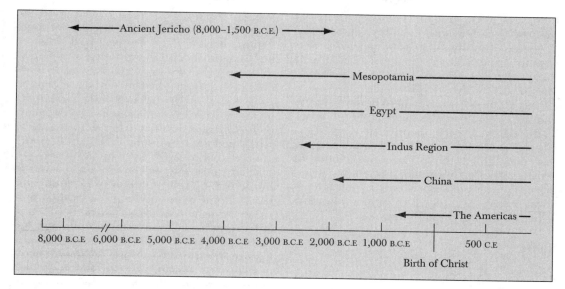

FIGURE 2–3   The Chronology of the First Cities

we shall find that cities in our own tradition also have held out the promise of "the good life." Certainly some progress has been made along that road. We shall find, however, that these cities, like their earlier counterparts, have had a tragic capacity for harboring the human indignities of coercive inequality, militaristic expansion, and war.

Crete and Greece

Western cities—those of Europe and North America—are relative latecomers in the urban story. Cities had been in existence for many thousands of years before urbanization took hold in the northern Mediterranean region on the island of Crete.

About 1800 B.C.E. urban settlements were established in Crete, probably by traders or migrants from the urban settlements of Mesopotamia. Little is known of these early cities, yet by all accounts they were thriving centers. A series of ornamental tiles found in the Palace of Minos depict what appears to be a typical city. Writes Sir Arthur Evans: "The

central features consisted of the towers and houses and a fortified town. . . . Also depicted were: trees and water, goats and oxen, marching warriors, spearmen and archers, arms and equipment, the prow apparently of a ship. . . ." (quoted in Mumford, 1961:121). Then for some reason the record breaks off inconclusively about 1400 B.C.E. (Carlton, 1977). Like Teotihuacan two centuries later, the cities of Crete were simply abandoned. Was this the result of some catastrophic volcanic eruption? No one knows for sure. In any event, it was not until seven centuries later that urban development appeared again in Europe, this time in Greece.

The early Greek polis, or city-state, did not follow the pattern of the cities of Mesopotamia and Egypt, which magnified the power of the elite at the expense of their other citizens. The fiercely independent Greek city-states— among them Athens, Corinth, and Sparta— experienced war, as well as peaceful rivalry symbolized by the Olympic games. Compared with earlier cities of the Near East, Greek cities were more egalitarian; in Lewis Mumford's phrase, they were cities "cut closer to the human measure . . . and delivered from the claims of quasi-divine monarchs" (1961:124).

Classes whose commercial influence reached outward from Sicily to northern Africa ruled these cities. The Greeks founded such cities as Messina in Sicily and Marseilles in France (Sjoberg, 1965). Unfortunately, however, in the end the Greek city-states turned on each other in the destructive Peloponnesian Wars (431–404 B.C.E.), leaving behind a remarkable legacy that highlighted the positive possibilities of urban civilization, including outstanding painting, sculpture, and architecture, as well as a political system and body of philosophy that influence the world to this day.

Rome

As Greek culture slipped into decline, another great civilization was gathering strength to the west. It was centered, perhaps more than any cultural system before or since, on a single city; indeed, the city's name is synonymous with the culture itself. As Aelius Aristedes claimed in the second century B.C.E.: "Rome! Everything is found here. All the skills which exist or have existed, anything that can be made or grown. If something can't be found here, then it simply doesn't exist!"

Aristedes was right. By the final centuries of the pre-Christian era, Rome was the dominant power of the Western world. By the time of Christ, the city on which the Roman Empire was based was gargantuan by all previous urban standards, approaching a population of approximately 1 million.

Rome displayed the same characteristics we have encountered in the earliest cities: a favorable ecological setting, the ability to produce an economic surplus, and a complex social structure. Also, like Greece, Rome was characterized by developed arts and sciences and by public monuments and buildings.

Yet Rome was an urban civilization almost exclusively based on the expression of militaristic power. For the several centuries during which the city thrived, Rome explored and revealed for all history the consequences of concentrating a city's resources almost entirely on the accumulation of power and wealth.

If the Greek conception of the good life was a city founded on the principles of moderation, balance, and human participation, the Roman conception was based on the celebration of sheer excess and unremitting domination. At its height the empire extended from Rome across the Mediterranean to northern Africa, from present-day Germany to the British Isles, from Egypt to the Near East; it included almost half the world's population (Gibbon, 1879; Stavrianos, 1983).

What can we say of the city that served as the center of this vast empire? In physical design Rome was similar to cities discussed earlier. At its center were a market, a forum, and a complex of monumental buildings. Radiating outward in orderly fashion across the breadth of the city—some 7 square miles overall—were major broad thoroughfares constructed according to a careful plan. Indeed, roads were one of Rome's greatest achievements. In all, over 50,000 miles of roads were constructed by the Roman work force. Extremely well built, they served as links between Rome and the empire's vast hinterland, from which the city drew tribute. Many of the major cities of Europe today—including London, York, Vienna, Bordeaux, Paris, and Cologne—were once provincial outposts of Rome.

Waterworks were another engineering achievement. The city had large public baths, fountains, hydrants along main streets, and a system of water drainage begun as early as the sixth century B.C.E. (Mumford, 1961). Perhaps most striking was the city's aqueduct system, completed during the second century B.C.E. and copied in many provincial cities founded by the Romans throughout Europe. These spillways brought fresh water, often from some distance, to the city, just as today's underground water system from upstate New York serves New York City.

The motive for all of this impressive engineering was ultimately to serve the interests of the ruling military and political elite. While the elite enjoyed incredible riches, Rome's poorer residents benefited little from the wealth that was brought continuously to the city, living in largely unplanned and squalid tenements.

At its height Imperial Rome was the center of a vast militaristic empire. The city, a mixture of magnificent buildings and squalid slums, contained carefully planned broad thoroughfares and an impressive water supply and drainage system. Here the Roman Forum, the heart of the city's ceremonial life, was crowded with temples, arches, statues, and public buildings.

[Where] the need was greatest, the mechanical facilities were least. Though the mass of the population might by day patronize at a small fee the public toilets in the neighborhood, they deposited their domestic ordure in covered cisterns at the bottom of the stairwells of their crowded tenements, from which it would be periodically removed by dungfarmers and scavengers. Even punctual nightly removal would hardly lessen the foul odor that must have pervaded the buildings. (Mumford, 1961:216)

This underside of Roman life had a further dimension—one that could hardly find sharper contrast with the Greek ideal of human dignity:

The main population of the city that boasted its world conquests lived in cramped, noisy, airless, foul smelling, infected quarters, paying extortionate rents to merciless landlords, undergoing daily indignities and terrors that coarsened and brutalized them, and in turn demanded compensatory outlets. These outlets carried the brutalization even further, in a continuous carnival of sadism and death. (Mumford, 1961:221)

The enduring, if horrible, example of Rome's "carnival of sadism and death" was the Circus. In the Cityscape box on page 46, Mumford describes this ritual around which the later city revolved.

Taken as a whole, Rome was a parade of contrasts: engineering excellence and technical achievement juxtaposed with human debasement and militaristic cruelty. Eventually, extended so far afield that it no longer could control its home base, and rotting from within, Rome sank into decline. It fell in 476 C.E. under the onslaught of northern invasion, and by the sixth century it had become a mere town of 20,000.

Decline: The Middle Ages

As Rome collapsed, so did the empire that had sustained urban life throughout much of Europe. With this eclipse came a period of about 600 years during which European cities

CITYSCAPE

Classical Rome: The Dance of Death

The existence of a parasitic economy and a predatory political system produced a typically Roman urban institution that embraced both aspects of its life and gave them a dramatic setting: the old practice of the religious blood sacrifice was given a new secular form in the arena.

Roman life, for all its claims of peace, centered more and more on the imposing rituals of extermination. In the pursuit of sensations sufficiently sharp to cover momentarily the emptiness and meaninglessness of their parasitic existence, the Romans took to staging chariot races, spectacular naval battles set in an artificial lake, theatrical pantomimes in which the strip tease and lewder sexual acts were performed in public. But sensations need constant whipping as people become inured to them: so the whole effort reached a pinnacle in the gladiatorial spectacles, where the agents of this regime applied a diabolic inventiveness to human torture and human extermination. . . . To make attendance at these spectacles even easier, as early as the reign of Claudius, 159 days were marked as public holidays, and as many as 93, a quarter of the whole year, were devoted to games at the public expense. Vast fortunes were spent on staging even a single one of these events. . . .

No body of citizens, not even the Athenians at the height of their empire, ever had such an abundance of idle time to fill with idiotic occupations. . . . after the hour of noon, in addition, the Roman workers, who had doubtless risen at daybreak, suffered no further demand on their time. The transformation of the active, useful life of the early Republican city into the passive and parasitic life that finally dominated it took centuries. But in the end, attendance at public spectacles, terrestrial and nautical, human and animal, became the principal occupation of their existence; and all other activities fed directly or indirectly into it. . . .

The gladiatorial games were first introduced into Rome in 264 B.C. by the consul Decimus Junius Brutus on the occasion of his father's funeral; but the Romans gave them a more utilitarian turn by employing the deadly contests as a popular means for the public punishment of criminals, at first presumably as much for an admonitory deterrent as an enjoyment. Too soon, unfortunately, the ordeal of the prisoner became the welcome amusement of the spectator; and even the emptying of the jails did not provide a sufficient number of victims to meet the popular demand. As with the religious sacrifices of the Aztecs, military expeditions were directed toward supplying a sufficient number of victims, human and animal. Here in the arena both degraded professionals, thoroughly trained for their occupation, and wholly innocent men and women were tortured with every imaginable body-maiming and fear-producing device for public delight.

Source: From *The City in History, Its Origins, Its Transformation and Its Prospects.* Copyright © 1961 and renewed 1989 by Lewis Mumford. Reprinted by permission of Harcourt, Inc.

either fell into a pattern of minimal survival or ceased to exist entirely. The commercial trade that had been the source of life to the empire and its cities was drastically curtailed. The danger of pillaging by barbarians increased.

Once-great cities, which had boasted populations in excess of 100,000, became virtually isolated hamlets. There evolved an almost singular concern for security. Surviving cities became fortified—surrounded by great walls—

a revival of an older urban feature that had been rendered unnecessary by the establishment of Roman control of nearly the entire continent.

The pattern of settlement typical of the fifth through the eleventh centuries was a mosaic of local manors, villages, and small towns in many ways reminiscent of the earliest urban settlements we considered at the beginning of this chapter. The dominance over a large hinterland so characteristic of Greek and Roman cities all but vanished. This is, of course, the essence of the image conveyed by the phrase "Dark Ages."

During this period arose a feudal system, in which a local lord provided security in exchange for service on his lands. In most cases, however, manors were situated in the countryside, weakening urban influence even further. A few highly fortified small cities and manor towns survived, but a delicate balance was struck in these settlements. Given the state of medieval technology, protection could be provided for only a limited population. A small population made a low level of production inevitable, and this, in turn, caused the city to stagnate.

Revival: Medieval and Renaissance Cities

The low point of urban life in Europe was reached in the ninth century (Roebucks, 1974). Then, around the eleventh century, a general "awakening" began to take place. The reasons for this change, which occurred gradually over several centuries, are numerous and complex, but a general development of urban trade and crafts was a key factor.

The Crusades (armed marches by Christian European groups against the possessors of "The Holy Land," where, more often than not, the Europeans found ultimate defeat) took place between 1096 and 1291; they contributed to a rebirth of trade routes linking Europe and the Near East. Pirenne (1952) contends that the reopening of trade began bringing new ideas and products to cities in Europe by the twelfth century. Mumford (1961)

turns the argument around and suggests that trade rebounded as cities once again became effective "stepping stones" across Europe and Asia. In any event, the growth of local trade began stimulating the long-dormant urban division of labor.

The emergence of a complex and competitive commercial class at the center of this trade, dominated from the eleventh century onward by craft guilds, contributed to a newly vibrant city life. However, the merchants alone did not dominate these cities. Many groups—including the church, the landed gentry, and the feudal royalty—vied for position. Small and self-contained, medieval cities allowed no single focus to dominate urban life in the way the military and political elements had dominated Rome.

As for their populations, medieval cities were small—both in relation to Roman cities (many of which supported more than 100,000 people) and in comparison with the industrial cities that would follow them. Although a few cities such as Paris and Venice were much larger in area, the physical dimensions of most medieval cities also were modest. Cities typically occupied a few hundred acres, about the size of a small town of about 5,000 people today. Walls surrounding the cities often were supplemented by a moat, as shown in Figure 2–4. Major roads connected the city gates to the center of the city—generally the cathedral, the marketplace, or major buildings such as the guilds or town halls. Mumford (1961) suggests that if any one center was of greatest importance, it was the cathedral, often towering over the rest of the city. Indeed, the importance of the church to the social life of medieval Europe is difficult to exaggerate:

... to be fully functioning human beings both urban and rural medieval people had to be members of the Roman Catholic Church. Religious minorities, notably Jews, were recognized as being mostly outside the mainstream of society.... [The] Catholic Church was the one, largely unchallenged church. To be cast out from it was the ultimate rejection of society, for without its acceptance, an individual was a spiritual leper whose situation was in some ways worse than

FIGURE 2–4 The medieval city, circa 1350, developed on a new site in response to the needs and patterns of the new trading system and for defense. The site was chosen at the intersection of rivers and roads, a natural route center that offered plentiful water, natural defenses, and an ample food supply from the surrounding agrarian area of the valley. The city was a trading and commercial center; craft industries produced goods for trade and for exchange with farmers of the surrounding area who supplied food, as well as many of the items involved in long-distance trade. Movement within the city was mainly pedestrian, so narrow streets with many angles were not constricting. Some wider, more open streets allowed passage of horse traffic involved in long-distance trade.

1: Cathedral
2: Market plaza
3: Guildhalls, craft and trade centers
4: Fortress of local lord
5: Defensive walls with turrets at intervals
6: Moat outside defensive walls

Source: Janet Roebuck, *The Shaping of Urban Society,* pp. 48–49. Copyright © 1974 by Janet Roebuck.

that of a physical leper, who was at least allowed to receive charity. (Roebuck, 1974:57)

The medieval city did not produce the sense of awe and massive scale that mark the modern Western city. Other than the cathedral and perhaps a palace, there were no tall buildings, and streets were narrow and winding rather than wide and straight as they are today. Paving of streets, done on a large scale in Rome during the empire, did not become common in medieval European cities until the twelfth and thirteenth centuries. Houses typically were built together—in rowhouse fashion—often with open space for cultivation in the rear. Despite the lack of such conveniences as indoor plumbing, the small population and relatively low density of these cities allowed life to proceed under conditions far more healthful than those of many postindustrial tenements today (Mumford, 1961).

Social life also thrived. The late medieval city was a true community, as Lauro Martines observes in the Urban Living box on page 50.

These European cities grew gradually—not only in population and area, but also with a renewed idea of the human possibilities of the city. The period from the twelfth century until about the sixteenth century was an age of general urban rebirth, or renaissance. First evident in Italian city-states such as Venice, Florence, Palermo, and Milan, this rebirth is easily linked to the humanistic conception of city life that flourished some 1,500 years earlier in Athens. During the Renaissance, the city gradually recaptured an interest in art, literature, and architecture.

The Renaissance humanists saw learning as the path to human virtue, dignity, freedom, and happiness—to becoming a perfect human being. The vehicles for attaining these goals were interpersonal dialogue and the

The city of Carcassonne in France remains an outstanding example of a medieval walled city. Compare this picture to Figure 2–4. The local lord's fortress is on the right and the cathedral is slightly to the left and above it. Such cities were characteristic of Europe for nearly 1,000 years after the fall of Rome (479 C.E.).

possibilities offered by the city. Yet there was an irony in this vision. In actuality, it was a vision of the perfected upper-class person. Indeed, humanists and nobility alike spoke disdainfully of the uneducated "masses" that surrounded them.

Although once again the city generated the ideal of full human development, the real contradiction of the era was that it was an ideal that the great bulk of the city's citizens had little chance to realize. Wealth, for example, was highly concentrated. In Lyon, a French city, in 1545, over half the wealth belonged to a mere 10 percent of the population (Hohenberg and Lees, 1985:147).

THE SECOND URBAN REVOLUTION: THE RISE OF MODERN CITIES

Within the walls of the Renaissance city, the seeds of another type of city altogether were being sown. The old feudal power structure was breaking down, giving people more freedom to live their lives where they chose; trade was becoming more important, increasing the available wealth. Cities were gaining rapidly in prominence.

Throughout Europe, commerce slowly began to replace agriculture as the dominant mode of making a living. A new middle class

URBAN LIVING

The Little World of the Renaissance City

Life in the Italian walled-in city about 1300 went on in a tight world of personal relations and public settings. Gossip and rumor rippled back and forth across the warp and woof of close family ties, inherited family friendships and animosities, numerous street acquaintances and peripheral contacts that were endlessly being renewed. These relations were especially dense for the rich citizens in politics, because such bonds were multiplied and vitalized by property and influence. . . . The personal–public texture of life in the Italian commune [city] lies beyond anything in our experience, but we catch glimpses of that vanished reality in the age's lyric poetry, which teems with personal allusions . . . references to streets, direct discourse, and dedications to friends. . . .

The same people walked the same streets daily. There was mutual instant recognition. . . . Every neighbor had his or her particular identity associated with a trade, a name, a reputation, a clan or family. Strangers were immediately picked out in the streets and doubtless stared at. Births, marriages, and deaths were neighborhood events—for the common knowledge and feeling of all.

Source: Lauro Martines, *Power and Imagination: City-States in Renaissance Italy* (New York: Knopf, 1979), pp. 76, 78.

began to rise to power. This class—the bourgeoisie (the French word means, literally, "of the town")—was composed of shopkeepers, traders, bureaucrats, government officials, and people engaged in commercial ventures of all sorts. As wealth increased in the cities, they began to attract ever more people who hoped to share in the obvious material benefits of this process.

By the mid-seventeenth century, feudalism was all but dead, and with it went the last remnants of the rural-centered life of the Middle Ages. In its place stood capitalism, a mode of life fundamentally grounded in the trade possibilities offered by the city. By the eighteenth century, the Industrial Revolution had begun, a process that fueled even more strongly the dominance of the city-based market economy.

The change was striking: City populations everywhere exploded (see Table 2–1). If the first urban revolution took place when cities first appeared some 10,000 years before, the second urban revolution occurred from about 1650 on: Europe became a continent of cities.

The preindustrial era had been characterized by low-efficiency technology and primitive health care. Both birth and death rates were high. In other words, people typically had many children, but many did not live to maturity. Even for those who did, life expectancy was much lower than today (usually under 40 years). As a result, natural population growth (the difference between the birth and death rates) was slow and frequently checked by massive numbers of deaths occasioned by outbreaks of plague. The Looking Back box on page 52 provides one vivid example.

But plague did not wreak its vengeance forever. In time a larger portion of the urban population enjoyed more wealth, more efficient means of production, and better health and sanitation conditions. Death rates fell dramatically, while birth rates remained high: What population experts call a demographic transition was underway. A major population explosion began throughout Europe, primarily centered in the cities. Although much urban growth resulted from migration—that is, from people coming to the city from the countryside—natural population growth was also extremely high. Together, both forces began to produce cities with population sizes undreamed of in antiquity. Recall that Rome, at its peak, contained around a million people. London in 2002 (see Table 2–1) contained seven times that number.

In European and North American countries, the urban demographic transition continued well into this century. Recently, however, a rising standard of living—making more children for "productive purposes" unnecessary—and effective means of contraception have begun to halt the trend. In most industrial nations, population growth has slowed as both birth and death rates have continued to decline. The situation is not so hopeful in many other areas of the world, however. As will be made clear in later chapters, overpopulation produced by an even more powerful demographic transition continues to create incredible suffering and threatens to overwhelm many nations.

Part of that explosive population growth can be found in the evolution of megacities

—metropolitan areas with populations of 10 million or more. By 2015, the number of megacities will be 22, with 16 of them in developing countries, including some of the poorest nations in the world (see Table 2–2). These huge urban areas are filled both with danger signs of overwhelming problems and with great promise in the now-visible stirrings of self-reliance. In the twenty-first century we will learn which potential dominates.

To conclude this chapter, we turn to a case study focusing on London, a city that many consider, perhaps with Paris and Rome, the greatest of European urban centers. As we examine this city of kings, queens, Shakespeare, Dickens, and Churchill, we shall see reflected all the stages of urban development we have just discussed.

❖ CASE STUDY ❖
London—The History of a World City

When a man is tired of London, he is tired of life; for there is in London all that life can afford.

Dr. Samuel Johnson (1709–1784)

There are certain great cities, suggests British urban geographer Peter Hall (1979:1), in which a disproportionate part of the world's most important business is conducted. These are the "world cities," such as London.

For nearly a thousand years, London has been a focus of European urban life. It is one of the three or four most important economic centers of the world. Its metropolitan area has a population of more than 12 million people, and over 8 million foreign tourists besiege it each year. Despite this vitality, the city has problems. Even though tourism annually brings in over $3 billion, the time-honored image of a relatively sedate city is changing rapidly. Some Londoners feel the quality of life is being destroyed as a fleeing middle class and a growing impoverished class changes the city's texture. They see "too many" foreign-born who come to stay without

TABLE 2–1   Population of Selected European Cities, 1700–2002 (in thousands)

City	1700	1800	1900	2002
Amsterdam	172	201	510	720
Berlin	—	172	2,424	3,290
Hamburg	70	130	895	1,688
Lisbon	188	237	363	663
London	550	861	6,480	7,394
Madrid	110	169	539	2,905
Naples	207	430	563	1,067
Paris	530	547	3,330	2,113
Rome	149	153	487	2,650
Vienna	105	231	1,662	1,543

Source: Adapted from T. Chandler and G. Fox, *3000 Years of Urban History* (New York: Academic Press, 1974); *The World Gazetteer*, accessed online at *www.gazetteer.de* on July 21, 2002.

LOOKING BACK

The Black Plague

Black Plague was actually an organism, *Bacillus pestis*, transmitted most often by fleas carried by rodents such as rats. It is perhaps difficult for most of us to imagine the effect of so great a pestilence, which in the course of only two years after its outbreak in Italy in 1347 killed at least one-fourth of the European population. The loss of life was even greater in cities and towns. Langer (1973:106–107) notes that during the 1347 outbreak the population of Florence was cut in half—from 90,000 to 45,000—while in Hamburg the loss of life was greater still. The effects of this event, and of subsequent plagues that menaced Europe until the seventeenth century, can hardly be exaggerated. Even so, we find a rebounding of population after each attack, and cities continued to grow.

regard for traditions and customs, and who fill up hospital casualty wards, police stations, and magistrate's courts. Shoplifting, once a rare occurrence, is now a common problem. People urinate in the streets, dress strangely, and often behave rudely.

More seriously, the city lost over 1 million jobs in recent decades. In the 1990s London's economy was stronger, although an occupational bipolarization continues, with high unemployment among the less skilled and less educated, and increased demand and good pay for business professionals. Most of London's middle class, however, has moved to the suburbs, leaving the city bereft of its traditional tax base and increasingly polarized into a home for the very rich and the poor. As we saw in Mr. Gawber's reaction to his new neighbors (see Chapter 1 box, The City in Literature), tension between whites and minorities still exists, although not with the violent confrontations of the mid-1980s.

So London remains, as Dr. Johnson put it, a mix of "all that life can afford." Why? What forces are at work in making a city a world city? To answer this question, we need to look at London's history.

Beginnings: 55 B.C.E.–1066 C.E.

London's story begins with Rome and Julius Caesar. After his conquest of Gaul in the first century B.C.E., Caesar was told of a large island to the north that had important natural resources. His expedition to the island in 55 B.C.E. met with little success, however: He encountered fierce resistance from the local Celtic tribes, and so he retreated to Rome to enjoy his other victories. But he brought back with him knowledge of the island.

A hundred years later, in 43 C.E., the fifth Caesar, the emperor Claudius, conquered the island. Claudius set up his main encampment at the first point upstream on the River Thames (pronounced "tems"; see the Looking Back box on page 54) where a bridge could be built, thereby allowing access across the river by troops to the south. The place was called "Londinium" (meaning "wild" or "bold" place), after the Celtic name for the area. A deep-water port, London's site facilitated the shipment of goods into the heart of England. The Romans built major roads in all directions and enclosed the city within a wall for protection. By 60 C.E., London was thriving: The Roman historian Tacitus wrote that the city was "famed for commerce and crowded with traders."

The Romans remained for nearly 400 years. By the beginning of the fifth century, Roman rule was being challenged continually by the remnants of the Celtic tribes (who had long before been forced into the nether regions of the country: Cornwall, Wales, and Scotland) and by invading tribes from northern Europe. Eventually, the cost of maintaining the British Isles, combined with the necessity of protecting the parts of the empire closer to Rome itself, became too great, and the islands were abandoned in 410 C.E. Virtually all remnants of the Roman occupation, including the Roman remains in London, were destroyed with great relish by the reemergent tribes. Nevertheless, the Romans left two legacies crucial to London's later history: the established city and a superior road system that linked it with the hinterland.

From the time of the Roman retreat until the Norman Conquest in 1066, Britain came under a variety of political overlords. Different tribes—the original Celts, Danes, Angles, Saxons, and Vikings—vied for control of the island, gaining and losing it numerous times. To take but one example, in 1013 the Danes conquered the city, driving out the Saxon king, Ethelred. Ethelred formed an alliance with King Olaf of Norway and together they quickly reattacked the city. Knowing that London Bridge was the key to London's southern supply route, they attached ropes to its huge pilings and sailed downstream, pulling the bridge in their wake (hence the origin of the eleventh-century song "London Bridge Is Falling Down"). Following the Saxon–Norwegian takeover, the Danes returned in 1016 and again they took the city. This seesaw pattern was typical.

Despite changing political fortunes, London thrived. Eager to maintain their success, its merchants usually threw in with whoever was in power, thus maintaining and strengthening London's importance as the economic center of England.

TABLE 2–2 Population of the World's Megacities, in Millions

	2002	2015 (projected)
Buenos Aires	13.0	13.0
Bombay, India	12.1	26.2
Seoul	11.2	13.0
Jakarta, Indonesia	10.8	13.9
Karachi, Pakistan	10.3	19.4
Manila	10.1	14.7
São Paolo, Brazil	10.1	20.3
Delhi, India	10.0	16.9
Metro Manila	9.9	12.6
Istanbul	9.2	12.3
Shanghai	9.0	18.0
Mexico City	8.7	19.2
Dhaka, Bangladesh	8.5	19.5
Moscow	8.4	9.3
Tokyo	8.2	28.9
New York City	8.0	17.6
Lagos, Nigeria	8.0	24.6
Cairo, Egypt	7.8	14.4
Tehran, Iran	7.7	10.3
Lima, Peru	7.6	9.4
London	7.4	7.6
Beijing	7.1	15.6
Bogota, Colombia	6.7	8.0
Kinshasa, Congo	6.3	9.4
Rio de Janeiro	6.0	11.9

Based on defined city borders.

Source: The World Gazetteer, accessed online at *www.gazetteer.de* on March 2, 2003.

The Medieval City: 1066–1550

The year 1066 brought political stability. The Norman invader, William the Conqueror, defeated the Saxon king, Harold, in the Battle of Hastings and marched on London. Finding the city well fortified and recognizing the vital importance of the trade connections it maintained elsewhere, William attacked the community of Southwark (pronounced "sutherk") at the opposite end of London Bridge. Leaving a standing army, he took the remainder of his forces to the smaller, less protected cities to the west and north. These

LOOKING BACK

"te Temmes"

accent

Why are the spelling and the pronunciation of London's river so different? Helene Hanff was offered this possible explanation:

Driving back to London we passed a village called Thame—pronounced as spelled, like "same" with a lisp—and the Colonel told me why the Thames is pronounced

Temmes. Seems the first Hanover king [George I] had a thick German accent and couldn't pronounce th. He called the river "te Temmes" and since the-king-is-always-right, everybody else had to call it the Temmes and it's been the Temmes ever since.

Source: Helene Hanff, *The Duchess of Bloomsbury Street* (New York: Avon, 1973), p. 75.

---

he systematically destroyed (ravaged might be a better word), always sending back news of his conquests. The message to Londoners was all too clear: Surrender or face utter devastation. Londoners opened the gates of the city and welcomed William as their king. Without a shot fired, William had gained his prize. By not sacking the city, William not only gained access to virtually all its wealth but also ensured that the city would be able to produce more wealth in the future. Slaughtered merchants trade with no one.

Twenty-five years before William's conquest, the Saxon king, Edward the Confessor, a devout Christian, had decided to build a great abbey west of the original City of London, around a sharp bend in the Thames. (Technically, then as today, the "City of London" is the original one-square-mile area encompassed by the Roman walls.) It was in this abbey, called Westminster (literally, "the church in the west"), that William chose to have himself crowned king of all England. He then took up residence in the nearby palace that had been constructed by Edward.

The site of William's coronation and residence was critical to the history of London for three reasons. First, an important political residence was established in the immediate vicinity of the financial capital, giving London the power of a "double magnet" as both a financial center and a political center. Second, the establishment of the City of Westminster to the west of the City of London meant that the land between would be filled with incoming people, thus "dragging" greater London in a westward sprawl out of the original Roman walled city. Third, the establishment of the royal residence in London inextricably tied London's local history to the nation's history. Henceforth, the history of London would be, to a large degree, part of the history of England.

For five and a half centuries, medieval London grew steadily. Nevertheless, it was an out-of-the-way place, an important, but not major, European city. This changed radically with the onset of world exploration. By 1550 London had become a world city.

The World City Emerges: 1550–1800

There are three reasons for the transformation of London. First, with the discovery of the Americas, London suddenly became a stop "on the way" for most northern European expeditions heading west to the Americas. It thus became a place where goods could be unloaded conveniently and transferred to the ships of other nations or processed in some manner for reshipment.

Second, because of its geographic isolation from the rest of Europe and the paucity of its natural resources, England became a seafaring nation, with the world's most efficient sailing fleet. Third, there was wool. Isolated from war-ravaged Europe for centuries, England was able to produce more of this precious material than any other country. With wool in ever-increasing demand, London quickly became the port where by far the largest proportion of the world's wool was traded, and London merchants established a virtual monopoly.

As a result of all these factors, London exploded in population, wealth, power, and influence. By the mid-1500s, the English Renaissance—comparable to those of Florence and Venice—had begun. Not only did commerce thrive; so did art, literature, music, and drama. It was the era of Henry VIII, Sir Thomas More, Elizabeth I, Roger Bacon, Sir Walter Raleigh, and, of course, Shakespeare.

Shakespeare, in fact, is a marvelous example of a city's nourishing effect on human creativity. In the late 1500s, Shakespeare arrived in London—the only place where serious dramatists could have their work produced. There he found patrons and competitors who pushed him to his peak. All his greatest work was written in London. As Oscar Wilde, the great nineteenth-century poet and playwright, put it, "Town life nourishes and perfects all the more civilized elements in man. . . . Shakespeare wrote nothing but doggerel lampoon before he came to London and never penned a line after he left."

It is important to see the link between a thriving city and the advance of cultural ideas. First, a dynamic city draws to it people from different backgrounds. As the population grows, the possibilities of permutations and combinations of ideas and lifestyles become legion. Second, a thriving city is usually a wealthy city, and there has been a very intimate historical link between wealth and

the development of cultural ideas. Simply, wealth supports leisure. Creative artists with wealthy patrons or buyers for their work can literally afford to develop their art in ways that would be impossible if leisure time were not available. In addition, the rich demand drama, architecture, and music, thereby enhancing the creative arts in another way.

People came to Renaissance London in droves. In 1500 the city was home to 75,000 people. By 1600 that number had nearly tripled to 220,000; by 1650 it had doubled again to over 450,000.

But London had no plan for accommodating these huge numbers of people. Housing became scarce and overcrowded, streets virtually impassable. The water became polluted, as—not surprisingly—did the streets themselves. As one historian notes:

> A whole network of officials, from the mayor down to the four [officials] attached to each ward, were continuously battling with the problems of street cleaning. People like William Ward, who caused great nuisance and discomfort to his neighbors by throwing out horrible filth onto the highway, the stench of which was so odious that none of his neighbors could remain in their shops, were prosecuted as public menaces. Many people defied regulations and simply emptied their slops into the street, or, like one ingenious fellow, piped them into the cellar of a neighbor. (Gray, 1978:133–34)

Then, in a single year, the city was hit twice by catastrophe. The first was directly connected with the unsanitary conditions we have just described. The Black Plague had visited London before, but as the Looking Back box suggests, never with the virulence of the epidemic of 1665–1666. The population of the city was nearly halved; more than 100,000 people died in the space of eight months.

Just as the city was beginning to recover, on the evening of September 2, 1666, someone upset a wood stove in Pudding Lane and the entire square-mile area of the original City of London burned to the ground in four days. The next Looking Back box on page 57 takes a closer look at the devastation of this London fire.

LOOKING BACK

The Great Plague of London, 1665–1666

There was no one way of dying. Some simply became sleepy and never woke up. The less fortunate endured an agonizing series of symptoms—shivering, violent vomiting, searing headache, fever and delirium—from which death came as a merciful deliverance. The . . . swellings, appeared in the groin and under the arms. Only if these tumours burst and let forth their evil might the stricken recover, but victims were driven crazy by the pain involved in lancing their sores. . . . [O]ne sign, a rash over the whole body, was regarded as a certain indication of approaching death, even though the patient was sometimes feeling perfectly well when he or she first noticed it. "The tokens," as these spots were called, are commemorated in what has now become an innocent children's rhyme:

Ring a ring a Roses,
A pocketful of posies,
'Tishoo, 'tishoo
We all fall down.

"A pocketful of posies" refers to the herbs people used to carry in order to ward off the plague. Sometimes the healthy were smuggled away from under the eyes of . . . watchmen, but doors marked with red crosses could only legally be opened to remove corpses on to the carts which trundled out at the dead of night to the pits. . . . There were gruesome stories about these carts; the drivers might fall dead on the way, leaving the horses to plunge where they would with their dreadful cargo, or to stand stock still in the streets awaiting discovery at dawn. It was all the town could manage to bury its dead.

Source: Robert Gray, *A History of London* (London: Hutchinson, 1978), pp. 170–71.

But, like the mythical phoenix, London rose from its own flames. Less than 40 years later, in 1700, the London area had a population of over half a million people and the city had been entirely, even spectacularly, rebuilt. It was more powerful than ever. By 1750 the population had grown to over 675,000; by 1800 it was nearly 900,000, almost twice the size of Paris.

Industrialization and Colonization: 1800–1900

The onset of the Industrial Revolution in the late 1700s spurred the growth of London as never before. London was already the center of British trade; what the city did not produce, it shipped; what it did not ship was simply not available for human consumption. To fuel its voracious industrial machine, England needed cheap raw materials in huge portions. Unable to supply all these materials itself, England, like many European nations of the period, colonized much of the globe as quickly as possible. Thus grew the British Empire, on which the sun never set and which, from its center in London, controlled the destinies of a quarter of the earth's population.

To accommodate the burgeoning empire and its industry, the city grew immensely. The docks expanded and provided huge numbers of jobs in the East End; the government civil service expanded to oversee the

LOOKING BACK

The Citty in Dreadfull Flames, 1666

This fatal night about ten, began that deplorable fire . . . in London.

After dinner I took coach with my wife and son and went to the Bank side in Southwark, where we beheld the dismal spectacle, the whole Citty in dreadfull flames neare the waterside. The fire having continu'd all . . . night (if I may call that night which was light as day for ten miles round about, after a dreadfull manner). . . . The conflagration was so universal, and the people so astonish'd, that from the beginning, I know not by what despondency of fate, they hardly stirr'd to quench it, so that there was nothing heard or seen but crying out and lamentation, running about like distracted creatures, without at all attempting to save even their goods. . . . Oh the miserable and calamitous spectacle! . . . God grant mine eyes may never behold the like, who now saw above 10,000 houses all in one flame; the noise and crackling and thunder of the impetuous flames, the shrieking of women and children, the hurry of people, the fall of Towers, Houses and Churches, was like an hideous storme, and the aire all about so hot and inflam'd that at the last one was not able to approach it, so that they were forc'd to stand still and let the flames burn on, which they did for neere two miles in length and one in bredth. . . . Thus I left it this afternoone burning, a resemblance of Sodom, or the last day. London was, but is no more!

Source: John Evelyn, *Diary*, 1666.

empire; growing industry provided still more jobs. London became like a huge, expanding mouth, swallowing up people by the millions. Nineteenth-century reformer William Cobbett called the city "The Great Wen" (literally, a tumorous cyst). By 1861 the population of London had risen to nearly 3 million. By 1901, the figure was almost 6.5 million. London's population had increased by more than 3 million in less than 50 years.

The city developed a level of poverty among millions of its residents that was unlike anything experienced before. Many—including Charles Dickens, Karl Marx, and Friedrich Engels—have described the suffering of the poor in nineteenth-century London, but few capture it as well as the French illustrator Gustave Doré, whose drawing accompanies this discussion.

The Modern Era: 1900 to the Present

After 1900, life improved. World War I united the country against a common enemy, and, ironically, the Great Depression of the 1930s helped equalize the suffering, as it cut the economic bottom out from under the country's middle and upper-middle classes. Then, in 1940, much of the city was destroyed once again. This time the culprit was Adolf Hitler's *Luftwaffe.*

Having overrun Europe in the late 1930s, Hitler believed that England was the key to toppling Western morale. He sought to destroy London's productive capacity, demoralize the population, and weaken England's will to resist. The first objective was largely accomplished; as the next Looking Back box on

The Industrial Revolution brought a tide of urban migrants by the millions to cities such as London. Misery and despair, a life of squalor living in unbelievable slum conditions, were the lot of many, as poignantly shown in this picture of London's Harrow Alley, drawn by French artist Gustav Doré in the 1870s.

page 59 explains, the second and third were never even approached.

After the war, the city regenerated itself once more. Rebuilt offices in the devastated city boomed, tourists came by the millions; and yet, much was lost in the war. The docklands and many of the factories were never repaired, and thousands of jobs were lost; the empire disappeared, and with it the immense wealth that made the city grow; more and more industry moved out of town.

Throughout most of the postwar period until the 1980s, Great Britain followed socialist policies to ensure basic housing, food, and medical services for all. Then—beset by a recession, high inflation, and burdensome government costs—voters elected a conservative government that embarked on a dismantling of Britain's socialist practices. Part of that effort was the elimination of the Greater London Council, which was responsible for maintaining the infrastructure of the London metropolitan area.

As the first city to develop an infrastructure able to sustain millions of people living and working in a relatively confined area, London can rightly be called the "mother of the modern megacity." That infrastructure—including water, gas and electricity supplies, sewage and waste disposal systems, an underground and suburban railway network—has since been copied by other large cities worldwide. However, although it was once a forerunner in creating a livable, modern metropolis, today London is lagging behind other world cities in managing and sustaining itself to meet the daily demands placed on it. With no coordinating administration to maintain the metropolitan infrastructure—especially in such environmental areas as air pollution and waste disposal—parochial interests so far have worked against an overall ecological policy (Girardet, 1994:12).

Race riots in the city's Brixton district in 1981 and 1985 demonstrated that its social fabric, as well, was unraveling. Londoners began to fear that the city had lost its ability to integrate diverse elements of society and survive social upheaval without shattering into fragments, a fear many still hold today (Porter, 1994).

Long-term unemployment was virtually unknown in London until the 1960s, when massive commonwealth immigration brought racial–ethnic minorities into the city's inner-city districts. Londoners such as Roy Porter (1994) viewed these areas as decaying and dangerous, filled with an emerging outcast group poorly integrated into the ties of workplace and neighborhood as unemployment remains two to three times above the city average. With an increase in crime and violence and a decrease in social services, many think London's future lies between dismal and dire. Commerce no longer serves as a unifying

LOOKING BACK

The Battle of Britain

From 7 September until 3 November 1940 London was attacked every night but one. . . . If the intention had been to stun the population into submission the bombardment proved entirely counterproductive. . . . Far from turning into gibbering neurotic wrecks in line with psychiatric predictions, Londoners actually began to shed their neuroses. Not only did total strangers risk their lives for one another; they even managed to talk to each other. As long as the bombs fell, all those nice distinctions of class and status which the English are wont to measure so carefully before committing themselves to anything as daring as a "Good morning" were swept aside. . . .

There is a photograph of St. Paul's rising unscathed above the smoke and fire which movingly symbolizes the town's indestructible spirit. Anyone in search of a miracle could do worse than ponder the survival of St. Paul's. Nearly all buildings around the cathedral [were] annihilated. . . . But the great church did not fall. Just what it meant to Londoners was movingly expressed by a woman from Bethnal Green who recorded her memories of 29 December 1940 thus: "I went up on the roof with some of the firemen, to look at the City. And I've always remembered how I was choked, I think I was crying a little. I could see St. Paul's standing there, and the fire all around, and I just said: Please God, don't let it go. I couldn't help it, I felt that if St. Paul's had gone, something would have gone from us. But it stood in defiance, it did. "

Source: Robert Gray, *A History of London* (London: Hutchinson, 1978), pp. 309–12.

---

force, and poor areas are becoming urban ghettos.

London's problems mirror those of many U.S. and other world cities, and its plight worries many Londoners: Homelessness, single-parent families, the isolation of the old, classroom violence, joblessness, rising crime, poverty, drug-dealing, neo-Nazi racial attacks—all these now-familiar troubles foretell alienation, antisocial behaviour and despair. Poverty and deprivation deepen, and fears rise of the emergence of a new, permanent underclass, resented by the rest, reinforcing polarisation. . . . As the able and the aspirant leave, quitting Greater London for cleaner, greener pastures elsewhere, the capital is being saddled with a disproportionate population of problem people—resource consumers rather than producers: the old, sick and disabled, broken and lone-parent families, the chronic unemployed, children in care, alcoholics, addicts, new immigrants (some illegal) and derelicts. (Porter, 1994:30)

In analyzing occupational and housing improvements in London in the 1970s and 1980s, Peter Congdon (1995) offered a more optimistic view. While acknowledging the city's problems, he also found a revitalization underway:

The continuing growth of financial, business and information services in the central city, and their deregulation in the 1980s, increased demand for . . . higher-income professional and managerial workers as a proportion of the London workforce. Despite the recent rise in regional unemployment [the city experienced] an improvement in average prosperity exceeding the national average. (Congdon, 1995:523)

London effectively blends its past and present, its modern buildings serving as a backdrop to the 11th-century Tower of London and complex along the Thames River. The city continues successfully to modernize to remain competitive, but its rich traditions and charm of bygone years remain an important part of London and are major attractions for millions of visitors each year.

Seven years later, mixed trends still were evident. *The Economist* reported that, in the second quarter of 2002, commercial property construction surpassed the previous peak reached in 1990. Yet, despite the fact that "cranes interrupt London's skyline in every direction," the demand for new office space was faltering by midsummer 2002.

Meanwhile, the construction of new private housing, partly in planned developments such as London Docklands, attracted higher-income groups. Continuing loss of manufacturing and of employment opportunities for the unskilled resulted in increased income inequality among Londoners. Also, despite new public housing for some lower-income city residents, a reduced municipal housing building program resulted in lengthening waiting lists for housing and rising homelessness, even as high-cost owner-occupied housing expanded elsewhere in London (Congdon, 1995:525).

Thus, even as London improves, the lower strata of its population are not necessarily better off.

Perhaps Dr. Johnson was right after all. With several trends occurring simultaneously, there is no one portrait of this city. London in the modern era is still as it was in Johnson's day: a world city that inevitably contains "all that life can afford."

❖ ═══════ ❖ ═══════ ❖

SUMMARY

Cities have been with us for 10,000 years. They began after the last Ice Age in favorable ecological settings in many areas of the world. Slowly and tentatively they established themselves, fueled by a surplus of goods and materials, whether developed by agriculture, trade, or military dominance. As they grew, they evolved a complex social structure—most particularly, a specialized division of labor and a hierarchical power structure. All these elements allowed cities, in time, to increase their dominance in human affairs. Thus began the first urban revolution.

The earliest cities, such as Jericho and Catal Hüyük, were scattered, independent units, often linked by trade but not much more. Sometime after 4000 B.C.E., however, the first urban empires began to appear. In Mesopotamia and later in Egypt, China, the Indus River Valley, and the Americas, systems of cities emerged. These became not only centers of culture but centers of regional domination as well. This link between city and empire was a central factor in the development of civilization for nearly 5,000 years. Urban empires pulled into their sphere diverse peoples, ideas, and great wealth and power. This was as true of Teotihuacan in North America as it was of Egypt in the Middle East.

Early Western civilization also centered around its cities—first those of Greece and then those of the Roman Empire. When the latter finally crumbled in the late fifth century C.E., most of the other cities of Europe—outposts in the Roman chain—lost their reason for being. The next 500 years—roughly from 500 to 1000 C.E.—were a decidedly anti-urban period. Many cities disappeared entirely. The few that managed to survive limped along, shadows of what they had been.

In the first few centuries of the second millennium C.E., a halting urban revival began. Slowly trade began to revive and the old feudal system began to break down as a new merchant class gained power. This revival reached its peak between 1400 and 1600 with the evolution of the Renaissance cities—most effectively symbolized by the Italian city-states of Florence, Venice, and Milan.

Then, around 1600, a turning point was reached. The old feudal social order was weakened beyond repair, and the merchant class, generating greater wealth through increasingly successful business ventures, began to control urban life throughout Europe. Seeing

new possibilities for a better life in material terms, people streamed into cities all over the continent. This influx, coupled with technological improvement and advances in health and sanitation services, created what is known as a demographic transition. Europe generally, but cities especially, exploded in population as death rates plummeted, birth rates stayed high, and migrants arrived by the millions. From 1650 on, cities—many huge in population and dominance—began sprouting all over Europe and in North America. This was the second urban revolution, spurred on primarily by the twin engines of capitalism and industrialization.

Today, cities exist in the farthest reaches of the globe. In many cases the growth of cities created immense problems and widespread suffering amid successes. Now, in areas of the world where the urban demographic transition first occurred (notably Europe and North America), urban growth has slowed dramatically. Unhappily, in other areas—as Chapter 13 explains—it has not.

Our case study of London illustrates, in the life of a single city, nearly all of these processes. London began as an outpost of the Roman Empire, achieved initial success, and then, with the Roman retreat in 410, fell into its own dark age—unheard of for centuries and the object of multiple invasions. It began to recover after the victory of William the Conqueror in 1066. For five centuries it built its prominence as the center of British life and, around 1600, blossomed into one of the greatest Renaissance cities in history. Its success was linked primarily to international trade. Through the next two centuries London grew and gained even greater control of world markets. Then, with the Industrial Revolution and intensive British colonization in the nineteenth and early twentieth centuries, the city exploded in population, undergoing a major demographic transition. Despite its incredible wealth-generating capacity, London has had massive problems that it has carried into this century. It now faces, as do many Western industrial cities, a future of declining population and industrial capacity.

CONCLUSION

The emergence of cities as a dominant force in human affairs is one of the crucial events of history. In many instances, cities have been the driving wheel behind the development of civilization. They have combined ideas in new ways, produced great wealth, wielded incredible power (often injudiciously and inhumanely), and become home to an increasing proportion of the world's population.

Yet, throughout history, cities have not always had the same character. As we suggested at the opening of this chapter, the city is largely synonymous with civilization itself. Each chapter in the story of human civilization has thus brought distinctive cities: cities of the early empires, the medieval city, the Renaissance city, and, most recently, the industrial-capitalist city.

Thus, there is both a constancy and a flux to city history. Together, these processes create urban living. We shall see both clearly evident again as we consider the development of North American cities in the next chapter.

CHAPTER 3

THE DEVELOPMENT
OF NORTH AMERICAN CITIES

Come hither, and I will show you an admirable
Spectacle! 'Tis a Heavenly CITY. . . . A CITY
to be inhabited by an Innumerable Company
of Angels, and by the Spirits of Just Men. . . .
Put on thy beautiful garments, O America, the
Holy City!

Cotton Mather,
seventeenth-century preacher

American urban history began with the small
town—five villages hacked out of the wilderness . . . each an "upstart" town with no past,
an uncertain future, and a host of confound-
ing and novel problems.

Alexander B. Callow, Jr. (1982)

To the visitor from London, the cities of
North America may seem to lack the rich texture that accumulates over centuries of history. In no city of North America, for example,
does a single building rival in age the Tower
of London—whose foundations were erected
in the eleventh century during the reign of
William the Conqueror. Even the current
Houses of Parliament and Buckingham
Palace—relative newcomers on the London
scene dating from the mid-nineteenth century—are older than all but a few urban structures in the United States and Canada.
Indeed, throughout Europe and much of the
non-Western world, one can find abundant
examples of exquisite old architecture that
suggests a vibrant, urban past that long pre-
dates the founding of Canada and the United
States.

However, if the cities of North America are
rather recent developments in the course of
world urban history, they have a fascinating
history of their own, spanning over 370 years.
This chapter examines this urban history from
the earliest settlements on the Atlantic coast,
literally "hacked out of the wilderness," to the
massive metropolitan regions of the new century, which contain more than 200 million
North Americans.

The first European settlements in North
America were founded in the early seventeenth century at the time when the medieval
city in Europe was being transformed by
industrialization. Perhaps not surprisingly,

the New World cities were founded specifically as trade- and wealth-generating centers to
fuel the growth of cities across the Atlantic in
Europe. The forces of postmedieval culture—
commercial trade and, shortly thereafter, industrial production—were the primary
shapers of urban settlement in the United
States and Canada. These cities, like the new
nations themselves, began with the greatest of
hopes. Cotton Mather was so enamored of the
idea of the city that he saw its growth as the
fulfillment of the biblical promise of a heavenly setting here on earth. Has that promise
been realized? To find out, this chapter examines the development of urban North America in terms of four phases:

1. *The Colonial Era.* This was the preindustrial
   period extending from the first settlements
   in the early 1600s to just after the ceding of
   Quebec to England and the U.S. Revolutionary War.
2. *The Era of Early Urban Growth and Westward
   Expansion.* Lasting from about 1800 to 1870,
   this transitional period saw the shift from an
   agricultural and trade-based way of life to an
   industrial economy.
3. *The Era of the Great Metropolis.* Running from
   1870 to 1950, this was the period of full
   industrialization.
4. *The Modern Era.* Extending from 1950 to the
   present, this has been a period of emerging urban regionalism and a postindustrial
   economy.

THE COLONIAL ERA: 1600–1800

If one could return to the North America of
the late sixteenth century, the only human
populations one would find would be those
of indigenous groups that Europeans dubbed
"Indians." These groups lived in many small
societies spread across the continent. Some,
such as the Cheyenne and the Sioux of the
western plains, were nomadic; others, like
the Hopi and the Navajo tribes of Arizona
and New Mexico, and the eastern Iroquois,
maintained seasonal or permanent settlements of up to 500 people.

Some cultures from Central America and Mexico (discussed in the last chapter) apparently spread into North America from the Southwest, moving as far east as the state of Mississippi. One such group was the Natchez, who lived in permanent settlements of perhaps 1,000 people and had considerable diversity and specialization of occupations, including priests and artisans. Until the Europeans arrived, the Natchez probably were the most "urban" people on the continent.

Beginnings

Although the Spanish founded St. Augustine in Florida in 1565, this settlement never became much more than an outpost. The seventeenth century, however, began a far-reaching transformation. The English settled in Jamestown, Virginia, in 1607. Jamestown, like St. Augustine, long remained little more than a village, but it established a pattern: There was a continent to be exploited. As word of successful British settlement in North America spread, more northern Europeans dared the dangerous voyage across the Atlantic. In 1620 the Puritans arrived in Massachusetts and established the Plymouth Colony. By 1630 some of their number had moved a few miles to the north, to a site with a fine harbor, and established the city of Boston. (The potential of a good river or seaport was a principal reason most cities were founded where they were.) In 1639 a group breaking away from the strict Puritanism of Boston founded the town of Newport in present-day Rhode Island. In 1624, the Dutch arrived at the tip of Manhattan Island and named their town New Amsterdam. By 1664, New Amsterdam had been ceded to the British and was named New York after King Charles II's brother James, the Duke of York.

Soon after, two more urban settlements joined the New World list. In 1680, the English established Charles Town (Charleston) on the eastern shore of what later would be the state of South Carolina. So impressed were they with this site that early Charlestonians boasted that the Ashley and Cooper

Rivers met at Charleston to form the Atlantic Ocean! Also impressive was the town founded by William Penn, leader of the Quaker religious group, at the point of junction of the Schuylkill and Delaware Rivers. In 1682 Penn christened it his City of Brotherly Love—Philadelphia.

Quebec city's European roots date to its founding in 1608 by Samuel de Champlain, making it the oldest city in Canada. Montreal—destined along with New York and San Francisco to become one of North America's most cosmopolitan cities—traces its European beginnings to 1642, when Paul de Chomedey established a settlement there that included dwellings, a chapel, a hospital, and separate schools for boys and girls, all within a protective stockade. Toronto, site of small French forts in the early eighteenth century, had a later start as a city. In 1793, Colonel John Simcoe, lieutenant governor of Upper Canada, selected the site as his capital because of its fine harbor, its strategic location for defense and trade, and the rich potential of its wilderness hinterland.

The Character of the Early Cities

These were the beginnings. With the exception of Newport (eclipsed in prominence by Providence in the nineteenth century), all of these settlements became important North American cities. During their earliest stages, however, they were so different from the cities we know today that they would appear virtually unrecognizable were we to visit them.

To begin with, they were exceptionally small, both in physical size and in population. New Amsterdam, for example, occupied only the southernmost tip of Manhattan Island, a far cry from the huge, five-borough City of New York that was incorporated in 1898. As for population, until the eighteenth century, neither New Amsterdam nor any of the other urban settlements of North America had populations approaching even 10,000. Not until the Revolutionary War did any of these places begin to develop the population sizes we associate with a city today.

Second, the small size of these settlements and the common ethnic and religious background of most of their population resulted in a very personalized urban existence. The town's inhabitants experienced a social life that was, in a real sense, collective, continually interacting with one another throughout their lives. Community life remained cohesive, as adults had daily contact with neighbors and other townsfolk during the week and expected to see one another each Sunday at church.

Third, the building patterns of early towns were unlike those common today. Boston was "one story structures, covered with thatch, and flung at random over the peninsula" (Bridenbaugh, 1964:9). The lack of regular street patterns in early Boston and New York gave both settlements the look of medieval towns. Even today that original pattern can be observed: Both central Boston and Manhattan below 14th Street still retain their initial pattern of irregular streets. Furthermore,

hard-surfaced streets were not commonly found in the United States until well into the eighteenth and nineteenth centuries. Only Philadelphia, settled half a century later than the others, was built from the beginning on the more familiar grid system now found in many North American cities (see Chapter 7, Figure 7–3).

Although many of these cities were founded as religious havens and had a medieval feel to them, such qualities were deceptive. Beneath the surface they were part and parcel of the change that was sweeping European urban civilization: They were unabashed trading centers bent on profit and growth. New Amsterdam was probably the most clearly commercial, but Puritan Boston and Quaker Philadelphia were no slackers when it came to money-making. The Looking Back box on page 67 shows how vigorously founder William Penn promoted his town of Philadelphia in a 1684 prospectus.

North America preindustrial cities were bustling port cities of commerce. Their concentrations of people and multitude of activities impressed visitors then, but they contained only about 5 percent of the total population. Not until the nineteenth century did any reach today's minimum standard of 100,000 for large cities, as this 1830's view of New York's Broadway suggests.

BROADWAY. NEW-YORK.

LOOKING BACK

Town Lots in Philadelphia: A Good Investment in 1684

Philadelphia . . . our intended Metropolis . . . is two Miles long, and a Mile broad, and at each end . . . upon a Navigable River. . . . From [August 1683 to August 1684] . . . the Town advanced [from 80] to Three hundred and fifty-seven Houses; divers of them large, well-built, with good Cellars, three stories, and some with Balconies. . . . There is also a fair [dock] of about three hundred foot square . . . to which a ship of five hundred Tuns may lay her broadside. . . . There inhabits most sorts of useful Tradesmen, As Carpenters, Joyners, Bricklayers, Masons, Plasterers, Plumers, Smiths, Glasiers, Taylers, Shoemakers, Butchers, Bakers, Brewers, Glovers, Tanners, Felmongers, Wheelrights, Millrights, Shiprights, Boatrights, Ropemakers, Saylmakers, Blockmakers, Turners, etc. . . .

There are Two Markets every Week, and Two Fairs every year. . . . Some Vessels have been here Built, and many Boats; and by that means a ready Conveniency for Passage of People and Goods. . . . The Town is well furnish'd with convenient Mills. . . . The Improvement of the place is best measur'd by the advance of Value upon every man's lot. . . . the worst Lot in the Town, without any Improvement upon it, is worth four times than it was when it was lay'd out. . . .

Source: William Penn, cited in Bayrd Still, *Urban America* (Boston: Little, Brown, 1974), pp. 16–17.

The underlying concept of all these cities was that they would serve as export centers for colonial raw materials going to the European home country. Boston, for example, supplied lumber for the ships of the British Royal Navy; for its part, Charles Town (Charleston) shipped rice and indigo back to the British Isles; New York and Montreal served as bases for the lucrative fur trade.

As time wore on, however, U.S. cities, distant from England geographically, became more and more independent. Colonial merchants began to compete with the British and established separate trade agreements with the West Indies and even with Europe. Enterprising craftspeople produced goods for local consumption equal in quality to those imported from England. On the civic front, more and more city governments, technically responsible to their "home offices" in Europe, found reason to cave in to local demands for more freedom in trade.

Through all this the cities prospered, attracting more and more diverse people. Although Boston was able to maintain its Puritan stamp for a time, New York attracted Germans, Jews, and Swedes; Philadelphia absorbed significant numbers of Germans, Irish, Welsh, and Dutch; and Charleston became home to groups of French Huguenots and Scots (Parrillo, 1996:40).

When Quebec was ceded to Britain in 1763, about 60,000 people—practically all of them Canadian-born French descendants—lived in the region. Ontario in the late eighteenth century was home to a comparable number of people, most of them from the United States, who were British loyalists, frontier farmers, and Quakers and Mennonites from Pennsylvania.

Many newcomers to the United States moved inland as the eighteenth century progressed, and numerous new, secondary cities, such as New Haven and Baltimore, were established. Although only a small fraction of the population lived in towns, an urban society was emerging along the eastern shore of what soon would become a new nation. By the late 1760s, the 13 colonies had at least 12 major cities and a total population (city and hinterland) of 2 million English, half a million of other European backgrounds, and nearly 400,000 slaves, almost all of whom were in the South (Parrillo, 1996:41–45). The major cities were rapidly losing their "backwater" status.

The Revolutionary War Era

Just as the events of the French Revolution centered on Paris, many significant events of the American Revolutionary era unfolded in cities. Most prominent were the Boston Massacre (1770), the Boston Tea Party (1773), the Philadelphia meetings of the Continental Congress (1774 and 1775), and the Constitutional Convention in Philadelphia (1787). In November 1775, American revolutionary forces occupied Montreal, but they withdrew the following spring after an unsuccessful siege of Quebec city by Benedict Arnold's troops; this failure ended efforts to secure Canada for the newly forming United States.

Although the struggle for U.S. independence did not take place entirely in cities, it was in many ways a city-instigated war. The bulk of the economic trade of the colonies was carried out in its cities. American merchants and colonists wanted freedom to pursue their life's interests as they saw fit, and in most cases economic interests were uppermost in their minds. The growth and development of the northern seaport towns generated numerous changes that affected labor relations, the distribution of wealth, the restructuring of social groups, and the emergence of the laboring class into the political arena. As historian Gary B. Nash (1979:383) notes,

This led, as the Revolution approached, to the rise of a radical consciousness among many and to an interplay between calls for internal reform and insurgency against external forces that adversely affected the lives of city people.

After the war, leadership of the new nation continued to be urban centered. New York became the first capital in 1789, and Philadelphia took over the title in 1790.

Despite this urban dominance, however, most of the population was not urban at this point. When the first census was completed in 1790, only 5 percent resided in urban places (places with 2,500 or more persons), and only 24 such places existed. Philadelphia was the largest settlement, with a population of only 42,000.

If the first phase of the urban history of the United States was marked by the establishment of a chain of important urban settlements on the East Coast, the next phase revealed a dramatic shifting of attention westward as the new nation began an expansion that, before the middle of the nineteenth century, would reach the Pacific Ocean.

GROWTH AND EXPANSION: 1800–1870

At the outbreak of the Revolutionary War, the western frontier of the northern colonies extended barely past the Hudson River, and the southern colonies reached outward only to the Appalachian Mountains. By the time the war was over, the territory of the United States extended roughly to the Mississippi River. The tremendous economic potential of this new region captured the interest of business leaders in established cities and, by the early decades of the nineteenth century, plans were under way to link the new territories with cities in the East. All this was decidedly competitive, as Constance Green notes:

The . . . Atlantic port cities were . . . increasingly aware that whoever captured the bulk of the Ohio valley trade would prosper at the expense of all other competitors. (1957:36)

The first of these links westward was established in 1818: The National Road (now

Interstate 40) was built, pushing through the Appalachians from the city of Baltimore. This trade route, along with Baltimore's large shipbuilding industry, caused that city to grow in size and wealth. Philadelphia attempted to keep pace, opening both canal and turnpike routes west, although with more modest success. Not to be outdone, New York opened the Erie Canal in 1825. Although it was not fully recognized at the time, the canal was to be the key to New York's increasing dominance over East Coast urban trade in the mid-nineteenth century. By cutting across upstate New York from the Hudson, the canal opened a water route to the entire Great Lakes region and much of Canada. Undaunted, Baltimore began another round in this interurban rivalry by opening a railroad line to Ohio in 1828. Other cities followed suit. Soon many railroad lines stretched westward, linking coastal cities to the hinterland.

By 1830, New York, Philadelphia, and fast-growing Baltimore had emerged as the main coastal cities, largely due to their control of the lion's share of commerce with the Ohio Valley. The remarkable rate of growth of these cities in comparison with Charleston, an original East Coast city still focused on tobacco and cotton production, is suggested in Table 3–1. As westward expansion proceeded, many new cities were incorporated. A glance at Table 3–2 shows that fully 39 major urban areas appeared between 1816 and 1876, the height of the westward expansion movement.

Canadian cities also benefited from new transportation links, especially in the 1850s. Toronto experienced rapid development with the coming of the Grand Trunk and Great Western railways and the signing of a trade treaty with the United States. From 9,000 in the 1830s, its population ballooned to 45,000 by 1861. Similarly, Montreal's railroad linkage to Toronto and initiation of shipping service with Europe brought its population to 270,000 by the end of the nineteenth century. Quebec city and its surrounding region numbered about 1 million by 1850, due mostly to rapid natural growth. Thereafter, lack of additional fertile lands in a favorable climate for this mostly agrarian economy prompted many French Canadians to migrate to work in the new industries in the United States.

Cities as Big Business

Economic gain was clearly the major objective of the urban growth of the early nineteenth century. As Europe had sought economic reward through colonization of the New World, so, in turn, did the cities of the East Coast seek to enrich themselves through expansion of trade networks with the West. Pittsburgh, Cincinnati, Louisville, Kansas City, Chicago, and other cities all attempted to gain their share of trade with their region and beyond. This competition and frenetic growth is portrayed in the Cityscape box on page 72.

TABLE 3–1   Population Growth of Selected East Coast Cities, 1790–1870

	1790	1810	1830	1850	1870
New York	33,131	100,775	214,995	515,500	942,292
Philadelphia	44,096	87,303	161,271	340,000	674,022
Boston	18,320	38,746	61,392	136,881	250,526
Baltimore	13,503	46,555	80,620	169,054	267,354
Charleston	16,359	24,711	30,289	42,985	48,956
Total U.S. urban dwellers	202,000	525,000	1,127,000	3,543,700	9,902,000
Total percent urban	5.1	7.3	8.8	15.3	25.7

Source: Statistics derived from U.S. Censuses in 1850, 1860, and 1910 (Washington, DC: U.S. Government Printing Office).

TABLE 3–2   Incorporation Dates of the 50 Largest U.S. Cities by Historical Period

Pre-1776 (3)	1776–1820 (7)	1821–1860 (25)	1861–1880 (8)	1881–1910 (7)
New York (1685)	Nashville (1784)	Boston (1822)	Denver (1861)	Virginia Beach (1887)
Philadelphia (1701)	Baltimore (1797)	St. Louis (1822)	Tucson (1864)	Long Beach, CA (1888)
Charlotte (1774)	Dayton (1805)	Detroit (1824)	Minneapolis (1867)	Oklahoma City (1890)
	New Orleans (1805)	Memphis (1826)	Seattle (1869)	Miami (1896)
	San Antonio (1809)	Jacksonville (1832)	Phoenix (1871)	Tulsa (1898)
	Pittsburgh (1816)	Columbus (1834)	Fort Worth (1873)	Honolulu (1909)
	Cincinnati (1819)	Cleveland (1836)	Fresno (1874)	Las Vegas (1909)
		Chicago (1837)	Indianapolis (1874)	
		Houston (1837)		
		Toledo (1837)		
		Austin (1840)		
		Milwaukee (1846)		
		Atlanta (1847)		
		Albuquerque (1847)		
		Kansas City (1850)		
		Los Angeles (1850)		
		El Paso (1850)		
		Sacramento (1850)		
		San Diego (1850)		
		San Francisco (1850)		
		San Jose (1850)		
		Portland (1851)		
		Oakland (1854)		
		Dallas (1856)		
		Omaha (1857)		

Source: Based on data from *Statistical Abstract of the United States 2001* and from *Encyclopaedia Britannica,* 2002.

The Beginnings of Industrialization

As Jaimie McPheeters's diary (see the City-scape box on page 72) makes obvious, as the nineteenth century wore on, in all the nation's cities one heard more and more the sound of machines. Although the major part of the North American Industrial Revolution would not occur until the latter part of the century, its beginnings were much earlier.

Surveying a country that offered them abundant raw materials, U.S. entrepreneurs lost no time after the Revolutionary War in adopting the new industrial techniques of Europe to establish a manufacturing base in the new nation. This process, in itself, gave birth to new and important cities inland. Secretary of the Treasury Alexander Hamilton played a

major role in the founding in 1792 of Paterson, New Jersey, at the site of the Passaic Falls, second only to Niagara Falls in its width and height. Pierre L'Enfant, the French-born engineer who would later plan Washington, D.C., designed a water raceway system to harness this water power for mills. As the first planned industrial city, Paterson quickly emerged as *the* cotton town of the United States and then as a locomotive-building center. Soon, New England emerged as the leader in textiles. Literary critic Van Wyck Brooks notes that by the 1830s around Boston, factory towns "were rising on every hand, in Eastern Massachusetts and New Hampshire—Lawrence, Lowell, Fitchberg, Manchester, Lynn. Every village with a water-fall set up a textile mill or a paper mill, a shoe factory or an iron foundry" (1936:4). Slowly, industrialization supported by private investment began to transform the developing continent, particularly in the North. As it did so, new tensions began to mount.

Urban–Rural/North–South Tensions

U.S. culture has always contained a streak of anti-urbanism. Some analysts link this sentiment to the popular image of North America as the "last frontier," the place where the confines of (urban) civilization could be left behind and adequate "space" found at last. Many of the country's original settlers came here specifically to escape Europe's rapid urbanization and to attain much-desired "room to breathe." As long as the early North American settlements remained small and kept their relatively homogeneous character, few tensions existed between urban and rural sections. Yet some of the founders of the United States worried greatly about how growing cities might transform the new nation. Thomas Jefferson, who was nurtured in the rural aristocratic tradition of Virginia, condemned cities as "ulcers on the body politic" and saw their growth as an invitation to all the corruption and evil that had befallen the Old World across the Atlantic. Commenting on an outbreak of yellow fever, Jefferson wrote the following to Benjamin Rush in 1800:

> When great evils happen I am in the habit of looking out for what good may arise from them as consolations to us, and Providence has in fact so established the order to things, as that most evils are the means of producing some good. The yellow fever will discourage the growth of great cities in our nation, and I view great cities as pestilential to the morals, the health and the liberties of man. (White and White, 1964:28)

As if in defiance of Jefferson's wishes, America's cities grew in number and prominence. To escape their influence, some people moved westward. The cities followed and brought with them the more mechanized existence of the industrial age. By 1850, many rural Americans were deeply alarmed about these developments. Agrarian periodicals regularly touted the superiority of country life over the deceitful ways of city life. The Looking Back box on page 74 suggests the tone and substance of this confrontation.

The debate on the pros and cons of city life soon took on a new and powerful dimension on the regional level: hostility between the North and the South. This conflict resulted from the fact that the unparalleled growth of U.S. cities between 1820 and 1860 was largely centered in the North. Cities such as New York, Philadelphia, and Baltimore simply outdistanced the conservative, slowly growing cities like Charleston and Savannah. The northern cities had the canal routes and the bulk of the railroad lines to the West, which produced tremendous increases in wealth and population. Moreover, they were dominating ever-greater shares of regional and national markets, outstripping the South in overall production as industrialization spread. The West, observes Arthur Schlesinger,

> was becoming steadily more like the Northeast, whereas the South, chained by slavery to agriculture, contained few sizable cities and those mostly at its edges. . . . Every year sharpened the contrast between the urban spirit of progress animating the one section and the static, rural life of the other. Few important industries existed below the Mason and Dixon line. . . . [The] Southerners, lacking the nerve centers for creative cultural achievement, fell behind in arts, letters and science. "It would have been surprising had they not desired secession," remarked Anthony Trollope, in America shortly after [the attack on] Fort Sumter. "Secession of a kind, a very practical secession, had already taken place." (1969:33–34)

The Civil War broke out in 1861. Although its causes were numerous, many historians believe that it was, in a very fundamental sense, a confrontation between urban and rural, industrial and agricultural values. The North's victory was a symbolic turning point. The world of Jefferson was dying. America's commitment to urban industrial expansion was now unchallenged. The stage was set for an

CITYSCAPE

Richard C. Wade said people searched for towns.

A City-Making Mania

Urban historian Richard C. Wade offers a glimpse of the incredible urban growth that characterized the early nineteenth century. Although the common conception is that towns and cities sprang up after land-hungry settlers had filled up a new region, notice Wade's assertion that towns actually preceded much of the westward movement of population. In fact, many who started west during this period went in search of urban—rather than rural—opportunities.

The towns were the spearheads of the American frontier. Planted as forts or trading posts far in advance of the line of settlement, they held the West for the approaching population. . . .

The speed and extent of this expansion startled contemporaries. Joseph Charless, the editor of the *Missouri Gazette*, who had made a trip through the new country in 1795, remembered the banks of the Ohio as "a dreary wilderness, the haunt of ruthless savages," yet twenty years later he found them "sprinkled with towns" boasting "spinning and weaving

establishments, steam mills, manufacturers in various metals, leather, wool, cotton and flax," and "seminaries of learning conducted by excellent teachers. . . ."

Not all the towns founded in the trans-Allegheny region in this period fared as well, however. Many never developed much beyond a survey and a newspaper advertisement. Others after promising beginnings, slackened and settled down to slow and unspectacular development. Still others flourished briefly then faded, leaving behind a grim story of deserted mills, broken buildings, and aging people—the West's first harvest of ghost towns. Most of these were mere eddies in the westward flow of urbanism, but at flood tide it was often hard to distinguish the eddies from the main stream. Indeed, at one time Wheeling, Virginia, St. Genevieve, Missouri, New Albany, Indiana, and Zanesville, Ohio were considered serious challengers to the supremacy of their now more famous neighbors.

Other places such as Rising Sun, Town of America, or New Athens, were almost wholly speculative ventures. Eastern investors scanned maps looking for likely spots to establish a city, usually at the junction of two rivers, or sometimes at the center of fertile farm districts. They bought up land, laid it out in lots, gave the place a name, and waited for the development of the region to appreciate its

urban explosion comparable to the one that had shaken Europe a century before.

THE ERA OF THE GREAT METROPOLIS: 1870–1950

The record number of small cities incorporated in the United States during the 50-year period that ended in 1870 had not yet acquired many of the urban characteristics most familiar to us: towering buildings,

populations in the millions, and blazing lights downtown. Two historical events would provide the impetus for this transformation: (1) the technological advance of industrialization and (2) the migration of millions of people to urban North America.

Technological Advance

Industrialization involved much more than simply a proliferation of factories in and around the enlarging urban areas. Several value. Looking back over this period one editor called it a "city-making mania," when everyone went about "anticipating flourishing cities in vision, at the mouth of every creek and bayou. . . ."

Louisville, 1849

Louisville
→ so
advanced

As evidence of the portrait just painted, here is a section from the diary of Jaimie McPheeters, a 15-year-old boy. In 1849, after hearing stories of the gold rush in California, Jaimie and his dad decided to leave Louisville, Kentucky, and head west. Just before he left, Jaimie's mother told him that when he returned, he could take his rightful place in "the cultural life of Louisville, and share in the city's advancement." This possibility prompted the following ruminations in Jaimie's diary. Clearly, even in 1849, Louisville was no "hick town."

Well, I thought, if you ask me, they've gone too far with this Louisville already. It was overdeveloped and blown up with commerce and business so you could hardly get across the streets any more without being run down by teamsters. Why, they had eight brickyards in Louisville in 1849—I saw it in a bragging pamphlet that was got up by some merchant or other that seemed to have a good deal of time on his hands. There were three pianoforte manufactures, too, and three breweries, two tallow-rendering houses, an ivory-black maker—for use in refining sugar, you know—eight soap and candle factories; three shipyards; two glue factories; and four pork houses that slaughtered upwards of seventy thousand hogs a year.

And if you were looking for steam machinery, they had twelve foundries that made the best on the river, or so the pamphlet claimed. There were rope factories, flouring mills, oil-cloth factories, three potteries; six tobacco stemmeries, a paper mill, and a new gas works that lit 461 street lamps over sixteen miles of main. Not only that, it had a gas holder measuring sixty feet in diameter and twenty-two feet high. People used to ride out Sundays to look at it, but the superintendent said it was a nuisance because he couldn't keep the children off. In the end, they were obliged to hire a watchman, but he was bullyragged so steady that he sort of went out of his head, so to speak, and they had to place him in a hospital that made a specialty of such cases.

Sources: Richard C. Wade, "Urban Life in Western America, 1790–1830," in *American Historical Review* (October 1958), pp. 14–30; and Robert Lewis Taylor, *The Travels of Jaimie McPheeters* (New York: Arbor House, 1985), p. 22.

inventions emerged that changed the face of the North American city. The construction of buildings with iron, and then steel, pushed the city skyward. In 1848 a five-story factory built with an iron frame had made news in New York; by 1884 a ten-story steel structure in Chicago had ushered in the era of urban skyscrapers. The success of these taller buildings was further ensured as another invention, the Otis elevator (devised in the 1850s) became widespread in the 1880s. By the end of the century, some buildings reached 30 stories; by 1910 a few were as high as 50. By 1913, New York had 61 buildings taller than 20 stories, and the famous city skyline was beginning to take form (Still, 1994:206–207).

As cities grew upward, they also pushed outward, aided by a new technology in street-level transportation. Prior to the Civil War, pedestrians had only horse-drawn vehicles to contend with. By the 1870s steam-powered trains were running on elevated tracks in New York. Soon after, "els" were built in other large cities. People's ability to move about certainly

LOOKING BACK

The Rural–Urban Debate

In 1811 a farmer near Lexing-ton [Kentucky] expressed the [rural–urban] conflict as con-temporaries saw it in a dia-logue between "Rusticus" and "Urbanus." The latter referred to the "rude, gross appear-ance" of his neighbor, adding: "How strong you smell of your ploughed ground and corn field. How dismal, how gloomy your green woods. What a miserable clash your whistling woodland birds are continu-ally making." Rusticus replied with the rural image of the town dweller. "What a fine smooth complexion you have Urbanus: you look like a weed that has grown up in the shade. Can you walk your streets without in-haling the noxious fumes with which your town is pregnant? . . . Can you engage in calm contemplation, when hammers are ringing in every direction—where there is as great a rattling as in a storm when the hail descends on our house tops?"

Source: Kentucky Reporter (Lexington), July 2, 1811. Cited in J. A. Callow and Alexander B. Callow, Jr. (eds.), *American Urban History* 2nd ed. (New York: Oxford Uni-versity Press, 1997), p. 105.

was enhanced, but the thunderous noise, bil-lowing smoke, and cascading sparks and cin-ders of these trains surely did little to preserve the peace and quiet of local neighborhoods or the quality of the environment.

In the 1880s the electric street trolley came into use. Still in operation today in Philadel-phia, Boston, and New Orleans, these devices also helped make mass transit a reality. Indeed, streetcars, and the subways that followed, were primarily responsible for making suburban life possible for millions. They allowed fast and in-expensive transportation beyond the city lim-its. Quick to see the possibilities of such transportation, real-estate speculators built housing tracts by the dozens. For example, be-tween 1870 and 1890 the suburbs of Roxbury, West Roxbury, and Dorchester, immediately surrounding Boston, witnessed the construc-tion of over 23,000 new houses (Warner, 1962). For the burgeoning middle class, an escape from the city's dirt and din was at last possible:

The . . . general satisfaction with suburbs came from their ability to answer some of the major needs of the day. . . . To middle class families [they] gave a safe, sanitary environment, new houses in styles somewhat in keeping with their conception of family life, and temporary neigh-borhoods of people with similar outlook. . . . In addition to benefiting [the middle class] the suburbs [also served that portion of the city's] population which could not afford them. The apparent openness of the new residential quar-ters, their ethnic variety, their extensive growth, and their wide range of prices from fairly inex-pensive rental suites to expensive single-family houses—these visible characteristics of the new suburbs gave aspiring low-income families the certainty that should they earn enough money they too could possess the comforts and sym-bols of success. (Warner, 1962:157)

Technology thus spawned the suburban dream in the late 1800s, enabling the middle class to move out of the city, separating their place of work from their place of residence. Unlike the more mixed pattern of the earlier walking city, the new housing tracts created homogeneous economic and social commu-nities that by and large excluded the poor (Palen, 1995:39–40). This pattern of social class segregation, and the attempt of many to escape to the suburbs, have remained two powerful aspects of urban history ever since.

Technological advance via the streetcar not only allowed cities to sprout suburbs, but also linked cities to one another with cheap transportation. At one time in the mid-nineteenth century, believe it or not, it was possible to travel from Boston all the way to New York and beyond simply by transferring from streetcar line to streetcar line. Such a system greatly stimulated interurban migration.

The Great Migration

The growing suburbs proved important in yet another way: They helped siphon off the incredible population growth of the era. The expanding industrial economy created opportunities for millions. Between 1870 and 1920, urban places (places with over 2,500 residents) in the United States increased their populations from just under 10 million to over 54 million. The country became, for the first time, a predominantly urban nation. (The United States passed the 50 percent urban population mark in 1913.) The rate of growth for many of the largest cities was nothing short of astonishing. By 1920 Chicago had over 12 times its 1870 population and was fast approaching the 3 million mark. New York, not yet a city of 1 million in 1870, was by 1920 approaching the 6 million mark.

Two demographic trends were primarily responsible for this striking increase in city dwellers: (1) depopulation of rural areas as people moved into cities and (2) immigration to the United States from abroad. The movement from the countryside to the city was brought about by automation—machinery was making old forms of hand-powered labor obsolete—and the possibility of greater wealth in the city. Between 1880 and 1890, nearly 40 percent of the nation's 25,746 townships actually lost population (Glaab, 1963:176). Unable to survive in the country and lured by the cities, thousands abandoned their farms to seek their fortunes elsewhere. As might be expected, migration was most intense in the Northeast and Midwest, where the largest cities were.

The absolute number of foreign immigrants to the United States was a bit smaller than the number of city-bound Americans who left rural areas during this period, but the changes wrought by immigrants from abroad were far greater. Representing dozens of different nationalities and ethnicities, they introduced staggering cultural diversity to the large cities of the United States. Glaab and Brown give some hint of the transformation:

> The influx of immigrants to the cities, particularly during the decade of the 1880's when over five million arrived in the United States, produced some striking statistics for individual cities. In 1890, New York . . . contained more foreign born residents than any city in the world. The city had half as many Italians as Naples, as many Germans as Hamburg, twice as many Irish as Dublin, and two and a half times the number of Jews in Warsaw. In 1893, Chicago contained the third largest Bohemian community in the world; by the time of the First World War, Chicago ranked only behind Warsaw and Lodz as a city of Poles. (1967:138–39)

One important effect of all this in-migration was the clustering together of cultural groups in distinctive city districts. The tremendous variety of these groups gave cities of the late nineteenth century a degree of diversity and excitement that was quite new in the United States—and would affect the character of the city from that time on. To travel the breadth of Chicago, Cleveland, Pittsburgh, or New York was—and still is today—to experience a succession of differing worlds, each characterized by its own shops and products, its own sounds and smells, its own language. Hence, in addition to upward and outward expansion and raw population growth, cultural heterogeneity became a third major characteristic of the new American metropolis.

Politics and Problems

With the enormous changes that reshaped cities in this period came equally enormous problems. How were the incoming millions to be fed, provided with water, electricity, jobs, and protection against unscrupulous exploitation? Only the city government was empowered to cope with these issues; however, the pressures against representing the public interest fairly were great. All the utility companies required franchises to use the streets—water and gas companies to lay pipes, electric companies to erect poles, and transit companies to lay iron rails. Local or out-of-town entrepreneurs offered to pay large sums for these lucrative franchises, and their bribes sometimes corrupted city officials.

Certain dictatorial political figures—"the bosses"—began to take control of many city governments. They got the job done, but in the process they usually lined their pockets with graft and kickbacks. By the turn of the century many city officials were as corrupt as any organized crime figure.

Outraged, citizens' groups demanded reform. In 1880 the Committee of One Hundred organized against a natural-gas monopoly and its illicit connection to Philadelphia's government. Other reform movements—in St. Louis, Milwaukee, Cincinnati, and New York—got under way. Progress was slow, however, because the bosses had developed an efficient "machine" that extended its tentacles into all layers of government and neighborhood life.

Another problem of the times was that large-scale immigration sparked an increasingly bitter reaction against newcomers. It was not just their numbers. By 1900, immigrants were more often from southern and eastern Europe, more likely to be Roman Catholic or Jewish than Protestant, and more likely to have darker eyes, hair, and skin tone than whites of northern and western European descent. Moreover, these newcomers often had manners and dress that made them stand out as "different." These "less desirable" immigrants added significantly to anti-city sentiment because, even more than earlier arrivals, they were overwhelmingly urban settlers. By 1910, in fact, over one-third of the inhabitants of the eight largest U.S. cities had been born abroad; another one-third were second-generation Americans. In sharp contrast, fewer than one in ten rural Americans

were foreign born at this time (Glaab, 1963:176). Within the city, people from "good stock" tried valiantly to get away from the newcomers. As a result, the wealthier suburbs often had a decided anti-ethnic and racist tinge to them.

The Quality of Life in the New Metropolis

The industrialization of the city reinforced the anti-urbanism campaign. Detractors saw life in cities as simply horrendous. Take Willard Glazier's impressions of Pittsburgh in 1884, presented in the next Looking Back box on page 77. Glazier finds Pittsburgh so harmful that he likens it to hell itself.

Some profited greatly in this age of great economic expansion. Tremendous fortunes were made and urban industrial empires became established. In 1892, the *New York Times* published a list of 4,047 U.S. millionaires; in 1901, J. P. Morgan founded U.S. Steel, the first billion-dollar corporation; and "by 1910 there were more millionaires in the United States Senate alone than there were in the whole nation before the Civil War" (Baltzell, 1964:110).

But times were not equally good for all. As the enormous mansion-retreats of the "robber-baron" industrialists rose across the urban fringe, the blight of the inner-city tenements became more and more conspicuous. With a steady stream of people entering the large cities of the North, property owners responded to the rising demand for housing by making the most profitable use of building space. New York tenements, denounced as "hideous" by Charles Dickens in 1842, had become even worse by 1900, as designs cheapened and more and more people moved into them. The word *tenement* now symbolized an airless, congested slum dwelling. By the turn of the century, perhaps 35 percent of New York City's population lived in such quarters, although the situation in most other industrial cities was somewhat more favorable. Despite periodic attempts at reform through

LOOKING BACK

[handwritten: Nice City at Night]
[handwritten: Iron]
[handwritten: William Glazier]

Industrial Pittsburgh, 1884

By all means make your first approach to Pittsburgh in the night time, and you will behold a spectacle which has not a parallel on this continent. Darkness gives the city and its surroundings a picturesqueness which they wholly lack by daylight. It lies low down in a hollow of encompassing hills, gleaming with a thousand points of light, which are reflected from the rivers, whose waters glimmer in the faint moonlight. . . . Around the city's edge, and on the sides of the hills which encircle it like a gloomy amphitheatre, their outlines rising dark against the sky, through numberless apertures, fiery lights stream forth, looking angrily and fiercely up toward the heavens, while over all these settles a heavy pall of smoke. It is as though one had reached the outer edge of the infernal regions, and saw before him the great furnace of Pandemonium with all the lids lifted. The scene is so strange and weird that it will live in the memory forever. One pictures, as he beholds it, the tortured spirits writhing in agony, their sinewy limbs convulsed, and the very air oppressive with pain and rage. . . .

. . . Failing a night approach, the traveler should reach the Iron City on a dismal day in autumn, when the air is heavy with moisture, and the very atmosphere looks dark. All romance has disappeared. . . . There is only a very busy city shrouded in gloom. The buildings, whatever their original material and color, are smoked to a uniform, dirty drab; their smoke sinks, and mingling with the moisture in the air, becomes of a consistency which may almost be felt as well as seen. Under a drab sky a drab twilight hangs over the town, and the gas-lights, which are left burning at midday, shine out of the murkiness with a dull, reddish glare.

In truth, Pittsburgh is a smoky, dismal city, at her best. At her worst, nothing darker, dingier or more dispiriting can be imagined. The city is in the heart of the soft coal region; and the smoke from her dwellings, stores, factories, foundries and steamboats, uniting, settles in a cloud over the narrow valley in which she is built, until the very sun looks coppery through the sooty haze. Her inhabitants are all too busy to reflect upon the inconvenience or uncomeliness of this smoke. Work is the object of life with them. It occupies them from morning until night, from the cradle to the grave, [except] on Sundays, when, for the most part, the furnaces are idle, and the forges are silent.

Source: Willard Glazier, *Peculiarities of American Cities* (1884), quoted in Charles N. Glaab, *The American City: A Documentary History* (Homewood, IL: Dorsey, 1963).

---

legislation, the urban housing problem remains a controversial issue to the present day (see Chapter 12).

Quality-of-life problems in the rapidly expanding industrial cities, unfortunately, were not limited to housing. Health hazards were great where high-density living was combined with inadequate sewerage and generally unsanitary conditions. Through the end of the nineteenth century, toilet facilities were grossly inadequate for immigrant tenement dwellers. Moreover, until the 1880s most Philadelphians drank water from the Delaware River, into which some 13 million gallons of sewage were being dumped weekly (Marshall, 1969:150). The frequency of epidemics was high. The

Chicago Times summed up the problem with appropriate bluntness:

> The river stinks. The air stinks. Peoples' clothing, permeated by the foul atmosphere, stinks. . . . No other word expresses it so well as stink. A stench means something finite. Stink reaches the infinite and becomes sublime in the magnitude of odiousness. (cited in Glaab and Brown, 1967:165)

Of course, attempts were made to remove many of these problems. Urban activists such as Jane Addams, awarded a Nobel Prize for the founding of Hull House (a settlement house) in Chicago (1889), attempted to help the situation of immigrants and improve living conditions. But for decades the battle was uphill. The cities were growing uncontrollably.

Trends Through 1950

Between 1883 and 1900, Toronto annexed adjacent villages and towns and doubled its area, again doubling its size through further annexation by 1920. In 1930, Toronto's metropolitan area included the central city, four towns (Leaside, Mimico, New Toronto, and Weston), three villages (Forest Hill, Long Branch, and Swansea), and five townships (Etobicoke, East York, North York, Scarborough, and York). Montreal annexed several cities, towns, and villages on its outskirts in the early twentieth century, thereby significantly expanding its municipal boundary as well.

The rush to cities slowed down considerably during World War I but resumed immediately afterward. One source of the new influx was returning soldiers who, after "seeing the world," no longer were content to stay at home. As a humorous popular song of the times asked: "How ya gonna keep 'em down on the farm after they've seen Paree?"

The other source was renewed immigration. Between 1870 and the start of World War I, over 20 million foreign immigrants disembarked on North American shores. The vast majority of them became city dwellers. When one adds to this the inmigration from the rural hinterland and natural population

increase by births, the shift is dramatic. The following statistic indicates the magnitude of the change: In 1870 only 25 percent of the U.S. population resided in cities; by 1920 the census reported that, for the first time, the urban way of life was the most common—51 percent were urban dwellers.

From a low of 110,000 in 1918 (the next-to-last year of the war), other countries increased their U.S.-bound human exports to 805,000 in 1921, over 222,000 of whom came from Italy alone (see Parrillo, 2003:184–86). However, such massive immigration was not to go on forever. Many ordinary Americans and political leaders became concerned about the ability of the United States to continually absorb the "tired, hungry, and poor" of foreign states. Such reservations were laced with a considerable degree of ethnic prejudice as well. By lobbying hard, anti-immigrationists were able to press the U.S. Congress in 1921 into passing a law limiting the foreign influx, particularly from southern, central, and eastern Europe. This was followed by legislation in 1924 restricting immigration even further.

The ultimate irony of the quota system, however, was that it did not stop migration to the cities, and it perhaps set the stage for even greater urban difficulties in the future. The industrial machine that had been developing since the late nineteenth century simply looked elsewhere for cheap labor and found African Americans in the South all too eager to find a better way of life. Between 1920 and 1929, more than 600,000 southern African Americans migrated to northern cities. By the end of the decade, Chicago's South Side and New York's Harlem had the largest concentrated black populations anywhere in the world. In Hartford, Baltimore, Washington, Philadelphia, Cincinnati, and Detroit, the black population grew enormously. Soon racial tensions developed in many northern cities, sometimes leading to riots, as in Detroit in 1925.

The next crisis happened with the stock market crash of 1929, which wiped out huge municipal investments, threw millions into destitution, and made local public projects virtually impossible to implement. Many cities became financially strapped to the point of bankruptcy. Seeing possible salvation in Franklin Roosevelt, 23 major cities supported the Democratic Party in the 1932 election, thereby ensuring his election. The next year the mayors of 50 cities met in Washington to found the U.S. Conference of Mayors and began lobbying efforts in their own behalf. They were not disappointed. The National Industrial Recovery Act appropriated $3.3 billion for much-needed public works and housing operations, and subsequent bills pumped billions more into housing construction, highway construction, and other relief for the cities. A fateful corner had been turned: As the thirties gave way to the forties, fifties, and sixties, cities became more and more dependent on the federal government. Despite many positive benefits of this connection, it was also to have major drawbacks.

THE NORTH AMERICAN CITY TODAY: 1950 TO THE PRESENT

Today's U.S. cities are in the process of three major changes: (1) people and businesses still abandon the central cities, continuing a suburbanization trend that began nearly 100 years ago, a process aptly called *decentralization;* (2) major population growth is occurring in cities in the South and West, the so-called *Sunbelt expansion;* and (3) the work typically performed in the central city is more and

more oriented to white-collar jobs, high technology, and services, as Canadian and U.S. cities adjust to the *postindustrial era.*

Decentralization

If the first three eras of North American urban history can be characterized as a time of "urban implosion," of ever-greater numbers of people converging on the central city itself, then the period since 1950 has seen the beginnings of a major "urban explosion," of people moving out from the core to the surrounding regions. One indication of this decentralization can be seen in the census data, shown in Table 3–3, for major northern cities between 1910 and 2000. Notice that all the cities in this table had become large metropolises by 1910 and that each grew rapidly in the following few decades. However, by 1950 that growth was slowing. By 1970 there was an actual decline in central-city populations and by the 1990s, seemed a full-scale central-city retreat was under way, although a few cities reversed this trend by 2000.

Many of these people, however, are not leaving the metropolitan region. They are moving to the suburbs near the cities. Table 3–4 on page 81 makes this clear by examining metropolitan area populations for selected cities across the continent, including those examined in Table 3–3. With few exceptions, suburbs are growing everywhere and have been doing so for over 30 years. Why?

TABLE 3–3   Population of Selected U.S. Northern Cities, 1910–2000 (in thousands)

	1910	1930	1950	1970	1990	2000
Baltimore	588	805	950	906	736	651
Boston	671	781	801	641	574	589
Chicago	2,185	3,376	3,621	3,367	2,784	2,896
Cleveland	561	900	915	751	506	496
Detroit	466	1,569	1,850	1,511	1,028	951
New York	4,767	6,930	7,892	7,895	7,323	8,008
Philadelphia	1,549	1,951	2,072	1,949	1,586	1,518

Source: U.S. Bureau of the Census.

Economic Considerations

By about 1950, more and more businesses, particularly in industry and manufacturing, were moving away from the industrial districts of central cities. The costs of refurbishing older buildings were high and, given high rents, expansion wasn't always possible. Further, some new assembly-line procedures required large, low-level structures rather than the multistory buildings characteristic of an earlier era. Concerns over rising crime rates, taxes, and traffic congestion also played their part in a proliferation of new "industrial parks" in the outer urban areas. Workers often moved from the central city to be near their relocated jobs. The result was a growth in suburban population and a decline in central-city population.

Economics is the driving force that prompts some urban critics to suggest governance changes. One view is to utilize regional planning, even regional government, to reduce sprawl, ghettoization, and economic competition among municipalities—often at their own expense by giving tax breaks to companies (Orfield and Rusk, 1998; Miller, 2002). Another proposal is to allow older cities to be "elastic cities" through annexation of suburbs. In capturing suburban growth, elastic cities promote greater economic progress for the entire metropolitan community and reduce fragmented local government that typically fosters segregation and poverty concentrations (Rusk, 1995:5–48).

Technology

As noted earlier, technological changes in energy (steam power) and building techniques (steel-frame skyscrapers) were important in the creation of a centralized metropolis in the nineteenth century. During the twentieth century the development of electric power, the widespread use of cars and trucks, the all-but-universal telephone, and—most recently—computer technology have been equally important in the decentralization of the urban area.

Unlike steam power, which must be used within the immediate area of its production, electric power can be transmitted over long distances. This makes it possible for both industries and residential areas to spread widely across the metropolitan area. Similarly, cars and trucks provide far greater flexibility in mobility and location than the rail transportation system that dominated the late nineteenth century. This has been especially true since the 1950s with the development of the interstate highway system and the ubiquitous outer-city "loops" (usually converted into a 200- or 400-level of the two-digit interstate highway number, such as Route 280 or Route 476) surrounding most major cities.

As rail lines pushed out of the cities in earlier decades, the first suburbs clustered around the railroad stations. But motor vehicles made it possible to live in a far wider area while still having access to the urban area as a whole. As late as 1920, the average commute was still only about 1.5 miles (B. Duncan, 1956). By 1960, however, this distance had grown to almost 5 miles (Hawley, 1971), and it is not uncommon today to travel 20 miles or more to work.

Taken together, these technological changes have changed the meaning of urban space. Because we move more easily across space—in minutes by car or milliseconds by telecommunications—physical proximity is no longer as necessary to tie together all the activities within the urban area. In fact, most of us who live in cities routinely think in terms of time ("We live about 40 minutes from the airport") rather than distance; we may not even know how many miles away the airport is.

Suburban Housing

Any consideration of urban decentralization during the last 50 years must include recognition of the tremendous proliferation of new housing, which is typically being constructed farther from central cities. This process is linked to transportation options and began in the late nineteenth century, but got perhaps its greatest push after World War II. At that time, millions of Americans returned from overseas to find their old neighborhoods in increasing disrepair (in the war effort many

TABLE 3–4   Population of Selected Metropolitan Areas, 1990–2000

	2000 Population (in thousands)	Change Since 1990 (in thousands)	Percent Change since 1990
Northern Cities			
Baltimore	2,553	+171	+7
Boston	3,407	+179	+6
Chicago	8,283	+862	+12
Cleveland–Lorain–Elvira	2,251	+49	+2
Detroit	4,442	+175	+4
New York	9,314	+767	+9
Philadelphia	6,101	+179	+4
Southern Cities			
Atlanta	4,112	+1,153	+39
Birmingham	921	+81	+10
Dallas	3,519	+843	+32
Houston	4,178	+856	+26
Miami	2,253	+316	+16
New Orleans	1,338	+52	+4
Orlando	1,645	+420	+34
Tampa–St. Petersburg–Clearwater	2,396	+328	+16
Western Cities			
Los Angeles–Long Beach	9,519	+656	+7
Phoenix–Mesa	3,252	+1,013	+45
Portland–Vancouver	1,918	+403	+27
Salt Lake City–Ogden	1,334	+262	+24
San Francisco	1,731	+128	+6
Seattle–Bellevue–Everett	2,415	+381	+19

Source: U.S. Bureau of the Census.

neighborhood maintenance projects had been shelved and the ability of private homeowners to maintain full upkeep was curtailed). In many instances, returning white soldiers also found minority groups, especially African Americans, living in or close to their former homes. (Many African Americans had migrated north during the war to operate the industrial machinery vacated by whites.) Finally, like almost all Americans, these men wanted their own place out of the congested city, a place with a little more room where they could raise their kids in clean air and send them to good schools, without fear of crime and other urban ills. This was, of course, the classic suburban dream.

What made its realization possible for millions was the federal government. The Federal Housing Authority and the Veterans Administration made low-interest construction loans available to veterans or to anyone else who could supply some assurance of their ability to repay. Millions of veterans took the FHA and the VA up on their offer and elected to build or buy new homes that, because of federal funding policies, were mostly built outside the central city, in suburban tracts.

The irony of this was that, like the immigration quota system, a well-meaning federal policy once again created major problems for cities over time. As the white middle class moved out to the separately incorporated suburbs, the cities lost even more of the tax base that departing industry was already eroding.

To add to the problem, the population that was left behind in the city core was increasingly composed of minorities and the poor. As industry abandoned the central city, many of these people were unable to find jobs and went on public relief. Thus the city was faced with an increasing demand for services and a shrinking ability to provide them. By the mid-1960s a true urban crisis—largely created by the decentralization phenomenon—was upon the country as a whole. Urban poverty was on the increase, minorities were justifiably angry over their standard of living, services were getting worse, and many cities were facing bankruptcy.

The Metropolitan Statistical Area (MSA)

As mentioned earlier, by 1910 decentralization was well under way in the United States. Cities were growing well beyond their traditional boundaries. In the cities of the North, for example, workers, unable to find adequate housing in the central city, spilled over into the surrounding towns and small cities. To take a single case, Boston's workers began to settle in Wakefield and Lynn to the north, in Wellesley and Natick to the west, and in Quincy and Braintree to the south. While technically these people were residents of their newly adopted local communities, on another level they were still clearly linked to Boston and under its sphere of influence.

Noticing this trend, the U.S. Bureau of the Census was faced with a problem: how to measure accurately the way cities were really growing. If it merely counted the residents of the central city—in this case, Boston—it would get a relatively small population count that would not reflect the fact that many of the people who lived in Braintree and Wakefield were really tied to Boston in a fundamental way. Consequently, the Census Bureau decided to count not only the central city and its population in its surveys, but the surrounding towns and cities that were obviously tied

to that central city as well. Thus was born the idea of the metropolitan area.

Since 1910 a series of terms have been used to designate such sprawling urban regions. From 1959 until 1983, the term *standard metropolitan statistical area* (or SMSA) was employed. Then, in 1983, the Census Bureau introduced the concept *metropolitan statistical area* (or MSA). An MSA is currently defined as including at least one city with 50,000 or more inhabitants, the county or counties containing the city, and any surrounding counties that have a high population density and a large proportion of inhabitants commuting to and from the central city. As of 2000, the Census Bureau recognized 273 MSAs within the United States, containing roughly three-fourths of the total population.

The Toronto Metropolitan Area

In 1953, Toronto created a federated form of government unique to North America to deal with the metropolitan phenomenon. Going beyond merely labeling a metropolitan area as such, this action created a consolidated governance system. The 13 municipalities of this metropolitan area formed a 25-member, elected Council of Metropolitan Toronto. Through united effort the Council succeeded in establishing a common property assessment and tax rate to deal with such regional problems as water supply, sewage disposal, mass transit, school building needs, housing for the elderly, parks, and urban development. This metropolitan governance approach is found in many European countries but is virtually nonexistent in the United States. Subsequently, the Council was modified to include 33 members but from only six municipalities.

Megalopolis and the Consolidated Metropolitan Statistical Area (CMSA)

French geographer Jean Gottmann was one of the first urbanists to look closely at the sprawling urban regions and to note the linkages between many independent urban municipalities.

The first such area, which he called "Megalopolis," was the unbroken urban region that emerged along the eastern seaboard of the United States, and he dubbed it the "BosWash corridor." In Cityscape on page 84 he describes this development.

The BosWash corridor was the first North American megalopolis, but not the last. Since the publication of Gottman's seminal book in 1961, other megalopolises have emerged— in Southern California ("SanSan") and across the northern Midwest from Chicago ("ChiGary") to Cleveland ("CleveAk"). Once again, such growth has not gone unnoticed by the Census Bureau, which coined the term *consolidated metropolitan statistical area* (or CMSA) to describe these areas. By 2000, 18 CMSAs were recognized as part of the urban landscape, including Dallas–Forth Worth, Denver–Boulder–Greeley, Detroit–Ann Arbor–Flint, Houston–Galveston–Brazoria, Miami–Fort Lauderdale, Milwaukee–Racine, and Seattle–Tacoma–Bremerton.

Nonmetropolitan Growth

The decentralization of the U.S. population has dispersed people outward from central cities not just to nearby suburbs, but to the outlying rural hinterland as well. Small towns and rural areas had steadily lost population for the first 70 years of this century. In the 1960s rural America lost 2.8 million people, but during the 1970s, the trend reversed itself as rural areas gained 8.4 million people, up some 15.4 percent. Between 1990 and 2000, the nonmetropolitan population increased by 5.1 million, a 19.7 percent increase (U.S. Bureau of the Census, 2002a).

No doubt improved transportation and communications are an important foundation of this change, and so too is the emergence of edge cities, to be discussed shortly. Yet Americans moving to small towns or rural areas also may be reacting to the problems of cities in the same way that those moving to the suburbs have done for decades: They are looking for a greater sense of security and reaffirming the value of simpler living. Still, the people moving to these areas are in no way traditionally rural. Most are well educated, have sophisticated tastes, and work in nearby cities. Local stores often spring up, supplying such items as French wines and the *New York Times Book Review.*

The Sunbelt Expansion

A glance back to Table 3–4 reveals the other main trend that is affecting contemporary U.S. cities. Although suburban population is growing everywhere, the table shows that it is growing fastest in the South and West. Figure 3–1 on page 85 drives home the point even more effectively, showing that the population of virtually every state below the Mason-Dixon Line and west of the Rocky Mountains increased considerably between 1990 and 2000.

During most of U.S. history the Northeast and Midwest regions and their cities dominated national affairs. No more. An immense power shift has occurred; the South has risen again and the West has also come into preeminence. Table 3–5 on page 86 illustrates just how dramatic the change has been by comparing the raw population figures and national rankings for the ten largest U.S. cities in 2000. New York, Chicago, Philadelphia, and Detroit still remained in the top ten but the latter two have lost significant population since 1950. If present trends continue, only New York and Los Angeles may appear on the next list. In addition, seemingly from nowhere, Houston, Dallas, San Diego, San Antonio, and, especially, Phoenix have leaped onto the top ten list. Why has this change occurred?

Snowbelt Debits/Sunbelt Assets

To begin with, the northern cities experienced the strains of age, and businesses found costs and taxes rising to the point where many were not willing to stay. Built around the cruder industrial machinery of the nineteenth century, these cities found their physical plants outmoded by newer, particularly "high-tech" industry. Renovation was exorbitantly costly. City streets were in disrepair.

CITYSCAPE

Jean Gottmann   Atlantic

Megalopolis: The BosWash Corridor

The Northeastern seaboard of the United States is today the site of a remarkable development—an almost continuous stretch of urban and suburban areas from southern New Hampshire to northern Virginia and from the Atlantic shore to the Appalachian foothills. . . .

. . . As one follows the main highways or railroads between Boston and Washington, D.C., one hardly loses sight of built-up areas, tightly woven residential communities, or powerful concentrations of manufacturing plants. Flying this same route one discovers, on the other hand, that behind the ribbons of densely occupied land along the principal arteries of traffic, and in between the clusters of suburbs around the old urban centers, there still remain large areas covered with woods and brush alternating with some carefully cultivated patches of farmland. These green spaces, however, when inspected at closer range, appear stuffed with a loose but immense scattering of buildings, most of them residential but some of industrial character. That is, many of these sections that look rural actually function largely as suburbs in the orbit of some city's downtown. . . .

Thus the old distinctions between rural and urban do not apply here any more. Even a quick look at the vast area of Megalopolis reveals a revolution in land use. Most of the people living in the so-called rural areas, and still classified as "rural population" by recent censuses, have very little, if anything, to do with agriculture. In terms of their interests and work they are what used to be classified as "city folks," but their way of life and the landscapes around their residences do not fit the old meaning of urban.

In this area, then, we must abandon the idea of the city as a tightly settled and organized unit in which people, activities, and riches are crowded into a very small area clearly separated from its nonurban surroundings. Every city in this region spreads out far and wide around its original nucleus; it grows amidst an irregularly colloidal mixture of rural and suburban landscapes; it melts on broad fronts with other mixtures, of somewhat similar though different texture, belonging to the suburban neighborhoods of other cities. Such coalescence can be observed, for example, along the main lines of traffic that link New York City and Philadelphia. Here there are many communities that might be classified as belonging to more than one orbit. It is hard to say whether they are suburbs, or "satellites," of Philadelphia or New York, Newark, New Brunswick, or Trenton. The latter three cities themselves have been reduced to the role of suburbs of New York City in many respects, although Trenton belongs also to the orbit of Philadelphia. . . .

This region indeed reminds one of Aristotle's saying that cities such as Babylon had "the compass of a nation rather than a city. . . ."

Source: Jean Gottmann, *Megalopolis* (New York: Twentieth Century Fund, 1961), pp. 3, 5–7.

Services were declining. Because of the financial burden they labored under, these cities could not offer tax breaks to businesses as liberally as they once had. Energy costs were skyrocketing. Superhighways (so vital to modern commerce) typically did not terminate conveniently in the industrial area. Union pay scales made labor very expensive.

The Sunbelt had few of these problems. With many cities industrialized only recently, they were able to build modern, efficient plants linked easily to superhighways. With stronger economies than their northern counterparts due to booming population growth, they could offer substantial tax breaks to businesses. Energy costs were also much lower. A less unionized labor force was an added attraction to businesses. The result was that businesses by the thousands deserted the North and headed for the cities of the South and West.

Private citizens also enjoyed many benefits living in the South and West. Sunbelt cities are warmer, cheaper to live in, and offer more jobs. Home heating and electricity typically cost twice as much in the Snowbelt cities as in the Sunbelt. Responding to such incentives, people head south or west.

The movement out of the North and Midwest is not only affecting whites. From Virginia to Texas (the states of the Old Confederacy), the black population increased 19 percent between 1970 and 1980, as more than a million more African Americans moved into the South than moved out. This was the first major reversal of the northward black migration pattern since it began after the Civil War, and the trend is continuing. The 2000 census showed 62 percent of all African Americans now living in the Sunbelt. Black migration to the South accelerated dramatically between 1990 and 2000; seven of the ten metropolitan areas that gained the most black residents in this period were in the South. But there is a difference between the earlier migration northward and the present one southward. Previously, most African Americans moving north were unskilled workers looking for any type of employment that would pay them more than the bare subsistence income they had earned in southern rural areas or cities. Today, most African Americans migrating southward are

FIGURE 3–1   State Population Changes (in percentages), 1990–2000
Source: U.S. Bureau of the Census.

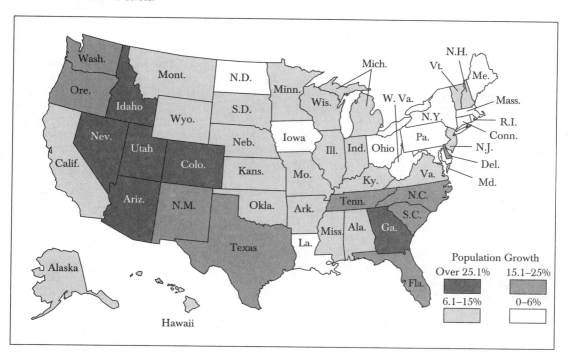

TABLE 3–5   The Ten Largest U.S. Cities in 2000 Compared with Rank in 1950 (population in thousands)

	2000		1950	
	Population	Rank	Population	Rank
New York	8,008	1	7,892	1
Los Angeles	3,695	2	1,970	4
Chicago	2,896	3	3,621	2
Houston	1,954	4	596	14
Philadelphia	1,518	5	2,072	3
Phoenix	1,321	6	107	96
San Diego	1,223	7	334	28
Dallas	1,189	8	434	21
San Antonio	1,145	9	408	24
Detroit	951	10	1,850	5

Note: Center city data only.

Source: U.S. Bureau of the Census.

of working age, and about one-fifth are college graduates, and thus they contribute to the growth of the black middle-class population in cities such as Atlanta, Charlotte, and Washington, D.C. Another 7 percent are aged 65 or older, moving south to retire (Frey, 1998).

Finally, many Sunbelt cities have been permitted, by law, to annex new territory, as the northern cities once did before municipal boundaries became rigid. Because of this territorial flexibility, Sunbelt economic and political boundaries are more congruent, and so far these cities have been able to avoid the financial straits of northern cities, becoming urban regions unto themselves. In contrast, most northeastern cities have the same boundaries that they had half a century ago and are surrounded by legally independent suburbs that wish no part of the problems of the old central cities.

The Sunbelt cities are on a growth spurt that resembles the one that Canadian and northern U.S. metropolises underwent in the period between 1870 and 1950. They are reshaping the face of urban North America. The process is feeding on itself. Business follows people; people follow business.

California provides just one example. For decades, people moving to the so-called golden land at the western edge of the continent tended to settle in that state's coastal cities—San Diego, Los Angeles, Santa Barbara, San Francisco—or their suburbs. Many are still doing so. However, in recent years the growth of California's inland cities has been nothing short of astounding. Growing as though there is no tomorrow are cities like Stockton, Bakersfield, Fresno, San Bernardino, Modesto, and Sacramento. Once again, it is quality-of-life issues that seem behind the change. Housing costs in coastal cities are astronomical, jobs are scarce (especially those that pay well), and smog and congestion are omnipresent. Inland, these problems are less intense.

BosWash Assets

Despite the Sunbelt expansion, the BosWash megalopolis remains a major part of U.S. urban life. It is a region where over 51 million people—almost one in five Americans—live. This 18 percent holds its share (19 percent) of the nation's wealth, compared with the 57 percent produced by the South and West, which contain 58 percent of the total population (Federal Reserve System, 2000). Nearly one-half of all investment capital available nationwide in 2000 was concentrated in the Northeast, where bank assets of $2.1 trillion accounted for 33 percent of the nation's total bank assets (U.S. Federal Deposit Insurance Corporation, 2002).

Why does this region still attract job-creating investments? With nearly one-fifth of the U.S. population on one-nineteenth of the land mass, it is the nation's most concentrated market region. Manufacturers in the BosWash corridor can reach over half the U.S. and Canadian industrial firms and retail sales outlets within 24 hours by truck. Also, the corridor states are, by air and sea, close to the 271 million people in the European Community countries. In addition, the 11-state region has the highest concentration of higher education institutions, sending 2.8 million students annually to 875 colleges and universities. Proximity to top colleges has influenced the location choices of high technology firms. Massachusetts's famous Route 128 (now called "America's Technology Highway") is near MIT and Harvard. New Jersey—with only 3.3 percent of the nation's population—has laboratories along Route 1 near Princeton University that do 9 percent of the research and development work in the United States (Parrillo, 2002:100–101).

Sunbelt Debits

Just as all is not negative in the Snowbelt, all is not rosy in the Sunbelt. A 2001 FBI report indicated that reported crime in the Sunbelt region constituted 64 percent of the total (41 percent in the South and 23 percent in the West), compared with 22 percent in the Midwest and only 14 percent in the Northeast. Pollution is increasing, water is running short (particularly in the Southwest), and population growth is just too great to absorb in many areas. Many of the fast-growth cities have not yet developed adequate infrastructure systems (roads, bridges, water and sewage systems) and the cost of doing so is rising rapidly.

Augmenting the population pressure is the influx of hundreds of thousands of Hispanics and Asians. San Antonio, now the nation's

ninth largest city, was the first with a Hispanic majority, but large Hispanic enclaves exist in every major city from Houston to Los Angeles. Some immigrants cross into the United States illegally in an attempt to escape the extreme poverty of their homeland (see Chapter 9) and to take part in the rich American Dream. The Immigration and Naturalization Service apprehended 1.4 million illegal aliens in 2001, but an estimated 150,000—the vast majority in the Southwest—elude detection each year (Parrillo, 2003:576). Typically, these aliens, many of whom are unable to speak English, have taken or have been forced into the worst jobs in the urban economy—the jobs that require long hours at low wages, with virtually no job security or chance for advancement, and involving dirty, physically punishing tasks under generally poor working conditions.

On another level, cultural and racial tensions between Hispanics and white Americans in the Sunbelt are mounting. Hispanics often are subjected to the same abusive treatment visited on African Americans in many cities and, in an earlier era, on Irish, Italian, and Jewish immigrants in the North. Housing problems also have become acute. Many Hispanic barrios in southwestern cities are beginning to resemble the impoverished slums of the developing world (Chapter 13).

Other difficulties are appearing. In the inland California cities mentioned earlier, the effects of rapid change and overcrowding are already beginning to show. Too few well-paying jobs are being created to keep up with the rising number of people seeking them. When the welfare rolls began to swell with unemployed, disgruntled citizens initiated several state referendums against illegal aliens and affirmative action policies. On another front, the great increase in automobile and industrial exhaust continues to create air pollution problems. A 2002 report revealed that, in California, air pollution kills more Californians each year than traffic accidents, homicide, and AIDS combined (Environmental Working Group, 2002). On a broader front, of the 25 U.S. cities identified in 2000 as having the greatest air pollution, 18 were in the Sunbelt (American Lung Association, 2000).

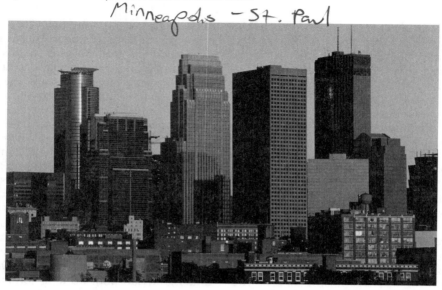

Minneapolis – St. Paul

Snowbelt cities such as Minneapolis–St. Paul, unlike Sunbelt cities, have high-density land use. The tight clustering of buildings—and therefore a closer proximity of shops, offices, and restaurants, not to mention apartment residences—places more activities within walking distance and therefore more crowds, congestion, and reliance on mass transit.

The pattern is nothing new. Throughout North American history, people have come to cities for the amenities they offered—jobs, education, the arts, and so on. When the cities become too crowded, a large percentage of people move on to what they perceive as greener pastures—the suburbs, the Sunbelt, anyplace where the streets are safer, the smog less oppressive, the cost of living lower, the jobs more plentiful. In time, these areas too begin to deteriorate as the "secret" of more comfortable living gets around and others descend on the area. California and other Sunbelt states are now beginning to experience this declining-quality-of-life problem. The question is: Where will we go, now that our older inner suburbs and our Sunbelt cities are experiencing the same deterioration and overload that the Snowbelt cities experienced not so very long ago?

Perhaps the answer is not to move at all but rather to attend to the problems of the city as they arise. Perhaps the urban core and all the amenities it has to offer could be salvaged if we were more attentive and less willing to pick up stakes and move the moment difficulties arise. Interestingly, this regeneration of the downtowns is happening in many cities, from Seattle and Portland in the West to Boston and Baltimore in the East.

THE COMING OF THE POSTINDUSTRIAL CITY

Almost 40 years ago, it looked as though our central cities were in an irreversible process of self-destruction. One of the enduring images of the mid-1960s appeared one evening on the television news as the screen behind CBS reporter Walter Cronkite showed thick, black smoke swirling all around the White House. Washington was in the throes of a major riot, as thousands of poor minorities reacted in desperation to their poverty, lashing out at our white-dominated society.

Dozens of U.S. cities experienced such riots in the 1960s. The National Advisory Commission on Civil Disorders studied 75 of these violent outbreaks and warned that the United States was "moving toward two societies, one black, one white—separate and unequal." Part of this problem showed itself in changing demographics. The central city was literally falling apart, and whites and the affluent were leaving for the suburbs. Industry was close behind as old factories became obsolete. Left in the decay were those who had little choice—the trapped and the poor, many of them minorities, increasingly embittered as the American Dream passed them by. It looked like the end of the city as we knew it, and many doubted that North American cities would ever rise again. In stark contrast, Canadian cities dealt with their problems more effectively, causing U.S. urbanist Jane Jacobs to refer to Toronto—by the 1960s a cosmopolitan city with a distinct racial–ethnic mix—as "a city that works."

In many cities today—despite the 1992 Los Angeles riot that left 58 people dead, 4,000 injured, and over $1 billion in property damage—the contrast with the earlier picture of older U.S. cities in disrepair is nothing short of amazing. All over the United States, new urban construction is in progress—from Pittsburgh to Seattle, from New York to Phoenix. Office towers are multiplying almost as fast as contractors can build them. Many residential areas of the city are being totally transformed as young urban professionals—the "yuppies"—move in, renovate old buildings or settle into new apartment complexes. Although many older cities, particularly smaller ones, are still hurting, the urban economy is alive once more. In most areas of the country, a true urban renaissance is under way as U.S. cities complete a shift to a postindustrial economy.

Deterioration and Regeneration

Since the mid-nineteenth century, U.S. cities had been industrial machines. They were the location of factories and their associated support industries. By and large, the people who worked in those industries lived in the city. But all that changed. As cities became more congested, more affluent people moved to the suburbs, leaving declining neighborhoods in their wake. With time, factories too fell into disrepair. Equally important, in the last few decades transportation services improved, making it more efficient for industries to locate outside of the central city on interstate loops. Together, as we have seen, these processes produced a city apparently rotting at the core, populated less and less by the rich and more and more by minorities and the poor.

But, as these last two chapters have shown, cities are remarkably resilient human creations with a built-in facility for regeneration because they are so vital to human life. Probably the city's most important trait, as we will discuss in detail in Chapter 7, is its ability to centralize and concentrate human affairs. Cities allow more efficient and intense activity in all areas of social existence: politics, religion, the arts and sciences, as well as the economy.

In the late 1960s, as central cities deteriorated or, worse, went up in smoke, scholars, politicians, and nearly everyone else wrung their hands and wondered what could be done. One voice suggested that we need do nothing: With time the city would save itself. That voice belonged to Edward C. Banfield, whose book *The Unheavenly City* (an obvious reference to Cotton Mather's wish for a "heavenly city" in the seventeenth century) created an enormous stir. The book, published in 1970, was controversial because of its basically conservative thesis that the city was too powerful an economic machine to remain down and out for long. Allow enough time and new businesses and people would see that they could get back into the central city and enjoy its great communicative advantages cheaply. They could buy up that land, renovate those deteriorated factories, houses, and apartment complexes, and thus avail themselves of the city's many benefits.

To some, Banfield's "do nothing" approach to urban destitution seemed callous and

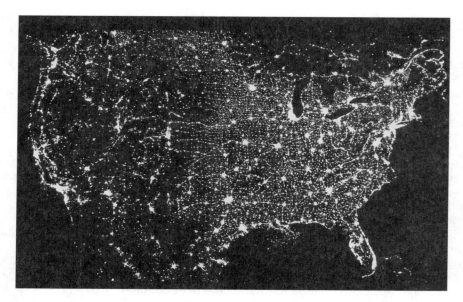

The night mosaic photographed from space illustrates the urban concentrations of people in North America more dramatically than could any artist or cartographer. The electric lights easily reveal where to find a megalopolis or metropolis and how much of the land is nonurban.

mean-spirited, and they roundly criticized him. And yet, well over three decades later, many of his predictions have come to pass. Cities across the nation are in the midst of a rejuvenation, and with little help from the federal government. The postindustrial city has arrived, and recent research suggests strongly that a general economic revitalization is under way (Teaford, 1990).

The reasons for this turnaround are two: (1) the growth of white-collar businesses tied to new technology, especially the use of microcomputers; and (2) a major shift in the way many industries do business. Regarding the first change—the growth of high-technology businesses—such organizations were more than happy to take over, renovate, or rebuild the structures left by departing heavy industry. They needed the central city location to maximize their efficiency.

As to the second element in the turnaround, many corporations are in the midst of a radical transformation, changing their

structure and operations. In the nineteenth century, major industries believed in a "beginning-to-end" process. That is, they oversaw and controlled their product from raw material to finished marketable item. This was true of most of the "giants," such as the Carnegie Corporation (steel) and the Ford Motor Company (which went so far as to raise sheep to produce wool for its cars' upholstery fabric!).

Now all that is changing. Big industries are divesting themselves of parts of their operations that are no longer profitable and are contracting out important products to other firms or to foreign companies. Thus, General Electric no longer makes microwave ovens or the ice makers that go into its refrigerators; these are being supplied by other firms in the United States, Korea, and Japan. Taking a more flexible approach, firms decide which parts of the production process they can perform profitably themselves and which would be more efficiently done by others (Prokesch, 1985).

Times Square

One of the best examples of an urban renaissance occurring in many North American cities is New York City's Times Square. Once the locale of sleazy porn stores and theaters and other seedy enterprises, it has undergone a facelift that is more than cosmetic. New hotels, theaters, and family-oriented businesses now dominate the area.

But such changes, which are happening all over the country, have important implications for the city: On the one hand, U.S. companies no longer require as many blue-collar workers or as many buildings geared to heavy industrial production. On the other hand, these corporations, which play so large a role in our urban scene, have created more white-collar jobs—jobs that depend on regular contact with other corporations, whether in the U.S. or abroad.

Naturally, many of the people employed by these postindustrial, high-tech industries want to live near their work and, while some (particularly those with families) continue to commute from the suburbs, many have opted to live in the central city. Illustrating this trend in the past several decades has been the process of gentrification, in which white-collar professionals have moved into and transformed older, decaying neighborhoods of many cities.

The Future

The postindustrial city will likely dominate North America's future, but what form will it take? Two trends are occurring simultaneously, and it is uncertain which will prevail in the twenty-first century. One trend is the appearance of edge cities, discussed more fully in Chapter 4. It is the evolution of edge cities on the fringe of older urban areas in the past two decades that helps explain the previously mentioned increases in population in nonmetropolitan areas. Joel Garreau (*Edge City*, 1991) suggests that North Americans have reinvented the city and that these new urban agglomerations are now the future. Numbering over 200 in Canada and the United States, these edge cities with their malls and office parks now dominate the nation's retail trade and office facilities.

The second trend is the revitalization of older cities, a significant process that shows no sign of stopping. More people, not fewer, are taking on the yuppie lifestyle, even as a new century begins. Since edge cities do not offer the residential ambience that young adults can find in a central city's brownstone houses, loft apartments, cozy restaurants and shops, the upgrading of many older city neighborhoods continues. In addition, the office building boom in many cities persists, to meet the needs of postindustrial corporations (Zipp and Cook, 1999).

Cleveland is a good example. In the 1960s and 1970s, this Ohio premier city was a symbol of urban despair. Severe social problems exploded into race riots in 1966 and 1968. Pollution was thick in the air and, in 1969, the Cuyahoga River actually burned for days because of the pollutants it contained. Cleveland's heavy industry was dying, its middle class was fleeing to the suburbs, and, by 1979, the city was on the verge of financial collapse.

A public–private partnership, forged by city government and business leaders in the early 1980s, breathed new life into the city. Perhaps the linchpin of the revitalization was the restoration of Cleveland's famous but abandoned landmark—the Terminal Tower commercial complex—into a rail transit station, a multilevel shopping center with upscale national stores, an 11-screen movie theater, a Ritz-Carlton hotel, and several highrise office buildings. The complex created over 3,000 permanent jobs and contributes more than $4 million in taxes to the city treasury (Greengard and Solomon, 1994:65).

Tourist attractions include the six-story Rock and Roll Hall of Fame and Museum, two new stadiums, and nearby Cedar Point amusement park with its 11 roller coaster rides (Herbert, 1996:72). Yuppies have turned abandoned warehouses into lofts and apartments. City residents can enjoy a lakefront park and trendy restaurants along the Cuyahoga River, where one can sit on the patios while barges and pleasure boats navigate the river. Although the city lost 5 percent of its population in the 1990s, that marked the smallest decline since the 1950s, and several hundred new homes sprout up each year,

reinforcing the spirit of urban revival that many residents feel (Schmitt, 2001:A1). To offset the city's loss of its former industrial base, Cleveland's leaders have rediscovered its waterfronts and made waterside development and amenities an important part of their economic strategy.

Strategy is exactly the right word. As the nation's central cities regenerate, many are engaging in a type of competition reminiscent of the interurban competition of the mid-1800s, when North American cities were growing by leaps and bounds. An increasing number of urban governments are hiring marketing professionals whose job it is to spiff up the city's image so that it can attract more businesses and tourists.

The Human Cost of Economic Restructuring

It is clear that the postindustrial process is not benefiting all of the city's residents. As gentrification progresses, the poorer residents of many city neighborhoods are simply displaced. Unable to pay the rising rents, they have to find somewhere else to live. Similarly, the fact that a few areas of our cities have become havens for the affluent has done little to change the very poorest areas of those cities: New York still has its Harlem and South Bronx, Chicago its South Side, Los Angeles its Watts, and Cleveland its Hough. Even more worrisome, the postindustrial economy is exacerbating the plight of the city's poor and unskilled.

This occupational restructuring creates a "skills mismatch" as our cities become ever more white collar. The cities' gradual shift away from manufacturing and goods processing eliminates many of the blue-collar jobs that were the first step up for millions of unskilled migrants and immigrants. The rising skill requirements of today's urban job market, demanding educated employees able to work with words and numbers in information-processing jobs, puts these new jobs out of reach for the urban poor. Thus, even as some urban neighborhoods improve, unemployment rates and welfare dependency among the unskilled remain high (Kasarda, 1990; Bauder and Perle, 1999).

In the 1980s several urban observers viewed postindustrial cities pessimistically (Bradbury, Downs, and Small, 1982; Berry, 1985; Downs, 1985). They saw the postindustrial city as increasingly characterized by two labor markets that fostered two dramatically unequal lifestyles —that of the well-paid white-collar professional and that of the low-paid service worker. Seeing these lifestyle inequities worsening in the foreseeable future, they concluded that the decline of the U.S. city was all but irreversible. Downs and his associates designed a computer simulation that pumped into Cleveland everything it seemed to need to reverse its inner-city problems—more jobs, better housing, improved transportation, the merging of city and county governments, and the restraint of suburban growth. Such improvements were much more than Cleveland could ever hope for realistically. Postindustrialism and the windfall of the urban upper classes may be flashy and hopeful on the surface but in reality, the critics contended, these "improvements" did not penetrate far beyond a small, favored group. In contrast, Roger Waldinger (1996) speaks of the interdependence between the city's affluent and poor, and of how the instability in the labor market and then the transformation of the ethnic division of labor is leading to positive developments, as he delineates in the case of the first postindustrial city, New York.

In conclusion, the postindustrial city is essentially the product of economic forces. Gentrification is all well and good as far as it goes, but not everyone agrees that the changes benefit all.

Historically, then, the North American city is engaged in a dynamic process that extends from its origins—those five communities "hacked out of the wilderness" in the seventeenth century—to the present configuration —much larger and still embroiled in rapid and significant change, as decentralization, the growth of the Sunbelt, and postindustrialization unfold. All these changes can be seen in the case study that closes this chapter, an analysis of North America's world city, New York.

❖ CASE STUDY ❖
New York—The "Big Apple"

Jim said everything was in New York. Jim said that he was happy, just standing in Grand Central Station, catching scraps of people's conversations. Jim said he would not mind standing all day on Sixth Avenue where they had the joke shops and the Orange Drinks, just watching the crowds go by. Jim said he would not mind standing all day in Radio City, where the French and British shops and the travel offices were, and the evergreens at Christmas and the tulips in the spring and where the fountains sprayed ceaselessly around Mr. Manship's golden boy and where exhibition fancy skaters salved their egos in the winter. If he grew tired of skaters, Jim said he would not mind standing and staring up and up, watching the mass of buildings cut into the sky.

John P. Marquand, *So Little Time* (1943)

Through almost all American history, New York has been the Great U.S. City. It symbolizes the United States to the world and, in many ways, reveals the rest of the world to the United States. New York not only represents the distinctive course of North American urban history, it is a timeless display of what urban life is all about. Here are just a few of the features that make it so outstanding.

First, New York is huge, an enormous concentration of population. Over 8 million people live within the city limits, and almost three times that many reside in the urban region that sprawls outward around the city. Second, it has the nation's greatest concentration of business and finance: About one-tenth of the largest U.S. corporations have headquarters in Manhattan, and a huge percentage of all stocks and bonds are traded there; in addition, it is a major location for most international businesses located in North America. Third, it is the largest U.S. port and has dominated American commerce since the early 1800s. Fourth, it is a mosaic of virtually every race and ethnic group in the world—over 50 different foreign-language newspapers are published in the city. Many of these groups have clustered together in such well-known districts as Chinatown, Harlem, Spanish Harlem, Little Italy, and the Lower East Side. Fifth, other New York districts are world-famous: Wall Street (finance), Madison Avenue (advertising), the garment district (center of the nation's clothing industry), Central Park (arguably the greatest urban park in the world), Fifth Avenue (for fashionable shopping and living), Greenwich Village (a longtime bohemian, student, and counterculture enclave), and Broadway (center of the most vibrant theater district in the world). Sixth, New York is also a key center of the arts, music, and publishing.

At street level New York abounds with crowds, traffic, musicians, vendors—multiple sights and sounds that bombard the senses. Indeed, the first experience of New York City is one many carry with them all their lives. On another level the city is deceptive. Its very size tricks us into thinking things are other than they are—something that the Urban Living box reveals about that grandest of illusion makers, Radio City Music Hall.

One cannot escape, however, the great contradictions, contrasts, and inconsistencies of New York life. The city is home to the richest and poorest of North Americans. Some of the worst social problems stand, literally, in the shadow of the proudest cultural achievements. Wealthy beyond belief in the private sectors, New York was on the verge of bankruptcy in the 1970s. Inevitably, perhaps, New York is the most loved and most hated city in the United States. Say outsiders, "A nice place to visit, but . . . I wouldn't want to live there." Some New Yorkers even boast about how awful it is—but most probably would never live anywhere else. In short, if something is to be found at all, it is to be found in New York. It is a world city par excellence. And, since September 11, Americans elsewhere have expressed a special bond for New York as the symbol of America united and defiant against terrorism.

New York, always at the center of U.S. life, has a varied history. Since its changes serve to illustrate the themes of North American

urban history generally, we shall look briefly at its development during each of the four phases discussed in this chapter.

The Colonial Era

New York was the earliest of the five major colonial settlements. Henry Hudson entered the river later named for him in the early autumn of 1609 on an expedition financed by the Dutch East India Company. Other explorers skirted the area in subsequent years and, by 1624, a small settlement, based primarily on the fur trade, was permanently in place on the southern tip of Manhattan Island. Peter Minuit arrived from Holland in 1626 as the settlement's first director general. In that same year he reached the world-famous agreement with the resident natives to trade ownership of the island for $24 worth of trinkets.

New Amsterdam, the center of the Dutch New Netherlands, prospered in the decades that followed: Houses were built and farmland was cultivated. A row of logs was put in place for protection along the northern edge of the settlement, which later became known as Wall Street. In 1638, a ferry service to Breukelen (later Brooklyn) began and the first settlers reached Staten Island. New Yorkers initiated a weekly market in 1648, and the first lawyer began practice in 1650.

In 1653 a charter granted by Holland allowed the town to organize a local government featuring a mayor and a city council. When the first survey was completed in 1656, the "city" had about 1,000 people living in 120 houses on 17 irregularly placed streets. Within a few years, some of the streets were stone-covered and a greater measure of security was provided by a town-watch (the earliest direct ancestor of New York's police force). Outside of town to the north were farms the Dutch called "boweries." This area, the point at which the irregular streets end (at about Houston Street today), was long known as "The Bowery." A farming village called Haarlem was established much farther up the island in 1658, at the end of a long dirt road known as "Broadway."

URBAN LIVING

All New York's a Stage

I'll tell you an old joke that will sum up Radio City Music Hall for you. It seems a man and his wife went to the Music Hall one Sunday afternoon, arriving toward the end of the film. When it ended, the house lights came up for a few minutes before the stage show and the man rose, murmuring to his wife: "I'm going to the men's room."

He located an exit on his floor—orchestra, loge, mezzanine, balcony or second balcony—but he couldn't find a men's room on it. He descended a staircase and looked on the next floor and couldn't find a men's room and descended another staircase. He walked along corridors and pushed open doors, he went along dark passages and up

and down steps, getting more and more lost and more and more frantic. Just as his need became intolerably urgent, he pushed open a heavy door and found himself on a small street lined with houses, trees and shrubs. There was no one in sight and the man relieved himself in the bushes.

All this had taken time, and it took him additional time to work his way back up to his own floor and locate his own aisle and section. By the time he finally reached his seat, the stage show had ended and the movie had begun again. The man slid into his seat whispering to his wife: "How was the stage show?" To which his wife replied: "You ought to know. You were in it."

Source: Helene Hanff, *Apple of My Eye* (New York: Doubleday, 1978), p. 129.

The first Jews arrived in the 1650s, establishing a long tradition that was to influence the city's history, and the first Quakers settled in the city in 1657. An English fleet anchored in 1664 and gained control of the town, renaming the settlement New York in honor of Charles II's brother, James, the Duke of York. The English commander continued a policy of religious freedom for all groups, reaffirming the tradition of religious tolerance initiated by the Dutch. Millions in later years would be drawn to this city where it was possible to worship and to express oneself as one chose.

In 1680, New York City began its climb to economic preeminence when it gained a monopoly on the sifting of flour for export. Docks multiplied, trade prospered, and support businesses of all sorts became established. The population grew steadily; from 4,000 in 1703, New York grew to 7,000 in 1723, and passed the 10,000 mark in 1737.

The first newspaper appeared in 1725; a stagecoach link to Philadelphia started in 1730; and the New York Public Library opened in 1731.

As this growth occurred, New York, like the other colonies, was beginning to resent ever more sharply the British impositions on trade. In 1765 the English government instituted the Stamp Act, placing a levy on all transactions. The colonists bitterly opposed it. Swayed, Parliament repealed the act in 1766, causing a New York group dubbed the "Sons of Liberty" to build a triumphant "Liberty Pole" in the city. The British took strong offense, an altercation followed, and some of the Sons of Liberty were killed. This was the first blood of the American Revolution.

When the revolution began, the British occupied New York for seven years. The war drove many New Yorkers temporarily out of the city, reducing its population by several thousand from a peak of 21,500. However, with the end of the war, the city leapt once more to life. George Washington was inaugurated as the first president of the United States in Federal Hall at the corner of Wall and Nassau Streets and, for a year thereafter (1790), New York served as the U.S. capital.

Growth and Expansion

By 1800 the city's population surpassed 60,000. The growth of New York during this second period continued to be spectacular. The population exceeded 96,000 by 1810 and 202,000 by 1830. Yet this was only a hint of things to come. Earlier, in 1792, a group of traders had met in the Wall Street area and planned what was to become the New York Stock Exchange. In 1807 the city approved its famous grid plan for street development. In 1825 the Erie Canal was completed, linking the Hudson with the Great Lakes and giving New York a long-sought trade advantage over its East Coast urban competitors. With direct access to the North American heartland, in the next few decades the city became the economic center of the United States.

In 1838 overseas steamship service began, establishing a connection with Europe that truly opened immigration. In 1840, for example, more than 50,000 people arrived in New York harbor from abroad, and most settled in the city. In 1846, the first telegraph line between New York and Philadelphia began operation. In 1848, a five-story factory (also a sign of things to come) opened its doors. Urban transportation improved with the introduction of the rail-mounted horsecar in 1850. This made "suburbanization" of the upper island more feasible by establishing a fare—a nickel—that was within financial reach of most New Yorkers. In 1853, New York hosted the nation's first "expo," symbolic of the grand optimism that by now was part of the city's character. In 1858, the plan for one of the greatest of urban landmarks—Central Park—was approved (though the park itself was not substantially completed until after the Civil War). In 1860, although still officially consisting of only Manhattan Island, the city boasted a population of 814,000, with another 250,000 nearby in Brooklyn, Staten Island, and Jersey City.

The Great Metropolis Emerges

After the Civil War, which temporarily slowed its growth, New York matured as a great metropolis. An unprecedented surge in the city's population occurred between 1870 and 1930, dwarfing all previous gains. Table 3–6 shows that New York City as a whole quintupled its population in the six decades after 1870. However, until January 1898, the five boroughs remained legally separate municipalities.

The period between 1870 and 1920 was an era of extensive foreign immigration to the United States, and New York was the major port of disembarkation for the entire country. Some nationalities arrived in huge numbers. For example, Chinatown began to take form in 1884; Italian immigration intensified after 1885; and Jews began to make their way through the Ellis Island immigration facility to the Lower East Side in large numbers after 1890. Many of these new urbanites went directly to work in industries that produced items such as garments and shoes. The excitement of arrival in New York is revealed in these comments by David Quizano, a Russian Jewish immigrant, and Vera Revendal, his Christian sweetheart, in Israel Zangwill's 1908 play *The Melting Pot:*

> [David] There she lies, the great Melting Pot— listen! Can't you hear the roaring and the bubbling? There gapes her mouth [he points east]—the harbor where a thousand mammoth feeders come from the ends of the world to pour in their human freight. Ah, what a stirring and a seething! Celt and Latin, Slav and Teuton, Greek and Syrian,—black and yellow—
> [Vera] Jew and Gentile—
> [David] Yes, East and West, and North and South, the palm and the pine, the pole and the equator, the crescent and the cross—how the great Alchemist melts and fuses them with his purging flame! (Zangwill, 1919:184–185).

As amazing as it sounds, by 1890 four out of five people living in the New York area were either born abroad or had foreign-born parents (Glaab and Brown, 1967). New York, like other American metropolises of the era, began to take on a characteristic "ethnic mosaic" pattern of settlement, as described by social reformer Jacob Riis in the Looking Back box on page 98.

This process of racial and ethnic mixture, however, has produced as much of a "pressure cooker" as a "melting pot." Indeed, the general economic opportunity New York provided during this period must be contrasted with the tensions that turned groups against each other, wages that were often appallingly low, and living conditions that were highly unfavorable to generations of immigrants. Although citywide residential density in 1890 was about 60 people to an acre, in immigrant areas densities reached alarming levels—as much as seven times greater. The frightful concentration continued to increase to almost 750 persons per acre—about 12 times the city average—in 1898 (Glaab and Brown, 1967). Today, the density of central Manhattan has fallen to about 100 persons per acre.

Sometimes, when immigrants mixed, the results were explosive. One area of midtown, from about West 15th Street to West 50th Street along Eighth, Ninth, and Tenth Avenues, was home to blacks and whites of different ethnic groups. During the work week

trouble was minimal, but on weekends in the summer, when much drinking and carousing occurred, violent fighting often broke out between groups. So intense were the confrontations that police nicknamed the area "Hell's Kitchen."

Governing this incredible and growing mass of people was difficult, at best. City Hall became increasingly corrupt as interest groups vied with one another for contracts, favors, and patronage. The greatest symbol of corruption in New York's history was that of political boss William "Boss" Tweed. In 1870, by means of $1 million in bribes to the New York State legislature and other groups, Tweed and his gang were able to gain complete political control over the city. It is estimated that they stole nearly $200 million in funds from the city treasury and garnered even more from kickbacks and payoffs. Finally exposed by the *New York Times* in 1871, Tweed was arrested and brought to trial. So confident was he that he would be acquitted that he haughtily said, in response to an allegation about his misappropriation of funds, "What are ya gonna do about it?" His confidence was misplaced. He went to jail in 1872. Nevertheless, extensive graft in city government continued to plague the city until well into this century.

Certain physical changes linked to technology contributed to the growth of the city during this period as well. In 1881, the Brooklyn

TABLE 3–6   Population of New York City, by Borough, 1870–2000 (in thousands)

	1870	1900	1930	1960	2000
New York City	1,476	3,437	6,929	7,782	8,008
Borough					
Manhattan	942	1,850	1,867	1,695	1,537
Bronx	37	201	1,265	1,425	1,333
Brooklyn	419	1,167	2,560	2,627	2,465
Queens	45	153	1,079	1,810	2,229
Staten Island	33	67	158	222	444

Note: The five boroughs were not officially incorporated as New York City until 1898.

Source: U. S. Bureau of the Census.

LOOKING BACK

The Crazy-Quilt Pattern of New York, 1890

Jacob Riis

A map of [New York], colored to designate nationalities, would show more stripes than the skin of a zebra, and more colors than any rainbow. . . . [G]reen for the Irish prevailing in the West Side tenement districts, and blue for the Germans on the East Side. . . . [I]ntermingled . . . would be an odd variety of tints that would give the whole the appearance of an extraordinary crazy-quilt. From down in the Sixth Ward . . . the red of the Italian would be seen forcing its way northward along the line of Mulberry Street to the quarter of the French purple on Bleecker Street and South Fifth Avenue. . . . On the West Side, the red would be seen overrunning the old Africa of Thompson Street pushing the black of the negro rapidly uptown.

. . . the Russian and Polish Jew, having overrun the district between Rivington and Division Streets, east of the Bowery, to the point of suffocation, is filling the tenements of the old Seventh Ward to the river front. . . . Between the dull gray of the Jew, his favorite color, and the Italian red, would be seen squeezed in on the map a sharp streak of yellow, marking the narrow boundaries of Chinatown. . . . Dots and dashes of color here and there would show . . . the Finnish sailors . . . the Greek pedlars . . . and the Swiss. . . . And so on to the end of the long register, all toiling together in the galling fetters of the tenement.

Source: Jacob Riis, *How the Other Half Lives* (New York: Hill and Wang, 1957), pp. 18–20. Originally published in 1890.

Bridge opened, and remains, along with the Golden Gate Bridge in San Francisco, one of the world's most beautiful. It was followed in 1903 by the Williamsburg Bridge and in 1904 by the first tunnel under the Hudson River connecting the city to the New Jersey shore. In 1906, the Pennsylvania Railroad also tunneled under the Hudson, establishing major rail transport in the heart of Manhattan at Penn Station. Subways soon followed. People now could live far from midtown and still get there cheaply and quickly.

At the lower end of Manhattan, the dazzling New York skyline began to take shape. Today, it is difficult to imagine New York without a forest of skyscrapers. Yet, before 1890, Manhattan below Central Park was completely covered by structures of less than five stories.

The first steel structure in New York appeared in 1889 and reached a "towering" 11 stories. From this point, New York grew upward as if the clouds had become great magnets. The number of buildings with 20 or more floors increased from 61 in 1913 to 188 in 1929. Indeed, half of all such buildings in the country were in New York (Armstrong, 1972).

Before the Depression stalled construction of office buildings, New York witnessed the completion of three famous architectural innovations that survive to the present day. The Chrysler Building, opened in 1930, is a marvelous 77-story example of Art Deco architecture—topped with six stories of magnificent stainless-steel arches. The following year marked the opening of the Empire State Building, which, at 102 floors, has symbolized New

York ever since. Rockefeller Center was begun in the same year. It was designed to include "everything" in one place, as urban critic Paul Goldberger observes:

> . . . skyscrapers, plazas, movement, detail, views, stores, cafes. It is all of a piece, yet it is able to appear possessed of infinite variety at the same time. . . . It was conceived as a place in which monumental architecture would spur both business and culture to new heights, and it has come remarkably close to fulfilling that somewhat naive goal. It is surely the parent of every large scale urban complex every American downtown has built since—from Atlanta's Peachtree Center to Hartford's Constitution Center to San Francisco's Embarcadero Center—and it is no insult to say that Rockefeller Center still remains far and away the finest such development ever built (1979:168–69).

New York Today

> New York? It'll be a great place if they ever finish it.

Short-story writer O. Henry

By the 1950s New York had grown from being a metropolis to being the center of that vast urban region that Jean Gottmann called a megalopolis. The 2000 census places the city at the heart of a vast metropolitan statistical area covering some 4,000 square miles with more than 21 million people. To illustrate the point another way, nearly one American in fourteen lives in the New York MSA.

From another perspective, however, this incredible region is a product of the decentralization that has affected so many cities in contemporary America. Bridges, highways, tunnels, cars, costs, and congestion—all led to a rapid move away from the city itself between 1970 and 1980, as New York City lost over 860,000 people (a loss greater than the entire central city population of San Francisco!). However, between 1980 and 1990, New York gained 251,000 inhabitants, and by 2000, the city had grown by another 685,000, due primarily to an influx of immigrants.

Economic Problems

By the late 1990s the nation as a whole had recovered all the jobs lost in the recession of the late 1980s and early 1990s, but the New York region regained only about a third of the 770,000 jobs it lost. The numbers reflected deep structural problems in this metropolitan region, especially in the concentration of the company headquarters of 46 of the nation's top 500 corporations. Many large businesses continue to shrink as corporate America merges, downsizes, and lays off workers. The merger of Chase Manhattan and Chemical Bank, for example, eliminated about 12,000 jobs (Johnson and Lueck, 1996). Then the destruction of the World Trade Center and its immediate surroundings caused a severe blow both to the corporate and neighborhood economies of lower Manhattan. The loss of or severe damage to 20 million square feet of office space, as well as the loss of tens of thousands of jobs, also directly affected 14,000 small businesses because there was less foot traffic and there were far fewer customers (Ploeger, 2002).

But major cities like New York are constantly changing. Just as immigration repeatedly remade the city throughout its history, so too have its economic fortunes rebounded despite the "gloom and doom" experts who sounded the city's death knell. New York and the other cities survived, and—despite recessions in the late 1980s, early 1990s, and early 2000s—they have worked their way back to financial solvency. Partially back, at least. And the city is back for many of the same reasons that Boston, Baltimore, and other cities are coming back: The postindustrial economy is remaking New York. New positions for highly trained professional workers, particularly in the information-processing and finance sectors, are available, along with lower-paying jobs in the service sectors of food, delivery, and tourism. Parts of the city, such as midtown, thrive as white-collar service centers where business professionals can remain in close contact with one another, have lunch, and socialize after work at a wide variety of places catering to their tastes. Once it is rebuilt, lower Manhattan will no doubt thrive again as well.

Until the advent of suburban shopping malls in the 1950s and 1960s, cities were the shopping meccas for almost everyone. By car, bus, and train, shoppers from the outlying towns would come to the city for all kinds of goods, for that was where the best and biggest stores, with the widest selections, were. Here, in New York City in the 1930s, shoppers crowd together during a popular sale at Macy's Department Store.

As in other cities, the proportion of people who work in postindustrial jobs is small—perhaps on the order of 10 percent. Many people are working in the service sector in restaurants, hotels, and retail stores, or as public employees (police, fire, transit, sanitation, social services). Manufacturing still plays a role, though. About 280,000 manufacturing jobs remain in businesses like apparel and printing, but a surprising number of new industrial enterprises have materialized, especially in computer software, video-production, recycling, and cargo shipping. A 1996 study issued by the Urban Research Center at New York University said that the average young manufacturing company in New York has only three employees, and that immigrants own nearly 41 percent of these businesses, compared with 12 percent nationwide. These 10,000 small companies range from older industries employing new methods of production, especially in garment manufacturing, to the high-technology loft shops of software makers in lower Manhattan and niche manufacturers serving immigrant neighborhoods (Johnson, 1996).

In pre–September 11 days, tourism soared, partly encouraged by the city's plummeting crime rate. Its 2000 total crime index for violent and property crimes put New York 160th out of 205 U.S. cities, making it the safest city among those with 1 million or more inhabitants (FBI, 2002). Retail sales went up, helped in part by the opening of numerous bank branches and chain stores. In fact, in mid-2002 a strong demand for store space bolstered the city's economy (Holusha, 2002). More feature films and television series are now shot in the city than at any time since the 1950s, and New York hosts the second largest concentration of motion picture activity. However, late 2002 saw air passenger arrivals, hotel occupancy, attendance at Broadway shows, ticket sales at tourist attractions like the Empire State Building, Ellis Island and the Statue of Liberty decline, adding to the city's woes in a time of a soft economy and budget deficits.

Nevertheless the 10 percent postindustrial workers in the information sector have a considerable impact on urban lifestyle. Throughout the city one can find clubs, coffee bars, chic shops, and trendy restaurants springing up, and attendance at concerts, museums, theaters, sports contests, and special events has risen as well. Rental housing is scarce and expensive, especially in Manhattan. Typical rents for nonluxury apartments in 2002 were $2,000 to $3,000 a month in Manhattan. A two-bedroom apartment in any "desirable" location (such as the Upper East Side or parts of the West Side) costs from $3,000 to $5,000 per month. To this frequently is added a "finder's fee"—usually two or three months' rent paid to the person who procures the apartment for the renter. And once-inexpensive lofts still sell on average for $700,000 (Hevesi, 1999:RE 1 Craigslist, 2003).

Upgrading the City

Construction is omnipresent. In the 1970s, the ill-fated twin towers of the World Trade Center in lower Manhattan boosted both the image and the economy of the city. In the 1980s, it was the construction of Battery Park City, a $1.5 billion, 92-acre commercial and residential complex that is home to the New York Mercantile Exchange, the Commodity Exchange, and American Express. There are also 2,000 apartments in eight buildings, a

Ritz-Carlton and an Embassy Suites hotel, four ferry slips, and a 15-screen multiplex theater (Dunlap, 1999). The site also includes a museum, parks, plazas, playgrounds, public arts, and schools. At 125th Street in Harlem, the neighborhood's first supermarket, the New Harlem USA shopping center and cinema multiplex, and the renovation of the Apollo Theater have improved the physical environment and quality of life (Pristin, 1999). In lower Harlem, the completion of 3,500 new apartments in rehabilitated buildings has revitalized commercial activity along 116th Street west of Malcolm X Boulevard. East New York, a once-devastated area in Brooklyn that was once dubbed the "murder capital of New York City," was transformed into a livable area of new multifamily homes and rental housing, with plans for 2,300 more new homes around a new mall. Perhaps, though, the most dramatic symbol of New York's revival is construction in the South Bronx. The image of the South Bronx as a lawless, burned-out, drug-infested area whose rampant crime rate inspired the movie *Fort Apache, the Bronx* no longer rings true (Oser, 1994; Purdy, 1994; Hevesi, 2001).

In a city full of surprises, few are as striking as the contrast between the 20-year-old image of the burned-out South Bronx and today's reality after what officials call the nation's largest urban rebuilding effort. With more than $1 billion in public dollars trained on the South Bronx since 1986, 19,000 apartments have been refurbished and more than 4,500 new houses have been built for working-class home buyers. More than 50 abandoned buildings that once stood like rotten teeth along major arteries like the Cross Bronx and Major Deegan expressways have been reclaimed as mid-rise apartment houses.

In spite of the wave of development that has swept through the South Bronx, large stretches, particularly the Mott Haven section, have been left behind, and there the ravages of crime, drugs, and decay continue unabated. Nevertheless, the progress is extraordinary considering the free-fall of the 1970s. Between 1970 and 1980, the population of the South

Bronx plunged by more than 40 percent as over 300,000 people left. In the next decade, the slide ended as the area gained about 26,500 people (Purdy, 1994; U.S. Bureau of the Census, 2002a).

Other signs of an urban renaissance are found everywhere. They range in scale from massive residential enclaves like Queens West and Riverside South, both loosely modeled after Battery Park City, to the Starbucks-style cafes that have sprouted up all over. The transformation of 42nd Street, once the center of sex and sleaze, into a family entertainment center with Disney as the linchpin, is simply amazing, and the renovation of Grand Central Terminal with upscale shopping malls is another positive sign.

Creation or restoration of parks offers another example of the improvement in the quality of life in New York. At Pier 25 in TriBeCa, for example, there is now a modest recreation area with miniature golf, volleyball, and a children's playground. Similar restorations at Pier 45 at Christopher Street and Pier 64 in Chelsea have made these areas available for recreation as well (A. Jacobs, 1995). Now these parks are being combined into the new Hudson River Park, 550 acres stretching from Battery Park City to 59th Street, with esplanades, waterfront activities, biking and roller blading paths, dog runs, athletic facilities, gardens, and sculptures. The success of the 1992 transformation of Bryant Park—once an unsafe, sequestered area for drug dealers—into one of New York's busiest public spaces, where thousands go day and night for lunch, concerts, outdoor movies, or simply to mingle, has surprised even members of the city's Planning Commission. It has become a "hot spot" for young adults, serving—in an odd manifestation of a small-town tradition—as Manhattan's town square (B. Weber, 1995).

On another front, over 130 <u>Business Improvement Districts, or BIDs</u>, exist in virtually every section of the city, from Harlem to Brighton Beach. More than 1,200 have been created in cities across North America in the last two decades, but their greatest impact has been in New York (in Times Square, for instance), where their numbers, size, and financial clout dwarf those of BIDs elsewhere. BIDs are self-taxing districts set up to clean, patrol, and upgrade their neighborhoods, providing services that were once the sole responsibility of city government. Cities, faced with budget problems, have welcomed the privatizing of municipal services. Once a majority of owners in a designated area agree, they work out a plan for services, which must be approved by the City Council. The city then collects an annual assessment (above the property taxes) from all property owners and turns the money over to the district. The resulting services and improvements—new sidewalks, signs, street lights, planters, wastebaskets, flags and banners, street sweepers, and unarmed uniformed security patrols—have reduced crime, cleaned up streets, and restored a sense of pride among merchants and the public (Lueck, 1994; Dickerson, 1999:1).

Changing Population

The exodus of people and firms has had a marked effect on the city's character and fortunes. Most of the outward movement has been by whites and the more affluent (although many of the most affluent seem to remain ensconced in their wealthy enclaves on Central Park West, Fifth Avenue, Park Avenue, and the Upper East Side). Since the end of World War II, over 3 million whites have left the central-city area. Minority migrants and immigrants have replaced them. In 1950 the population of the five boroughs was 87 percent white, 9 percent black, and 3 percent Hispanic. By 2000 the city's profile had shifted to 34 percent non-Hispanic white, 28 percent black, 27 percent Hispanic, and 11 percent Asian (Sachs, 1999; U.S. Bureau of the Census, 2002b).

Although many minorities work in the information processing and service sectors, unemployment and poverty are high within the city's African American and Hispanic American communities. The Community Service Society of New York reported that about 20 percent of New York City residents lived in poverty in

2001. Poverty was highest among Hispanic residents at 28 percent; 30 percent of New York's children were poor (double the national rate), as were 19 percent of the city's elderly. All of these rates were above the national average (Community Service Society, 2002).

In the midst of the difficulties, some continue to try to improve their lives, placing their faith in an improving neighborhood. Many new-style New York homeowners of lower-income status, tired of their urban lifestyle but not of the city—investing their life savings and adding faith, determination, and hard work—have helped revitalize parts of run-down neighborhoods that only a few years ago seemed hopelessly lost. Whether moving into new housing improved by others or employing "sweat equity" to upgrade a run-down dwelling, a surprising number of lower-income New Yorkers have been successful in these efforts. Their combined efforts are giving a much-needed facelift to some of the city's worst neighborhoods.

Beyond the Devastation

On that infamous day of September 11, New York City suffered the worst tragedy in its history. In addition to the heartbreaking loss of so many innocent lives were the severe economic losses. As the NYC Chamber of Commerce (2002) reported, these losses included billions of dollars of damaged or destroyed private capital and public infrastructure; thousands of dislocated workers; millions of dollars of lost sales due to business interruption; and significant disruption to the financial services industry that makes New York the capital of the global securities and banking markets.

City Comptroller William C. Thompson, Jr. (2002) issued a detailed report on the extent of those losses in just one year's time. Among the report's findings:

- The economic cost to the city from the attacks on September 11 totaled between $83 billion and $95 billion, the final figure dependent on the number of jobs eventually relocated out of the city permanently.

- The attacks destroyed 13 million square feet of prime office space—equal to the entire office space inventory in the central business districts of Atlanta or Miami.
- It will cost $21.8 billion to replace the buildings, infrastructure, and tenant assets lost as a result of September 11.
- Job losses attributable to September 11 cost the city more than $17 billion in lost wages. New York City is down a total of 146,000 jobs as result of the attacks, with 83,000 fewer jobs than before September 11 and the loss of a projected 63,000 jobs that would have resulted from economic growth.
- The attacks cost the city nearly $3 billion in lost taxes and nearly $500 million in unreimbursed expenses. Roughly half of the $6 billion budget gap that had to be closed to balance fiscal year 2003 was attributable to September 11.

Sudden unemployment and business losses fell not just on the many small businesses dependent on customers who worked at or visited the World Trade Center, but also on those dependent on tourism—including hotels and restaurants, theaters, the taxi industry, airlines, and airport-related industries. A study by the Center for an Urban Future found that LaGuardia and Kennedy Airports suffered larger economic losses than most other major hub airports in the country. Those losses permeated almost every aspect of these airports' business, from cargo and passenger traffic to hotel vacancies, causing the elimination of 16.5 percent of all airport-related jobs—10,000 jobs—in the city since September 11. That is by far the largest percentage loss of any industry in the city, including the securities industry, which lost 9 percent of its jobs (Kennedy, 2002).

Although the federal government helped, with its Federal Emergency Management Agency (FEMA) providing $901 million in aid through August 2002, New York City still faced a $251 million shortfall. With state support and pledged federal funding to meet remaining expenses and to rebuild the lower Manhattan area, the city is in a position to deal with its most immediate needs. However, its reduced revenues from payroll, sales, and

The winning, innovative design for reconstruction of the World Trade Center site includes new buildings, a 1,776-foot spire/transmission tower, a museum, a memorial park in the void leaving intact the footprints of where the towers once stood, and a street-level promenade, leaving visible the impressive slurry wall that holds back the Hudson River.

user taxes will present budget deficit worries for the next several years (Thompson, 2002).

When the Lower Manhattan Development Corporation, the state agency created to supervise the rebuilding of ground zero, first received competing designs from architectural firms, the public reaction was highly negative, criticizing them as too conventional and uninspiring. The second round of proposals produced more imaginative concepts and audacious designs, resulting in the selection of a proposal from Daniel Libeskind in February 2003. This design combines commercial

buildings with cultural, performing arts, and transportation centers all linked to a memorial park and pedestrian walkway. Its beautiful and dynamic composition will, advocates say, "re-assert New York's cosmopolitan identity" and "re-establish New York's skyline as the most thrilling in the world" (Muschamp, 2002).

And so New York goes on, with its successes and failures, its ability to symbolize simultaneously all that is great and tragic about all cities. To many, New York is the quintessential city, as Peter Berger suggests in the Urban Living box on page 105. If New York fails, in some sense cities everywhere fail, but if it succeeds, it offers hope for all.

❖ ——————————— ❖ ——————————— ❖

SUMMARY

The development of North American cities has been, in its own way, as dynamic and varied as that of European cities. Neither Canada nor the United States began as an urban nation; in fact, that idea would have been anathema to many of either country's founders. Nevertheless, in three and a half centuries, that is what both have become.

The process of urbanization began just as European feudalism was breathing its last. Begun as places of religious and political freedom, the new colonies rapidly established themselves as major trading centers. By 1700, coastal villages were becoming bustling towns. By the late eighteenth century, these small cities began to develop into major urban areas. They traded up and down the coast and with Europe and became rich by establishing links with the vast and rich heartland of the country. Inland cities appeared. By the middle of the nineteenth century, industrialization was transforming the northern cities of the United States and, to some degree, their Canadian and newer midwestern counterparts, into manufacturing centers. The South, still operating on the "small city" pattern associated with agriculture, fell behind. With victory for the North, the Civil War effectively ended the small- versus large-city "debate" in the United States.

URBAN LIVING

In Praise of New York

Peter Berger praises N.Y.

Much of the rest of the country sees New York as one gigantic agglomeration of social ills: crime, poverty, racial hatred, mismanaged and corrupt government—not to mention dirt, pollution, and traffic congestion of virtually metaphysical dimensions. . . . And yet, despite all this, New York City continues to be a magnet and even an object of love, sometimes fierce love. People, especially young people, continue to come in large numbers, irresistibly drawn to the city by expectations of success and excitement. And New Yorkers themselves, although they, too, frequently share the negative views of their own city, nevertheless continue to be inexplicably, perhaps dementedly, attached to that putative cesspool of perdition in which they reside. Such ambivalence suggests that the reality of New York is more complicated than its symbolic imagery.

. . . New York . . . is not only a vast and vastly important city, but the city par excellence, the prototypical cosmopolis of our age. . . . Every urban experience [that people] have had before has been, in a way, an anticipation of New York. . . . Wherever skyscrapers reach upwards toward the clouds, wherever masses of cars stream back and forth over steel-girded bridges, wherever heterogeneous crowds pour through subways, underground concourses, or cavernous lobbies encased in glass—there is a bit of New York. . . . The mystique of New York City is, above all, the mystique of modern urban life, concentrated there more massively than anywhere else.

Source: Peter Berger, "In Praise of New York," excerpted from *Commentary*, February 1977 by permission; all rights reserved.

After 1870, North American cities, particularly in the North, the Midwest, and Lower Canada, exploded into metropolises of millions. Trade and industry were the driving wheels behind this development. More and more jobs generated more and more wealth. Drawn to this opportunity, millions came from abroad, resulting in the ethnic–racial–religious mosaic that characterizes so many North American cities. With this influx came great problems, particularly in the United States. Quality of life began to deteriorate, and poverty and exploitation became rampant. New technological advances enabled many to escape to streetcar suburbs. Consequently, cities began to spread over the countryside. Losing revenue because of this exodus, and greatly hampered by the Depression, cities began to depend on federal assistance.

After World War II, decentralization accelerated. People and businesses departed the central cities, leaving the innermost areas increasingly populated by the poor and minorities (unable to escape because of poverty or prejudice) and by service-oriented or professional businesses. Huge metropolitan regions became more the norm, replacing earlier central-city cores.

In the older Snowbelt cities of the United States, decentralization had particularly disastrous results. When the cities lost people and businesses, billions in tax and sales revenues and hundreds of thousands of jobs were lost as well. Many cities faced a continual threat of bankruptcy. The South and West, however, experienced an urban boom. Sunbelt cities were the direct beneficiaries of northern cities' problems with their old industrial systems, poor inner-city transportation for products, and deteriorating services. The Sunbelt cities built new plants, surrounded by efficient superhighways; they provided good or brand-new service systems; and they offered lower costs—particularly for energy and labor. Some Sunbelt cities were able to expand their physical boundaries—for example, in Texas, one of the states with greatest urban expansion, suburbs were annexed almost as fast as they appeared, thus keeping the tax and business base within the city jurisdiction.

In a contemporary trend that may turn out to be the most important of all, North American cities are rapidly developing a postindustrial economy based on high technology, white-collar jobs, and services. As a result, in recent years cities have been rebuilding the deteriorating office and housing stock left from earlier decades and improving many other amenities that define the quality of urban life. Older cities once in the throes of economic disaster are rebounding, although problems clearly remain, particularly with the poorer residents. Serving as white-collar service centers, these cities have attracted young, relatively affluent professionals whose presence has had great impact. Another trend is the formation of edge cities on the fringes of established metropolitan areas.

The evidence suggests that all three trends—decentralization, the move to the Sunbelt, and the growth of a postindustrial economy—will continue in force in the new century. As a result, northern cities such as New York will continue to adapt to a changing economic structure and a new population. Meanwhile, the Sunbelt picture is not as rosy as it once was. The population boom, in many instances, has been too much to cope with, crime rates are high, and racial tensions are on the rise as Hispanics move up from Mexico and Latin America and African Americans move back to the South. Furthermore, even in cities where postindustrialization is in full sway, there is no indication that the new-found wealth of the few who are participating in this lifestyle will spread to the urban population as a whole. On the contrary, it appears that the gap between the urban rich and poor is widening, not narrowing.

CONCLUSION

It seems evident that in the three centuries since urbanization took hold in the New World, North Americans have not built Cotton Mather's hoped-for "Heavenly City." Nevertheless, there are signs that cities are being revitalized, if only partially, as we begin the twenty-first century. Whether this rebuilding process will continue or whether the North American version of the urban experiment will come, as it did in the late 1960s and early 1970s, to resemble Edward Banfield's "Unheavenly City" more than likely will depend on the decisions made by the people living in these cities in the next several years. If we continue to see the city as something to "use," but not something to be collectively concerned about, the outlook probably is not very bright. If, on the other hand, we see the city as a human creation and thus subject to understanding and human control, then we might be justified in being more optimistic about the outcome.

Chapters 2 and 3 have provided an overview of the long path that cities have followed from their origins thousands of years ago until a few decades ago. The new patterns of urban and suburban development are significantly different and so widespread that they clearly will be important factors for the foreseeable future. In the next chapter we will examine these newest components of urban life.

CHAPTER 4

CITIES AND SUBURBS OF THE TWENTY-FIRST CENTURY

We can't always predict the future, but we do invent it. Today's decisions affect tomorrow's realities, just as we are living out the decisions made by preceding generations. For example, the change in public preference from urban to suburban living owes much to federal legislation in the late 1940s and 1950s that provided low-cost builder and buyer loans, as well as to a massive highway-building program that made it easier to live away from city jobs and activities. That growth in middle-class suburban housing, and the subsequent exodus of many businesses to suburban campuses or shopping malls, eroded the cities' economic vitality and tax base, which, in turn, worsened the quality of urban schools and the quality of life for many city dwellers who remained. The suburban lifestyles that most North Americans favor today, as well as the problems besetting many U.S. cities, are the result of social forces unleashed two generations ago. So too will the decisions of recent decades affect urban and suburban lifestyles for decades to come.

Four patterns in particular—sprawl, edge cities, gated communities, and common-interest developments—have grown so fast and had such a strong effect on urban areas that we can discuss both their current influence on the quality of life as well as their importance for the foreseeable future.

URBAN AND SUBURBAN SPRAWL

Stretching across North America—from the West Coast to the East Coast, from Toronto to Miami, from Vancouver to Tucson—are large metropolitan areas fused into a series of megalopolises. Gobbling up the land are strip malls and large suburban tracts of cookie-cutter housing of such striking similarity that they are creating an unvarying sameness everywhere, blurring traditional regional differences. Within this vast homogeneous panorama, one could be almost anywhere on the continent and find few visual clues as to locale.

What Is Sprawl?

Sprawl is the term used to describe spread-out or low-density development beyond the edge of services and employment. It separates where people live from where they work, shop, and pursue leisure or an education, thereby requiring them to use cars to move between these zones. This type of development results from decades of unplanned, rapid growth and poor land-use management. *Sprawl* thus identifies the cumulative effects of development that is automobile-dependent, inefficient, and wasteful of natural resources.

As people move farther from core cities and into outlying regions, so do all the trappings of urban life: stores, offices, factories, hospitals, crime, congestion, and pollution. Developments claim more and more open land as the population increases and disperses. One town looks like another, stores on the highways erect signs to shout out their wares to the fast-moving traffic going by, and every activity requires a separate trip by car (see the Critical Thinking box on page 109).

According to the Regional Plan Association, if the office space needed for each 5 million increase in population were built only in suburban office parks it would cut a swath a half-mile wide and 54 miles long. However, in a large city with skyscrapers, 200 acres would fulfill the same need. The reason is that each million square feet of suburban office space requires, on average, 80 acres (25 of those acres for parking lots) as compared with 1 acre in a large city, half of which is for an office plaza. In smaller cities, the same 1 million square feet would take up about 6 acres, with the construction of 25-story buildings with landscaping and parking lots (Caldwell, 1973:45–56).

Two striking examples of suburban sprawl-development patterns consuming far more land than urban development patterns are in Pennsylvania and Arizona. Since 1950, Pennsylvania has lost more than 4 million acres of farmland to sprawl—an area larger than Connecticut and Rhode Island combined. The city of Phoenix now covers some 600 square miles,

CRITICAL THINKING

James
Howard
Kunstler

Something Is Wrong

Americans *sense that something is wrong* with the places where we live and work and go about our daily business. We hear this unhappiness expressed in phrases like "no sense of place" and "the loss of community." We drive up and down the gruesome, tragic suburban boulevards of commerce, and we're overwhelmed at the fantastic, awesome, stupefying ugliness of absolutely everything in sight—the fry pits, the big-box stores, the office units, the lube joints, the carpet warehouses, the parking lagoons, the jive plastic townhouse clusters, the uproar of signs, the highway itself clogged with cars—as though the whole thing had been designed by some diabolical force bent on making human beings miserable. And naturally, this experience can make us feel glum about the nature and future of our civilization.

When we drive around and look at all this cartoon architecture and other junk that we've smeared all over the landscape, we register it as ugliness. This ugliness is the surface expression of deeper problems—problems that relate to the issue of our national character. The highway strip is not just a sequence of eyesores. The pattern it represents is also economically catastrophic, an environmental calamity, socially devastating, and spiritually degrading.

. . . We reject the past and the future, and this repudiation is manifest in our graceless constructions. Our residential, commercial, and civic buildings are constructed with the fully conscious expectation that they will disintegrate in a few decades. This condition even has a name: "design life." Strip malls and elementary schools have short design lives. They are expected to fall apart in less than fifty years. Since these things are not expected to speak to any era but our own, we seem unwilling to put money or effort into their embellishment. Nor do we care about traditional solutions to the problems of weather and light, because we have technology to mitigate these problems—namely, central heating and electricity. Thus in many new office buildings the windows don't open. In especially bad buildings, like the average Wal-Mart, windows are dispensed with nearly altogether. This process of disconnection from the past and the future, and from the organic patterns of weather and light, done for the sake of expedience, ends up diminishing us spiritually, impoverishing us socially, and degrading the aggregate set of cultural patterns that we call civilization.

Source: James Howard Kunstler, "Home from Nowhere," *The Atlantic Monthly* 278 (September 1996), 43–66. Reprinted by permission of the author.

an area larger than the state of Delaware. In the next 50 years, sprawl is expected to consume more than 3.5 million acres of California's Great Central Valley, the nation's prime greengrocer (Purdum, 1999). Elsewhere, trends are similar. Between 1970 and 1990, metro New York's population grew only 5 percent, but consumed 61 percent more land, while metro Chicago's population grew by just 4 percent, but consumed 46 percent more land.

Opponents cite figures for the loss of rural land that vary from about 400,000 to 1.4 million acres a year. Advocates counter that there is no shortage of empty land in the United

States, that 95 percent of the land is undeveloped, and that the rate of land development is an infinitesimal .07 percent a year. Although that is a low figure, it does mean that during the lifetime of a child born today, the developed area of the nation would double. Which side's figures are accurate? Actually, they both are. The problem is that this development is concentrated in a relatively few areas, close to the big cities (Pedersen, Smith, and Adler, 1999:24).

Why Do We Have Sprawl?

Sprawl is like that cartoon snowball rolling down the hill, growing in size and momentum, becoming practically unstoppable. In the past half-century, government policies on taxation, transportation, and housing—nurtured by society's embrace of *laissez faire* development—subsidized virtually unlimited low-density development. And the more this development occurred, the more people clamored for it.

A house in the suburbs became, for many, the personification of the ideal lifestyle. Massive road-building projects and community planning designed around the car encouraged people to abandon the cities for the greener pastures of suburbia. As these nonmetropolitan areas grew in population, a new phenomenon—the shopping center—came into existence, with large department stores from the city serving as anchors for the variety of retail enterprises along the indoor corridors. Office and industrial parks followed, either lured by tax incentives, induced by management preferences, or prompted by the relocation of competitors. Whatever the reason, the snowball effect generated more and more growth farther and farther away from cities into outlying regions. As a result, much of the natural landscape around the largest cities in Canada and the United States has been transformed.

Where Does Sprawl Occur?

Sprawl occurs everywhere. It is most obvious and grows most spectacularly in the rapid growth areas of the South and West. For instance, on the periphery of Denver, farmland is yielding to sprawl at a rate of 90,000 acres per year. Significantly, though, land development is no longer proportional to population growth. Studies show that a 1 percent increase in population results in 10 to 20 percent growth in land consumption (Florian, 1999:24). West Palm Beach, Florida, for example, experienced a 15 percent population increase between 1990 and 1996 but a 25 percent decrease in population density during the same period.

Yet sprawl doesn't occur only because of population growth. Cincinnati, which lost 15 percent of its population between 1970 and 1980, then another 10 percent between 1980 and 1996, nonetheless increased its land area from 335 square miles in 1970 to 573 square miles in 1996. Metro Cleveland's population declined by 11 percent between 1970 and 1990, but it still consumed 33 percent more land. Also, between 1990 and 1996, Akron, Ohio, experienced a 37 percent decrease in population but a 65 percent increase in developed land area use (Florian, 1999:25).

An important study, *The Dark Side of the American Dream* (1998), conducted by the Sierra Club, an environmentalist group, identified the 30 most sprawl-threatened cities (see Table 4–1). Some cities—such as Phoenix, Spokane, Boise, and many California cities—are not in this group because they evolved as sprawled cities from the beginning and are thus not sprawl-threatened. However, most of these qualify for a "dishonorable mention" because of their continuing patterns of sprawl.

The Problems of Sprawl

Most people don't realize all the negative aspects of sprawl. To them it is the means of owning a house on a large lot and enjoying the convenience of one-stop mega-mall shopping. Yet these suburbanites pay a price in air pollution, traffic congestion, and visual blight. Longer commutes take time away from families, increase gasoline consumption as well as wear and tear on cars, cause traffic congestion, and increase instances of road rage. For example, the typical worker in Atlanta drives 37 miles round trip to work, while those in

TABLE 4–1   The Most Sprawl-Threatened U.S. Cities

Large Cities (Population: 1 million or more)		Medium Cities (Population: 500,000–1 million)
1. Atlanta, GA	11. Detroit, MI	1. Orlando, FL
2. St. Louis, MO	12. Baltimore, MD	2. Austin, TX
3. Washington, DC	13. Cleveland, OH	3. Las Vegas, NV
4. Cincinnati, OH	14. Tampa, FL	4. West Palm Beach, FL
5. Kansas City, MO	15. Dallas, TX	5. Akron, OH
6. Denver, CO	16. Hampton Roads, VA	
7. Seattle, WA	17. Pittsburgh, PA	
8. Minneapolis–St. Paul, MN	18. Miami, FL	
9. Fort Lauderdale, FL	19. San Antonio, TX	
10. Chicago, IL	20. Riverside–San Bernardino, CA	

Small Cities (Population: 200,000–500,000)	Dishonorable Mention
1. McAllen, TX	1. Los Angeles, CA
2. Raleigh, NC	2. San Diego, CA
3. Pensacola, FL	3. Phoenix, AZ
4. Daytona Beach, FL	
5. Little Rock, AR	

Source: From *The Dark Side of the American Dream,* © 1999 Sierra Club Books. Reprinted by permission.

Dallas drive 30 miles, and in Los Angeles the daily drive is 21 miles (Florian, 1999:25). When people complain that it takes an hour and a half to go 30 miles, some suggest that the answer is more highways. But the building of more roads and the widening of others results in the cutting down of more trees, creating an ugly and desolate landscape devoid of vegetation and full of strip malls.

We pay a high social price for sprawl as well. By spreading residences, medical and commercial offices, and industries throughout a region on large tracts of land, we increase residents' dependence on automobile transportation. Everything and everyone is too spread out to make public transportation economically feasible. With insufficient coordination of work sites and highways, traffic congestion results. Nor can everyone get around by car: A lifestyle that requires a car discriminates against poor families, the elderly, the disabled, and the young. Suburban

teenagers, for instance, usually lack sufficient activities in their town but are unable to travel to locations where such diversions do exist. Suburban parents thus spend a large part of their time chauffeuring their children to stores, cinemas, juvenile activities, and other events.

Green space advocates, disparagingly called "tree-huggers" by developers and business interests, have long deplored the decades-old growth pattern that consumes large expanses of prime farmland and woodland. In recent years, however, other individuals, groups, and organizations—realizing the costs and consequences of sprawl—have suggested that these costs may outweigh the benefits. Joining their ranks are low-income housing advocates, social service organizations, church leaders, and others concerned about urban decay and poverty (McMahon, 1997:4). Those seeking to curb sprawl base their concerns around environmental damage, loss of farmland and historic centers, financial costs, and transportation issues.

Environmental Damage

As new structures arbitrarily emerge in scattered fashion across the countryside, they disrupt wildlife habitats and fragment rural regions once abounding in farmland, fields, forests, lakes, and ponds. An example of the latter is the runoff from streets, parking lots, lawns, and farms that empties pollutants and sediment into waterways, degrading water quality and smothering habitat. In *The Dark Side of the American Dream*, the Sierra Club gave two examples of this problem:

> Around the Chesapeake Bay, sprawl is gobbling up open space and forest lands quickly. According to the Chesapeake Bay Foundation, more than 90,000 acres are consumed by sprawl each year in the bay states. Today, 4 to 5 times more land is used per person than 40 years ago. As a result, toxins and sediments are flowing into the bay in increasing amounts and upsetting the delicate balance of the watershed's ecosystem. Sprawl is undermining progress in cleaning up the Chesapeake Bay and protecting habitat for fish and wildlife.

> The Sonoran Desert is the largest desert in North America, covering about 120,000 square miles. Daily summer temperatures exceed 100 degrees Fahrenheit. Most parts of the desert receive less than 10 inches of rainfall a year. But, far from being a parched and barren wasteland, the Sonoran Desert is one of the most botanically diverse deserts in the world. More than 2,500 plant species and various desert animals call the Sonoran Desert home.

> Today, more than 80 percent of Arizona's population lives in the Sonoran Desert, which includes the rapidly growing areas around Phoenix and Tucson. For the natural habitat of the Sonoran Desert, which evolved gradually over millennia, the rapid changes brought by man-made development, including fragmented habitats, new competition for food and water by imported non-native species, and changes in air and climate conditions, could pose a very serious threat. (Sierra Club, 1999)

Sprawl has also had disastrous consequences involving the destruction of wetlands and building on flood plains. Wetlands act as natural sponges that soak up and store rain and runoff. When they are bulldozed over and asphalted under, water that would have been stopped or slowed is free to flood. With few exceptions, floods are most frequent, and loss of life and property are greatest, in counties that have lost the most wetlands—especially in the past 30 years.

According to the Federal Emergency Management Agency (FEMA)—the government entity responsible for disaster response and prevention—the number of floods, flood deaths, and property losses caused by flooding is increasing. Nationwide, floods killed over 900 people between 1988 and 2001, and cost an average of $4.3 billion each year during the same period. And FEMA believes that a principal cause of this increased flooding is poor planning and unwise development that destroys the wetlands and open space that protect communities.

Worsening pollution is another negative effect that sprawl has on the environment. In Seattle, for example, experts blame development around Puget Sound for the polluted water and habitat destruction that resulted in the proposed Endangered Species listing of chinook salmon. Another form of pollution is found in the suburbanized areas of Las Vegas, the fastest-growing city in the United States. This mid-sized city, which increased its population by 84 percent between 1990 and 2000, gains a new resident every nine minutes. As a result, the city now has serious air- and water-quality problems (Sierra Club, 1999).

Loss of Farmland

Sprawl threatens farmland all across the North American continent. A 1996 report by the American Farmland Trust, in an analysis of 181 major land resource areas, identified an alarming 70 percent of "prime or unique" farmland as now in the path of rapid development. On average, 400,000 farm acres a year disappear to make way for residential and commercial centers. Between 1970 and 1990, almost 20 million acres of rural land were developed nationwide. Texas lost more "prime and unique" farmland than any other state—nearly a half million acres from 1982 to 1992. Along the East Coast, writes the Sierra Club:

This aerial view of Las Vegas shows the spread-city phenomenon occurring in the U.S. Sunbelt area. Like other Sunbelt cities in which climate and work opportunities attract many, its rapid growth strains the existing infrastructure and water supply and gobbles up the land, as its sprawling development pattern increases dependence on the automobile.

Even places like Vermont, a state with a powerful rural legacy, are not immune to development pressures. The very name of the state, "Vermont," is practically synonymous with rural life in this country. Its rural personality is largely responsible for the area's economic health as millions of tourists visit Vermont each year and produce billions of dollars in revenue for state coffers.

Yet, beginning in the 1980s, as more and more people moved to Vermont in search of a better quality of life, development (often in the form of malls and superstores) began to slice up this bucolic countryside. In just two years, the state lost 10 percent of its farmland. (Sierra Club, 1999)   *Vermont*

Anti-sprawl advocates argue that this contagious, so far unstoppable, march across fertile, high-quality farmland is quickly undermining the nation's agricultural productivity. Furthermore, the trend is a worldwide phenomenon, with cities growing outward and absorbing peripheral farmland in their inexorable drive to accommodate their burgeoning populations. As the world population expands from 6 billion to 9 billion in the twenty-first century, we may require more arable land for agriculture, not less.

In contrast, others argue that negative claims about sprawl and vanishing farmland are vastly overstated. People's freedom to choose low-density suburban living arrangements over high-density living arrangements, they contend, is a positive aspect of life. Moreover, as the late economist Julian L Simon noted in *Hoodwinking the Nation* (1999), much farmland is left idle to limit crop surpluses. James Legacy (2000) adds that the introduction of new crops in developing nations such as Nigeria has markedly increased local food crop production. However, he cautions, we should nonetheless carefully examine our land use policies so that marginal agricultural lands get used for housing and roads, while our best farmlands are kept in agriculture.

Loss of Historic Treasures

The centrifugal shift of businesses and residences into outlying areas takes people away from the older, established central cities, downtowns, and neighborhoods where so much of the heritage of both Canada and the United States is concentrated. These areas then lose their economic health, and the buildings and other historical reminders that define these once bustling places fall into disrepair. Sprawl thus robs cities of character, as abandoned factories, boarded-up homes, and decaying retail centers dominate the urban landscape. Smaller, older cities in the northeastern United States are especially vulnerable to this process, but even newer cities can be victims. For example, historic Spokane, Washington, once called "The City Beautiful," is reeling under the pressures of growth, with 54,000 newcomers expected in the next 20 years. Many city residents—believing that sprawl and automobile dependency were taking over and crushing the city's charm—banded together to form the Spokane Horizons project to develop a comprehensive plan to address issues like parking, new roads, and infrastructure capacity while calling for a healthy downtown and surrounding neighborhoods.

As explained in *The Dark Side of the American Dream*, the loss of historically important centers to sprawl is not limited to cities:

> Lancaster County [Pennsylvania] has been called "the Garden Spot of America, a kind of Eden on the East Coast, the idyllic farmscape where the Amish retreat from the modern world" (*Boston Globe*, Michael Grunwald). The county also produces hundreds of millions of dollars in farm products and hosts thousands of tourists every year who come to enjoy the area's beauty and experience a piece of American history.
>
> But Lancaster is beginning to take on the cast of the rest of suburbia. While an agricultural protection program is in place, the county has lost about 4,800 acres to development since 1980—or 68 square miles over a ten-year period to house 60,000 people, according to the National Trust for Historic Preservation (NTHP).

To add insult to injury, Walmart has proposed building five stores which the Amish and other dedicated citizens are trying to prevent from happening. Lancaster County has in fact been named one of the most endangered historic sites in the world by the NTHP because of the devastating effects of sprawl.

Financial Costs

Conventional wisdom says that development strengthens the municipal tax base. That may have been true in the 1980s, but by the 1990s local officials had discovered that increases in tax revenues were eaten up by costs to their communities for delivering new services (including water and sewer lines, schools, police and fire protection, and roads) to people who lived far away from the existing infrastructure. Here are some examples:

- Between 1970 and 1995, Maine spent over $338 million building new schools while the number of public school students declined by 27,000.
- Fresno, California, has doubled in size since 1980, producing $56 million in yearly revenues, but the cost of services has risen to $123 million (not including costs for roads and sewers).
- From 1970 to 1990, Minneapolis–St. Paul closed 162 physically adequate schools in urban and central suburban areas and opened 78 brand-new schools in the outer suburbs.
- Providing services to new development has grown so costly in Prince William County, Virginia, near Washington, D.C., that even though the county has the highest property-tax rate in the Commonwealth, every new house brings a $1,688 shortfall (Sierra Club, 1999).

A Maryland study predicts that, in the first two decades of the twenty-first century, sprawl will cost state residents about $10 billion more for new roads, schools, sewers, and water than would be necessary if growth were more concentrated. Similar studies in California, New Jersey, Florida, and elsewhere have demonstrated a direct relationship between sprawl and the spiraling costs of government (McMahon, 1997:4). These additional costs don't occur only in the growing communities. As people flock to the outlying suburbs, cities—their tax base eroded—must raise taxes on the remaining taxpayers to pay for city services.

Traffic Problems

Because sprawl, by definition, is low-density, automobile-dependent development on the edge of service and employment areas, it generates longer commutes and greater traffic congestion. In Atlanta, where motorists now lead the nation in miles driven per person per day, air pollution is so bad that the area has lost federal funding for failing to meet clean-air standards. Cars zipping along highways, or worse, cars stuck in traffic jams, spew millions of tons of carbon dioxide and other greenhouse gases into our atmosphere each year. The 1999 Sierra Club report identified time wasted in traffic (beyond normal commuting time) in 1994, as part of its study of the effect of sprawl. The top five cities in time squandered because of traffic congestion were (1) Riverside–San Bernardino; (2) Washington, D.C.; (3) San Francisco–Oakland; (4) Los Angeles; and (5) Houston. Other findings were:

- Detroit drivers wasted 57 hours per person in traffic.
- Baltimore drivers spent 138 percent more time in traffic than in 1982.
- Cleveland drivers spent 260 percent more time in traffic than in 1982.
- Dallas drivers wasted 55 hours per person caught in traffic.
- San Antonio drivers wasted 30 percent more time in traffic than they did in 1990.
- Riverside–San Bernardino drivers wasted 75 hours caught in traffic, highest in the country. (Sierra Club, 1999)

The problem is most acute in Southern California, where traffic congestion is growing by about 3 percent a year, as measured by the number of miles of clogged freeways. The congestion will get worse as this region of 19 million absorbs a projected 7 million new residents in the next 20 years—the equivalent of twice the population of Chicago. The Southern California Association of Governments predicts that if population trends and transportation spending continue at their current pace, average rush-hour speeds will drop from about 35 mph to 15 mph in the region's urban centers by 2010. The term *rush hour*, whether in Southern California or elsewhere, is in actuality no longer accurate. Where once the rush hour was exactly that—typically an hour between 7 and 8 A.M. and another between 4 and 5 P.M.—today the peak traffic periods last from 6 through 9 A.M. and from 3 until 7 P.M. (Martin, 1999).

Harm to Cities

Sprawl may be primarily a suburban phenomenon, but it has a powerful urban counterpart. People are only beginning to realize that it wastes generations of investment in urban infrastructure—that abandoned buildings in the city, clogged highways, and the new megamalls in farm fields have something in common: Although seemingly unrelated, they are all the direct results of sprawl. As Jeff McLaughlin (1999) observes:

> Sprawl is not just a 20-minute drive in a $40,000, 12-miles-per-gallon sport utility vehicle to buy a half-gallon of milk. Sprawl is also a 20-minute wait by a core-city resident for a dilapidated municipal bus that will lug its passenger over potholed streets to a "convenience store" for that half-gallon of milk.

Sprawl hurts cities in several ways: (1) It erodes the city's tax base as people flock to the suburbs, forcing cities to raise taxes on remaining taxpayers to pay for city services. (2) It destroys downtown commerce by pulling shoppers from once-thriving locally owned stores and restaurants to large regional malls. (3) It increases unemployment and concentrates poverty in urban centers. (4) It robs cities of character as abandoned factories, boarded-up homes, and decaying retail centers dominate the landscape (Sierra Club, 1999).

Atlanta's afternoon rush-hour traffic snarls at what commuters refer to as "spaghetti junction"—the intersection of Interstates 85 and 285. Many of these drivers are heading from their jobs to homes in suburban Gwinnett County. In two decades, Gwinnett's population has more than tripled to exceed 465,000. Atlanta's phenomenal growth, and lack of adequate mass transit, are the main reasons why the area suffers from traffic congestion, air pollution, and urban sprawl.

Solutions to Sprawl

Sprawl by definition is a regional problem, and solving the problem requires convincing people that comprehensive, rational planning and strategies to combat it are in their self-interest. "Smart growth" public policies seek ways to stop the bulldozing of forests and farms and instead encourage reinvestment in cities and urbanized towns. An increasing number of community leaders, concerned citizens, environmental groups, and government officials are exploring alternative growth and development approaches to sprawl, some of which are still on the drawing boards while others are gaining more widespread adoption.

Land Purchases

In the 1960s, the federal government began setting aside a percentage of its royalties from offshore oil drilling to acquire or expand recreational land and open space. Now, through referendums and local or state government initiatives, efforts to protect open space and slow suburban sprawl are growing. In November 1998, New Jersey voters approved a $1 billion referendum to raise the gasoline tax to set aside half the state's remaining 2 million acres of open space over the next 10 years. Earlier, voters in Monroe County in Pennsylvania approved a $25 million bond referendum to purchase undeveloped land over a ten-year period. Voters in Austin, Texas, approved an increase in water rates to protect thousands of acres of environmentally sensitive land around the city. Maryland's newly established Smart Growth and Neighborhood Conservation Program includes $71 million to buy agricultural, forest, or natural areas that are in danger of development. Elsewhere, in Florida and Michigan, for example, communities are also purchasing land to prevent development.

Urban Growth Boundaries

Oregon and Washington require all communities to designate official boundaries in order to separate urban areas from their surrounding greenbelt of open lands, including farms, watersheds, and parks. The intent is to funnel growth to areas with existing infrastructure while protecting the wide diversity of natural resources wrapped around these population centers. Portland, Oregon—featured in this chapter's case study—has had an urban growth boundary in place since 1975. Although Portland has grown almost 50 percent in population since then, it has consumed only 2 percent more land. Home prices are lower than in other major West Coast cities, and builders support the growth boundaries because there is less red tape and more flexible zoning within the designated growth areas. As a result, Portland is one of the healthiest and most livable cities in the United States (McMahon, 1997). Other cities that have been successful in this approach are Boulder, Colorado, and the California cities of San Jose, Morgan Hill, Napa, and Santa Rosa (Sierra Club, 1999).

Revitalizing Existing Cities and Towns

The rejuvenation of once-thriving cities and towns—where mass transit, existing infrastructure, and high-density living can support growth—will attract new residents and limit urban flight. Many communities are preserving their unique architecture through restoration and are utilizing good planning to restore a sense of community, improve livability, and enhance economic vitality. Through innovative public–private redevelopment strategies, they are creating vibrant urban environments that reconnect to their histories and cultural identities. Chattanooga, Tennessee, cleaned up its once seriously polluted river, the Tennessee, and created a riverfront park and a promenade that now attract both wildlife and people. Suisun, California, in the San Francisco Bay area, converted an area containing a polluted waterway, decaying warehouses, and a high-crime neighborhood of dilapidated houses into a charming place filled with shops, affordable homes, and a canal for boating. As part of its smart growth plan to encourage revitalization by drawing people to the inner city, Maryland gives at least $3,000 to people to buy a home in areas closer to their places of work.

Transit-Oriented Approaches

Some proposed solutions for relieving traffic congestion focus on building more highway lanes, using "smart corridors" with synchronized traffic lights to move vehicles through congested areas, adding carpool or high-occupancy vehicle (HOV) lanes, or building more rail lines alongside the highways that connect cities and suburbs. While these proposals may alleviate traffic congestion somewhat, they do nothing to slow sprawl. Indeed, they may intensify it. Instead, planners seek to strengthen ridership on public transit by encouraging or requiring more compact mixed-use development around transit stops. Some companies, worried that congested roads and long commutes hurt their ability to hire and retain workers, have taken such steps. Bell South is consolidating 75 scattered work sites (with 13,000 workers) into three near the Atlanta rapid transit system. Adobe Systems recently moved its headquarters to downtown San Jose and pays 300 workers $30 monthly subsidies to ride mass transit. In upscale South Denver, businesses—finding it difficult to get low-wage workers to commute from other parts of the city because of the traffic congestion—are lobbying to get "working-wage" housing built (Jones, 1999). In Vancouver, British Columbia, sprawl spread eastward and carpeted the Fraser River Valley with dozens of suburbs; as a result, rush-hour traffic headed out of the city over Lion's Gate Bridge was routinely backed up for three miles. Unable to stop the sprawl, planners sought to reduce the traffic congestion. Determined to avoid further "Los Angelization," regional leaders rejected the idea of building more highways as the backbone of their local transportation network. Instead, they set up an extensive transit system—utilizing trains and ferries, but anchored by 1,000 buses (20 times the number in the Atlanta region) that drive the system and account for 80 percent of all transit travel. Significantly, as more suburbanites and commuters converged on the Vancouver metropolitan region, area planners opted to spread the population around by creating self-sustaining job centers in the suburbs to the east. They did so through SkyTrain, an 18-mile automated light-rail train. Its elevated electric cars—colored white and trimmed in the red, blue, and yellow colors of the province—zip along into the suburbs of East Vancouver, Burnaby, New Westminster, and Surrey, taking passengers to and from their homes or work in far less time than on the clogged highways. Metrotown, once a suburban warehouse district on the wane, has become SkyTrain's busiest station, as office buildings, apartments, movie theaters, and a mall now ring the station (Turner, 1997; Manuel, 1997).

These four approaches—land purchases, growth boundaries, revitalization, transit solutions—and other grass-roots efforts at comprehensive land-use planning to designate growth and nongrowth areas are essential to revitalizing our urban cores and protecting our open space, outdoor lifestyles, and farmland. If public policy invests money, effort, and vision into our communities rather than into sprawl, and stops subsidizing new roads, utilities, and development at the expense of our urban centers, the public will have more options to make environmentally responsible lifestyle choices.

EDGE CITIES

Not since the expansion of small cities into huge metropolises a century ago have we seen as profound a change in our urban world as the emergence of edge cities. An *edge city* is a new, sprawling, middle-class, automobile-dependent center typically located at the fringe of an older urban area, at the intersection of major highways, where little except villages or farmland existed three decades earlier.

In the second half of the twentieth century, North Americans went through three waves of centrifugal movement away from the older cities. First came the suburbanization of North America, most notably after World War II, as people moved into new homes beyond city boundaries. Next came the malling of North America, particularly in the 1960s and 1970s, when we moved our stores out to where we lived. And now, says Joel Garreau (1991), we have moved our means of creating wealth, the essence of urbanism—our jobs—out to where most of us have lived and shopped for two generations. This has led to the rise of edge cities, resulting in profound changes in the ways we live, work, and play. Garreau describes the new urban form this way:

> For some who recognize the future when they see it, but always rather hoped it might look like Paris in the 1920s, the sprawl and apparent chaos of Edge City makes it seem a wild, raw, and alien place. For my sins I once spent a fair chunk of a Christmas season in Tysons Corner, Virginia, stopping people as they hurried about their holiday tasks, asking them what they thought of their brave new world. The words I recorded were searing. They described the area as plastic, a hodgepodge, Disneyland (used as a pejorative), and sterile. They said it lacked livability, civilization, community, neighborhood, and even a soul.
>
> These responses are frightening, if Edge City is the laboratory of how civilized and livable urban America will be well into the next century. Right now, it is vertigo-inducing. It may have all the complexity, diversity, and size of a downtown. But it can cover dozens of square miles, and juxtapose schools and freeways and atria and shimmering parking lots with corporate lawns and Day-Glo-orange helicopter wind socks. Its logic takes a while to decode.
>
> Will we ever be proud of this place? Will we ever drag our visiting relatives out to show off our Edge City, our shining city on the hill? Will we ever feel—for this generation and the ones that follow—that it's a good place to be young? To be old? To fall in love? To have a Fourth of July parade? Will it ever be the place we want to call home? (Garreau, 1991:8–9)

It is the evolution of edge cities in the past quarter-century that helps explain the increases in population in nonmetropolitan areas, as discussed in the previous chapter. Garreau suggests that North Americans have reinvented the city in recent decades and that these new urban agglomerations are now the future. Numbering over 200 in the United States, these edge cities with their malls and office parks now dominate the nation's retail trade and office facilities. The City in Literature box on page 120 offers further insight into the edge city phenomenon.

Edge cities are appearing in Canada as well as in the United States, but apparently for different reasons. Unlike the United States, the Canadian government does not provide suburb-enhancing tax deductions for home mortgages, and it has greater control over planning and development. In Canada also, there is a greater emphasis on mass transit; a relative lack of freeways; vibrant, bustling urban centers; and a relative lack of racial problems. Nevertheless, edge cities are flourishing. Toronto, for example, has only 46 percent of the area's market. The rest is found in the nine edge cities growing up around it. These are Midtown–Yorkville and North York–North Yonge to the north; Mississauga, the Downsview Airport area, and the Etobicoke–427 area to the west; and the Don Valley Parkway–401 area, Markham–404 area, Eglington–Don Mills area, and Scarborough to the east.

What Garreau calls edge cities have become the dominant form:

> By any functional urban standard—tall buildings, bright lights, office space that represents white-collar jobs, shopping, entertainment, prestigious hotels, corporate headquarters, hospitals with CAT scans, even population—each Edge City is larger than downtown Portland, Oregon, or Portland Maine, or Tampa, or Tucson. Already, two thirds of all [North] American office facilities are in Edge Cities, and 80 percent of them have materialized in only the last two decades. (Garreau, 1991:5)

Characteristics and Commonalities

Garreau identified over 200 new edge cities in the United States and Canada, giving him a comparative base for analysis. Garreau

concluded that this fledgling urban form, despite a sprawling, apparently chaotic evolution, actually possesses specific characteristics. A full-blown edge city contains

- At least 5 million square feet of leasable office space;
- At least 600,000 square feet of retail space (the equivalent of an average mall of three large stores and 80 to 100 shops and boutiques);
- An increasing population each weekday morning, marking it as primarily a work center, not a residential suburb;
- A local perception as a single-end destination for mixed use—jobs, shopping, and entertainment. (Garreau, 1991:425)

What one cannot find, however, is a clearly defined territorial boundary, for edge cities do not have the same look (the compactness of closely adjacent buildings and high pedestrian traffic), political organization (elected officials or civic codes), or even visual clues of older cities (signs, edges) to mark their perimeters. As Garreau explains:

> The reasons these places are tricky to define is that they rarely have a mayor or a city council, and just about never match boundaries on a map. We're still in the process of giving each Edge City its name—a project, incidentally, that could use more flair. In New Jersey, for example, there is one with only the laconic designation "287 and 78." The reason there are no "Welcome to" signs at Edge City is that it is a judgment call where it begins and ends. (1991:6)

A common feature of edge cities is that they have sprouted far from the old downtowns, in locales where, 30 years ago, little existed save villages and farmland. They typically evolve adjacent to two or more major highways, usually with shopping malls serving as anchor points. Figure 4–1 on page 122 shows two of the more densely concentrated Edge City regions—the New York and Los Angeles areas.

Types of Edge Cities

Edge cities fall into one of three major categories: (1) *uptowns*, built on top of pre-automobile

THE CITY IN LITERATURE

Atlanta's Edge Cities — Tom Wolfe

He looked away from the buildings and out over the ocean of trees. Since Atlanta was not a port city and was, in fact, far inland, the trees stretched on in every direction. They were Atlanta's greatest natural resource, those trees were. People loved to live beneath them. Fewer than 400,000 people lived within the Atlanta city limits, and almost three quarters of them were black; if anything, over the past decade Atlanta's population had declined slightly. But for the past thirty years all sorts of people, most of them white, had been moving in beneath those trees, into all those delightful, leafy, rolling rural communities that surrounded the city proper. By the hundreds of thousands they had come, from all over Georgia, all over the South, all over America, all over the world, into those subdivided hills and downs and glens and glades beneath the trees, until the population of Greater Atlanta was now more than 3.5 million, and they were still pouring in. How fabulous the building booms had been!! As the G-5 banked, Charlie looked down. . . . There was Spaghetti Junction, as it was known, where Highways 85 and 285 came together in a tangle of fourteen gigantic curving concrete-and-asphalt ramps and twelve overpasses. . . . And now he could see Perimeter Center, where Georgia 400 crossed 285. Mack Taylor and Harvey Mathis had built an office park called Perimeter Center out among all those trees, which had been considered a very risky venture at the time, because it was so far from Downtown; and now Perimeter Center was the nucleus around which an entire edge city, known by that very name, Perimeter Center, had grown. . . .

Edge city . . . Charlie closed his eyes and wished he'd never heard of the damn term. He wasn't much of a reader, but back in 1991 Lucky Putney, another developer, had given him a copy of a book called *Edge City* by somebody named Joel Garreau. He had opened it and glanced at it—and couldn't put it down, even though it was 500 pages long. He had experienced the *Aha!* phenomenon. The book put into words something he and other developers had felt, instinctively, for quite a while: namely, that from now on, the growth of American cities was going to take place not in the heart of the metropolis, not in the old Downtown or Midtown, but out on the edges, in vast commercial clusters served by highways.

Source: Excerpt from "Atlanta's Edge Cities," from *A Man in Full* by Tom Wolfe. Copyright © 1998 by Tom Wolfe. Reprinted by permission of Farrar, Straus & Giroux LLC.

settlements, such as Pasadena, California, or Arlington, Virginia; (2) *boomers*, the typical edge city located at the intersection of two major highways and almost always centered on a mall, such as most of those in Figure 4–1; and (3) *greenfields*, a master-planned city by one developer on thousands of farmland acres, such as Irvine, California, and Las Colinas, near the Dallas–Fort Worth airport.

Because boomers, the most common form of edge cities, have grown so profusely throughout North America, urbanists identify three subcategories of them [see Figure 4–2 on page 124]. The strip boomer city is usually only a few hundred yards wide but extends for miles along a major highway. Most representative are the strips along Route 1 in Princeton, Route 128 near the Mass Pike outside Boston, and I-270 in Montgomery County, Maryland, in the Washington, D.C.

region. All three suffer severe traffic congestion because of their extended shapes. The node boomer city is relatively dense and contained, such as The Galleria area near Houston, Tysons Corner in Virginia, and the Midtown–Yorkville and North York–North Yonge areas in Toronto. The pig-in-the-python boomer city is a cross between the previous two types. It is a strip that develops one or several nodes along it, such as the Lodge Freeway in Southfield, northwest of Detroit, or King of Prussia, Pennsylvania, northwest of Philadelphia. (Garreau, 1991:115)

Evolving Middle-Class Centers

The majority of metropolitan North Americans now work, shop, and live in and around the 200-plus "new hearths of our civilization." Shopping malls function as the village squares for these new urban centers. Adjacent are the hotels, office buildings, and corporate headquarters, whose tall buildings are not side by side as in a downtown, but instead are located on campuslike settings of grass and trees, gazing at one another at a respectful distance. Surrounding this broad center of employment and shopping are the single-family suburban homes whose occupants now outnumber those living next to the old downtowns.

The rise of edge cities is essentially a function of social class, not race. They are evolving in metropolitan areas with low black populations (Denver, Minneapolis, Seattle, Toronto) as well as in metropolitan areas with high black populations (Atlanta, Chicago, New York, Washington). In the latter, middle-class African Americans (presently about one-third of the total U.S. black population) are just as likely to be part of edge cities as are middle-class whites. Just as the skin of the middle-class North American comes in various hues—brown, black, shades of tan, and white—so too do edge cities reflect this reality.

The edge city, however, has been criticized as plastic and sterile, lacking in livability, civilization, community, neighborhood—in short, having little urban soul (Garreau, 1991:8). It is, however, an unfinished new city form and we do not yet know if, in its maturity, this ugly duckling will emerge as a splendid swan. Whatever its ultimate shape, we do know that the

> Edge City acculturates immigrants, provides child care, and offers safety. It is, on average, an improvement in per capita fuel efficiency over the old suburbia–downtown arrangement, since it moves everything closer to the homes of the middle class.
>
> That is why Edge City is the crucible of [North] America's urban future. Having become the place in which the majority of [North] Americans now live, learn, work, shop, play, pray, and die, Edge City will be the forge of the fabled [North] American way of life well into the twenty-first century (Garreau, 1991:8).

And edge cities are appearing worldwide as well. They now mark the fringes of Bangkok, Beijing, London, Paris, and Sydney. Increased affluence, the desire for more individual transportation, greater use of computers and telecommunications requiring air climate control, and the existence of world financial centers requiring trading floors of at least 20,000 square feet are some of the important elements shaping the growth of edge cities in urban areas throughout the world.

Three Edge City Variations

Not all edge cities are alike, nor does their evolution occur for the same reasons everywhere. The following examples illustrate how the edge city can serve as its own motivation, emerge as a solution to a problem, or simply become the problem.

Edge City as Motivator

By 1990, Oshawa Centre, one of the oldest shopping malls in Ontario, Canada, was showing its age. Originally built for the town's blue-collar population, the place was dark and ugly, some of the stores had outdoor-facing windows and doors plastered with newspaper and cardboard, and its sales and rental value were declining. Not anymore. The Toronto-based Cambridge Shopping Centres purchased it in 1991 for $145 million. It did so because Garreau had written in *Edge*

FIGURE 4-1A

THE LOS ANGELES AREA

▲ Old Downtowns
● Edge Cities
○ Emerging Edge Cities

San Gabriel Mountains

Santa Ana Mountains

Santa Monica Mts.

Pacific Ocean

10 Miles
16 Kilometers

Valencia

Warner Center/
West Valley

San Fernando Valley/
Sherman Oaks/
Van Nuys

Burbank/
North Hollywood

Pasadena

San Bernardino

Ontario Airport/
Rancho Cucamonga

Riverside

South Valley/
Covina

Downtown

Mid-Wilshire

Miracle Mile

Beverly Hills/Century City

West Los Angeles

Marina del Rey/Culver City

LAX/El Segundo

South Bay/Torrance/Carson

Fullerton/La Habra/Brea

Anaheim/Santa Ana

Westminster/
Huntington Beach

Long
Beach

South Coast Plaza/
John Wayne Airport

Irvine
Spectrum

Newport Beach/
Fashion Island

San Clemente/
Laguna Niguel

Ventura/
Coastal Plain

THE NEW YORK AREA

▲ Old Downtowns

● Edge Cities

○ Emerging Edge Cities

FIGURE 4-1B

123

The Strip Boomer City

The Node Boomer City

The Pig-in-the-Python Boomer City

FIGURE 4–2

City that shopping malls usually function as the village squares of the new urban centers. "So, taking that theory," said Ronald Charbon, Cambridge's director of strategic market information, "we said, 'Where are the next edge cities going to occur? Where is the next wave of growth going to occur in the greater metropolitan Toronto area? And are any of our shopping centres sufficiently located to capitalize on that growth?'" (cited in Berman, 1997).

Using census tracts and surveys, Cambridge amassed a population profile of the area, discovering that areas surrounding Oshawa were white-collar and that projections of the area's growth rate were almost three times that in the Greater Toronto Area. So the company took the gamble, invested $40 million in a major facelift, and recruited upscale stores. However, that was only one part of a sophisticated strategy to turn Oshawa Centre into the village square that Garreau described. Cambridge secured government approval to construct six modest-sized office towers over a 25-year period. The Oshawa Centre is thus in the midst of a massive transformation from a jerry-built suburban mall into a mixed-use development that includes retail, business, government, and community services, all inspired by Garreau's book.

Edge City as the Solution

Since incorporating in 1956, Schaumburg, Illinois, has been what Judy Pasternak (1998) called "the ultimate faceless postwar suburb." Located 26 miles northwest of Chicago, the town is home to nearly 74,000 people living in townhouses and subdivisions and shopping in one or more of the 65 shopping centers that line its streets. Along its expressway, glassy office towers provide a solid employment base. The one thing lacking in Schaumburg is that it has no center, no downtown, no place to walk to or for people to gather. In fact, it hadn't had a town center since 1875.

That is now changing. The local government tore down a faded strip mall on a 30-acre site to make way for a downtown center called "Town Square." But this place is no small-town core like the downtowns of older suburbs that developed around train depots generations ago. There are no retail stores lining Main Street. In fact, there is no Main Street. Instead, a supermarket and a cluster of retail stores border a large parking lot, giving this area the look of a shopping center. Nearby is a new library, a brick clock tower, a green wrought-iron gazebo, a pond, curved benches, and a chain restaurant. "It's plastic," grumbled one store owner. Others, however, are more optimistic, hoping that this shopping area—with plenty of parking, strolling amenities, and mixed-use development—will allow community to blossom where none had existed before (Pasternak, 1998).

Edge City as the Problem

The more that Tysons Corner, Virginia—one of Joel Garreau's prime examples of an edge city—continues to grow and thrive economically, the more it remains an object of derisive commentary by architects, city planners, design critics, and urban scholars. Indeed, finding ways to "fix" Tysons Corner has been the goal of several planning studies sponsored by academic institutions, professional groups, and Fairfax County, home to this edge city. Tysons Corner today is larger, in both geographic size and employment, than many U.S. central cities, with more than 80,000 jobs and 12,000 residents sharing a few hundred acres of former farmland. Moreover, five new office building projects that will add 10,000 jobs (and perhaps almost as many automobile trips) are under construction, and zoning allows for an additional 20 million square feet of commercial space. Incredibly, though, Metrorail does not go there, making road transit the only means of transportation (Lewis, 1999).

Clearly, mass transit would greatly alleviate the traffic congestion. During weekday rush hours and weekend shopping times, backups are horrendous. Recommendations include creating an elevated rail system looping around Tysons Corner and introducing a link between Tysons and the regional Metrorail network. But much more is needed. Tysons is not pedestrian-friendly, for there are few

This view of Tysons Corner, Virginia, shows the new edge city we now build. It has no defined borders or recognizable center, and its various buildings are not conveniently near one another. All the commercial activities and none of the charm of a city—the pedestrians, the architecture, the cultural attractions—can be found here. A car is a necessity in edge cities and, as a result, traffic congestion is unavoidable.

sidewalks or signalized crosswalks—critical for safely traversing the extraordinarily wide, traffic-choked roads—making walking around Tysons virtually impossible.

Even if traffic congestion could be reduced and pedestrian traffic encouraged, the aesthetic and visual deficiencies, the visual chaos and formlessness would still remain. In the interest of bringing a bit of visual order to Tysons Corner, a county task force developed a plan a few years ago to address streetscapes, pedestrian walkways, site planning of buildings, and open space. Still, Tysons has no civic focus, or heart, and so planners propose a "town center" as a way to "give Tysons more soul." Such an undertaking is still several years away, however. In the meantime, Tysons continues to be emblematic of how poorly we have planned, zoned, and developed much of the landscape girdling our cities since the end of World War II (Lewis, 1999).

GATED COMMUNITIES

Gated communities in the United States can be traced to the late 1800s, when upper-income gated developments in New York's Tuxedo Park and private streets in St. Louis sprang up, as wealthy citizens sought to "insulate themselves from the troublesome aspects of rapidly industrializing cities" (Blakely and Snyder, 1997:4). However, these communities, and the fenced compounds built in the twentieth century by members of the East Coast and Hollywood aristocracies, were different from today's gated communities. They were unique places for unique people. Although a few other exclusive gated communities began to appear—such as Sea Pines on Hilton Head Island, South Carolina, in 1957—they remained rare until the late 1960s and 1970s, when master-planned retirement developments first appeared. These were the first places where average Americans could wall themselves off from the rest of society.

Beginning in the 1980s, gated communities increased rapidly—not only in retirement villages, but in resort and country club developments, then in middle-class suburban subdivisions, setting off a quiet but important trend that continues today. In the mid-1980s, gated communities were rare on Long Island, New York, but by the mid-1990s they had become common, with a gatehouse included in almost every condominium of more than fifty units. Elsewhere, there are now entire incorporated cities that feature guarded entrances; one example is Canyon Lake, 60 miles east of Orange County in California.

Over 20,000 gated communities, or fenced neighborhoods, containing more than 3 million units—approximately 9 million people—now exist in the United States. The greatest number of these developments is in suburban areas of the Southeast and Southwest, but older, inner-city neighborhoods are also experiencing this phenomenon. Many gated communities have been built in metropolitan areas across the country, including Los Angeles, Phoenix, Dallas, Houston, Chicago, New York, and Miami. In fact, 80 percent of new urban housing developments are gated (Blakely and Snyder, 1997). This pattern is occurring in Canada as well. In Toronto, three older gated areas—Palmerston Avenue, Fairview Boulevard, and Wychwood Park—are city jewels that enjoy high real estate values.

Suburbanites, however, are gating just as fast as urbanites. In Southern California, for example, about 100 such communities were built in San Fernando Valley in the 1980s and, in that same decade, the number of gated communities doubled in Orange County. What makes gated communities different from typical twentieth-century suburbs, which usually also involve economic and social segregation?

Gated communities are actually defended by walls, with access control either by electronically operated gates or 24-hour guards, and grounds patrolled by private security forces. Residents enjoy their own pay-as-you-go services. They share responsibility for common areas and for enforcing the numerous rules and regulations, often through homeowner associations, rather than relying on conventional elected local governments for many common services.

Gated communities obviously segregate people living within their walls from others even more profoundly than the most exclusive suburban jurisdiction can, and they thus accentuate patterns of segregation. While there are a variety of approaches to living barricaded lives, the reasons residents choose them usually center around fear of crime and attempts to produce economic and physical security, free from the problems of traffic and noise.

Types of Gated Communities

In their study of the development and social impact of this rapidly growing phenomenon, Edward J. Blakely and May Gail Snyder (1997) suggest that they fall into one of three categories: "lifestyle," "prestige," and "security-zone" communities. Although these categories are helpful for analysis and understanding, there is actually much overlap between them, as each contains some elements of the others. Still, each caters to a different housing market and has a different approach to developing a sense of community within its walls. Moreover, each variety promotes a particular combination of four social values: the "sense of community" (preservation and strengthening of neighborhood bonds); "exclusion" (separation and protection from the outside); "privatization" (the desire to privatize and internally control public services); and "stability" (homogeneity and predictability).

Where sense of community is a primary value motivating the residents of gated communities, it reflects all five aspects of community: shared territory, shared values, a shared public realm, support structure, and a shared destiny. Exclusion helps define shared territory by separating community members from outsiders. Privatization reflects a desire to protect a shared destiny through increased local control. Stability suggests shared values and support structures, and retaining stability is also a way of predicting shared destiny. (Blakely and Snyder, 1997:122)

Lifestyle Communities

Lifestyle communities are an expression of conspicuous consumption and a new leisure class. They emphasize amenities and include retirement communities, such as the nationwide chain of Leisure Worlds, that offer senior citizens the chance to engage in a wide variety of activities close to their homes. Another type are golf and leisure communities, where the gates cordon off the leisure resources for the exclusive use of community residents. Blackhawk Country Club near San Francisco and Rancho Mirage in California's Coachella Valley cater to people with special interests, like golf or tennis. Lifestyle communities attract those who want separate, private services and amenities within a homogeneous, predictable environment.

Prestige Communities

Prestige communities are status-oriented enclaves, such as those in affluent Pacific Palisades or Marblehead in San Clemente, primarily containing the rich and famous, the affluent, the top one-fifth of Americans. These communities emphasize exclusion and image; the gates symbolize the eminent status of their residents. Prestige communities attract those seeking a stable neighborhood of similar people where property values will be protected. For these residents, concerns about separation and privatization of services are secondary.

Security-zone Communities

Security-zone communities are "enclaves of fear" primarily concerned with protection, and are a defensive measure reflecting a fortress mentality with walls, gates, closed streets, and various security systems. In these enclaves, often located in inner-city and lower-income neighborhoods, residents band together to shut out their neighbors in the hope that the gates will protect them from crime, traffic, and outsiders. Security-zone communities seek to strengthen and protect a sense of community, but their primary goal is to exclude the places and people their residents perceive as threats to their safety and quality of life.

Some municipalities have taken action against gated communities. In Fort Collins, Colorado, they have been banned as "disruptive to a sense of community." Four suburbs of Dallas also barred them on the grounds that their residents have security that is denied to others (Cantor, 1998).

A Sense of Community

For several decades, social observers have noted a loss of community in modern life—what Robert MacIver (1962) referred to as "the great emptiness." In *Habits of the Heart* (1985), Robert N. Bellah and his associates reported that traditional communities, where individuals have permanent emotional bonds, were yielding to "lifestyle enclaves," where relationships are often based on such superficial similarities as consumption style or leisure interests. Such enclaves diminish social life, say the authors, and all residents can do is compare their own material gains with those of their neighbors to piece together some idea of "how they are doing." Robert B. Reich (1991) expressed concern that wealth was rapidly polarizing society because the well-to-do were effectively seceding from society by walling themselves into privately policed fortress communities. In their study of gated communities, Blakely and Snyder also lamented the loss of community:

> The fabric of civitas, communal commitment to civic and public life, has begun to rip. . . . The borders of the gated communities are emblematic of the proliferation of boundaries being set and hardened as communities fragment, looking inward. (Blakely and Snyder, 1997:176)

As communities turn inward, motivated by security and other social needs, do the residents find what they seek? Critics, including Blakely and Snyder, charge that they do not—

Gated communities, such as this one at Dana Point, California, are a rapidly growing phenomenon. Segregated from the outside world with walls, fences, electronically operated gates and/or 24-hour guards, residents essentially live barricaded lives. Such communities typically cater to a housing market emphasizing prestige, lifestyle, or security-zone neighborhoods that promise a sense of community, exclusion, private control of public services, and the stability of homogenization.

that gated communities reflect the social fragmentation and civic atrophy currently plaguing society. Because these barricaded neighborhoods exclude the lower classes not only from living in these residences (through prohibitive housing costs) but also from even casually passing by, they limit social contact among different members and groups of society. Such class separation is often *de facto* racial segregation, and this social distance can weaken further the civic bonds among societal members. According to Andrew Stark, a University of Toronto professor and author of *Public Pastures, Private Arrangements* (1998), a comprehensive look at the impact of gated communities, "Americans . . . are renegotiating the character of the lives they live together and raising larger questions about the meaning of community" (in Cantor, 1999).

According to various studies, the quality of community does not improve in gated developments. Even though residents move to such places in the belief that they will find their nostalgic idea of community, they do not. In fact, these communities promote privacy within privacy; there are no front porches to

induce interaction, and residents tend to stay in their own backyards and not visit one another. As a result, Blakely and Snyder found that gating often does not provide what people are seeking. Although residents often expressed some satisfaction about life within these enclaves, they also expressed much disappointment, especially about the lack of a sense of shared community. In comparison with nonresidents, members of gated communities do not find stronger ties with one another.

As to whether gated communities actually serve as a deterrent to crime, the statistics are mixed. Formidable fencing and gates, by design, restrict access and therefore provide both a physical and psychological barrier for criminals. However, the effectiveness of gates and fencing depends on the nature of the property and the people living in it. In the security-zone communities, one study found declines in crime right after closure of the gates, but no decline was sustained for more than a short time. Among lifestyle communities, Blakely and Snyder found that many had the same problems as other urban communities. In some cases, the gates fostered a false sense of security; police reported that crime was as likely to come from people living within the gates as from outside.

COMMON-INTEREST DEVELOPMENTS (CIDS)

Gated communities are often called common-interest developments (CIDs). However, not all CIDs are segregated communities (although many are), and not all gated areas are CIDs (although most are). There is a close relationship between the two phenomena, but they are not the same thing. CIDs—which require membership in a self-governing homeowners' association—include suburban planned-unit developments of single-family homes, urban condominiums, and housing cooperatives, and they have become familiar sights throughout North America. Moreover, the rapid spread of CID housing is the largest and most dramatic privatization of local government functions in North American history. Currently, over 200,000 of these developments exist in the United States, housing some 42 million people, or nearly one-eighth of the population (Vanderpool, 1999:2).

Builders find CID housing profitable because it is a mass-produced commodity and enables them to concentrate more people on less land. Buyers are willing to accept smaller lots and narrower streets because the development contains open spaces and desirable amenities, including facilities owned in common by all residents—such as swimming pools, gyms, parks, golf courses, social centers, often even exclusive access to shopping centers and their own schools. Public officials are willing to issue building permits for these high-density, designed communities, with their private infrastructure, because they add taxpayers at minimal public cost.

Residents must belong to homeowner associations, pay monthly fees, and live under the rule of residential private governments. These governments perform functions for their residents that were once the province of local government, providing, for example,

police protection, trash collection, and street maintenance and lighting. In one sense, this community design is a logical, evolutionary step in the suburban ideology of territorial control (housing-market segmentation, single-use zoning, inaccessibility to mass transit, cul-de-sacs). However, some critics think that the emergence of this new civic culture undermines the diversity and vitality of cities. The Critical Thinking box on page 131 takes a closer look.

In *Privatopia* (1994), Evan McKenzie wrote that millions of affluent homeowners were being "encouraged to secede from urban America, with its endless flux and ferment, its spontaneity and diversity and its unpredictable rewards and hazards" and "beckoned to a privatized, artificial, utopian environment where master-planning, homogeneous populations, and private governments offer the affluent a chance to escape from urban reality." However, said McKenzie, they pay a heavy price, for they surrender a good deal of their freedom and privacy. CID residents live under the rule of their corporate board of directors, an elected group of neighbors enforcing a set of restrictions created by the developer to ensure that the master plan will never be altered. This private government operates outside the constitutional limits that bind local authorities, because the courts often accept the legal fiction that CID restrictions are private, voluntary arrangements among individuals. In truth, they are nonnegotiable regulations, drafted by the developer's lawyers and imposed on all residents, as the Urban Living box on page 132 explains.

Just as urban renewal frequently uprooted lower-income people from their homes, so too have CID developments. Perhaps the most publicized of these displacements has been on Daufuskie Island, South Carolina. Here, amid the dirt roads crisscrossing the five-by-two-mile island, the black Gullah population has owned land for generations, and the people lived in an open community, going anywhere and sharing in each other's good fortune and helping one another in bad times. Now, developers of the gated communities of Haig Point and Daufuskie Island Club and Resort have made more than half

CRITICAL THINKING

Common
Interest Developments

CIDs Threaten Urban Culture

For those who live outside CIDs, in America's beleaguered cities, the rapid spread of CIDs threatens to transform urban culture in ways some find deeply disturbing. This "secession of the successful," as Robert Reich calls it, deprives urban America of a vast amount of human and economic resources. It promotes a two-class society of haves and have-nots, the former enjoying a privatized set of what were formerly public services, and the latter struggling to survive in cities faced with increasing responsibilities and shriveling revenues.

The city, Lewis Mumford tells us, is "a structure specially equipped to store and transmit the goods of civilization." Cities are dense concentrations of a society's population, wealth and power—assets which, for 6,000 years, have enabled cities to create, reflect, amplify, and communicate whatever a society has to offer to the world.

Conservative scholar Charles Murray views CIDs as symbols of an emerging caste society in which the affluent, freed from dependency on public institutions, may come to regard cities as "an urban analog of the Indian reservation"—places of deprivation and dysfunction for which they feel no responsibility.

Urban theorist Mike Davis, in *City of Quartz*, paints the picture of a privatized Los Angeles, architecturally redesigned to physically separate the two classes and protect the rich from the rest. He saw in this separation the potential for "approaching Helter-Skelter," even before 1992 brought the most intense urban riot in American history.

CIDs are, in a sense, a privatized, master-planned version of the village-centered life that our species led for millennia, and that many romanticize today. For the rest of us, CIDs may speed the decline of cities as centers of cultural, political, and economic power. Cities may come to resemble the future Los Angeles of *Blade Runner*—desperate holding pens, struggling to provide mere physical security and unable to afford other social services to all. . . .

It is time to ask whether corporate builders should be allowed to continue spreading CIDs across the country, guided only by the calculus of private profit, or whether we should have an open, public discussion of the consequences—before the metropolis becomes a necropolis.

Source: Evan McKenzie, "Trouble in Privatopia," *The Progressive* 57 (October 1993), 30–36.

the island off-limits to them, as warning signs at nearly every fork in the road make clear. In 1990, the National Council of Churches —with 25 million members—charged that the developers of resort and residential communities on Daufuskie (as well as on Hilton Head Island) were committing "cultural genocide" by dislodging black residents through conflicts with developers and resulting higher property taxes. The conflict has also been the

subject of national news shows, lawsuits, and numerous newspaper stories. In 1992, the National Association for the Advancement of Colored People (NAACP) threatened to file a class-action suit against Beaufort County and developers on Daufuskie Island for driving black families off their land. At present, much of the island remains undeveloped, most of the public roads are still unpaved, and the pace of homebuilding had slowed by

URBAN LIVING

CID Violations of Personal Freedom

The stories below, all reported in various news stories, do not merely reflect isolated neighborhood conflicts. They are examples of business as usual in walled, private, urban and suburban enclaves called common-interest developments (CIDs). For some, CID living means having to fight to defend a semblance of privacy and personal freedom, while the few residents who enforce the rules enjoy a degree of personal power over their neighbors that the constitution denies to public officials.

- In Monroe, New Jersey, a homeowners' association sued a married couple because the wife, at age 45, was three years younger than the association's age-48 minimum for residency. The judge ruled in favor of the association, ordering the 60-year-old husband to sell, rent the unit, or live without his wife.
- In Ashland, Massachusetts, a CID board informed a Vietnam veteran that he could not fly the U.S. flag on Flag Day. He called the press, the story appeared on the front page of a local newspaper, and under public pressure, the board backed down.
- In Boca Raton, Florida, an association took legal action against a homeowner for having a dog weighing more than 30 pounds, in violation of association rules. A court-ordered weighing revealed that the dog

was just an ounce over the weight limit. The association persisted with the suit nonetheless—determined to pay an attorney and use the courts to exclude the dog from the development for even that infraction.

- In Santa Ana, California, a condominium association issued a citation to a 51-year-old grandmother for violating one of its rules. Her offense? "Kissing and doing bad things" while parked one night in the circular driveway. She acknowledged kissing a friend good night, but retained an attorney and threatened legal action against this invasion of her privacy.
- In a development near Philadelphia, a couple bought a home and brought their sons' metal swing set with them. A year later, the association told them to take it down, despite the absence of any written rules on swing sets. When they challenged this order, the association passed a rule prescribing that all swing sets must be made of wood, in keeping "with what the overall community should look like." The family then submitted a petition from three-fourths of the homeowners supporting their swing set, along with data from the Environmental Protection Agency warning against the danger to children (theirs were aged two and four) from the poisonous chemicals found in pressure-treated wood used for outdoor swing sets. The association's response was to impose a daily fine of ten dollars until the set was removed, and to refuse offers to compromise, such as painting the swing set in earth tones.

late 1999. Future development, however, is a virtual certainty.

Planners, sprawl opponents, and urban sociologists often cite Portland, Oregon, as a growing city that successfully controls its growth and development. Portland thus serves as an appropriate case study for the various themes and problems discussed in this chapter.

❖ CASE STUDY ❖
Portland, Oregon

Virtually all cities in western North America have undergone boom periods that gobbled up the land, strained the infrastructure, and resulted in congestion, dirty air, and tax-strained school systems. Yet Portland enters the twenty-first century as a healthy, vibrant city displaying few of the problems found in other urban places. Years ago, Portland determined to defy the boom mentality, and set out to consciously plan its future. This effort reflects the city's long history of concern for urban quality of life and commitment to the common good (Egan, 1996).

The Physical Setting

Portland stands in a choice location, surrounded by natural beauty and resources that, as the first Looking Back box on page 134 reports, greatly impressed its founders. Situated about 100 miles from the Pacific Ocean at the confluence of the Columbia and Willamette Rivers, Portland is surrounded by a combination of water and lush greenery rarely found in urban settings. Snow-capped Mount Hood, Oregon's highest point (11,235 feet), is 48 miles away, and Mount Rainier, Mount St. Helens, and Mount Adams in Washington are all visible from the city. Also nearby is the spectacular Columbia Gorge and Multnomah Falls (850 feet). The city thus offers cosmopolitan living coupled with a variety of nearby outdoor activities such as camping, canoeing, fishing, hiking, hunting, mountain climbing, and skiing.

Portland includes some of this outlying natural beauty within the city limits. Also known as "The City of Roses" for its large International Rose Test Gardens and the second-largest all-floral parade in the United States (after Pasadena), Portland has a magnificent park system including some 200 green spaces. The city boasts the largest forested municipal park in the nation (5,000 acres) and the world's smallest dedicated park, Mills End Park (24 inches). Three other important areas are the elm-shaded South Park blocks in the downtown area, McCall Waterfront Park, and Washington Park, home of the Rose Test Gardens, where more than 500 varieties of roses bloom, as well as of the Oregon Zoo (known for its recreated African rain forest) and the Japanese Garden. Portland is also the only U.S. city to have an extinct volcano, Mount Tabor, within the city limits.

History

Several gold rushes drew immigrants along the Oregon Trail, stimulating Portland's early growth. Deep water and abundant natural resources soon made the settlement a popular and prosperous port and commercial center, handling the farm and forest produce of the Cascade Range, Willamette Valley, and Columbia Basin.

As with many Old West centers, Portland had its seamy side, with vice and violence figuring into its late-nineteenth-century scene. A clever entrepreneur named "Sweet Mary," the proprietor of a brothel, eluded taxes and flouted city laws by operating her business on a barge that ran up and down the Willamette River, legally outside Portland's jurisdiction. Others, like John "Bunco" Kelly—profiled in the next Looking Back box on page 135— were even more devious.

By the turn of the century, Portland had become a tamer place, and the city had eliminated most of the seedy activities of its busy waterfront. About this time Simon Benson, a teetotaling lumber baron, walked through one of his mills and noticed the smell of alcohol on his workers' breath. When he asked why they drank in the middle of the day, they replied that there was no fresh drinking water to be found downtown. To resolve this situation, Benson built 20 fresh-water drinking fountains in the downtown area, now known as Benson's Bubblers. Beer consumption reportedly fell by 25 percent after the fountains were installed. Those water fountains still bubble for locals and visitors alike along Portland's downtown streets. Yet Portlanders still love their beer: Today the city has 37 microbrewery outlets, more than any other U.S. city.

Urban Decline and the Planners' Response to Sprawl

In the 1960s, Portland fell victim to the same ills afflicting other U.S. cities. Its economy nosedived as industries closed. Shuttered mills and empty warehouses dotted the waterfront. People began moving away, unemployment rose, and those who remained found

LOOKING BACK

A Quarter, a Penny, and a Name

In 1843, Tennessee drifter William Overton and Massachusetts lawyer Asa Lovejoy beached their canoe on the banks of the Willamette River. Overton, impressed by the natural beauty of the area, saw great potential in the mountain-ringed, timber-rich land and decided to stake a claim to 640 acres. However, he lacked the 25 cents required to file. So he struck a bargain with Lovejoy: In return for a quarter, Overton would share the claim with his friend.

After laying out a town plan, clearing trees, and building roads, Overton soon lost interest in the site and moved on, selling his half of the claim to Francis S. Pettygrove. The new partners, however, could not agree on a name for their budding settlement. Lovejoy insisted on naming the site after his hometown of Boston, while Pettygrove was equally adamant about his native Portland, Maine. They decided to flip a coin, now known as the "Portland Penny," to settle the argument. Pettygrove won on two out of three tosses and Portland, Oregon, became a reality.

---

their standard of living sliding downward. One after another, downtown stores went belly up as the central business district slipped into a serious economic decline. The bus system lost so much business that it, too, went bankrupt.

But the stage was set for Portland's revival when Republican governor Tom McCall signed a new state law in 1973 requiring all of Oregon's cities to devise plans to limit urban sprawl and to protect farms, forests, and open space. Portland responded with the strictest laws in the nation. Ignoring lawsuits and pressures from commercial and development interests, Portland's leaders drew a line around their metropolitan area, banning any development beyond that point (much as London had done during its post–World War II reconstruction). The plan's intent was to force jobs, homes, and stores into a relatively compact area served by light rail, buses, and cars.

Automobiles, of course, are a major cause of the urban sprawl besetting most cities. Portland bucked the trend by tearing up its downtown riverfront freeway, converting the

area, along with abandoned warehouse sites, into one of the city's most-used parks, named for McCall. It also limited downtown parking spaces and created an award-winning mass transit system. The integrated transit system includes buses and the MAX, an urban light rail line, as well as a downtown transit mall and Fareless Square, the 300-block downtown free-ride zone. All are popular; for example, about 80,000 riders commuted daily on MAX in 2001–2002, far exceeding planners' expectations. No Portlander is forced to ride MAX or Tri-Met buses, but 75 percent of those who do, own cars but choose a public transit option instead. So successful has the MAX been that an 18-mile Westside extension was opened in 1998 and then a 5-mile extension in 2001. Portland is one of the few regions in the country where transit ridership is growing faster than vehicle miles traveled (TriMet, 2003). The city also applauds bike travel, placing brightly colored bikes and bike racks throughout the city for anyone to use.

Portland also enacted a downtown development plan inspired by the ideas of Jane

LOOKING BACK

Portland's Dark History

Most cities have a dark side to their history, replete with a gallery of colorful characters. Portland was home to an infamous hotelier, Joseph "Bunco" Kelly, notorious in the late 1800s for kidnapping young men and selling them to ship captains. In many port cities throughout the world, bar owners and hotel operators relied on the shanghai trade to supplement their businesses. Kelly was one of the best. Paid by unscrupulous captains to intoxicate potential crew members, Kelly would deliver his drunken quarry to waiting ships. The unfortunate men would wake up the next day, stranded at sea and forced to work for indefinite periods of time.

In one attempt to make a quick buck, Kelly delivered to a ship a dime-store Indian heavily wrapped in blankets. When the captain learned the next morning that his new crew member was made of wood, he became enraged and threw it overboard. The artifact was recovered by two men operating a dredge nearly 60 years later.

Probably Kelly's most outrageous act followed the boast that he could gather a full crew in less than 12 hours. After a ship's captain challenged him, Kelly ran across a group that had stumbled upon the open cellar of a mortuary. Thinking the cellar was part of the Snug Harbor Pub, the men had each consumed cups of embalming fluid, which they had mistaken for liquor. When Kelly found them, several had died and others were dying. Claiming the dead were merely unconscious from too much drink, Kelly sold all 22 to the captain, whose ship sailed before he discovered the truth.

Jacobs, August Heckscher, William H. Whyte, and James Rouse (all of whom will be discussed in Chapter 14). All new buildings, including garages, must be people-friendly at street level. Blank walls are banned in favor of stores, offices, and eating establishments. Further, Portland set aside 1 percent of public construction funds to enhance the physical attractiveness of the area through outdoor public art.

In 1996, Portland enacted an even stricter plan for its three-county metropolitan area. The city envisions adding 500,000 new residents—in essence, another Portland—in the existing urban boundaries of its 362-square-mile metropolitan borders within 20 years. This may mean more apartment buildings and townhouses in previously single-family neighborhoods. To keep "big box" stores from springing up in industrial areas, Portland's new plan limits retail outlets to 60,000 square feet and restricts the number of parking spaces a new store may have, in a further effort to encourage use of mass transit. As part of their ambitious crusade to stop sprawl by limiting job growth, Portland officials in 1999 imposed a $1,000-per-job "growth impact fee" on the Intel Corporation if its new jobs exceed an imposed limit (Hayward, 1999).

In becoming "the reigning model for growth management in the United States," Portland followed the visionary guide set for it by Lewis Mumford back in 1938, when he declared, "I have seen a lot of scenery in my life, but I have seen nothing so tempting as a home for man than this Oregon country. . . . You have the basis here for civilization on its highest scale" (cited in Stephenson, 1999).

Portland's popular Tom McCall Waterfront Park attracts pedestrians at all hours of the day and is the site of numerous special events, such as the Rose Festival, Dragon Boat Races, and annual carnival. Many U.S. cities have rediscovered and revitalized their waterfronts, attracting residents and tourists alike, thereby enhancing the quality of life and ambience of the city.

Portland Today

Portland stands today as a model city. It has a dense downtown containing about twice the work force it had 20 years ago. Yet, despite its growth, Portland has retained its nineteenth-century small city block design, which yields a pedestrian-friendly city core. The central business district (CBD) is virtually a walker's paradise, beckoning strollers to pass along the tree-lined streets on brick walkways and to stop to enjoy fountains, benches, and small parks along the way. Pedestrians may shop at over 1,100 retail stores; enjoy many outstanding coffee houses and restaurants; visit one of the city's microbreweries; or browse in any one of the numerous bookstores—including Powell's City of Books, with the largest number of volumes (nearly 1.5 million) in the United States.

The city's economy is healthy, helped in large measure by the silicon forest of high-tech office campuses and factories—such as Intel and Hewlett-Packard—that grew inside the metro area. Nowhere are there signs of the industrial or residential abandonment that scar cities elsewhere (Abbott, 1995:3). New major department stores—Nordstrom's and Saks Fifth Avenue—enhance the central business district. Recreational activities include comedy clubs, ballet, opera, symphonies, modern dance, theater, a planetarium, hockey and baseball teams, and the Portland Trail Blazers professional basketball team.

In terms of aesthetics, amenities, economy, land use, and planning, most people applaud Portland as "a city that works," an appellation once only applied to Toronto. As Michael Burton, the metropolitan area's executive director, said in a message to Portland residents:

We have been careful stewards of the land and have fought to protect our natural resources against the urban sprawl that has plagued almost every other metropolitan area in this country. We have worked hard to maintain our enviable quality of life. (quoted in Egan, 1996)

Will Portland, with a 2000 metropolitan population of 1.9 million, maintain its urban growth boundaries to protect the surrounding countryside? Although metropolitan Portland has grown by about 44 percent since 1980, the urbanized area has expanded by only 2 percent (O'Meara, 1999:10). An anticipated population increase of 500,000 people in just 20 years will surely test both its resolve and its ability to balance big-city excitement and small-town charm. But if the planners and city leaders have their way, the answer will be yes.

❖ ———————— ❖ ———————— ❖

SUMMARY

Four patterns of land development—sprawl, edge cities, gated communities, and common-interest developments—became so widespread by the end of the twentieth century that they will most likely affect both urban and suburban lifestyles for at least the first few decades of the twenty-first century.

Sprawl refers to low-density land development beyond the edge of services and employment. Sprawl uses up large tracts of land (even when cities decline in population), increases residents' dependency on automobiles, creates traffic congestion and pollution, and wastes natural resources. Solutions to sprawl include purchasing and preserving open space, setting urban growth boundaries, revitalizing existing cities and towns, and pursuing transit-oriented approaches.

The past three decades have seen the evolution of more than 200 edge cities in North America and elsewhere, located at the fringes of older cities. Their sprawling land use and auto dependency stand in marked contrast to the compact land use of older "walking" cities. Not clearly marked by territorial boundaries but usually situated near two major highways,

edge cities fall into three categories: uptown, boomer, and greenfield. Boomer cities are by far the most numerous and have three subcategories: strip, node, and pig-in-a-python. Essentially middle-class entities that cut across racial lines, edge cities have a shopping mall as their anchor point, and provide more jobs, shops, and entertainment than older cities do.

Although gated communities first appeared in the United States in the late 1800s and a few other such exclusive locales came into existence in the 1950s, it was only in the late 1960s and 1970s, when retirement communities materialized, that average Americans began to wall themselves off from society. The 1980s marked a rapid increase in gated communities, both in urban and suburban locales, and now over 8 million people live in them. Categories of gated communities are lifestyle, prestige, and security-zone. Critics charge that this residence pattern contributes to social fragmentation, does not really deter crime, and does not provide any real sense of community.

Common-interest developments (CIDs) may or may not include gated communities. These master-planned developments require monthly fees for shared amenities and membership in a homeowners' association, which has broad regulatory powers over residents—powers that critics charge invade both the privacy and the constitutional rights of individuals.

CONCLUSION

Although Canada has stronger central government controls over land use than the United States, both countries are experiencing sprawl, edge city development, and an increase in exclusive communities. Some areas have more successfully contained these growth patterns than others, but they predominate nonetheless. What do these popular choices bode for the future of older cities and for the social cohesiveness of Canadian and U.S. societies?

Generations ago, zoning and planning boards throughout Canada and the United

States generated building and density code variances to preserve the position of the privileged; so economic and social segregation are by no means new social phenomena. However, gated communities go much further in their exclusivity, for they create physical entry barriers. Moreover, they privatize not only individual space, but community space as well. The common-interest developments do even more: They privatize civic responsibilities (police protection) and communal services (street maintenance, entertainment, and recreation). This new development creates a private world that requires residents to share little with their neighbors outside their barricades or even with the larger political system.

The recent evolution of edge cities and exclusive communities is still new, but already the dominance of these urban forms in North America suggests a need for further research. But this is only part of the urban picture. The next five chapters will examine how social scientists—sociologists, psychologists, geographers, anthropologists, and political economists—have come to analyze cities as living entities. Reading these chapters, you will discover that the urban story gets even more interesting.

CHAPTER 5

URBAN SOCIOLOGY
The Classic Statements

Once humans learned to harness the machine, the resulting social upheaval dramatically changed virtually everything. Nowhere were the changes more pronounced than in European cities. The emerging factory system drew in unheard-of numbers of people, with the result that the cities exploded with population. In 1816, for example, Germany had barely 2.5 million urbanites; by 1895 the number had passed 13 million. During the nineteenth century, London grew from 861,000 to a monumental 6.5 million.

Imagine such radical change: Overwhelmed by incoming migrants, cities could not provide adequate food, safe housing, sanitary facilities, medical care, or enough jobs. As a result, poverty, disease, malnutrition, and crime were on the rise. City streets no doubt seemed chaotic. This was the context in which urban sociology emerged. In the Looking Back box on page 142, Friedrich Engels (1820–1895) vividly describes the appalling slum conditions that industrialization brought to Manchester, England.

THE EUROPEAN TRADITION: 1846–1921

Sociology was born in Europe, a child of the Industrial Revolution. Given its start by August Comte (1798–1857), it was nurtured by the sociologists who followed—including Karl Marx, Friedrich Engels, Ferdinand Tönnies, Emile Durkheim, Georg Simmel, and Max Weber—who sought to explain the great transformation wrought by urbanization and industrialization.

Karl Marx and Friedrich Engels: From Barbarism to Civilization

Karl Marx (1818–1883) spent most of his adult life in England during the heyday of the Industrial Revolution. Marx was among the first of the classical sociologists to offer an analysis of the transformation of European society.

Marx argued passionately that the economic structure of society is "the real foundation . . . [that] determines the general character of the social, political, and spiritual processes of life" (1959:49; orig. 1859). By this he meant that the economic system serves as the base on which the social institutions of family, religion, and the political system take form. Although he conceded many causes of social change (such as technological advances), Marx contended that societal transformation primarily results from *conflict* between those who control the process of economic production (capitalists) and those who supply the necessary labor (proletariat). Thus, to argue that social problems such as poverty and unemployment are the fault of individuals is a form of *false consciousness* since, as Marx saw it, the flaws of capitalism are the causes of these and other problems.

But Marx and his colleague Engels held that the city has special importance. People, they said, live as "generic, tribal beings" in preindustrial, traditional societies. Only with the rise of the city does productive specialization begin to free individuals to act on their own. It is in cities, then, that the state emerges so that people take on a political role as citizens, deliberately planning their own environment and using new scientific skills. Thus, to Marx and Engels, the rise of the city amounted to nothing less than a transition from barbarism to civilization:

Marx + Engels

> The greatest division of material and mental labour is the separation of town and country. The antagonism between town and country begins with the transition from barbarism to civilization, from tribe to State, from locality to nation, and runs through the whole history of civilization to the present day. . . . (1846:143)

However, Marx and Engels made it clear that not every city was liberating in this way. Under what they called "Asiatic modes of production" some cities remained chained to the bonds of the primitive community—with its limited division of labor, common property, and lack of individualism. As a result, these cities depended entirely on the agricultural surplus, and the functions of these cities—military, religious, or bureaucratic—lacked the dynamic drive of a commercial economy (Germani, 1973:20).

Even in industrial cities, however, Marx and Engels held that the social evolution of humans was not yet complete since a capitalist elite controlled the economy. Seeing firsthand the destructive aspects of early industrial capitalism, Marx and Engels believed that the historical process would further evolve with a worldwide anticapitalist revolution that would usher in socialism. Only in this final evolutionary phase would workers become aware of the real cause of their problems, unite and act together to transform society into a new and just order.

Ferdinand Tönnies: From *Gemeinschaft* to *Gesellschaft*

In his masterwork, *Gemeinschaft and Gesellschaft* (1887), the German sociologist Ferdinand Tönnies (1855–1936) described two contrasting types of human social life: *gemeinschaft,* or "community," which characterized the small country village; and *gesellschaft,* or "association," which characterized the large city. Within the village, Tönnies maintained, social life forms a "living organism" in which people have an essential unity of purpose, work together for the common good, and are united by ties of family and neighborhood. Such is not the case in the city, in which social life is a "mechanical aggregate" characterized by disunity, rampant individualism, and selfishness, even hostility. Among city dwellers, a belief in the common good is rare; ties of family and neighborhood are of little significance.

The typology of *gemeinschaft* and *gesellschaft* has had a lasting influence on urban sociology because it was one of the first theories to understand human settlements by means of a continuum. At each "pole" of the continuum was a specific, "pure" type of settlement. Using such a formulation, one could classify any actual settlement at some point along the continuum as having a certain measure of *gemeinschaft* qualities and a certain degree of *gesellschaft* qualities.

In Tönnies's conceptions of *gemeinschaft* and *gesellschaft,* we can observe the influence of Karl Marx, a fact Tönnies openly acknowledged in citing "Karl Marx' masterful analysis of industrial development" (Tönnies, 1887:64). In fact, Tönnies's idea of community finds its counterpart in the "primitive community" and "primitive mode of production" that Marx and Engels had written about 40 years earlier.

Gemeinschaft

Tönnies used the concept of *gemeinschaft* to characterize the rural village and surrounding land worked communally by its inhabitants. Social life was characterized by "intimate, private, and exclusive living together," and members were bound by common language and traditions. They recognized "common goods—common evils; common friends—common enemies" and carried within them a sense of "we-ness," of "our-ness." Thornton Wilder expresses this sense of village togetherness eloquently in his play *Our Town*; see the analytical commentary about the play in the Cityscape box on page 144.

Gesellschaft

In the character of the modern city Tönnies saw a wholly different style of life, in which the meaning of existence shifted from the group to the individual. Where *gemeinschaft* expresses a sense of "we-ness," *gesellschaft* is more rational, more calculating. By its very nature, *gesellschaft* conditions people to be primarily concerned with their own self-interest, to "look out for Number One," in contemporary terms. In *gemeinschaft* the "natural" social institutions of kinship, neighborhood, and friendship are predominant; in *gesellschaft* these forms of association tend to decline. In the City in Literature box on page 145, Englishman Robert Crowley's sixteenth-century poem conveys Tönnies's sense of what *gesellschaft* is like.

1st manufacturing city in the World

textile

not clean

crowded

LOOKING BACK

Friedrich Engels

Working-Class Manchester, 1844

Friedrich Engels, the son of a wealthy German manufacturer, went to Manchester, England, in 1842 to learn the textile business. During his early years there, he gathered material for his first book, *The Condition of the Working Class in England*, in 1844. This excerpt from that work vividly describes Manchester's appalling slum conditions.

Here one is in an almost undisguised working-men's quarter, for even the shops and beer-houses hardly take the trouble to exhibit a trifling degree of cleanliness. But all this is nothing in comparison with the courts and lanes which lie behind, to which access can be gained only through covered passages, in which no two human beings can pass at the same time. Of the irregular cramming together of dwellings in ways which defy all rational plan, of the tangle in which they are crowded literally one upon the other, it is impossible to convey an idea. And it is not the buildings surviving from the old times of Manchester which are to blame for this; the confusion has only recently reached its height when every scrap of space left by the old way of building has been filled up and patched over until not a foot of land is left to be further occupied.

. . . Right and left a multitude of covered passages lead from the main street into numerous courts, and he who turns in thither gets into a filth and disgusting grime, the equal of which is not to be found . . . and which contain unqualifiedly the most horrible dwellings which I have yet beheld. In these courts there stands directly at the entrance, at the end of the covered passage, a privy without a door, so dirty that the inhabitants can pass into and out of the court only by passing through foul pools of stagnant urine and excrement. . . . Below it on the river there are several tanneries which fill the whole neighborhood with the stench of animal putrefaction. Below Ducie Bridge the only entrance to most of the houses is by means of narrow, dirty stairs and over heaps of refuse and filth. . . .

The view from [Ducie] Bridge . . . is characteristic for the whole district. At the bottom flows, or rather stagnates, the Irk, a narrow, coal-black, foul-smelling stream, full of debris and refuse, which it deposits on the shallower right bank. In dry weather, a long string of the most disgusting blackish-green slime pools are left standing on this bank, from the depths of which bubbles of miasmatic gas constantly arise and give forth a stench unendurable even on the bridge forty or fifty feet above the surface of the stream. . . .

Passing along a rough bank, among stakes and washing-lines, one penetrates into this chaos of small one-storied, one-roomed huts, in most of which there is no artificial floor; kitchen, living and sleeping-room all in one. In such a hole, scarcely five feet long by six broad, I found two beds—and such bedsteads and beds!—which, with a staircase and chimney-place, exactly filled the room. In several others I found absolutely nothing, while the door stood open, and the inhabitants leaned against it. Everywhere before the doors refuse and offal; that any sort of pavement lay underneath could not be seen but only felt, here and there, with the feet. . . .

Enough! The whole side of the Irk is built in this way, a planless, knotted chaos of houses, more or less on the verge of uninhabitableness, whose unclean interiors fully correspond with their filthy external surroundings. And how could the people be clean with no proper opportunity for satisfying the most natural and

Chapter 5 Urban Sociology   **143**

ordinary wants? Privies are so rare here that they are either filled up every day, or are too remote for most of the inhabitants to use. How can people wash when they have only the dirty Irk water at hand, while pumps and water pipes can be found in decent parts of the city alone? In truth, it cannot be charged to the account of these helots of modern society if their dwellings are not more clean than the pig sties which are here and there to be seen among them. The landlords are not ashamed to let dwellings like the six or seven cellars on the quay directly below Scotland Bridge, the floors of which stand at least two feet below the low-water level of the Irk that flows not six feet away from them; or like the upper floor of the corner-house on the opposite shore directly above the bridge, where the ground-floor, utterly uninhabitable, stands deprived of all fittings for doors and windows, a case by no means rare in this region, when this open ground-floor is used as a privy by the whole neighbourhood for want of other facilities!

As for the rest, the filth, debris, and offal heaps, and the pools in the streets are common . . . and another feature most injurious to the cleanliness of the inhabitants, is the multitude of pigs walking about in all the alleys, rooting into the offal heaps, or kept imprisoned in small pens. Here, as in most of the working-men's quarters of Manchester, the pork-raisers rent the courts and build pig-pens in them. In almost every court one or even several such pens may be found, into which the inhabitants of the court throw all refuse and offal, whence the swine grow fat; and the atmosphere, confined on all four sides, is utterly corrupted by putrefying animal and vegetable substances. . . .

Such is the Old Town of Manchester, and on re-reading my description, I am forced to admit that instead of being exaggerated, it is far from black enough to convey a true impression of the filth, ruin, and uninhabitableness,

the defiance of all considerations of cleanliness, ventilation, and health which characterise the construction of this single district, containing at least twenty to thirty thousand inhabitants. And such a district exists in the heart of the second city of England, the first manufacturing city in the world. If any one wishes to see in how little space a human being can move, how little air—and such air!—he can breathe, how little of civilisation he may share and yet live, it is only necessary to travel hither. . . .

Everything which here arouses horror and indignation is of recent origin, belongs to the industrial epoch. The couple of hundred houses, which belong to old Manchester, have been long since abandoned by their original inhabitants; the industrial epoch alone has crammed into them the swarms of workers whom they now shelter; the industrial epoch alone has built up every spot between these old houses to win a covering for the masses whom it has conjured hither from the agricultural districts and from Ireland; the industrial epoch alone enables the owners of these cattle sheds to rent them for high prices to human beings, to plunder the poverty of the workers, to undermine the health of thousands, in order that they alone, the owner, may grow rich. In the industrial epoch alone has it become possible that the worker scarcely freed from feudal servitude could be used as mere material, a mere chattel; that he must let himself be crowded into a dwelling too bad for every other, which he for his hard-earned wages buys the right to let go utterly to ruin. This manufacture has achieved, which, without these workers, this poverty, this slavery could not have lived.

Source: Friedrich Engels, *The Condition of the Working Class in England,* trans. by W. O. Henderson and W. H. Chaloner (New York: Macmillan, 1958).

CITYSCAPE

Here is a closeness [handwritten annotation]

Our Town: *The Spirit of* Gemeinschaft

Thornton Wilder's play *Our Town* is an acclaimed classic for many reasons, including its poignant portrayal of "ordinary life-cycle events." However, to many people, its real charm lies in the insights it provides into life in a typical small town, where people live in what we may appropriately call a *gemeinschaft* community.

The play opens with the "Stage Manager" telling the audience about "our town," Grover's Corners, a small village in New Hampshire. He asks the audience to imagine the layout of the town and the life of its inhabitants.

To orient us, he points out what first appear to be differences—where, for example, the Polish immigrants live. They migrated to Grover's Corners to work in the mill, he tells us, as did a few "Canuck" families. Next he tells us where the various churches are: Catholic, Congregationalist, Presbyterian, Methodist, Unitarian, and Baptist, in that order. He does not tell us that such differences may separate people's lives somewhat, but they by no means isolate them from one another. Almost intuitively we know this, however—a fact reaffirmed through our learning that everyone here knows quite a bit about almost everyone else. They don't necessarily like everyone, or always approve of certain people's behavior (such as excessive drinking, for example), but there is a closeness, an intimacy, among the people nevertheless. This is how it also was in the medieval city—Weber's ideal form of *gemeinschaft*—where class differences, disagreements, even conflict existed within a close-knit community dominated by traditional values and continuity.

To help us understand some of this tradition and continuity, the Stage Manager informs us that the town's earliest tombstones—dating back to 1670—are engraved with names such as Grover, Cartright, Gibbs, and Hersey. These are the same family names as among the townspeople in 1901, the year in which the play takes place. Emphasizing this theme of stable relationships in daily life, he tells us, "On the whole, things don't change much around here." He also offers bits of other information—the nonexistence of burglars and the daily visits by nearly everyone to the grocery store and the drug store on Main Street. These manifestations of mutual trust, daily routine, familiarity, and regular social interaction suggest a cohesiveness of community that is the essence of *gemeinschaft*.

As the play unfolds about this ordinary small town, one where "nobody remarkable ever come out of it, s'far as we know," we learn about more than just some events in the lives of George Gibbs and Emily Webb, or of their family, friends, and neighbors, both alive or deceased. We witness the way life once was in simpler times in North American small towns—a way of life that no doubt still exists in whatever small towns still remain. But for most of us—living in a *gesellschaft* environment—it is a bygone reality, not ours.

One way to distinguish easily the difference between *gemeinschaft* and *gesellschaft* is to consider, when people ask "How are you?"—do they really want to know? Tönnies's communal relation—*gemeinschaft*—is built on broad concern for the other as a person, and such a question has significance beyond convention, beyond politeness. In the contrasting

THE CITY IN LITERATURE

The City as Gesellschaft

And this a city
  In name but in deed
It is a pack of people
  That seek after meed
    [profit].
For officers and all
  Do seek their own gain
But for the wealth of the
  Commons

No one taketh pain.
And hell without order
  I may it well call
Where every man is for himself
And no man for all.

—Robert Crowley (1575)

[handwritten notes: Tonnie's sense of what Gesellschaft is like; All want the # for every man for himself; Robert Crowley]

case—*gesellschaft*—each person is understood in terms of a particular role and service provided (as teacher, computer programmer, or butcher). In the city the question "How are you?" is usually asked only out of politeness: We don't know other people well and, what's more, we usually don't want to know them well.

Gemeinschaft and *Gesellschaft* in History

Tönnies believed that the study of European history revealed a gradual, and generally irreversible, displacement of *gemeinschaft* by *gesellschaft.* He saw the rapid rise of cities in Europe during the nineteenth century as the inevitable emergence of *gesellschaft* as the dominant form of social life. Although he thought it inevitable, Tönnies obviously did not think this transformation altogether good: For him, the unity and human concern of *gemeinschaft* was gradually lost in *gesellschaft.*

Tönnies's ideas contain the beginning of a sociology of the city. He was among the first to see urban life as distinctive and worthy of study. Moreover, his use of contrasting pure types is a pattern that numerous other urban sociologists followed.

Emile Durkheim: Mechanical and Organic Solidarity

Like Tönnies, the French sociologist Emile Durkheim (1858–1917) witnessed the urban revolution of the nineteenth century. He, too, developed a model of contrasting types: mechanical solidarity and organic solidarity are analogous to Tönnies's *gemeinschaft* and *gesellschaft.*

Mechanical solidarity refers to social bonds that are constructed on likeness, on common belief and custom, on common ritual and symbol. Such solidarity is "mechanical" because the people who participate in it—people living in family units, tribes, or small towns—are almost identical in major respects and are united almost automatically, without thinking. Each family, tribe, or town is relatively self-sufficient and able to meet all life needs without dependence on other groups.

In contrast, organic solidarity describes a social order based on individual differences. Characteristic of modern societies, especially cities, organic solidarity rests on a complex division of labor, in which many different people specialize in many different occupations. Like the organs of the human body, people depend more on one another to meet various needs. A lawyer depends on other people—say, restaurant owners and grocers—to supply food, and is able to specialize in legal activity. Similarly, of course, the restaurant owner and the grocer need not study law, for the same reason.

In this complex division of labor, Durkheim saw the possibility of greater freedom and choice for all of society's inhabitants. Although Durkheim acknowledged the problems that cities might create—impersonality, alienation, disagreement, and conflict—he argued for the ultimate superiority of organic over mechanical solidarity: "[The] yoke that we submit to [in modern society] is much less heavy than when society completely controls us [as it does in rural society], and it leaves much more place open for the free play of our initiative" (1893; 1964:131).

Durkheim and Tönnies: A Comparison

[handwritten annotation: — they looked at processes that produced the city]

While Durkheim agreed with Tönnies's conclusion that history was characterized by a movement from an emphasis on one type of social order to another—from mechanical solidarity (or *gemeinschaft*) to organic solidarity (or *gesellschaft*)—there are important differences in their ideas. For instance, Durkheim took exception to labeling the tribal or rural environment alone as "natural." Rather, he asserted that "the life of large social agglomerations is just as natural as that of small groupings."

This assertion reveals that Durkheim did not share Tönnies's negative view of modern society. In fact, Durkheim reversed Tönnies's terminology and labeled *gemeinschaft* "mechanical" and *gesellschaft* "organic." Although Tönnies saw little hope for truly humane life in the city (he cited parents' admonition to their citybound children to beware of "bad *gesellschaft*"), Durkheim was more optimistic. Durkheim saw the increasing division of labor characteristic of modern urban societies as undermining traditional social integration and creating a new form of social cohesion based on mutual interdependence. Contractual agreements among individuals or groups

clearly express this interdependence. Still, Durkheim cautioned, no society can exist entirely on the basis of contract: At the very least, there needs to be a moral foundation on which we agree about how to enter into and execute all contracts fairly.

Durkheim thus provides an important counterpoint to Tönnies. Although both theorists recognized that cities were associated with the growth of social differentiation and individuality, Tönnies feared the undermining of the very fabric of social life, whereas Durkheim saw the possibility of continuing social cohesion and greater human development. Yet the effects of the city on individuals extend beyond these two visions.

Georg Simmel: The Mental Life of the Metropolis

Both Tönnies and Durkheim described the broad societal processes that produced the modern city. Although they made passing reference to the mental characteristics of city dwellers—the city dweller was more impersonal, more rational, freer—they did not look systematically at the social psychology of city life. That task was undertaken by another German, Georg Simmel (1858–1918).

Like his contemporaries, Simmel saw in the rise of the modern world a cause for concern: How was the individual to maintain a spirit of freedom and creativity in the midst of the city's "overwhelming social forces"? In his famous essay "The Metropolis and Mental Life," Simmel suggested that the personality would learn to "accommodate itself" to the urban scene (Simmel, 1905, 1964).

The City's Characteristics

To Simmel, the unique trait of the modern city is the intensification of nervous stimuli with which the city dweller must cope. Unlike the rural setting, where "the rhythm of life and sensory imagery flows more slowly, more habitually, more evenly," the city constantly bombards the individual with an enormous kaleidoscope of sights, sounds, and smells. To

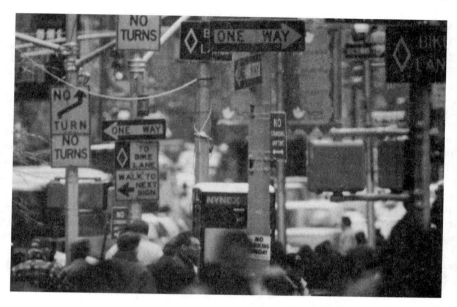

Whenever we walk along a city street, we encounter an abundance of stimuli, far more than we can absorb. This intensification of nervous stimuli—from the many signs, sounds, movements, and crowds of people—forces us, says Simmel, to discriminate carefully, to tune in what is important and to tune out what is not.

avoid being overwhelmed by such stimulation, the individual learns to discriminate carefully—to tune in what is important and tune out what is irrelevant. In time, urban people become more sophisticated and intellectual, more rational and calculating than their rural counterparts.

Such rationality means that urbanites are highly attuned to time. Cities, Simmel observed, are marked by the ever-present clock and wristwatch. "If," he continued, "all the clocks and watches in Berlin would suddenly go wrong in different ways, even if only by one hour, all economic life and communication of the city would be disrupted for a long time" (1964:413). In addition to the rational organization of time, Simmel saw the rationality of the city expressed in its advanced economic division of labor (here he echoed Durkheim). Social life in the city is the interplay of specialists.

But perhaps the most powerful means of conveying the message of urban rationality was Simmel's discussion of the importance of money. "The metropolis," he stated, "has always been the seat of a money economy." Why is money so important in urban life? One reason is that the advanced division of labor requires a universal means of exchange. Money performs this critical function. As Simmel wrote (1964:414), "Money is concerned only with what is common to all: It asks for the exchange value, it reduces all quality and individuality to the question: How much?"

The Individual's Response

How, asks Simmel, is the urbanite to behave in the midst of such powerful stimulation and unending demand for rational response? Or, on a more practical level, can you really stop to help everyone you see on the street who is in some sort of trouble? Simmel believed not. Consequently, he reasoned, the urbanite adapts to city life by developing what he called a "blasé" attitude, a social reserve, a detachment. Put simply, in the city we respond with our head rather than our heart. We learn to adopt a matter-of-fact attitude about the world around us. We simply don't care; we don't want to "get involved," as is shown dramatically in the examples in the Urban Living box on page 150.

Even worse, Simmel speculated that the cultivated indifference necessary to living in the city may harden into a measured antagonism. "Indeed, if I do not deceive myself," he wrote, "the inner aspect of this outer reserve is not only indifference, but, more often than we are aware, it is a slight aversion, a mutual strangeness and repulsion, which will break into hatred and fight at the moment of a closer contact, however caused" (1964:415–16). Perhaps each of us can recall feeling some anger about the way someone unknown to us was behaving in a city—someone who broke into a line ahead of us, for example, or someone who approached us in a city park, demanding spare change.

Like Durkheim, Simmel could see freedom in the separateness fostered by city living. The urbanite, he thought, can transcend the pettiness of daily routine and reach a new height of personal and spiritual development. But Simmel also detected in the city's freedom a haunting specter. "It is obviously only the obverse of this freedom," he wrote, "if, under certain circumstances one nowhere feels as lonely and lost as in the metropolitan crowd."

Feeling like a cog in a giant machine, some people maintain their sense of individuality in a city by doing something "odd," by "being different" and thereby standing out. It is this sense of alienation that Simmel would use to explain the motivation for the graffiti craze in so many cities, a process that has defaced buildings, signs, subway trains, and public monuments. For many of these vandals, their signed logos raise them out of their anonymity and shout out, "I'm not just another face in the project among a million others. I exist. I am here!"

In the end, then, Simmel appears to side more with Tönnies than with Durkheim in his evaluation of the city. Although he depicted the city as the setting where the great historical contest between true human liberation and alienation would occur, his analysis left little doubt that he believed the second option was likely to be victorious.

Max Weber: The Historical and Comparative Study of Cities

Tönnies, Durkheim, and Simmel all analyzed a single type of city. That is, they developed their theories by "reading" the main trends of European urban history and the main elements of life in the cities they knew.

German sociologist Max Weber (1864–1920) believed that any theory that took account of cities in only one part of the world at one point in time was of limited value. This concern proved to be his major methodological contribution to urban sociology.

Die Stadt

Weber demonstrated his approach in his famous essay "*Die Stadt*" ("The City"), which first appeared in 1921. Surveying cities of Europe, the Middle East, India, and China, Weber developed a definition of what he called the full urban community:

> To constitute a full urban community, a settlement must display a relative predominance of trade–commercial relations, with the settlement as a whole displaying the following features: (1) a fortification; (2) a market; (3); a court of its own and at least partially autonomous law; (4) a related form of association; and (5) at least partial political autonomy. (1966:80–81)

This definition illustrates what Weber called an *ideal type*, a model constructed from real-world observation that highlights the crucial elements of some social phenomenon. Weber was well aware that many cities would not contain all of the elements in his definition. In such cases, the city simply would not be a "full urban community" in his sense. We shall examine the characteristics of such a community in more detail.

If you encountered this stranger lying unconscious on your campus or in a suburban mall parking lot, the probability is high that you would help him or get help. In the city, however, where sleeping vagrants, drunks, and addicts often abound, you might easily ignore him and avoid getting involved, as several people here are doing.

First, Weber's urban community is based on trade or commercial relations. In rural areas, people are more or less self-sufficient, growing their own food, providing their own clothing, and so on. Trade and commerce are of limited importance there. Not so in the city. Weber clearly agreed with Tönnies, Durkheim, and Simmel that economic self-sufficiency is nearly impossible in cities; people are economically interdependent, linked by Durkheim's organic solidarity. Indeed, the economic aspects of city life are so important that a distinct mechanism of exchange—the market—evolved to facilitate them.

Second, an urban community is relatively autonomous. Weber specified that a true city has a court and law of its own and at least partial political autonomy. It also must be militarily self-sufficient, having a fortification system and army for self-defense if and when necessary. Such autonomy is essential if urban dwellers are to identify the city as theirs, as a place demanding their allegiance in the way that the small town receives the allegiance of its inhabitants.

Third, Weber said that the urban community must have "a related form of association." By this he meant that city living must involve social relationships and organizations through which urbanites gain a sense of meaningful participation in the life of their city.

The "Full Urban Community" in History

Like Durkheim, Weber believed that cities could be positive and liberating forces in human life. Unlike Durkheim, however, Weber did not see much hope for twentieth-century cities. Indeed, he thought only the fortified, self-sufficient cities of the medieval period deserved the title of "full urban community." Only in these cities had there existed

Urban Apathy: The Death of Kitty Genovese and Other Rather Unnerving Events

NY, Times / March 1964

On March 14, 1964, a grim item appeared in a tiny story on page 26 of the *New York Times*. It reported the murder of Kitty Genovese near her home in the Kew Gardens section of New York's Borough of Queens. What seemed at first to be a report of a crime without particular public significance exploded into a major controversy when the *Times* reported two weeks later that dozens of Ms. Genovese's "neighbors" had observed her attacker stab her repeatedly during a period of half an hour without coming to her aid or even calling the police until after she was dead! In an editorial the following day, the *Times* posed a frightening question: "Does residence in a great city destroy all sense of personal responsibility for one's neighbors?"

The death of Kitty Genovese thus became symbolic of the argument that the city was an unhealthy setting that lacked even a rudimentary sense of human community.

But it didn't stop with Kitty Genovese. Hers is only the most celebrated case. On the night of November 30, 1984, the same thing happened in Brooklyn. A woman was attacked in the Gowanus Apartments, a New York City housing project. As she was beaten, she began screaming and continued her cries for 20 minutes. Many heard her—no one came to her rescue. Finally, her assailants dragged her into the lobby of a building and shot her dead. It was only then that someone deigned to call the police (*New York Times*, December 2, 1984).

The same year, the same indifference to the victims of urban crime surfaced again, this time in St. Louis. In one case a man was

---

the commercial relations, autonomy, and social participation that he believed to be the defining characteristics of urbanism.

With the rise to preeminence of the nation as a political entity in the seventeenth, eighteenth, and nineteenth centuries, Weber claimed, cities had lost their military and, to a large extent, their legal and political, autonomy—necessary elements for identifying with the city as a psychological "home." People came to identify with other units of society—the nation, country, business or, as recognized by Tönnies and Simmel, with themselves alone.

By recognizing medieval cities as examples of the full urban community, Weber hoped to show that "the good life" had existed in cities and might flourish again. Yet, by suggesting that a pinnacle of urban culture had been

realized before in history, Weber implied that history might not necessarily be progressive (Sennett, 1969:6–10).

The City and Culture

Weber stood apart from his colleagues who tended to see the city itself as the cause of the distinguishing qualities of urban life. In contrast, Weber's analysis, fueled by his broad understanding of cities in other cultures and at different points in history, suggested that cities are intimately linked to larger processes—to particular economic or political orientations, for example. If a society's character is different, the nature of its cities will be different. Thus, feudal or Chinese societies would not produce the same type of urban life that European industrial capitalism does.

robbed at gunpoint while dozens of people looked on. When the man approached the onlookers afterwards and asked why they hadn't helped him, they replied that they just "didn't want to get involved." In another incident a woman was attacked by three men at Busch Memorial Stadium during a Cardinals baseball game. She screamed for help. No one responded. She said later: "I was shocked more than hurt. I just sat there and screamed and not one soul stopped. I saw all these legs going by, and I thought about reaching out and grabbing somebody." Said Sgt. Frank Baricevic of the St. Louis Police of these disturbing incidents: "Police departments are only as good as the people they protect. If [people] don't want to get involved, if they don't want to cooperate, then we're in trouble" (*New York Times*, August 18, 1984).

More recently, people's actions were a little different. On a bridge into downtown Detroit in September 1995, Deletha Word banged her car into another driven by Martell Welch. With dozens of other cars stopped on the bridge, Welch pulled Word out of her car, ripping off some of her clothes, and pushed her down on the hood to beat her. One of Welch's friends then held her down while Welch got a car jack that he used to smash up her car. The woman broke free and ran to the outside railing of the bridge, where she threatened to kill herself. "Jump, bitch, jump!" yelled Welch's friends, and she dropped off the bridge. Two men, Lawrence Walker and Orlando Brown, jumped off the bridge in a vain attempt to save her. Word's body was recovered miles downstream that day—minus a leg, which had apparently been cut off by the propeller of a passing boat. Some reporters called the crowd's failure to respond reminiscent of Kitty Genovese's murder. Yet this time several motorists did call 9-1-1 on their cellular phones, and 26 people came forward to help police track down the suspect (Stokes and Zeman, 1995).

The European Tradition: An Evaluation

The ideas of Marx, Engels, Tönnies, Durkheim, Simmel, and Weber form the core of classical urban sociology, and have had an enormous impact on the field ever since. It is important, however, to balance their contributions with their limitations.

Contributions

Perhaps the most important contribution of the classical theorists was their insistence that the city is an important object of sociological study. Marx, Engels, Tönnies, and Durkheim all clearly analyzed the contrasts between rural and urban life. Simmel and Weber went a step further by actually developing theories of how cities worked.

Second, all six theorists recognized that *there is something distinctive about the city and the way of life it creates.* They all saw the city as increasing human choice, emphasizing rationality, being characterized by a complex division of labor, and creating a unique experience for its inhabitants. This concern with the city's unique qualities has been, as the next section will demonstrate clearly, a major focus of the discipline ever since.

Third, taken together, these theorists suggested the main concerns of the discipline. Marx and Engels emphasized economics and the problems of inequality and conflict. Tönnies, Durkheim, and Weber all considered the social structure of the city. Simmel suggested the importance of the urban experience.

Finally, all six Europeans made the evaluation of cities a fundamental element in their work. Each made quite clear what he thought beneficial and what he considered detrimental to the city's ability to produce a humane life for its population.

Limitations

Three generations later, we can easily see how the central ideas of these theorists were an outgrowth of the times and cities in which they lived. Cities were quickly replacing villages and countryside as the main arena of life. For all their excitement, one could hardly argue that these rapidly growing cities provided a good life for many of their inhabitants. Little wonder, then, that three of these theorists (Tönnies, Simmel, and Weber) saw the cities of their day as threats to long-cherished human values. Durkheim, Marx, and Engels had mixed responses to the changing cities. Durkheim acknowledged the problems of alienation and conflict in the cities but also saw the ultimate superiority of the new industrial age. Marx and Engels saw not the city, but the capitalist economy, as a social evil.

Of course, one can only speculate on how the theories of these men might have changed had they been able to witness the growth of suburbs, major efforts at urban planning, reforms in many of the most overtly exploitative practices of turn-of-the-century cities (such as child labor), the rise of labor unions, the civil rights movement, and the recent collapse of communism in an economically bankrupt Soviet Union and a fettered Eastern Europe.

Also, the theorists show some disagreement in their interpretations. The contrast between Tönnies and Durkheim is most instructive. Tönnies saw *gemeinschaft* as humane and *gesellschaft* as brutal. Using his terms of mechanical and organic solidarity, Durkheim reversed the interpretation: The tribal or country life was cloying, undeveloped; the life of the city, in contrast, was liberating and full of potential for development.

On another level, Simmel thought the social–psychological adaptations he studied were a product of the great city itself. He implied that all metropolises would produce similar mental processes. Weber disagreed.

He argued that only certain historical and cultural conditions produced the type of city that Simmel observed (modern capitalist cities, for example) and that other historical and cultural conditions would produce very different types of urban social–psychological adaptation.

Similarly, Marx and Engels maintained that the human condition in cities was the result of the economic structure and that a different economic system would produce a different city with different social interaction patterns.

With the evidence available at the time, it was impossible to judge such contradictory claims, although later chapters will show that Weber's position on this issue was closer to the truth.

URBAN SOCIOLOGY IN NORTH AMERICA: 1915–1938

About the time of World War I, urban sociology began to develop in the United States. From the outset, the discipline's character was somewhat different from that in Europe, with U.S. researchers showing greater concern with actually going out and exploring the city. At the same time, many of the themes of the European tradition were carried into North American sociology.

The era in which this sociology developed is noteworthy. The early twentieth century in North America, as in Europe, was a period of industrialization and rapid urban growth. A mounting flow of immigrants—most of whom settled in cities—ensured that, by 1920, the United States would become a predominantly urban society. In short, the Grover's Corners of North America (as described in the last Cityscape box) were rapidly giving way to the expanding industrial metropolis.

No city typified this explosive growth better than Chicago. A crude outpost in 1830, by 1900 Chicago was approaching a population of 2 million and was expanding both upward and outward. The first steel-frame building—a marvel of the age—opened its doors in Chicago in 1884, towering an incredible ten stories above the ground! By the close of World War I, Chicago boasted a population of almost 3 million. Immigrants from Europe and migrants from the countryside were everywhere. Like hundreds of exploding North American cities, Chicago was billowing the black, smoky flag of prosperity, creating its share of severe problems as it went. It was in Chicago that the main elements of U.S. urban sociology took form.

Robert Park and Sociology at the University of Chicago

Although U.S. universities had offered courses in "social science" as far back as 1865, sociology first gained intellectual respectability when the University of Chicago invited Albion W. Small (then president of Colby College) to found a sociology department in 1892 (Faris, 1967). Within the next 30 years the department attracted several notable scholars. One of the most outstanding was Robert Ezra Park (1864–1944).

Leaving a newspaper job in 1915 to join the department, Park established the first urban studies center in the United States. His interest in urban matters had both European and North American roots. In his early years he had studied with the Russian sociologist Kistiakowski (who held much the same view of social change as Tönnies) and with Georg Simmel. Park was also deeply influenced by *The Shame of the Cities* (1906), a book by U.S. journalist Lincoln Steffens suggesting that serious urban problems were everyone's responsibility. An excerpt from this critique appears in the Critical Thinking box on page 154.

Although he was aware of both the bad and the good, there can be no question that Park had an almost unbounded fascination with the city. Not only did Park guide several generations of students in explorations of all aspects of Chicago, but he served as first president of the Chicago Urban League. Dedicating his life to relentless personal exploration of the city, Park later wrote:

> I expect that I have actually covered more ground, tramping about in cities in different parts of the world, than any other living man.

> Out of all this I gained, among other things, a conception of the city, the community, and the region, not as geographical phenomenon [sic] merely, but as a kind of social organism. (1950, p. viii)

A Systematic Urban Sociology

Park presented the program he used to guide urban sociology at the University of Chicago in his classic article "The City: Suggestions for the Investigation of Human Behavior in the Urban Environment" (1967; orig. published 1916). First, he argued that urban research had to be conducted by disciplined observation, in much the same way that anthropologists studied other cultures. Second, he conceived of the city as a social organism with distinct parts bound together by internal processes. Urban life was not chaos and disorder (stereotypes of Chicago during the Roaring Twenties notwithstanding) but rather tended toward an "orderly and typical grouping of its population and institutions" (1967:1). He wrote:

> Every great city has its racial colonies, like the Chinatowns of San Francisco and New York, the Little Sicily of Chicago, and the various other less pronounced types. In addition to these, most cities have their segregated vice districts . . . their rendezvous for criminals of various sorts. Every large city has its occupational suburbs, like the stockyards in Chicago, and its residential enclaves, like Brookline in Boston, the so-called "Gold Coast" in Chicago, Greenwich Village in New York, each of which has a size and character of a complete separate town, village, or city, except that its population is a select one. (1967:10)

This notion of the city's orderliness led Park to urge his students to develop detailed studies of all segments of the city's population— not only industrial workers, real-estate officials, and VIPs, but also migrants, hobos, musicians, prostitutes, and dance hall workers. The conviction that all "parts and processes" of the city were linked was at the heart of Park's new social science, which he termed "human, as distinguished from plant and animal, ecology." Finally, Park also saw the city as a "moral as well as a physical organization"

Lincoln Steffens

The Shame of the Cities: Who's to Blame?

When I set out on my travels, an honest New Yorker told me honestly that I would find that the Irish, the Catholic Irish, were at the bottom of it all everywhere. The first city I went to was St. Louis, a German city. The next was Minneapolis, a Scandinavian city, with a leadership of New Englanders. Then came Pittsburgh, Scotch Presbyterian, and that was what my New York friend was. "Ah, but they are all foreign populations," I heard. The next city was Philadelphia, the purest American community of all, and the most hopeless. And after that came Chicago and New York, both mongrelbred, but the one a triumph of reform, the other the best example of good government that I had seen. The "foreign element" excuse is one of the hypocritical lies that save us from the clear sight of ourselves. . . .

When I set out to describe the corrupt systems of certain typical cities, I meant to show simply how the people were deceived and betrayed. But in the very first study—St. Louis—the startling truth lay bare that corruption was not merely political; it was financial, commercial, social; the ramifications of boodle were so complex, various,

and far-reaching that one mind could hardly grasp them. . . .

And it's all a moral weakness; a weakness right where we think we are strongest. Oh, we are good—on Sunday, and we are "fearfully patriotic" on the Fourth of July. But the bribe we pay to the janitor to prefer our interests to the landlord's, is the little brother of the bribe passed to the alderman to sell a city street, and the father of the air-brake stock assigned to the president of the railroad to have this life-saving invention adopted on his road. We are pathetically proud of our democratic institutions and our republican form of government, of our grand Constitution and our just laws. We are a free and sovereign people, we govern ourselves and the government is ours. But that is the point. We are responsible, not our leaders, since we follow them. We let them divert our loyalty from the United States to some "party"; we let them boss the party and turn our municipal democracies into autocracies and our republican nation into a plutocracy. We cheat our government and we let our leaders loot it, and we let them wheedle and bribe our sovereignty from us. . . . The people are not innocent.

Source: Lincoln Steffens, *The Shame of the Cities* (New York: McClure, Phillips, 1904), pp. 2–3, 7–9.

and carried evaluative judgments of urban living deep into his sociology.

Park's Image of the City

What was it about the city that so fascinated Park? First, like Weber, Park saw in the modern city a commercial structure that owed "its existence to the market place around which it sprang up." Like Marx, Weber, and Durkheim, he saw in modern city life a complex division

of labor driven by industrial competition. With Tönnies, Park believed that this market dominance would result in the steady erosion of traditional ways of life. The past emphasis upon "family ties, local associations . . . caste, and status" would yield inevitably to a *gesellschaft*-like system "based on occupation and vocational interests."

Second, Park perceived the city as increasingly characterized by *formal social structures*, best exemplified by large-scale bureaucracies such as police departments, courts, and welfare agencies. In time, he reasoned, these would take the place of the more "informal" means (such as neighborhood interaction) by which people had historically organized their everyday lives. Similarly, politics would develop a more formalized tone. Park contended that

> the form of government which had its origin in the town meetings and was well suited to the needs of the small community based on primary relations is not suitable to the government of the changing and heterogeneous populations of cities of three or four millions. (1967:33)

The city dweller, unable to take account of all the issues at stake in the operation of a complex city, would have to rely on "the organization represented by the political boss and the political machine or other civic organizations such as voter leagues."

As an ex-newspaperman, Park could hardly have been expected to omit the media from his description of the formalization of city life. The face-to-face oral network by which information flowed in the village ("gossip" is the more precise, if less scholarly, term) would be replaced by reliance on impersonal mass media. Such was the significance of the city newspaper, and, soon after that, radio and television and, eventually, the Internet.

The third dimension of Park's image of the city, showing the effects of his studies with Simmel, was his emphasis on the psychosocial dimension of urban life. Park suggested that life within the city would become *less sentimental* and *more rational*. Deep-seated sentiments and prejudices would give way to calculation based on self-interest. At the same time, however, Park was aware that the erosion of traditional sentimental ties in the city might give rise to new social bonds in the form of interest groups. In this, there is a clear Durkheimian quality to his argument: Ties based on likenesses (mechanical solidarity) are replaced by bonds based on the interdependence of differentiated parts (organic solidarity).

Freedom and Tolerance in the City

As a social reformer, Park recognized that the modern city revealed problem upon problem; but, like Durkheim, Park was fascinated with what he saw to be the possibilities for freedom and tolerance in the city. He wrote:

> The attraction of the metropolis is due in part to the fact that in the long run every individual finds somewhere among the varied manifestations of city life the sort of environment in which he expands and feels at ease; he finds, in short, the moral climate in which his peculiar nature obtains the stimulations that bring his innate dispositions to full and free expression. It is, I suspect, motives of this kind which have their basis, not in interest or even in sentiment, but in something more fundamental and primitive which drove many, if not most, of the young men and young women from the security of their homes in the country into the big, booming confusion and excitement of city life. (1967:41)

In short, what Tönnies saw as steady disorganization, Park saw as potential for greater human experience. He continued:

> In a small community it is the normal man, the man without eccentricity or genius who seems most likely to succeed. The small community often tolerates eccentricity. The city rewards it. Neither the criminal, the defective, nor the genius has the same opportunity to develop his innate disposition in a small town that he invariably finds in a great city. (1967:41)

Summing up, we see in the ideas of Robert Park a new emphasis upon the doing of urban research and on-site investigation of the city quite unlike the more abstract theorizing of Tönnies, Durkheim, and Simmel, and unlike the historical work of Marx, Engels and Weber. Park's main contribution was his demand that we get out there and see how the city actually works.

Louis Wirth and Urban Theory

If the European theorists produced a great deal of theory but conducted little actual research, early Chicago sociologists did just the opposite. During the 20 years that followed the publication of Park's urban studies program in 1916, Chicago sociologists produced a wealth of primarily descriptive studies. Not until 1938 was this imbalance rectified, when Louis Wirth (1897–1952) published his famous essay "Urbanism as a Way of Life."

Wirth's great contribution to urban sociology was the patient and systematic organization of the insights of previous urban sociologists into the first truly sociological theory of the city. By a *theory* of the city, we mean that Wirth began his analysis by isolating several factors that he argued were *universal social characteristics* of the city. He then proceeded to systematically deduce the consequences of these factors for the character of urban social life. He said, in effect (as all good theorists do): If this condition is present, then that condition will result.

Wirth began with a definition of the city as a (1) large, (2) dense, permanent settlement with (3) socially and culturally heterogeneous people. Let us examine what conditions of urban social life follow from each of these elements.

Population Size or Scale

Wirth believed, first, that large population size alone produces great diversity in the cultural and occupational characteristics of a city. This diversity partly results from (1) the simple fact that larger numbers of people coming together logically increase the potential differentiation among themselves, and from (2) the migration of diverse groups to the city (as in Chicago, where Wirth was writing). No one has better captured this sense of urban diversity than Walt Whitman in his 1855 poem "Song of Myself," an excerpt from which appears in the City in Literature box on page 157.

Second, the condition of cultural diversity produced by a large population has the additional effect of creating a need for formal control structures, such as a legal system. Third, a large, differentiated population supports the proliferation of specialization, and an occupational structure based upon differing occupations (artist, politician, cabdriver)

emerges. Fourth, specialization organizes human relationships more on an "interest-specific" basis that Wirth described as "social segmentalization":

> Characteristically, urbanites meet one another in highly segmental roles. They are, to be sure, dependent on more people for the satisfactions of their life needs than are rural people . . . but they are less dependent upon particular persons, and their dependence upon others is confined to a highly fractionalized aspect of the other's round of activity. This is essentially what is meant by saying that the city is characterized by secondary rather than primary contacts. The contacts of the city may indeed be face-to-face, but they are nevertheless impersonal, superficial, transitory, and segmental. (1964:71)

In other words, rather than understanding others in terms of who they are, the urbanite typically conceives of others in terms of what they do, in terms of their roles and what they can do to advance one's own ends. The qualities of rationality and sophistication are simply additional ways of suggesting that urban ties become, in essence, relationships of utility. Lastly, even with the stabilizing constraint provided by formal controls and professional codes of conduct, Wirth could not escape the conclusion that large population size carried with it the possibility of disorganization and disintegration, a fear shared by all the European theorists.

Population Density

The consequence of population density is to *intensify* the effects of large population size on social life. Rather than manifesting the quality of sameness one might associate with the countryside, the city becomes separated into a mosaic of readily identifiable regions or districts. (Here we can see the direct influence of Wirth's teacher, Park.) Both economic forces (such as differing land values) and social processes (such as attraction and avoidance based on race and ethnicity) tend to produce fairly distinct neighborhoods and districts.

For example, many U.S. cities have a predominantly Italian area (such as Boston's

THE CITY IN LITERATURE

The City—From *Song of Myself*

Walt Whitman

The pure contralto sings in the
  organ loft . . .
The married and unmarried
  children ride home to their
  Thanksgiving dinner . . .
The deacons are ordain'd with
  cross'd hands at the altar;
The spinning-girl retreats and
  advances to the hum of the big
  wheel . . .
The lunatic is carried at last to the
  asylum, a confirm'd case . . .
The jour printer with gray head and gaunt
  jaws works at his case . . .
The machinist rolls up his sleeves—the
  policeman travels his beat—the gate-keeper
  marks who pass . . .
The opium-eater reclines with rigid head and
  just-open'd lips;
The prostitute draggles her shawl, her bonnet
  bobs on her tipsy and pimpled neck;

The crowd laugh at her blackguard oaths,
  the men jeer and wink to each other . . .
The President, holding a cabinet council,
  is surrounded by the Great
  Secretaries;
On the piazza walk three matrons
  stately and friendly with twined
  arms . . .
Patriarchs sit at supper with sons and grand-
  sons and great-grandsons around them . . .
The city sleeps . . .
The old husband sleeps by his wife, and the
  young husband sleeps by his wife;
And these one and all tend inward to me,
  and I tend outward to them,
And such as it is to be of these, more or less,
  I am.

Source: Walt Whitman, "Song of Myself," in *Leaves of Grass*, 1855.

North End), a Chinatown (such as San Francisco's), and a high-income area (such as Chicago's North Shore). Similarly, major cities frequently have a garment district and a financial district (such as New York's Wall Street). Wirth called this process of separating the city into districts "ecological specialization." In the Cityscape box on pages 158–159, Charles Dickens vividly portrays some of these districts.

Density also operates on the social–psychological level. Exposed to "glaring contrasts . . . splendor and squalor . . . riches and poverty," Wirth argued, city dwellers develop a mental shorthand, a mental mapping of the city, its regions, and its inhabitants. This insight (drawn from Simmel) helps us understand the urbanite's tendency to stereotypical and categorical thinking, and the reliance on grasping the city through visible symbols and uniforms (clothing, cars, fashionable

street addresses). The implication is clear—population density fosters a loss of sensitivity to the "more personal aspects" of others—and suggests why people in the city sometimes seem "cold and heartless."

As suggested earlier by Durkheim and Simmel, Wirth contended that the "juxtaposition of divergent personalities and modes of life" results in a *greater toleration of differences*. Along with this, physical closeness tends to *increase social distance* among urbanites. Forced into physical proximity, city dwellers characteristically close off or tune out those around them. (On a small scale, this happens when people, busily chatting, enter a crowded elevator and abruptly become silent, staring up at the numbers on the elevator wall.)

Again echoing Simmel, Wirth suggested that high density may cause an increase in antisocial behavior. Wirth posited that "the necessary movement of great numbers of

CITYSCAPE

The Streets of London

In this scene from *The Old Curiosity Shop*, Charles Dickens describes walking through London one morning in 1840:

The town was glad with morning light; places that had shown ugly and distrustful all night long, now wore a smile; and sparkling sunbeams dancing on chamber windows, and twinkling through blind and curtain before sleeper's eyes, shed light even into dreams, and chased away the shadows of the night. . . . Bright and happy as it was, there was something solemn in the long, deserted streets, from which like bodies without souls all habitual character and expression had departed, leaving but one dead uniform repose, that made them all alike. All was so still at that early hour, that the few pale people whom they met seemed so much unsuited to the scene, as the sickly lamp which had been here and there left burning was powerless and faint in the full glory of the sun.

Before they had penetrated very far into the labyrinth of man's abodes which yet lay between them and the outskirts, this aspect began to melt away, and noise and bustle to usurp its place. Some straggling carts and coaches rumbling by first broke the charm, then others came, then others yet more active, then a crowd. The wonder was at first to see a tradesman's window open, but it was a rare thing soon to see one closed; then smoke rose slowly from the chimneys, and sashes were thrown up to let in air, and doors were opened, and servantgirls, looking lazily in all directions but their brooms, scattered brown clouds of dust into the eyes of shrinking passengers, or listened disconsolately to milkmen who spoke of country fairs, and told of waggons in the mews, with awnings and all the things complete and gallant swains to boot, which another hour would see upon their journey.

This quarter passed, they came upon the haunts of commerce and great traffic, where many people were resorting, and business was already rife. . . .

This throng of people hurried by, in two opposite streams, with no symptom of cessation or exhaustion; intent upon their own affairs; and undisturbed in their business speculations, by the roar of carts and waggons laden with clashing wares, the slipping of horses' feet upon the wet and grassy pavement, the jostling

individuals in a congested habitat causes friction and irritation."

Heterogeneity

In completing his theory of urbanism, Wirth suggested several consequences of social difference, or heterogeneity. First, "social interaction among such a variety of personality types in the urban milieu tends to break down the rigidity of caste lines and to complicate the class structure." Consequently, there tends to be a heightened social mobility in the city as the inertia of family background weakens under the force of personal achievement.

Second, social mobility is typically accompanied by physical movement. "Overwhelmingly the city dweller is not a homeowner and since a transitory habitat does not generate binding traditions and sentiments, only rarely is he a true neighbor." Remember Kitty Genovese in an earlier Urban Living box?

Finally, the concentration of diverse people leads inevitably to further depersonalization. Against a background of commercial mass production and consumption, personal relations are eroded by an emphasis on money. Thus, Wirth repeated Simmel's earlier view of the city as a "pecuniary nexus."

of the more impatient passengers, and all the noise and tumult of a crowded street in the high tide of its occupation. . . .

They withdrew into a low archway for shelter and watched the faces of those who passed, to find in one among them a ray of encouragement or hope. Some frowned, some smiled, some muttered to themselves, some made slight gestures, as if anticipating the conversation in which they would shortly be engaged, some wore the cunning look of bargaining and plotting, some were anxious and eager, some slow and dull; in some countenances were written gain; in others loss. . . .

Again this quarter passed, they came upon a straggling neighbourhood, where the mean houses parcelled off in rooms; and windows patched with rags and paper, told of the populous poverty that sheltered there. The shops sold goods that only poverty could buy, and sellers and buyers were pinched and griped alike. Here were poor streets where faded gentility essayed with scanty space and shipwrecked means to make its last feeble stand, but tax-gatherer and creditor came there as elsewhere, and the poverty that yet faintly struggled, was hardly less squalid and manifest than that which had long ago submitted and given up the same. . . . [Here were] children, scantily fed and clothed, spread over every street, and sprawling in the dust—scolding mothers, stamping their slip-shod feet with noisy threats upon the pavement—shabby fathers, hurrying with dispirited looks to the occupation which brought them "daily bread" and little more. . . .

At length these streets, becoming more straggling yet, dwindled and dwindled away. . . . [Then] part cottages, two and two with plots of ground in front, laid out in angular beds with stiff box borders and narrow paths between, where footstep never strayed to make the gravel rough . . . then fields, and then some houses, one by one, of goodly size with lawns, some even with a lodge where dwelt a porter and his wife. Then came a turn-pike, then fields again with trees and haystacks, then a hill, and on top of that the traveller might stop, and—looking back at old Saint Paul's [Cathedral] looming through the smoke, its cross peeping above the cloud (if the day were clear), and glittering in the sun, and casting his eyes upon the Babel out of which it grew until he traced it down to the furthest outpost of the invading army of bricks and mortar whose station lay for the present nearly at his feet—might feel at last that he was clear of London.

Source: Charles Dickens, *The Old Curiosity Shop* (London: Chapman and Hall, 1841).

These three dimensions of Wirth's theory—size, density, and heterogeneity of population—interact to produce the unique way of life he termed "urbanism." Clearly, Wirth was pessimistic about urbanism as a way of life. He saw the city as an acid that, in time, dissolved traditional values and undermined the formation of institutions and meaningful relationships. Like Park, he touted the possibilities for greater freedom in the city, but he also worried that urbanism's positive aspects inevitably would be compromised by the disorganization he saw in turbulent Chicago. Only by massive efforts at urban planning, he imagined, could people create a humane urban environment.

The U.S. Tradition: An Evaluation

We must not be too quick to accept these judgments. Like their European colleagues, Chicago sociologists were responding to one kind of city, a North American city moving into the high gear of industrialization. Neglecting historical or cross-cultural comparisons limited the significance of their work. How would their evaluations of the urban environment have changed had they, like

Weber, looked at cities in history or in cross-cultural perspective?

Chicago sociology may be skewed for yet another reason. Park's insistence on on-site study, coupled with his interest in urban disorganization and problems, led him and his colleagues to concentrate on the "seamy side" of city life. A glance at the group's classic publications, brilliant though many of them are, reveals this bias: Nels Anderson, *The Hobo* (1923); Ernest Mowner, *Family Disorganization* (1927); Harvey Zorbaugh, *The Gold Coast and the Slum* (1928); Frederich Thrasher, *The Gang* (1929); Clifford Shaw and Henry McKay, *Social Factors in Juvenile Delinquency* (1931); Paul Cressey, *The Taxi Dance Hall* (1932); Norman Hayner, *Hotel Life* (1936); and Edwin H. Sutherland, *The Professional Thief* (1937). Although there are many other aspects of city urban life that might be explored, Wirth based his theory heavily on the evidence supplied by such studies.

Limitations notwithstanding, the Chicago group made great contributions. Park deserves lasting credit for his rejection of armchair theorizing in favor of studying the city firsthand. The second key contribution was Wirth's first true urban theory, which became a persuasive document that dominated the field for the next 20 years. All in all, Chicago sociologists were almost solely responsible for the early growth of urban sociology in the United States (Lofland, 1985; J. Thomas, 1983).

THE CLASSIC THEORIES AND MODERN RESEARCH: MYTHS AND REALITIES

Is the city a heaven or a hell? A place where the best attributes of human life emerge or a place where people inevitably "go bad"? The seventeenth-century English poet Abraham Cowley thought he knew the answer when he wrote: "God the first garden made, and the first city, Cain." But was he right? The weight of the classic tradition—European and North American—is on Cowley's side. Despite qualifiers and hopeful asides, only Durkheim was mostly optimistic. Wirth's theory symbolizes this verdict. On the one hand, he suggested that people in the city are more tolerant. But on the more negative side, he asserted that city people are impersonal and detached from meaningful relationships. He concluded that the city tends toward social pathology (crime, violence, mental illness), a tendency only made worse as urban density increases.

Are these observations correct? More than 60 years have passed since the publication of Wirth's urban theory. Since then a great many social scientists have investigated cities and urban life to gather additional evidence.

Tolerance in the City

Early urban theory contended that the characteristic aloofness and social diversity of the city produced an atmosphere of tolerance that contrasted with the jealous parochialism of the village and small town. Indeed, for most of us, our urban experiences are linked somehow to the unusual and the unexpected, which we take in stride because, well, because we're in the city!

Most researchers who have looked closely at the relationship between urban life and tolerance conclude that this contention is only partially valid. Although greater tolerance of others' lifestyles and attitudes is more prevalent in cities than in rural areas, factors other than the city may account for this difference. For example, sociologists have known for some time that higher levels of wealth and education are associated with higher levels of tolerance. If greater percentages of wealthy and highly educated people live in the city than in other environments, as is generally the case, then urban tolerance may be as much a product of these factors as it is of the city itself. Urban tolerance also exists because many city dwellers prefer anonymity and privacy, thereby encouraging a "live and let live" attitude (Fischer, 1971; Karp, Stone, and Yoels, 1991).

Another factor that may lend itself to greater tolerance in the city is migration. One research study found that tolerance increased among those moving to a city, regardless of the size of the destination community (Wilson, 1991). Perhaps geographic mobility—moving to a more heterogeneous locale—enhances one's mental mobility as well in relating to strangers.

It should be noted, too, that people who live in the East and West, in or out of cities, are more tolerant of others than are people who live in the Midwest or the South. In other words, it seems that cultural beliefs (such as the "laid-back" attitude of Californians) are more important in determining tolerance levels than the mere fact that people live in a city.

In summary, Wirth was only partly correct when he suggested that cities generate tolerant attitudes. People in cities do have more tolerant attitudes than people who live elsewhere; yet this difference appears to be declining with time and is partly a product of other factors, like wealth and regional differences.

Impersonality in the City

The dominant characteristics of urban relationships, concluded most of the classical theorists, would be loneliness, indifference, and anonymity. At its most basic level, this argument is built on numerical logic. As the number of people interacting increases, attention becomes distributed more broadly so that impersonality inevitably must rise. Wirth summarized this argument by saying: "Increase in the number of inhabitants of a community beyond a few hundred is bound to limit the possibility of each member of the community knowing all the others personally" (1964:70).

Yet the "urban anonymity" thesis fails to recognize that many urbanites are not the lonely lot that Wirth and others implied. For example, as early as the 1940s, William F. Whyte's *Street Corner Society* (1943), a study of an Italian immigrant area in an eastern city, revealed the existence of strong family, neighborhood, and friendship ties. Soon after that, other studies (Bell and Boat, 1957; Greer, 1962; Bruce, 1970) confirmed that primary ties were not incompatible with city

living. Indeed, in some areas of the city—ethnic neighborhoods, for example—such ties appear to be as intense and intimate as any in rural areas. In a study of a Korean neighborhood in New York City, Ill Soo Kim (1981:319) found that urbanites who had yet to master English were forced to rely on one another, remaining a close-knit community.

Ethnicity is not the only bond among urban dwellers. Kinship, occupation, lifestyle, and other personal attributes also form the basis for group ties (Suttles, 1972; Street et al., 1978; Fischer, 1984). For example, many cities contain districts of college students, elderly people, homosexuals, artists and musicians, and wealthy socialites. More broadly, people with interests in common, wherever they may live, may remain in close contact with one another through an interactional network, utilizing the telephone, restaurants and bars, and special meeting places.

But perhaps these are the exceptions. What of the lonely crowd living in all those high rises, the people who don't know any of their neighbors? Doesn't Wirth's theory accurately describe them? Recent research suggests that this notion, too, may be exaggerated. The fact that one does not necessarily know (or want to know) one's urban neighbors does not mean that the urban dweller has no personal relationships. Indeed, what seems to be significant about the urban environment is not the lack of ties of attachment but how these ties vary. That is, cities seem to encourage alternative types of relationships more than other environments do.

The city, then, frees people from the often stifling intensity of less dense settings. But it gives them many options for connecting with others. This is an exercise in the positive freedom Durkheim saw in the city.

Even the most "private" urban dwellers usually have meaningful personal relationships. Karen Franck (1981) found that, although good friendships develop slowly in the city, urban friendships seem to become more intimate and more highly valued than those in rural settings. Friendship in the city also tends to be more varied, broadening people's

In a city we are almost never alone, but we may well be lonely. Most face-to-face contacts are impersonal, superficial, and segmental. However, research shows that although city dwellers have far more of these secondary relationships, they also have just as many meaningful primary relationships as nonurbanites.

perspectives and opportunities. Think of urban people you know. Most have friends and relatives, but not always in the same building or neighborhood. To expect urban friendship and intimacy to be localized, as they usually are in the village or small town, is to misunderstand urban living (Macionis, 1978; Freudenberg, 1992).

Other means for urban connectedness abound. The telephone, as well as e-mail, makes possible extensive contact without face-to-face interaction. Consider, too, the proliferation in cities in recent years of voluntary associations, such as film societies, singles bars, health and natural food centers, karate clubs, meditation and yoga centers, "stop smoking" groups, and physical fitness centers. Participants in such organizations, living throughout the urban area, often establish primary relationships with one another.

In *The Urban Neighborhood* (1968), Suzanne Keller suggested that urban "neighboring" varies markedly—from active and intense relationships to impersonal nods. While working-class people usually live in "tighter"

neighborhoods, upper-middle-class people typically have networks of friends dispersed over a wide area. Similarly, people with children tend to be more "localized" in their orientation than single people "on the move." Here, Keller echoes Herbert Gans (1962b), who, in a stinging critique, concluded that the "impersonality" that Wirth saw in the city *as a whole* characterizes, at best, only the most poverty-stricken and down-and-out of the city's residents.

Even when coherent social networks are absent in low-income urban neighborhoods, they can develop. In Kalamazoo, Michigan, for example, the city's Building Blocks program generated street-level social capital by identifying small project areas and intensively using students as front-line organizers. The key to this program was organizing around inclusiveness through empowerment and use of the residents' "assets," and straddling apparent divisions between self-interest and collective interest, self-help and cooperation. Initial success built on further success, and the trust, once established, also built on itself, leading eventually to an interactive community (Cummings, 2000).

Wirth's mistake, and that of other classic theorists, was to allow the most visible aspects of city life, its *public* demeanor, to become the basis of his theory about urban living in general. Although, following Park, he did acknowledge the neighborhood element in city life, he tended to focus his attention on "street behavior." Wirth saw, of course, the hustling, competing, apparently lonely crowd. By not examining more closely the *private* lives of the city's citizens, he inadvertently distorted urban life into a stereotype of impersonality.

We are led, then, to the conclusion that the early study of both rural and urban places suffered from what might be called a "misplaced concreteness" (Cahnman and Heberle, 1971). Early analysts took polarized constructions such as *gemeinschaft* and *gesellschaft*, or mechanical and organic solidarity, as synonymous with such real, concrete settings as actual villages and cities. While the overall social order of the city may place greater emphasis on *gesellschaft* characteristics, and while the village may tend more toward *gemeinschaft* characteristics, it is incorrect to assume that either *gemeinschaft* or *gesellschaft* exists in any absolute, concrete sense. There is an important difference between the statement that one commonly sees more strangers in cities and the statement that cities are impersonal. In some ways they are; in other ways, they most certainly are not.

Density and Urban Pathology

Perhaps the most provocative idea put forth by the classical theorists—particularly Simmel, Park, and Wirth—was that human beings react to increasing population density with psychological disorder (such as mental illness) or antisocial behavior (crime or aggression, for instance).

One source of support for this hypothesis is our own common sense. Probably all of us have experienced some measure of frustration and aggression in crowded settings—trying to push our way through a turnstile at a

For city residents, the streets are the "rivers of life," where people-watching and social interaction are the everyday norm. This privatization of public space—setting up crates or chairs on the sidewalk, sitting on front stoops or on a bench, playing games, or holding a street fair—is the urban equivalent to the suburbanites' front and back yards combined, and often a lot more interesting.

football stadium, or fuming as thousands of cars coalesce in a massive traffic jam. It is easy to assume that the place where this occurs—the city—is responsible for our feeling. But are we reacting to the condition of urban crowding, or are we merely experiencing a sense of frustration not very different from what we might feel if our car broke down along a lonely country road?

A second source of the alleged linkage between density and pathology is research that appears to have some bearing on the quality of urban life. For example, J. B. Calhoun (1962:139) found that high density in rat populations produced a reaction he termed a "behavioral sink"—an environment where aborted pregnancies, higher infant mortality,

Pathology — Studies causes, effects & nature of disease

homosexuality, and cannibalism abounded. Although Calhoun made no attempt to suggest that human beings would respond in similar fashion to conditions of crowding, Edward Hall argued that such a connection is not only plausible but accurately describes urban life. "The implosion of the world population into cities everywhere," Hall wrote, "is creating a series of destructive behavioral sinks more lethal than the hydrogen bomb" (1966:155). Hall warned that if no corrective measures were taken, people in densely crowded areas could "destroy the city," an idea we explore in the Cityscape box on page 165.

Hall realized that different groups of people—whites and blacks, for example—might have different cultural expectations about spatial behavior. Yet he appeared to believe that all of these different reactions have a biological basis, and that the human species, like rats, has a genetically given need for a certain amount of space. He asserted that if that built-in barrier is transgressed—in a crowded apartment or on a dense city block—pathology results.

There are at least two problems with this argument. First, no one yet has been able to locate any genetic code for spatial behavior in humans. Until such a linkage can be demonstrated, projecting onto human beings living in cities what we know about animal pathology and overcrowding is highly questionable. It may well be, for example, that people's perceived needs for space are entirely *learned* and that they react negatively to violations of their learned spatial expectations much as they would to an insult to their learned religious beliefs.

Second, as evidence for his thesis, Hall points to the high incidence of "social problems" (illness, crime) in densely settled areas of the city. Frequently, those cited are lower-class and ethnic areas. But such associations may be spurious rather than causal. By this we mean that illness, crime, and crowding may appear together because all are caused by some other factor(s), such as poverty, unemploy-

ment, and racial discrimination. Moreover, subsequent research has shown that, when such factors are taken into account, there is little or no evidence that crowding has any of the negative effects posited by Hall (Michelson, 1976; Fischer, 1984; Bagley, 1989; Lepore and Evans, 1991; Rousseau and Standing, 1995).

Urbanites do contend with crowded conditions, such as crammed elevators and subway cars; with rambunctious cabdrivers, the frustrations of traffic, and intense competition for parking spaces. However, people have one distinct advantage over rats: superior adaptability. First, we live and work on many levels, so we are not continually milling together on the ground. Second, we have codes of urban conduct that guide us to wait in line for the bus; keep to the right when walking; alternate merge or stop at red lights when driving. Cities have bicycle, foot, and horse paths connecting parks and open space that make movement safer and more pleasant. Freeways permit faster travel to and from downtowns, while traffic circles, one-way streets, and coordinated traffic lights ease the traffic flow in crowded areas.

Still, what of the fact that some researchers find that crowding does heighten aggression in some people? Perhaps an analogy with listening to music may explain the matter. When you listen to music that you like, turning the volume louder enhances the experience. However, if you don't like that music, an increase in the volume only makes the experience more unpleasant. For people with a good support system and a high level of life satisfaction, crowding has little effect, except perhaps temporarily affecting one's mood. On the other hand, if people are already in unpleasant circumstances, have aggressive tendencies, or feel alienated or frustrated, then crowding may well generate further negative reactions. The point is that crowding in and of itself does not result in pathological behavior, but rather other factors people bring to that situation may have that effect (Verbrugge and Taylor, 1980; Aiello et al., 1983; Bonnes et al., 1991).

Tom Wolfe, the Pump House Gang

O Rotten Gotham! Sliding into the Behavioral Sink

Journalist Tom Wolfe spent some time with Edward Hall in the late 1960s. He put his impressions of Hall's thesis into his own inimitable style.

I just spent two days with Edward T. Hall, an anthropologist, watching thousands of my fellow New Yorkers short-circuiting themselves into hot little twitching death balls with jolts of their own adrenalin. Dr. Hall says it is overcrowding that does it. Overcrowding gets the adrenalin going, and the adrenalin gets them hyped up. And here they are, hyped up, turning bilious, nephritic, queer, autistic, sadistic, barren, batty, sloppy, hot-in-the-pants, chancred-on-the-flankers, leering, puling, numb—the usual in New York, in other words, and God knows what else. Dr. Hall has the theory that overcrowding has already thrown New York into a state of behavioral sink. . . . Among animals, the sink winds up with a "population collapse" or "massive die off." O rotten Gotham. . . .

It got to be easy to look at New Yorkers as animals, especially looking down from some place like a balcony at Grand Central at the Rush Hour Friday afternoon. The floor was filled with the poor white humans, running around, dodging, blinking their eyes, making a sound like a pen full of staring rats or something. . . .

"If it weren't for this ceiling"—[Dr. Hall] is referring to the very high ceiling in Grand Central—"this place would be unbearable with this kind of crowding. And yet they'll probably never 'waste' space like this again."

They screech! And the adrenal glands in all those poor white animals enlarge, micrometer by micrometer, to the size of cantalopes. Dr. Hall pulls a Minox camera out of a holster he has on his belt and starts shooting away at the human scurry. The Sink! . . .

We really got down in there by walking down into the Lexington Avenue line subway stop under Grand Central. We inhaled those nice fluffy fumes of human sweat, urine, effluvia, and sebaceous secretions. One old female human was already stroked out of the upper level, on a stretcher, with two policemen standing by. The other humans barely looked at her. They rushed into line. They bellied each other, haunch to paunch, down the stairs. Human heads showed through the gratings. The species North American tried to create bubbles of space around themselves, about a foot and a half in diameter—

"See, he's reacting against the line," says Dr. Hall.

—but the species Mediterranean presses on in. The hell with the bubbles of space. The species North American resents that, this male human behind him presses forward toward the booth . . . breathing on him, he's disgusted, he pulls out of the line entirely, the species Mediterranean resents him for resenting it, and neither of them realizes what the hell they are getting irritable about exactly. And in all of them the old adrenals grow another micrometer.

Dr. Hall whips out the Minox. Too perfect! The bottom of The Sink!

Source: Tom Wolfe, *The Pump House Gang* (New York: Bantam, 1969), pp. 233–35.

Finally, in global context we see that culture also mediates the experience of city living, influencing how we are affected by population density. For example, Bombay, India, has an extremely high rate of urban crowding but an extremely low homicide rate; to cite another example, Turks—whose cultural behavior favors closer interpersonal interaction—do not respond negatively to increased crowding conditions (Baldassare, 1979; Bagley, 1989; Rustemli, 1992).

URBAN LIVING

How City Dwellers Cope—and Cope Well

How is it possible, given the fast pace and obvious stresses of urban life, that city residents can maintain mental health comparable to that of country folks? One explanation offered by experts: The relationship between stress and mental and physical pathology is dependent not so much on the nature of the stress as on the individual's perception of it. The brain has been called a stimulus-reduction system, a means to reduce, in order to comprehend, the nearly infinite number of stimuli that reach the senses at any given moment. It is an aspect of the brain that seems tailor-made for life in the city.

An out-of-towner caught in midtown Manhattan at rush hour, for example, may feel under enormous pressure and strain. But the New Yorker, with his stimulus-reduction mechanism operating at full steam, hardly feels any special stress at all. By the same token, the big-city residents may ignore the loud, the profane, the drunk and the demented—phenomena that might compromise the mental equilibrium of the uninitiated.

And there are statistics to back up such theories. A recent survey of the National Center for Health Statistics sought to find the incidence of stress-related, chronic health problems, such as hypertension and heart disease, among those over 65 years of age. The results: 47.6 per 100 for farm residents; 47.5 for small-town residents; 40.5 for city residents.

Urban Malaise

A last hypothesis put forth by most of the classical theorists concerned "urban malaise." They suggested that, conditions of density aside, the urban environment created loneliness, depression, and anxiety more readily than did other types of settlement.

This contention, too, has been challenged by later research. Leo Srole (1972) questioned 1,660 New Yorkers in the 1950s and 695 people from the same group again in the 1970s. Not only did Srole find that the mental health of New Yorkers was slightly better than that of rural residents; he also found that mental health, especially of women, had improved dramatically over the interval between the two samples. Other researchers reported similar results (Fischer, 1973; Freedman, 1978; Hackler, 1979; Kadushin, 1983).

In a review of global studies on the effects of cities on children, Thomas Weisner (1981) concluded that urban living does not subject children to more stress than do other types of environments. He noted that children moving to the city from the country did experience some increase in stress. However, such an increase in stress is regularly observed in people who have had other major catastrophic changes in their lives—such as the death of a loved one, the loss of employment, or moving from one place to another.

Apparently, then, the city doesn't create greater psychological distress. In fact, the higher population density of urban places may well have positive effects, such as making more people socially accessible to each other (Verbrugge and Taylor, 1980). When it comes to city dwellers dealing with their environment, as the Urban Living box above suggests, it seems that the vast majority do quite well.

Overall, much of the recent evidence fails to support many of the specific claims made by the classic theorists about urban living. The city is clearly not a heaven; but neither is it the hell some thought it to be. The city is more tolerant than other types of settlement, it is not as impersonal as many thought it was, and it does not produce greater rates of malaise or other pathologies. On the basis of what we now know, there is reason for more optimism than is shown by most classic theorists. The reality, in short, is both more complex and more hopeful than the myths.

The New Urban Sociology

All this research has produced a shift in the way many urbanists approach their subject matter. As we have just seen, the classical hypotheses about the city advanced by Simmel, Wirth, and others have not stood the test of careful scrutiny. Some have been shown to be false; others require serious modification. Such findings occasioned the creation of what John Walton (1981) called "the new urban sociology."

Instead of an emphasis on the role of technology or urban ecology, this newer approach directs attention to social conflict, inequality, and change as they affect cities, and does so within a global context. No single theory captures the new urban sociology, although neo-Marxists and conflict theorists predominate. We will explore this important approach in Chapter 9.

SUMMARY

The context in which urban sociology emerged was one of remarkable change. Indeed, it was ferment associated with the Industrial Revolution that was responsible for sociologists noticing the city as an object of study in the first place. What have we learned from them?

First, they suggested specific aspects of the city for urban sociologists to focus on; second, they attempted to analyze the nature of the city in general. In the latter instance, they had successes and failures. On the positive side

they correctly saw in the city elements of social life not prominent elsewhere. They saw the city as having more specialized occupations, more formalized interaction patterns, more rationality, and a rapider tempo of life. On the negative side, they erred in some of their specific claims about the nature of the city. They were right about greater tolerance, but they exaggerated the city's impersonality, and they seem, on the whole, to have been wrong about urban pathology. The context in which they wrote played a significant role in these misperceptions. Seeing cities growing by millions of inhabitants with seemingly unconquerable problems, they reasoned that the city itself must be the cause of these ills.

A second limitation is the narrowness of all early theory. Marx and Engels saw cross-cultural differences in how civilization evolved in Western compared with Eastern cities, but concentrated on the economic system as the basis for all attributes of an urban society. Tönnies and Durkheim employed the comparison of oppositional types but did not consider the city in concrete historical settings. Simmel added the social–psychological dimension, although he too considered only cities of one time and place. Weber argued for the importance of exploring cities in cross-cultural and historical perspective, but wrote little about the modern city (perhaps a subtle way of indicating that he—like all his colleagues except Durkheim—also saw it in a negative light).

Park and Wirth both provided breakthroughs. Park demanded that on-site city research be an integral part of urban sociology, thereby providing the mechanism for getting behind the surface impressions of the urban environment. Ironically, his focus on urban problems and his lack of a comparative historical frame led him to the same negative conclusions about the city as others. Wirth then tried to build a theory of the city by linking together the suggestions of his colleagues. A major difficulty was that he built his theory on Park's skewed data base and on the somewhat misleading evaluations of the European tradition.

Recent research has shown that many of the specific claims made by Wirth and his colleagues were incorrect. Early work saw the city as the cause of greater impersonality, poorer mental health, and various forms of stressful or pathological behavior. The new urban sociology, which has emerged in the wake of the classical urbanists' failing theories, sees the city as existing in a complex historical, cultural, and economic setting. All these elements play a role in how the city operates, and all must be carefully examined by systematic research.

CONCLUSION

What we take from the classical tradition is its interest in urban studies per se and its combined model of urban analysis. A useful urban analysis must (1) examine the city on both its social–structural and psychosocial dimensions, (2) study actual cities in historical and comparative perspective, (3) attempt to build an overarching theory of the city, and (4) evaluate cities in terms of the quality of human life. It will be the task of the remaining chapters to do justice to this tradition.

SOCIAL PSYCHOLOGY
The Urban Experience

What makes cities so stimulating? Why do they pull from us reactions of either stout admiration or powerful aversion? Georg Simmel's answer was that the city is a tremendous concentration of buildings, images, and people that intensifies stimulation as no other form of human settlement does. Everywhere you turn—around a corner, breaking through a crowd, entering the subway—the city demands a response.

How do we make sense of this coming-at-you-from-all-sides, sometimes in-your-face creation that is the city? Simmel answered that we learn to categorize the city's elements, paying attention to some things and ignoring others. University of Chicago sociologist Louis Wirth agreed, suggesting that we mentally "map" the city. Unfortunately, neither theorist said much about how this mapping process works. But, drawing on later research, this chapter sketches the outlines of this process—the characteristic elements of the social psychology of the city.

THE PHYSICAL ENVIRONMENT

We react to the city in two ways—as a physical setting and also as a social environment. First, we will consider how people perceive their physical surroundings and try to make sense out of them.

Kevin Lynch: The Image of the City

To explore how people made sense of the city's physical complexity, urbanist Kevin Lynch interviewed urbanites in Boston, Jersey City, and Los Angeles. In each city, Lynch showed his respondents a map of several square miles of the central city and asked them to describe it in their own terms. Most could offer a personal *image of the city* that Lynch defined as the individual's "generalized mental picture of the [city's] external physical world" (1960:4).

Before we continue, take a moment and think of the city you know best. On a piece of paper, draw as detailed a map of it as you can, putting in everything of importance that you can recall. This exercise will make the following discussion far more meaningful.

Building an Image

Most of Lynch's respondents developed their image of the city in a similar fashion. First, their images emerged as part of a two-way process: (1) They made distictions among the various physical parts of the city, and (2) they organized these parts in a personally meaningful way.

For example, Figure 6–1 shows downtown Boston, where the large park known as the Boston Common and Public Garden separates various downtown districts from one another. To the west of the park is the residential Back Bay area, with its characteristic three- and four-story apartment houses. To the north is the wealthier Beacon Hill district, where one finds the State House. To the east and south is most of Boston's central business district, full of high-rise office buildings, stores, and entertainment facilities.

To a person living, say, in a small apartment house just west of the Garden and the Common, the park area may be the dominant element in an image of the city because the person may go there frequently for walks, getting to know every bench, fountain, and footpath. But this same individual may know little about the rest of downtown.

On the other hand, to another Bostonian living nearby, the park may have little significance. Working in the high-rise offices on the east side of the park, this person may have little desire to use the Garden. In this case, the distinct image might be of the downtown buildings, including where the good restaurants are, and of all the shortcuts for getting from one building or street to another.

Common Elements of Images

Lynch discovered that people built their urban images from five common elements. *Paths,* he explains, are "channels along which the observer customarily . . . moves. They may be streets, walkways, transit lines, canals, railroads." *Edges,* the boundaries between two

FIGURE 6–1 Downtown Boston

Source: Kevin Lynch, *The Image of the City*, 1960. MIT Press, Cambridge, Mass.

areas, include shores, walls, wide streets, or breaks between buildings and open space. *Districts* represent medium-to-large sections of the city. Examples in Boston that people commonly noted were "Back Bay," "Beacon Hill," "the Common," "the shopping district." *Nodes* stand as points of intense activity, such as a railroad terminal, a square, or a street-corner hangout. Nodes are often the places to which "paths" lead. Finally, Lynch's subjects built their images around *landmarks*—physical reference points including buildings, signs, stores, domes, gas stations, or hills.

At this point, look back at the map you drew a few minutes ago. Were you thinking in terms of Lynch's categories?

Lynch also found that most people incorporate many of the same elements in their images; that is, what is a path or edge to one person is a path or edge to many others. Looking back at Figure 6–1, virtually every Bostonian recognizes the Charles River as a major edge separating one large district of the city ("downtown") from another (Cambridge). Similarly, most people also mention "Mass. Ave." to the west and the Southeast

Expressway to the east as key edges. Main paths are Beacon Street, "Comm. Ave.," and Boylston and Tremont Streets. Commonly mentioned nodes include Copley Square (site of the "BPL," the Boston Public Library), North Station (a railroad and subway terminal), and Park Street Station. Although it is below ground, Park Street Station is another classic example of an urban node: The junction of Boston's three main subway lines is constantly abuzz with activity.

Although Lynch discovered that people in every city appear to use the same elements in constructing their images, he also found that some cities stimulate their residents to form more complex images than other cities do. In Boston, virtually everyone Lynch interviewed could identify *numerous* paths, edges, nodes, districts, and landmarks. In Jersey City, by contrast, even long-term residents could identify only a few such elements, often confessing confusion and uncertainty about what existed in different parts of their own city. Perhaps most illustrative of their weak image of their city was the residents' frequent mention of the looming, overpowering New York City skyline to the east as a landmark. In his summary findings about Jersey City, Lynch emphasized its nondescript character:

> When asked for a general characterization of the city, one of the most common remarks was that it was not a whole, that it had no center, but was rather a collection of many hamlets. The question: "What first comes to mind with the words 'Jersey City'?," so easy to answer for Bostonians, proved to be a difficult one. Again and again, subjects repeated that "nothing special" came to mind, that the city was hard to [characterize], that it had no distinctive sections. . . .

Many remarks came out about the indistinguishability of the physical scene:

> "It's much the same all over . . . it's more or less just common to me. I mean, when I go up and down the streets, it's more or less the same thing—Newark Avenue, Jackson Avenue, Bergen Avenue. I mean, sometimes they're more or less just the same; there's nothing to differentiate them." (1960:29–31)

In Los Angeles, Lynch found, residents have an even less sharp image of their city

because of the great sprawl and uniformity of cross streets, which make it difficult to locate anything with confidence. Although the area studied was comparable in size to the other two cities, it included little more than a central business district. Those interviewed, most of whom worked there, could describe just a few landmarks in any specific detail: the "ugly" black and gold Richfield Building and the pyramid atop City Hall. The strongest element of all was Pershing Square,

> an exotically landscaped open space in the heart of the downtown, reinforced by its use as an outdoor political forum, camp meeting, and old people's hangout. Along with the Plaza–Olvera Street node (involving another open space), Pershing Square was the most sharply described element, with its immaculate central lawn, fringed first by banana trees, then by a ring of old people sitting in solid ranks on the stone walls, then by busy streets, and finally by the close files of downtown buildings. (1960:36–37)

Even so, many Angelenos were uncertain of the precise location of Pershing Square. Moreover, most residents of the city could identify only paths, and often confused one with another. When asked to describe or symbolize Los Angeles as a whole, residents found it hard to respond, simply describing their city as "spread-out," "spacious," "formless," or "without centers." Lynch offered one person's comment as illustrative of this diffused urban image:

> "It's as if you were going somewhere for a long time, and when you got there you discovered that there was nothing there, after all." (1960:41)

The "Imagability" of Cities

It was the difference in the clarity of urban images offered by his subjects that led Lynch to suggest that cities differ markedly in imagability. This concept is important for two reasons. First, a clear urban image gives people a working knowledge and emotional security about their city. (However, as the Urban Living box reveals, recent terrorist acts make many people feel less secure in cities.) A strong urban image makes acquisition of knowledge relatively easy

URBAN LIVING

Living with Terrorism

All of us have become sensitized to the vulnerability of cities to terrorist attacks. Masumoto City in 1994 and Tokyo in 1995 fell victim to chemical terrorism with use of the toxic gas sarin on defenseless civilians in subways. The 2001 attacks on the Pentagon in Washington, D.C., and on the twin towers of the World Trade Center in New York City, with their horrific losses of life and mass destruction, still reverberate in the minds of hundreds of millions of people worldwide. In October 2002, Chechnyan terrorists took more than 750 people hostage in a Moscow theater, resulting in the deaths of nearly 200 rebels and hostages, killed mostly by gas used during a rescue attempt.

These and other incidents remind us all too often that urban centers attract terrorists. The large concentrations of people—as well as the tall buildings, symbolic monuments, and infrastructure of bridges and tunnels—are all tempting targets to those intent on inflicting maximum damage and deaths. People once avoided cities for fear of becoming victims of violent crimes. Now many fear, not just being in major cities, but even living near one in the event of biological, chemical, or nuclear attack.

Seeing concrete barricades at many important locations and undergoing bag searches at concerts, sporting events, and airports are part of our new reality. For some, living or working in tall buildings, or viewing the cityscape from high-perched observation decks, holds little appeal. Others, refusing to allow their lives to be ruled by fear, continue their daily urban routines and lifestyles.

Whether they respond by avoidance or defiance, however, urbanites recognize that their world is a different one than the one that existed before September 11. That realization is also part of the social psychology of urban life.

and sets people at ease emotionally. Second, a comprehensible urban environment "heightens the potential depth and intensity of the human experience" (1960:5). It invites us to experience more, to involve ourselves more in the life of the city. Lynch concluded that "imagability" is one of the essential aspects of a positive urban environment. Lynch's conclusions have been replicated in later studies of both large and small cities as well as in cities in other countries (Lynch, 1984).

Stanley Milgram: More on Mental Maps

One of the most intriguing aspects of Lynch's work is his discovery that even people living in the same city construct very different mental images of their surroundings. Most people's maps mix details with distortions as well as large gaps. To understand why mental maps are so distinctive, psychologist Stanley Milgram explored how New Yorkers and Parisians understood their cities. In both cases, he found that people construct mental maps *based on their personal experience, their interests, and their knowledge of the socially recognized "important areas" of the city* (Milgram, 1972; S. Duncan, 1977; see also Thill and Sui, 1993; Kulhavy and Stock, 1996).

The Individuality of Mental Maps

Figure 6–2 presents drawings of two people's mental maps of Manhattan. Painter Susan Rowland's Manhattan emphasizes details of the

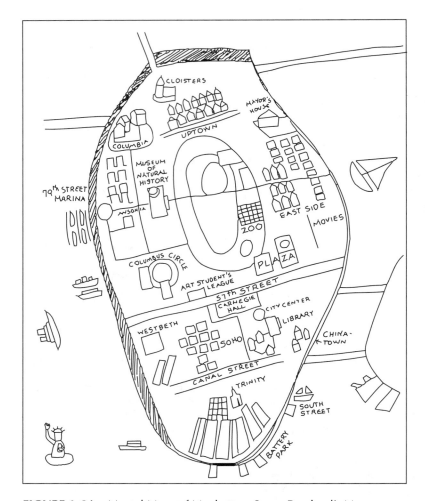

FIGURE 6–2A   Mental Maps of Manhattan: Susan Rowland's Map

Source: Susana Duncan, "Mental Maps of New York," *New York,* Dec. 18, 1977, pp. 233–35. Alexandria Milgram.

Upper West Side where she lives, the Upper East Side, and artistic and cultural centers such as the "Cloisters," "SoHo," "movies," the "library." New York's famed midtown area is virtually absent. In contrast, teacher Cynthia Blanchard's Manhattan emphasizes the Harlem district where she lives. Featured prominently are swimming pools, parks, and high-rise apartment buildings. Missing, save for one or two items, are midtown and lower Manhattan.

No one, Milgram found, can re-create the complexity of the whole city. Moreover, everyone's images constantly evolve as urban experiences deepen or as the city changes. Figure 6–3 illustrates this process with two mental maps of London drawn by U.S. student Tom Jermain. In his first map, drawn two weeks into a ten-week stay, Jermain presents London's center city with almost no detail at all, and the few areas he does note are misplaced and distorted in size. In the second map, drawn eight weeks

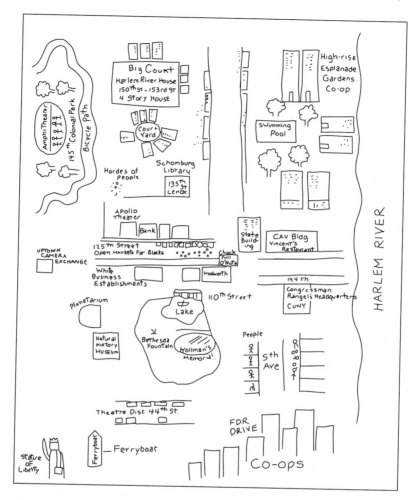

FIGURE 6–2B Mental Maps of Manhattan: Cynthia Blanchard's Map

Source: Susana Duncan, "Mental Maps of New York," *New York,* Dec. 18, 1977, pp. 233–35. Alexandria Milgram.

later, we see that London has come alive to this visitor, and he offers far more detail, as well as greater geographical accuracy. In short, with time, most people succeed in comprehending the city and using it effectively.

Multiple Urban Realities

What all this suggests is that there are as many Seattles, for example, as there are people living there. More broadly, each of these active

mental maps contributes to the larger urban dynamic that is the full Seattle.

But mental maps are not completely a matter of individual differences. Donald Reitzes (1983) demonstrated that race played a key part in how residents understood Atlanta. Whites, he found, preferred quieter, more serene areas of the city, while African Americans were more attracted to busy, noisy, and exciting places. In large measure, such racial

FIGURE 6–3A Tom Jermain's Changing Mental Maps of London

Source: Tom Jermain. Reproduced with permission.

differences are probably reflections of class standing and affordability. Overall, white people are more affluent than black people are, and well-off families are more able to secure a quieter, more relaxed environment.

In sum, the city is a dynamic, creative, ongoing admixture of experiences, as Chicago urbanist Robert Park (1916; 1967:1) eloquently stated:

> The city . . . is something more than a congeries of individual men and of social conveniences—streets, buildings, electric lights, tramways, and telephones . . . something more, also, than a mere constellation of institutions and administrative devices—courts, hospitals, schools, police, and civil functionaries of various sorts. The city is . . . a state of mind.

In the Cityscape box on page 178, novelist Alfred Kazin describes his return to his old neighborhood in the Brownsville district of New York. Present in his image of the city are all of Lynch's visual categories, complex interpretations of sound and smell, as well as evidence of his own social background.

THE SOCIAL ENVIRONMENT: *GESELLSCHAFT*

Living in the city demands that we deal with more than the physical environment. We must also contend with large numbers of *people*, most of whom we don't know and probably don't want to know. How do we cope with what Ferdinand Tönnies (Chapter 5) called

FIGURE 6–3B   Tom Jermain's Changing Mental Maps of London
Source: Tom Jermain. Reproduced with permission.

the city's *gesellschaft* characteristics—its vast numbers and characteristic anonymity?

The Pedestrian: Watching Your Step

Standing on the sidewalk during rush hour along Canal Street in New Orleans; State Street in Columbus, Ohio; or Kearny Street in San Francisco, anyone can observe the "faceless crowd" of urbanites going about their daily business. Taking such a detached perspective, the city's people seem almost like sheep, an undifferentiated, robotlike herd. But is this really so?

Sociologist Erving Goffman (1971) believed city life is an orderly routine, one that allows people to meet their personal needs while surrounded by an unknown mass of others. He reminds us that people on the street are there for a reason. We travel the city to get to work, to enjoy a restaurant, to meet a friend, to catch a subway, or perhaps just to take a walk. Just because the observer cannot perceive such motives is no reason to think they don't exist.

Goffman then explains that pedestrians observe an intricate set of social rules. There is a traffic code for the sidewalks, just as there is a code for automobiles using the streets. Goffman notes that pedestrian traffic in U.S. cities sorts itself into two opposing streams, with the dividing line somewhere near the middle of the sidewalk. Within each stream, people "watch their step" in a variety of ways: First, they keep themselves at least slightly aware of

CITYSCAPE   Alfred Kazin

The Streets of Brownsville

All my early life lies open to my eye within five city blocks. . . . On Belmont Avenue, Brownville's great open street market, the pushcarts are still lined on each other for blocks, and the din is as deafening, marvelous, and appetizing as ever. . . . When I was a boy, they . . . reached halfway up the curb to the open stands of the stores; walking down the street was like being whirled around and around in a game of blind man's bluff. But Belmont Avenue is still the merriest street in Brownsville. As soon as I walked into it from Rockaway, caught my first whiff of the herrings and pickles in their great black barrels, heard the familiarly harsh, mocking cries and shouts from the market women—"Oh you darlings! Oh you sweet ones, oh you pretty ones! Storm us! Tear us apart! Devour us!"—I laughed right out loud, it was so good to be back among them. . . .

Chester Street. . . . The way home.

On my right hand the "Stadium" movie house—the sanctuary every Saturday afternoon of my childhood, the great dark place of all my dream life. On my left the little wooden synagogue where I learned my duties as a Jew and at thirteen, having reached the moral estate of a man, stood up at the high desk before the Ark (Blessed Be He, Our Lord and Our Shield!) and was confirmed in the faith of my fathers. . . .

The block: my block. It was on the Chester Street side of our house, between the grocery and the back wall of the old drugstore, that I was hammered into the shape of the streets. Everything beginning at Blake Avenue would always wear for me some delightful strangeness and mildness, simply because it was not of my block, the block, where the clang of your head sounded against the pavement when you fell in a fist fight, and the rows of store lights on each side were pitiless, watching you. . . . [I recall] smelling the sweaty sweet dampness from the pool in summer and the dust on the leaves as I passed under the ailanthus trees. . . .

We worked every inch of it, from the cellars and the backyards to the sickening space between the roofs. Any wall, any stoop, any curving metal edge on a billboard sign made a place against which to knock a ball; any bottom rung of a fire escape ladder a goal in basketball; any sewer cover a base. . . . Our life every day was fought out on the pavement and in the gutter, up against the walls of the houses and the glass fronts of the drugstore and the grocery—in and out of the fresh steaming piles of horse manure, the wheels of passing carts and automobiles, along the iron spikes of the stairway to the cellar, the jagged edge of the open garbage cans, the crumbly steps of the old farmhouses still left on one side of the street.

Source: Alfred Kazin, *A Walker in the City* (New York: Harvest Books, 1969), pp. 11–12, 17, 25–26, 30–31, 39–40, 83–84.

obstacles, such as mailboxes, lampposts, or groups stopped on the sidewalk. Second, they casually note the speed of people in front of or behind them, gauging their own speed accordingly to avoid collisions. Third, to move faster or slower than the stream, people move to the outside of the lane. Fourth, people utilize various strategies to avoid collisions, perhaps making coughing noises or shifting packages to alert a careless walker to impending contact.

Fifth, people scold one another for breaking any of these rules. After someone brushes by, one pedestrian may loudly protest: "Why don't ya look where you're going?" Such reactions show us that people know the rules for pedestrian behavior and call others to task for any transgressions. In essence, a tacit contract exists among users of public space, who come to trust each other to act like competent pedestrians (Wolfinger, 1995).

Rules of pedestrian traffic vary from culture to culture, of course. This variety can puzzle—and even intimidate—a traveler, as the Urban Living box on page 180 explains.

Escalators represent another example of cultural variety. In the United States, passengers pile on all together, making passage by anybody behind almost impossible. In England and in many other European nations, however, escalator passengers ride on the right side, leaving a lane on the left for anyone wishing to pass. Taking their first ride on London escalators, North Americans who place themselves on the left-hand side of a ramp are often a bit puzzled to hear people behind them ask, "Please move over." Conversely, Britons riding a U.S. subway escalator can be quite puzzled at the "rudeness" of locals who jam up the ramp so no one can pass.

Finally, even in that most dense and anonymous of urban worlds, the subway, people evolve mechanisms for ordering and personalizing their experience. The second Urban Living box on page 180 offers a look at the subway at rush hour.

Together, these examples reveal that street behavior is not nearly as chaotic as it might appear at first glance. City dwellers may have to deal with larger numbers of people, often in crowded conditions, but urban life is not necessarily difficult or dehumanizing.

A World of Strangers

Besides coping with the city's sheer numbers, urbanites also must learn to deal with anonymity, since we live in what Lyn Lofland (1985) calls "a world of strangers." Lofland argues that we look for visual clues in order to classify strangers in much the same way that we make sense of the city's physical environment.

Appearance and Location

First, we identify strangers in terms of their *appearance* and their *physical location* within the city. That is, we give strangers "the once-over," noting their clothing, hairstyle, jewelry, what they're carrying, and how they're walking. We also let location speak for people: For example, in a district of office buildings and expensive restaurants, we expect different types of people than in a district full of all-night movie houses or pornographic bookstores.

Lofland concedes that there is nothing uniquely urban about such tactics. Even in small towns, people judge each other by appearance and by "which side of the tracks" they call home. The point is simply that in big cities, our reliance on clues like appearance and location becomes essential. After all, the odds of running into someone one knows in midtown Manhattan or Chicago's downtown "loop" are small, indeed.

Worth noting is that using spatial location as a clue to people's identities is a modern practice. In preindustrial cities, public spaces such as the town square usually had many uses: for schooling, religious services, parades, shopping, general loitering, and even executions. In short, because virtually *anybody* might be found there, location provides few clues about who strangers are. In the part, then, citizens put great stock in appearance, as illustrated in the Looking Back box on page 182.

In modern industrial societies, however, the rules change. Although dress still plays a part in identifying strangers, costume is no longer the central clue it once was. Dress codes have relaxed and people from all walks of life, without fear of censure, wear almost any sort of finery. There are important historical reasons for this change.

In the preindustrial city, only the wealthy could afford clothes of silk and satin and jewelry made from gold and silver. With the Industrial Revolution, however, mass production made many types of dress much more

John Macionis

Saigon: Learning to Cross the Street All Over Again

The first morning after we arrived in port, we left the ship early and made our way along the docks toward the center of Ho Chi Minh City—known to an earlier generation as Saigon. After looking us over—a family of U.S. visitors—the government security officers waved us through the security gates without so much as glancing at our papers. But we paused nonetheless, coming face to face with dozens of men crowded just beyond the gate, all operators of cyclos—bicycles with a small carriage attached to the front—which are the Vietnamese equivalent of taxicabs. "No, thanks," I stated firmly, breaking eye contact, and making a firm gesture with my arm. In New York, it is hard enough to find a cab; here, we spent the next twenty minutes fending off persistent drivers who cruised alongside us pleading for our business. The pressure was uncomfortable.

Let's cross the street, I suggested. We turned to the traffic and immediately realized that there were no stop signs or signal lights. In fact, there was no break at all in the steady stream of bicycles, cyclos, motorbikes, and small trucks that rattled along the rough roadway. What to do? Then the answer came, in the form of a tiny woman who walked right next to us and plunged out into the traffic without so much as batting an eye. She simply walked at a steady pace across the street; drivers saw her coming and made room for her. To us, she appeared to part the waves of vehicles as if she had some mysterious power.

We took a deep breath. From several yards back, we walked right into the traffic keeping eyes straight ahead. Amazing! It worked. Such are the rules of the road in Vietnam.

Source: Based on travel by John Macionis to Vietnam, 1994.

Anne Petry

The Subway at Rush Hour

A crowd of people surged into the Eighth Avenue express at 59th Street. By elbowing other passengers in the back, by pushing and heaving, they forced their bodies into the coaches, making room for themselves where no room had existed before. As the train gathered speed for the long run to 125th

Street, the passengers settled down into small private worlds, thus creating the illusion of space between them and their fellow passengers. The worlds were built up behind newspapers and magazines, behind closed eyes or while staring at the varicolored show cards that bordered the coaches.

Source: Ann Petry, *The Street* (Boston: Houghton Mifflin, 1998), p. 27.

affordable. Further, a rising standard of living allowed more and more people to purchase and display such goods. The film *Hester Street* offers an example: In one scene from this view of New York back in 1900, Jake, a Russian-Jewish immigrant, takes his family to Central Park. Making more money than he ever did in the old country, Jake is wearing a modestly priced but very fashionable suit. As he parades around the park, he exclaims proudly: "Look at me! I'm a real American! Who could tell if I was a Jew or a Gentile?"

If dress means less to us in modern cities, then, location means more. We recognize that industrial cities are composed of numerous distinct districts, for business, warehousing, residence, and entertainment. In business districts, we expect to encounter businesspeople and we expect them to act in a businesslike manner.

For example, Huntington Avenue marks the boundary between two major districts of Boston (look back at Figure 6–1). On the north side of the street are the upper-middle-class Back Bay and Fenway areas that include Symphony Hall, the Museum of Fine Arts, numerous expensive shops and art galleries. But just across the street begins the lower-class, predominantly African American Roxbury district, with run-down housing and down-scale shops.

To position oneself at the corner of Huntington and Massachusetts avenues near Symphony Hall when the Boston Symphony Orchestra is playing is a remarkable sociological experience. On one side of the street are men sporting formal black-tie dress and women are decked out in ermine and pearls. Yet just 20 feet away are people in threadbare and tattered clothes. Strangers on both sides of the street are well aware that they inhabit two different social worlds, and few people move from one to the other.

Of course, such patterns don't mean that some people can't "work the system." We all know that it is possible for us to pass ourselves

In a city many people share public space. Whether in small groups or alone, on a lunch or work break or resting from sightseeing, they gather wherever there is some pleasant sun and a place to sit. Steps and low walls are two popular choices, and there they either ignore others or else partake in that favorite urban pastime: people-watching.

LOOKING BACK

Clothes Make the Man

Lyn Lofland

To a degree unknown to moderns, the resident of the preindustrial city literally "donned" his identity. The Roman citizen, for example, expressed the fact of his citizenship by wearing as decreed by law, the white toga. A "gentleman" in the Colonial cities of America was known by his "periwig." . . .

Urban elites everywhere struggled to differentiate themselves from their "inferiors" not only by the design of their dress, but by the materials as well. The cap of the medieval Frenchman was made of velvet for the elites, rough cloth for the poor. In Elizabethan England, [Gideon Sjoberg reported that] "Commoners were prohibited by law from wearing clothing fashioned from gold or silver cloth, velvet, furs, and other 'luxury' materials." Hair length also indicated status. Among the Franks, only the elite had long hair. . . .

The clothing of outcaste groups . . . was often regulated by law. . . . [T]he Parsi minority in the Persian city of Yezd were forced, until the 1880s, "to twist their turbans instead of folding them, [were] denied various colors, and [were] prohibited rings, umbrellas, and other items."

Occupation, too, was signaled by dress. The lawyers of medieval France, for example, were distinguished by their round caps . . . and the executioners of the period were forced to wear a special coat of red or gold so that they would be readily recognizable in a crowd. . . . Each of the various types of itinerant peddlers of Peking . . . wore a distinctive costume as did the clergy of twelfth century Europe and the members of religious sects in numerous preindustrial cities.

Source: Lyn H. Lofland, *A World of Strangers* (Prospect Heights, IL: Waveland Press, 1985), pp. 45–46.

off as something we are not by manipulating the way we dress and act. A narcotics agent may infiltrate a drug ring, and a social scientist may live anonymously in an area in hopes of learning the inside story of people's lives. Sometimes people intentionally "perform": A sighted person may don dark eyeglasses, hold a sign saying "blind," and beg; sedate, middle-class suburbanites may come into the city to "swing" at night, retiring at evening's end to their normal routine.

Privatizing Public Space

Lofland (1985:118–23) suggests that another way we reduce the vastness and complexity of a city is to transform areas into private or semiprivate space. People can claim a street corner as a hangout; a tavern (such as television's "Cheers") can become a club to its regular patrons; and musicians can transform a section of a park into an outdoor performance arena. Such "home territories" are rarely intentional; usually, they result from unplanned, uncoordinated actions that end up spatially segregating certain types of people. The city is full of such patterns: yuppies appropriate plazas, skid row vagrants lay claim to benches and steam grates, gay people come to think of a neighborhood as "their own." Outsiders entering such spaces soon pick up cues of dress and behavior that indicate they are on semiprivate ground.

On a larger scale, whole urban districts can become home territory or "turf" to a specific group. Most residential neighborhoods have a dominant character, perhaps based on class, race, ethnicity, and age. Although cities are largely impersonal, they are also (in Robert Park's phrase) "mosaics of small worlds." Within *gesellschaft*, in short, the city reveals many *gemeinschaft*-like subsocieties.

Class, Race, and the Urban Experience

People have devised strategies for making sense of the city. But this hardly means that the urban experience is the same for everyone, since traits such as class, age, gender, race, and ethnicity shape our lives in the city as they do elsewhere.

The next Cityscape box on page 185 offers four very different urban experiences. In the first passage, Kathryn Forbes re-creates her "Mama's" image of turn-of-the-century San Francisco. Though by no means rich, Mama and her family were beginning to realize the dreams they had brought with them from Norway. Next, Jonathan Raban speaks about the difficulty he has in keeping from going "soft"—a bit crazy—"in a soft city." He writes as a "marginal man"—a freelance writer, unmarried, living alone, with few friends and no local family. Third, though she was poor, Clara Rodriguez tells of growing up in a stable and vibrant community, one that was largely cut off from the city as a whole. Eventually, she would witness the South Bronx collapse in urban decay—but her childhood memories convey a far different reality. Finally, an African American migrant from the South, Lutie Johnson, struggled for years to free herself and her son from the grasp of the ghetto. Every time she made some progress, she saw it disappear in exploitation or cruelty. On this particular night she walks home and sees a robbery. She begins to realize that she may never get out and that life on the street amounts to a powerful barrier—built on race and class—that stands between her and her dreams.

The City as *Gesellschaft:* A Reassessment

Many early urban theorists feared that people could never cope with the city's sheer physical size, its large population, and its anonymity. Yet, we *have* learned to cope. We contend with physical size by creating our personal mental image of the city. We deal with the complexities of street life by observing codes of behavior and seeking out clues to the identity of strangers. And, of course, our own social characteristics place us within some part of the city. While urban life may not always be pleasant, these factors work to make it meaningful.

THE SOCIAL ENVIRONMENT: *GEMEINSCHAFT*

Then, too, the city abounds with personal relationships. Only the most extreme of urban isolates—Jonathan Raban's "marginal man," perhaps—live according to the stereotype of *gesellschaft*. For most, interpersonal bonds provide a basis for social and psychological security in the city.

Urban Networks

The study of interpersonal ties is called *network analysis*. As we shall see, urban networks may or may not involve organized social groups, nor need they be defined by locality.

London Couples

In an early study of networks, Elizabeth Bott (1957) examined the relationships of married couples in London. A key finding, illustrating the effects of social class on the urban experience, was that working-class partners each maintained their own networks, while middle-class spouses participated in a single network. Subsequent studies of the connection between conjugal role segregation and social networks suggest that other factors than absence of a kin network—such as the support system provided by the network or even the availability of other groups—affect marital solidarity (Blood, 1969; Wimberley, 1973; Dasgupta, 1992). Such findings do not discount the role of class, however. The next Urban Living box on page 188 offers a closer look at Bott's marriage networks.

Washington, D.C. Street-Corner Men

Eliot Liebow (1967) completed a classic participant observation study of poor African American men who frequented a street corner—"Tally's Corner"—in Washington, D.C. Most of these men, Liebow found, believed until their late teens that they would become adult breadwinners and husbands. Driven by this ideal, many married and fathered children. Unfortunately, most of the men had few skills and little education and ended up with little more than menial jobs.

Many men came to hate the idea of performing degrading work. In time, many stopped working: Some were fired, some just quit. In any case, the men soon realized they could barely provide for themselves, much less a family. This failure was evident to their wives and children and a deep source of personal pain and family tension. To make matters worse, the government offered to provide public assistance to wives and children—but only if no father were living in the home.

Men crushed by their plight could find some comfort "hanging out" together. At Tally's Corner, people commiserated and didn't ask embarrassing questions. There, a man could forget failure and get by from day to day. Before long, most men were spending more time there than at home. The next Urban Living box explains that networks supplied the heart and soul of life on "Tally's Corner."

Boston Neighborhoods

Many urban relationships are set in neighborhoods. Distinguished by physical or social boundaries, neighborhoods contain people who share important social characteristics such as social class, race, and ethnicity.

In a study of Boston's predominantly Italian West End neighborhood in the 1950s, Herbert Gans (1982) suggested that, despite the many differences among residents of an urban neighborhood, many *gemeinschaft*-like relations exist.

At the time of Gans's research in the 1950s, the West End was a low-income, low-rent district adjacent to the elite Beacon Hill area. Traditionally home to immigrants, over the years the West End had been dominated by various categories—including Italians, Jews, Poles, and Irish, as well as a handful of artists and bohemians.

Most casual observers of the West End concluded that it was a chaotic slum. Yet living in the area revealed a different—more accurate—picture. There, Gans found as much *gemeinschaft* as might be found in many nonurban environments, as the Urban Living box on page 190 suggests. This doesn't mean that everyone knew everyone else personally, but it does mean that most West Enders forged strong ties with family, neighbors, and friends.

Other researchers have reached similar conclusions after investigating other cities. For example, Gerald Suttles (1968) reported strong interpersonal ties among Italians in Chicago's Addams area, and Joseph Howell (1973) provided a similar description of life in an inner-city Washington, D.C. neighborhood. Finally, a complex study by Fischer et al. (1977) found important interpersonal networks operating throughout the Detroit metropolitan area. In sum, though they may be hidden to the casual observer, personal relationships may be every bit as important to urban neighbors as they are to people living in rural communities.

Friendships

Yet many urban relationships do not involve neighbors. More affluent urbanites especially—many of whom move from city to city to establish their careers—are not linked to neighborhoods in any traditional sense. Yet friends they have. Recent studies show that such people typically forge friendships at work, with people with whom they have lunch or a drink and dinner, or with friends they meet more casually, say, at a concert or in the park. The point is that such friendships may be maintained among people who

CITYSCAPE

The Varieties of Urban Experience

Mama's San Francisco

In those days, if anyone had asked Mama unexpectedly, "What nationality are you?" I believe she would have answered without hesitation, "I am a San Franciscan."

Then quickly, lest you tease her, she would add, "I mean Norvegian, American citizen."

But her first statement would be the true one.

Because from the moment she was to step off the ferryboat, confused and lonely in a strange land, San Francisco was to become suddenly and uniquely her own.

"It is like Norvay," the Aunts and Mama had declared.

And straightaway she'd taken the city to her heart.

Mama learned so many things about San Francisco. She could tell you how to get to Telegraph Hill; what time the boats came in at Fisherman's Wharf; the names of the young boys who tended the teeming crab kettles along Bay Street; and where to find the blue and yellow lupines at Land's End.

The cable cars were an endless delight, and Mama's idea of a perfect Sunday afternoon was for Papa to take us riding on them from one transfer point to another.

Papa would tell of the time Mama took out her citizenship papers and astounded the solemn court by suddenly reciting the names of the streets. "Turk, Eddy, Ellis, O'Farrell," Mama had said proudly, "Geary, Post, Sutter, Bush, and Pine."

Papa said the clerk had quite a time making Mama understand that such knowledge was not necessary for citizenship.

And if anyone ever asked us where we were born, Mama instructed us we should say "San Francisco": Didn't copies of our birth certificates, neatly framed and hung on the wall of Papa's and Mama's room, testify to that proud fact?

"After all," Papa used to tease her, "after all, San Francisco isn't the world."

But to Mama it was just that. The world.

The Marginal Man

I live here on a corner of the square in a borrowed flat, without property, at haphazard. By comparison with the right family and neighborhood life of the small town, I have few attachments or continuities. My existence is lax and unshaven. I have no proper job, just an irregular series of commissions and assignments, the chores and errands of a middle class hobo. . . . Freelance writers . . . tend to drift to the peripheral fringe of things, habitual onlookers and overhearers. My flat is pitched on the western edge of my private version of London, a place to make forays from, scavenging eastwards for material and odd jobs. I am on the rim, both geographically and socially; and this marginal position suits me very well. . . .

Cities are scary and impersonal, and the best most of us can manage is a fragile hold on our route through the streets. We cling to friends and institutions, exaggerate the importance of belonging, fear being alone too much. The freedom of the city is enormous. Here one can choose and invent one's society, and live more deliberately than anywhere else. Nothing is fixed, the possibilities of personal change and renewal are endless and open. But it is hard to learn to live as generously as real citizenship demands. I spot in others the same mouselike caution which keeps me hugging the edge of the pavement, running from bolthole to bolthole,

(continued)

unequipped to embrace that spaciousness and privacy of city life which so often presents itself as mere emptiness and fog.

For me a city day is a succession of guarded moves, as if one was crossing a peat bog. . . . [We] need to hold on tight to avoid going completely soft in a soft city. So much of metropolitan life is just the slowing of symptoms of fright. In the city one clings to nostalgic and unreal signs of community, takes forced refuge in codes, badges and coteries; the city's life, surface and locomotion, usually seems too dangerous and demanding to live through with any confidence. The mad egotism of the man who stops you in Soho Square to tell you he is John the Baptist, or the weird rural delusions of another tramp nearby who fishes hopefully through a grating at the corner of Old Compton Street ("Caught anything?" "I had some good bites."), seem not unlikely consequences of the exercise of the freedom of the city. Its discontinuities give one vertigo; few people who aren't criminals or psychopaths will risk themselves on the rollercoaster ride of change and incongruity which the city offers. So much of city life is an elaborate process of building up defenses against the city—the self a fortified town raised against the stranger. We hedge ourselves in behind dreams and illusions, construct make-believe villages and make-believe families.

Life in the South Bronx

The South Bronx in New York City has always been home to me. As a young girl growing up there, I was surrounded by a stable family and a sense of community, even though the area was viewed as a place where only "the poorest of the poor" lived.

My earliest recollection of my neighborhood is of an energetic and alive community with a great deal of social interaction. I recall being wheeled with my sister in a huge baby carriage in front of what the *New York Times* would subsequently call those "solid, grimy five-story tenements." My parents would stop to converse with neighbors, part of a network of people who knew each other well and who helped each other.

My South Bronx had a richness of life, a dynamism and stability of relations that few other places have. However, as I matured, I came to understand that the world beyond my community's boundaries had a different view of us. That world saw us as "different" and poor and was often instinctively hostile or afraid of us. Yet, I never felt poor, deprived, or disadvantaged. I also never understood what inspired hostility toward those I held dear.

At an early age I came to puzzle over this contradiction, why the view from within was so different from the view from without; why hostility, fear, or disrespect should exist without cause. This developed in me a basic curiosity about the view of those affected and the factors that affected them.

The world within which I grew up was not all roses and pastels (a festive Puerto Rican dish). My childhood was as full of traumas, joys, and disappointments as the next person's. There were the usual struggles to survive that all people who have little money or who have strong differences of culture, color, and language experience. Life was hard, but life was manageable.

As I was growing up, I witnessed my community and others like it destroyed by forces over which we had little control: drugs,

live a considerable distance apart (Macionis, 1978; Wolfe, 1983).

It was industrial technology that broke up the communities of old, with new opportunities pulling people away from the towns of their birth. Yet technology also provides new means to stay in touch: the telephone has served this purpose throughout this century, and computer technology will surely support countless "on-line" relationships in the new century.

urban renewal, and housing abandonment. . . . The dynamism and stability of the communities of the South Bronx [were] destroyed by external forces.

Not all Puerto Ricans fled; some fought to maintain their neighborhoods, fought drug dealers, and organized to get support from the city and federal governments. Currently, the decline has slowed and signs of revitalization have appeared. The South Bronx has bottomed out, but the history lived there will remain a bitter chapter for all concerned.

Lutie Johnson's New York

A man came suddenly out of a hallway just ahead of her—a furtive, darting figure that disappeared rapidly in the darkness of the street. As she reached the doorway from which he had emerged, a woman lurched out, screaming, "Got my pocketbook! The bastard's got my pocketbook!"

Windows were flung open all up and down the street. Heads appeared at the windows—silent, watching heads that formed dark blobs against the dark spaces that were the windows. The woman remained in the middle of the street, bellowing at the top of her voice.

Lutie got a good look at her as she went past her. She had a man's felt hat pulled down almost over her eyes and men's shoes on her feet. Her coat was fastened together with safety pins. She was shaking her fists as she shouted curses after the man who had long since vanished up the street.

Ribald advice issued from the windows:

"Aw, shut up! Folks got to sleep."

"What the hell'd you have in it, your rent money?"

"Go on home, old woman, 'fore I throw somp'n special down on your rusty head."

As the woman's voice died away to a mumble and a mutter, the heads withdrew and the windows were slammed shut. The street was quiet again. And Lutie thought, no one could live on a street like this and stay decent. It would get them sooner or later, for it sucked the humanity out of people—slowly, surely, inevitably.

She glanced up at the gloomy apartments where the heads had been. There were row after row of narrow windows—floor after floor packed tight with people. She looked at the street itself. It was bordered by garbage cans. Half-starved cats prowled through the cans—rustling paper, gnawing on bones. Again she thought that it wasn't just this one block, this particular street. It was like this all over Harlem wherever the rents were low. . . .

And she began thinking of Pop unable to get a job; of Jim slowly disintegrating because he, too, couldn't get a job, and of the subsequent wreck of their marriage; of Bub left to his own devices after school. From the time she was born, she had been hemmed into an ever-narrowing space, until now she was very nearly walled in and the wall had been built up brick by brick by eager white hands.

Sources: Kathryn Forbes, *Mama's Bank Account* (New York: Harcourt, Brace, 1943), pp. 39–40; Jonathan Raban, *Soft City* (London: Hamish Hamilton, 1974), pp. 222–27, 230; Clara E. Rodriguez, "The Puerto Rican Community in the South Bronx: View From Within and Without," in Beth B. Hess, Elizabeth W. Markson, and Peter J. Stein, *Sociology* 5th ed. (Boston: Allyn and Bacon, 1996), p. 507; and Ann Petry, *The Street* (Boston: Houghton Mifflin, 1998), pp. 228–29, 324–25.

Scenes

One of the city's hallmarks is its diversity of people, meaning that not everyone has some traditional location—such as a neighborhood —in which to develop interpersonal ties. In

fact, many people *invent* places where they get together. John Irwin (1977) calls such places "scenes."

Scenes include bars, clubs, discos, or areas of a city taken over by a group (much as San

URBAN LIVING

Two Types of Marriage Networks

Segregated Marriage Networks

At one extreme was a family in which the husband and wife carried out as many tasks as possible separately and independently of each other. There was a strict division of labor in the household, in which she had her tasks and he had his. He gave her a set amount of housekeeping money, and she had little idea of how much he earned or how he spent the money he kept for himself. In their leisure time, he went to cricket matches with his friends, whereas she visited her relatives or went to a cinema with a neighbor. With the exception of festivities with relatives, this husband and wife spent very little of their leisure time together. They did not consider that they were unusual in this respect. On the contrary, they felt their behavior was typical of their social circle.

Joint Marriage Networks

At the other extreme was a family in which husband and wife shared as many activities and spent as much time together as possible. They stressed that husband and wife should be equals: all major decisions should be made together, and even in minor household matters they should help one another as much as possible. This norm was carried out in practice. In their division of labor, many tasks were shared or interchangeable. The husband often did the cooking and sometimes the washing and ironing. The wife did the gardening and often the household repairs as well. Much of their leisure time was spent together, and they shared similar interests in politics, music, literature, and in entertaining friends. Like the first couple, this husband and wife felt their behavior was typical of their social circle, except that they felt they carried the interchangeability of household tasks a little further than most people.

Source: Elizabeth Bott, *Family and Social Network* (London: Tavistock, 1957), pp. 52–53.

Francisco's Haight-Ashbury district was inundated by hippies in the 1960s or Bryant Park in New York City by yuppies in the late 1990s). Many who participate in scenes devote a considerable amount of time and energy to them.

Most scenes are part-time. They usually occupy the hours away from work (a favorite restaurant where taxi drivers go for lunch, or a gymnasium frequented by boxers in the evening). Second, to "make the scene" suggests that participants are in some sense "on stage," emphasizing only one particular aspect of themselves—their ability to dance or their knowledge of literature, for instance.

Further, scenes are of four main types. Most cities have *lifestyle scenes* that attract writers, musicians, gays, or political radicals. On summer evenings in Toronto, for example, young people from all over the metropolitan area descend on Yonge Street, often remaining until the wee hours of the morning. On foot or in cars with stereos blaring, they eat, talk, yell, buy records, and generally hang out up and down a dozen city blocks.

The *local scene* is more exclusive. A local bar, for example, may attract a particular crowd and may even discourage "outsiders" from coming in.

The *open scene* is more fluid in terms of clientele, yet it too provides the opportunity

URBAN LIVING

The Networks of Street-Corner Men   Eliot Liebow

[The most important people in a man's network are those] with whom he is "up tight": His "walking buddies," "good" or "best" friends, girl friends, and sometimes real or putative kinsmen. These are the people with whom he is in more or less daily, face-to-face contact, and whom he turns to for emergency aid, comfort or support in time of need or crisis. He gives them and receives from them goods and services in the name of friendship, ostensibly keeping no reckoning. Routinely, he seeks them out and is sought out by them. They serve his need to be with others of his kind, and to be recognized as a discrete, distinctive personality, and he, in turn, serves them the same way. They are both his audience and his fellow actors.

It is with these men and women that he spends his waking, nonworking hours, drinking, dancing, engaging in sex, playing the fool or the wise man, passing the time at the Carry-out or on the street-corner, talking about nothing and everything, about epistemology or [Muhammad Ali], about the nature of numbers or how he would "have it made" if he could have a steady job that paid him $60 a week with no layoffs.

So important a part of daily life are these relationships that it seems like no life at all without them. Old Mr. Jenkins climbed out of his sickbed to take up a seat on the Coca-Cola case at the Carry-out for a couple of hours. "I can't stay home and play dead," he explained, "I got to get out and see my friends."

Source: Eliot Liebow, *Tally's Corner* (Boston: Little, Brown, 1967), pp. 163–64.

---

for personal relationships. Bars without a well-defined clientele fall into this category. As Sherri Cavan writes:

> Public drinking places are "open regions": Those who are present, acquainted or not, have the right to engage others in conversational interaction and the duty to accept the overtures of sociability proffered to them. (quoted in Irwin, 1977:35)

Finally, the *specialized scene* involves activities such as tennis, barbershop harmony, amateur theater, chess, skateboarding, and countless other activities. Like the local scene, these provide a sense of in-group solidarity with others who share some special interest. Yet specialized scenes have a degree of openness and population fluidity that local scenes cannot have.

Perhaps one of the best-known specialized scenes among college students, especially those attending a city college or university, are the clubs. These typically crowded gathering places have a DJ or band, a dance floor, a bar, and room to sit or stand. In Boston some of the more popular clubs are Aria, Avalon, Club Nicole, Roxy, and the Sweetwater Cafe. Other clubs cater to different types of clientele, such as African Americans, Hispanic Americans, or yuppies. But all club people come to listen and dance to the music and, of course, to enjoy some good times with old or new friends.

Temporary Networks

Many urban dwellers use another type of network to make initial or short-term personal contact in the city. Examples of such networks

URBAN LIVING

Boston's Thriving West End

Everyday life in the West End was not much different from that in other neighborhoods, urban or suburban. The men went to work in the morning, and, for most of the day, the area was occupied largely by women and children—just as in the suburbs. . . . In the afternoon, younger women could be seen pushing baby carriages. Children of all ages played on the street, and teenagers would "hang" on the corner, or play ball in the school yard. . . . Many women went shopping every day, partly to meet neighbors and to catch up on area news in the small grocery stores, and partly to buy foods that could not be obtained in the weekly excursion to the supermarket. On Sunday mornings, the streets were filled with people who were visiting with neighbors and friends before and after church. . . .

On the whole . . . the various ethnic groups, the bohemians, transients, and others [lived together] without much difficulty, since each was responsive to totally different reference groups. . . . [For example] as Italians like to stay up late, and to socialize at high decibel levels, the bohemians' loud parties were no problem, at least to them. . . .

Many West Enders had known each other for years, if only as acquaintances who greeted each other on the street. Everyone might not know everyone else; but, as they did know something about everyone, the net effect was the same, especially within each ethnic group. Between groups, common residence and sharing of facilities—as well as the constant struggle against absentee landlords—created enough solidarity to maintain a friendly spirit. Moreover, for many families, problems were never far away. . . . Thus when emergencies occurred, neighbors helped each other readily; other problems were solved within each ethnic group.

For most West Enders, then, life in the area resembled that found in the village or small town, and even in the suburb.

Source: Herbert Gans, *The Urban Villagers* (New York: Free Press, 1982), pp. 14–16.

---

are "lonely hearts" clubs, dating agencies, public ballrooms, call-in radio talk shows, dial-a-prayer, and suicide hot lines.

Sometimes such networks serve people who are extremely lonely or desperate. Just as frequently, they serve people who are quite happy with their lives. People who participate in late-night talk shows need not be lonely, after all; they may be working late, or just interested in speaking their mind.

Identifying with the City

The ability to know and identify with an entire city probably ended in the Middle Ages. With the dawning of the modern age, Western cities began a relentless increase in population, as well as an expanding division of labor, resulting in the large, diverse cities we find today.

Still, most people have some sense of knowing their city, although such knowledge often is based on clichés and stereotypical images that outsiders also may share. Thus, beer has made Milwaukee famous in the same way that sun defines Miami and the entertainment industry has elevated Los Angeles and Hollywood. St. Louis has its arch and Toronto its CN Tower ("world's tallest freestanding structure!"). And, while Stratford-on-Avon has its

Social researchers deflated the myth of urban alienation by documenting the pervasiveness of social networks among virtually all city dwellers, rich and poor alike. One does not need the formal trappings of social organizations to enjoy intimate ties with others. A street corner or public bench can easily serve to create a *gemeinschaft* environment.

Shakespeare, Hannibal, Missouri, is proud to be the boyhood home of Mark Twain (Samuel Clemens).

In addition, identification with the modern city is fostered by sports teams ("Minneapolis–St. Paul—Home of the Twins, Vikings, and North Stars!") and by important local events (St. Patrick's Day in Boston, the Rose Parade in Pasadena, Inauguration Day in Washington, D.C.). One of the most famous urban rituals is Mardi Gras, which practically defines New Orleans to many outsiders. This event's vital importance to residents of the city (not to mention its attraction for a million or so tourists each year) is reflected in the next Urban Living box on page 192.

Historical events—both negative and positive—also help to define the urban experience. The San Francisco earthquake of 1906 and the assassination of President John F. Kennedy in Dallas in 1963 are examples of costly and tragic events that remain alive in people's minds, while the ride of Paul Revere through Boston and the First Continental Congress in Philadelphia are Revolutionary War events well known centuries later by most of the cities' present-day inhabitants.

The City as *Gemeinschaft:* A Reassessment

A wealth of research supports the conclusion that the vast majority of urbanites are "well-connected" in their cities. On the one hand, most are engaged in a variety of networks. Families, neighborhoods, friendships, scenes, and even temporary contacts are examples. Similarly, most city residents have a sense of identification with their city. We conclude, then, that, while they may not always be readily apparent, characteristics of Tönnies's *gemeinschaft* —personal relationships and a sense of belonging—do flourish in the city.

URBAN LIVING

Mardi Gras: New Orleans's Great Urban Festival

Christmas is hardly over when Carnival opens, and it goes on for two months, more or less, depending on the date of Lent. During its last week it gathers momentum, with ever grander balls and street parades, shimmering floats in the daytime processions, and night floats whose gold and scarlet hues are caught by flambeaux in the hands of [participants].

Eventually comes Mardi Gras itself—Fat Tuesday, the day before Ash Wednesday—the supreme fete celebrated by thousands in costumes ranging from ornate to casual, by "marching clubs," and by truck and wagon parties, with competitions among weirdly masked contestants dancing on the corners. In the midst of all this moves Rex, official King of all the Kings for the day, a crown on his head, a rhinestone encrusted scepter in his hand, leading his parade while his Queen waits on a draped reviewing stand. And throughout the day will be heard on every side that foolish but memory-stirring song which is Mardi Gras' theme:

> "If ever I cease to love, if ever I cease to love,
> May the fish get legs and the cows lay eggs—
> If ever I cease to love!"

This is a day of gusto and illusion, of buffoonery and satire, of the brilliant and the ridiculous. Fat Tuesday brings the sparkle of delighted eyes, the tap of feet in jazz rhythm, the bubbling of champagne, the magic of the hot dog (with Creole dressing), the fun of wondering who it is that is talking to you. By and large it is a day marked by pleasant behavior. Obstreperous drunks are few, fisticuffs negligible. Through the decades New Orleans has learned how to have a good time within reasonable bounds. . . .

Bands are blaring along the route. Slowly the floats move along, the path being cleared by police on horses or motorcycles. Mothers hold their children up to see better, or fathers carry them on shoulders or in boxes fixed on the ends of poles. As each float passes, its maskers reach into bags holding the throw-outs: beads, whistles, and other trinkets for the crowd. "Throw me something!" "Gimme something, Mister!"—and the gifts fly in a shower as the float moves by. There is no Carnival excitement to match that of reaching out and catching a gift, no disappointment like that of realizing that the man in front of you has the longer reach. . . .

The day is one of smells—of popcorn, beer, cotton candy, dust stirred by jigging feet, and people. It is a panorama of the life of New Orleans—Creole, American, black, white, brown—compressed into twenty-four hours, with something of everything that the old city has meant. There is French *joie de vivre*, the endless capacity for a good time, the willingness to let others have theirs. To appreciate it requires humor, a relaxed mood, and an aspirin. . . .

Source: Harnett T. Kane, *Queen New Orleans* (New York: Bonanza, 1949), pp. 331–32, 341–42, 346.

THE TEXTURE OF THE CITY

Most cities convey a unique impression—a look and feel that Gerald Suttles (1984) terms a "texture." New York is the "Big Apple," a city of energy, hustle, and fear; Boston is relaxed, "cultural," and intellectual; Los Angeles is "laid back," the heart of the "new America." While these are stereotypical impressions, many people share them.

But to what extent are such images real? Suttles argues that a city's texture is grounded in its history, architecture, street names, and even the nicknames for certain parts of town. Together, these elements add up to an objective reality, not just one individual's impression.

A visitor to Hollywood, for example, can actually see the footprints and handprints of the stars in the cement in front of Grauman's Chinese Theater, use a map to visit the homes of the stars, and see the huge "Hollywood" sign overlooking the city. Who knows? If you're lucky, you might even end up face to face with a famed actor at a restaurant. Stars, money, and fame are all part of Hollywood's texture as "Tinsel Town."

Another city, Detroit, has been battling its image as the country's "least wonderful town" (Barron, 1985). With the decline of the automobile industry in the 1970s, the flight of affluent people to the suburbs, and the collapse of its center-city areas, Detroit gained a reputation as unsafe and unpleasant—a violent cultural wasteland. As both cause and effect, Detroit's population plummeted by 44 percent between 1950 and 1990 (Jackson, 1996). It then lost another 77,000 people between 1990 and 2000, bringing its total population below 1 million for the first time since the early twentieth century.

How does a city overcome such a reputation and population loss? City officials put more police on the streets and made concerted efforts to rebuild neighborhoods. Yet, by 2002, Detroit remained—for the third year in a row—the most dangerous of 327 U.S. cities, as measured by the six basic crime categories of murder, rape, robbery, aggravated assault, burglary, and motor vehicle theft (Morgan Quitno, 2002). However, the city is also experiencing a cultural renaissance, with a restored Detroit Opera House and with appealing exhibits at the Henry Ford Museum, the Detroit Historical Museum, and the Museum of African American History in the Detroit Cultural Center. In addition, the Detroit Institute

Ethnic pride parades and street fairs, such as the International Food Festival on Ninth Avenue in New York City, are popular means by which a city not only celebrates its diversity, but also provides a rich variety of activities not to be found in any other setting. Regardless of one's own background, such events are a source of interest and enjoyment.

of Arts is one of the nation's biggest art museums and contains exceptional Diego Rivera murals. Moreover, for just fifty cents, the People Mover elevated train takes riders on a 2.9-mile loop of the downtown to numerous shops, hotels, as well as Greektown, a popular restaurant district (Meredith, 1996b).

But perhaps the best indicator of Detroit's future potential to change its textural image is General Motors' 1996 purchase of the flashiest landmark in the city's skyline, the Renaissance Center. This downtown complex of five glass towers—one soaring 73 stories and housing the 1,400-room Westin Hotel—has some 2.2 million square feet of office and retail space. GM's move back to the central city promises to spur the renewal of this troubled city, persuading other companies to locate downtown as well and to revitalize the urban economy.

Portland, Oregon, (see case study in Chapter 4), already has a strong positive image based on a revitalized downtown, new housing and businesses, and a rebuilt waterfront (W. Turner, 1985). Visitors delight in strolling down tree-lined shopping streets, observing the many fountains, and traveling safely by bicycle. Portland is prospering as one of the vibrant new cities of the West: no wonder that, during the 1990s, its population has increased by some 40,000 annually.

In short, our senses do not deceive us when we get a different feeling from one city than from another. Although urban areas share many common elements, their individuality is quite real.

HUMANIZING THE CITY

People have devised ways to humanize life in today's urban environment, just as they did in the towns and villages of the past. Even when struggling with poverty, most people have found ways to maintain positive personal relationships. Although some homeless people live on the margins in almost complete isolation, most urban poor generate a social network to help them cope.

Virginia Schein (1995) conducted in-depth interviews with 30 single mothers receiving public assistance. All were working or had some work experience. She found that, for many, a network of family, friends, and teachers provided both emotional support and resources, enabling the women to battle their fears and to struggle onward, despite many hardships in their daily lives. Arlene, a 34-year-old mother of three, had just earned an associate college degree in business administration

and moved off public assistance benefits to start a job as a customer service representative. Never, she explained, could she have done so without family support:

> I told my sister when I graduated that I owed much of it to her. My sister helped me out with the baby-sitting. She would pick them up [my kids] from day care, feed them supper, and give them baths. Then she would bring them to my house, put them to bed, and wait for me to get home, usually around 9:30. (1995:102)

For others, support came from nonfamily members, as another woman explained:

> It was like a three-ring circus. I have the [two] children, five classes, driving back and forth. It was quite a struggle to juggle all of that. I realized that I couldn't do this all on my own. I could ask for help and not feel disgraced. . . .
>
> I realized that there are people out there that care. They helped me. Then it got better. I knew there were people that I could call, that I had the support that I needed, that these people understood what I was going through. (1995:99)

— Church

Renata, a 37-year-old mother of two teenagers who did not finish high school, spoke of the positive support she received from her church:

> I just got tired of trying to fix things and nothing would get fixed. Things would change and I couldn't change them back. I started going to church and I ended up going and going. I started going a year ago and am getting to know a lot of people. I was the type that stayed home all the time. I went to work, came home, went to work, came home. I didn't associate with many people on the block. I had one neighbor on one side and a girlfriend on the other and that was it. Now I go to church every Sunday, I sing in the choir, and I talk to people all day long.
>
> One woman said, "You look so good, you have a glow, it's your aura. I don't know what it is but you look so different." A little old lady

Arlene got lots of family support from sister

URBAN LIVING

Helping Each Other in the Ghetto   Carol Stack

Cecil (age 35) lives in The Flats with his mother Willie Mae, his oldest sister and her two children, and his younger brother. Cecil's younger sister Lily lives with their mother's sister Bessie. Bessie has three children and Lily has two. Cecil and his mother have part-time jobs in a cafe and Lily's children are on aid. In July of 1970 Cecil and his mother had just put together enough money to cover their rent. Lily paid her utilities, but she did not have enough money to buy food stamps for herself and her children. Cecil and Willie Mae knew that after they paid their rent they would not have any money for food for the family. They helped out Lily by buying her food stamps, and then the two households shared meals together until Willie Mae was paid two weeks later. A week later Lily received her second ADC check and Bessie got some spending money from her boyfriend. They gave some of this money to Cecil and Willie Mae to pay their rent, and gave Willie Mae money to cover her insurance and pay a small sum on a living room suite at the local furniture store. Willie Mae reciprocated later on by buying dresses for Bessie and Lily's daughters and by caring for all the children when Bessie got a temporary job.

Source: Carol Stack, *All Our Kin* (New York: Harper & Row, 1974), p. 37.

that lives up the street also said, "You should have started going to church a long time ago —you look good." It all gives me a little more confidence each day. If I can make it this day, then I can make it the next day and the next one and the next one. (1995:102–103)

In a classic study, Carol Stack (1974) stressed the ingenuity of poor African Americans in the inner-city area of a large midwestern city. Most of the men, she learned, were recent migrants from the South whose search for better jobs had resulted, at best, in low-paying, menial jobs. Most of the women struggled to raise their children with no steady source of income. Despite the odds against them, Stack discovered, these poor people had responded to their plight by constructing a diffuse family structure that allowed them to maintain a stable community and meet everyone's basic needs.

The network was a means to respond to an immediate crisis, as people shared clothes, food, and rent money. But each time help was given, a debt was incurred. The helping families and individuals, sure to be in need of assistance themselves in time, expected that those they had helped would assist them in turn. As these obligations spread, the residents established a massive network of "cooperation and mutual aid" (1974:28–31). The expanding network became one extended family, a fact suggested by the common practice of referring to the community as "all our kin." In the Urban Living box, Stack describes how one particular network evolved.

Residents, Stack found, shared virtually everything, from clothes to food to child care responsibilities. Sometimes fathers of children lived at home and sometimes, when they could not support their families, they did not. Even then, fathers frequently contributed what they could to the upbringing of their children. When mothers had to work, they turned to their own mothers or to neighbors for help with the children. Thus, an informal day-care system evolved that ensured that children always would have the attention of at least one caring adult. Through this reciprocal aid system, people gave what was needed and expected that their kindness would be repaid later on. Or, as one woman put it,

> Sometimes I don't have a damn dime in my pocket, not a crying penny to get a box of paper diapers, milk, a loaf of bread. But you have to have help from everybody and anybody, so don't turn no one down when they come round to help. (Stack, 1974:32)

Those who don't "play fair" by reciprocating are quickly sanctioned, as documented by other researchers, including Doug A. Timmer, D. Stanley Eitzen, and Kathryn D. Talley, who conducted in-depth interviews of the homeless in Tampa, Denver, and Chicago. As one once-homeless woman explained:

> For six months I took [my sister] in my apartment without [the Housing Authority] knowin' about it and helped her out, fed her, bought things for her. We had holidays together. And I threw this in her face three weeks ago and told her, "This is the way it is, you know. I helped you and now you can't help me. Then you can forget about me." So we haven't called each other at all. And I won't call her. 'Til doomsday. I won't call her. Even if she comes lookin' for me, she won't find me. (Timmer et al., 1994:113)

Through this system of cooperation and mutual support, in spite of the conditions that hem them in, the people in study after study have invented ways to meet at least their basic needs and to soften the blow of their poverty. Such positive adaptation is a prime example of how people can make their urban experience, even under the harsh conditions of poverty, more humane.

SUMMARY

Living in cities alters our perceptions. There is an urban experience because we react to the city as a physical and social environment. Such reactions represent a social psychology of the city.

We make sense of the city by ordering it. Kevin Lynch observed that we trace the physical landscape, identifying paths, edges, districts, nodes, and landmarks. In part, such distinctions arise from the physical form of the city itself (streets, after all, are "natural" paths) and, in part, from our personal needs and creativity (people invent "back street" paths to get from one place to another more quickly). To this basic insight, Stanley Milgram contributed a deeper understanding of the process of "mental mapping."

A similar ordering occurs as we respond to the city's social aspects. On the one hand, we cope with the city's *gesellschaft* characteristics (large numbers and high density) by inventing rules of behavior for riding the subway, standing in line, or walking in the street. We also size up strangers from their dress, demeanor, and location in the city. Nevertheless, despite many common strategies, we all react individually to the city. Our social characteristics—whether we are rich or poor, immigrant or native, mainstream or marginal —have much to do with the nature of our urban experience.

On another level, we have developed complex ways of establishing meaningful relationships in the city. Urban networks are a prime example. Personal networks take many forms, including kinship, neighborhood, street-corner friendships, or people frequenting some "scene." Most of us also identify with our city as a whole, merging traits of our particular city (a key industry, a winning sports team, or an important historical event) with our own personal urban experience. All these mechanisms lend a *gemeinschaft*-like character to the urban experience.

Next, there is the notion of urban texture. Recent research has shown that there is much truth in people's comments that, based on its history, architecture, location, and people, each city "feels" a little different.

Last, the investigations of Virginia Schein and Carol Stack show how people, even those facing the most desperate conditions, can humanize the city and turn it into a meaningful experience.

Together, all these elements of the urban experience provide us with a sense of order and security in this largest of human agglomerations, and they make the city meaningful, usable, and often enjoyable.

CONCLUSION

The city is a big place. It has more people, more buildings, more paths, more nodes, more possibilities for interaction and relationship than any other form of settlement. As Georg Simmel argued many years ago, cities demand a lot of mental work from those who wish to make sense of them. In the end, such extra mental effort may be the unique element that creates the sophistication for which urban dwellers are noted.

GEOGRAPHY AND SPATIAL PERSPECTIVES

Making Sense of Space

If you happen to be endowed with topographical curiosity, the hills of San Francisco fill you with an irresistible desire to walk to the top of each one of them. Whoever laid the town out took the conventional checkerboard pattern of streets and without the slightest regard for the laws of gravity planked it down blind on an irregular peninsula that was a confusion of steep slopes and sandhills. The result is exhilarating. Wherever you step out on the street there's a hilltop in one direction or the other. From the top of each hill you get a view and the sight of more hills to the right and left and ahead that offer the prospect of still broader views. The process goes on indefinitely. You can't help making your way painfully to the top of each hill just to see what you can see. . . .

This one is Nob Hill. . . . Ahead of me the hill rises higher and breaks into a bit of blue sky. Sun shines on a block of white houses at the top. Shiny as a toy fresh from a Christmas tree, a little cable car is crawling up it. Back of me under an indigo blue of mist are shadowed roofs and streets and tall buildings with wisps of fog about them, and beyond, fading off into the foggy sky, stretches the long horizontal of the Bay Bridge.

Better go back now and start about my business. The trouble is that down the hill to the right I've caught sight of accented green roofs and curved gables painted jade green and vermillion. That must be in Chinatown. Of course the thing to do is take a turn through Chinatown on the way down toward the business district. . . .

John Dos Passos,
"San Francisco Looks West"

In a basic sense, cities are things—complex physical entities. Cities exist within geographic and climatic settings that naturally shape them. The hands and minds of human beings, of course, also play a part as people react to a city's physical setting. San Francisco is an excellent example—people have started with an exciting geography and a pleasant climate, added a host of their own creations (diverse neighborhoods, clattering cable cars, a lively Chinatown, and bridges that span sparkling waters) to produce a particularly enticing urban experience. This chapter explores the interrelationships between a city and its physical setting.

URBAN GEOGRAPHY

Some cities, like San Francisco, straddle hills. Others, like St. Louis, Tucson, or Oklahoma City, stretch across flat plains. No matter what the topography of the land, however, a city's design reflects its physical environment.

Take, for example, Los Angeles, San Francisco's massive neighbor 500 miles to the south. Originally a Spanish mission outpost, for decades Los Angeles remained a series of scattered communities surrounded by mountains in the relatively flat, near-desert region of California's southwest.

In the 1920s, however, coincident with the rise of the movie industry, Los Angeles began to grow rapidly. As its population surged upwards, the city became a bowl-shaped collection of outlying suburban communities. At first, public transport—electric trains and streetcars—linked the new settlements with Los Angeles. With the arrival of the mass-produced private automobile, public transportation ridership swiftly declined, as commuters preferred the convenience and privacy of driving themselves to and from the city. This heavy reliance on automobiles fostered ever-expanding urban sprawl throughout the region and gave us Los Angeles's incredible freeways. Says Jan Morris:

These remain the city's grandest and most exciting artifacts. Snaky, sinuous, undulating, high on stilts or sunk in cuttings, they are like so many concrete tentacles, winding themselves around each block, each district, burrowing, evading, clambering, clasping every corner of the metropolis as if they are squeezing it all together to make the parts stick. They are inescapable, not just visually, but emotionally. They are always there, generally a few blocks away; they enter everyone's lives, and seem to dominate all arrangements. (Morris, 1976:30)

As Los Angeles expanded, people settled the mountains themselves, with streets "forever ribbing and probing further into [the] perimeter hills, twisting like rising water ever higher, ever deeper into their canyons, and sometimes bursting through to the deserts beyond" (Morris, 1976:28).

Ironically, the city's increasing population, its heavy reliance on the automobile, and its geography combined to produce an unexpected but monumental environmental problem: smog. Although it is by no means the only city beset by this threat to health, Los Angeles's smog problem has been particularly serious because the surrounding hills trap noxious fumes in the bowl-shaped region where most of the city's people live. Only recently has the problem lessened, thanks to California's "toughest in the nation" pollution laws. Despite its air quality problems, the Los Angeles area continues to grow—from about 3 million in 1980 to about 3.7 million in 2000—and the automobile continues to reign supreme.

The Location of Cities

Geography and climate, then, provide the physical conditions to which urbanites must adapt. In fact, certain physical characteristics usually determine whether an area becomes a city at all.

Look at Figure 7–1, which shows the geographical location of the 32 most populous urban areas in North America. All but one are located on waterways. They are either seaports (Los Angeles, New York, Vancouver), lakeports (Chicago, Milwaukee, Toronto), or on major rivers (Cleveland, Memphis, Montreal). The advantage of such sites for stimulating trade is enormous. However, even cities on less important waterways (Phoenix, Dallas, Denver) are where they are because, at least initially, there was enough water to support their populations.

The sole exception to the waterway thesis is Atlanta. Yet its site, too, was determined by a geographical consideration: In the 1840s Atlanta was selected as the southern terminus of the Western and Atlantic Railroad because of its centrality to the rest of the South. Thus, even Atlanta illustrates that environmental considerations play a key role in locating a city. With this in mind, we can consider briefly the sites of five other cities: Houston, Miami, Montreal, Salt Lake City, and Washington, D.C. What products and activities do you associate with each?

Houston

Located near the East Texas oil fields, this city has been booming since the 1950s. Its metropolitan population more than doubled between 1970 and 2000 to nearly 4.5 million. Because of oil—every major oil company has offices in Houston—and cheap shipping of oil via the Gulf of Mexico, the city has become the second busiest port in the country (after New York), and the nation's largest port in international tonnage. Considered by many as the "energy capital of the world," Houston is home to more than 5,000 energy-related companies. Since 2000, the city has ranked first in the nation in new business growth (Houston, 2002).

Miami

Although it is a port, Miami is best known for tourism and as a mecca for retirement. The winter climate is ideal, with temperatures hovering near the 80s, nearly unlimited sun, and endless beaches. "Fun in the Sun" is the city's motto. In recent years, however, Miami has become a major market for specialized goods, thanks in large measure to its large Cuban-American community. Because of the Cubans' economic success, the city has become attractive to wealthy Latin Americans. They fly to Miami, stay in or near Little Havana, speak nothing but Spanish, and buy numerous U.S. goods—clothes, computers, stereos—from Cuban merchants at prices much lower than they would pay at home. Such visitors are crucial to maintaining the city's economy (Miami, 2002).

Montreal

Built on and around a mountain slope located at the junction of the St. Lawrence and Ottawa river systems in the southwestern corner of Quebec, Montreal is North America's fifteenth largest metropolitan area, containing a 1999 population of 3.4 million people. Although Montreal has a strong, diversified industrial base, service dominates its economy. Many national and international service companies are headquartered there, especially in the banking, culture, finance, telecommunications, and transportation sectors. Montreal

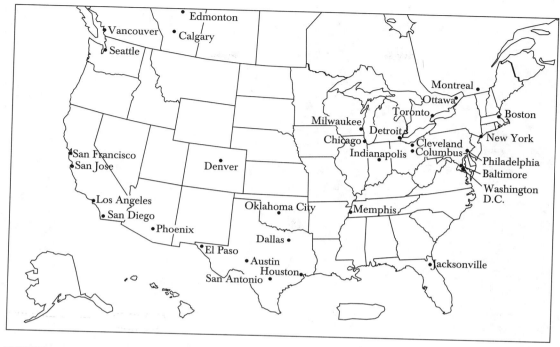

FIGURE 7–1   Geographical Location of the 32 Most Populous North American Metropolitan Areas, 2000.

Source: U.S. Bureau of the Census, 2002a, Table 48, p. 47.

also accounts for one-fourth of all corporate research and development expenditures in Canada (twice its share by population). Long, cold winters have prompted an expansive and delightful underground network of shops, restaurants, and theatres that people enjoy year-round. Montreal also is home to four professional sports franchises, a ballet company, an opera company, and a symphony orchestra (Montreal, 2002).

Salt Lake City – Mormons

Situated at the foot of a mountain range near the forbidding and barren Great Salt Lake in Utah, Salt Lake City might seem an unlikely urban site. Yet the Mormons thought otherwise. Migrating westward in the mid-nineteenth century, looking for a place where they could practice their religion freely, the Mormon leaders saw the Salt Lake region as the place God had set aside for them. In a sense, the region's remoteness was the key to its founding. But, as it turned out, the location is more hospitable than it appeared at first glance. Salt Lake City became a point of rest and departure for westward migration, and the salt proved to be a valuable resource, so the city became the only area within hundreds of miles able to support a large population, numbering over 1.1 million in 2000 (Salt Lake City, 2002).

Washington, D.C. – Potomac River Basin

Here we have a very different case. Its founders did not look on Washington as an economic center. The issue was politics—wishing to avoid choosing between Philadelphia and New York as the permanent U.S. capital. In addition, Washington represented a symbolic link between two great regions: the

Must Satisfy BASIC environmental considerations

Cities experiencing their greatest growth during the automobile age have, like Houston pictured above, massive freeway approaches and interchanges as well as generally wider streets and more car-friendly services (parking, drive-in facilities) than older cities. They are typically situated in warm climes, on fairly level land, with port access less necessary.

North and the South. Once the Potomac River basin (water again!) became the site of the U.S. capital city, the nation's emergence as a world power generated a vast government bureaucracy, hundreds of foreign embassies, countless special interest groups, and a vast array of hotels, restaurants, and national landmarks that make this urban area unique. Its population, however, has steadily dropped, from 757,000 in 1970 to 572,000 in 2000 (Washington D.C., 2002).

Why Cities Are Where They Are

Both environmental *and* social factors play a role in siting an urban area. On the environmental side, any setting, in order to become a city, must fulfill a number of basic conditions. First and foremost, it must be a *minimally*

hospitable environment. It cannot be infested with disease-producing organisms, be subject to extreme heat or cold, or exist on a floodplain. In addition, any city has to have *access to adequate supplies of food, water, and building materials.* This is not to say that cities cannot overcome limitations in some sites, but settlers' ingenuity and technology must be up to the task. For example, gas and oil heat have made winter survival in northern cities possible for millions, just as air conditioning moderates the extreme heat of southern urban areas. Similarly, water and other resources can be imported. Las Vegas, situated in the Nevada desert, is perhaps the best example of an "impossible" city brought to life by modern technology.

Once basic environmental conditions have been met, social factors come into play. We will discuss seven such factors, using the five cities just discussed as illustrations.

1. Some cities are situated at a *natural crossroads* for a region. Montreal, for example, is the most important port on the St. Lawrence River and Seaway, lying between the Atlantic Ocean to the east and the Great Lakes to the west. Other examples are St. Louis and Chicago, the latter nicknamed "the crossroads of the nation." Such crossroads facilitate the concentration of people, services, and, especially, trade goods.

2. Other cities develop because they are located at what economists call *"break-of-bulk"* points. These are locations where a good—the "bulk"—is transferred from one type of transportation to another, say, from truck to ship. Houston is a break-of-bulk point for oil. In such places, goods often are warehoused for a time or processed in some way to make the next leg of the trip more economical. When this happens, a city develops a set of subindustries that deal with storing or processing. In Houston, oil to be shipped from the city often is stored in huge tanks, later to be refined into gasoline or heating oil. James Heilbrun gives another example:

> Probably the most often cited case of a city that has attracted industry because it is a transshipment point is Buffalo. An enormous flour-milling industry developed there because grain could be carried

Buffalo - flour milling

Montreal
fur trade
petroleum

inexpensively across the Great Lakes from the grain belt of the North Central States, unloaded at Buffalo, the easternmost port that could be reached before the St. Lawrence Seaway was built, there milled into flour, and then shipped by rail to the large East Coast markets. (1974:65)

Furthermore, the break-of-bulk function of cities is an enduring feature. The Urban Living box describes two cases separated by more than a century. Note the striking similarities between Charles Dickens's description of 1860 London and Vincent Parrillo's comments about contemporary Seattle.

3. Another major reason for a city's location is access to some valuable *raw material.* Montreal's early history rested heavily on its colonial fur trade; today, this city remains an important shipping center, handling the millions of gallons of petroleum processed each day by Montreal-Est refineries. Similarly, Houston and its refineries are near the East Texas oilfields; San Francisco boomed in the mid-nineteenth century because it was the closest port to the Sierra Nevada gold mines; and Pittsburgh's greatness is largely due to its proximity to coal mines that afforded cheap power for its steel mills.

4. Miami suggests another reason for a city location. Here we have an *amenity city* located in a particular place because it provides certain surroundings—sea, surf, sand, and sun—not easily available elsewhere. In its recent guise as "Latin America's supermarket," this predominantly Spanish-speaking city boasts a complete array of North American goods for sale. And much the same is true of Orlando (home of Disney World) and many other Florida cities. Similarly, Las Vegas offers the attraction of gambling to westerners, as Atlantic City does to people on the East Coast, and as Monte Carlo does to Europeans. Other amenity cities are Hot Springs, Arkansas, and Bath, England (both renowned for their hot mineral waters), and Innsbruck, Austria (a world-class skiing city).

5. Washington, D.C. is an example of an *administrative or political city,* a city established primarily for governmental purposes, as was Ottawa, Canada's national capital. Two recently constructed international examples are Canberra, Australia, and Brasília, Brazil.

6. Closely related historically to the administrative function has been a city's *strategic*

military location. That is, many cities have been situated in easily defensible spots (Athens, Quebec City), and others (London) have been sited because they offered military access into a whole region.

7. Finally, cities can be located for *religious or educational reasons.* Salt Lake City prospered as the home of Mormonism. In a similar way, *Islam* Mecca in Saudi Arabia is the fountainhead of Islam, and Jerusalem is a focal point of no fewer than three major world religions: Christianity, Islam, and Judaism. University cities, such as Cambridge in England, Ithaca in New York (home of Cornell University), and Berkeley in California (site of one of the main campuses of the University of California) are cities that have achieved prominence for educational reasons.

A combination, then, of geographic–climatic conditions and social–economic factors explains why cities are where they are. Where many advantages come together, a city typically gains special importance. New York's prominence rests on its location as a natural port, an easily defended island, a gateway to a huge hinterland rich with raw materials, a natural break-of-bulk point, and a crossroads for people. The Critical Thinking box on page 205 offers another thought about New York.

Finally, if the balance between a city's physical environment and people's social or economic needs and interests shifts, the city must adapt or else it will decline. History is strewn with the ruins of cities unable to adapt, including the ancient Egyptian capital of Luxor and the recently found Mayan city of El Mirador. On the other hand, cities sometimes survive great geographic–economic disasters. San Francisco is the best-known U.S. case, having recovered from the calamity of the 1906 earthquake to become one of the most vibrant U.S. cities.

THE SHAPE OF THE CITY

Once cities begin, what determines the form or physical shape they take? The answer depends on what the city's social and economic functions are.

URBAN LIVING

Break-of-Bulk in Two Cities

In the following passage Charles Dickens describes London's River Thames in early morning, as seen from a small boat traveling downstream.

Nineteenth-Century London

Early as it was, there were plenty of scullers going here and there that morning, and plenty of barges . . . and we went ahead among many skiffs and wherries, briskly.

Old London Bridge was soon passed, and old Billingsgate market with its oysterboats and Dutchmen, and the White Tower and Traitor's Gate, and we were in among the tiers of shipping. Here, were the Leith, Aberdeen, and Glasgow steamers, loading and unloading goods, and looking immensely high out of the water as we passed alongside; here, were colliers by the score and score, with the coal-whippers plunging off stages on deck as counterweights to measures of coal swinging up, which were then rattled over the side into barges; here, at her moorings, was tomorrow's steamer for Rotterdam . . . and here tomorrow's for Hamburg, under whose bowsprit we crossed.

In the next passage, Vincent Parrillo describes a similar morning, only this time more than a century later and in a major U.S. port.

Late-Twentieth-Century Seattle

Even to the casual observer, the Port of Seattle is a busy place, filled with freighters, tugboats, barges, commercial fishing vessels, and pleasure craft. Geographically closer to Asia than any other major U.S. port, its natural deepwater harbor attracts commercial shippers from throughout the Pacific Rim. It is one of the largest U.S. container ports, one of the leading distribution centers on the West Coast, and the top U.S. port in container tonnage exports to Asia (over 6 million metric tons annually). Today ships from Japan, Singapore, and Taiwan are anchored at the docks, each by one of 28 commercial marine terminals.

At these terminals the container cranes transfer auto parts; bamboo baskets; electronic, household, and plastic products; foods; tools; and a variety of other products to an on-dock intermodal rail facility for direct shipment to inland destinations. Elsewhere, toplifts and forklifts transfer shipments to the 1.5 million square feet of warehouse storage space in the Terminal 106 Complex, to other outdoor storage areas, or to the waiting trucks at the 20 loading docks.

Everywhere the eye turns, one sees the bustling activity of workers: Longshoremen, stevedores, crane and forklift operators, grain terminal operators, truckers, railway men, foremen, and supervisors—are all unloading, storing, or loading the imports or exports passing through this port.

Source: Charles Dickens, *Great Expectations* (London: Chapman and Hall, 1860), from Chapter 54; and based on travel of Vincent N. Parrillo to Seattle, 1991.

To begin, consider that Athens is spread around the natural hilltop of the Acropolis; Edinburgh is sited around a massive outcropping in Scotland; and Paris and Mexico City were situated on islands. These examples suggest that defense was one of the prime interests of these city dwellers. Durham, in northern England, provides another example. Founded about 1000 C.E., Durham is situated atop a high, steep peninsula formed by

[handwritten margin note: Steep slope Wear peninsula; Wear River]

The New York City Skyline—A Cast of Thousands

No one could look at [the New York City skyline] without asking: "Who built it?" If you consult the library books, you'll be told that the Empire State Building was designed by Shreve, Lane & Harmon, and that Rockefeller Center was created by Corbet, Harrison & MacMurray, Hood & Foulhoux, Reinhard and Hofmeister. Yes, but who? What senior member of the firm drafting

plans for the Lever Building said, "Suppose we used green glass?" . . . Who of the Seagram architects first said tentatively, "What about bronze?"

. . . Whose pencil drew the spectacular sweeping curve of 9 West Fifty-seventh Street? Who built it? Anon., that's who. Nobody built the New York skyline. Nobody by the thousands.

Source: Helen Hanff, *Apple of My Eye* (Garden City, NY: Doubleday, 1978), p. 54.

---

the Wear River. The sides of the escarpment are extremely difficult to scale, even if one could get across the river. Naturally protected on three sides, the founders of Durham only had to defend the narrow fourth side, and so here they built their heavily fortified castle.

The Radiocentric City

The importance of defense prompted preindustrial people to build cities in the form of a great container, protected by natural geographic features (Durham's steep slope) and human constructs such as walls, moats, castles, or battlements. Urbanists characterize such cities as *radiocentric,* because they radiate outward from a common center.

A wonderful example of this urban form is preindustrial Baghdad in Iraq (see Figure 7–2). Set within an outer wall with four fortified gates, the inner core of the city—containing the ruling caliph's palace and the mosque—was further protected by two rings of densely packed residential quarters where the city's poor people lived. Along the main access roads leading from the gates to the core, arcades or shops provided easy shopping access for Baghdad's inhabitants.

But not all radiocentric cities have a perfectly radial shape. Ming Peking (see Figure 8–1) was heavily walled and moated for defense, yet took the shape of a series of rectangles and

FIGURE 7–2   The Radiocentric City: Baghdad circa 146–762 C.E.

Source: From *An Urban Profile of the Middle East*, by M. Hugh Roberts. Copyright © 1979 by M. Hugh Roberts. Reprinted with permission of St. Martin's Press, LLC.

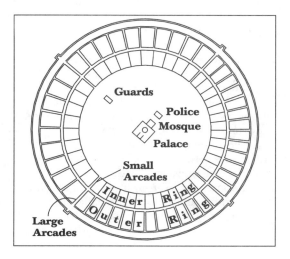

Hans Blumenfeld said cities can grow 3 wa[ys]

squares attached to and within one another. These shapes reflect the Chinese cosmology of the 1400s, which led planners to arrange the city on the points of the compass—north, south, east, and west.

Other considerations encourage cities to develop a radial shape. As any city grows, people want to be as close to the center as possible to make travel easier. Because a circle places the most people closest to the center, many cities grow as subcommunities in a ring-like fashion around a central core. As anyone who has gazed out an airplane window at night knows, most cities look like huge wheels with central spokes radiating outward. The spokes—highways and rail lines—suggest another reason for the city's generally radial form. Because the shortest route to the center of a circle is a straight line, people build access roads to the city as directly as possible. That practice suggests the origin of one of history's best-known sayings: "All roads lead to Rome."

The Gridiron City

Despite the common radial pattern of most of the world's cities, the downtown areas of well-known North American cities—Atlanta, Chicago, Los Angeles, Montreal, New York, Philadelphia, Toronto, Vancouver—are not of a radiocentric design. Indeed, while radiocentric center cities are the rule in much of the world, that form is the exception in North America.

Closer to home, we find *gridiron* cities, composed of straight streets crossing at right angles to create many regular city blocks. This form is typical of cities built after the Industrial Revolution—because only then did cities place such importance on economic activity. A city gridiron plan facilitates the movement of people and products throughout the city. This form is also an efficient way to divide land—and sell it as real estate. Figure 7–3 shows William Penn's 1682 plan for selling lots in Philadelphia.

However, grid patterns do not always result from careful planning. Typically, when a settlement begins, merchants favor a main-street

location that allows people to shop and move from one store to another along the street. Furthermore, open-ended streets serve business well because they allow room for growth as well as easy access to and from the shopping area. The U.S. and Canadian Midwest and West are full of such Main Street towns. If, in time, another major street crosses the original street, we see the beginnings of a gridiron around "four corners" that may well expand from there.

City Growth: Horizontal, Vertical, and Interstitial

How, exactly, do cities expand? According to urbanist Hans Blumenfeld, cities can grow in any of three ways: (1) outward (expanding horizontally); (2) upward (expanding vertically); or (3) toward greater density (expanding interstitially). Which pattern predominates depends primarily on a society's technology, says Blumenfeld:

> As long as intra city traffic moved only by foot or hoof, possibilities of horizontal and vertical expansion were strictly limited. Growth was mainly interstitial, filling up every square yard of vacant land left between buildings until the city became a solidly built-up amorphous mass of brick. With the advent of the elevator and the steel frame, the vertical growth of skyscrapers began, leaving interstices of half-developed and vacant lots. Suburbs spread out horizontally along streetcar and bus lines and around suburban railroad stations, surrounded by wide-open spaces. But with the development of the private automobile, these interstices between the suburbs began to be filled in, tending to make the outskirts as amorphous as the central area, though less densely settled. (1964:31)

City Shape and Quality of Life

Some scholars link the shape of cities to the quality of urban life. Max Weber, whose ideas are discussed in Chapter 5, praised medieval cities because in them, enclosed within city walls, people could easily identify with the city as their social world. Today's tall, gridiron

FIGURE 7–3   The Gridiron City: William Penn's Philadelphia Plan, 1682.

cities work against such positive identification by being very open, and also by placing so much emphasis on economic activity. Today's urbanites, in other words, are preoccupied with "How much is it (the street, the house, the job) worth?" Other human concerns—maintaining the old neighborhood, religious ties, and an identification with the city as a whole—have fallen by the wayside.

URBAN ECOLOGY: THE CHICAGO SCHOOL

> There are forces at work within the limits of the urban community . . . which tend to bring about an orderly and typical grouping of its population and institutions. The science which seeks to isolate these factors and to describe the typical constellations of persons and institutions which the cooperation of these forces produce is what we call human, as distinguished from plant and animal, ecology. (Park, 1916)

Robert Park, dean of the Chicago sociologists discussed in Chapter 5, used cities as a laboratory to study social life. Research by Park and his colleagues generated the science of human ecology.

The Ecological Theory of Urban Development

the study of living things + their environment

Drawing on the approach of plant and animal ecology, which studies the relationship between living things and their environment, Park investigated how human beings live in their urban world. Park believed that the evolutionary struggle for survival was evident in social life in the form of *competition for scarce resources* such as food, clothing, shelter, and land. This competition conferred on the city the characteristic diversity Park called "natural" areas: business districts, ethnic neighborhoods, skid rows, and rooming-house areas.

For Park, urban competition is not only economic; it is also about *power*. People compete for control of parks, streets, and ethnic districts—and above all for the prestige that comes from living in a fashionable neighborhood or having an impressive occupation.

Boston grew from a small, walled colonial city to an important city of commerce, annexing such adjoining municipalities as Brighton, Charlestown, Dorchester, Roxbury, and West Roxbury between 1868 and 1874. Today it is a large metropolis, utilizing its waterways to full advantage both commercially and recreationally.

Beyond competition, Park noted that large-scale *population movements* also influence urban development. Most of the immigrants who came to Park's Chicago and other growing North American cities a century ago had little education, few skills, and were exceedingly poor. With few options, they poured into over-crowded housing in the center cities and took low-paying jobs in factories. Marie Jastrow, recalling her father's arrival in New York, gives an illustration in the Cityscape box.

Jastrow's father and his family did not stay on lower Manhattan's Hester Street forever. With time, most immigrants learned skills, made money, and moved to better housing (Jastrow's family moved to Yorkville in New York's East 80s). As they did in cities across the continent, they left their old neighborhoods to the next poor group to enter the city. The Chicago sociologists called such population movements *invasion–succession*.

The Concentric Zone Hypothesis

To Park, competition and population movement shaped and reshaped cities. In this process, claimed Park, the city as a whole took on broad, characteristic patterns. In the mid-1920s, one of Park's students, Ernest W. Burgess, suggested that the city develops somewhat the way a tree does, growing outward in a series of concentric rings or zones over time.

CITYSCAPE

The New World—New York, 1905

My father crossed the Atlantic and landed on Ellis Island at the beginning of October 1905, well aware of the ordeal that awaited him. He had heard stories. The threat of deportation haunted every [poor] immigrant. . . .

Eyes, ears, chest—the entire person was scrutinized by doctors. Some were rejected. Those who were turned away fell into the depths of despair, waiting, without hope, for the first ship to take them back.

Hour after hour the examination went on. At last my father found himself on American soil, a silent, solitary figure. He had passed the inspection. Now, for the first time, he was alone, separated from his fellow travelers. It was a painful aloneness. . . .

A policeman walked by and stopped. What was this lonely figure doing in the cold afternoon, sitting in the park? An immigrant, no doubt, just off the ship. . . .

"Are you expecting anyone?" The officer spoke some German. My father shook his head. No, he expected no one, he knew no one. But he would appreciate help in locating a room.

"Can you pay?"

"Yes," Papa again shook his head. "But not much." He hesitated a moment. "The room has to be cheap."

The policeman smiled, writing something on a slip of paper.

"Go to this address. Tell them that Officer Schmidt gave you this." My father looked at the address he had just received. . . . He wondered how to get to the address he was holding in hand, but dared not ask.

Officer Schmidt was becoming impatient. "What is it? Can't you read?"

"Yes, I can read," said my father, "but, if you would be so kind to give me directions, I do not know this city."

"Of course, you just got in," laughed the officer. "I'll take you to the streetcar on that corner. You give this address to the conductor, he will let you off on the right street."

"Thank you," said my grateful father. "I shall never forget this—how you helped me on my first day in America."

. . . The Hester Street tenement where my father lived for the first few months stood in the midst of a heavily populated immigrant area. It was the first stopover for many Jewish families. No one arrived here with more than token funds. They had nothing, these people, but dreams and hopes for the better future this new land could offer. None spoke English, very few spoke any language but Yiddish. It is easy to see why they clustered together and found comfort in the nearness of their countrymen.

The six-story structures in that street were planned for thirty-six tenants, six to a floor. Actually, counting the boarders that were crowded into every available corner "to help pay the rent," no landlord knew how many people lived in his building. But no one counted, as long as the rent was ready on the first of every month.

Source: Marie Jastrow, *A Time to Remember* (New York: Norton, 1979), pp. 21–24, 36.

Although Burgess assumed that economic competition was central to urban life, he, like Park, saw other social forces at work. Moving to a suburb, for example, is not just an economic consideration; it also confers prestige, suggesting that people have "made it."

The lights of a city such as Toronto at night offer strikingly beautiful visual images while simultaneously illustrating its ongoing life and activities after dark. Toronto's strategic location on the shore of Lake Ontario enhances its economic vitality, making this metropolitan area home to over 6 million people—one-fourth of Canada's total population.

Burgess described the city in terms of <u>five main zones</u> (see Figure 7–4, right side). In his words:

This chart represents an ideal construction of the tendencies of any town or city to expand radially from its central business district—on the map "The Loop" (I). Encircling the downtown area there is normally an area in transition, which is being invaded by business and light manufacture (II). A third area (III) is inhabited by the workers in industries who have escaped from the area of deterioration (II) but who desire to live within easy access of their work. Beyond this zone is the "residential area" (IV) of high-class apartment buildings or of exclusive "restricted" districts of single family dwellings. Still farther, out beyond the city limits, is the commuters' zone—suburban areas, or satellite cities—within a thirty- to sixty-minute ride of the central business district. (1984:50; orig. 1925).

Burgess illustrated his model by applying it directly to the Chicago of his day (Figure 7–4,

left side). Once we take the "halving effect" of Lake Michigan into account (the heavy line shows the city's edge by the lake), Burgess's theory did a creditable job in explaining the location of the city's districts. The most valuable land (Zone I) was contained within "The Loop" downtown, which was the exclusive preserve of business. In Zone II, the "zone in transition," stood factories and slums, the latter overflowing with down-and-out roomers and ethnic groups of various sorts including Italians (Little Sicily) and Chinese (Chinatown). The third zone, the "zone of workingmen's homes," was predominantly inhabited by second-generation migrants, the descendants of earlier Chicago immigrants who had taken the first step in escaping the inner city by moving out of the slums. Here, too, was the "two-flat" area, where two families occupied duplex houses, instead of four or more as was so often the case in the slums. Zone IV was the "residential zone," dominated by residential

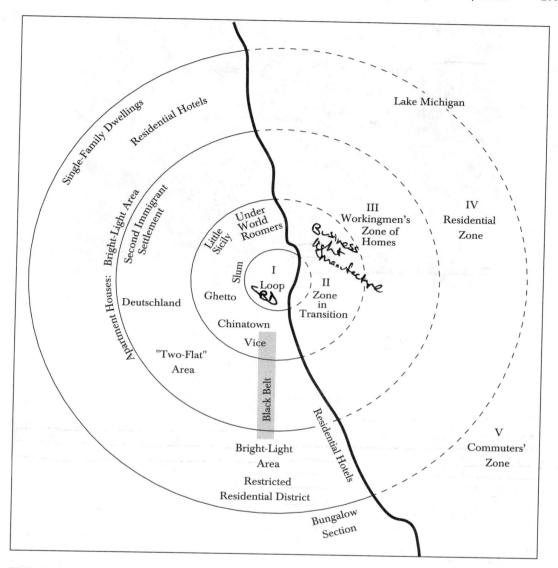

FIGURE 7–4   Chicago's Concentric Zones

Source: From "The Growth of the City," in Robert E. Park and Ernest W. Burgess, eds., *The City.* Copyright © 1967 University of Chicago Press, p. 55, chart II. Reprinted by permission of the University of Chicago Press.

hotels, apartment areas, and, most important, single-family homes. In this zone, too, existed a relatively wealthy "restricted residential district," an area that excluded people with "undesirable" ethnic or racial traits.

Criticisms of the Chicago School

Although he based his model on Chicago, Burgess thought his zonal hypothesis would describe any city. But do other cities and towns

This 1906 photo, taken in Los Angeles at the intersection of Main and Fourth Streets, is similar to others taken in eastern U.S. cities in that period. However, LA's rapid population growth in the post-automobile age over miles of flat, near-desert land resulted in a spread city heavily dependent on freeways and private transportation unlike the older cities of the Northeast.

conform to the concentric zone pattern? Certainly some do. In a study of 318 U.S. metropolitan areas, Schwirian, Hankins, and Ventresca (1990) found that, between 1950 and 1980, longitudinal movement toward the Burgess model typically occurred among "industrially based, older, larger, more dispersed metropolitan communities" in the Northeast.

However, critics question the Chicago School's reliance on the concepts of unrestrained competition and population movements (Berry and Kasarda, 1977:6). Although sometimes these forces play a key role in how groups "settle out" in U.S. cities, Mark La Gory and his associates (1980) studied 70 urban areas and concluded that these forces are more powerful in some times and places than in others. Life in early industrial cities was especially competitive, for example, much more so than in medieval cities. Similarly, immigration was more pronounced between 1880 and 1920 in North America than it is today; in Mexico and other poorer nations, the opposite is true.

A third criticism is that Burgess's model implicitly assumes that cities everywhere are based on transportation systems like the railroad. This, we know, is simply not the case.

Finally, some critics dismiss the ecological theory as "too biological." That is, the principles of plant and animal ecology do not do a very good job of explaining human activity. People, unlike plants, are thinking creatures who reflect and act creatively on their urban environment. Ecological theory pays little attention to the role of choice in the evolution of the city (Berry and Kasarda, 1977). Such criticism has diminished the importance of Park's ecological approach and of Burgess's concentric zone model over time. In their place, a host of alternative theories and models suggest that the forces shaping land use are more complex than Park or Burgess suspected.

German - Deutschland   Ghetto - Chicago
Black Belt - Chicago

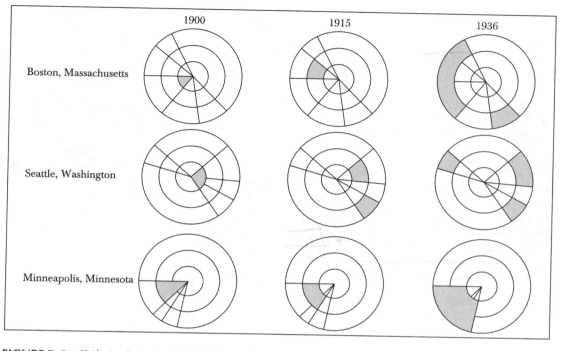

FIGURE 7–5   Shifts in the Location of Fashionable Residential Areas in Three American Cities, 1900–1936. Fashionable areas are indicated by shading.

Source: Adapted from Homer Hoyt, *The Structure and Growth of Residential Neighborhoods in American Cities* (Washington, DC: Federal Housing Administration, 1939), p. 115, figure 40.

URBAN ECOLOGY: OTHER THEORIES

Soon after the emergence of the Chicago School, two other ecological growth theories achieved prominence. The sector and multiple nuclei theories addressed some of the shortcomings of the Park and Burgess approach.

The Sector Theory

Homer Hoyt (1939) made the first major attempt at modifying the zonal hypothesis. He noticed that a fair number of city districts did not conform to the purely concentric model suggested by Burgess. Even in Burgess's Chicago (Figure 7–4), unusual areas like the "Deutschland Ghetto" (the home of German

immigrants) and the "Black Belt" obviously cut across zones.

This observation led Hoyt to study, block by block, residential patterns in 142 cities. The scope of Hoyt's study was a major advance over Burgess's work, which was based almost exclusively on Chicago. Hoyt also examined cities in three different time periods: 1900, 1915, and 1936, adding an important historical dimension. Figure 7–5 graphically presents Hoyt's findings concerning high-prestige, fashionable areas in three of his cities.

First, Hoyt found, upscale districts formed sectors of varying size. Second, although he noted a rough concentric shape to the cities, many sectors took a pie-shaped form rather than resembling an entire ring, as Burgess had suggested. Third, lower-income districts

Homer Hoyt - pie shaped ring

often abutted and sometimes even surrounded fashionable districts. (A classic example is Harlem's "Striver's Row," a wealthy, two-block oasis of pristine houses surrounded by buildings approaching utter collapse.) Fourth, as time passed, Hoyt found a tendency for sectors to move out of the city radially, along a path begun by the sector in earlier years (Seattle provides a good example).

Fifth, in the later periods, cities revealed two or three fashionable areas in different places. Hoyt noted that factors other than competition and population movement influenced this process. For example, Hoyt observed that the wealthy neighborhoods in many cities stand on "high ground" (Boston's Beacon Hill, for instance), indicating a preference by the wealthy to be "above" the city's poorer residents. Elsewhere, he found high-prestige sectors located for aesthetic reasons—on waterfronts, for example. In still other cities, he found such districts located along main transportation lines that facilitated easy access to the center city.

The Multiple Nuclei Theory — Chauncey Edward Ullman Harris

Although Hoyt's study was a major advance over the work of the Chicago ecologists, it was limited by a focus on residential sectors. Hoyt imagined that industry, too, moved radially outward from the center city—upriver, or along railroad lines, for instance—but he never investigated this hunch.

In 1945 Chauncy Harris and Edward Ullman broadened Hoyt's findings with another theory of urban land use. They argued that as the contemporary city grew, it diversified, developing many distinct sectors of activity. Figure 7–6 graphically portrays this multiple nuclei theory.

Harris and Ullman noted that modern cities typically have a major central business district (the CBD is sector 1 in Figure 7–6), but that, in addition, city-specific historical, cultural, and economic factors generate various additional districts as well. For example, wholesale light manufacturing (2) might be near the CBD, with low-income residences (3) in various separate districts nearby. A medium-income residential area (4) might abut the CBD and give way on its outer edge to a high-income residential area (5). Between the two might exist a secondary business district (7) and, farther out, a completely separate residential suburb (8). Heavy manufacturing (6) might lie a relatively large distance from the CBD and evolve an industrial–residential suburb (9) nearby.

Why do multiple nuclei develop? First, certain types of activities require certain types of facilities. For example, heavy manufacturing requires a great deal of space. A century ago, space was plentiful downtown. In recent years, however, space near the CBD became hard to find and expensive. As a result, much heavy manufacturing moved from the CBD to outlying industrial areas where land was readily available and taxes were often lower. In Chicago, for example, heavy manufacturing once located in the CBD is now on the south side of the city, in or around Gary, Indiana.

A second cause of multiple nuclei is the fact that some activities are incompatible, so that people seek to keep distance between them. For example, "porno" districts that feature X-rated movies, peep shows, and "gentlemen's clubs" may be distasteful to owners and customers of more "respectable" businesses. As a result, areas such as Boston's "Combat Zone" typically stand off as distinctive, highly centralized districts with few other businesses nearby. Over the course of this century, zoning laws have reinforced the separation of incompatible districts.

Third, some urban activities are better off away from the CBD. As we have seen, many city residents "escape" to the suburbs motivated by the desire for quiet and prestige. Similarly, some land-intensive activities, such as automobile salvage or golf courses, cannot afford a CBD site; hence, they locate at some distance from it. Additionally, many city firms have relocated near the beltways that surround so many U.S. cities as trucking has assumed a key role in interstate transportation.

Perhaps the most important contribution of Harris and Ullman's theory is that it seriously questions the notion that urban land use is predictable at all. Burgess's zonal hypothesis and, to a lesser extent, Hoyt's sector theory both implied certain inevitable patterns of land use. In contrast, Harris and Ullman's multiple nuclei theory suggests that a mix of historical, cultural, and economic situations shapes and continues to reshape every city. Even the core CBD might fall into decline, as it has in recent decades (Ullman, 1962).

Social Area Analysis

Eshref Shevky
Marilyn Williams
Wendell Bell
L. A. & San Fran.

In studies of Los Angeles and San Francisco, Eshref Shevky and Marilyn Williams (1949) and, later, Shevky and Wendell Bell (1955) took a new tack, attempting to describe urban land use in terms of the social characteristics of urbanites. These researchers examined traits such as *social ranking* (roughly, amount of prestige), *family type* (number of children, type of house, whether mother worked or not), and *how important people considered their ethnicity*. Examining official census tracts for all parts of the city, they noted that a tract's population shared such characteristics to a high degree. Homogeneous districts they called "social areas." In San Francisco, for example, they found that groups in some areas measured low on social rank and family status but high on ethnicity. That is, people in this area typically had low prestige, lived in large families occupying multiple-dwelling housing, and were of identifiable ethnic or racial background. Conversely, people in other areas measured high on social rank and low on family status and ethnicity. By combining these social characteristics in every possible manner, Shevky, Bell, and Williams argued that as many as 32 distinct social areas might be found in cities. Furthermore, they suggested that such social traits are the foundation of urban social structure:

> In the impersonal setting of the city . . . social standing does not rest on any intimate evaluation

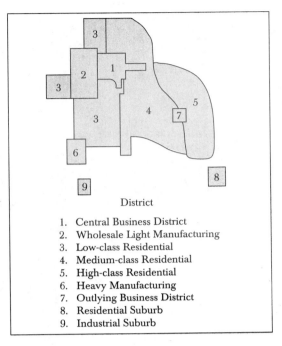

District

1. Central Business District
2. Wholesale Light Manufacturing
3. Low-class Residential
4. Medium-class Residential
5. High-class Residential
6. Heavy Manufacturing
7. Outlying Business District
8. Residential Suburb
9. Industrial Suburb

FIGURE 7–6   The Multiple Nuclei Theory

Source: From Chauncy O. Harris and Edward L. Ullman, "The Nature of Cities," *The Annals*, 242 (Nov. 1945), American Academy of Political and Social Science. Used by permission of American Academy of Political and Social Science.

of persons nor any discriminating appraisal of differences within groups. Instead, certain easily recognizable traits, such as houses and possessions, become symbolic of rank. . . . As every occupation is evaluated and generally accorded honor and esteem on a scale of prestige in society, so every residential section has a status value which is easily recognized by everyone in the city. Even a casual visitor in Los Angeles could name a half dozen places representative of the exclusive sections on the westside and along the foothills of the Santa Monica and San Gabriel Mountains. (Shevky and Williams, 1949:61–62)

In the Critical Thinking box on page 217, Jan Morris applies this theory to Hollywood.

But even if everyone understands these social characteristics, do they really shape land use? In a study of ten U.S. cities, Van Arsdol, Camilleri, and Schmid (1958a, 1958b, 1961)

Paterson, New Jersey—the first planned U.S. industrial city—typifies an old manufacturing city. In classic sector theory patterning, many of its factories lined the railroad tracks, and its fashionable district moved eastward along Broadway to the high ground of Manor Hill. No longer thriving, the city struggles to maintain a solid economic base.

found social rank, family status, and ethnicity useful in identifying social areas in six of the cities, but of limited use in the four others. They suggested that other traits, too, would have to be measured if social area analysis were to prove widely useful in understanding city form. Indeed, other researchers have included additional variables in their studies, such as the physical composition of census tracts as crime level predictors (Bell, 1982), family structure and social control (Sampson, 1986), zip codes and community characteristics (Pittman and Andrews, 1986), and family and school characteristics and substance abuse (Ryan, et al. 1999).

Like all the approaches we've discussed, social area analysis has been strongly criticized. One problem is that this approach is not theoretical but merely gives a description of cities' areas (Hawley and Duncan, 1957).

That is, social area analysis cannot predict where groups will settle or explain why groups have settled where they have. Recall that Park and Burgess noted the ecological forces of competition and population movements causing concentric rings to develop. Likewise, Harris and Ullman attributed the unique form of each city to historical, cultural, or economic factors.

In short, social area analysis, too, offers limited insights into urban land use. As a result, another, more sophisticated technique came on the scene and provided some important results.

Factorial Ecology

Factorial ecology uses computer technology to sort through the social traits of an urban population. This approach differs from social

CRITICAL THINKING

Hollywood—Home of the Stars

Nostalgia blurs the realities of Hollywood, the Versailles of Los Angeles, and peoples it forever with the royalty of another era, the Astaires, the Tracys, the Garbos, and nobles of even earlier vintage. Now as always the tourist buses circumnavigate the Homes of the Stars, and the tours peddle their street plans on Sunset Strip. Now as always Hollywood feeds upon narcissism, cosseted in sycophancy and sustained by snobbery. Scattered over the Hollywood Hills, and over the Santa Monica Mountains into the San Fernando Valley, the houses of the movie people stand sealed and suspicious in the morning, the only sounds the swishing of their sprinklers, the snarling of their guard dogs, or perhaps the labored breathing of their gardeners: and in their garages the cars are profligately stacked, Jag beside Merc, Rolls upstaging BMW.

Source: Jan Morris, "Entering L.A.: Historical Monument," *Rolling Stone,* July 1, 1976, p. 32.

These 3 factor accounted for 86% of residential patterning of the city

area analysis because, rather than beginning with a few preselected social characteristics (such as social rank), it analyzes *all* characteristics that might be important to urban life, including density and spatial arrangements (O'Brien and Roach, 1984). Those that "work" are the "factors" we are looking for.

Basic Findings   *Whangarei = New Zealand*

Ronald J. Johnston (1976) used factorial ecology to examine Whangarei, a city in New Zealand, taking eight important social characteristics and doing a computer analysis of each of Whangarei's 22 census-tract areas. His results indicated that some areas of the city had high concentrations of male workers in professional or managerial occupations, who held university degrees and earned high incomes. These traits were so strongly linked to one another that Johnston combined them into a single factor called *socioeconomic status* (similar to Shevky, Bell, and Williams's social rank). Johnston also found residential areas of the city that were home to unmarried people over age 16 living in rental housing. This led him to designate *family status* as a second important factor. And, although of less importance, *ethnic factors* also played a part in determining where people lived in Whangarei. Taken together, these three factors—socioeconomic status, family status, and ethnicity—accounted for 86 percent of the residential patterning of this city.

Johnston's findings have been confirmed by others investigating cities in other countries. For example, in a study of Copenhagen, Pedersen (1967) found socioeconomic status, family status, and population mobility to be key factors that explained city residence; and, in a study comparing Helsinki and Boston, Sweetser (1965) identified socioeconomic status and family status as major factors in both cities and ethnicity as important in Boston.

A Synthesis Theory: Berry and Rees

Do these findings make earlier theories about concentric circles, sectors, and multiple nuclei obsolete? No, say sociologists Brian Berry and Phillip Rees (1969). In fact, factorial ecology shows that all these approaches have been partially correct. The problem was that no earlier theory captured the full complexity of what was going on with urban land use, which Berry and Rees depict in Figure 7–7.

They began by asking what would happen if each of the major social characteristics uncovered by factorial ecology—socioeconomic status, family status, and ethnicity—were the only force at work in the city. They concluded that if socioeconomic status were operating alone, cities would tend to divide themselves into sectors (Figure 7–7A). That is, of course, precisely what Homer Hoyt observed in his study as the pie-shaped outward movement of elite groups. But while Hoyt restricted his observations primarily to wealthy groups, Berry and Rees contended that this outward sectoring would characterize all urbanites, whether rich or poor.

Second, if family type were operating alone, differing demands for space would cause people to arrange themselves in concentric zones (Figure 7–7B), as Park and Burgess suggested. Single adults and those with few children would tend to cluster in the innermost circle, near their work and the attractions of the CBD (I). Those with more children (and fewer workers) would characterize the second circle (II), and groups with the most children and fewest workers would settle in the outermost circle (III).

Third, were ethnicity to operate alone, minorities (the shaded areas of Figure 7–7C) would tend to be segregated in various ethnic communities throughout the city—for example, in Chicago's South Side, New York's Harlem, San Francisco's Fillmore, and Miami's Little Havana, as the next Cityscape box on page 220 explains.

In truth, of course, no social characteristic ever operates in isolation. Many influence one another, generating a complex land use pattern. In Figure 7–7D, Berry and Rees show what might result from the effects of socioeconomic status, family status, and ethnicity working together. To take a few examples, beginning at the bottom right, you would be likely to find in the outermost area of a North American city white people of high socioeconomic status with a lot of children, and families with few working adults. (Thus the shorthand of "H III W," where "H" stands for a high income, "III" for numerous children, and "W" for white racial background.) In the next area, closer to the CBD, you also would be likely to find white people of high socioeconomic status, but this group probably would have fewer children and more working adults (H II W). Moving to the sector on the left, you would be likely to find, in the outermost district, white people of middle socioeconomic status with many children and few working adults (M III W). Moving toward the center-city area on the same sector, however, the next area might be a segregated African American neighborhood of low socioeconomic status (B). You could interpret the rest of Figure 7–7D in the same way.

Berry and Rees knew that particular minorities are often segregated from others and thus develop subsectors of their own, replicating the citywide pattern on a smaller scale. Figure 7–7E illustrates this process, showing, within the segregated area, the subgroups with low fertility and high number of working adults nearest the center city (I) and the subgroups with high fertility and fewest working adults farthest out (III).

As the city changes over time, as shown in Figure 7–7F, what Berry and Rees call <u>tear faults</u> develop. Given existing districts and neighborhoods within the city, however, the tear faults are not always symmetrical, resulting in the pattern shown in Figure 7–7G.

Finally, in time, new technology and competition for valuable CBD space produce multiple centers of industry and shopping districts away from the original downtown, as suggested by Harris and Ullman (Figure 7–7H). Also developing are suburbanized industrial workplaces (1), industrial satellites (2), and separate areas of heavy industry (3).

Figure 7–7I puts all these forces into play. It depicts sectors, inner circles, segregated areas (with their own inner circles), tear faults occasioned by city growth, and the decentralization of industry (symbolized by the "L" areas that mark lower socioeconomic people "pulled out" from the center-city area to be near the industries for which they work).

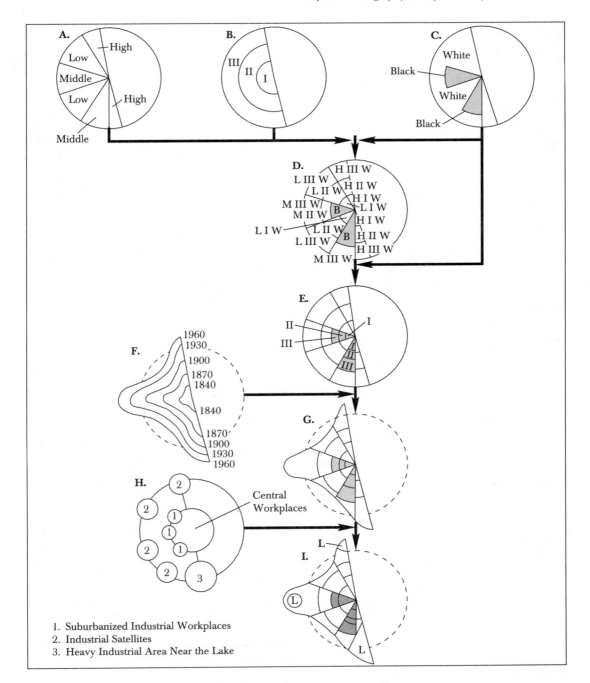

FIGURE 7–7   An Integrated Model of Urban Land Use

Source: Adapted from Brian J. L. Berry and P. H. Rees, "The Factorial Ecology of Calcutta," *American Journal of Sociology* 74 (March 1969), figure 13. University of Chicago Press. Reprinted by permission of the University of Chicago Press.

CITYSCAPE

Miami's Little Havana

The center of Little Havana lies along 8th Street in Southwest Miami. It is one of several areas in Miami and its environs in which substantial numbers of Cuban Americans reside. As is typical in areas that served as initial enclaves for a particular group (Chinatown in San Francisco, for example) the current population of Little Havana is older and poorer than other, later Cuban concentrations in the Miami area. . . .

Along 8th Street, for a stretch of several miles, are homes and apartments occupied primarily by Cuban families. Many of the homes have characteristically Cuban features such as decorative Spanish tiles, Catholic shrines in the backyards, and fences enclosing the front yards. There are many Cuban-owned stores, restaurants, and financial institutions catering largely, but not exclusively, to co-ethnics. . . . Some shops offer special wearing apparel such as guayaberas: lightweight, short coats traditionally worn by Cuban men. There are a number of botanicas selling religious goods, including potions for recalling saints and spirits and aerosol cans whose contents are guaranteed to improve one's love life. Many small grocery stores sell Cuban food products and almost all the pharmacies in Little Havana have signs in their windows announcing that they send medicine to Cuba. Local churches offer masses in Spanish and English.

A dozen or more daily and weekly Spanish-language newspapers are available at Little Havana's newsstands or from coin-operated boxes. Some of the newspapers are primarily oriented to news about Cuba and the Cuban population in the United States, whereas others focus on Latin America as a whole. The area is also served by WQBA, one of several Spanish-language radio stations, but the one that has historically claimed to be La Cubanisma (the most Cuban). Little Havana also contains a number of outdoor cafes and outdoor tables, where a mostly elderly male clientele gathers during the day and evening to play cards and dominos under black olive trees. A focal point in Little Havana is Domino Park, where older men play dominos throughout the day, smoke cigars, and talk about the old days in Cuba.

A number of Little Havana's restaurants offer traditional Cuban dishes such as chicken and yellow rice. Some of the restaurants are inconspicuous neighborhood eateries, others are highly ornate. The most famous among the latter is probably the Restaurant Versailles, "the mirrored palace," which was designed to closely resemble several once-popular night spots in Havana. . . .

Walking down Southwest 8th Street gives a former Cuban a feeling of being transported back in time to the Havana of yesterday. Little Havana in Miami is, in many respects, a copy of Havana in Cuba. Murals of the latter, complete with street signs, decorate the walls of restaurants, keeping alive memories of life in Cuba.

Source: From *Urban Enclaves: Identity and Place in America* by Mark Abrahamson. Copyright © 1996 by Worth Publishers. Used with permission of W. H. Freeman and Company/Worth Publishers.

Obviously, even Figure 7–7I is an idealized portrait that fits no actual city. Yet Berry and Rees contend that, once the additional effects of local geography (a mountain or lake may limit development in some direction) or history (a government grant may fund a low-income housing project in a place not accounted for by the model) are taken into account, this model can be applied to any city—at least in North America—and can provide an explanation for where types of people and business activities locate.

Criticisms of Factorial Ecology

Although factorial ecology remains the "state of the art" approach in explaining urban land use, significant questions and problems remain. Some critics question the method itself. For example, Ronald J. Johnston (1976) argues that computers may distort (or even create) some of the patterns researchers find. Moreover, the census tracts used in factorial ecology are not always socially defined neighborhoods. Thus, people with particular traits in common (say, ethnicity) may see themselves as a community, a fact missed by researchers using government data that shows them living in different census tracts. Then, too, there are certainly errors in census data, known to miss significant numbers of migrants, homeless people, and poor people.

Other criticism focuses on how well this method may apply to cities around the world. Berry and Rees may have found similar processes at work in Chicago and Calcutta, but these cities have much technology and economic activity in common. Perhaps, factorial ecology works for Western cities and others undergoing Western-style "modernization." But what about cities of the Middle Ages, where religious values were paramount? And what of more traditional cities shaped by cultural values unfamiliar to westerners? There, perhaps socioeconomic status, family status, and ethnicity may play a smaller role, or even no role at all, in the urban ecology (London and Flanagan, 1976).

In a factor analysis of Rabat-Sale, a principal metropolitan area of Morocco, Janet Abu-Lughod (1980) found that "social caste," a combination of ethnicity and social class characteristics, played the dominant role in determining where everyone lived in the city. Similarly, in a study of Tel Aviv in Israel, Borukhov and his associates (1979) found that in addition to socioeconomic and family status, "religious orthodoxy" figures in where people live in that city.

Finally, rising in opposition to factorial ecology has been the Marxist-based school of radical urban geography. These geographers believe that urban land use patterns in the modern era are mostly the result of capitalist market forces. They have been joined by scholars in the field of political economics and in what is called "the new urban sociology" to advance an alternative approach to the study of land use in cities. We examine their approach both in the section below and in Chapter 9.

THE LOS ANGELES SCHOOL AND POSTMODERNISM
[handwritten: — rejection of Chicago School]

Partly as a spinoff from the multiple nuclei theory, but more importantly as a rejection of the Chicago School, a new perspective—dubbed "the Los Angles School"—has emerged in recent decades. Focusing on the five-county region of Southern California (Los Angeles, Ventura, San Bernardino, Riverside, and Orange counties), its emphasis is on multi-centered, dispersed patterns of growth.

Perhaps the origins of this new perspective lie in the vivid depiction of the Los Angeles area by Rayner Banham (1973, 2001). He identified four basic "ecologies" that differed markedly from those advanced by the Chicago School. These were (1) surfurbia (the beach cities along the coast); (2) the foothills (the private enclaves of the privileged in such areas as Beverly Hills and Bel Air); (3) the plains of Id (the endless central flatlands); and (4) autopia (the freeways that exist as "a single comprehensible place" and "coherent state of mind"). Banham was partly harsh in his description of the "plains of Id," describing them as "gridded with endless streets, peppered endlessly with ticky-tacky houses clustered in indistinguishable neighborhoods, slashed across by endless freeways that have destroyed any community spirit that may have once existed." *[handwritten: boulevards, bou leu]*

Douglas Suisman (1990) reasoned that the city's boulevards, not its freeways, give form to its structure and communities. As surface streets—rather than the self-contained freeways

[handwritten at bottom: Rabat - Sale = Morocco]

with their on-off ramps—these boulevards connect different sections of the metropolis, provide an organizational framework for local travel destinations, and serve as a "filter to adjacent residential neighborhoods." For Suisman, boulevards are the defining element of the city's public space in its linkage between municipalities.

Edward W. Soja (2000) helped bring a postmodern perspective to this school of thought in his argument that Los Angeles is a decentralized metropolis with a fragmented power structure that is becoming increasingly pliant and disorganized. Although the center may hold as a strategic surveillance point for social control, radiating outward is a complex, highly fragmented mishmash of "wedges" and "citadels" separated by boulevards acting as corridors. With global capitalism serving as an underlying rationale, Soja views Los Angeles as resembling "a gigantic agglomeration of theme parks." Moreover, he suggests that the worldwide future of urbanism will resemble Los Angeles (Miller, 2000).

Michael J. Dear, a leading advocate of the Los Angeles School, shares Soja's belief about the city serving as a prototype for fragmentation and social differentiation in a global economy and postmodern culture. He adds that, as a consequence of physical sprawl, the city's "decentered politics" is one way that the city serves as a herald of the future. He describes the L.A. region as "split in many separate fiefdoms, with their leaders in constant battle." With over 100 municipalities in Los Angeles County (total population nearly 10 million), there are many problems of political representation. These include city–county government disputes, slow-growth/no-growth movements, and the difficulties associated with minority-group political participation. As a result, many alliances—formal and informal, legal and illegal—form to press their claims. Either autocratic—even corrupt—power will result, or else there will be "polarization along class, income, racial and ethnic lines" (2000:14–15).

Are the postmodernists correct in saying that cities are developing in a way that is no longer rational or manageable according to the old logic of urban development advocated by the urban ecologists? Is the evolution of Los Angeles that they describe the wave of the future? Only time will tell. Yet, with the Census Bureau projecting the Los Angeles region to increase by another 6 million by 2020 (essentially by the size of three Chicagos), its ongoing growth and development as the second largest metropolitan area in the United States is more than just an academic question.

SUMMARY

People founded cities at particular geographical sites that, at a minimum, supported a population's physical needs. Other human needs—political, religious, educational, and economic—also have played a role in locating cities.

Indeed, such factors helped forge two basic city shapes. Radiocentric cities have a tendency to emerge where religious and political forces are of central interest to a population; gridiron cities spring up when economic concerns predominate.

Robert Park and Ernest W. Burgess (the Chicago School) saw competition and population movement as responsible for shaping cities. Burgess's concentric zone model illustrates their ideas. But critics raised questions as to whether a biologically determined competition could explain people's behavior, and they pointed out numerous exceptions to the zonal hypothesis.

Recognizing the difficulties of the Chicago theory, Homer Hoyt suggested that many cities were organized in sectors, and that the prime cause of such sectoring was socioeconomic status. This was a helpful contribution but, like the Chicago model, it ultimately failed to account for the complexity of urban life.

An additional contribution was Harris and Ullman's multiple nuclei theory. This model abandoned any idea of a deterministic pattern of urban development: It held zones, sectors, and even the CBD as variable, with city form changing over time.

Social area analysis is an approach distinguished by its lack of theory. Its originators, Shevky, Bell, and Williams, simply examined the major social traits of the urban population. While their technique produced accurate descriptions of who lived where in cities, it had no ability to explain why people lived where they did. With earlier explanations of urban land use (the concentric zone, sector, and multiple nuclei theories) discredited as being too simple, urban ecology was at an impasse until the arrival of factorial ecology. This technique analyzes the significance of all factors that researchers think might be influential in urban land use. Its major finding has been that the social characteristics initially examined by social area analysis—socioeconomic status, family status, and ethnicity—do account for most of the residential land uses in cities studied thus far.

This discovery led Berry and Rees to hypothesize that the earlier theories all held a part of the truth. Cities do take the shape of concentric zones, sectors, and multiple nuclei according to the socioeconomic status, family status, and ethnic traits of their residents. While the Berry and Rees model does seem to apply to most cities in the contemporary Western world, there is doubt that it can account for the full range of historical and cross-cultural urban life.

The Los Angeles School is a recently evolved approach that uses a critical spatial perspective and postmodern viewpoint to understand the spread-city phenomenon. Besides more accurately explaining urbanism in Southern California than the urban ecologists could, its emphasis on political fragmentation and social differentiation calls our attention to the problems of governance and community within a metropolitan area increasingly impacted by global capitalism.

CONCLUSION

Urban land use is extremely complex. This chapter has traced increasingly sophisticated efforts to capture this multifaceted reality. We can be pleased with major advances, particularly in our understanding of how cities in the Western or modernizing world organize space, but more needs to be done. The recent evolution of edge cities is still new, but already the dominance of this urban form in North America suggests a need for further research. While we certainly need to pursue all leads in the field of urban human ecology, urbanists also need to consider the powerful influence that different cultural traditions and values have on city life. It is to this topic that we turn in the next chapter.

CHAPTER 8

COMPARATIVE URBANISM
The City and Culture

PROLOGUE: SIX MONTHS
IN IBADAN

Ibadan
/ Peace Corps

All her life Dorothy McAllister had lived in Boston. As her plane rose over Logan Airport, she glanced back at the city, marveling at what she saw—a thriving downtown with skyscrapers, interlocking highways and bridges overflowing with cars, factories coughing refuse into the air, and endless crowding of building upon building, from harbor to horizon, some ten miles in all directions. In most of the housing below lived families much like her own—Dad off to work on the subway or in the car in the morning, Mom taking care of the kids and working full- or part-time. Across town there were relatives—aunts, cousins, and grandparents—whom she saw occasionally. Whatever awaited her, she thought as the plane banked out over the Atlantic and Boston disappeared from view, would be only a variation on this common theme—for Boston was the very model of the great city.

She was wrong. Four days later, after delays, frustrating airline inefficiency and bureaucratic rigmarole, she arrived in Ibadan for six months with the Peace Corps. A major city in Nigeria, Ibadan was not like Boston at all. As her plane approached, she saw no skyscrapers, no network of superhighways, no clusters of factories, and, beyond the central city itself, nothing like Boston's residential suburbs. In their place were endless cultivated fields containing crops that looked unfamiliar to her (Ibadan grows yams, maize, cassavas, plantains, and cocoyams).

After Dorothy landed, the shock was even greater: This city's daily routines were so unlike those she knew as to be nearly incomprehensible. For instance, she found out that few men worked in offices. Over half went instead to work the farms outside the city. (She knew no one in Boston who was a farmer!) And they didn't ride; they walked. While some returned at night, many stayed away for days, even weeks. Men who were not farmers typically engaged in a trade, such as blacksmithing.

Most women worked at handicrafts, such as pottery or weaving. Heavy machinery was conspicuously absent and, except for one or two small firms, factories simply did not exist.

The main market of the city, where the farm produce and crafts were traded, was run predominantly by women, and the businesses of Ibadan in no way resembled the competitive free-enterprise system of Boston. Women traditionally traded in only one product, rarely branching out or expanding. Furthermore, vendors seemed to know just about everyone with whom they traded, and their success was as dependent on their personal relations with customers as on their business sense. This city didn't seem as cold and impersonal as those Dorothy had known before.

Family life, too, had little resemblance to what Dorothy knew in Boston. Mothers, fathers, and children lived together with relatives and tribal allies, often numbering over a thousand and linked by their land holdings, ancestry, and common religious heritage. Power and prestige within this "family" were distributed by age and sex. Some men were deemed more important than others, not as a result of being successful in business, but simply by virtue of being older. Wives (a man could have as many as four if he could support them) held status according to whether they had been married first, second, or later.

Finally, among these people there was a stronger identification with the city itself than was true in Boston. The king was the center of city life and, over the generations, all of Ibadan's descent groups had made pacts with the royal family. Every descent group had access to the king through local meetings and representatives on the king's council. Little distinction was made among descent groups in terms of prestige.

Months later, as her plane rose over Ibadan's central district and market and the city's fields came into view for the last time, Dorothy thought back about her earlier departure from Boston. She could not have imagined, then, a city as different as Ibadan; and yet, there it was, thriving and alive in the late twentieth century. She had learned that cities are not necessarily all variations on a single theme. They can be as different as night and day.

Intimate open-air markets are common in many parts of the world. Much more frequently than in the urban Western world, city life—such as here at Bara Bazaar in northern India—is based on kinship and ethnic ties. While the men work their farms or produce their crafts, the women sell the products in the market place, often knowing just about everyone with whom they do business.

THE CITY AND CULTURE

Why this difference? The answer is *culture.* Despite Louis Wirth's contention (see Chapter 5) that their size, density, and heterogeneity make cities characteristically impersonal, transient, and anonymous, it is not always so. Ibadan—a large city now with more than 1.8 million people—contradicts Wirth's characterization on virtually every count. In overlooking the importance of culture in urban life, Wirth failed to recognize that *the city is not an entity unto itself.* It reflects the larger culture of which it is a part. ~~Wirth said~~

In short, cities reflect and intensify the world's cultures. North American culture, with its emphasis on free enterprise and the nuclear family, creates cities such as Boston with skyscrapers downtown (which maximize trade advantages) and single-family dwellings all around the city. The culture of the Yoruba (the people who comprise the bulk of Ibadan's population) emphasizes personalized trade relations, handicrafts, and an extended family, and generates cities that are quite different.

Cities are never completely self-defining. They are human creations that display the same variety as all human culture. This chapter is about that all-important link between the city and culture. We can fully understand a city only by exploring the cultural patterns found throughout the larger society.

city's were impersonal

THE CITY AND THE HINTERLAND

. . . those that are good manners at the court are as ridiculous in the country as the behavior of the country is most mockable at the court.

Shakespeare, *As You Like It*, III, 2

Interdependencies

Shakespeare noted something that everyone knows: Country and city ways are often quite different. Yet we must be wary of overgeneralization. For example, in Ibadan, with the city's fields so close by and farmers such a large part of the city's population, it is virtually impossible to distinguish between city and country ways (Lloyd, 1986). Indeed, in any location, city and country are not independent of each other at all, but rather have a symbiotic relationship.

Consider this oft-forgotten connection: *Much of the population of the city initially came from the hinterland.* Throughout history, the migration of people seeking a better life transformed city and country alike. To take but one example, during the great expansion of European cities in the nineteenth century, England changed from an almost completely rural society to a nation in which over 60 percent of the population lived in cities. Table 8–1 presents these population shifts in England and Wales during the second half of that century. In 40 years, the number of towns nearly doubled, the urban population more than doubled, and the rural population noticeably decreased.

The relationship between the city and its hinterland involves much more than just the dynamics of migration, however. There is also a reciprocal dependence on the resources each supplies. Because a large proportion of city dwellers (even in Ibadan) engage in specialized occupations other than agriculture, the hinterland must supply the city's food. Many of the specialty occupations of the city—such as weaving or steel manufacturing—depend on the hinterland's raw materials. Conversely, the hinterland obtains many of its goods—the clothes made by weavers, tractors made with the steel—from the city.

But perhaps the most important link between city and hinterland (Shakespeare notwithstanding) is the reciprocal shaping of lifestyles. Migrants who swell the city's ranks bring to the city their cultural traditions. The result is a living kaleidoscope of human behavior, ranging all the way from groups who devotedly try to continue living as they did in the "old country" (New York's Hasidic Jews, for example) to the various "hyphenated" Americans (Asian-Americans, Hispanic-Americans) who maintain only some of the old ways in their new urban setting.

At the same time, other rural influences, including traditional folk music, art, and literature, are constantly altering the city's character. Country music, in fact, is exclusively played on at least one radio station in nearly every major U.S. city, and "country rock" is a peculiar rural–urban musical confluence.

Very common in North American and European cities (less so in African cities like Ibadan) is the human cultural hybrid—the urban person who takes a little bit from many of the originally rural lifestyles that exist in the city and integrates them into a new lifestyle altogether. Such a person was Mayor Fiorello La Guardia of New York, as described in the Looking Back box on page 228. Perhaps it would be fair to say that a little bit of La Guardia exists in most city dwellers today.

This influence works in two ways, however. Just as the city receives much from the countryside, it typically returns the favor, radiating outward an influence far beyond its borders. In fact, many sociologists think that this influence, in modern times, far outstrips the hinterland's effect on urban affairs.

TABLE 8–1   **Urban and Rural Population in England and Wales, 1851–1891**

	Urban		Rural
	Number of Towns	**Total Population**	**Total Population**
1851	580	8,990,809	8,936,800
1861	781	10,960,998	9,105,225
1871	938	14,041,404	8,670,862
1881	967	17,636,646	8,337,793
1891	1,011	20,895,504	8,107,021

Source: Adapted from Adna Weber, *The Growth of Cities* (New York: Columbia University Press, 1899), Table XVIII.

LOOKING BACK

Mayor Fiorello La Guardia of New York

To put it sociologically, La Guardia was a marginal man who lived in the edge of many cultures. . . . Tammany Hall may have been the first to exploit the vote-getting value of eating gefullte fish with the Jews, goulash with the Hungarians, sauerbraten with Germans, spaghetti with Italians, and so on indefinitely, but this unorthodox Republican not only dined every bit as shrewdly but also spoke, according to the occasion, in Yiddish, Hungarian, German, Serbian-Croatian, or plain New York English. Half Jewish and half Italian, born in Greenwich Village yet raised in Arizona, married first to a Catholic and then to a Lutheran but himself a Mason and an Episcopalian, Fiorello La Guardia was a Mr. Brotherhood Week all by himself.

Source: Arthur Mann, cited in E. Digby Baltzell, *The Protestant Establishment* (New York: Vintage, 1964), p. 29.

Urban Dominance

"I cannot see that London has any great advantage over the country," said Mrs. Bennett, "except the shops and public places. The country is a vast deal pleasanter, is it not . . . ?"

Jane Austen, *Pride and Prejudice,* 1813

[handwritten: Argued that country was better than city]

Thus Mrs. Bennett, engaged in a verbal duel with some of London's high society, defended her rural environment in the early part of the nineteenth century. Her championing of the country was not well received. Everyone present—her own daughters included—subsequently told her that, like it or not, London had numerous advantages over the countryside, among them a greater diversity of people and, well, there was just so much more to do in London.

Right or wrong, Mrs. Bennett was wiser than she knew, for her allusion to what she saw as the city's one advantage—its shops and public places—suggests why the city's influence has spread so far beyond its physical boundaries. As Louis Wirth argued, the city's importance

. . . may be regarded as a consequence of the concentration on [it] of industrial, commercial, financial, and administrative facilities and activities, transportation and communication lines, and cultural and recreational equipment such as the press, radio stations, theaters, libraries, museums, concert halls, operas, hospitals, colleges, research and publishing centers, professional organizations, and religious and welfare institutions. (1964:63)

Indeed, North American cities have maintained cultural dominance over society far out of proportion to the number of city dwellers since the coming of European settlers in the seventeenth century. Moreover, as we described in Chapter 3, the importance of early eastern settlements, most notably Boston, Charleston, Montreal, Newport, New York, and Philadelphia, was supplemented by that of newer cities as the population moved westward to such places as Chicago, Kansas City, St. Louis, and Toronto. In the Far West, especially following the completion of the transcontinental railroad to San Francisco in 1869, towns and cities continued to stand at the center of social life. This fact was observed by Josiah Strong, who commented in 1885, "It is the cities and towns which frame state constitutions, make laws, create public opinion, establish social usages and fix standards of morals in the West" (206).

[handwritten: Josiah Strong said
he said → towns & cities stand at
the create in center of social life]

North American growth is thus intertwined with the story of the development of cities. Cities—consistently the centers of an expanding market, the loci of advances in communication, and the sources of leadership in politics, fashion, and the arts—have a long linkage with cultural firsts: the first daily newspaper (Philadelphia, 1784), the first stock exchange (New York, 1792), and the first telephone system (Boston, 1877; linked to New York in 1884, to Denver in 1911, and to San Francisco in 1915).

Such a pattern of urban dominance over the broader society is hardly limited to North America. We find a description of the same phenomenon in Alexis de Tocqueville's historical account (1856/1955) of the French Revolution of 1789. Beginning in the 1600s as the feudal system weakened, French life increasingly became centralized in Paris. As a result, when the Revolution erupted in Paris, it quickly carried the rest of French society along with it.

Tocqueville noted that, in times past, Paris had been "no more than the largest town in France . . . [but by] 1789 things were very different; it [was] no exaggeration to say that Paris was France" (1955:72). The city controlled the nation's economic, intellectual, and political lifeblood. This urban dominance was also evident as one left Paris for the countryside. Inquiring as to the political climate of the outlying areas, English observer Arthur Young heard time and again: "We are only a provincial town; we must wait till Paris gives us a lead" (Tocqueville, 1955:74).

That is exactly what Paris did. It is one of the remarkable facts of history that the cultural ideas ("Liberty! Equality! Brotherhood!") that were to transform France and much of Western civilization, in conjunction with the American Revolution a decade earlier, were largely city born.

Urban dominance is thus a central pattern of the modern and historical world. Sometimes, however, urban influence is not so welcome, as the people of Grafton County, New Hampshire, have decided. Their views are described in the Cityscape box on page 230.

In other instances urban dominance is more subtle, as in the case of "Springdale" (a pseudonym), a small town in upstate New York. With its quiet streets and surrounding rural countryside, it would seem a world apart from the city. The appearance is deceiving.

While residents of the town display a great deal of pride in their traditions of independence and self-sufficiency—values they associate with small-town life—they also have come to recognize that these sentiments are beginning to ebb away. The average Springdaler, wrote sociologists Arthur Vidich and Joseph Bensman, who studied the town in the late 1950s,

> . . . sees that the urban and metropolitan society is technically and culturally superior to his own community. He sees this in his everyday life when he confronts the fact that his community cannot provide him with everything he needs: almost everyone goes to the city for shopping and entertainment; large numbers of people are dependent on the radio and television; and everyone realizes that rural life would be drastically altered without cars and refrigerators. (1968:79)

It may be edge cities and not older cities that impact on many rural landscapes today, but this is merely a newer form of urban dominance. Nor are these the only links that bind the residents of Springdale to the larger urban society. Their lives are influenced by outside specialists from organizations such as the state agricultural extension service, as well as by their own college-trained professionals. Additional organizations that serve to "import" the culture of the urban society include such national organizations as the Odd Fellows and the Kiwanis Club. Perhaps more important, the economic and political life of the town is shaped more by state and federal agencies than by local entities. Taxes, education for the town's children, and the price of local farmers' milk are all increasingly subject to outside forces that are mostly city based. Vidich and Bensman concluded that, despite the desires and pretensions of the townspeople, most "plans and decisions that refer directly to the community are made from a distance by invisible agents and institutions"

CITYSCAPE

The Invasion of the City Slickers
New Hampshire.

[What city people who move to the country] bring along is a series of unconscious assumptions. It might be better for rural America if they brought a few sticks of dynamite, or a can of arsenic.

Take a typical example. Mr. and Mrs. Nice are Bostonians. They live a couple of miles off Route 128 in a four-bedroom house. He's a partner in an ad agency; she has considerable talent as an artist. For some years they've had a second home in northern New Hampshire. The kids love it up there in Grafton County.

For some years, too, both Nices have been feeling they'd like to simplify their lives. They look with increasing envy on their New Hampshire neighbors, who never face a morning traffic jam, or an evening one, either; who don't have a long drive to the country on Friday night and a long drive back on Sunday; who aren't cramped into a suburban lot; who live in harmony with the natural rhythm of the year; who think the rat race is probably some minor event at a county fair.

One Thursday evening Don Nice says to Sue that he's been talking to the other partners, and they've agreed there's no reason he can't do some of his work at home. If he's in the office Wednesday and Thursday every week, why the rest of the time he can stay in touch by telephone. Sue, who has been trapped all year as a Brownie Scout leader and who has recently had the aerial snapped off her car in Boston, is delighted. She reflects happily that in their little mountain village you don't even need to lock your house, and there is no Brownie troop. "You're wonderful," she tells Don.

So the move occurs. In most ways Don and Sue are very happy. They raise practically all their own vegetables the first year; Sue takes up cross-country skiing. Don personally splits some of the wood they burn in their new woodstove.

But there are some problems. The first one Sue is conscious of is the school. It's just not very good. It's clear to Sue almost immediately that the town desperately needs a new school building—and also modern playground equipment, new school buses, more and better art instruction at the high school, a different principal. Don is as upset as Sue

(1968:81). Thus, just as Springdalers now go periodically to the world of the city, the world of the city has subtly transformed, for better or for worse, Springdale and communities like it.

THE CITY AND CIVILIZATION

Cities have always been the fireplaces of civilization, whence light and heat radiated out into the dark, cold world.

Theodore Parker,
nineteenth-century U.S. preacher

The reason for the city's increasing dominance in modern affairs, as we have hinted already, is that everything human—art, music, business, traditions, what we love and hate—converges there. The city does not create a way of life all its own but rather provides the setting where any way of life, any cultural tradition, can intensify and recreate itself in a manner not possible in other settings. For example, Socrates, Plato, and Aristotle all lived in Hellenic Athens, sharing ideas and challenging each other. This simply would not have occurred had when they discover that only about 40 percent of the kids who graduate from that high school go on to any form of college. The rest do native things like becoming farmers, and mechanics, and joining the Air Force. An appalling number of the girls marry within twelve months after graduation. How are Jeanie and Don, Jr., going to get into good colleges from this school? . . . Pretty soon Sue and Don join an informal group of newcomers in town who are working to upgrade education. All they want for starters is the new building ($2.8 million) and a majority of their kind on the school board.

As for Don, though he really enjoys splitting the wood—in fact, next year he's planning to get a chainsaw and start cutting a few trees of his own—he also likes to play golf. There's no course within twenty miles. Some of the nice people he's met in the education lobby feel just as he does. They begin to discuss the possibility of a nine-hole course. The old farmer who owns the land they have in mind seems to be keeping only four or five cows on it, anyway. Besides, taxes are going up, and the old fellow is going to have to sell, sooner or later. (Which is too bad, of course. Don and Sue both admire the local farmers, and they're sincerely sorry whenever one has to quit.)

Over the next several years, Don and Sue get more and more adjusted to rural living—and they also gradually discover more things that need changing. For example, the area needs a good French restaurant. And it needs a much better airport. At present there are only two flights a day to Boston, and because of the lack of sophisticated equipment, even they are quite often canceled. If Don wants to be sure of getting down for an important meeting, he has to drive. Sue would be glad of more organized activities for the kids. There's even talk of starting a Brownie troop.

In short, if enough upper-middle-class people move to a rural town, they are naturally going to turn it into a suburb of the nearest city. For one generation it will be a nice and truly rustic suburb, with real farms dotted around it, and real natives speaking their minds at town meeting. Then as the local people are gradually taxed out of existence (or at least out of town), one more piece of rural America has died.

Source: Text excerpt, "The Invasion of the City Slickers" reprinted from Noel Perrin, "Rural Area: Permit Required," in *Country Journal* (April 1980), pp. 34–35. Copyright © 1980 *Country Journal*. Reprinted by permission of *Country Journal* and Noel Perrin.

they all lived in rural hamlets, cut off from one another.

Nowhere is this process of intensification represented more clearly than in the suggestion that the city encapsulates a whole culture. Throughout history, writers have seen the city as capturing the essence of human civilization. Indeed, Euripides, the classical Greek playwright, maintained: "The first requisite to happiness is birth in a great city." The Critical Thinking box on page 232 illustrates not only the connections among our most common words about cities and civilization,

but also the linkage between city and culture as expressed in the writings of some of history's most important urbanists.

Is the city truly synonymous with civilization? To find out, let's examine in more detail the ideas of Oswald Spengler and Lewis Mumford.

Oswald Spengler

Oswald Spengler (1880–1936) was a German philosopher who saw in cities the drama of the rise and fall of civilization. He contended that cities developed, ultimately dominated a

CRITICAL THINKING

The City and Civilization

City Words

Those of us who live in the city should be grateful to our language, because the words that have to do with the city are usually flattering. We city dwellers, at least in ancient days, were supposed to be more *civil* in our manners and more *civilized* in our ways than others, for both of these words *civil* and *civilized* are the eventual children of the Latin term *civis* which meant "one who lives in a city." All city folks, you see, were regarded as automatically cultured and well housebroken. And from ancient Latin we have borrowed the word *urbs* which also meant city, and we used it to create the word *urbane* which describes the smooth manners that were presumed to be characteristic of *metropolitan* society. The Greek parts of the word *metropolitan* are *metro*, "mother," and *polis*, "city," so a *metropolis* is the "mother city" or the chief or capital city of a country, and he who lives in a *metropolis* is supposed to inherit the sophisticated ideas and manners that go with such a center. And from the

Greek *polis*, "city," we inherited our word *politic*. If you are *politic*, you are expedient, shrewd, discreet, and artful in your address and your procedure, which sounds dangerously like a city slicker!

City Culture

> Just as the beginning of Western Civilization is marked by permanent settlement of formerly nomadic peoples . . . so the beginning of what is distinctly modern in our civilization is best signaled by the growth of great cities. (Louis Wirth, 1938)

> The city is . . . the natural habitat of civilized man. (Robert Park, 1916)

> [The city is] the most precious invention of civilization, second only to language itself in the transmission of culture. (Lewis Mumford, 1961)

> All great Cultures are town-Cultures. . . . World history is city history. Peoples, states, politics, religion, all arts, and all sciences rest upon one phenomenon . . . the town. (Oswald Spengler, 1928)

Source: City Words extract: Wilfred Funk, *Word Origins* (New York: Bell, 1978), pp. 97–98.

society, and then declined, carrying with them the culture built over generations and centuries. The cyclical element in Spengler's theory (generally considered too simplistic by contemporary social scientists) is less important for our purposes than his belief that "all great cultures are town-cultures" and that "world history is city history."

Spengler believed strongly that human civilization takes on distinctive qualities in the city. At some point in its development, the "soul" of the city emerges: "Out of the rustic group of

farms and cottages . . . arises a totality. And the whole lives, breathes, grows, and acquires a face and inner form and history" (1928/1969: 65–66). Spengler believed that the countryside never has a soul in this sense; it is a "landscape" at most, never a "world."

Moreover, the city senses its own power and uniqueness:

> . . . it is a place from which the countryside is henceforth regarded, felt, and experienced as "environs," as something different and subordinate. From now on there are two lives, that of

the inside and that of the outside, and the peasant understands this just as clearly as the townsman. . . . The new Soul of the City speaks a new language, which soon becomes tantamount to the language of the culture itself. (1969:66, 68)

Thus, the essence of ancient Egypt was symbolized by Thebes, ancient Greece by Athens, the Roman Empire by Rome, Islam by Baghdad, and prerevolutionary France by Paris. Indeed, Spengler believed that whole periods of European civilization were manifest only in cities. Is it not true, he asked, "that the Renaissance style flourished only in the Renaissance city, the Baroque only in the Baroque city?" (1969:68).

Modern sociologists generally view Spengler's contribution to urban sociology as modest because few accept his cyclical ideas of historical change. Yet he correctly sensed the connection between city and civilization, an idea developed extensively by a U.S. urbanist whose work we will discuss next.

Lewis Mumford

Lewis Mumford (1897–1952) traced the cultural importance of cities through Western history. Based on historical and comparative evidence, he argued that the city has indeed been at the very center of Western civilization from its beginnings.

Mumford believed that, of all creatures, only human beings seem to be aware of themselves as fundamentally distinctive. We can think, invent, and wonder about such things as life, death, sex, and god(s). In the course of human evolution, Mumford reasoned, people attached these thoughts to places. The earliest centers of this kind were probably caves and places of burial. These sites were symbolic centers to which wandering groups could return periodically to ponder the mysteries they wished to understand. Thus began civilization. "In the earliest gathering about a grave or a painted symbol, a great stone or a sacred grove, one has the beginning of a succession of civic institutions that range from the temple to the astronomical observatory,

from the theater to the university" (Mumford, 1961:9).

As time passed and technology improved, some people began living at these places permanently: The shrine became a camp, then a village, and finally a town. Mumford (like Spengler) suggests that, at a certain point, the cultural ideas, the people, and the place all jelled as the city emerged (see the Critical Thinking box on page 234).

Thenceforth, the story of civilization became the story of urban history. Yet we must be careful here. We often assume that civilization automatically means progress—that what exists today is somehow a better form of what went before. Neither Spengler nor Mumford meant to suggest this notion of cultural evolution; rather, their idea was that the city was culture "writ large," the living embodiment of a society's or epoch's ideas. Cities did not inevitably progress. In them, as already mentioned, Spengler saw the rise and fall of civilization; and, like Max Weber before him (Chapter 5), Mumford believed that cities better than today's existed in the past—in Hellenic Athens, for example.

Similarly, despite Spengler's and Mumford's claims, we should not link all of civilization to cities, powerful as they may be in concentrating culture. Anthropologists have long insisted that we must look carefully at the lives of all of a society's people. Culture and civilization are just as real in the countryside and the small village, although they may be in other forms.

From Mumford and Spengler, then, we learn that, although the city and civilization are not precisely synonymous, the city has a unique power to intensify and symbolize culture. Any city will dynamically and intensely reflect the characteristics of its surrounding culture; however, because cultural patterns vary so widely, cities may be markedly different from one another. In the following case studies we will read about two cities, Peking during the Ming Dynasty (1368–1644 C.E.) and Hellenic Athens of the fifth century B.C.E.—capitals of vastly different civilizations and separated by more than 1,500 years.

CRITICAL THINKING

The Crystallization of the City

. . . This new urban mixture resulted in an enormous expansion of human capabilities in every direction. The city effected a mobilization of manpower, a command over long-distance transportation, an intensification of communication over long distances in space and time, an outburst of invention along with a large-scale development of civil engineering, and, not least, it promoted a tremendous further rise in agricultural productivity. . . . When all this happened, the archaic village culture yielded to urban "civilization," that peculiar combination of creativity and control, of expression and repression, of tension and release, whose outward manifestation has been the historic city. From its origins onward, indeed, the city may be described as a structure specially equipped to store and transmit the goods of civilization, sufficiently condensed to afford the maximum amount of facilities in a minimum space, but also capable of structural enlargement to enable it to find a place for the changing needs and the more complex forms of a growing society and its cumulative social heritage. The invention of such forms as the written record, the library,

the archive, the school, and the university is one of the earliest and most characteristic achievements of the city. . . .

What happened . . . with the rise of cities, was that many functions that had heretofore been scattered and unorganized were brought together within a limited area, and the components of the community were kept in a state of dynamic tension and interaction. In this union, made almost compulsory by the strict enclosure of the city wall, the already well-established parts of the protocity—shrine, spring, village, market stronghold—participated in the general enlargement of concentration of numbers, and underwent a structural differentiation that gave them forms recognizable in every subsequent phase of urban culture. The city proved not merely a means of expressing in concrete terms the magnification of sacred and secular power, but in a manner that went far beyond any conscious intention it also enlarged all the dimensions of life. Beginning as a representation of the cosmos, a means of bringing heaven down to earth, the city became a symbol of the possible.

Source: Excerpts from Lewis Mumford, "The Crystallization of the City" in *The City in History: Its Origin, Its Transformation, and Its Prospects.* © 1961 and renewed 1989 by Lewis Mumford. Reprinted with permission of Harcourt, Inc.

❖ CASE STUDY ❖
Ming Peking

Situated on the northern seacoast, China's capital city is centered around the Forbidden City and Tiananmen Square, the world's biggest public square, with an area of 98 acres. Now a city of 12 million people, Beijing (formerly called Peking) has a 3,000-year history and contains fascinating remnants of its glorious past.

Established in northeastern China to protect the country from invaders from the north, Beijing grew into a city at least several centuries before the birth of Christ. During the thirteenth century C.E., when the Yuan (Mongol) emperor ruled China, Kublai Khan transformed Beijing into a capital city. Soon after the overthrow of the Yuan by the Ming Dynasty in 1368, the Emperor Yung Lo spared no expense in turning the city into a monument to all of Chinese culture and to himself as symbolic head of that culture. It was a massive job. Wagonloads "of a specially chosen marble were brought a distance of 1,500 miles from Uyn-nan and this precious material was used to renew and extend the palace and to clothe the city's roads and bridges with fresh dignity and beauty" (Loewe, 1964:241).

Physical Structure

The design, deliberately created to symbolize everything vital to Chinese life, arranged the whole city on a perfect north–south axis, around which were temples and altars. Perhaps no better example exists of Lewis Mumford's idea of the city as a physical container, for Ming Beijing literally revealed the city within the city, surrounding the all-important core where the emperor lived (see Figure 8–1).

The city was about 25 square miles in area and was composed of two major sections, each roughly rectangular in shape. Beijing's southern section, known as the Outer City or Chinese City, contained most of the city's population, probably about 320,000 people at the end of the thirteenth century (Chandler, 1987:356).

The northern section, however, was of quite another character. Known by the name Tartar City or Inner City, this area was surrounded by a massive wall about 50 feet high and just as thick. Indeed, whereas in the West the words for *city* are linked to the words for *civilization* and *politics*, in Chinese the word for *city* literally means "wall," indicating in yet another way that the city was a container of major cultural significance (Murphy, 1984:189). All city streets were arranged in a gridiron, with gates through the wall arranged symmetrically.

Centrally located within the walls of the Tartar City was another area, called the Imperial City. Protected by yet another wall, and including about 5 square miles of parklike land complete with artificially constructed lakes and hills, this was the focus of the political and religious power and splendor of Ming civilization. In the midst of this constructed urban tranquility, and surrounded by a moat and yet another defensive wall, were the palaces and

residences—facing south—of the emperor. This was called the Purple City by the Chinese and later dubbed the Forbidden City by Europeans on their realization that access was gained only by the emperor's personal decree. Just to the north was a large, artificially constructed mound of earth, Coal Hill, on which stood temples prominently visible above the city.

Symbolism

Ming Peking was based on elaborate Chinese cosmology (Wright, 1977). The temples and altars were religious symbols of the sun, earth, and, most important, heaven.

Chinese astronomers had discovered long before Peking was built that the center of the heavens was the North Star, around which everything revolved. On earth—the human universe—the Chinese believed that everything revolved around the "Son of Heaven," the emperor. As the northernmost major city of China, Peking thus became the emperor's capital. The importance of the north was also evident in the city's location on a north–south axis and by the fact that the emperor could be reached only by traveling north along the Great Processional Way. Even the name of the emperor's city, the Purple City, was chosen because the North Star gave off a purple hue in the night sky.

The symbolism did not stop there, however. The colors and height of all buildings had cultural meaning. Peasants, lowly and unimportant, were allowed only houses of one story and could paint their roofs only a dull gray. In the Imperial City various functionaries couldn't have houses of more than one story either, but to signify their higher status they were allowed roofs painted green, red, or purple, depending on their role. Only in the Forbidden City itself were buildings allowed to be more than one story. Their roofs were painted a bright gold-yellow, symbolizing the life-giving (sunlike) qualities of the emperor's rule. As an ancient Chinese text proclaimed, the emperor's role was "to stand in the center of the earth and stabilize people within the four

FIGURE 8–1   Ming Peking

Source: Adapted from Roderick MacFarquhar, *The Forbidden City* (New York: Newsweek Books, 1972), p. 46.

seas." He did this within the Forbidden City, "the place where earth and sky met, where the four seasons merge, where wind and rain are gathered in, and where yin and yang are in harmony"[1] (MacFarquhar, 1972:79).

Given his importance, it is little wonder that the emperor had everything for the "good life" within a stone's throw. The construction of the Forbidden City was a marvel of urban design, as can be seen by carefully examining the buildings shown in Figure 8–2. Note especially the buildings in the center—the emperor's sole preserve. The first group, the buildings immediately to the north of the Supreme Imperial Gate, are buildings of state: the Hall of Supreme Harmony was reserved for special state occasions, such as the New Year's ceremony and the emperor's birthday; the smaller Hall of Central Harmony was the place where the emperor prepared himself and waited for functions; the Hall of Protecting Harmony was for the reception of visitors and for day-to-day governance. The second group of central buildings—to the north of these state buildings —were the emperor's residences. Entering by the Gate of Heavenly Purity, one found the Palace of Heavenly Purity, the emperor's quarters; next was the Hall of Vigorous Fertility, which, its name notwithstanding, was where official seals were stored; finally, the Palace of Earthly Tranquility, where the empress lived (MacFarquhar, 1972).

Ming Peking is a striking example of the city's ability to intensify culture. Peking was a symbolic world, a whole city built on the cultural themes of harmony with nature, security (city within city), and power. Each "layer of the onion" reemphasized the whole and led to the vital, omnipotent center, the emperor.

This particular symbolism probably means little to us, but we can imagine what it meant to the Pekingese. In a similar manner, our cities transmit and magnify our culture. What

[1]The two competing forces of nature in Chinese philosophy.

is important in our culture is "writ large" in Boston, Birmingham, and Boise. We don't have cities within cities or predominant religious symbolism, like Peking. We have, as Dorothy McAllister saw as she flew over Boston on her way to Ibadan, commercial skyscrapers, fast-moving automobiles on superhighways, and private single-family houses. What might such constructions say about what is culturally important to us?

❖ ━━━━━━━ ❖ ━━━━━━━ ❖

❖ CASE STUDY ❖
Hellenic Athens

There is small risk of exaggerating the differences between Ming Peking and Hellenic Athens, situated on the rocky northern coast of the Mediterranean. During a period of barely two generations in the fifth century B.C.E., between about 480 and the start of the Peloponnesian Wars in 431, a civilization took form which Mumford has described as "a far richer efflorescence of human genius than history anywhere else records, except perhaps for Renaissance Florence" (1961:167). Imagine an almost simultaneous development of the arts of painting, sculpture, and architecture; the realization of a rationally structured democracy; and the birth of a body of philosophy that remains at the center of Western thinking today. At the heart of this Golden Age was the city of Athens. "Justly or not," wrote Eric Carlton (1977:77), "Athenian culture has become almost synonymous with the Greek achievement."

The Preclassical Period

Four migrating tribes settled Athens as early as 2000 B.C.E., and eventually the Greek peninsula came under the control of feudal overlords who called themselves, perhaps with not the greatest modesty, the *aristoi* (or aristocracy; literally, "the best people"). By the eighth century

FIGURE 8–2 The Forbidden City

Source: Roderick MacFarquhar, *The Forbidden City* (New York: Newsweek Books, 1972), p. 73.

B.C.E., these overlords were in charge of several hundred independent Greek city-states, or *poli* (the source of our contemporary word *political* and of the urban suffix *-polis*). Over the next two centuries the city-states grew rich, as technology and overseas trade improved and military conquests multiplied.

Ironically, it was this very success that led to the aristocrats' downfall. The improvement of trade created a wealthy middle class that began to demand participation in city rule, and the martial victories evolved a warrior class with both the skills and arms to take over the city-states. In a series of coups d'état between 660 and 550 B.C.E., they did just that in many trade and maritime city-states, earning in the process the name *tyrannos* (Burn, 1970).

Tyrants or not, the preeminence of warriors during this period was to prove fortuitous. Early in the fifth century B.C.E., a series of Persian invasions threatened the Greek peninsula. Together, Athens and her rival city-state, the more militaristic Sparta, finally routed the invaders in 479 B.C.E., setting the stage for what many regard as the city's—and perhaps even Western history's—greatest moment.

The Golden Age

In the fifth century B.C.E., the city of Athens had a population of roughly 150,000 (Bowra, 1977) and was not much more than 1 square mile in size. We can best understand Athenian life in the Golden Age as the celebration of human possibilities. "Men come together in the city to live," exclaimed Aristotle in a timeless salute to the human possibilities of city life, and "they remain there in order to live the good life." What was this "good life"? In his famous funeral oration in honor of Athenian victims of the Peloponnesian Wars, Athenian statesman Pericles conveyed its essence: The Greek ideal, he said, began with the principle of democracy "which favors the many instead of the few."

The Athenian belief in democracy was grounded historically, for the city-states that preceded the Golden Age were independent units. Indeed, so independent were they that one cannot speak of one "nation," even at the apex of Greek culture. Each city-state pursued its own ends and believed that no one had the right to dictate otherwise.

This fierce sense of independence also characterized the Greek citizen. In 600 B.C.E., with dissatisfaction rife, Athens was on the verge of revolution. To avert this, Solon, an aristocrat, was chosen as arbitrator. He immediately proposed a reorganization of the Athenian constitution that allowed all "free citizens" (excluding women, slaves, and foreigners) a place in the city's governing body, the Assembly. He established the People's Council, numbering some 400, with the charge of preparing the Assembly's agenda. Members were chosen from the four main Athenian tribes (a hundred each), thereby preventing dominance by any one group. Finally, government officials were made accountable to the Assembly for their work each year. Political participation was mandatory for all citizens; without regard to "obscurity of conditions," each was required to take part in the public life of the city.

Athenian democracy was a brilliant innovation, affording all free citizens participation in government. It also allowed the citizen the right to live as one chose within that overarching system. Classical Athens did not stand as a monument to an all-powerful god or to a ruling family, but rather to all free citizens. In one of the great dramas of the age, Sophocles' *Antigone*, we find this statement (which could well serve as a critique of Ming Peking): "A city that is of one man is no city."

The ideals of human development and versatility were vital to Hellenic civilization. A primary cultural value was that all citizens should strive for refinement, although without extravagance, and pursue individual well-being— a fusion of the well-tutored body, mind, and spirit. Athenians developed the body through constant work, exercise, and sport, including the Olympic Games, in which individuals from different city-states competed for the glory of their state. Continual dialogue provoked the mind. In their leisurely society citizens often spent much of the day talking about the deeper matters of life. Plato's dialogues between the great philosopher Socrates and his friends are an excellent example. Edith Hamilton beautifully summarizes one such dialogue in the Urban Living box.

Athenians even managed the life of the spirit differently. For example, no system of formal or mystical religion placed the gods at great distance from the people of the city. In Peking the priests were "specialists" sequestered within the walls of the Forbidden City, but in Athens the "priest was just another conscientious layman whose amateurism was not even dignified by prophetic presumptions; his religious duties were simply his civic duties" (Carlton, 1977:226). This ideal of participation meant that temples such as the Parthenon were always open to people, who typically marked their religious observances informally, frequently outdoors.

Indeed, as Greek civilization entered the Golden Age, the gods themselves became less abstract and more like human beings. They were the objects of jokes, criticism, and bargains, but—all the same—they were used as models for human development. As William Chase Greene (1923:226) noted, the Olympian gods "became the symbol of something nobler in human nature," something within the reach of human endeavor.

A tripartite focus on body, mind, and spirit was the unique combination that formed the crux of Athens's success. By developing serious interests in all three areas, the Athenian indirectly kept any one area from becoming all-absorbing. This focus kept more practical areas of life—politics or economics, for example—in check. Too much politics breeds overemphasis on power and control; too much economics cultivates obsession with wealth and material goods. For a brief period, the citizens of Athens avoided these pitfalls.

Behind the Glory

Athens's moment at the pinnacle of urban history was not to last; it was undermined eventually by the culture's own egocentrism and exploitative practices. The wealth and leisurely pace of Athens in its Golden Age rested in large measure on the goods and services of others. During its successful expansion before the fifth century B.C.E., Athens had conquered many other city-states and regions. From them Athens extracted tribute in materials, taxes, and people—many of whom became slaves; Mumford (1961) has estimated that one-third of the city's population held this unhappy status. Women, too, were excluded from citizenship and were relegated to household duties. Themselves hesitant to enter into the service of others, the elite Athenian citizens benefited from the widespread use of such human servants (Gouldner, 1971).

Elitism reared its head in yet another, more immediately destructive, way. The Athenians refused citizenship to foreigners, many of whom, as traders, had become permanent residents. This robbed the citizenry of potentially invigorating new ideas, forcing the foreign population into an exclusive concern with economic matters. Demoralized, these traders devoted their energies to moneymaking and material consumption. In time, they became indifferent to government so long as they were free to make a profit. By the end of the fourth century B.C.E., profit making had become the center of city life, and the older idea that economic activity was simply a means to a more holistic life—so central to the health of the city—began to wane (Mumford, 1961:150–55).

Finally, as the Golden Age reached its climax, Athenians came to see their city as the most civilized in the world and themselves as the apotheosis of humanity. They believed they could learn from no one. The city became static, and demoralization spread further (Mumford, 1961).

Into this setting came the Peloponnesian Wars, begun in 431 B.C.E. between Athens and Sparta. Soundly defeated, Athens surrendered in 404 B.C.E. In total confusion and in public contradiction of all their democratic ideals, in 399 B.C.E. the Athenians tried Socrates and condemned him to death for "undermining the state by his endless public questionings."

The handwriting was on the wall. In 338 B.C.E., the Athenians put up belated opposition to an invasion force led by Philip of Macedon. Their defeat at the Battle of Chaeronea has been called "the death of the free polis."

URBAN LIVING

An Afternoon with Socrates

The most charmingly leisured of Plato's dialogues is, perhaps, the *Phaedrus.* "Where are you bound?" Socrates asks Phaedrus, to which the young man answers that he is going for a walk outside the wall to refresh himself after a morning spent in talk with a great rhetorician: "You shall hear about it if you can spare time to accompany me." Well, Socrates says, he so longs to hear it that he would go all the way to Megara and back rather than miss it. With this, Phaedrus begins to be doubtful if he can do justice to the great man: "Believe me, Socrates, I did not learn his very words—oh, no. Still, I have a general notion of what he said and can give you a summary." "Yes, dear lad," replies Socrates, "but you must first of all show what you have under your cloak—for that roll I suspect is the actual discourse, and much as I love you, I am not going to have you exercise your memory at my expense." Phaedrus gives in—he will read the whole essay; but where shall they sit? Oh, yes, under "that tallest plane-tree, where there is

shade and gentle breezes and grass on which to sit or lie." "Yes," Socrates answers, "a fair resting place, full of summer sounds and scents, the stream deliciously cool to the feet, and the grass like a pillow gently sloping to the head. I shall lie down and do you choose the position you can best read in. Begin." A number of hours are spent under that plane-tree, discussing "the nature of the soul—though her true form be ever a theme of large and more than mortal discourse"; and "beauty shining in company with celestial forms"; and "the soul of the lover that follows the beloved in modesty and holy fear"; and "the heavenly blessings of friendship"; and "all the great arts, which require high speculation about the truths of nature"; and men who "are worthy of a proud name befitting their serious pursuit of life. Wise, I may not call them, for that is a great name which belongs to God alone—lovers of wisdom is their fitting title." That is the way two gentlemen would while away a summer morning in the Athens of Plato.

Source: Edith Hamilton, *The Greek Way* (New York: Norton, 1993), pp. 114–15.

After that, Athens became a satellite in the Macedonian Empire until the Roman overlords arrived in 148 B.C.E.

❖ ══════════ ❖ ══════════ ❖

MING PEKING AND ATHENS: A COMPARISON

The culture that prevailed in classical Athens was of a radically different character from that of Ming Peking. Without doubt, the cities had certain parallels: substantial inequality; large areas of poor housing; crowded, winding streets; and important central monuments

and public buildings. There were all-important differences, however. Chinese civilization rested on a fundamental cultural belief in a godlike emperor that gave an unmistakable stamp to Peking. Monuments and buildings dwarfed the common individual as they simultaneously magnified the pomp and majesty of the emperor and his elite. Indeed, what clearer indication of a distant, exclusive power structure could there be than a citadel in the form of Peking's Forbidden City?

Athens seems, overall, more humane in character. The Greek cultural ideals of citizen participation stamped that city with a human scale,

Athens today is strongly shaped by its culture and history. Even the physical environment reveals that social reality, as seen above. Looming above the city from its craggy hilltop site sits the Acropolis—built in the second half of the fifth century B.C.E. as the citadel of ancient Athens. Particularly prominent are the pillars of the Parthenon—the temple of Athena, patron goddess of the city.

encouraging openness, communication, and development among its free citizens. Such ideals can be seen in all Athens's public buildings—in the theaters (where, not by accident, the audience sat above the performers, not the other way around), in the public forums, in the temples, in the gymnasia, in the marketplace. These buildings were not monuments to an absolute emperor; rather, Athens was much more a celebration of the "good life," an ideal that was evident in spite of important failings in practice.

In comparing Hellenic Athens and Ming Peking, we see just how different cities in different cultures can be. But this comparison shows us more: Athenian success at encouraging citizen participation and in developing the very best in human nature by a process of dialogue and growth shows us what the city can be. We are prompted to ask, in other words, how or why one city might be better than another. If we agree, for example, that democracy, equality, and continual mental, bodily, and spiritual development are ideals for which human beings should strive, Athens provides

us with a real-life case where those ideals were encouraged. What, then, might we do to encourage the further manifestation of positive cultural values in our own modern-day cities? (See the next Cityscape box.)

THE CULTURE OF CAPITALISM AND THE CITY

Nineteenth-century London certainly was not like either Ming Peking or Hellenic Athens. Dominated by feverish economic activity, it was the forerunner of the modern city described by U.S. urbanist Louis Wirth in Chapter 5.

But Friedrich Engels, who first saw London in 1842—the year he met Karl Marx and began their long collaboration—gave an interpretation radically different from that of Wirth. Whereas the Chicago urbanist imagined he was describing the essential characteristics of all large, modern cities, Engels was aware that he was looking only at a certain cultural setting, a city intensifying the tremendous power

CITYSCAPE

The Capitalist City: 1850

London is unique, because it is a city in which one can roam for hours without leaving the built-up area and without seeing the slightest sign of the approach of open country. This enormous agglomeration of population on a single spot has multiplied a hundred-fold the economic strength of the two and a half million inhabitants concentrated there. This great population has made London the commercial capital of the world and has created the gigantic docks in which are assembled the thousands of ships which always cover the River Thames. . . . All this is so magnificent and impressive that one is lost in admiration. The traveller has good reason to marvel at England's greatness even before he steps on English soil.

It is only later that the traveller appreciates the human suffering which has made all this possible. . . . It is only when he has visited the slums of this great city that it dawns upon him that the inhabitants of modern London have had to sacrifice so much that is best in human nature in order to create those wonders of civilisation with which their city teems. The vast majority of Londoners have had to let so many of their potential creative faculties lie dormant, stunted and unused in order that a small, closely-knit group of their fellow citizens could develop to the full the qualities with which nature has endowed them. . . . Hundreds of thousands of men and women drawn from all classes and ranks of society pack the streets of London. Are they not all human beings with the same innate characteristics and potentialities? Are they not all equally interested in the pursuit of happiness? And do they not all aim at happiness by following similar methods? Yet they rush past each other as if they had nothing in common. . . .

No one even thinks of sparing a glance for his neighbor in the streets. . . . We know well enough that this isolation of the individual—this narrow-minded egotism—is everywhere the fundamental principle of modern society. But nowhere is this selfish egotism so blatantly evident as in the frantic bustle of the great city. The disintegration of society into individuals, each guided by his private principles and each pursuing his own aims has been pushed to its furthest limits in London. [emphasis added]

. . . Here men regard their fellows not as human beings, but as pawns in the struggle for existence. Everyone exploits his neighbor with the result that the stronger tramples the weaker under foot. The strongest of all, a tiny group of capitalists, monopolise everything, while the weakest, who are in the vast majority, succumb to the most abject poverty.

What is true of London, is true also of all the great towns, such as Manchester, Birmingham and Leeds. . . . The observer of such an appalling state of affairs must shudder at the consequences of such feverish activity and can only marvel that so crazy a social and economic structure should survive at all.

Source: Friedrich Engels, *The Condition of the Working Class in England,* trans. by W. O. Henderson and W. H. Chaloner (New York: Macmillan, 1958), pp. 30–31.

of Western industrial capitalism. Note especially the passage in italics in the Cityscape box: What Wirth saw as a consequence of a large, differentiated population, Engels interpreted as cultural forces at work.

Engels was mightily disturbed by what he saw. If Hellenic Athens with its cultural ideas of developing the whole person was the city's zenith, surely Engels believed nineteenth-century London to be its nadir. Yet the characteristics of both cities reflect the dominant ideals and activities of the larger culture. In the same way that Greek culture produced cities in which economic activity was regarded as of decidedly secondary importance, Western culture under the influence of capitalism spawned cities where economic gain was an unrestrained obsession.

The Capitalist City

As a means of livelihood, capitalism is very old. A rich capitalist life flourished in the fifth century B.C.E. in Athens, and no doubt such activity is centuries older. Significant commercial activity aimed at the accumulation of profit also took place on an increasing scale in medieval Europe, especially after the eleventh century. Mumford noted that "so marked was this influence that . . . Alain of Lille could say: 'Not Caesar now, but money, is all'" (1961:411).

If capitalism itself was not new, the unparalleled energy with which the spirit of commerce and profit began to assert itself in the sixteenth century C.E. certainly was. Apparently, several factors prompted this change. First, the feudal order of the Middle Ages began to erode as merchants, primarily in cities, gained power. Desiring to broaden their market, these merchants established trade routes among cities all over Europe in the period between 1200 and 1500. Goods began to pour into these cities, and people in the countryside began to get wind that a better life—or at least a life with more material amenities—could be had in cities. Major urban population growth ensued and fueled increased economic vitality (Heilbroner and Milberg, 2001).

Gradually, from the sixteenth century onward, the economic interests of life came to dominate Western European cities. Capitalism set the principal cultural theme, with the new order organized around a rather different set of economic relationships than its feudal predecessor. No longer bound to lords and manors, individual workers could sell their labor to whoever would pay the highest wages. Second, under these conditions economic activity became increasingly competitive. Because

everyone was striving for profits, workers had to outdo each other in some way to get the greatest economic benefits. When industrialization arrived in the mid-eighteenth century, capitalism's hold over Western cities was greatly enhanced.

The Industrial Revolution

Like capitalism, *industrialism*—the process of manufacturing goods in large quantities for mass consumption—had existed in Western society to a limited degree before the eighteenth century. However, it was only after the adoption of capitalism on a large scale that the influence of industrialism began to grow. For all intents and purposes, large-scale industrialism began in England about 1750.

One important reason that English society proved so amenable to industrialism was the penchant, particularly evident in the upper middle classes, for engineering and guiding economic activities by the most scientific methods available. If efficient methods were not available, the innovative British invented them. Perhaps the most famous example of an invention that changed the economic order was James Watt's steam engine. This machine, perfected by 1775, had literally hundreds of applications, from textile manufacturing to flour mills to the mass production of the common pin. Its ability to save hand labor and contribute to the mass production of items was nothing short of remarkable, and in very little time entrepreneurs put this invention into widespread use. By 1781, Matthew Boulton, Watt's partner in a steam-engine manufacturing company, was claiming that "the people of London, Birmingham, and Manchester [are] all 'steam mill mad.' " From then on, the Industrial Revolution was in full force. Other inventions, such as Arkwright's spinning jenny and Maudslay's automatic screw machine, revolutionized other areas of production. "The Revolution . . . fed upon itself. The new techniques . . . simply destroyed their handicraft competition around the world and thus enormously increased their own markets" (Heilbroner and Milberg, 2001:75–77).

For the city dweller, the most important change was the invention of the factory.

> The factory may be singled out as the agent which gives [the industrial–capitalist] city its structural form and social purpose. By the word "factory" I mean more than an industrial enterprise: the factory is the locus of mobilized abstract labor, of labor power as a commodity, placed in the service of commerce as well as production. Accordingly, the term applies as much to an office building and a supermarket as to a mill and a plant. Once the factory becomes an element of urban life, it takes over the city almost completely. (Bookchin, 1996:51)

With the domination of the factory, the very symbolism of the city changed. The city in feudal Europe had been, above all, a Christian city, symbolically dominating the region with its Gothic cathedral. (A striking example is Venice, spread out around St. Mark's Cathedral, built in 1176.) The capitalist era, as Mumford remarked, turned the culture of feudalism on its head, transforming "six of the seven deadly sins [gluttony, pride, covetousness, envy, lust, and anger] into cardinal virtues (sloth became perhaps an even greater sin)" (1961:346). The church declined as the focal institution of society; in the place of spires appeared smokestacks, and the public plaza became a growing central business district.

> If capitalism tended to expand the market and turn every part of the city into a negotiable commodity, the change from [small-scale handicraft] to large-scale factory production transformed the industrial towns into dark hives, busily puffing, clanking, screeching, smoking for twelve and fourteen hours a day, sometimes going around the clock. The slavish routine . . . became the normal environment of the new industrial workers. None of these towns heeded the old saw, "All work and no play makes Jack a dull boy." [They] specialized in producing dull boys. (Mumford, 1961:446)

In short, the dominant capitalist cultural theme, in conjunction with industrial mechanization, created a new emphasis in urban consciousness. In describing a typical schoolroom in "Coketown," a fictionalized English factory city of the nineteenth century, Charles Dickens explained the main ingredient of this consciousness, presented in the next Cityscape box.

Urban Life as Economics

"You are never to fancy!" With this phrase Dickens summarized what so worried Engels about the capitalist city: It reduced everything in life to objective facts and quantity. Other aspects of life—subjectivity, quality, art, music, politics, religion, and creative thought—were downplayed or consciously eradicated.

This new consciousness not only transformed how city people acted; it transformed the physical structure of the city itself, thereby intensifying the capitalist theme even further. Land, once merely a place to live, became real estate:

> If the layout of a town has no relation to human needs and activities other than business, the pattern of the city may be simplified: the ideal layout for the business [person] is that which can be most swiftly reduced to standard monetary units for purchase and sale. The fundamental [urban] unit is no longer the neighborhood . . . but the individual building lot, whose value can be gauged in terms of front feet: this favors an oblong with narrow frontage and great depth, which provides a minimum amount of light and air to the buildings, particularly the dwellings, that conform to it. Such units turned out equally advantageous for the land surveyor, the real estate speculator, the commercial builder, and the lawyer who drew up the deed of sale. In turn, the lots favored the rectangular building block, which again became the standard unit for extending the city. (Mumford, 1961:421–22)

So strong was this pattern in the physical form of the city after the sixteenth century that even cities with mountainous geography (such as San Francisco), which might have benefited from a switchback or zigzag pattern to facilitate moving up and down the terrain, were subjected to a grid pattern.

Murray Bookchin used even stronger language to suggest the extent to which the modern Western city has been shaped by the industrial-capitalist system:

CITYSCAPE

"Nothing but the Facts, Ma'am"— Capitalist–Industrialist Consciousness

"Now, what I want is, Facts. Teach these boys and girls nothing but Facts. Facts alone are wanted in life. Plant nothing else, and root out everything else. You can only form the minds of reasoning animals upon Facts: nothing else will ever be of any service to them. This is the principle on which I bring up my own children, and this is the principle on which I bring up these children. Stick to Facts, Sir!"

The scene was a plain, bare, monotonous vault of a schoolroom, and the speaker's square forefinger emphasized his observations by underscoring every sentence with a line on the schoolmaster's sleeve. The emphasis was helped by the speaker's square wall of a forehead, which had his eyebrows for its base, while his eyes found commodious cellerage in two dark caves, overshadowed by the wall. The emphasis was helped by the speaker's mouth, which was wide, thin, and hard set. . . .

"Thomas Gradgrind, Sir. A man of realities. A man of facts and calculations. A man who proceeds upon the principle that two and two are four, and nothing over, and who is not to be talked into allowing for anything over. Thomas Gradgrind, Sir—peremptorily Thomas—Thomas Gradgrind. With a rule and a pair of scales, and the multiplication table always in his pocket, Sir, ready to weigh and measure any parcel of human nature, and tell you exactly what it comes to. It is a mere question of figures, a case of simple arithmetic. . . .

"Girl number twenty," said Mr. Gradgrind, squarely pointing with his square forefinger, "I don't know that girl. Who is that girl?"

"Sissy Jupe, Sir," explained number twenty, blushing, standing up, and curtseying.

"Sissy is not a name," said Mr. Gradgrind. "Don't call yourself Sissy. Call yourself Cecilia."

"It's father as calls me Sissy, Sir," returned the young girl in a trembling voice, and with another curtsey.

"Then he has no business to do it," said Mr. Gradgrind. "Tell him he mustn't. Cecilia Jupe. Let me see. . . .

"Give me your definition of a horse."

(Sissy Jupe thrown into the greatest alarm by this demand.)

"Girl number twenty unable to define a horse!" said Mr. Gradgrind, for the general behoof of all the little pitchers. "Girl number twenty possessed of no facts, in reference to one of the commonest of animals! Some boy's definition of a horse. Bitzer, yours. . . ."

"Quadruped. Graminivorous. Forty teeth, namely twenty-four grinders, four eye-teeth, and twelve incisive. Sheds coat in the spring; in marshy countries, sheds hoofs, too. Hoofs hard, but requiring to be shod with iron. Age known by marks in mouth." Thus (and much more) Bitzer.

"Now girl number twenty," said Mr. Gradgrind. "You know what a horse is. . . ."

["But Sir," said Cecilia Jupe, blushing] . . . "I fancy . . ."

"Ay, ay, ay! But you mustn't fancy," cried the gentleman, quite elated by coming so happily to his point. "That's it! You are never to fancy!"

Source: Excerpt from Charles Dickens, *Hard Times* (London: Oxford University Press, 1955; orig. published 1854), pp. 1, 3–5, 7.

Every esthetic urban pattern inherited from the past tends to be sacrificed to the grid system (in modern times, the factory pattern par excellence), which facilitates the most efficient transportation of goods and people. Streams are obliterated, variations in the landscape effaced without the least sensitivity to natural beauty, magnificent stands of trees removed, even treasured architectural and historical monuments demolished, and wherever possible, the terrain is leveled to resemble a factory floor. The angular and curved streets of the medieval city which at every turn delighted the eye with a new and scenic tableau, are replaced by straight monotonous vistas of the same featureless buildings and shops. Lovely squares inherited from the past are reduced to nodal points for traffic, and highways are wantonly carved into vital neighborhoods, dividing and finally subverting them. (1996:90–91)

Assets and Debits

On one level, the capitalist city has unquestionably been successful in generating a higher material standard of living for a larger proportion of its population than any other urban system in history. For example, only 10.8 percent of the U.S. population in metropolitan areas was below the poverty line in 2000, compared with 13.4 percent in nonmetropolitan areas. Useful material goods and technological innovations are omnipresent, and, given the "hands-off-the-individual" value that is so central to capitalism, there is a very real degree of political freedom, and other kinds of freedom, too, for residents of such cities. They can vote, come and go as they please, and (if they have the money) live where they like.

But there are debits as well: Millions of poor families live in cities, and districts that are unprofitable have fallen into shocking decay. Within such areas, as we will see in later chapters, people suffer incredibly. Similarly, the dominant focus on material goods and technological innovations often means that many people are preoccupied with the newest CD or DVD player or the latest car, and less mindful of social and environmental needs that require attention.

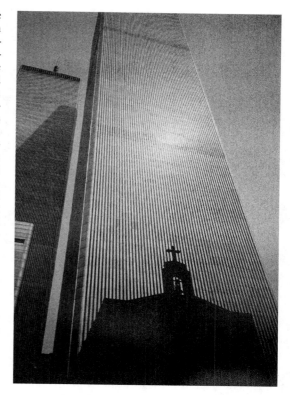

The glass and steel façade of a World Trade Center skyscraper once towered above a church in silhouette in downtown New York. The size and positioning of both these buildings suggested the relative importance of economics and religion in contemporary Western society, unlike the medieval era when church steeples were the highest visible points in cities.

Finally, even freedoms have their problematic side. The freedom to accumulate wealth, prestige, and power has meant, over the years, that some individuals in our cities have much more of these scarce resources than others. With wealth primarily in the hands of a few (the richest 5 percent of the U.S. population controls 47 percent of the wealth), there is a tendency for these people to control both the economic and political spheres of life to such a degree that others are effectively cut off from any true success or representation.

Problems such as these led to a reaction: a second type of modern city, established around and intensifying yet another set of cultural themes, those of communism.

To get a sense of the contemporary communist city, we return to Peking. The Looking Back box gets us acclimated. It records the first visit to the city by Liang Heng, a young Red Guard supporter of Chairman Mao Zedong, during the turmoil of the Cultural Revolution of the 1960s.

Standing on the Meridian Gate of the old Ming Imperial City (Figures 8–1, 8–2), looking out over the millions assembled in Tiananmen Square, Mao established the People's Republic of China on October 1, 1949. It was on this historic spot that Liang Heng gazed in rapture as a dedicated revolutionary in the late 1960s.

Today, five decades after Mao made that fateful pronouncement, Peking is a different city. Its feudal and imperial past has been almost completely eradicated. Even its name has been changed—to Beijing (the old name, *Peking*, was a Western transcription of *Beijing*). On the site of the old dynasties has arisen what is the most important communist city in the world, now that communism no longer dominates Russia and eastern Europe.

Modern Beijing thus provides us with a final illustration of the consequences of different cultural themes in urban places. The great walls that protected the city and the emperor in the Ming period are gone. In their place is a city-encircling highway, while below ground the city's modern subway system provides 25 miles of track along two major lines. The Forbidden City is now a museum open to all, surrounded by great new buildings of state: the Great Hall of the People, the Historical Museum, and the Mausoleum that holds Mao's remains. The sixteen multistoried hotels in Beijing easily dominate the old buildings of the emperor. Replaced, too, are many of the old, sonorous names of the imperial years. For example, the Pavillion of Pleasant

Sounds has given way to People's Road and Anti-Imperialist Street.

The contrast is jarring on yet another level, especially when seen in comparison with capitalist cities. Beijing has no extreme poverty, no seedy sections of town, no prostitutes, no beggars, virtually no crime, very little pollution, and nearly pristine streets. What makes all this possible is a modern cultural tradition that sees political control of almost all aspects of life by the state, as well as the political responsibility of the individual to others, as the cornerstones of the good life.

The Emergence of Modern Beijing

The Communists did not gain control of China easily. Ironically, it was the expansion of capitalist nations and their cities in the nineteenth century that made it possible.

In 1644, the Ming rulers who had built Imperial Peking were replaced by the Ch'ing Dynasty. Like their Ming predecessors, the Ch'ing emperors were not interested in contact with the outside world; but it did not follow that the world was uninterested in China. In the late 1700s and early 1800s—not coincidentally the time of the industrial-capitalist revolution—various European countries made overtures to China in hopes of finding yet another trade market, for they desired China's silk, tea, and silver. When the emperor rebuked them, tensions grew. The Europeans became determined to find a way to open China to trade, and the Chinese were just as determined to keep them out.

The denouement came in the mid-nineteenth century. For many years, the British had been smuggling India-grown poppies into China. Converted into opium and mixed with tobacco for smoking, the poppies gave rise to China's infamous opium dens, which served an estimated 2 million addicts by 1835. Finally, enraged, an imperial commissioner from Beijing seized and destroyed over 2.8 million pounds of opium in Canton in 1839. It was a fateful decision. Later the same year the English launched the so-called Opium War as a punitive action. They won hands down; the resulting treaty

LOOKING BACK

Peking! Home of the Glorious Revolution!

Peking was cold to my sneakered feet, and the wind was like knives, but to me it was heaven. The avenues seemed five or six times as broad as those in [my home city of] Changsha, the buildings cleaner and more splendid, if a bit austere. I immediately demanded to be taken to Tian An Men Square, and tired as they were, my friends took me, watching with amusement as I stared at everything that was legend—the Great Hall of the People, the Monument of the Heroes of the People, the Historical Museum. Like every other Red Guard coming to Peking for the first time, I took my oath in front of the huge picture of Chairman Mao, lifting my "Little Red Book" in my right hand, sticking out my chest and reciting proudly, "Chairman Mao, Liang Heng has finally come to your side. I will always be loyal to you. I will always be loyal to your Thought. I will always be loyal to your Revolutionary line." I could have stayed there all night. . . .

Source: Liang Heng and Judith Shapiro, *Son of the Revolution* (New York: Vintage, 1984), pp. 114–15.

---

opened five Chinese ports to unrestricted trade and established the British colony of Hong Kong. In 1860 another war and treaty forcibly opened more Chinese ports to European trade.

Severely weakened, the ruling dynasty lost the Sino-Japanese War in 1895 and, during the anti-foreigner Boxer Rebellion of 1900, fled Beijing. Chinese insurgents held Peking for 55 days against an eight-nation "relief force." The insurgents' inevitable defeat placed China almost completely under foreign domination. In 1911, Dr. Sun Yat-sen overthrew the remnants of the dynasty and proclaimed a Chinese Republic. Chiang Kai-shek succeeded him in 1927, but power struggles throughout the country meant that the government remained ineffectual.

Angered by the disadvantageous trade relations that the republic still tolerated with foreign countries, in 1934 China's fledgling Communist Party under Mao Ze-dong undertook the 6,000-mile Long March to China's hinterlands to escape Chiang Kai-shek's army. The Communists returned in 1948 and, after a six-week seige, occupied Peking. The People's Republic was proclaimed the following year.

Urban Life as Politics

The Communists vowed to free China from centuries of domination of the many by the few and from exploitation by foreign countries. To do this they transformed nearly all of Chinese life into an expression of the new political ideas. The job of the state was to provide equally for everyone; the job of the individual was to contribute to the state's success by participating unselfishly in the state-linked neighborhood units, school classes, factories, and party committees (Bonavia, 1978). Only by collectivizing everything, the Communists believed, and by constantly reminding everyone of the dangers of backsliding into individualism, was true progress to be attained.

The key concept in all this was *tzu-li kengsheng* —"self-reliance" or "regeneration through one's own efforts." In developing this concept, the party divided each city into districts (Beijing has nine), each district into neighborhoods, and each neighborhood into smaller residential areas. Each residential area developed its own "residents' committee," designed to link each individual with the city authorities and vice versa. It became the job of these

Tiananmen Square is the world's largest square (98 acres). Its northern Gate of Heavenly Peace, from which the square takes its name, has a balcony where ancient imperial edicts were read and where Chairman Mao proclaimed the People's Republic of China in 1949. The Museum of the Chinese Revolution and Chinese History, Qianmen Gate, Monument to the People's Heroes, Mao's Memorial Hall, and the Great Hall of the People, seat of China's congress, are at the square, also site of the 1989 massacre of protestors.

committees to oversee local services—security, fire, sanitation—and to keep political responsibility uppermost in peoples' minds (Sidel, 1974).

Study groups developed unceasing political awareness in which all neighborhood residents participated (there also were study groups in schools and factories). The tasks of these groups were three: (1) to communicate to all citizens the importance of participation in all areas of life; (2) to chastise political troublemakers of all kinds, such as "revisionists," "factionalists," "ultra-Leftists," "capitalists," and "imperialists"; and (3) to examine constantly through group self-criticism each individual's performance (Sidel, 1974; Bonavia, 1978). As one influential Chinese citizen put it:

> If a person truly loves his neighbor or truly is his brother's keeper, then he has a moral and social duty to correct his brother's shortcomings. If truly no man is an island and the actions of each person directly affect the lives of all others, then the "group," however defined, has a real and direct stake in controlling the actions of its members. (Victor H. Li, quoted in Sidel, 1974:59)

Thus, any form of extreme individualism in the Western sense would be seen as a selfish act. In modern China, says a Beijing scholar,

> [a] student may express his individual personality to the full, yet still study for the sake of the revolution. But a student in the grip of [Western-style] individualism studies only to build up his own career. "Individual interest" is respected in China, but an individualistic outlook, which leads a person to exploit others for his own benefit, is not proper. (Chou I-Liang, paraphrased in Terrill, 1975:386)

It is difficult to imagine more contrasting views of city life than those outlined above and those held by people of contemporary Western cities.

The Difficulties of Urban Life

Beijing's population in 1949, the year of the declaration of the People's Republic, was less than 2.5 million. (Today it is over 6.6 million and bursting at the seams.) Successful in feeding and housing its people, China nevertheless remained saddled with a primitive industrial system and an inferior educational system that left it in desperate need of trained personnel (China was an almost entirely peasant society until the 1950s). Its standing as a world-class economic power remained elusive, and the nation was not able to provide widespread high-quality education.

To curb these problems, in 1959 Mao initiated the "Great Leap Forward," an unsuccessful crash program aimed at improving industry and production. He also launched the "Great Proletarian Cultural Revolution" in 1966 to eliminate "revisionism." Ironically, the overzealous youth movement associated with the Cultural Revolution, the Red Guards (of which Liang Heng was a passionate member), closed the universities, impaired production, and brought many Chinese cities to an almost dead stop until they were finally brought under control by the army.

Economic Reform

With Mao's death in 1976, a great power struggle emerged in Beijing for the control of the party—a struggle won by Deng Xiaoping and his followers. The new leaders de-emphasized the more extreme elements of Maoism, and since 1978, the Chinese leadership has been trying to move from a sluggish Soviet-style centrally planned economy to a more market-oriented economy but one that is still within a rigid political framework of Communist Party control. To this end the authorities switched to a system of household responsibility in agriculture in place of the old collectivization, increased the authority of local officials and plant managers in industry, permitted a wide variety of small-scale enterprise in services and light manufacturing, and opened the economy to increased foreign trade and investment. The result has been a quadrupling of the gross domestic product (GDP) since 1978.

One long-term threat to continued rapid economic growth is the deterioration in the environment, with increasing air pollution and soil erosion and a steady fall in the water table, especially in the north. China continues to lose arable land because of erosion and economic development; furthermore, the regime gives

insufficient priority to agricultural research. The government plans to intensify efforts to stimulate growth through spending on infrastructure—such as water control and power grids—and poverty relief and through rural tax reform aimed at eliminating arbitrary local levies on farmers (CIA, 2002).

A Rising Consumerism

Visitors to Beijing today find a city alive with energy. In one section of the city—just south of the old Forbidden City—is a shopping section for the capital's citizens. Beneath billboards advertising Toshiba TV sets are department stores filled with goods, with no shortage of lookers and buyers. One reason for this increasing consumerism is the additional spending money generated by the new policies encouraging individual enterprise. For example, in another part of the city is a farmers' market where workers from a local commune sell surplus vegetables not needed for the commune or for state consumption. They are allowed to keep the profits from such transactions. Some young people, selected by the government to go abroad to teach Chinese in a North American college, earn Western salaries —astronomical by Chinese standards. When they return to Beijing, they are allowed to keep the money they have saved and are thus able to afford better apartments in new sections of the city and to provide their families with a variety of consumer goods.

All this change—a movement "from Marxism to Mastercard"—has its critics. Many powerful Communist Party members see the revolution of Mao being "sold out," and, as an indication that the policies of Deng and his successors are not all positive, they cite extensive evidence that corruption is now beginning to appear in many areas of Chinese life as people scramble for the accoutrements of a consumer society. They charge that the current policies generate self-centeredness and a kind of Western decadence. Nonetheless, Jiang continues the open-door policy, and China and its cities once again are in the throes of major social change.

❖ ━━━━━━━━━ ❖ ━━━━━━━━━ ❖

Through the global economy and pop culture, cultural diffusion impacts on any city and its culture, yet few would think this is a scene anywhere in North America, not even in Chinatown. In Beijing, China, a delivery rider rests on his tricycle in front of a billboard promoting Pepsi, featuring pictures of pop singers Janet Jackson, Guo Fucheng, Wang Fei, and Ricky Martin.

SUMMARY

Ramona thought about the city.
—I have to admit we are locked in the most exquisite, mysterious muck. This muck heaves and palpitates. It is multidirectional and has a mayor. . . . Our muck is only a part of a much greater muck—the nation-state—which is itself the creation of that muck of mucks, human consciousness.

Donald Barthelme, *City Life*, 1970

The city does not exist by itself, but is linked intricately to the broader society of which it is a part. Any city's physical and social forms are shaped by the cultural values of that society and by its historical epoch. For example, although there is some truth in the old idea that the ways of the country and the city are distinct and "ne'er the twain shall meet," recent research has shown that cities and their hinterlands are bound together in a complex interdependence that allows each to have significant influence over the other.

Cities are not entirely synonymous with civilization. They are symbolic centers that concentrate, intensify, and re-create the cultural forces found throughout the society. In the cities we compared and contrasted in this chapter—Boston and Ibadan, Ming Peking and Hellenic Athens, nineteenth-century industrial-capitalist London and contemporary industrial-communist Beijing—we found significant differences. These differences attest to the importance of culture in shaping the social and physical environment of the city. Only by studying cities in a comparative manner can we understand this urban variability. As Brian Berry said, "The most fundamental axiom of . . . urban sociology is that the urban landscape is a mirror reflecting the society that maintains it" (1985:96).

CONCLUSION

If urban variety is so marked, what is left as distinctively urban? What do all the cities we've considered in this chapter have in common? To answer this question, we certainly must go beyond the factors of size, density, and heterogeneity proposed by Louis Wirth. We propose a new definition of the city, one that acknowledges the importance of the cultural dimension that Wirth neglected: In comparison with other types of permanent human settlement, *a city is a relatively large, dense settlement that has a complex social structure that greatly reflects, intensifies, and re-creates cultural values and forms.*

A few comments are necessary to clarify this definition. The first set of characteristics—"a large, dense settlement"—are Wirth's; he seems quite right about them. The next characteristic—"a complex social structure"—is from V. Gordon Childe (1950). You may recall that Wirth also suggested that the city is composed of "socially heterogeneous individuals." By this he meant that people of different racial, ethnic, and religious backgrounds tend to mingle in the city. Anthropological research has shown that this is more accurately descriptive of modern Western cities (to which people of different countries migrate) than it is of their nonindustrial counterparts (such as Ibadan and Beijing). Yet, even if social heterogeneity is not characteristic of all cities, nearly every urbanist has noted that the city has a more complex division of labor and a more sophisticated political system (if only to handle the large numbers and density) than do other forms of human settlement. Such complexities are what we mean by "a complex social structure."

Finally, the idea that any city is a reflector, intensifier, and re-creator of cultural values and forms is a direct outgrowth of this chapter. In the final analysis, the nature of any city lies in its unique ability to interpret a particular set of cultural values in a distinctive form. By "cultural values" we mean those shared beliefs and ideas that characterize any social group of long duration. By "form" we mean the typical round of everyday activities and arrangement of urban space that characterize any city. Thus, because the cultural values of the Greeks during Athens's Golden Era (the fifth century B.C.E.) regarded moneymaking as secondary and a holistic life as primary, we found that the daily life of the city was dominated by dialogue, politics, recreation, and ritual. While the Greeks surely went to the agora (the market) to trade, they just as frequently went there to talk and relax. Even their buildings reflected this cultural emphasis. The Acropolis, where the most important buildings of Greek civilization were located (the Parthenon, the Erechtheum, the Propylea, the Temple of Athena Nike), sits on a hill overlooking the rest of the city. The agora, lesser in importance, lies at the bottom of the hill. All this appears reversed when we consider the form of contemporary capitalist cities such as those of North America. Here the round of daily activities focuses on the economic. Most people spend the bulk of their day getting and spending, and planning for more of the same. Dialogue, politics, recreation, and ritual come later—in the evenings, on the weekends, during the two-week vacation. The city's physical layout reflects this cultural priority. Streets are arranged on a grid for easy movement and buying and selling, and the most important buildings—at least those that dominate the skyline of any major North American city—are those of commerce.

In such comparative observations lies a crucial lesson about studying cities: Quite simply, if we don't understand the relationship between the city and culture, we can't properly understand the city. As alluded to in our discussion of the emergence of modern Beijing, we also need to consider the role of economic power in dictating quality of life and urban land use. It is to this perspective that we turn in the next chapter.

THE NEW URBAN SOCIOLOGY
The City and Capitalism

Ecology = relationship between organisms + their environment

In the early 1970s, an alternative theoretical approach to urban ecology began to take form. In part, this development was a response to what its proponents saw as deficiencies of the earlier urban ecology model described in Chapter 7. But it was also a response to the turmoil of the times. The late 1960s and early 1970s were a period of upheaval in both the United States and Europe, prompting a more critical and political outlook on society. Not surprisingly, many scholars were led to reexamine the assumption that geography and technology were the main factors shaping urban life.

These "new" urbanists highlighted the distribution of wealth and political power in the city. They noted that the wealthiest people lived on the most desirable land and enjoyed the greatest access to the city's services. Is it any accident, they asked, that the city's best schools are situated in the city's richest neighborhoods? Or that new superhighways tear through old urban neighborhoods, with patent disregard for poor residents, to better serve the city's elite and those who have fled to the wealthy suburbs? Their answer was a resounding "No!" On the contrary, they concluded, "the structure of the city is to be explained by the pursuit of profit, which is the *raison d'être* of capitalist society, modified by the actions of the State, which has the functions of preserving and legitimizing this society" (Hall, 1984b:32).

This alternative approach has come to be known as "the new urban sociology" (Gottdiener, 1994). In truth, however, most of its theoretical arguments are quite old, drawing heavily on the ideas of Karl Marx (1818–1883). What is new is their application to the city and, more specifically, to recent trends such as globalization of the economy, economic restructuring in the United States, and the proliferation of megacities and edge cities.

The heart of this new approach is a central reliance on *political economy theory* and its application to urban life. That is, urban life is to be understood in terms of the social structures and processes of change that benefit some groups at the expense of others (Gottdiener and Feagin, 1988).

Before we examine some of the major aspects of this new perspective—which is rapidly becoming the dominant view in the field—we will review some earlier contributions to political and economic analysis, which draw on the ecological model discussed in Chapter 7.

URBAN ECONOMICS: THE TRADITIONAL PERSPECTIVE

People who know cities often have an image of a vibrant downtown, a place where the action is, where the buildings are taller and the lights brighter. That is, indeed, an accurate image of North American, European, or "westernized" cities. Approaching a major city at night along a dark highway, one sees first the distant glow of the city lights even before making out the evening skyline. Barring an electrical blackout, large areas of the center city are never dark. Why? Why shouldn't the "action" be everywhere? Why should the tall buildings be concentrated in a single area?

Central Place Theory

To begin to answer these questions, realize that the city is the only place where everything human comes together. Compared with the fixed life of rural areas or the small town, the city's possibilities are practically limitless. Indeed, the city is the place where the mix of people and ideas makes the creation of new things easy. The city, by its very nature, promotes "interaction and fusion" (Mumford, 1961:568).

Note, further, that as one approaches the center of the city, the level of human activity becomes more intense. The greatest action is, literally, in the center, where people contact each other more frequently. There, in the "downtown," one finds the greatest economic advantages that cities can offer.

The Economic Advantages of Cities

Cities tend to be located where important *goods or services* are available in abundance (Winston-Salem, Raleigh, and Durham, North Carolina, are in the heart of tobacco-producing country) or where goods and services can be obtained easily (New Orleans is near the mouth of the Mississippi River). In either case, a prime location means that cities obtain, produce, and distribute their goods and services more cheaply than smaller settlements can. To ship heating oil to Albany, New York, costs a certain amount, but to further transport that oil to the small town of Ticonderoga, 100 miles away, adds additional transportation and handling costs. _formed, collected into a mess_

Second, cities play host to what economists call *agglomeration industries*. Take Detroit, home of the automobile industry. Because the major U.S. car manufacturers have their home bases there, the city also attracts various subindustries to serve them—companies manufacturing car paints or engine pistons, for example. The Big Three automakers share these subindustries, which benefits everyone involved, including the customer, who ultimately buys the car for less. Other examples of famous agglomeration industries are the entertainment industry in Los Angeles and Hollywood, meatpacking in Chicago, country music in Nashville, and the fashion industry in New York. In each case, the presence of agglomeration industries keeps production costs lower than they might be in a smaller settlement.

A third economic advantage of cities, particularly those based on a free-enterprise system, is that _competition_ among various producers works to keep costs down and quality up for various goods and services. Because so many businesses of the same type exist in cities, no business can charge a great deal more than its competitors for the same product. To do so, in a competitive environment, would simply mean that customers would go elsewhere to find a better deal, with predictable consequences for the company's future. For the same reason, if one business offers poor quality goods at the same price at which a competitor sells a better product, which firm will prosper?

But what about a business in a small town with little competition? There businesses typically offer less value to their customers, since

it's too inconvenient and expensive for most local people to go to the city to get the lower price or the better product.

Competition also explains why so many businesses of the same type tend to cluster together in the city. In fact, most cities have entire districts devoted solely to the computer, stereo, camera, automobile, fashion, baking, or entertainment businesses. The reasons for such proximity are easy to understand. Businesses of the same type that are located near one another can (1) know what their competitors are up to by simply walking across the street; (2) provide a single locale where customers can easily engage in comparison shopping, and (3) share agglomeration services, thereby making the products cheaper for everyone.

Fourth and finally, cities can offer higher-quality products at lower prices because they stand amidst a *greater population*. This means that urban businesses have a larger available work force than do their rural counterparts; thus, other things being equal, they can hire the more qualified people. Just as important, urban companies benefit from a larger pool of customers.

For these four reasons, the city has marked economic advantages over the hinterland. Once established, a city may operate as a "magnet" or a "growth machine," becoming more and more productive as it draws raw materials and people from all around (Mumford, 1961; Molotch, 1976).

Within the city, economic advantages increase as one nears the city center; for this reason, people who stand to benefit from those advantages want to locate near there. This principle points up why we find at the city's center a *central business district* (CBD), and why, at the city's center, the action truly is greater, the buildings taller, and the lights brighter.

The Urban Hierarchy

Basic economic advantages also help explain why some cities grow much larger than others. The largest cities are just more centrally located relative to important goods or services. Chicago is a major urban center because

Perhaps nowhere in North America is the global economy as visible as in the daily loading and unloading of container shipments onto or off trucks and ships at its seaports, such as here in Seattle. While many import and export goods are finished products on their way to wholesalers, many others are parts destined for assembly in factories in nations other than the ones in which they were manufactured.

of its location at the southern end of Lake Michigan and also because of its centrality to the nation's population. A century ago, Chicago thrived as the ideal location for shipping goods from the heavily settled Northeast to all other regions of the nation. Similarly, Chicago was a natural stopover for people heading westward. In comparison, Milwaukee, another major Great Lakes port, has less geographic centrality. Therefore, as Chicago developed into a major city, Milwaukee evolved into a second-tier urban area.

That cities should arrange themselves into hierarchical order should come as no surprise. Common sense suggests as much—all Iowans know, for example, that Des Moines is a more important city than the college town of Fairfield. It was not until the 1930s, however, that German geographer Walter Christaller incorporated this pattern into urban theory (1966; originally published 1933) Christaller suggested that the more important a city's economic function to a region, the more its population will increase. In turn, the city's hinterland

—smaller cities, towns, rural areas—becomes dependent on the large city for many goods and services that their smaller populations cannot support. Of course, this makes the city grow even more.

Christaller also suggested that, all else being equal, cities (especially smaller ones) space themselves in order that they do not cut into each other's markets. That is, cities emerge at "distance intervals," so that each serves a local hinterland. The upstate New York area provides an example: Stretched along the New York State Thruway, at least 75 miles apart, are the major urban areas of Buffalo (2000 population: 293,000), Rochester (220,000), Syracuse (147,000), Utica–Rome (300,000), and Albany–Schenectady–Troy (876,000). Each of these areas serves a distinctive hinterland and a series of smaller cities.

All of this means that, over a fairly large geographical region, we expect cities to be distributed by size. Most numerous will be smaller, *local* cities (Geneva, New York, for example); next up the scale will be fewer but larger

He said cities space themselves at

regional cities (such as Rochester); and, more significant, a smaller number of large, *national* cities (Pittsburgh and Philadelphia), and, finally, a very few, very large *world* cities like New York, Paris, and Tokyo. North America's world city, New York, is centrally located within the populous Northeast and affords easy access to the entire United States and Europe. There one can discover virtually anything from Indonesian restaurants to dozens of Broadway, off-Broadway, off-off-Broadway, and local theater groups. In most smaller cities, of course, Indonesian restaurants are nowhere to be found and theatergoers must be content with pre-Broadway trial runs, post-Broadway tours, or small local theater offerings. This is why, over the last century or two, people have sometimes referred disparagingly to lower-order cities as "one-horse towns." Or, as essayist Alexander Woollcott put it back in the 1930s: "A hick town is one where there is no place to go you shouldn't be."

The General Pattern of Land Use

> This vertical place is no more an accident than the Himalayas are. The city needs all these tall buildings to contain the tremendous energy there.
>
> Edward Field

Imagine you are traveling through the countryside toward any North American city. At the beginning of the trip, there are fields and perhaps some scattered farms or houses. As you approach the city, built-up residential areas appear, increasing in density as you near the city's center.

A Theoretical Model

Is this pattern typical of North American cities you know? If you think it is, economist William Alonso (1971) would say that this perception is no accident. Cities do use their land in a patterned way.

In building a model, Alonso described the ideal case, assuming that (1) the city existed in a completely flat, featureless place; (2) it had a single CBD; (3) efficient transportation existed

in all directions; and (4) every person in the city was motivated by economic self-interest.

Alonso was well aware that, in real life, many of these assumptions might not hold. For example, San Francisco exists on hills, the Minneapolis–St. Paul metropolis has two CBDs, Philadelphia's subway system runs only to certain parts of the city, and the Mormons who founded Salt Lake City were hardly motivated by purely economic interests. Similarly, Alonso knew that other factors such as ethnic relationships, politics, and history all play a role in urban life. Nevertheless, Alonso's model helps us see how *economic concerns* shape city land use. Only those who can pay the most will locate in the city's center. This is why the downtown is primarily a business district, with whatever residential property exists there taking the form of smaller apartments typically piled high on a small amount of land.

Overall, Alonso's model suggests a city with two major districts: (1) a CBD in the middle occupied by businesses of various types (offices, industries, warehouses) and (2) the surrounding, mostly residential areas. Circling the residential district would be yet other rings, containing businesses that require even more land and where rents are even lower. In such urban fringe areas, we might expect to find drive-in theaters, junkyards, cemeteries, and golf courses. (If one ever found a CBD golf course, however, one could bet that the cost of going nine holes would be expensive, indeed!) Farther out still, as population dwindles away, we would begin to find little except farms.

Figure 9–1 summarizes Alonso's model of urban land use. As it shows, businesses pay the highest rents to be near the CBD. As the distance from the CBD grows, the number of businesses declines until, at some point, they cease altogether. This means that, despite the lower rents, it is not economically feasible to operate a business there since it requires giving up the trade advantages of being in or near the CBD.

Most residents cannot afford the high rents of the CBD and so they live some distance away. As distance increases, rents continue to drop, but, at some point, no matter how low the rent, transportation problems in terms of time and money become so great that virtually no city workers choose to live there. People engaged in agriculture and other land-intensive pursuits can least afford to pay CBD rentals; hence their businesses appear only a considerable distance from the CBD.

The Case of the Inner-City Poor

At this point you may be agreeing with Alonso's general conclusions but wondering why most inner cities in North America also have many poor neighborhoods. If Alonso is correct, poor people, unable to afford high rents, should be living a long distance from the CBD.

Let's take a closer look. With little disposable income, poor people are unable to pay high rents. But they also cannot afford the high costs of travel from a remote area. Therefore, many poor people do pay higher rents in order to live near the CBD. But to do so, they have to live in high-density housing, perhaps sharing an apartment with another family.

On the other side of the coin, more affluent families can and do accept the higher cost of commuting from outside the CBD. But they do so mostly because they demand a great deal of space, which only a suburban neighborhood can provide within their budgets. And, no doubt, many find additional "value" in having few poor people as neighbors.

Criticisms of the Basic Theory

Some scholars, like Michael P. Todaro, question whether free enterprise, in the sense assumed by the proponents of the economic theory we have just discussed, really exists at all. To them, consumers are too powerless to set the agenda for a society's economic production. The Critical Thinking box on page 260 takes a closer look at this question.

To illustrate this criticism, consider "Blackston," a pseudonym for a poor black area of a major eastern city. There, Betty Lou Valentine (1980) compared supermarket prices

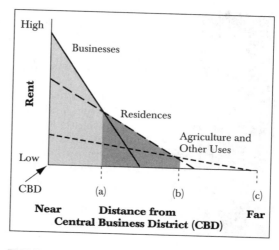

FIGURE 9–1 The Economics of Urban Land Use

with those in surrounding, higher-income white neighborhoods. She found that poor African Americans paid *significantly higher prices* for their groceries in Blackston than more affluent whites living elsewhere did. Why? Supermarket owners in Blackston think of African Americans as "captured customers." Because of the expense and inconvenience of going to white neighborhoods (most black families in Blackston do not own cars) and because of the overt prejudice they encounter when they do, most blacks have little choice but to do their shopping locally. Knowing this, Blackston supermarket owners can charge more than store owners whose customers can easily climb in their cars and shop elsewhere. The point is that, to the extent that people cannot really choose where to shop, the free-enterprise system is an ideal rather than a reality.

Valentine's observation that people of color often encounter overt prejudice illustrates a second problem with Alonso's economic model: People do not live by bread alone. Important noneconomic factors also influence urban land use. People in some neighborhoods may actively resist any "undesirables" who seek to move nearby. This resistance often extends beyond personal attitudes,

CRITICAL THINKING

Does Free *Enterprise Really Exist?*

In economic theory, the basic questions of what and how much to produce are assumed to be determined by the aggregate preferences of all consumers as revealed by their market demand for different goods and services. Producers are assumed simply to respond to these "sovereign" consumer preferences and, motivated by the desire to maximize profits, they are assumed to compete with each other *on equal terms* in the purchase of resources and the sale of their products. . . . The ultimate rationale for the efficacy of this theory or model of economic activity is Adam Smith's famous notion of the "invisible hand" of capitalism, which postulates that if each individual consumer, producer and supplier of resources pursues his or her own self-interest, they will, "as if by an invisible hand," be promoting the overall interests of society as a whole.

Unfortunately, the facts of economic life in both the developed and the less developed nations of the world are such as to render much of [this] theory of negligible importance. . . . Consumers as a whole are rarely sovereign about anything, let alone with regard to questions of what goods and services are to be produced, in what quantities and for whom. Producers, whether private or public, have great power in determining market prices and quantities sold. The ideal of competition is typically just that—an "ideal" with little relation to reality. Finally, the so-called "invisible hand" often acts not to promote the general welfare of all, but to lift up those already well-off while pushing down that vast majority of the population which is striving to free itself from poverty, malnutrition, and illiteracy.

Source: Michael P. Todaro, *Economic Development,* 7th ed. (Boston: Addison-Wesley, 1999), p. 14.

---

influencing zoning laws and the practices of real estate agents that can keep people from housing they may be able to afford. In an examination of the affluent suburb of Brookhaven on Long Island, Roger Williams (1978) reported widespread resistance to a proposed low-income housing project that would allow some poor families to live in Brookhaven. This resistance, often tinged with racism, soon surfaced in local politics:

> In a local election campaign last fall, Bob Hughes, the Republican candidate for town supervisor, warned against the "teeming hordes" who would descend on Brookhaven if it provided low-income housing. "It's the pull-up-the-gangplank syndrome," says [a] county official.

"I'm here, so don't let anybody else in—especially any of those people" (1978:18).

A third type of criticism points out that Alonso's economic theory applies to only a limited range of cities. For example, anthropologist Richard Fox (1977) argues that the capitalist–industrial city (on which the economic theory is based) is only *one* of at least five major city types that have existed historically. Other types noted by Fox include regal–ritual cities (with political and religious concerns at their core), administrative cities (with many government activities), colonial cities (that manage a colonial region for another nation), and mercantile cities (with trade as their principal concern). Of these, only the last operates on similar economic principles to the modern Western city. In the others, people are not making decisions based on the economic principles assumed by Alonso.

None of this is to say that Alonso's theory is wrong. But, clearly, it is limited in its utility and is but one model of how the free market makes use of land. Let's look at a different model of land use as a prelude to examining a newer, more dominant economic model, as delineated in the new urban sociology.

Urban Areas as Theme Parks

Since the 1960s, one dominant land use pattern has been the transformation of public space into packaged, thematic environments (Sorkin, 1992; Gottdiener, 2001). While some of this is apparent in the presence of theme parks like Disney World and Dollywood, or tourist cities like Las Vegas, or megamalls like the enormous one in West Edmonton, Canada, less noticeable to many Americans is a similar pattern in many North American cities.

Some themed public space areas, however, are well known and prosperous, like Baltimore's Harborplace and New York's South Street Seaport. Many other cities have rediscovered their own waterfront areas and have redeveloped them with parks, restaurants, stores, and various activities. Although each city's waterfront view may vary somewhat, one finds a generic similarity existing among all such areas in all cities. Similarly, historic districts—from San Diego's Gaslamp Quarter to Boston's Faneuil Hall marketplace—have their own unique charm, but their redevelopment to lure patrons to their shops, restaurants, and entertainment locales results in a somewhat homogeneous design.

Perhaps though, the epitome of themed urban space is not in the rebuilding of an old urban environment, but rather in the building of an artificial city environment as a theme park *away from* the city (such as Disney's Main Street). Built at a cost of $3 billion

and opened in 1993, another such entity is CityWalk in Universal City, California. Originally intended to encourage traffic between Universal Studios' theme park and its Odeon Theatre to generate additional profits, it became not just a spectacular success in that regard, but its own destination as well for millions of visitors. Promoted as possessing "all the glitz and excitement of an actual urban boulevard, but with none of the problems associated with real city life: no carjackers, no panhandlers, no grime, no graffiti, no hookers, no muggers—yet also with no mall roof to block out the sunny skies or night time stars," CityWalk claims that, "for once, walking outside in the 'city' is completely safe" (Wayne, 2002). Designed by Jon Jerde, the same architect who created the massive Mall of America in Minnesota, CityWalk features outrageous architecture that uses every visual trick imaginable to wow the passing crowds, along with numerous street performers (mimes, magicians, musicians, and entertaining street vendors). In Orlando, Florida, Universal Studios offers a smaller CityWalk combination of shops, restaurants, cinemas, live entertainment, and nightclubs as a gateway between its two theme parks, Universal Studios and Islands of Adventure.

Whatever entertainment value private themed environments may have, critics warn of their dangers. Michael Sorkin (1992), for example, says that they are not benign imitations, but instead manipulative structures designed to maximize behavior control and eliminate authentic interaction as found in traditional public space. Mark Gottdiener believes that, in the aftermath of the cold, faceless public space left behind by the modernist era, the forces of capitalism have staged a "vengeful return of meaning and symbolism" to create "material space for the realization of consumer fantasies" through imitation and simulation (2001:34, 70). The problem with this is that we lose our reality as we buy into a visual theme, turning our landscape inside out, becoming convinced that all places are the same in the built environment that excludes other forms (Zukin, 1993).

POLITICAL ECONOMY: THE "NEW" PERSPECTIVE

By the end of the 1960s, an increasing number of social scientists found that the traditional economic model, as well as conventional theories of urban ecology, no longer accounted for many important changes in cities. In North American cities, one had to look beyond the city itself to understand the dramatic decline in industrial jobs; the movement of millions of people from the cities to the suburbs; the movement from the Snowbelt to the Sunbelt; and the intensifying financial problems of so many cities. Some other paradigm seemed necessary to explain the new urban realities, thus setting the stage for the political economy approach.

Several assumptions served as the foundation for the new approach. First, any city exists within the larger political structures of county, state, and nation. Beyond that, international political processes—such as oil embargos, trade agreements, hostilities—can affect urban life on a local level. Second, local economies do not operate independently but connect to one another to forge state, national, and international economic networks. Most important, the new breed of social scientists began to discount the notion that "natural processes" shape the physical form and social life of cities in favor of the belief that political and economic institutions—including banks, governments, and international corporations—shape urban life.

One key focus is the role of investment decisions in shaping cities. Who makes decisions that direct a city's economy? And for what purposes? In addition, the political economy approach investigates how conflicts—between labor and management, between racial and ethnic populations, and between social classes—have shaped the physical and social character of cities.

The new political economy viewpoint drew together geographers and philosophers as well as sociologists specializing in the investigation of urban development. Drawing on the ideas of Karl Marx, such thinkers as Henri Lefebvre, David Harvey, Manuel Castells, and

Allen Scott argued that urban changes must be understood in the light of historical economic and political forces.

Henri Lefebvre: Redefining the Study of Cities

French philosopher Henri Lefebvre (1902–1991) sparked the application of the critical and Marxian perspective to studying the city. Drawing from the writings of Karl Marx and his associate Friedrich Engels, Lefebvre (1970, 1991) applied the economic categories of capital, labor, profit, wages, class exploitation, and inequality to explain the unevenness of urban development. In doing so, he helped develop many ideas about cities to which Marx and Engels never did devote much attention. He thus became a seminal source of new thinking about the city, suggesting that urban development was as much a product of the capitalist economic system as was any manufactured good.

Two Circuits of Capital

To advance his concept, Lefebvre made a distinction between two types of investment capital. He identified the commonly studied economic activity—investment to hire workers to manufacture a product to sell at a profit to be used for more investment—as the *primary circuit of capital*. Thus, in a capitalist system the main flow of money is from investors into materials and labor costs to create a manufactured good whose sale generates profits for still more manufacturing ventures. This continual circulation of manufacturing capital generates much wealth for investors but is also what pumps the national economy. Hence Lefebvre named this circular money flow the *primary* one.

To examine the unevenness of urban development, Lefebvre identified another important profit-oriented economic activity—real estate investment—as the *second circuit of capital*. Investment in land, he maintained, almost always leads to profit and serves as an important means for acquiring wealth. One buys property expecting it to appreciate in value or develops land for residential or commercial purposes—both of which yield a profit. The circuit becomes complete when the investor takes that profit and invests it in more land-based projects.

Within a city, he suggested, profit-seeking motives determine the stability, decline, or rejuvenation of various areas. Lefebvre's focus on real estate investment pushing city growth in certain ways was a turning point that influenced subsequent theories and analyses of the dynamics of urban development.

Space as Part of Social Organization

Lefebvre made a second important contribution with his assertion that space is more than just a social "container"; it is also closely linked to behavior. That is, we construct our surroundings to meet particular needs and objectives; our surroundings, in turn, affect our subsequent behavior. People thus organize their daily lives and actions—whether cultural, economic, educational, or social—within constraints or opportunities of the built environment. We need to think of planners and developers, then, as important architects of social life. Lefebvre added that comparable social systems organize space similarly, so that edge cities or suburbs in Australia, Canada, or the United States, for example, closely resemble one another.

The Role of Government

Venturing further into territory uncharted by Marx, Lefebvre also considered the actions of government, from the national level down to the local level, as a critical factor shaping a city's use of space. Governments are empowered to make various decisions that affect city shape and urban life—decisions that range from condemnations of structures, claims of eminent domain, provision of funding, approving new roads or alterations to roads, supervising urban renewal, and responding to zoning appeals. The federal and state governments also collect taxes from, and distribute resources to, various lower-level political units (states, counties, and municipalities). The government also directly owns a great deal of urban land (fire, police, and government

buildings; parks, roads) and exercises control over the rest (zoning, tax valuation). With all these forms of social control over space utilization, governments can strike deals to attract corporations to a certain locale or take many other actions to encourage development or redevelopment of an area.

Further, Lefebvre distinguishes between two definitions of space: *abstract space* and *social space*. The first is what businesspeople, investors, and government have in mind when they discuss the dimensions of size, location, and profit. The second is what individuals who live, work, and play in an area think about their environment. Often, Lefebvre claims, government and business talk about abstract space—plans, say, to build a shopping mall or construct a low-income housing project—paying little attention to the ideas of local people. The resulting conflict, continues Lefebvre, is much the same as (but not identical to) the class conflict discussed by Marx.

These three ideas of Lefebvre—two circuits of capitalism, space as a component of social organization, and the role of government in managing space—were highly influential in charting the course others would take. Most new theories in urban development trace their origins to this French philosopher, although many later theorists do not agree with all of Lefebvre's arguments. We will now turn to some of these later urbanists and present their contributions to an urban political economy.

David Harvey: The Baltimore Study

The prominent English geographer David Harvey (1992; 1973) illustrates Lefebvre's ideas in a Marxist analysis of how the capitalist real estate system operated in Baltimore, directly shaping many of the city's problems concerning social inequality. He divided Baltimore into real estate submarkets that included the inner city, white ethnic areas, the low- to moderate-income African American area of West Baltimore, areas of high turnover, middle-income areas in Northeast and Southwest

Baltimore, and other upper-income areas. Each of these areas revealed a distinctive pattern of buying and selling, as reflected in the amount of up-front cash or investment through private loan transactions, bank financing, and government insurance. Each physical environment generated different levels of commitment by community banks, private financial institutions, and government agencies, which, in turn, influenced potential developers, speculators, homeowners, and renters.

Harvey's detailed analysis revealed that urban development is not a monolithic growth process. Instead, it occurs unevenly. This second circuit of capital varies in its investment arrangements from place to place, influenced by different combinations of social factors, profit potential, and conflict. For example, banks showed no interest in lending to the inner-city poor, who, of necessity, financed their housing transactions by cash payment, private loans, and/or government programs. White ethnics also had trouble securing bank financing; instead they financed their housing purchases through community-based savings and loans associations. Both inner-city and white ethnic areas had difficulty obtaining Federal Housing Authority (FHA) or Veterans Administration (VA) insurance, unlike Baltimore's middle-income sections. People in more affluent sections rarely resorted to FHA guarantees and made far greater use of commercial and savings banks. Also, with their political and economic power, they could repel speculative incursions into their neighborhoods, unlike residents of poor or working-class neighborhoods.

Thus, Harvey demonstrated how discrimination by investment capitalists in the housing market affects the dynamics of buying, selling, and neighborhood transition. He also showed the role of government in shaping a city's use of space: West Baltimore rose above other poor areas in the city as a result of multiple government renewal programs. Essentially, Harvey's Baltimore study disclosed how the priorities of the second circuit of capital, aided by government programs, link directly to central city decay and the suburbanization

of the population. Actions by real estate investors—more so than actions by industrial capitalists, he maintained—lead to areas of the city becoming run-down and abandoned.

Urban change, claims Harvey, reflects the changing needs of a capitalist economy. That is, capitalists build a physical city appropriate to the city's needs at one point only to destroy it later, usually in the course of some crisis. Different segments of the urban population—investors (finance capital), store owners (commerce capital), manufacturers (industrial capital), financial analysts, as well as white- or blue-collar workers—have different priorities and goals. Capital interests, motivated by profit making, and labor, seeking to protect and enhance its standard of living, often engage "in a series of running battles over a variety of issues that relate to the creation, management, and use of the built environment" (Harvey, 1992:268).

Unwilling, therefore, to risk their profits by granting too much power to workers, the capitalist class seeks government intervention to secure the type of urban development that serves its narrow interests. This strategy explains widespread urban blight; finance capital has little reason to invest in poor neighborhoods, preferring instead the greater profits found in high-rent districts. This reluctance to aid decaying urban areas, claims Harvey, is precisely why government intervention is so important. But public urban renewal projects seem to operate only to restore the area's profitability in order to attract finance and commerce capital once again, in the process doing little for the poor. Harvey's contribution, then, lies in revealing how the actions of finance capital (rather than industrial capital) affect a city's fortunes.

Manuel Castells: Updating Marx

Manuel Castells—while influenced by Lefebvre's writings—maintained a more orthodox Marxist approach to the study of cities. His special contribution (1982, 1985) was extending Marxist analysis beyond the traditional

David Harvey's study disclosed how some Baltimore neighborhoods fared better than others because of priorities set by real estate investors and government programs. His conclusion was that these decisions, more than those by departing industrialists, are closely linked to decaying areas of a city, prompting abandonment and relocation to another area.

conflict between labor and capital to explicitly urban patterns. He also highlighted the conflict between local government and the working class arising from local administration of various social welfare programs. Although the national government funds such programs as needs-based income, housing, and health care benefits for the poor, local or city governments typically administer them. City residents seeking these resources often become entangled in conflict with city agencies.

Welfare Capitalism

Castells views welfare capitalism—the government providing worker subsidies—as an important social movement affecting urban life. To him, key issues such as housing, education, mass transportation, health, and welfare make sense only within the context of disputes arising over their administration by city government agencies. Such government activity to provide resources to the working class, to Castells,

represents an effort to "extend" capitalism, and gives rise to new urban struggles and patterns of conflict unknown in Marx's time.

In one sense, changing economic conditions since the early 1980s have lessened the impact of Castells's analysis. The once expansive welfare states found in the advanced industrialized countries of the Western world are cutting back. Recessions, aging populations, tax revolts, budget deficits, and fiscal crises all have curbed government spending and, in some cases, have led to dismantling of welfare programs. Thus, local governments administer fewer subsidizing programs than they once did.

On the other hand, however, the 1996 welfare reform legislation in the United States empowered the states and local municipalities to set their own guidelines for administration of federal funds. Perhaps people's struggles to receive the more limited aid available under decentralized regulations may intensify the conflict between the working class and local government that Castells identified.

Modes of Development

Examining industrial growth in suburbs, Castells adapted one of Marx's concepts to fit the information age. Whereas Marx had stressed the *mode of production*—the things needed to produce goods and services, such as land, tools, knowledge, wealth, or factories— Castells (1991) introduced the concept of the *mode of development.* The key element in the industrial mode of development, he explained, was discovering and applying new sources of energy. In today's informational mode of development, however, the key element is developing new forms and sources of information. One obvious consequence of this shift is that corporate decisions about location no longer rest on proximity to raw materials or to a large, unskilled labor pool, as they once did.

Castells's focus was the differential effect of emerging high-tech businesses on segments of the urban region. Specifically, he found that high-tech production disproportionately occurred in suburban rather than central-city communities. Such companies typically have facilities on the periphery of cities, thereby accelerating the pace of outward movement and sparking the rise of edge cities. Influencing choice of suburban locations is the need for large-batch production facilities combined with automated subsidiary plants, access to a freeway system, and the typically suburban locale of research and design centers and military installations for testing and marketing defense-related products.

Allen Scott: Business Location and the Global Economy

Another English geographer, Allen J. Scott (1980, 1988), offers additional non-Marxist insights into the impact of changes in the production process on urban space. His approach is not a comprehensive theory of the built environment but a study of the relationship between a city's fortunes and the globalization of the economy. Further, in rejecting the urban ecology approach, Scott suggests

that the economic interests of powerful transnational corporations—not a biological model of species competition over territory— determine urban growth patterns.

Horizontal Integration

Over the course of this century until about 1970, cities evolved into metropolitan regions as corporations changed in their economic organization. Once, companies were small entities with all their functions centralized in one location. Gradually, many industries absorbed or consolidated with competitors, sometimes taking the form of an *oligopoly* (the domination of a market by a few producers). Then they maintained headquarters in a major city with easy access to banking, marketing, and other necessary services—but they located their production plants, distribution centers, and sales divisions elsewhere, in locales most advantageous to them. In time, many companies gained control over the manufacture of all parts that went into their final product, as when auto companies manufactured not just the engine, frame, and body of the automobile but also batteries, headlights, radios, upholstered seats, window glass, and bumpers as well. Some companies even obtained ownership of raw materials needed for the manufacturing process. With their separate functions thus spatially dispersed, companies maintained a national network of command and control to reduce costs and maximize profits. This economic structure is called *horizontal integration.*

One way to maximize profits is to minimize shipping costs in the total manufacturing process. Not surprisingly, while horizontal integration was predominant, the specialized production facilities were mostly located near the main assembly plant—virtually all auto parts plants were within 150 miles of "Motor City," or Detroit, the automobile manufacturing center. Close proximity of these subsidiary agglomeration industries not only kept shipping costs low but also created an economically interdependent metropolitan region. As the companies prospered, so too did the cities.

Vertical Disintegration

Beginning in the 1970s, large corporations, while still maintaining some horizontal integration (especially of manufacturing, marketing, and administration activities), began to unload their production support companies (*vertical disintegration*). In other words, instead of manufacturing materials or parts needed for the production process themselves, they awarded contracts to suppliers through a process of competitive bidding. Competitiveness among subcontractors resulted in lower costs because of the elimination of overhead costs in maintaining inventory stocks and offset concerns about shipping expenses. The advent of computer manufacturing or computer assisted manufacturing (CAM) enhanced the coordination of this system of production, enabling companies to keep track of all needs and to order "just-in-time" parts more easily.

A significant consequence of vertical disintegration was the creation of many new supplier companies locating where labor and energy costs were low, either in North America or abroad. Scott sees this last development as the climax of vertical disintegration: the ability of large companies to conduct business on a global scale. In short, businesses have become transnational or multinational, investing their capital and locating their manufacturing, marketing, and administration anywhere in the world that best suits their needs. Suppliers may now be anywhere: perhaps in the non-unionized, low-energy-cost Sunbelt or, better yet, in extremely low-wage countries in poor regions of the world.

How has this affected older industrial cities? For most of them, plant closings meant the loss of thousands of jobs, an out-migration of workers and their families seeking jobs elsewhere, and a depressed economy. Loss of an industrial base adversely affected the city's commercial base, as stores no longer had the same customers as before. In contrast, the Sunbelt exploded in industrial development and population growth. As virtually every northeastern U.S. city steadily shrank in population in the second half of the twentieth century, the fastest-growing cities were those in the Sunbelt (see Chapter 3).

No longer dominated by manufacturing, older cities have shifted to providing greater employment opportunities in business services. Most have not fully recovered and are still experiencing population decline. A few cities, however, such as New York, London, and Tokyo, now function as "highly concentrated command posts in the organization of the world economy." They are also important locations of finance, specialized service firms, and innovation sources, and serve as markets for the products and innovations produced (Sassen, 1991:3–4).

New economic realities thus shape the production process and in turn affect urban growth patterns—a subject we will now explore further through two sociological approaches, one examining local conditions and the other viewing global conditions.

John Logan and Harvey Molotch: Urban Growth Machines

John Logan and Harvey Molotch (1987) employed political economy theory in an effort to identify *who* the central decision makers in North American cities are and to determine *why* they do what they do. In concentrating on the battles between pro- and anti-growth factions, their study is essentially an application of Lefebvre's categories of abstract space and social space that we discussed earlier.

Urban growth coalitions—typically made up of bankers, businesspeople, corporate property owners, developers, politicians, and investors —seek to spark population growth, increase the market value of land, and stimulate the city's economy through investment and development. To accomplish these goals, they pressure the city government to create a "good business climate" (cleanliness, safety, tax incentives, low-interest loans, relocation assistance). They also seek to enhance and promote the image of the city, promoting its attributes (such as cultural and recreational activities, sports teams, landmarks, and night

Another example of the global economy can be found in the manufacturing plants of North American multinational corporations located in other countries, such as this plush toy plant in Shanghai, China. Benefiting from a cheaper, non-union labor force and generous tax incentives, companies find more profit in paying higher shipping costs from abroad than in higher U.S. expenses for wages, employee benefits, and taxes.

life). Their focus on quality of life, however, only extends to what Lefebvre termed "abstract space" issues involving the high profits that accompany urban growth.

By contrast, most local residents have a "social space" view of their community, and they may oppose growth as being against their best interests. City residents may wish to protect the "character" of their neighborhood, preserve older buildings, limit traffic flow, and maintain parks and other open spaces.

Advocates of urban growth point to its advantages—more jobs, additional tax ratables, increased economic activity—and they are often correct in doing so. What also accompanies growth, however, is environmental degradation, higher rents, more crime, greater traffic congestion, and an infrastructure unable to handle an increased population. Tensions in the growth machine materialize as community groups seek to block a proposal or

at least to lessen its negative impact on their community and the environment.

Logan and Molotch also point out how the global economy influences many changes in the city. Local political action is less effective than it once was because the deindustrialization of North American cities has caused the flight of industrial capital. The "new international division of labor" may benefit some people (major corporations and their stockholders reap huge profits from the new global economy), but ordinary people in cities back home are weakened by a loss of jobs. Thus, local people have less power to oppose the corporate agenda, just as corporations have more power to get their own way.

At the heart of all contemporary urban land use, then, there is a focus on the most profitable use of materials and labor. The question that corporate executives ask is simply: "If we do this, will we make money?" Concerns for

Corporate headquarters once typically located in major North American cities, and many still do. In recent decades, however, some moved part or all of their operation to suburban campus locations, lured by local tax abatements and other economic incentives. This Hewlett-Packard office building—with its tree-lined courtyard, benches, and volleyball court—typifies this pattern.

the welfare of the worker, the neighborhood, and the city's poor simply take a back seat (if they exist at all). This "profit-bias" has international roots and consequences, as Peter Hall explains:

> In the modern world, newly industrializing countries undermine the traditional economic bases of older nations and regions. In the latter, skilled workers in declining industries lose their jobs and end up in unskilled service occupations. Entrepreneurs react to the threat of competition by closing older inner city plants and concentrating production in rural areas, where unionization is weaker and wages are lower. Multinational enterprises centralize their control functions in a few of the world's cities, where they can displace other functions to other cities and suburbs. Because profit seeking and competition are inherent and incessant, this process of change is never ending. (1984b:33)

In the end, urban political economy presents an alternative to what its proponents see as the biased approach of the older urban ecology model; in the newer model, there is an assumption that profit making and capitalism are the natural forces that shape cities.

THE GLOBAL ECONOMY

Economic forces always affect cities. As discussed in Chapter 3, for example, the Industrial Revolution redefined urban life and greatly increased city population size. At the midpoint of the twentieth century, the typical North American city was an industrial center. White-ethnic, blue-collar neighborhoods peppered the urban landscape, built around the factories in which residents worked. In other parts of the city, its middle class resided. Then, in the 1950s and 1960s, the exodus of the middle class—soon followed by many businesses and industries—created a fiscal crisis from which some cities have never recovered.

By the 1970s manufacturing was in decline nationwide, and the transfer of much economic production to other countries dramatically changed the older cities. Gone were most of the jobs that earlier migrants and immigrants used as a path to economic security. Gone too were the ties that bound central-city workers to their local employers. Also gone was a sizable portion of the cities' tax base.

Forced to restructure their economies away from manufacturing, North American cities evolved into service centers, specializing in advertising, corporate management, finance, and information processing. In particular, cities expanded those business services required by the finance capitalists who head up investment activity for the global economy (Sassen, 1991). Next, the 1980s and 1990s bore witness to *economic restructuring* and the globalization of the economy that spawned still other changes in metropolitan regions. This transition produced a new generation of cynics sounding the death knell for cities, but as explained in the Critical Thinking box on page 271, this view ignores the essential role that cities play in today's world.

Such changes are evident in the present-day character of the urban labor force. The demand for many of the entry-level factory jobs traditionally held by urban poor with limited education and skills dropped dramatically, countered by a rising demand for computer-literate workers with verbal and quantitative skills. The reason was that, although some corporate headquarters moved outside the central cities, the latter continued to provide a necessary concentration of firms and jobs necessary to run the advanced corporate economy (Sassen, 1994:76).

In turn, this efficient agglomeration of specialized product services became a vital link in the evolving global economy, to which we now turn.

A World System

With its macrosocial view, the political economy approach to understanding cities' conditions fits nicely into a world-system perspective. This emphasis views capitalism as evolving through a long, historical process that draws increasing areas of the world into a single economic and political system (Wallerstein, 1979; 1997). This system operates as a hierarchy so that countries at various stages of development constitute the "core," the "semiperiphery," or the "periphery." Within that framework, cities occupy a place in the world urban hierarchy that greatly affects growth patterns within each city. The impact of the global economy on U.S. cities is discussed in the next Critical Thinking box on page 272.

The Hierarchy of Countries

The more economically developed countries (Canada, Japan, the United States, the nations of Western Europe) constitute the "core" of this world system and are home to the transnational corporations that dominate the global economy. The headquarters of transnational corporations, located in large cities within rich countries, carry out high-level decision-making that guides the world's economic forces. Because so many employees are well-paid professionals, these cities benefit in the quality of housing and of economic and social enterprises that spring up to cater to their tastes.

Countries in the "semiperiphery"—such as Argentina, Hungary, Poland, and South Korea—have close ties with the richest nations. Yet these countries play a secondary role in global economic matters. Most of the transnational corporate employees in these countries are lower middle class. For the most part, their somewhat lower standard of living brings a less grand variety and quality of activities to the urban scene than found in the "core" countries' cities.

Countries in the "periphery" are the poor, less-developed countries in Africa, Asia, and Latin America. Jobs in these countries typically pay little and offer little opportunity to advance. These transnational corporate workers are typically rural migrants living in slums or shantytowns and struggling to survive. The impact of the global economy on the cities of "periphery" countries is more negative than positive. Although a small, affluent elite exists in virtually all cities, most urban residents of

CRITICAL THINKING

Cities and the World Economy   Saskia Sassen

If cities were irrelevant to the globalization of economic activity, the center could simply abandon them and not be bothered by all of this. Indeed, this is precisely what some politicians argue—that cities have become hopeless reservoirs for all kinds of social despair. It is interesting to note again how the dominant economic narrative argues that place no longer matters, that firms can be located anywhere thanks to *telematics* [telecommunications and computer technologies that allow for instantaneous transmission of information over short and long distances], that major industries now are information-based and hence not place-bound. This line of argument devalues cities at a time when they are major sites for the new cultural politics. It also allows the corporate economy to extract major concessions from city governments under the notion that firms can simply leave and relocate elsewhere, which is not quite the case for a whole complex of firms. . . .

In seeking to show that (1) cities are strategic to economic globalization because they are command points, global marketplaces, and production sites for the information economy; and (2) many of the devalued sectors of the urban economy actually fulfill crucial functions for the center, [we should re-emphasize] the importance of cities specifically in a globalized economic system and the importance of those overlooked sectors that rest largely on the labor of women, immigrants, and, in the case of large U.S. cities, African Americans and Latinos. In fact it is the intermediary sectors of the economy (such as routine office work, headquarters that are not geared to the world markets, the variety of services demanded by the largely suburbanized middle class) and of the urban population (the middle class) that can and have left cities. The two sectors that have stayed, the center and the "other," find in the city the strategic terrain for their operations.

Source: **Saskia Sassen**, *Cities in a World Economy.* (Thousand Oaks, CA: Pine Forge Press), 1994, p. 124.

---

these third-tier countries live at the lower end of the socioeconomic scale. Their cities thus offer even fewer of the usual social amenities of a city, except for those catering to tourists or the small local elite. Integration into the global market encourages informal enterprises within local urban economies, but often at the cost of a serious erosion of wages and employment conditions (Portes et al., 1997:246).

Thus, the three tiers of countries in the world system are unequal yet interdependent. The system operates mostly in the interest of the richest nations, while providing far less to the majority of the world's people who live in

less economically developed nations. The quality of urban life in each of the three tiers reflects this world-system hierarchy (see Figure 9–2 on page 274).

Of the many transnational corporations involved in this system, the "Just Do It!" Nike Corporation makes a product familiar to most readers of this book. Nike designers, researchers, executives, and other white-collar employees live and work in the large cities of the core countries and receive excellent salaries and benefits. Yet Nike workers—the people who actually make the shoes—inhabit peripheral countries such as China, Vietnam,

CRITICAL THINKING

The Impact of the Global Economy on U.S. Cities

... [New York] was the preeminent city of the time; it housed the headquarters of major corporations and the nation's financial center and served as the country's locus of transportation and communication—it was the nation's major link to the rest of the world. Until the middle of the twentieth century, almost all of the United States' international flights arrived in and departed from New York, and the international publishing and financial institutions that were located in the United States' were almost exclusively headquartered in New York.

The world economy has grown in the past fifty years or so, with the economy of each nation increasingly influenced by events occurring outside of its borders. Decisions that greatly affect millions of people are now routinely made in "global cities." These are the cities—such as London, Paris, and Tokyo—in which almost all of the world's economic activity is integrated and coordinated. The awesome efficiency of modern transportation and communication has made it possible for executives in the headquarters of a multinational corporation to control its production, sales, and marketing activities all around the world. The headquarters may be in London, production facilities may be in Taiwan, advertising may be centered in Atlanta, and the primary sales market may be Mexico City.

As ties between the United States and other nations have strengthened, the number of U.S. cities serving as important links to the world system has increased. In addition to New York, Los Angeles has become an important link to the Pacific Rim nations, Miami to the nations of South America, and so on.

In an apparent paradox, the rising preeminence of the local in the postmodern city has been facilitated by the appearance of a global capitalism. The emergence of post-Fordism [i.e., an increasingly flexible, disorganized regime of capitalist accumulation] has resulted in an accelerated flow of global capital, and an endless search for cheap labor supplies on an international scale. These trends have connected the local ever more effectively to the world-wide developments of post-Fordism; what happens in downtown LA tomorrow may result from yesterday's fluctuations in local labor markets in East Asia. At home, the consequences have been a rapid deindustrialization especially in the snowbelt, and (re)industrialization in the sunbelt. Los Angeles, in perhaps a typically postmodern way, is experiencing both simultaneously. Within its limits, the city has vestiges of a major automobile manufacturing industry, as well as in the glittering towers of corporate high-techdom. LA is an "informational city" with, at the same time, a proliferation of minimum-wage, part-time service industry jobs (e.g., fast food outlets) and a massive informal sector (street vendors on freeway off-ramps; can recycling efforts from the backs of trucks; etc.). In social terms, the postmodern metropolis is increasingly minoritized and polarized along class, income, race and ethnic lines. The disadvantaged classes are overwhelmingly people of color. Their family lives are increasingly disrupted by the demands of a flexible, disorganized workplace (for example, the pressure on both parents to work, or the need for families to crowd together to be able to afford housing). These trends have been aggravated by the strong dose of privatism, as well as the practical effects of privatization, that emerged during the Reagan era and show few signs of abating.

Sources: Mark Abrahamson, *Urban Enclaves: Identity and Place in America* (New York: St. Martin's Press, 1996), pp. 10–11; Michael J. Dear, *The Postmodern Urban Condition* (Malden, MA: Blackwell, 2000), p. 15.

Potsdamer Platz, once a no-man's land between East and West of weeds and barbed wire, is the symbolic heart of modern Berlin. The 82-acre development is a cluster of a new mass transit system, sleek corporate high-rises, shopping malls, and theaters. The district was developed mainly with global capital from corporations such as Sony, Asea Brown Boveri (an international conglomerate), and DaimlerChrysler for the sites of their European headquarters.

and Indonesia. The shoes or sneakers you wear may well have been made by young children living an impoverished existence, working long hours for little pay, in hot, crowded factories. In 1998, Nike CEO Philip Knight admitted that the brand had become "synonymous with slave wages and arbitrary abuse," and pledged to do something about it. While conditions have improved somewhat, wages remain at about $45 a month for a 66- to 77-hour work week (Schmidt, 1999).

The Role of Cities

Cities serve as important nodes in the global network, linking together money (investment capital), people (human capital), production (industrial capital), and commodities (commercial capital). Instant communications, electronic cash transfers, rapid transportation, and the relative ease of shipping by tankers or cargo jets make cities key elements of the global economy. As such, they are locked in a reciprocal relationship: They help shape the world system and, in turn, the world system shapes them. Today, it is the importance of a city's role in the world system that largely determines its prospects for growth and prosperity (Gugler, 1996:2–4).

Cities are no longer independent entities whose fortunes rise or fall according to what happens in a limited, local region. The prevailing view is that place no longer matters—that modern technology allows firms to locate anywhere, making cities irrelevant to the globalization of economic activity. One expert, however, disagrees. Saskia Sassen (1994:76) argues that cities offer an infrastructure concentration and servicing that are key dynamics in providing the capabilities for global control. Although some components of the financial district—notably in foreign currency markets—may exist in cyberspace, international cities such as New York, London, and Tokyo are examples of another aspect of the global economy: urban economic cores of banking and service activities. They are "transterritorial

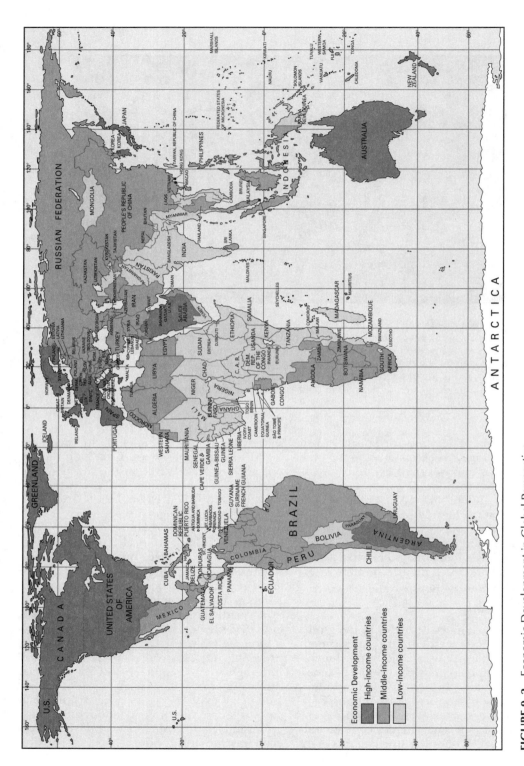

FIGURE 9–2 Economic Development in Global Perspective

Source: From Macionis's *Sociology*, 9th ed. (2003), using data from United Nations Development Programme (1995) and The World Bank (2002). Map projection from *Peters Atlas of the World* (2002).

The global economy manifests itself in virtually all cities. It is practically impossible, for example, to go to any urban locale worldwide and not find McDonald's, Burger King, Pizza Hut, Kodak film, American cigarettes, Coke, or Pepsi. Foreign sales are an important part of all multinational corporate profits.

centers constituted via digital highways and intense economic transactions" within "a specific complex of industries and activities." Thus, these three cities stand at the apex of the global urban hierarchy because they are the financial capitals of the nations that dominate the world economy. On a smaller scale, Miami and Toronto—as significant regional sites—illustrate the locational concentration of certain industries and activities embedded in the new international corporate sector (1994:96–97). Their financial districts are of recent vintage, their expansion a response to the dynamics of globalization.

The place of cities in the world economy, then, is as "command points, global marketplaces, and production sites for the information economy." Some intermediate sectors of the economy—the ones not geared to world markets but providing services to the mostly suburbanized middle class—may have left, but cities provide strategic terrain for the operations in a globalized economic system (Sassen, 1994:124).

URBAN POLITICAL ECONOMY: FOUR PRINCIPLES

Although various urban political economists still emphasize different aspects of economic activity and mix the disciplinary viewpoints of economics, geography, political science, and sociology in one fashion or another, they all now agree on four principles as the foundation for studying and analyzing cities and urban life.

1. *A city's form and growth result not from "natural processes," but from decisions made by people and organizations that control wealth and other key resources.* Rejecting the ecological model, urban political economists view cities as benefiting or suffering from investment decisions made by financial and business organizations. Thus, cities are products of broader economic forces and trends, as well as of the technologies employed by businesses.

2. *Urban forms and urban social arrangements reflect conflicts over the distribution of resources.* Urban life, claim political economists, is an

Maquiladoras

Toluca, Mexico

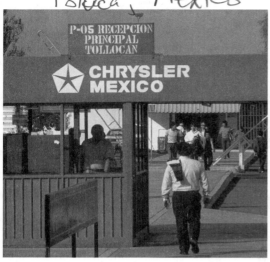

The *maquiladoras*'system locates primary manufacturing near the U.S. border to allow multinational companies to use cheap labor and ship finished goods back to the United States. Here workers enter and exit past a control booth at a Chrysler maquiladora plant in Toluca, Mexico, one of nearly 100 U.S. owned and operated companies on the South Texas/Mexico border.

ongoing struggle between rich and poor, between powerful and powerless, between management and labor, between the needs of vast businesses and the desires of local communities. As the next Critical Thinking box on page 277 suggests, such ongoing confrontation often brings a sense of paralysis to people living within today's cities.

3. *Government continues to play an important role in urban life.* Local government plays a key role in allocating resources and mediating conflicts among various groups vying for support. Decisions about zoning, tax incentives, and spending priorities, for example, still have much to do with a city's (a) business locations, (b) housing and resident population types, and (c) public space activities. And, significantly, because cities exist within a larger society, the federal government—with its enormous resources and regulatory powers—is a key influence on urban life, both directly through its spending programs and indirectly through its management of the prime interest rate for loans and its rules governing investors.

4. *Urban growth patterns significantly result from economic restructuring.* The globalization of the economy has changed the face of many North American cities as manufacturing has given way to service industries. Further, corporate mergers and takeovers have created vast conglomerates, in the process eliminating many medium-sized firms and the jobs they provided. Downsizing, by which corporations strive to achieve a leaner, less costly organizational structure, has also reduced the number of middle-management positions. Together, these dimensions of economic restructuring have dramatically reshaped cities, fostering growth or decline in metropolitan regions throughout North America and around the world.

THE URBANIZATION OF POVERTY

The world's poor once huddled mostly in rural areas, but no longer. Now, they live mostly in cities and, by 2015, the poorest cities will house three-quarters of the world's population (Piel, 1997). This urbanization of poverty creates problems that affect the quality of life for all residents—problems that cities so far have been unable to resolve.

The Developing World

In virtually every less-developed country (LDC), poverty—once found primarily in the villages of traditional agricultural societies—has moved to the cities of those countries. Significantly, however, the poverty of the world's poor is not the recognizable socioeconomic institution found in industrialized countries. This new form of poverty traps these unfortunate people in nations that have solved the first economic problem (the production of material goods), but not yet the second (the sufficient, if not equitable, distribution of the goods their industries produce). Food and consumer goods are not the only areas of deprivation. These cities lack sufficient housing, piped water, sewerage, public transportation, schools, police protection, doctors, hospitals, and other necessary amenities and defenses of urban

"symbolic economy
"public culture"
is old

Sharon Zukin
The Cultures of Ci

CRITICAL THINKING

Public Culture and Scarce Resources

. . . [O]utright competition has dramatically changed the public sphere. Chronic fiscal crisis has so weakened public institutions and the members of their work force that their sense of mission has narrowed to saving their own jobs. Groups that interact in the same representative institutions, from city councils to boards of education, have radically different agenda that breed immobilism and distrust. The social practices of a public culture seem outmoded because they are "modern," along with the unquestioned hegemony of downtown and the pretended invisibility of class and ethnic cultures. The very concept of public culture seems old because it requires transcending private interests; it has been replaced by new rules of privatization, globalization, and ethnic separation. If every culture can set the rules—is individually hegemonic—it makes no sense to think of a transcendent common culture.

Yet what cities still do have in common is a "symbolic economy"—a continual production of symbols and spaces that frames and gives meaning to ethnic competition, racial change, and environmental renewal and decay. Despite the power of real estate developers, their architects, and members of public commissions, no single vision mobilizes this symbolic economy. Indeed, like the competing claims to embody "representations" of different cultures, the preeminence of culture since the 1970s has occurred despite the absence of vision, powerlessness of old elites to control the conditions of everyday urban life, and unprecedented debates over what should be built (or unbuilt) and where. A deep chasm lies between the post-1970s appreciation of visual culture and the absence of a master vision to control the chaos of urban life. This gap offers opportunities for both access and exclusion, for both elitism and democratization.

Source: Sharon Zukin, *The Cultures of Cities* (Cambridge, MA: Blackwell, 1995), p. 265.

---

life (Piel, 1997). See the Urban Living box on page 279 for one profile of urban poverty.

What is intimidating about the urbanization of poverty in LDCs is its scale. Between 1950 and 1990, as the first wave of industrialization came to poor, preindustrial countries, their cities expanded by 1 billion inhabitants, through migration from villages and through natural increase. Already exceeding the total population of cities in industrialized countries, cities in poor countries will increase by another 2 billion in the next fifteen years, according to the projections of demographers. These cities cannot now provide for the billion who have arrived during the past four decades, let alone the 2 billion yet to come.

At present, 30 percent of households in Latin America lack piped water and sanitation. In the cities of Asia, 50 percent lack those amenities; in Africa, where the cities are smaller but the fastest growing, 70 percent lack amenities. When the predicted 2 billion new urban poor arrive, these percentages will no doubt increase (Piel, 1997).

Housing is no problem for most urban poor in LDCs, as they had previously built their own shelters in their villages. Since most city land already belongs to someone else, they build their makeshift dwellings in the less desirable locales—the lowlands and even wetlands around the city, or hillsides too steep for ordinary buildings. These shantytowns go by many names: *citas miserias, bustees, bidonvilles,*

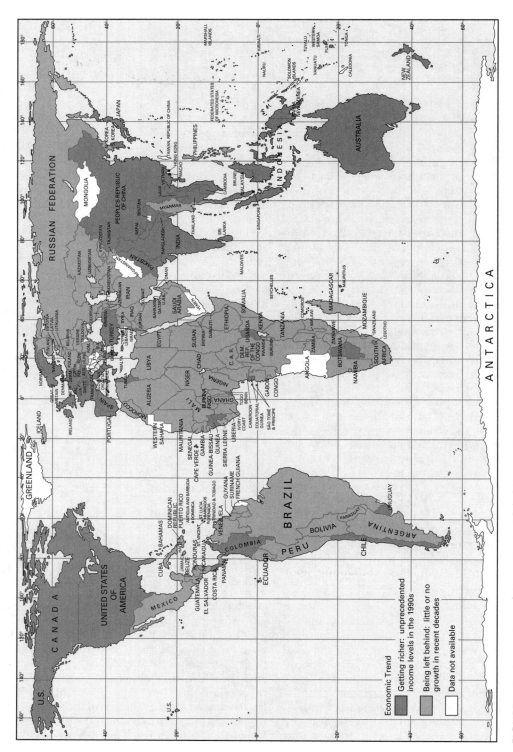

FIGURE 9–3 Prosperity and Stagnation in Global Perspective

Source: United Nations Development Programme; updated in Macionis's *Sociology* (2003).

Economic Trend

Getting richer: unprecedented income levels in the 1990s

Being left behind: little or no growth in recent decades

Data not available

URBAN LIVING

India: A Different Kind of Poverty

[handwritten: Macionis went to Madras]

The statistics show that India is one of the poorest nations of the world, with average incomes less than $1,500 per year. Unfortunately, India is home to one-third of all the world's hungry people.

But statistics do not prepare North Americans to face the reality of poverty in India. Most of the country's 900 million people live in conditions far worse than do those we label as "poor" at home. A traveler's first experience of Indian life is sobering and sometimes shocking. Arriving in Madras, one of India's largest cities with 7 million inhabitants, a visitor immediately recoils from the smell of human sewage that hangs over the city like a malodorous cloud. Untreated sewage also renders much of the region's water unsafe to drink. The sights and sounds of Madras are strange and intense—as motorbikes, trucks, carts pulled by oxen, and waves of people choke the streets. Along the roads, vendors sit on burlap cloth hawking fruits, vegetables, and cooked food. Seemingly oblivious to the urban chaos all around them, people work, talk, bathe, and sleep in the streets. Tens of millions of homeless people fill the cities of India.

Madras is also dotted by more than a thousand shanty settlements, containing about half a million people, many of whom have converged on the city from rural villages in search of something better. Shantytowns are clusters of huts constructed of branches, leaves, and discarded material. These dwellings offer little privacy and lack refrigeration, running water, and bathrooms. The visitor from the United States understandably feels uneasy entering such a community, since the poorest sections of our own inner cities seethe with frustration and, oftentimes, explode with violence.

But, here, again, India offers a sharp contrast because its people understand poverty differently than we do. No restless young men hang out at the corner, no drug dealers work the streets, and there is surprisingly little danger. In the United States, poverty often means anger and isolation; in India, even shantytowns are built of strong families—children, parents, and sometimes elderly grandparents—who extend a smile and a welcome.

In traditional societies like India, ways of life change slowly. To most Indians, life is shaped by *dharma*, the Hindu concept of duty and destiny that encourages them to accept their fate, whatever it may be. Mother Teresa, who won praise for her work among the poorest of India's people, went to the heart of the cultural differences: "Americans have angry poverty," she explained. "In India, there is worse poverty, but it is a happy poverty."

Perhaps we should not describe as "happy" anyone who clings to the edge of survival. But the sting of poverty in India is eased by the strength and support of families and communities, a sense that existence has a purpose, and a world view that encourages each person to accept whatever life offers. As a result, the visitor comes away from a first encounter with Indian poverty in confusion: "How can people be so poor, and yet apparently content, vibrant, and so joyful?"

Source: Based on John Macionis's research in Madras, India, November 1988.

geccondus, favelas, and *pueblos jovenes.* With a stubbornness and resistance to bureaucratic oppression, the residents struggle to survive, and do so utilizing a reciprocal exchange system to help one another cope with extreme poverty (Lomnitz, 1997). Others live an even worse existence as homeless city dwellers. Sadly, many of them are the young, as the Urban Living box on page 281 reveals.

The Developed World

Less developed Countries

Unlike the LDCs, the more-developed countries (MDCs) of Asia, Europe, and North America have maintained urban societies for generations, if not centuries. Although their cities have contained large numbers of poor people for that same period of time, only in recent years have greater concentrations of the poor clustered in urban areas than elsewhere. This pattern is more pronounced in Canada than in the United States.

Canada

In a comparative demographic profile of poverty throughout Canada, the Canadian Council on Social Development (2000) reported that images of poverty as a rural phenomenon are out of date. Roughly seven out of every ten poor Canadians live in an urban area. Among Canada's largest urban centers, Montreal, Ottawa, Toronto, Vancouver, and Quebec City had the highest rates of poverty for children under the age of 15. Families supported by one income earner are more likely to be poor in certain urban areas than in others. For example, in Thunder Bay, Oshawa, Kitchener, and Calgary, the proportion of poor one-earner families is much lower than in Cape Breton, Saint John, Montreal, and Hamilton. Also, the effect of unemployment on poverty rates varies in urban areas. Vancouver and Windsor, for instance, had nearly identical unemployment rates, but the rate of poverty in Vancouver was 31 percent while in Windsor it was 20 percent.

Similarly, the rate of poverty among senior citizens living in urban areas varies significantly. Less than 8 percent of elderly persons in Saskatoon, Gloucester, and Nepean live in poverty—less than in Burlington (21 percent) and Quebec City, Trois-Rivieres, and Hamilton, and Winnipeg (15–16 percent). Reasons may be related to the cost of living in these different urban areas, and to the source of income for seniors. In some urban centers, today's seniors are likely reaping the benefits of local economies that offered them good wages and benefits before they retired.

United States

Central cities do not house the majority of the U.S. poor, as one-third live in suburban areas and nearly one-fifth live in nonmetropolitan areas (U.S. Bureau of the Census, 2002b). However, central cities contain the highest concentrations of poverty, and their poverty rate has been above the national average since the early 1970s. Two major reasons account for this poverty concentration in the centers of large U.S. cities. First, many of the more affluent residents moved to the suburbs, leaving the poor behind. Second, as more jobs moved out to the suburbs, employment opportunities for city residents dwindled (O'Hare, 1996:27). Douglas Massey (1990) sees this geographic (and social) segregation by income levels as intensifying in the coming decades. Furthermore, a growing concentration undermines efforts to prevent and reduce urban poverty.

The homeless are perhaps the most visible of a city's poor, and their numbers have grown in the United States and in other developed countries as well (Kraft, 1995). Estimates of the number of U.S. homeless range from 230,000 to 750,000. Despite nearly $5 billion pumped into programs designed to combat homelessness between 1993 and 1999 (compared with just $1.5 billion between 1987 and 1993), the U.S. Department of Housing and Urban Development (HUD) hasn't made a dent. According to the U.S. Conference of Mayors, the demand for emergency shelter hasn't declined once in the two decades the group has been tracking it and, in fact, demand increased by 13 percent in 2001 over 2000 (U.S. Conference of Mayors, 2002). Ironically, the high numbers of homeless are sustained in good times and bad. As downtowns become more prosperous, higher-priced apartments replace tattered, low-rent refuges, including many old single-room occupancy hotels (SROs) that had provided flophouse-quality housing to many people living on the edge of poverty.

URBAN LIVING

Latin American "Street Children": Living on the Edge

Perhaps the greatest tragedy in Latin American cities has been the appearance of millions of "street children"—or *meninos de rua*. Like the tip of an iceberg, the presence of the street children suggests problems that run far deeper: poverty that stunts the lives of children who labor long hours each day, who work as prostitutes, or who fall victim to hunger and disease. Seventy-five percent of the Latin American population and nearly 70 percent of those at or below the poverty line now live in urban areas (World Bank, 2002b).

According to a study by the Institute for Human Development (INPRHU), approximately 15,000 children between the ages of 7 and 14 live on the streets of Managua, Nicaragua (Scheid, 1995). In Mexico City, the number approaches 40,000 (Robberson, 1995). San Salvador harbors 2,000 street children, and an estimated 5,000 street children struggle in Guatemala City, most of them between the ages of 7 and 14 (Casa Alianza, 2002). Both São Paolo and Bogotá each have tens of thousands of street children, many of them girls who begin working as prostitutes as early as age seven (Farah, 1996).

In some countries—like El Salvador and Guatemala—the street children are orphans of the civil war that ravaged their countries. Others come from broken or crowded homes where there is not enough to eat, and where physical and sexual abuse are commonplace. Just a couple of decades ago, the public looked on street urchins with a mixture of annoyance and affection. In Brazil they were known as *moleques*, that is, ragamuffins, scamps, or rascals. They were streetwise kids who were cute and cunning, sometimes sexually precocious, and invariably economically enterprising. Making themselves useful in a variety of ways, honest and otherwise, they were reminiscent of Aladdin, the Arabian Nights character portrayed by Disney. Today, however, most people look on them as public pests who should be forcibly removed from the urban landscape (Human Rights Watch, 2002).

Many of these young people live in and around the cities' sprawling public markets, where it is easy to scavenge food. A few work at shining shoes, cleaning windshields, or selling anything from candy to their bodies, but most beg or steal to survive.

Many cannot resist the temptation of cheap drugs to obliterate their hunger and cold. A few years ago, glue was the drug favored by street kids, but solvent and paint thinner are cheaper and easier to come by. A solvent-soaked rag, easily clenched in a palm, is also much more discreet than plastic bags of glue, which police have been known to seize and dump on the children's hair and clothes. All solvents have the desired effect: They stop the hunger pains and numb the physical and psychological effects of the brutality of the security forces. Inhaling the fumes produces hallucinations and escape, but the long-term effects are devastating: irreversible brain damage, paralysis, kidney or liver failure and, eventually, death. About 90 percent street youth in Latin America are estimated to be everyday users of inhalants (Casa Alianza, 2002).

In other countries, the story is much the same. In the eyes of too many people, street children are not even human, and so they are dispatched in much the same way one would step on a cockroach. It's a form of social cleansing, ridding the streets of social vermin who lie amid the rubbish, or under parked cars, curled up inconspicuously on the concrete until someone comes along and kicks them. And people rarely stop to wonder why they are there in the first place.

CRITICAL THINKING

A Bold Initiative

While shelters can provide a clean and safe environment for a homeless family, the shelter system should not be simply a way station until permanent housing is secured. To address the needs of these families, shelters also must provide a variety of services and programs that enable families to build sound, independent living skills, complete their education, and obtain job training before moving to permanent housing. Not shelters, but rather Residential Education Training (RET) Centers—or American Family Inns—are required to deliver such a service intervention plan. Through RET Centers, desperately needed services such as health care, counseling, and substance abuse treatment can be economically and efficiently provided. Educational programs such as living skills workshops for adults or after-school accelerated learning programs for children are immediately accessible and responsive to the needs of parents and children. Homes for the Homeless has developed and has continued to refine the RET Center model over the past five years as a response to the changing characteristics of homeless families.

American Family Inns have proven to be a successful mechanism to start families on a secure path to independent living. *Approximately ninety-four percent of all families who have participated in the services offered by HFH's RET Centers have maintained their residences once placed in permanent housing.* When compared to New York City's return-to-shelter rate of fifty percent for formerly homeless families, RET Centers offer a successful solution by addressing the severe complexities of the poverty faced by homeless families.

The dramatic changes in the composition and characteristics of homeless families over the last several years highlight the emerging fact that homelessness is not simply a housing issue. Rather, the trends illustrate that homelessness is merely a symptom of a debilitating poverty affecting a very young and vulnerable population. Policymakers and service providers must meet the challenge of this complex issue with bold initiatives such as the RET Center model. Only then will it be possible to break the cycle of poverty and homelessness which is now plaguing the poor urban family.

Source: "A Bold Initiative" excerpted from *The Cycle of Family Homelessness: A Social Policy Reader,* Appendix B. New York: Institute for Children and Poverty, 1998.

Frustrated at the lack of progress, and pressured by angry residents and merchants over the continued presence of street dwellers and increasingly aggressive panhandling by many of them, local leaders have turned to evicting the homeless. Instead of dealing with the causes—including mental illness, mothers in poverty, and teen vagrancy—they are attempting to drive them away by new laws and tighter restrictions on panhandling and sleeping in public places. The National Law Center

on Homelessness and Poverty (Associated Press, 1999) reported that at least 234 cities have used police to forcibly remove the homeless from certain sections of town.

The changing global economy has eliminated many low-skill jobs that once enabled the cities' poor to extricate themselves from poverty, and the current crackdown on homelessness does nothing to address its causes. Until policies are implemented aiming at causes, not symptoms, of urban poverty and homelessness, experts warn that the problem could get worse (Cohen and Tharp, 1999). See the Critical Thinking box on page 282 for one approach to resolving this problem.

SUMMARY

The conventional ecological analysis of cities and urban life highlights the advantages of particular locations and the various economic benefits cities offer over the hinterland. Living in cities allows people to get more goods of higher quality more cheaply. These economic advantages, economists like Alonso argue, are sufficient to explain recurrent patterns in urban land use: For example, businesses predominate at the center (the CBD), surrounded by residential areas and, farther out, agricultural areas. Even so, this theory may be descriptive only of Western (primarily North American) cities and, in any case, it ignores various noneconomic forces (such as race prejudice) that also affect urban land use.

By the 1960s, many social scientists came to the conclusion that the urban ecology model could not address changing patterns of urban life. French philosopher Henri Lefebvre was a major influence on the political economy perspective and contributed ideas about the primary and secondary circuits of capital, space as a form of social organization, and the role of government. David Harvey's Marxist analysis of Baltimore revealed that finance capital, not industrial capital, was the key shaper of neighborhood quality. Manuel Castells updated Marx by explaining welfare capitalism as a new form of class conflict probability and by discussing modes of development in lieu of modes of production. Allen Scott discussed horizontal integration and vertical disintegration as a basis for understanding business relocation in the global economy. John Logan and Harvey Molotch, drawing on Lefebvre's distinctions between abstract space and social space, examined the tensions arising between urban growth advocates and residents of the current built environment who may oppose the proposed new use of that space.

Economic restructuring changed older cities from a manufacturing base to a service industries base. Urban economic changes need to be understood in the context of an evolving world system of economic interdependence that places nations in a global hierarchy. This hierarchy consists of the "core" of highly developed countries, the "semiperiphery" of less-developed countries, and the "periphery" of the least developed countries. Within the ever-expanding global network, cities are locked in a reciprocal relationship, serving as important nodes linking together wealth (investment capital), people (human capital), production (industrial capital), and commodities (commercial capital).

Although political economists go in different directions, depending on their disciplinary viewpoints and areas of focus, they agree on four basic principles of political economy. First, decision-makers controlling resources—not natural processes—shape city form and growth. Second, conflicts over distribution of resources also shape city form and social arrangements. Third, government continues to play a role in affecting urban patterns. Fourth, economic restructuring is a key influence in urban growth patterns.

Just as the world is becoming more urbanized, so too is poverty. In developing countries, poverty takes a different form than in developed countries, because the equitable distribution of goods does not match the production of material goods. The rapid growth of urban poor—1 billion over the past 40 years and a projected 2 billion in the next 15—creates a serious problem for developing world cities in attempting to provide both the necessities and amenities for this burgeoning population. Developed world countries, such as Canada and the United States, are experiencing greater geographic segregation based on income levels, placing greater burdens on their cities to cope with large concentrations of the poor. Poverty results in serious problems of homelessness in MDCs, while the wretched conditions in the many shantytowns in LDCs mark their housing problem.

CONCLUSION

The economic trends that have produced major changes in economic and employment opportunities in North American cities will continue. So will the increased integration of poor countries and their cities into the world economy. Globalization is a process that no one can stop or reverse. Therefore an understanding of global political economy remains essential in any study of cities and urban life. This perspective addresses the rapid changes occurring worldwide and thus offers a comparative approach that is lacking in the ethnocentric U.S. urban ecology model.

Urban political economy, however, has two important limitations (Pahl, 1989; Walton, 1993). Large-scale concepts, such as Castells's modes of development, do not fully explain the differences between cities that are in the same mode of development. That is, global political and economic forces do not fully determine the character of all cities and neighborhoods; local variations do exist. For one thing, individuals do not respond like a ball in a pinball machine, reacting to the force of a flipper by going in another direction. They reflect, interpret, and react on their own. One danger in the political economy approach is in ignoring the individual factor—something researchers now realize and are striving to overcome.

Peter Hall (1984b:34) suggests further that urban political economy is as much defined by what it omits as by what it stresses. On the one hand, there is much to be recommended in the political economists' critique of urban ecology. On the other hand, the political economy approach does not deal very extensively or very deeply with cases where capitalist cities have been successful at raising the general standard of living of the city as a whole. Nor does it offer much insight as to the weaknesses of socialist cities in meeting the needs of many of their people. In the future, Hall sees both the conventional ecological and the new political economy approaches forming a critical dialogue that focuses on each other's strengths and limitations. In the end, of course, we can look forward to gaining an even more sophisticated understanding of urban land use.

Meanwhile, despite limitations, political economy has now become a dominant perspective in urban studies, inspiring many scientific investigations of cities throughout the world. These studies examine not only present-day patterns but also the future of cities—a subject we will turn to at the end of this book. Next, though, we will look at the anatomy of the city in terms of cities' social classes, minority populations, and problems in the areas of housing, education, and crime.

CHAPTER 10

SOCIAL CLASS
Urban and Suburban Lifestyles

What's your stereotype of a person from the city? As likely as not, you find this a difficult question to answer, because, well, there are so many kinds of people in the city. Exploring the extent of urban diversity is the task at hand. Here, we investigate how urban patterns are linked to social class; in Chapter 11, our attention turns to race and ethnicity.

In this "anatomy" of the North American city, we shall find that our cities are a study in paradox. While some urbanites clearly experience "the good life," others continually fall victim to a host of problems (the focus of Chapter 12), including poor housing, poverty, unemployment, discrimination, and crime. Our first task is to consider the causes and consequences of all these variations. Later, in Chapter 14, we will explore what has been done and what might be done to create a more humane urban environment.

URBAN DIVERSITY: MULTIPLE VIEWS

Imagine sitting in Union Square in downtown San Francisco noting the different types of people who walk by. A well-dressed young woman carrying an attaché case hurries past, as if she is late for her next appointment. An old man, unshaven and in shabby dress, reclines on the grass enjoying the warm sun; occasionally he removes a brown bag from his coat pocket, unscrews the top of a bottle inside, and raises it for a quick drink. Nearby, four long-haired young men in bright floral shirts and jeans engage in a serious discussion about the state of the nation. A short distance away, an African American woman plays a guitar as she offers Christian messages to anyone who will listen. For a moment, she attracts the attention of a group of Chinese-American children, 10 or 11 years old, who playfully skip their way through the square. A middle-class couple emerges from the City of Paris department store carrying a large assortment of packages. They buy ice cream from a street vendor, stroll into the square, and collapse wearily but happily on the soft grass.

Similar scenes play out daily in all the major North American cities. This brief portrait suggests the essence of urban life: tremendous human variety, which is sometimes troubling, sometimes exhilarating, but always interesting. Clearly, urban people in North America live very diverse lives. Although their lives may touch for a moment in Union Square, they are propelled onward by different interests, experiences, and life circumstances.

This chapter examines a wide range of urban lifestyles. By *lifestyle*, we mean the patterned ways of living that distinguish people in the urban arena. These lifestyles reflect structural characteristics such as social class, age, gender, and racial and ethnic background. As we go along, we shall keep in mind a central question: How much do factors such as social class shape our lives as urban people and how much are our lives the product of the city itself? This debate—over whether our particular social traits or the city itself is the primary cause of the distinctive patterns of urban living—lies at the heart of the whole notion of urban lifestyles.

Louis Wirth: Urbanism as a Way of Life

The champion of the view that the city itself shapes the lifestyles of city dwellers was the University of Chicago theorist Louis Wirth, whose work we highlighted back in Chapter 5. In his classic 1938 essay "Urbanism as a Way of Life," he identified *urbanism* as that "distinctive . . . mode of life which is associated with the growth of cities." To Wirth, the city worked its magic by forcing people to encounter one another in a special way: In the city, large numbers of heterogeneous people come into contact in dense settings, generating a new type of behavior and awareness—an urban way of life. City dwellers become rational, self-interested, specialized, somewhat reserved, and highly tolerant.

Harvey Cox (1965) captured Wirth's point brilliantly in his description of his own experiences. Of his boyhood days in a village, Cox wrote:

During my boyhood, my parents never referred to "the milkman," "the insurance agent," "the junk collector." These people were respectively, Paul Weaver, Joe Villanova, and Roxy Barozano. All of our family's market transactions took place within a web of wider and more inclusive friendship and kinship ties with the same people. They were never anonymous. In fact, the occasional salesman or repairman whom we did not know was always viewed with dark suspicion until we could make sure where he came from, who his parents were, and whether his family was "any good." (1965:37)

His later life in the city was, however, quite different:

Now, as an urbanite, my transactions are of a very different sort. If I need to have the transmission on my car repaired, buy a television antenna, or cash a check, I find myself in functional relationships with mechanics, salesmen, and bank clerks whom I see in no other capacity. These contacts are in no sense "mean, nasty, or brutish," though they tend to be short . . . unifaceted and segmental. I meet these people in no other context. To me they remain essentially just as anonymous as I do to them. (1965:37–38)

As Wirth understood it, the essence of urban living was being *cosmopolitan*—literally, "belonging to all the world." Robert Merton (1968:447–53) drew a useful distinction between "local" and "'cosmopolitan'" lifestyles. The life of the localite centers in the immediate area. Typically born in the area in which they live, localites are bound up within social relations and life commitments encapsulated within that specific territory. Cosmopolites, on the other hand, are more rootless and think in terms of wider possibilities. They are more likely to move on (perhaps to new jobs or a better home). Whether rich or poor, cosmopolites display a certain degree of detachment, have a somewhat blasé attitude toward their immediate surroundings, and show a sophistication in matters of taste and friendship not typical of localites. Although Merton acknowledged that cosmopolites and localites could exist anywhere, there is little doubt that the cosmopolitan attitude is found more frequently among

city dwellers and the localite attitude is more typical in small towns or rural areas.

But are cosmopolitanism and localism set off as clearly as Merton thought they were? For one thing, cosmopolitanism is found in many small college towns, such as Gambier, Ohio. Then, too, Chicago, Toronto, and most other large cities contain residential enclaves where localism abounds—Italian neighborhoods, Vietnamese communities, perhaps a Chinatown, or maybe an old upper-class area. If this is the case, then possibly the city doesn't produce a distinctive way of life at all. So argues Herbert Gans, the most outspoken critic of the Wirthian position.

Herbert Gans: Urbanism as Many Ways of Life

Herbert Gans (1968) contends that the city is a kaleidoscope of many lifestyles, only some of which resemble the cosmopolitanism described by Wirth. Further, Wirth's key variables—size of population, density, and social heterogeneity—cannot account for most of these lifestyles. Rather, Gans suggests, urban diversity is a product of specific social characteristics, such as class, age, and gender.

Exploring lifestyle diversity in North American cities, Gans identified four types of urban lifestyles: the cosmopolites, the unmarried or childless, the ethnic villagers, and the deprived or trapped. We shall consider each in turn.

The Cosmopolites

This first lifestyle seems most like Wirth's notion of the urban sophisticate. Cosmopolites are people who choose to live in the city because of its cultural diversity and because the city offers the range of activities, experiences, contacts, and friends they enjoy. Usually highly educated and displaying "sophisticated taste," cosmopolites choose a residential area with people like themselves, yet remain detached from most of their neighbors, valuing privacy and being selective about their friendships.

Gans claims the clearest examples of cosmopolites are intellectuals, artists, musicians, writers, and students. Some are affluent—affluence

Many young urban professionals ("yuppies"), who may also be "dinks" (dual income, no kids), find much in the city to enjoy. Eating out and going to a concert, the theater, or clubs are favorite pastimes. You'll also find many in the parks—roller blading, strolling, jogging (as here in San Francisco), sitting, reading, or sunning themselves—enjoying "down time" outdoors.

always increases the range of available choices—but this is not always the case. Cosmopolites congregate in New York's Upper West Side but also in Greenwich Village (where income is perhaps half as high). New Orleans's French Quarter and San Francisco's Nob Hill are other examples.

The Unmarried or Childless

This second urban lifestyle (which, Gans notes, frequently overlaps with the cosmopolite category) includes single adults or couples without children who live in city apartments rather than in the single-family residences found farther out in the urban area. Apartments are easier to maintain and less expensive for people who don't need a lot of space. This category typically includes young people just out of high school

or college and newly married couples with city-centered careers. These are the *yuppies*—young urban professionals—and the couples sometimes termed *dinks*—dual income, no kids. Yuppies and dinks have been responsible for the gentrification of urban neighborhoods—the upgrading of housing and the opening of new restaurants, fitness centers, specialty stores, and boutiques (Sassen, 1991).

Also included in this grouping are people whose children have grown up and left home. Of course, many pass through this category as part of the life course; but others may choose a single lifestyle for their whole lives. With the continual decentralization of families to the suburbs and the progressive evolution of cities into white-collar, information- and service-oriented centers, the proportion of singles in the central-city population has been steadily increasing to perhaps one-third of all residents. See the Urban Living box on page 289

Undoubtedly, Wirth's characteristics of high rationality and self-interest predominate for some people in this category. Also, as increasing numbers of African Americans move into the professional ranks, they, too, find pleasure in this lifestyle.

The Ethnic Villagers

Not everyone lives as do the couples profiled in the Urban Living box. Ethnic villagers show almost none of the so-called typical urban characteristics noted by Wirth. Explains Gans, "The 'ethnic villagers' are ethnic groups which are found in such inner-city neighborhoods as New York's Lower East Side, living in some ways as they did when they were peasants in Europe or Puerto Rican villages" (1968:37). The ethnic villagers sustain many rural life patterns in the city, claiming a local area, emphasizing traditional religious beliefs and family ties, and displaying suspicion of outsiders. Most ethnic villages are old, having been settled for some time by successive generations of the same families.

Ethnic villagers often earn low or moderate incomes. They know one another. In addition to New York's Lower East Side, Little

URBAN LIVING

DINKS Dine Out

Rich Parke, a patent attorney, and Liesbeth Severiens, associate publisher for two banking-industry magazines, are both in their mid-30s and have no children. The New Yorkers spend more than $20,000 a year eating out—and that doesn't include business meals. Dinner checks during their twice-a-week forays to five local restaurants average $65. On weekends, when they tend to dine with other couples and patronize trendy spots, the check is usually higher. Their weekly lunch expenses average $70, and restaurant breakfasts add $50 to their dining-out budget.

Mike and Judy Zeddies live in Chicago's upscale Lincoln Park neighborhood. He's a food broker; she's the art director at a local print shop. They're in their early 30s, too. The Zeddies guess they spend "a good $200" dining out each week. With dining patterns similar to those of Parke and Severiens, their grand total is about $12,000.

Bev Bajus is operating officer of the American Dietetic Association and its foundation. She lives in Chicago during the week. Her husband, Don, lives in Minneapolis, where he's a partner in a computer character animation studio. Both are over 50. They spend weekends together, generally alternating between the two cities.

"Dining out is a form of entertainment and adventure for Don and me," says Bajus. "Friends have similarly hectic schedules and dinner is often the only convenient time for socializing. Also, most of our friends share a similar love affair with food."

About 24 million married-couple households had no children living at home in 1995, and that number could top 30 million in 15 years, according to *American Demographics* magazine. It's a strong market for restaurateurs to pursue. While not all DINKs are affluent, they generally have more disposable income than their counterparts with children. . . .

"A lot of our dinner dining decisions revolve around the time factor," says Janet Janis, a Chicago bank vice president in her early 30s. "Cooking at home requires planning. You have to have gone to the store or gotten something out of the freezer. Around 8 o'clock, Dave and I look at each other and say, 'What are we going to do about eating?' And we sure aren't about to start cooking a meal at that time of the day. So we pick up the telephone, call a bunch of local restaurants and ask about the waiting times."

Source: Reprinted from Susie Stephenson, "DINKs dine out (advice on marketing restaurants to dual-income/no-kids couples)," *Restaurants & Institutions*, April 1, 1997, vol. 107, no. 8, p. 78(4). Reprinted by permission of Reed Publishing USA.

Italy, and Chinatown, such "tight" neighborhoods are found in Philadelphia's Kensington (Polish) and "South Philly" (Italian) districts, Cleveland's multiethnic West Side, Boston's Irish South Boston area ("Southie"), and Los Angeles's Mexican-American barrio. The next Urban Living box on page 290 provides

two firsthand accounts of life in urban ethnic villages.

The Deprived and Trapped

The remaining category contains people who differ from all the others in having very few choices about where or how to live. The

URBAN LIVING

The Ethnic Villagers

New York:
The Jewish Lower East Side

The streets were ours. . . . It was a prospect not always amiable or ever free from terror, but it drew Jewish boys and girls like a magnet, offering them qualities in short supply at home: the charms of the spontaneous and unpredictable. In the streets a boy could encircle himself with the breath of immigrant life, declare his companionship with peddlers, storekeepers, soapboxers. No child raised in the immigrant quarter would lack for moral realism: just to walk through Hester Street was an education in the hardness of life. To go beyond Cherry Street on the south, where the Irish lived, or west of the Bowery, where the Italians were settling, was to explore the world of the gentiles—dangerous, since one risked a punch in the face, but tempting, since for an East Side boy the idea of the others, so steadily drilled into his mind by every agency of his culture, was bound to incite curiosity. Venturing into

gentile streets became a strategy for testing the reality of the external world and for discovering that it was attractive in ways no Jewish voice had told him. An East Side boy needed to slip into those gentile streets on his own. He needed to make a foray and then pull back, so that his perception of the outer world would be his own, and not merely that of the old folks, not merely the received bias and visions of the Jews.

When he kept to the Jewish streets, the East Side boy felt at home, free and easy on his own turf. Even if not especially friendly or well mannered, people talked to one another. No one had much reason to suppose that the noisiest quarrel between peddler and purchaser, or parents and children, was anything but a peaceful ritual.

Boston: The Italian West End

To most of the West Enders, the area had been home either since birth or marriage. Some were born in the West End because this was where their parents had settled when they first came to America or where

cosmopolites and the unmarried or childless usually choose their locale; ethnic villagers live in their neighborhoods "partly because of necessity, partly because of tradition." But for those who suffer intense poverty (many of whom face the additional handicap of racial discrimination), there is little chance to escape. As Gans puts it, the deprived are the very poor, the handicapped, those in broken family situations, and those of nonwhite racial background who "must take the dilapidated housing and blighted neighborhoods to which the housing market relegates them" (1968:37–38). The Urban Living box on page 294 poignantly describes the plight of one

such family, the Tomalsons, who desperately want to move out of their Manhattan neighborhood so their daughters can grow up in a better environment.

The trapped, a category of urbanites similar to the deprived, are those who wish to move from deteriorating neighborhoods but lack the financial means to do so. Often such people have lived in what was once a desirable neighborhood, only to be left behind as industry or minorities "invaded" the area. At the extreme, they live a prisonlike existence, trapped both by their fear of a new environment that may seem strange and hostile and by their own limited income. Many are North they had moved later in life. Others came as adults in the Italian "invasion" of the West End during the 1930s. Many of them had grown up in the North End and had moved at the time of marriage in order to take advantage of better and larger apartments in the West End. In any case, almost all of the West Enders came to the area as a part of a group. Even their movements within the West End—that is, from the lower end to the upper—had been made together with other Italians at about the same time. . . .

. . . West Enders were in the West End because this is where they "belonged." . . . While they do want to be left alone, they are not averse to the aural or visual closeness of their neighbors. As everyone knows everyone else's activities and problems anyway, they know that it is impossible to hide anything by physical privacy. As one West Ender put it:

> I like the noise people make. In summer people have their windows open, and everyone can hear everyone else, but nobody cares what anybody is saying; they leave their neighbors alone. In the suburbs, people are nosier; when a car comes up the street, all the windows go up to see who is visiting whom.

While the image of the suburb is overdrawn, it is true that in the West End, where people knew so much about each other, there was no need for prying. A feeling of privacy could be maintained in the midst of high density.

In addition, hearing and seeing their neighbor's activities gave the West Enders a share in the life that went on around them, which, in turn, made them feel part of the group. . . . West Enders, living mainly in the group, have an insatiable appetite for group experience. . . .

I was told by one social worker of an experiment some years back to expose West End children to nature by taking them on a trip to Cape Cod. The experiment failed, for the young West Enders found no pleasure in the loneliness of natural surroundings and wanted to get back to the West End as quickly as possible. They were incredulous that anyone could live without people around him.

Sources: New York extract: Irving Howe, *World of Our Fathers* (New York: Harcourt, Brace, Jovanovich, 1976), pp. 256–57; Boston extract: Reprinted with permission of The Free Press, a Division of Simon & Schuster Adult Publishing Group from *The Urban Villagers* by Herbert J. Gans. Copyright © 1982 by Herbert J. Gans. Copyright © 1962 by The Free Press.

America's rapidly growing population of elderly people. In the Urban Living box on page 295, Barbara Myerhoff describes the entrapment of a group of elderly Jews living in Venice, California, a declining Los Angeles beach community.

The trapped and deprived, that familiar image of the urban poor, do not constitute the majority of urbanites. The proportion of urban poor ranges from about one-sixth in New York, the largest U.S. city, to more than one-fourth in a smaller city like Newark, New Jersey. Also, keep in mind that images of poverty as primarily an urban phenomenon are incorrect. In 2000, about 42 percent of

those living in poverty resided in central cities; 36 percent lived in metropolitan areas outside central cities, and 22 percent lived in rural areas (U.S. Bureau of the Census, 2001). Not so in Canada, however, where about seven of every ten poor families lives in an urban center with a population of 100,000 or more (Canadian Council on Social Development, 2000).

The Disaffiliated

An additional lifestyle we can add to Gans's analysis is the disaffiliated. Examples include the tramp, the hobo, the wino, the drug addict, or the wandering "bag lady." Also, as a result of

Ethnic villagers live in tight-knit communities where they find a strong social support network and meaningful personal relationships that envelop and protect them from the impersonality of the city. In highly visible Chinatowns, above the street-level commercial enterprises that lure tourists, live many of the community's inhabitants.

the 1975 Supreme Court ruling (*O'Connor v. Donaldson*) stating that mental patients who pose no obvious danger to anyone cannot be confined against their will, tens of thousands of formerly confined men and women were released into the streets. In some parts of the United States, the mentally ill constitute about 22 percent of the homeless population, the largest segment of the disaffiliated (National Coalition for the Homeless, 2002).

Most of us encounter such people from time to time, perhaps sleeping on benches in parks or bus stations, standing in doorways along skid row streets, or panhandling on busy walkways. It is all too clear that they inhabit the edges of society, and we usually assume they are cut off from work and family, weeks away from their last job or even their last square meal—a familiar stereotype. However, there is more going on.

Recent decades have seen a new type of homeless person. Efforts to revitalize cities with new construction on the edges of the central business districts, or downtowns, destroyed many of the old single-room occupancy hotels (SROs) that had provided housing to many people living on the edge of poverty. Between 1970 and 1990, for example, Chicago and New York lost about 70 percent of their SROs and Los Angeles more than half (Hoch and Slayton, 1989; Koegel, 1996). In addition, the loss of low-cost housing due to urban renewal or gentrification forced many out of their neighborhoods, thereby increasing the demand on remaining low-income housing, pushing up rents beyond what many could afford.

As a result, the National Coalition for the Homeless (2002) reported that about 600,000 people were homeless—many of them in female-headed families, the fastest-growing segment of the homeless population. Current estimates identify about 40 percent of all homeless as families, 40 percent as single men, and 14 percent as single women. Twenty-two percent are mentally ill, while 34 percent are drug or alcohol dependent.

Particularly disturbing is the fact that 75 percent of the homeless family population are children, the most vulnerable members of our society. The average age of the homeless child is six (U.S. Conference of Mayors, 2001). Homeless children are nine times more likely to repeat a grade and four times more likely to drop out of school than other children (Institute for Children and Poverty, 1993b:1). Only four out of ten heads of these families have any work history and, even then, most jobs are either part-time or short-term, held less than six months (ICP, 1994:2). Also significant is that 68 percent of these parents lack a high school diploma (Whitman, 1995:32). Limited schooling and little work experience are the all-too-typical attributes of the impoverished, but the added factor of homelessness denies these families any stability or community support.

There are some hopeful signs. The Urban Institute (usually respected by both conservatives and liberals) predicts only small future increases in the numbers of homeless. Indeed, officials at many city shelters across the country have reported stable or declining shelter populations in recent years. An effective strategy to help the homeless is to turn shelters into transitional housing, where social service professionals can directly address people's health and job problems (Mathews, 1992:29). Homes for the Homeless, for example, offers comprehensive programs such as Crisis Nursery, Together in Emotional Strength (TIES), and the Residential Educational Training (RET) Center, all of which address the multifaceted issues at the core of homelessness: education, health care, domestic violence, substance abuse, and job training.

Despite these promising signs, however, the root causes of homelessness—lack of education, inadequate low-income housing, and poverty—are unlikely to go away soon.

Urban Characters

Cities contain more than a simple range of lifestyles. They also are home to a category of people whose lives are in some way distinctive: the strange people, the ones you can't figure out, the oddballs, the characters. Here is William H. Whyte's recollection of a stroll in Manhattan:

> On a stretch of Fifth Avenue recently, the following [street acts] could be caught: steel drum player at 60th Street; flutist at 59th; mime at 58th; two girl folksingers at 54th; the Krishnas at 53rd; a trio playing Bach at 49th. There are [also] acrobats, musicians, one-man bands, violinists, Karate groups [and] animal acts. (1974:27)

And that isn't all. Within a few blocks in any direction New Yorkers would be likely to run across "Preacher Willie," the "Husband-Liberation Man," or "Mr. Magoo," the freelance traffic director. If you walk along Market Street in San Francisco, over through Union Square, and catch the cable car to Ghiradelli Square and Fisherman's Wharf, in all probability you will see dozens of street acts, sidewalk crusaders, and would-be star entertainers.

It's not that city living makes people strange. It is just that the chances of a city dweller encountering a character are much greater than they are for the resident of a small town. Add to that the fact that urban anonymity can make people "act out" in a way they never would in settings where they are well known. The city thus provides a safe haven for people who flout convention or tweak the public's nose (T. Wilson, 1986).

Wirth and Gans: A Comparison

The preceding discussion of prominent urban "types" as discerned by Gans is only a partial list. Obviously, there are countless variations of all these lifestyles. And that is the point. So many urban lifestyles exist that it makes little sense to claim, as Wirth did, that the city produces a relatively uniform type of human being.

The rather hard-nosed, calculating person Wirth hypothesized as the typical urban dweller does appear—most frequently in the cosmopolite and unmarried or childless categories. But even among these people, Wirth's variables of population size, density, and heterogeneity appear to have limited effect. For instance, many cosmopolites can buy the space they need to fend off what they believe is excessive density, just as many ethnic villagers positively thrive in high-density neighborhoods.

URBAN LIVING

The Deprived: "We've Got to Get Out of Here"

[Mrs. Tomalson] "We both worry a lot about the kids at school. Every time I hear about another kid shot while they're at school, I get like a raving lunatic. What's going on in this world that kids are killing kids? Doesn't anybody care that so many black kids are dying like that? It's like a black child's life doesn't count for anything. How do they expect our kids to grow up to be good citizens when nobody cares about them?

"It's one of the things that drives George crazy, worrying about the kids. There's no way you can keep them safe around here. Sometimes I wonder why we send them to school. They're not getting much of an education there. Michelle just started, but Julia's in the fifth grade, and believe me, she's not learning much.

"We sit over her every night to make sure she does her homework and gets it right. But what good is it if the people at school aren't doing their job? Most of the teachers there don't give a damn. They just want their paycheck and the hell with the kids. Everybody knows it's not like that in the white schools; white people wouldn't stand for it.

"I keep thinking we've got to get out of here for the sake of the kids. I'd love to move someplace, anyplace out of the city where the schools aren't such a cesspool. But," she says dejectedly, "we'll never get out if George can't find a decent job. I'm just beginning my nursing career, and I know I've got a future now. But still, no matter what I do or how long I work at it, I can't make enough for that by myself."

George, too, has dreams of moving away, somewhere far from the city streets, away from the grime and the crime. "Look at this place," he says, his sweeping gesture taking in the whole landscape. "Is this any place to raise kids? Do you know what my little girls see every day they walk out the door? Filth, drugs, guys hanging on the corner waiting for trouble.

"If I could get any kind of decent job, anything, we'd be out of here, far away, someplace outside the city where the kids could breathe clean and see a different life. It's so bad here."

Source: Lillian B. Rubin, *Families on the Fault Line* (New York: HarperCollins, 1994), pp. 227–28.

Thus, while cities do act on us in much the way Wirth claimed, we need to keep several limitations in mind. First, few urban lifestyles are found exclusively in the city; and, second, the determinants of these lifestyles are largely people's general social characteristics rather than the city itself. That is, cosmopolites live as they do because they are relatively wealthy and highly educated; likewise, the lives of the deprived and the trapped reflect poverty, a lack of skills and schooling, and, often enough, racial or ethnic discrimination. We can make a similar argument for any other lifestyle on the list.

Wirth's mistake was in generalizing too much from the urban conditions of the time in which he lived. Observing the incredibly rapid growth of North American and European cities early in this century, Wirth became convinced that the city was a powerful force that would come to dominate human life. A generation later, Gans and others could see that this simply wasn't happening; urban diversity continued to flourish. Today,

URBAN LIVING

The Trapped: "Number Our Days"

Signs of what was once a much larger, more complete Yiddish ghetto remain along the boardwalk. Two storefront synagogues are left, where only a few years ago there were a dozen. There is a delicatessen and a Jewish bakery. Before there were many kosher butcher stores and little markets. Only three Jewish board-and-care homes and four large hotels are left to house the elderly. The four thousand or so elderly Jews in the neighborhood must find accommodations in small, rented rooms and apartments within walking distance of the Center. A belt, roughly five miles long and a mile wide, constitutes the limits of the effective community of these Eastern European immigrants, nearly all of whom are now in their middle eighties and up. . . . Muggings, theft, rape, harassment, and occasional murders make it a perilous neighborhood for the old people after dark.

A decade ago, census figures suggest that as many as ten thousand elderly Eastern European Jews lived in the neighborhood. Then Yiddish culture flourished. . . .

In the late 1950s, an urban development program resulted in the displacement of between four and six thousand of these senior citizens in a very short period. It was a devastating blow to the culture. "A second Holocaust," [one] called it. "We've only got a few more years here, all of us. It would be good if we could stay till the end."

Source: Barbara Myerhoff, *Number Our Days* (New York: Touchstone, 1980), pp. 5–7.

we can conclude that *urbanization*—the clustering of population in some areas—does not necessarily generate *urbanism*—a single, distinctive way of life.

Claude Fischer: A Subcultural Theory of Urbanism

Despite Gans's critique, many argue that there *is* something different about the city and its people. Claude Fischer (1975) offered what he called a "subcultural theory of urbanism." Fischer conceded that much urban variety reflects factors such as class, age, and family status. Yet Fischer claimed that the city generates a level of *intensity* that does not exist elsewhere—intensity produced by a combination of Wirth's ecological variables.

Fischer explained that large numbers, density, and social heterogeneity do not define but *intensify* the subcultural characteristics that people possess, producing the more visible variety and sharper contrasts of the urban experience. In other words, class, age, family type, and other traits do define people's lives, but to imply, as Gans does, that these characteristics produce the same effects in a city of 10 million that they do in a town of 15,000 is simply wrong. The city magnifies these effects in a special way.

How? Because their large numbers in a city allow various types of people to form a "critical mass." Once in a city, people find out about one another, establish their own meeting places, create their own rituals, and attract still more people. Examples are the entertainment community in Hollywood, the country music people in Nashville, or the gay community in Columbus, Ohio. "Specialized" places rarely exist in nonurban areas simply because the critical mass of people of any one type simply isn't there (often enough, because they have moved to a city to benefit from precisely the "critical mass" Fischer describes). In short, Fischer's theory draws together Wirth's emphasis on the ecological forces of the city with Gans's emphasis on the characteristics of urban dwellers themselves, showing that both play a role in shaping urban lifestyles.

LIFE BEYOND THE CITY LIMITS: A BRIEF HISTORY OF SUBURBS

> When a city dweller packs up and moves his family to the suburbs, he usually acquires a mortgage, a power lawn mower, and a backyard grill. Often, although a lifelong Democrat, he also starts voting Republican.
>
> *Newsweek*, April 1, 1957, p. 42

Thus far we have said little about lifestyles found in the fastest-growing urban region of all: the suburbs. The 2000 census placed the U.S. population at some 281 million people, up about 31 million (or 12 percent) from the 1990 census. In contrast, the population of U.S. suburbs was some 141 million in 2000, up about 20 million (or 17 percent) since 1990. In 2000, 50 percent of the U.S. population lived in suburbs. With the numbers of suburbanites growing faster than the total population since the 1990 census, a majority of people now live in suburbs.

And the popularity of suburbs extends well beyond those who live there. Polls show that 60 percent of New York City residents, 48 percent of people in Los Angeles, and 43 percent of Bostonians would move out of their city if they could (Scheider, 1992:33).

Yet, like central cities, suburbs are quite diverse. Although stereotypes of suburban dwellers (as in the quotation above) were once somewhat truthful, the suburban picture now is much more complex. For one thing, U.S. suburbs are no longer almost exclusively white, as they were only a couple of decades ago. Analysis of 2000 census data from all 330 metro areas in the continental U.S. shows that while minorities were 18 percent of the total suburban population in 1990, their presence had risen to 25 percent by 2000. As the total

suburban white population grew by 5 percent in the decade, black suburbanites grew more rapidly, by 38 percent, and the numbers of Hispanics and Asians in suburbs exploded, up 72 percent and 84 percent respectively (Lewis Mumford Center, 2001c).

Furthermore, as we discussed in Chapter 3, the suburbs are pushing even farther out. New, outer-ring suburbs are spreading like wildfire, and older, inner-ring suburbs are beginning to decay. But that is getting ahead of the story. To understand the suburbs of today, we need to take a quick look at the suburbs of the past.

Suburbs and the Gilded Age

Most people are vaguely aware that suburbs grew rapidly after World War II. But suburbs are much older than that. Suburban settlement has been a continuous part of U.S. history since the seventeenth century, although its significance grew over time.

One big push came in the mid-nineteenth century, as railroads stretched outward from the central city carrying an increasing number of affluent and fashionable people to their new summer residences in outlying settlements. Of fashionable Philadelphians, E. Digby Baltzell writes:

> The early suburbanites usually spent only the summer months in the country, the more wealthy in their country houses and their less affluent friends in various popular boarding houses. With the improvement of rail service in the last few decades of the nineteenth century, large suburban estates began to multiply, suburban developments were built, and many families remained the year round. (1979:197)

In the 1870s the Pennsylvania Railroad proposed to sell land in the area of the Bryn Mawr Station (about 10 miles west of Philadelphia) and offered it to wealthy prospective suburbanites. In 1881, George W. Childs (himself the owner of a fabulous country estate at Bryn Mawr) and A. J. Drexel built what was probably the nation's first suburban development, in nearby Wayne. Baltzell records that "they erected fifty modern homes which included

Although their numbers were fairly small, the movement of affluent urbanites in the late nineteenth century to suburban areas not too far from the city conferred a quality of prestige on suburban living that persists today. Here, a New Jersey family, wearing their Sunday best, plays croquet on the well-mowed lawn behind their house.

Sambass Werner

spacious lawns, ample shade trees, and such conveniences of the city as water, sewer, and gas mains" (1979:204).

Such suburban residence in the United States clearly was limited to the rich, and few people today appreciate just how rich many were. For instance, in 1900 Peter Arrell Brown Widener built one of the most grandiose suburban residences (in Elkins Park, just to the north of Philadelphia), and it remains today as a monument to the excesses of the Gilded Age. Built on 300 acres, Lynnewood Hall has 110 rooms, formal French gardens, and, while owned by the Wideners, contained "one of the finest private art collections in the world" (Baltzell, 1979:212). The wealth of the early suburban residents has remained an important source of suburban prestige ever since.

Streetcar Suburbs

Sam Bass Warner studied the growth of the suburbs of Roxbury, Dorchester, and West Roxbury to the south of central Boston. From 1850 to 1900 these communities increased in population from 60,000 to about 227,000 (1962:35). The key to this increase was the streetcar, which carried people beyond the bounds of the old "walking city" of Boston, making frequent stops at stations that soon became centers of suburban housing. Suburban living and streetcar service, Warner concluded, "moved together"—the more there was of one, the more there was of the other. Later, crosstown service filled in the area between the original suburbs and downtown. By 1900, the old "walking city" was surrounded by a mosaic of "streetcar suburbs," which contained about half of the population of greater Boston (Warner, 1962:3).

The process repeated itself across North America. As urban subway and elevated systems pushed ever farther from the central city early in this century, suburbs appeared everywhere. And this growth has not abated. A ride on subway or elevated lines with stops at stations along the way invariably shows major shopping and residential units close by the transit station itself and, as one moves outward on the line, residential tracts of progressively newer design.

The Arrival of the Automobile

Central cities still claimed 65 percent of the total urban population in 1910. But by World War I, suburbs were growing faster (Farley, 1976:4). Decentralization was under way, and nothing did more to encourage people to move outward than the automobile. Before cars were common, suburbs were long corridors, stretching out along the streetcar tracks that led from the city core. Suburban settlement spread all around the city, however, as cars made every part of the region accessible to commuters.

The first automobile (the Duryea) appeared in the United States in 1893. Mass production began soon afterward, in 1908, with Henry Ford's Model T, the first "affordable" car, selling for about $500 (which was still most of a year's wages for the average worker). As Table 10–1 shows, from 120,000 cars in 1909, manufacturers were turning out 4.5 million cars each year by 1929.

TABLE 10–1 Automobiles Manufactured in the United States (Selected Years)

Year	Number of Vehicles
1905	24,000
1909	120,000
1916	1,500,000
1922	2,270,000
1929	4,455,000
1950	6,666,000
1980	6,376,000
1990	6,231,000
2001	4,882,000

Source: Adapted from Gary A. Tobin, "Suburbanization and the Development of Motor Transportation," in B. Schwartz, ed., *The Changing Face of the Suburbs* (Chicago: University of Chicago Press, 1976), pp. 101–104; and U.S. Bureau of the Census, *Statistical Abstract of the United States* 2002, Table 1010, p. 645.

With the paving of more and more roads, the percentage of people living in suburbs moved ever upward. From 1900 to 1940, growth was moderate. World War II stalled new construction, but after the war a virtual "suburban fever" seized the nation.

The Postwar Era: 1945–1970

Once the Great Depression and World War II were in the past, North America's suburbs exploded. Suburban growth had its roots in prosperity, the long-term desire of most middle-class people to have a place of their own away from the crush of the city. Add to this fact the beginning of the postwar baby boom (families have always preferred suburbs), as well as the rush of many white people to escape the declining and increasingly minority-occupied housing of the central cities.

Government weighed in, as well, using tax money to construct metropolitan expressways, offering low-interest loans to developers to build on vacant land, and providing Veterans Authority (VA) and Federal Housing Authority (FHA) loan guarantees that put a mortgage within the reach of a far greater number of people. All across North America, new housing developments appeared. None, however, illustrates "suburban fever" better than Levittown on New York's Long Island.

Some 30 miles east of Manhattan, Levittown rose from potato fields. Begun in 1947 by developer Abraham Levitt and his sons, it was originally planned as 2,000 rental units for veterans. However, the project escalated to 6,000 units within a year, and after the construction of the last house by 1951, Levittown contained 17,447 homes (Wattel, 1958:287).

The houses (almost all of which were sold, not rented) were small and strikingly uniform in appearance:

> The original Levittown house was designed in the "Cape Cod" manner, with 720 square feet of space on the first floor. A concrete slab . . . served as the ground floor; there was no cellar. The heating unit (oil) was located in the kitchen. In addition to the kitchen, the first

floor contained two bedrooms, a bath, a living room, numerous closets and a stairway which led to the unfinished (expansion) attic. Homes were situated on plots of 6,000 square feet or slightly larger. All interiors were exactly alike, four facades with assorted colors were used to vary the exteriors. (Wattel, 1958:291–92)

Retail businesses were quick to follow the flow of population into these bedroom communities, and local shopping malls increasingly became part of suburban living. Although a suburban shopping center broke ground as early as 1907 in Baltimore and another shortly afterward in the Country Club district of Kansas City, in 1946 only eight such centers existed in the entire United States (Jackson, 1973). By 1960, the number soared to 3,800 and then tripled again to 13,000 "malls" by 1970 (King, 1974:102; Tobin, 1976). No wonder that, by 1970, there were as many people working in the suburbs as there were in the central cities (Rosenthal, 1974).

1970 to the Present

Today's suburbs, particularly those closest to the city, no longer fit the white, middle-class, family-with-kids stereotype. More and more, suburbs are home to minorities, the working class and poor, and the aged.

Minorities

Following the federal fair housing legislation of 1968, middle-class minorities—mostly African Americans—moved into the suburbs in increasing numbers. Suburbs have become more and more racially diverse, and there now exist many stable multiracial neighborhoods (Lee and Wood, 1991:37). Yet this population shift did not end residential racial segregation. Most of this migration operated as an invasion–succession process, with blacks replacing whites, eventually yielding a black suburb.

Minority suburbanization is most pronounced in metropolitan regions of 500,000 or more, where the minority population grew from 19 percent in 1990 to 27 percent in 2000. These suburbs are now 12 percent Hispanic, 9 percent black, and 5 percent Asian. The change is even more substantial in some areas. For example, blacks are now more than 20 percent of the suburban population in such areas as Atlanta, Fort Lauderdale, Miami, New Orleans, Richmond, and Washington, D.C. Hispanics exceed 25 percent of the suburban population in Miami, Los Angeles, Riverside, and San Diego (Lewis Mumford Center, 2001c).

Population Trends

Analysts once expected the suburban boom to subside. After all, suburbs seem to involve a decided compromise: gaining a bigger house, a lawn, and better schools, but having to commute to work in the central city. In addition, the center cities still offer more exciting elements of urban life—the variety, night life, arts and entertainment, ballparks, universities, and the best of most other things: hospitals, shopping, and restaurants.

However, the suburban trend continues. The main reason, noted earlier, is that the central city is no longer where everybody works. Countless businesses have moved out to the suburbs in the past few decades, so that more than twice as many of the nation's commuters now travel from suburb to suburb each day as travel from suburb to central city.

In addition, recent decades have seen the suburbanization of virtually everything that used to be found only in the center city. What is sometimes termed the "malling of America," with suburb after suburb developing its own shopping and cultural centers, means that suburbs now outpace the center city for both amount of goods available and dollars spent (Kowinski, 2002). Across the United States and Canada, malls now number more than 60,000—about one mall for every 7,000 people. Some, like the King of Prussia Mall, some 20 miles from downtown Philadelphia, are vast cities unto themselves, where one can find virtually anything, including theatres and musical entertainment. Many people wonder why they should ever want to live anywhere else.

Politics

Given this shift of population and economic strength, it should come as no surprise that suburbs have gained enormous political clout in recent years. Because suburbia now contains the majority of voters, the reapportionment of congressional districts following the 1990 census transferred political power from the cities to the suburbs. In the years since then, legislators, reflecting the fiscally conservative views of suburban constituencies, have displayed less support for central-city needs and more interest in trimming the size of centralized government, taxes, and the deficit.

Beginning with the Reagan administration in 1981, Republicans have championed a policy called "the New Federalism." The idea is to divest the federal government of as many public support programs as possible and to return these services to the states, where people are closer to the problem. In 1996, a Republican-controlled Congress—with the approval of Democratic president Bill Clinton—added welfare programs to the list of federal divestment. This change pitted the cities against the suburbs for available funds, a competition that decidedly favors the suburbs to this day.

Furthermore, past antipoverty programs have been largely funded via taxes paid by people living in suburbs. Will suburban officials vote to place taxes on themselves and their constituents in order to support the inner-city poor? The prospects for the center city, in other words, are not very bright under the New Federalism. Assuming they lose various financial battles with suburban representatives at the state level, city governments—already struggling with financial problems—would need to raise new revenues or further curtail services. In the process, the quality of life in central cities could deteriorate further, ethnic and racial tensions may intensify, and another exodus of the middle class outward might take place.

SUBURBAN LIFESTYLES

Suburbs share increasing population and rising political power. But they are not all alike in other respects. Across North America, a variety of different suburban types now exist, reflecting sharply contrasting lifestyles. Here we can trace suburban lifestyles as they evolved over the last century.

The Aristocratic Life

A century ago, suburban residence symbolized the lifestyle of the well-to-do. Thus, the people joining the nation's first country club (1882) in Brookline, Massachusetts, took to heart the advice wealthy Bostonians gave their children: "Boston holds nothing for you except heavy taxes and political misrule. When you marry, pick out a suburb to build a house in, join the Country Club, and make your life center about your club, your home and your children" (recalled by Supreme Court Justice Louis Brandeis in Mumford, 1961:495).

Fabulous estates such as Lynnewood Hall—called the Versailles of America—clearly set off the lifestyle of early suburbanites from others. The idea was to emulate the country ways of European aristocracy, as Pierre Lorillard II did better than almost anyone.

In 1886, Lorillard (heir to a tobacco fortune) inherited some 600,000 acres and, at a cost of $2 million, created a millionaires' colony north of New York. Tuxedo Park was "a kind of country club *cum* family resort where some two or three hundred of New York's Best People who were growing tired of resort hotels at Saratoga or Richfield Springs might come to hunt, fish, and skate" (Baltzell, 1979:357).

> At Tuxedo Park Lorillard produced almost a caricature of the Victorian millionaire's mania for exclusiveness. In less than a year, he surrounded seven thousand acres with an eight-foot fence, graded some thirty miles of road, built a complete sewage and water system, a gate house which looked like "a frontispiece of an English novel," a clubhouse staffed with imported English servants, and "twenty-two casement dormered English turreted cottages." On Memorial Day, 1886, special trains brought seven hundred highly selected guests from New York to witness the Park's opening. (Baltzell, 1964:122–23)

By offering his club members property within Tuxedo Park for purchase, Lorillard created, as Baltzell suggests, a sort of Levittown for aristocrats.

Yet, as streetcar lines and then roads choked with automobiles appeared early in this century, new housing rippled outward from cities and, with it, a new image of the suburban lifestyle began to take hold. Its roots were the same—to live "the good life"—but the magnitude of the change ensured that the vision would be watered down.

The New Suburbia

After World War II, suburbs were redefined as homes for the masses as the Tuxedo Parks of North America yielded to the standardized "Cape Cods" found at Levittown. By the mid-1950s, the picture of the new suburban lifestyle had turned sour. Most authors seemed to agree with influential sociologist David Riesman, who confessed at the outset of his essay "The Suburban Sadness" that he was "one who loves city and country, but not the suburbs" (1958:375).

First Impressions

Criticism centered on several alleged traits of the middle-class suburban way of life, particularly the powerful tendency toward conformity. Just as suburban houses were similar in appearance, critics imagined that so too were the lives within them. Suburbanites were young, had small children, ate crunchy breakfast cereal, socialized eagerly with each other (coffee klatches in the morning, barbecues in the evening), and obsessively copied each other in tastes and styles in an endless effort to "keep up with the Joneses." Always thinking *of* themselves, but rarely *for* themselves, suburbanites fashionably looked to the experts: Dr. Spock explained child care to mothers, and Dale Carnegie (*How to Win Friends and Influence People*) guided husbands to success within the company. The Eisenhower landslides of 1952 and 1956 (Ike did extremely well in the suburbs) furthered the assumption that, once in the suburbs, Democrats molted into Republicans. If the frenetic activity of the

suburban lifestyle ever did allow one to settle down a bit, it was only for a moment, only until the next move—for families allegedly picked up stakes every few years in their treadmill-like search for success and happiness.

Journalists as well as sociologists were unrelenting in their attack. John Keats blasted suburban developments in his best-selling book *The Crack in the Picture Window* (1956) and named his major characters John and Mary Drone (their neighbors included the Faints and the Amiables), making it absolutely clear that the people of suburbia were as prefabricated as their two-car garages. Another study (also a best-seller), by Gordon, Gordon, and Gunther, was the not-so-subtly titled *The Split Level Trap* (1960). But most influential of all was William H. Whyte's best-seller, *The Organization Man* (1956), a study of Park Forest, Illinois, which documented the "wanderings" of the rootless corporate executive. To cap it all off there was folksinger Pete Seeger's popular rendition of Malvina Reynolds's "Little Boxes," presented in the City in Literature box on page 302.

Taking a Closer Look

Was this harsh assessment really the truth about suburbs? Many thought not, claiming that much of the work reflected sloppy research and preconceived notions—an attack by intellectuals and journalists on a way of life that was much more complex than they imagined. Some critics, like Herbert Gans (1968), who actually moved into the second Levittown, in New Jersey, concluded that many so-called observers of suburbia were interested in little more than selling a nasty "suburban myth."

It is true that young, middle-class white couples with children populated many of the suburban developments of the late 1940s and the 1950s (Wattel, 1958). But the attack on suburbia seems more rooted in a broader fear on the part of journalists and intellectuals that the United States was becoming a homogenized "mass society" surrendering the U.S. ideal of the rugged, independent, and individualistic pioneer. Certainly the United States has lost a great deal of its former frontier spirit; but should we blame this on the suburbs?

"Little Boxes"

Malvina Reynolds

Little boxes on the hillside,
Little boxes made of ticky tacky,
Little boxes on the hillside,
Little boxes all the same.
There's a green one and a
    pink one
And a blue one and a yellow one,
And they're all made out of ticky tacky,
    And they all look just the same.

And the people in the houses
All went to the university,
Where they were put in boxes
And they came out all the same.
And there's doctors and
    lawyers,
And business executives,
And they're all made out of
    ticky tacky,
And they all look just the same.

And they all play on the golf
    course
And drink their martinis dry,
And they all have pretty
    children
And the children go to school,
And the children go to
    summer camp
And then to the university,
Where they are put in boxes
And they come out just the
    same.

And the boys go into business,
And marry and raise a family
In boxes made of ticky tacky
And they all look just the same.
There's a green one and a
    pink one
And a blue one and a yellow
    one,
And they're all made out of
    ticky tacky
And they all look just the
    same.

Suburban living comes in many forms, depending on the age of the community and the income level of its residents. Some areas have a considerable amount of open space and houses situated on large properties, whereas in other neighborhoods houses sit on small lots with hardly any property space. To urbanites, suburbia is a place of boring uniformity, but to suburbanites it is a place of quiet, comfort, and safety.

Contemporary Suburbia: Complexity and Diversity

Even if the suburban stereotype once had some truth, the influx of people of various backgrounds in recent decades has generated quite a suburban mix. Suburbs vary widely in terms of average income, racial composition, average age, and length of residence.

Middle-Income Family Suburbs   Darien, Connecticut, and Levittown, New York, are probably closest to the suburban stereotype. Life centers around the family, but little evidence exists of frantic neighborhood socializing. As Peter Muller describes how people live there:

> The management of children is a central . . . concern, and most local social contact occurs through such family-oriented formal organizations as the school PTA, Little League, and the Scouts. . . . Neighboring is limited and selective, and even socializing with relatives is infrequent. . . . The insular single-family house and dependence on the automobile for all trip making [accommodate the development of a] network of self-selected friends widely distributed in suburban space. (1981:72)

In suburbs such as these, few people are poor, most are white, and almost everyone has at least finished high school.

Upper-Income Suburbs   These communities resemble the old aristocratic suburbs of yesteryear. They include Grosse Pointe Shores near Detroit, Kenilworth and South Barrington near Chicago, Valley Forge in Pennsylvania, and California's Beverly Hills. Their populations tend to be somewhat older, and fewer women work for income. Families have large houses, usually built on large properties, and center their social lives around churches and exclusive country clubs.

Although the older elite suburbs long resisted the entry of racial, ethnic, and religious minorities, the newer affluent suburbs—typically located at the outer suburban edges—accept anyone with the right-sized bank account. Perhaps the best example of economic elitism prevailing over ethnic prejudice is Beverly Hills, California, where wealthy Arabs and rich Jews live harmoniously as neighbors—a far cry from their counterparts in the Middle East.

Working-Class Suburbs   Just a few miles to the north of San Jose, California, the suburb of Milpitas stood in stark contrast to suburbs like Darien or Grosse Pointe Shores. In 1960 Bennett Berger published an account of the lifestyles of 100 residents of Milpitas, most of whom were employed in blue-collar jobs at a nearby Ford assembly plant. His study revealed that these families were not of very high status, weren't looking to "get ahead," identified themselves as Democrats, paid little attention to "experts" like Dr. Spock, and spent most of their time with relatives. Perhaps most important, Berger found that the men and women of Milpitas at that time were very much the same as working-class people living in the central city. By 2000, the demographics of Milpitas had changed considerably, with a 52 percent Asian American, 31 percent white, and 17 percent Hispanic American population. About 75 percent of its people earned $50,000 or more in 2000, with only 23 percent in working-class occupations (U.S. Bureau of the Census, 2002b).

Working-class suburbs multiplied rapidly after World War II, when working-class families moved outward along with many industries. Muller describes the dominant interests of most:

> [Suburban] working-class, ethnic-centered neighborhoods are characterized by a broad social interaction of informal groups congregating at such local meeting places as the church, tavern, street corner, or door stoop. Local group acceptance and integration is the dominant social value, and communal life stresses the availability of a satisfying peer-group society, similar neighborhoods, maintaining easy access among people well-known to each other, and collective defense of neighborhood respectability. (1981:74–75)

Today, many of these older blue-collar suburbs are suffering from a loss of jobs as industries have closed or moved factories abroad.

With an eroding industrial and commercial tax base, many of these suburbs are deteriorating physically, and property taxes are on the rise. Not surprisingly, many of the more affluent residents are packing up and moving farther out. There, they hope to find a newer version of their dream home and, perhaps, a lower tax rate.

Suburban Cosmopolitan Centers In marked contrast to Milpitas (and different even from Darien and Grosse Pointe Shores) are communities like Princeton, New Jersey, home of Princeton University. Composed mainly of academics, professionals, writers, actors, artists, and students, these communities resemble the university areas, bohemian enclaves, and cosmopolite residential neighborhoods of central cities. Their population is usually deeply interested in "high culture," and theaters, music facilities, and elegant, unusual restaurants are found there in abundance.

Minority Suburbs Most suburbs are now racially diverse and becoming more so all the time. Even so, some suburban communities remain racially segregated. Some African Americans seek out racially homogeneous communities as a deliberate choice. Some affluent new African American suburbs attracting middle-class families who prefer socializing in a racially homogeneous environment are Rolling Oaks near Miami; Brook Glen, Panola Mill, and Wyndham Park near Atlanta; and Black Jack, Jennings, Normandy, and University City near St. Louis. Similarly, black residents in suburban Prince George's County in Maryland, who comprise 63 percent of the county's total population, find comfort in living in affluent but predominantly black communities or subdivisions. Here, Barron Harvey, professor of accounting at Howard University, explains moving from a white, upper-middle-income suburb in Fairfax County, Virginia, to Prince George's County:

> We always wanted to make sure our child had many African-American children to play with, not just one or two. We always wanted to be in a community with a large number of black

professionals, and to feel part of that community. We never really felt like we were part of Fairfax. (Dent, 1992:20)

More often, though, black suburbs result from invasion–succession. That is, after some minorities enter a community, whites begin to leave. Eventually most whites are gone, creating a segregated black suburban community analogous in many ways to its center-city counterpart, the black ghetto.

Muller (1981) distinguishes three subtypes of black suburbs. The first is what he calls the "spillover" community, such as Glenarden, Maryland, adjacent to Washington, D.C. These suburbs are direct outgrowths of center-city black ghettos that move, over time, beyond the center city. Significant spillover suburbs of blacks presently exist in Cleveland, St. Louis, Chicago, Atlanta, Miami, Los Angeles, and New York and are becoming more and more prevalent throughout the country. The income level of spillover communities is high relative to other black suburbs because, like whites departing from the center cities throughout this century, those blacks moving outward tend to be middle class, wishing to leave poorer neighbors behind.

"Colonies," such as Kinloch, Missouri (96 percent black in 2000), just outside St. Louis, represent a second type. Often these isolated communities originally arose as shantytowns outside the city proper and, in recent decades, white suburbs grew up around them. Colonies are poor areas with deteriorating housing and large numbers of people living below the poverty level (about 60 percent, in Kinloch's case). Few members of the community have much schooling, and most work in low-skill jobs. The outlook for them is as bleak as it is for center-city ghetto residents.

Only somewhat better off is the "satellite city," exemplified by Chester, Pennsylvania, about 10 miles downriver from Philadelphia. Originally an industrial city, Chester was a place of thriving shipbuilding and metalworking. No more. Both industries have fallen on hard times, leaving Chester and its black population—about three-fourths of the suburb's 37,000 residents—high and dry. Their poverty level is half that of Kinloch's, and their outlook only a bit brighter.

In 2000, 49 percent of all U.S. Hispanics lived in suburbs, up from 46 percent in 1990. The ten metropolitan areas with the most Hispanic suburbanites are in just five states: California (Los Angeles–Long Branch, Riverside–San Bernardino, San Diego, Orange County, San Francisco, Oakland); Florida (Miami); Texas (Houston); Arizona (Phoenix–Mesa); and Nevada (Las Vegas). Such cities now have what are in essence Hispanic suburbs (Lewis Mumford Center, 2001c).

Monterey Park near Los Angeles is an Asian suburb, its population over two-fifths Chinese American. This is the exception, however, because Asians—a diverse racial category of many cultures—typically move to predominantly white suburbs. As the most affluent U.S. minority group, with a median family income of $56,316 in 1999, more Asians (58 percent) live in suburbia than any other racial or ethnic category.

The continuing influx of Asian and Hispanic immigrants, together with the tendency of many to settle directly in the suburbs, suggests that suburbs will become more diverse in the years to come. Clearly the old stereotype about suburbia no longer fits very well.

In the past two decades, many African Americans, part of a growing black middle class, have realized the American Dream by owning a house in suburbia. While some live in integrated neighborhoods, others prefer to live in mostly-black communities, finding greater comfort for themselves and their children in a homogeneous racial setting.

The Exurbs

Exurbs are the newer ring of settlement beyond the old suburbs. By and large, the exurban population is white, relatively wealthy, highly educated, and professional. Although it would be misleading to say that this region's residents are all the same, there seems little doubt that, depending on the locale, they are much more likely to resemble the residents of Grosse Pointe Shores, Darien, or Princeton than other suburban groups.

In 1957, A. C. Spectorsky published the first account of these people, based on his observations (none too systematic, it should be noted) of an exclusive residential area on the fringes of the New York City metropolitan area. Spectorsky called this outlying area an "exurb," and the name has stuck. Moreover,

his book *The Exurbanites* has proven prophetic, for what was a small trend in 1957 has become quite a stampede in recent years. Then, the exurbanites settled heavily in counties such as Fairfield (Connecticut), Rockland and Westchester (New York), and Bucks (Pennsylvania). Today there are exurban counties surrounding every major city, from Marin near San Francisco to Forsyth near Atlanta.

As Spectorsky noted, however, living in what seems like a rural place a long way from center city does not prevent exurbanites from being city people at heart. For one thing, their lifestyle is like that of the cosmopolite—very highbrow—but transplanted into the rustic, rural charm of some outlying nook-of-a-village. When not commuting to and from "The City," they remain in touch through their cell phones, PCs with modems, and fax machines in their home offices. Exurbanites

William Dobriner fears exurbs will overrun all little towns

CITYSCAPE

The Natural History of a Reluctant Suburb

What it means for a long-established village to be suburbanized can be seen from the recent history of a community called here, for reasons of tact, "Old Harbor." It is a real place, in the general New England area, on the Atlantic Coast. Over 300 years old, Old Harbor lies at the foot of a curving valley between two green necks of land stretching into the sea.

In its early years, Old Harbor served as the local nexus of an agrarian and colonial society. Its grist mills ground local grain into flour through the power of the impounded waters of the tide ponds and mill dams. The natural harbor drew shipping from all over the east coast. Whaling ships worked out of the home port, and coastal shipping from ports as far away as the West Indies unloaded hides, rum, cattle, cord-wood, charcoal, etc., on Old Harbor's busy wharfs. Over the [centuries] . . . the village prospered but remained comparatively changeless in some fundamental ways—it continued to be a Yankee village of industrious merchants, seamen, farmers, and craftsmen. . . .

By the middle of the nineteenth century . . . change was imminent. In 1867 the railroad came to the village and became a serious competitor with marine transportation, and thereafter the harbor declined as a vital force in the village's economy. Even more ominous was the fact that 36.6 miles from the village lay the borders of a city . . . showing a capacity for incredible growth and its influence was extending beyond its borders. . . . In writing to a relative in 1872, one villager noted, "There has been a very curious thing this summer, I must have

seen 15 or 20 strangers in town during July and August."

The first invaders of Old Harbor were members of the new industrial aristocracy who emerged in the decades after the Civil War. . . . By the turn of the century, Old Harbor had become their carefully guarded preserve. They bought the old farms and cleared away acres for their summer playgrounds and gigantic estates. They fenced off two- and three-hundred-acre parcels and created separate dukedoms populated by communities of servants and laborers.

By the early 1920s, the township in which Old Harbor is located was undergoing rather intensive immigration from the metropolitan area. The city was going through one of its growth spasms, and the population was spilling over the city limits into the adjacent counties. Old Harbor was one county removed, but this was the decade in which the automobile drastically changed the character of American society and culture. [Soon] a few miles to the south of the Village, in "Old Harbor Station," the railroad terminus, a new and rather singular figure stood on the platform waiting for the 8:05 to the city: the commuter, the classic suburbanite, with his freshly pressed tight trousers, starched white collar, and morning paper folded neatly under his arm.

After the Second World War, population that had been trapped in the city during the war years exploded into the county neighboring Old Harbor. In ten years, the number of people in this "rural" county passed a million and made it one of the most rapidly growing areas in the United States. . . . In the ten years from 1945 to 1955, Old Harbor Township doubled its population, and the village itself has now absorbed between two and three times the number it had in 1940. In just ten years, a 300-year-old village, with many of the descendants of the original founders still living there, underwent a social shock that wrenched it from whatever remained of the patterns of the past. . . .

No longer is there enough space in Old Harbor. You can't park your car on Main Street any more, there may not be room in church if you arrive late on Sunday, classrooms are "overcrowded," and you have to wait your turn for telephones to be installed in your new house. . . . [But] the fundamental schism between the world of the old-timers and the world of the newcomers makes a problem that is less obvious but both more important and harder to cope with.

The temper of the suburbanite "community" may be summarized in the way the suburbanites talk about Old Harbor:

I came to Old Harbor because there is still some green around here and yet I can still get to the airport in 45 minutes. It's a nice place to live—the schools are good. . . . I like being near the water. It is hard to say how long we'll be here. I would like to be based further south, but as a place to live Old Harbor is fine.

I can't think of Old Harbor as my own town or anything like that. Most of my friends live closer to the city and I work there. . . . I guess I sleep more of my time here than anything else, but it's a good place for the kids. I've got a lot of contacts and interests outside.

But an old-timer says:

They [the suburbanites] don't know what's going on around here. They don't care. But I do; this is my town. I used to fish down at the tide basin. Now they're talking of tearing it down. I went to school here. All my friends live around here. It's crazy what's happening. I can

look out my shop window and can't recognize 49 out of 50 faces I see. There was a time I knew everybody. It used to be our town. I don't know whose it is any more. . . .

This is the real issue that splits the suburbanite and villager communities apart. For the suburbanites, Old Harbor is another commodity; it is a product that can be rationally consumed; it is a means by which they hope to achieve a complex series of personal goals. For the villagers, on the other hand, Old Harbor is not a means to anything; it is simply an end in itself.

Yet the future lies with the metropolis and not the village. You can see it in the new super expressways that slice through Old Harbor's meadow-lands. You sense the shift in internal balance in the village by the domination of the suburbanites at school board meetings. You know it on an autumn's evening, in the crisp sea air, and in the deepening twilight around the mill pond. The great shuddering bulk of the mill squats in the hollow, intimidated by the headlights of the commuters as they race down and through the valley, dreary from the city and hungry for home. Pencils of light search into the gaping slats and crudely intrude upon the embarrassment of the mill's decay—the rusting gears, the splintered shaft, the rotting timbers, and marsh slop heaped up by the last high tide. . . . Up along the darkening necks the lights are going on in the new split levels and "contemporaries" tucked into the ridges. The lights go on and off as the night rolls in. They seem to be winking at the senile mill as it sits and broods in the gathering darkness.

Source: Reprinted with the permission of Simon & Schuster Adult Publishing Group from *Class in Suburbia* by William M. Dobriner. Copyright © 1963 by Prentice-Hall, Inc., copyright renewed © 1991 by William M. Dobriner.

devour books, theater, and art, and (if they can) they raise horses. For Spectorsky, they are indeed an intriguing mix of high tech, high culture, and rustic charm.

Why are so many people moving still farther out from the center city? Recent research points up a variety of expected reasons: Some move there to be near a job, others to retire from one; many have family and friends in the area, others comment that they "like to live in the country and have some open space around me" or, sometimes, "because I want to get out of the city" (Fuguitt, 1984). For others, it is simply where they can find affordable housing. In short, the exurb, like the suburb before it, is yet another step in the unending quest for greener pastures.

But some worry about the rise of exurbia, fearing that it will overrun what is left of North America's small towns. William Dobriner noted these fears back in 1963. In the Cityscape box on pages 306–307, he describes the fate of "Old Harbor"and reviews almost all of the suburban story.

Urban Culture and the Suburbs

Finally, what about Wirth's ecological variables —large numbers, density, and social heterogeneity—shaping the suburbs? Do suburbanites adapt to the flow of people in the same way that central-city people do?

Obviously not. Wirth's factors are much weaker in the suburbs (and weaker still in the exurbs). Although more people live in the suburbs than in the center city, their dispersion over a wide area reduces their contact with one another; housing density is lower, and much more open space exists for daily life; and the intentional planning of some suburbs means that their residents have much in common.

More than in the center city, then, lifestyles in the suburbs reveal the effects of social factors such as class and ethnicity. In other words, whereas much of the inner city's diversity, intensity, and change follows from its unavoidable mix of peoples, the suburbs are more "laid back."

But even if the city's ecological characteristics are weaker in the suburbs, suburbanites are still affected by the city. As Spectorsky noted, in a fundamental sense all suburbanites are "of" the city. Many work there and "bring the city home" with them. And the urban media, politics, economy, and problems affect virtually everyone. As the Cityscape box shows so well, even the exurbanites are "city slickers" through and through.

SUMMARY

If stereotypes about urbanites contain some truth, they also contain distortions. Research points again and again to the existence of pronounced urban variety—a range of lifestyles that defies easy description. This is as true of the suburbs as it is of the center city.

In center cities, claimed Herbert Gans, at least five major lifestyles coexist. The cosmopolites, to take just one example, are as different from the disaffiliated as can be imagined. Such diversity significantly weakens Louis Wirth's hypothesis that the city's unique ecological characteristics—large numbers, density, and social heterogeneity—produce a single, characteristic lifestyle. Refuting Wirth's hypothesis, Gans argues that sociocultural characteristics—such as class, age, gender, and race—are the real architects of people's lives.

Countering this claim, Claude Fischer replied that Wirth was not all wrong. In his view, the city's ecological traits do affect people's lives, but not quite in the way Wirth suggested. Rather than producing an effect directly, Fischer argues, large numbers, density, and heterogeneity intensify other characteristics to produce pronounced urban lifestyles.

But what of the outer city, the fastest-growing urban region? This question led us to the suburbs. For decades, the suburbs were berated for producing a single lifestyle: dull, middle-class people, rubber-stamped by a dehumanized physical and social environment of chilling mediocrity and sameness.

A brief review of the history of the suburbs saw them emerge in the late nineteenth century as country estates and small enclaves for the well-to-do—people anxious to escape the immigrant lifestyles and industrial commotion of the inner city. With the invention of the automobile in the twentieth century, however, the suburbs changed. People moved there in ever-increasing numbers, especially after World War II. By 1970, more people lived in suburbs than in central cities.

A close look shows the suburban stereotype—of white middle-class families with children and white-collar jobs living in "little boxes"—to be decidedly biased. Even in the heyday of the new suburbia, life was never as one-dimensional as the critics would have it. The last three decades witnessed a marked increase in suburban diversity as large numbers of the aged, the working class, and minorities moved to these outlying areas. This migration has produced a lifestyle complexity that rivals that of the inner city. There is every reason to believe that this complexity and diversity will continue to increase into the next century as immigration and decentralization continue.

Suburbs fall into recognizably distinct types. There are middle-income suburbs, exclusive upper-income suburbs, working-class suburbs, minority suburbs, and—increasingly in the South, Southwest, and West—Hispanic suburbs. Social class appears more significant than race and ethnicity in suburban settlement patterns as more and more African Americans, Asians, and Latinos move into the newer suburbs. An exception to this pattern so far is the growth in the past three decades of yet another urban ring, the exurbs, which lie beyond the original suburban tracts. By and large, the exurbs are being inundated by affluent white urbanites, looking, as had their parents before them, to leave the problems of the city behind as they search for more living space.

Two other patterns caught our attention. First, it is no longer true that the center city is the place where all the amenities of urban life exist. Some suburbs have developed into true "minicities," offering all the goods, services, and entertainment that once drew people to the city's center. Second, there is a serious political battle looming between the center cities and the suburbs over monies for programs and services. While the suburbs were small, the center cities held the purse strings. Now, with the growth of the suburbs, political power has shifted, and suburbs are looking after themselves to the detriment of the center cities. This confrontation has been augmented by the policies of a more conservative Congress and administration, with its desire to rid the federal government of programs that it thinks can be better handled at the state level. Unfortunately, the true losers in this encounter are most likely to be the inner-city poor, who will find, as funds dry up or are diverted to suburban programs, that center-city governments no longer have the ability to help them.

CONCLUSION

In the end, then, three distinct sets of variables are responsible for urban lifestyles. Wirth's ecological variables (large numbers, density, heterogeneity) have their strongest effect in the central city but get weaker as one moves out of the city through the inner suburbs and, ultimately, to the exurbs. Gans's sociocultural variables (class, age, race, and so on) have a major effect in any type of settlement; however, in the central city they are intensified because of the existence of "critical masses" of diverse people. In the inner suburbs and particularly in the exurbs and beyond, sociocultural variables act more independently to shape lifestyles.

Behind the overarching pattern of urban lifestyles, however, lies much more than a preference for living in a certain location. Economic and political factors, as well as racial and ethnic prejudice, all play key roles. These factors have always been crucial in the organization of urban life, so it is fitting that we devote the next chapter to a consideration of them.

CHAPTER 11

RACE, ETHNICITY, AND GENDER
Urban Diversity

"I'm off to make a new life in the city!" Words such as these have echoed throughout history, in countless languages, throughout the world. Everywhere and always, cities have been immigrant-luring magnets. This basic fact explains why so many cities display striking diversity—in people, their neighborhoods, and their ways of life. Indeed, part of the excitement of a city lies in precisely this heterogeneity, the range of urban choices, the countless activities and opportunities.

Especially in the major immigrant-receiving nations—Britain, Canada, and the United States—racial and ethnic diversity has long been a common trait of cities. This chapter focuses on social diversity in North America and the ways in which race, ethnicity, and also gender continue to play a vital part in shaping urban life.

CITIES AND IMMIGRANTS

In the United States, home to more immigrants than any other country on earth, cities remain mosaics of ethnic communities. At times, minorities even become the majority, as in Milwaukee back in 1850, when that city contained 6,000 Germans and 4,000 native-born citizens (Parrillo, 2003:160). At the height of the "Great Immigration" between 1880 and 1910, roughly 1 million immigrants came to these shores

annually, and seven out of ten of them settled in cities. Not surprisingly, in most cities in the northeastern United States, foreign-born people comprised two-thirds to three-fourths of the population. In 2000, by contrast, as seen in Table 11–1, the cities with the highest percentage of foreign-born residents were Miami at 59.5 percent, Los Angeles at 40.9 percent, San Francisco at 36.8 percent, and New York at 35.9 percent—proportions significantly higher than in 1990, but still far lower than those at the beginning of the twentieth century (U.S. Bureau of the Census, 2002b).

Certainly their greater presence affects cities' economies, but are immigrants a benefit or a problem for cities? That question—whether on a national, state, or local level—is a fiercely debated one. A two-year study published by the National Academy of Sciences for the U.S. Commission on Immigration Reform found that immigrants add about $10 billion annually in net economic output due to the increased supply of labor and resulting lower prices, and that a typical newcomer pays $80,000 more in taxes than he or she receives over the course of a lifetime. However, immigrant households are costly at first because they tend to be younger and have school-age children using the public schools (National Center for Policy Analysis, 1997). Critics argue that some states and urban centers receive the lion's share of immigrants,

TABLE 11–1   Racial/Ethnic Population in Metropolitan Areas, 2000 (by percent)

City	Asian	African American	Hispanic	Foreign-Born
Boston	5.5	7.2	5.9	25.8
Chicago	5.2	19.0	17.1	21.7
Dallas	4.6	15.2	23.0	24.4
Detroit	2.8	23.3	2.9	4.8
Houston	5.9	17.5	30.0	26.4
Los Angeles	13.5	9.9	44.6	40.9
Miami	1.9	20.0	57.3	59.5
New York	10.1	23.7	25.1	35.9
Philadelphia	3.8	20.3	5.1	9.0
San Francisco	25.1	5.6	16.8	36.8
Washington, D.C.	7.7	26.6	8.8	12.9

Source: U.S. Bureau of the Census.

and their concentrated presence strains a community's social fabric and places an economic burden on those areas in education, health, and welfare costs (Clark, 1990; McCarthy and Vernez, 1997). George Borjas (2001) maintains that, while immigrants in general may enrich the nation, their high numbers and the growing proportion of poorly educated, low-skill workers have negative consequences that require a reexamination of our immigration policy objectives.

Ethnic Enclaves and Ethnic Identity

When we take account of the racial and ethnic variation of the U.S. population, today's cities display highly visible racial and ethnic diversity that is actually increasing. Like the European immigrants of previous generations, the new immigrants create their own ethnic enclaves and distinctive social institutions. The very size of cities allows for large concentrations of ethnic peoples. Cities thus continue to be mosaics of small worlds, abuzz with different sights, sounds, and smells reflected in ethnic celebrations, parades, restaurants, street fairs, stores, and other cultural activities. For some people, of course, cities—or at least certain neighborhoods in cities—are to be avoided precisely because of these differences, which they equate with danger and disorder.

The shifting pattern of ethnic and racial immigration underlies much of the complexity of today's cities. Table 11–2 shows that, from 1861 to 1960, the vast majority of legal immigrants to the United States were white people from Europe and Canada. During this period, differences between immigrants and people already in this country were mostly ethnic. That is, various whites—say, the Irish, Italians, and Jews—differed in cultural traditions but not in race. Since 1960, however, the bulk of our legal (and illegal) immigrants have been people of color from Asia and Latin America. Racial diversity, as well as ethnic differences, compound the problems of acceptance and rejection.

Ethnic Change

A city's spatial structure reflects ethnic subcultures as immigrants arrive and, through a process known as *chain migration,* settle near friends and relatives. A vibrant ethnic community evolves—with leaders, institutions and organizations, stores, clubs, and same-language media—to help newcomers put down roots and "make it." At the same time that this pluralism manifests itself, however, the forces of assimilation also take hold. Immigrants seek to be part of their adopted country and try to become "American." Despite the challenges of learning a new language and, for some, barriers based on skin color, virtually all immigrants gradually identify more and more with their new country, where they expect to spend the rest of their lives.

Herbert Gans (1962b, 1982) noted that tight "ethnic villages" built by first-generation European immigrants did not always hold up when members of the second and third generation moved from the "old neighborhood" in the central city to leafy (and less ethnic) patches of the suburbs. Of course, such outmigration makes room for new immigrants, an invasion–succession process that refreshes urban pluralism even as assimilation draws others into the mainstream.

New York City

For most of the nation's history, New York has stood as a symbol of racial and ethnic diversity. More than a generation ago, E. Digby Baltzell noted:

> Even today [New York's] citizenry, almost half of whom are foreign born or the children of foreign born, includes more blacks than most cities in Africa, a greater concentration of Jews than at any other time or place. . . . More Puerto Ricans than any other city outside of San Juan, more persons of Italian descent than most cities in Italy, and more [Irish] than Dublin. (1964:ix)

New York still holds first place as the nation's leading destination of immigrants. In

TABLE 11–2   Legal Immigrants to the United States, 1861–2000 (by percent)

Region of Birth	1861–1900	1901–1930	1931–1960	1961–1990	1991–2000
Europe	90	79	58	18	15
Canada and Newfoundland	7	11	16	5	2
Asia	2	3	5	31	31
Latin America	0	5	17	34	38
Africa	—	—	1	2	4
Other	1	2	3	10	10

Source: U.S. Immigration and Naturalization Service.

2000, about 86,000 immigrants entered New York City, compared with about 71,000 coming to Los Angeles (U.S. Immigration and Naturalization Service, 2002:59). At present one in three New Yorkers is foreign-born. Brighton Beach, Brooklyn, is known as "Little Odessa"—a place where tens of thousands of Russians live in the largest Russian immigrant community in the world. New York City also has this nation's largest concentration of Haitians, most of them living in the Brooklyn neighborhoods of La Saline, Flatbush, Bedford-Stuyvesant, Bushwick, and East New York.

Dominicans were the single largest immigrant category coming into the city during the 1980s and 1990s, at a rate of about 20,000 a year, pushing their total numbers in the city to over 406,000. Other Caribbean immigrants include Jamaicans and Guyanans. About a third of the Guyanans are of Asian Indian descent, but most Guyanans are of African ancestry and tend to live in culturally mixed neighborhoods.

The Asian Indian community in Queens, numbering over 109,000, may be the largest in the country. Indians have the highest median income of any new ethnic group, probably because 80 to 90 percent are professionals who spoke English before arriving. Lower Manhattan's Chinatown is five times the size it was in 1965, both in size and numbers, and is now home to about 100,000 people. Chinatown has now all but swallowed up New York's Little Italy, with more than two-thirds of the buildings on the Little Italy stretch of Mulberry Street now Chinese-owned. More than 90 percent of the independent greengroceries in New York City are Korean-owned, as are over 15,000 small businesses, including import-export companies, manicure shops, gift shops, and fish markets. Over 86,000 Koreans now live in New York City, and they are typically highly educated professionals from urban areas such as Seoul.

Los Angeles

Dubbed the "Ellis Island of the 1990s," Los Angeles increased its population by 17.4 percent from 1980 to 1990, and by an additional 6 percent between 1990 and 2000, mostly due to foreign immigration (U.S. Bureau of the Census, 2002a). Today, nearly half of all residents in Los Angeles city are Hispanic, and almost two-thirds of these are Mexican Americans. The city now has more people of Mexican ancestry than any other city in the Western Hemisphere except for Mexico City and Guadalajara. Salvadorans and Guatemalans are two other heavily represented populations.

African Americans comprise 11 percent of the city's population, followed by Asians at 10 percent. Included among the Asians are 63,000 Chinese, 101,000 Filipinos, 92,000 Koreans, 37,000 Japanese, 25,000 Asian Indians, and 20,000 Vietnamese. In addition, 13,000 Native Americans represent 0.4 percent of the Los Angeles population. Found there also are tens of thousands of Iranians.

RACIAL AND ETHNIC MINORITIES

The early history of people of color in North American cities is primarily the story of people of African descent living in the United States. Their influx into Canada occurred in small numbers in the nineteenth century, but increased significantly as more and more people from the Caribbean and the United States moved north during the twentieth century. Native peoples in both Canada and the United States have seldom lived in the white people's cities, and an Asian presence did not become significant in most locales until the second half of the nineteenth century.

African Americans

From the time of the first census in 1790 until the beginning of the twentieth century, about 90 percent of the U.S. black population lived in the South, mostly in rural regions. Overall, just one in four African Americans lived in an urban area. A few southern cities had sizable black populations (ranging from 25 to 50 percent of the total) in the late 1800s, a time that the black population of northeastern cities had yet to reach even 5 percent.

The Lure of the North

The promise of schooling and better work lured black migrants to the North after 1900. By 1910, 10 percent of the African American population lived in the North. Full implementation of the segregationist Jim Crow laws in the South, economic hard times, and the boll weevil's destruction of cotton crops prompted many more to head north in the next decade, raising the northern black population from 850,000 in 1910 to 1.4 million in 1920.

Hostility to labor unions in the North and *de facto* **segregation** (unequal treatment of people based on social customs and traditions) created a dual society there, just as *de jure* **segregation** (unequal treatment established by law) had done in the South. But northern blacks were an urban people, some poor, others

working class or even middle class. Black churches formed the bedrock of the segregated racial community. Although African Americans did earn more money in the North, in 1914 their earnings did not exceed four-tenths of white earnings (Higgs, 1980:125).

The Great Migration

World War I and the restrictive legislation that followed it put an end to the Great Immigration from Europe, initiating the Great Migration from the South. As cities such as Chicago, New York, and Boston grew into industrial metropolises, African Americans saw greater opportunity there than in the agricultural South. The push–pull factors spurring migration included the decline of southern agriculture as well as farm mechanization on the one hand, and northern industries' shortage of labor and active recruitment of black workers from southern states on the other.

During the 1920s, the net black out-migration from the South amounted to almost 1 million people. Slowing during the Great Depression of the 1930s, the massive relocation of blacks accelerated once again as industrial production rose during World War II. Migration remained high until the 1970s, when urban decentralization and minority movement to the suburbs slowed the process. Note, for example, in Table 11–3, that Baltimore, Washington, D.C., St. Louis, Atlanta, Los Angeles, San Jose, and San Francisco experienced a decrease in their African American populations between 1990 and 2000. Most other cities showed only modest gains. The dramatic increase in New York City was primarily the result of a large influx of Dominican, Haitian, and Jamaican immigrants.

In Baltimore, Detroit, Atlanta, and New Orleans, blacks are the majority population, as is the case in other cities including Birmingham, Alabama (73.5 percent); Gary, Indiana (84.0); Jackson, Mississippi (70.6); Macon, Georgia (62.5); Memphis, Tennessee (61.4); Newark, New Jersey (53.5); Richmond, Virginia (57.2); and Savannah, Georgia (57.1). While it is conceivable that blacks may achieve a majority in

TABLE 11-3   African American Population in Selected U.S. Cities

Region	City	1990	2000	2000 as Percent of Total Population
Northeast	Boston	157,234	175,921	20.2
	New York	1,185,340	2,830,010	25.4
	Philadelphia	674,126	698,380	43.7
	Baltimore	444,910	432,860	63.0
	Washington, D.C.	424,202	376,117	45.1
Midwest	Cleveland	251,143	265,237	44.0
	Detroit	812,812	818,434	71.3
	Indianapolis	171,821	213,225	25.3
	Chicago	1,138,970	1,143,232	33.7
	Milwaukee	191,102	227,384	34.4
	St. Louis	239,894	228,411	42.0
	Kansas City, MO	181,920	195,941	27.3
South	Atlanta	262,113	256,251	61.5
	Jacksonville, FL	159,358	214,898	29.2
	New Orleans	308,631	329,241	64.5
	Houston	464,087	507,389	24.7
	Dallas	311,439	337,285	23.1
	San Antonio	69,768	78,363	6.6
West	Denver	56,747	63,876	11.5
	Phoenix	59,980	89,913	4.3
	San Diego	104,924	105,794	7.7
	Los Angeles	565,105	529,121	12.0
	San Jose	43,961	40,407	3.3
	San Francisco	76,944	62,677	8.1
	Seattle	54,106	58,938	7.7

Source: U.S. Bureau of the Census.

other major cities as well, the fact that African Americans represent about 13 percent of the total U.S. population makes it statistically improbable that black majorities will appear in most other major cities. In fact, in Inglewood, California, and Washington, D.C., blacks were a majority in 1990, but were not in 2000 (U.S. Bureau of the Census, 2002).

To some, the city seems a dangerous place where only the strongest and most calculating survive. That image applies only to certain sections of cities, and in those locales, as explained in the Urban Living box on page 316, being "streetwise" is a valuable asset.

Residential Segregation Patterns

African American migrants, like earlier European immigrants, settled in the least desirable central-city neighborhoods. For the Europeans, this residential segregation reflected mostly lower resources and group preferences (Lieberson, 1963; Douglas Massey, 1985; Lieberson and Waters, 1988). As these immigrants gained education and income, they assimilated and moved out of these traditional ethnic enclaves.

Unlike the Europeans, however, many African Americans have remained confined

URBAN LIVING

Street Wisdom

Typically, those generally regarded as streetwise are veterans of the public spaces. They know how to get along with strangers, and they understand how to negotiate the streets. They know whom to trust, whom not to trust, what to say through body language or words. They have learned how to behave effectively in public. Probably the most important consideration is the experience they have gained through encounters with "every kind of stranger." Although one may know about situations through the reports of friends or relatives, this pales in comparison with actual experience. It is often sheer proximity to the dangerous streets that allows a person to gain street wisdom and formulate some effective theory of the public spaces. As one navigates there is a certain edge to one's demeanor, for the streetwise person is both wary of others and sensitive to the subtleties that could salvage safety out of danger.

The longer people live in this locale, having to confront problems on the streets and public spaces every day, the greater chance they have to develop a sense of what to do without seriously compromising themselves. Further, the longer they are in the area, the more likely they are to develop contacts who might come to their aid, allowing them to move more boldly.

This self-consciousness makes people likely to be alert and sensitive to the nuances of the environment. More important, they will project their ease and self-assurance to those they meet, giving them the chance to affect the interaction positively. For example, the person who is "streetdumb," relying for guidance on the most superficial signs, may pay too much attention to skin color and become needlessly tense just because the person approaching is black. A streetwise white who meets a black person will probably just go about his or her business. In both cases the black person will pick up the "vibe" being projected—in the first instance fear and hostility, in the second case comfort and a sense of commonality. There are obviously times when the "vibe" itself could tip the balance in creating the subsequent interaction.

Source: Excerpt from Elijah Anderson, *Streetwise.* Copyright © 1990 by University of Chicago Press. Reprinted with the permission of the University of Chicago Press.

and isolated in racial ghettos, particularly in the Northeast and Midwest, where 36 percent of all African Americans live. Through a variety of individual and institutional actions, a persistently high level of black–white segregation remained throughout the twentieth century, revealing the extent of racial stratification in U.S. society (Massey, 1999; St. Clair and Clymer, 2000).

Between 1870 and 1920, segregation in the cities of the North was slight. By 1965, Karl and Alma Taeuber's classic study of racial segregation revealed a dramatic climb in the segregation index. To measure that segregation, the Taeubers developed what they called an *index of dissimilarity*, which they applied to each neighborhood. Their index ranged from a low of zero, meaning the neighborhood reflected the same proportion of blacks and whites as in the entire city, to a high of 100, meaning that no racial mixture was found. Overall, in 1960, the average segregation index for 207 large cities was 86.2, with scores ranging from a not-so-low 60.4 (San Jose, California) to 98.1 (Fort Lauderdale, Florida).

Since the Taeubers' research findings, other researchers have used the index of dissimilarity to track trends in residential segregation. Since the 1970s, racial residential segregation has slowly but steadily decreased in the United States. In 1980, the black–white metropolitan segregation index was 73.9, and it dropped to 65.1 in 2000. However, it still remains fairly high between blacks and whites in cities and suburbs. In 2000, the average white person in metropolitan America resided in a neighborhood that was 80 percent white and 7 percent black. In contrast, the typical black individual lived in a neighborhood that was only 33 percent white and as much as 51 percent black (Lewis Mumford Center, 2001a).

Of the 50 metropolitan areas with the largest black populations, the ten with the highest levels of segregation (in descending order) were Detroit, Milwaukee, New York, Chicago, Newark, Cleveland, Cincinnati, Nassau–Suffolk (N.Y.), St. Louis, and Miami. All but New York and Miami experienced modest segregation declines since 1990, and most are "Rustbelt" metro areas where black–white segregation has been particularly resistant to change. At the other end, the ten metro areas with the least black–white segregation were all Sunbelt regions in North and South Carolina, Florida, California, and Virginia. Despite signs of progress in the South, several cities in this region also display persistent segregation. For example, New Orleans is above the national average, and segregation in the city of Atlanta has risen in the past 20 years and is much higher than the national city average (Lewis Mumford Center, 2001a).

In recent decades, as the black middle class moved out of central cities into mostly inner-ring suburbs, they left behind an isolated black poor concentrated in decaying neighborhoods of high crime and unemployment (Wilson, 1987). Researchers have long known that ethnic and racial residential segregation interacts with social class and the family life

cycle to shape the entire urban area (Shevky and Bell, 1955). Many social scientists, particularly those using the political economy model, emphasize the economic roots of racial segregation (Logan and Stearns, 1981; Logan and Molotch, 1987; Jargowsky, 1996).

Still, beyond economic differences, racial prejudice also plays an important role as many whites flee a neighborhood when blacks move in. Similarly, African American preferences for moving to mostly black suburbs also contribute to segregation. Evidence also points to active, if unacknowledged (by the white community at least) attempts to keep blacks from buying homes in white urban neighborhoods.

Prior to the civil rights and open housing laws of the 1960s and 1970s, realtors included in their code of ethics a regulation that prohibited selling homes to buyers not sharing the racial and ethnic characteristics of neighbors (Helper, 1969). Most whites believe that passage of fair housing and antidiscrimination laws mostly eliminated institutional discrimination in housing (Farley et al., 1993). However, recent studies show that, even now, African Americans stand a one-in-two chance of being discriminated against in a rental and a one-in-five chance of being discriminated against in the sale of a home (Galster, 1990; 1996).

A common method is *steering*, in which rental or real estate agents direct, for example, an African American couple to a city area populated by others of their race or else refrain from telling them about available property in a white area. Another strategy to discourage the African American buyer is asking a much higher rent or purchase price than a white family would pay (Downs, 1981). Such subtler forms of discrimination occur much more frequently than the highly publicized but infrequent instances of vandalism or firebombing of a home newly acquired by people of color in a white neighborhood.

Whatever the circumstances, such practices combine to create a *dual housing market*. White resistance to housing desegregation results in practices that make housing differentially available to people based on their race. Despite the continued increase in income of the growing black middle class, racial segregation persists for most African Americans.

The Truly Disadvantaged

For the trapped African American poor left behind in the inner city, the future is bleak. Among those lacking the necessary schooling and communication skills required for work in the service and information sectors of the economy, unemployment rates may be as high as 80 percent (Kasarda, 1993). These "truly disadvantaged," in the words of William J. Wilson (1987), are poor people who rely on welfare assistance and the underground economy to survive.

Unlike the immigrant poor of the past, today's poor inner-city residents face social isolation. The exodus of middle- and working-class two-parent black families removes essential role models and reduces community resources. Furthermore, outsiders avoid these neighborhoods, leaving them plagued by massive unemployment, crime, and schools that do not promote achievement. Consequently, area residents—women and children on welfare, school dropouts, single mothers, and aggressive street criminals—live virtually cut off from the larger society. Gary Orfield noted the magnitude of this isolation:

> To a considerable extent the residents of city ghettos are now living in separate and deteriorating societies, with separate economies, diverging family structures and basic institutions, and even growing linguistic separation within the core ghettos. (1988:103)

Besides being isolated, the ghettoized poor have poor quality schools, limited medical care, high infant mortality, and high rates of substance abuse and violent crime. Current social indicators offer little cause for optimism, for such problems have structural causes that our society has yet to overcome.

Hispanic Americans

By far the fastest-growing nonwhite category in the United States is Hispanics—Mexicans, Puerto Ricans, Cubans, Central and South Americans, and others of Spanish origin—and they now constitute the nation's largest minority. In the majority of U.S. cities with a population exceeding 100,000, Hispanics outnumber African Americans. These cities include Albuquerque, Dallas, Denver, Houston, Las Vegas, Los Angeles, New York, Phoenix, Salt Lake City, San Diego, San Francisco, and Tucson. In 12 other large cities, Hispanics are a majority of the population, outnumbering all other categories combined (see Table 11–4).

The Census Bureau term "Hispanic" wrongly suggests a single category of people. In truth, Hispanics differ in their race, cultural backgrounds, social class, and length of residence in North America. Some, most often Mexican Americans, live in rural areas, particularly in the U.S. Southwest. Others, such as many Cuban Americans, live in suburbs. Some, such as Central and South Americans, have been in North America for only a few years, while others, notably Puerto Ricans and the *Hispanos* of the U.S. Southwest, have lived all their lives on the U.S. mainland. Although Hispanics live in all 50 states and in all Canadian provinces, many categories tend to cluster in one geographic area. Florida is home to over 70,000 Nicaraguans and about three-fourths of all Cubans. Almost two-thirds of all Puerto Ricans live in the Northeast (primarily New York and New Jersey); California and Texas, by contrast, contain three-fourths of all Mexican Americans (Lewis Mumford Center, 2001a). We now take a closer look at Hispanic diversity.

Puerto Ricans

As U.S. citizens, Puerto Ricans enjoy open migration privileges between their island and the mainland. Before World War II, the poor living conditions on the island offered strong push factors that impelled people to migrate:

> If someone had looked around at the potential sources of new [urban] immigration . . . his eye might well have fallen on Puerto Rico . . . in the middle 1930's [it was] a scene of almost unrelieved misery. (Glazer and Moynihan, 1970:86)

After 1945, postwar prosperity and regular air flights to the mainland brought as many as 50,000 Puerto Ricans per year to the United States. Most came to New York. Why? Anthropologist Elena Padilla explained in 1958:

> For years now Puerto Ricans have been hearing about New York City, have read about it in the local papers, heard about it on the radio, and seen some of its scenery. . . . New York is regarded as a place where many Puerto Ricans live and where they have improved their conditions of life, their health, and their general welfare. Many . . . have known New York migrants who have returned to Puerto Rico and boasted of their "good life" in New York. (1958:21–22)

Glazer and Moynihan (1970) noted that often men migrated first, leaving their wives and children in Puerto Rico until they secured enough resources to support the entire family. (This is a common pattern in all poor nations, as Chapter 13 explains.) In other cases, women, often with children (but unmarried or separated), moved from the island, hoping for work or at least welfare support until they could find employment.

Upon a newcomer's arrival, friends and extended kin provided support services to help ease the adjustment to mainland city life. Despite this, life in New York was significantly different from Puerto Rican life and created particular hardships. Padilla (1958) suggests that this "culture shock" involved unfamiliar patterns of behavior, differing attitudes and values, and, perhaps most significantly, unexpected individualism. Often expecting others to make sacrifices to aid them, many migrants were disappointed at the degree of individualistic self-interest shown in the city.

By 1960, some 900,000 Puerto Ricans lived within the continental United States, about 600,000 residing in New York City. The center of the New York Puerto Rican community became East Harlem, also known as Spanish Harlem (97th Street to about 125th Street between Third and Fifth Avenues). Until the late 1970s, however, continuous shuttle migration (migrants returning to the island and new arrivals coming to the mainland) inhibited an

TABLE 11–4   Hispanic Majorities in Selected Cities of 100,000 or More—Percent of Total City Population, 2000

Brownsville, TX	91.3	Miami, FL	65.8
Corpus Christi, TX	54.3	Oxnard, CA	66.2
El Monte, CA	72.4	Pomona, CA	64.5
El Paso, TX	76.6	Salinas, CA	64.1
Hialeah, FL	90.3	San Antonio, TX	58.7
Laredo, TX	94.1	Santa Ana, CA	76.1

Source: U.S. Bureau of the Census.

organized community life. Hometown clubs —voluntary organizations based on one's place of birth—offered social opportunities to celebrate life cycle events (birthdays, first communions, confirmations, weddings). But because they drew members from scattered New York neighborhoods, they did not operate as community centers. Only the annual Puerto Rican Day parade, begun in 1958, served as a focal point of group identity. By the late 1970s, greater neighborhood organization was evident, as more people put down roots in the city.

In the 2000 census, over 3 million people living on the mainland United States identified themselves as Puerto Rican. New York City, where most Puerto Ricans once lived, now is home to only one in four. New York State's Puerto Rican population—64 percent of the mainland total in 1970—fell to 34 percent in 2000, as members of this group continued their migration into other states. Those other states with large shares of the Puerto Rican population are Florida (16 percent), New Jersey (12 percent), Pennsylvania (8 percent), Massachusetts (7 percent), Connecticut (6 percent), with Illinois and California at about 5 percent each (U.S. Bureau of the Census, 2002a).

Migration has brought limited success to Puerto Ricans. About 26 percent earned family incomes exceeding $50,000 in 2000, while almost 31 percent earned between $25,000 and $50,000. These statistics are a marked improvement over previous years, yet more Puerto Ricans live in poverty than all other

Hispanics, as shown in Table 11–5. Furthermore, like African Americans, Puerto Ricans experience racial discrimination and are, after blacks, the category most segregated from whites. The reason, Massey and Bitterman (1985) argue, is racism. Since a significant percentage of Puerto Ricans have dark skin, they tend to live in cities near blacks. Since whites often shun blacks when choosing residences, "Puerto Ricans become bystander victims of [whites'] racial prejudice, leading to their residential segregation in society" (Massey and Bitterman, 1985:306).

Another factor contributing to Puerto Rican poverty is a high level of female-headed families. In recent years women have headed over one in three Puerto Rican families, compared with one in five Mexican-American families. Yet nearly two-thirds of Puerto Rican youths graduate from high school, a share higher than the one in two for Mexican Americans (U.S. Bureau of the Census, 2002a). Perhaps as educational attainment improves (13 percent now graduate from college), future earnings for this group will also improve.

Mexican Americans

Over 20 million Mexican Americans lived in the United States in 2000, with most living in the West (57 percent) and South (33 percent). Mexican Americans make up 30 percent of the Los Angeles population, 27 percent of Houston, 21 percent of San Diego, and 18 percent of Chicago (U.S. Bureau of the Census, 2002b).

Although most are new arrivals, Mexican Americans have been a significant presence in the United States for over 150 years. Generally accorded greatest prestige are the *Hispanos*, descendants of families who resided in the Southwest prior to the Mexican-American War in 1848. Immigration from Mexico picked up around the turn of the century, and descendants of these more "recent" residents occupy a middle status. Below them are the most recent arrivals, many of whom prefer to be called *Chicanos*, a name that implies both a political consciousness and cultural pride in their Mexican heritage.

New arrivals typically live in crowded urban barrios in California and Texas. Poverty is common, although life is better than the destitution they left behind in Mexico. Aiding their adjustment is the Mexican-American tradition of family support, which continues (although somewhat weakened) in large cities. Today's urbanites tend to follow nuclear-family instead of extended-family residence patterns and to have less male dominance, higher intermarriage rates, and more diverse occupations (Parrillo, 2003:441).

Fertility for Mexican-American women is nearly twice as high as for the non-Hispanic population. This higher fertility rate, together with high levels of migration by mostly young people, suggests further significant population increases in the urban Mexican-American population. However, women of Mexican ancestry born in the United States show much lower fertility rates than do women born in Mexico, illustrating the effect of cultural assimilation on family size (del Pinal and Singer, 1997:26–27).

Mexican Americans face a number of disadvantages. Discrimination in employment and housing, coupled with a lack of English language skills, limits opportunities for many. Some adolescents, with little hope for the future, turn to street gangs for a sense of belonging and importance. The Urban Living box on page 322 shows what gang membership means to *Chicana* women in East Los Angeles.

Despite the challenges, about 45 percent of Mexican Americans have made it into the middle class, with annual family incomes exceeding $35,000. Over one-third are working class, and the remainder are poor (U.S. Bureau of the Census, 2002a). Most in poverty live in central cities, where school dropout rates run as high as 45 percent and drug use and gang violence are everyday realities (Chavez et al., 1989; del Pinal and Singer, 1997). For this segment, urban life is a far cry from the opportunities many hoped for.

Central and South Americans

About 100,000 immigrants from Central and South America enter the United States each year, almost one-third of them from El Salvador and Colombia (U.S. Immigration and Naturalization Service, 2002). Nearly 700,000

TABLE 11–5   Income Levels of Hispanic Americans, 2000

	All Hispanics	Mexicans	Puerto Ricans	Cubans	Central and South Americans	Other Hispanics
Median family income	$31,663	$31,123	$30,129	$38,312	$33,105	$34,935
Percent of families in poverty	20.2	21.2	23.0	15.0	16.3	18.1
Percent of persons in poverty	22.8	24.1	25.8	17.3	16.7	21.6

Source: U.S. Bureau of the Census.

Central Americans live in the Los Angeles–Long Branch metropolitan area, over 200,000 in the Washington, D.C. region, and nearly that number in Miami. New York and Houston each contain over 150,000 Central Americans. With a population of about 650,000, Salvadorans constitute the majority of Central Americans in most cities, followed by Guatemalans, who number about 370,000. From the Caribbean, Dominicans are another significant urban presence, particularly in New York, where they are the second-largest Hispanic group, numbering over 400,000 (Parrillo, 2003:462). Most are working-class people living in central cities.

Since 1981, more than 250,000 Colombians also have settled in the United States. Although they are dispersed throughout the country, sizable Colombian communities exist in New York, Miami, and Los Angeles. Colombians are a mixture of educated professionals and low-skilled peasants seeking a better life in North America's cities.

Asian Americans

Like Hispanics, Asians in North America reflect a wide range of distinctive cultures. They are a highly urban population, with 96 percent living in metropolitan areas in 2000, compared with 81 percent of the total population. However, they are more likely than African and Hispanic Americans to live in suburbia; almost half do so, in fact. Most numerous are the 2.7 million Chinese Americans, followed by the 2.4 million Filipino Americans, 1.9 million Asian Indians, and the

1.2 million each Vietnamese and Koreans (Lewis Mumford Center, 2001b). Most of the newer immigrants from these ethnic groups reside in larger cities such as Los Angeles, New York, and Chicago (described further in the Case Study at the end of this chapter).

Chinese Americans

The first Asians to come to the United States, Chinese immigrants arrived in the San Francisco area about 1850. In the frenzy of the California gold rush (beginning in 1849), the building of the transcontinental railroad, and the rise of West Coast textile manufacturing, Chinese immigrants found jobs waiting, and they constituted 25 percent of the labor force in 1860 even though they were only 9 percent of the population (Gibson, 1877:51–52). When the economy turned sour in the 1870s, however, whites felt a growing economic threat from the Chinese, and a period of marked hostility ensued. During this period the American Federation of Labor conducted an incessant and racist anti-Chinese campaign, complaining bitterly about the "Yellow Peril."

Violence erupted in several western cities. In 1871 in Los Angeles, angry mobs massacred 21 Chinese; in Denver anti-Chinese riots wreaked havoc in the streets in 1880. At Rock Springs, Wyoming, in 1885, a mob attacked and murdered 28 Chinese, wounded many others, and drove hundreds more from their homes. In Tacoma, Seattle, Oregon City, and many smaller towns, angry mobs forcibly expelled Chinese residents, with considerable loss and destruction of property (Parrillo, 2003:298).

Women in the Gangs of Los Angeles

In the traditional Mexican culture, it is undesirable but certainly more acceptable for boys to be out roaming the streets; it is never appropriate behavior for females. Therefore, Latinas who either join a gang or in any way affiliate themselves with the *cholo* lifestyle, are subsequently stigmatized by the more traditional Mexican community. . . . In the present field investigation, parents and members of extended family who were interviewed had nothing but negative remarks concerning the "*Cholas*"—the gang girls.

On the other hand, the young women had completely rejected the hardworking ethic, the good wife and mother role model so common among Hispanic women, for the *Cholo* lifestyle. They, in turn, had nothing positive to say about the more traditional women either. . . .

There has been historically and frequently a good deal of bad blood between barrio residents and law enforcement. Then if there is also friction at home, the gang subculture is skillful at socializing many youths to their value system. For many of these teens—not just the females—their Mexican self-concept has already been altered. They recognize that they do not belong to the mainstream Anglo culture, but they know they do not belong to the Mexican culture either. Those who have ever traveled to Mexico to visit grandparents and other relatives have soon learned that they are considered outsiders in their ancestral land as well. Their speech is ridiculed and they are called "*pochos*." Thus, Mexican values about home and family do not carry very much weight for some youngsters.

Different individuals experience varying degrees of cultural conflict. Those who experience severe marginalization are easy targets for the gang paradigm, especially if parental influence is lacking or not respected by the youngster. Young women living on the margins of both cultures are easy prey.

Frequently such young women are confronted with a double standard at home. In many Mexican culture homes, it is normal for boys to be treated more leniently than girls, enjoying more privileges, being allowed to stay out later, and even dominating their sisters who must often iron their shirts to perfection and wait on them at the dinner table. In the traditional Mexican family, the joys of motherhood and family security are highly prized. Typically, Mom always seems happy and both she and Dad are primarily concerned with providing for the children. The family is sacred. In the traditional Mexican family, Mom also stays at home and cooks

---

In 1882, the United States curbed the immigration of all Asians with the passage of the Chinese Exclusion Act. Canada took similar action in 1923 (partly to quell U.S. criticism that Chinese were entering the United States by way of British Columbia). The U.S. Congress passed broader anti-immigration laws in the 1920s that ended virtually all Chinese immigration. Congress ended the ban in 1943; however, only about 100 Chinese entered the United States annually until 1965, when a more liberal immigration law opened the door much wider.

In response to hostility in the late nineteenth and early twentieth centuries, some Chinese moved eastward; others banded together in low-rent urban enclaves, usually situated near major means of transportation (shipping docks or railroad terminals). These became the Chinatowns that, even today, still and sews—even today with the economy virtually forbidding this practice any longer. In some Mexican homes, Mom has to work; nevertheless, she returns to the nest and puts in another shift cooking, washing, ironing, and nurturing.

Many young women are fed up with this double standard and expressed their exasperation vociferously. Given a few other displeasures and grumblings about home, and with the pressures provided by poverty-stricken environments, they become likely targets for gang recruitment. In addition, in many of the homes, Dads were not always present and if they were, they were not necessarily able to provide very much of anything for their children. Some Moms were not at all happy with cooking and sewing. Others were themselves in gangs at one time.

Many of these youngsters have witnessed or experienced beatings, and a number of forms of parental violence.

Connie: "Mom always got between me and my Dad and she'd catch the belt in her hand sometimes so it wouldn't hit me again. Sometimes my Dad would get so mad he'd start swinging at both of us. One time my older brother beat me up till I was black and blue."

In the traditional Mexican family, "spare the rod; spoil the child," is still very much in style. The gang girls often reported other kinds of abuse as well.

. . . In this investigation, Latina gang and non-gang affiliated seemed to function in large measure as auxiliary, or as accomplices to males, going along with criminal activity committed by the males. Girls' crimes appeared to be still largely "traditionally female" prostitution, shoplifting, running away, fighting with other girls, and drug-related crimes. Actual scuffles among these young women involved knife assaults and/or scratching and kicking types of fights which reportedly occurred frequently sometimes against other women and often against males as well. . . .

In the current research, most gang girls came from less conventional Mexican families. They seemed to be from more dysfunctional families, sometimes from *cholo* families. Many of their parents were at one time themselves gang-members, or associates of one kind or another. Other gang-affiliated females came from homes with parents who have given up, or who never cared very much in the first place. . . .

Much of the current study concurs with older studies. The gang has been and still appears to be a welcome source of support for *cholas*. Ironically, in view of the ill treatment, the infidelities and abuses the women receive at the hands of the males, it is surprising that so many women, gang as well as non-gang affiliated, found the gang members so appealing. . . .

Source: Francine Garcia-Hallcom, *An Urban Ethnography of Latino Street*, 1997. www.csun.edu/~hcchs006/gang.html.

---

attract immigrants. In these enclaves, the Chinese pooled their resources to provide economic assistance to one another. During much of this century, however, Asians faced formidable social barriers. Kept within the limits of racial ghettos by prejudice and discrimination, many Chinese never learned to speak English, further limiting their opportunities.

Since 1965, the Chinese-American population has quintupled. Chinatowns—such as

those in San Francisco, Los Angeles, and New York—are, paradoxically, both tourist attractions and slum communities. Filled with overcrowded, dilapidated buildings and troubled by the problems of youth gangs and high rates of tuberculosis, they nonetheless retain historical, picturesque, and commercial importance. The streets mark off the sections of regional origins and dialects of their residents, much as in any early-twentieth-century

Little Italy. In New York, the largest Chinese enclave in the Western Hemisphere, Burmese Chinese concentrate on Henry Street, Taiwanese on Centre Street, Fukienese on Division Street, and Vietnamese Chinese on East Broadway (Kwong, 1987).

Chinese Americans currently present a bipolar occupational distribution. About 30 percent are in professional and technical positions, twice the rate among whites. However, the Chinese are also overrepresented as low-skilled, low-paid service workers, with 24 percent in this category compared with 7 percent of the white labor force. Although median family income among Chinese Americans is above the national average, they are likely to have more wage earners in the family. That fact, rather than higher-paying positions, accounts for most of the difference.

Japanese Americans

The Japanese attack on Pearl Harbor in Hawaii on December 7, 1941—killing thousands of U.S. servicemen, sinking several ships, and destroying the naval base—generated fear and hostility against second- and third-generation Japanese Americans. Within months, U.S. troops—acting under a presidential order—relocated more than 110,000 people of Japanese ancestry (most of them U.S. citizens) to military detention centers inland. Significantly, this action occurred only on the West Coast, not in Hawaii, where the Japanese were more fully integrated into the society. As a result of this policy, Japanese Americans—not one of whom had been convicted of any treasonous act—suffered not only anger and humiliation but a crushing economic setback. Their forced relocation obliged most to sell their homes, land, businesses, and possessions for dimes on the dollar.

With low annual immigration, Japanese Americans represent a steadily declining share of Asian Americans, and now number about 800,000. Most are U.S.-born and have high educational and income levels, higher even than white people. Outgroup marriage now exceeds 50 percent, making Japanese Americans the most structurally assimilated

nonwhite group (Barringer et al., 1993:144; Awanohara, 1990:16).

Korean Americans

In metropolitan Los Angeles, where about 200,000 Korean Americans now live, 40 percent of adult males operate their own businesses (Awanohara, 1991a:36). Nationwide, Korean self-employment is higher than in any other racial or ethnic category, including whites: 1 in 9 Korean Americans is a business owner, compared with 1 in 15 among whites and 1 in 67 for African Americans (Yoshihashi and Lubman, 1992:A1). So deeply entrenched is self-employment in the Korean immigrant ethos that one survey reported that 61 percent of South Koreans planning to emigrate to the United States expect to go into business for themselves even though few had done so in their homeland (Awanohara, 1991a:36–37).

In Los Angeles, Korean Americans have cornered the wig and liquor businesses. In Washington, D.C., Philadelphia, and New York City, Koreans are especially visible as grocery-store owners and fruit-stand operators. Korean greengrocers now sell more than three-fourths of New York City's produce (Min and Kolodny, 1994).

Asian Indians

The Asian Indian presence in North America has increased dramatically in the past several decades. Census tallies reported about 300,000 Asian Indians in Canada in 2001 and 1.9 million in the United States, twice the number a decade earlier. With overpopulation a serious problem in India (one in six of the world's people live there!), high migration rates are likely to continue.

Hindi speakers constitute the largest group of Asian Indian immigrants, followed by Gujarati, Punjabi, and Bengali speakers. Asian Indian immigrants also arrive from East Africa and Latin America, particularly from the Caribbean and Guyana, where earlier generations had first gone as indentured plantation laborers (Awanohara, 1991b:35). Almost three-fourths of the immigrants are in professional or managerial occupations; the remainder most often operate convenience stores, gas stations, and family-managed hotels and motels. Consequently, most Asian Indians settle in large metropolitan areas, most significantly in Chicago; New York; San Jose; Washington, D.C.; and Central New Jersey (U.S. Immigration and Naturalization Service, 2002).

Vietnamese Americans

Barely noted by the Census Bureau in 1970, over 1.9 million Vietnamese lived in the United States and over 110,000 in Canada in 2000. They are the largest Asian group in Texas; but by far the largest concentration of Vietnamese—some 150,000 people—is in "Little Saigon" in Orange County, California, where the language, signs, shops, offices, and music all convey a distinctly Vietnamese character. Similarly, Anaheim, California, now has its own Little Saigon (Lee 1998; Matsuoka, 1990:341). San Jose is home to over 105,000 Vietnamese Americans, and the Houston–Galveston–Brazonia megalopolis contains another 64,000 (U.S. Bureau of the Census, 2002b).

The "Model Minority" Stereotype

Despite their cultural diversity, many Asian Americans have a record of educational achievement, high income, and overall success in Canadian and U.S. metropolitan areas. Dubbed a "model minority" because of their accomplishments, Asian Americans often display success in a variety of occupational roles: Chinese engineers, Japanese financiers, Filipino nurses, Korean entrepreneurs, and Vietnamese restaurateurs abound, reinforcing this positive stereotype. Yet the reality is not entirely favorable:

> Beneath a thick crust of scientists, professionals, and entrepreneurs are thicker layers of struggling families—peddlers and waiters and office cleaners and sweater stitchers who eke out a bare living by dint of double jobs and the presence of multiple wage earners. (Chua-Eoan, 1990:33)

Many Southeast Asian refugees remain on welfare, hampered by language difficulties, poor education, and weak job skills. Not all Asian students perform well in school. The criminal activities of Asian drug rings, extortion gangs, and youth gangs are often a brutal menace.

In short, there is some truth to the "model minority" stereotype; but, like other generalizations, it conceals as much as it reveals about a complex category of people.

Native Americans

Throughout their history right up to about 1950, few Native Americans lived in cities. Most resided in rural areas, on or near reservations. In recent decades, however, a steady migration to cities has brought more than half of all Native Americans to urban areas.

The largest groups of natives are the Cherokee (281,000) and the Navajo (269,000). Census data indicate there were 2.5 million Native Americans in 2000, up from 800,000 in 1970. Some of this increase is due to a birth rate almost twice the national average, and some is due to the fact that more people now claim Native American ancestry on census forms.

About 43 percent of U.S. natives reside in the West and another 31 percent in the South, although several hundred thousand live in various metropolitan areas across the country. Table 11–6 provides details.

TABLE 11–6   Native American Population Living in Metropolitan Areas, 2000

Albuquerque	17,444	Oklahoma City	17,743
Boston	2,365	Omaha	2,616
Chicago	10,290	Philadelphia	4,073
Cleveland	1,458	Phoenix	26,696
Dallas–Fort Worth	6,472	Portland, OR	5,587
Detroit	3,140	San Antonio	9,584
Denver	7,290	San Diego	7,543
Houston	8,568	San Francisco	3,458
Jacksonville	2,474	Seattle	5,695
Los Angeles	29,412	Tucson	11,036
Minneapolis	8,378	Tulsa	18,551
New York	41,289		

Source: U.S. Bureau of the Census.

As always, migration to cities is prompted by the desire for a better life—most reservations are economically depressed, offering few jobs, little schooling, and inefficient services provided by the Bureau of Indian Affairs. Yet for most natives the city has not delivered much.

Although not living in ghettos, about three-fourths of urban Native Americans do live in poorer neighborhoods. Those lacking schooling and job skills generally experience the same poverty they left behind but without the tribal support system. Research suggests that Native Americans who migrate to cities are more likely to be working than those who remain behind on the reservations, but it takes five years for urbanites to show any income gains (Snipp and Sandefur, 1988).

Some urban migrants experience culture shock in their unfamiliar environment. Aware of their standing as a minority, newcomers may seek out other Native Americans, usually of the same tribe, often by frequenting a local bar. Drunkenness is as serious a problem in the cities as it is on reservations. The problem is a cultural clash: Native Americans find that their emphasis on consensus, equality, and communal use of property do not fit with the competitive life of North American cities. With few role models to point the way, some gravitate to skid row and an existence centered around the bottle and the bar. Others gradually adapt to urban living, but often holding a low-paying job. Only those who manage to gain economic security are likely to move from the central city into a racially mixed suburb. Even there, most natives try to preserve their ethnic identity, and they tend to interact little with non-natives (Weibel-Orlando, 1991).

WOMEN AND THE CITY

Women's lives in the city reflect the power of gender as well as class, race, and ethnicity. Economic changes as North American cities have industrialized and, more recently, entered the postindustrial era have greatly affected the lives of women.

Work

As both Canada and the United States industrialized, poor women, mostly from immigrant families, went to work in urban factories in low-skill jobs for low wages. In fact, women were the main work force in many textile mills and garment factories.

In the mid-nineteenth century, millions of Irish flocked to North American cities to seek their fortunes. The number of Irish households headed by women was high, approaching 20 percent, often because many husbands died from industrial accidents. In such cases, women commonly expanded their households to include other relatives or boarders to help meet living expenses. Then, too, of some 2 million Irish who came to the United States between 1871 and 1910, most were women, unlike the common pattern by which males migrated first. Many unmarried women migrated to U.S. cities, primarily to seek domestic work as maids or jobs in textile mills (Diner, 1983:73–74). For Irish women, then, the city was a place of continual hard work and economic security.

Most other immigrant women also sought work in cities. In Chicago, the needs of immigrant women and their families prompted Jane Addams to found Hull House, beginning the U.S. settlement home movement. The Case Study of Chicago at the end of this chapter looks more closely at Jane Addams's role in women's lives.

A very different story centers on middle- and upper-class women, usually born to prosperous U.S. merchants and industrialists. Men placed them on a pedestal, as towers of moral strength and refinement, as if to balance their own competitive world of work. Prevailing values in the nineteenth and early twentieth centuries held that the nature of women was to please and the nature of men was to achieve. By the 1920s, the expanding number of middle-class families only reinforced the notion that a woman's place was as housewife and mother, as keeper of home and hearth (Freeman, 1975; Ryan, 1979).

For the most part, this attitude prevailed among the middle class until World War II, when a labor shortage drew women into the work force, filling factory positions vacated by men now in uniform. From 25 percent in 1920, the percentage of women working increased to 36 percent during the early 1940s. But a postwar recession and soldiers returning to their former jobs resulted in the firing of 2 million women within 15 months after the war ended. Then, as the suburban decade of the 1950s ensued, the "Ozzie and Harriet" generation (named after the popular sitcom) resumed the pattern of women's lives' being confined to the house.

By 1970, however, change was under way, due to the increasing costs of a middle-class lifestyle (including the soaring costs of sending children to college), along with a wide range of new employment opportunities for women in the city's information and service economy. The dual-career family became the norm. By 2000, the female labor force participation rate reached 66 percent, way up from 46 percent in 1980. Mothers, too, joined the labor force: In 1975, 45 percent of mothers of children under age 18 with a husband at home worked for pay; by 2000, that share had increased to 71 percent (U.S. Bureau of the Census, 2000a).

Urban Space

A key focus of recent feminist urban research is the extent to which cities use space to meet the needs of women (Mazey and Lee, 1983; Spain, 1992; Garber and Turner, 1993). For example, how does the urban environment support the needs of today's working woman? One answer is that a host of specialized services have emerged, providing child care, household cleaning, lawn care, and shopping assistance to the working woman. Moreover, fast-food and takeout restaurants, laundries, and dry cleaners carry out tasks for which she often has little time. Large merchandising stores and supermarkets, as well as malls and mini-malls, make shopping efficient by minimizing time spent going from store to store.

Another issue concerns the allocation of public space. In a male-dominated society, planners typically allocate most open space to male-oriented activities such as sports, giving little consideration to the needs of women. More attention needs to be given to creating safe environments to protect children at play, providing less-constrained places for women to walk or jog, and creating housing that promotes more contact with neighbors, especially for children. Finally, researchers suggest that spatial arrangements should not segregate the sexes, thereby reinforcing traditional ideas about gender, but should allocate space to help all individuals' lives (Doreen Massey, 1994).

The Public Sphere

More women than ever before hold elected public office; tens of thousands now serve as mayors or members of city councils across North America. Among major cities where women have served as mayor are Chicago, Phoenix, Portland, Oklahoma City, San Antonio, San Francisco, and San Jose. As women become more active and visible in the public arena, they seek to shape and redirect policies affecting women's daily lives in the city. The fact that large cities have a large share of women who make extensive use of urban facilities and services—including transportation and child care—makes an urban policy responsive to women's needs imperative.

To date, even though many women now participate in decision-making, they have had limited success in putting on the political agenda key issues that challenge male dominance. As the number of women leaders increases, however, this situation is likely to change.

In concluding this chapter, we present a case study of what was, for a century, the "second city" of the United States—its greatest inland metropolis, Chicago. Chicago's development illustrates all the issues raised in this chapter. As Jurgis and Ona Rudkis (Chapter 1

Railroad commuters are a familiar part of any large city's work force. Once their ranks were mostly male but, with almost half the labor force now female, so too is the proportion of commuters. The greater presence of women has led to changes in the texture of urban space and in services and activities catering to their needs.

Looking Back box) and Robert Park and the University of Chicago sociologists (Chapter 5) found out, Chicago has been a city in which class, race, ethnicity, and gender have played a central part in people's lives.

❖ *CASE STUDY* ❖

Chicago, "City of the Big Shoulders"

Hog Butcher for the World,
Tool Maker, Stacker of Wheat,
Player with Railroads and the Nation's
    Freight Handler;
Stormy, husky, brawling,
City of the Big Shoulders:
They tell me you are wicked and I believe
    them, for I have seen your painted women
    under the gas lamps luring the farm boys.
And they tell me you are crooked and I
    answer: Yes, it is true I have seen the
    gunman kill and go free to kill again.
And they tell me you are brutal and my reply
    is: On the faces of women and children I
    have seen the marks of wanton hunger.

And having answered so I turn once more to
    those who sneer at this my city, and I give
    them back the sneer and say to them:
Come and show me another city with lifted
    head singing so proud to be alive and
    coarse and strong and cunning.
Flinging magnetic curses amid the toil of
    piling job on job, here is a tall bold slugger
    set vivid against the little soft cities;
Fierce as a dog with tongue lapping for
    action, cunning as a savage pitted against
    the wilderness,
        Bareheaded,
        Shoveling,
        Wrecking,
        Planning,
        Building, breaking, rebuilding,
Under the smoke, dust all over his mouth,
    laughing with white teeth,
Under the terrible burden of destiny
    laughing as a young man laughs,
Laughing even as an ignorant fighter laughs
    who has never lost a battle,
Bragging and laughing that under his wrist is
    the pulse, and under his ribs the heart of
    the people,
        Laughing!

Laughing the stormy, husky, brawling
laughter of Youth, half-naked, sweating,
proud to be Hog Butcher, Tool Maker,
Stacker of Wheat, Player with Railroads
and Freight Handler to the Nation.

Carl Sandberg, "Chicago"

Carl Sandberg captures much of the flavor of turn-of-the-century Chicago in this poem he wrote in tribute to the city in 1916. Not everyone, of course, shared his enthusiasm. Visiting Chicago in the 1850s, Swedish novelist Frederika Bremer decried it as "one of the most miserable and ugly cities," a place where people come "to trade, to make money, but not to live" (cited in Glaab and Brown, 1967:85–86). Rudyard Kipling, visiting the Chicago of the Gay Nineties, was more direct: "Having seen it," he wrote, "I urgently desire never to see it again. It is inhabited by savages" (cited in Rokove, 1975:22).

What is it about Chicago that draws such powerful and divergent responses from observers? Perhaps it is that the most powerful themes in the United States concern wealth, prestige, power, and the drama by which they are gained or lost. Chicago, which rocketed to prominence in barely 50 years, clearly exhibits such themes. This "city of the big shoulders," at once brash and breathtaking, is a magnifier of U.S. wealth and poverty without equal.

Early Chicago

In 1673, the future site of Chicago, where the Chicago River joins Lake Michigan, caught the attention of early explorers Jacques Marquette and Louis Joliet as a possible water link between Lake Michigan and the Mississippi.[1] The area remained under Indian and French control for almost a century until the English took charge in 1763. Shortly thereafter, it passed into the hands of the new United States of America. Early in the next century,

Native Americans vacated the area and the U.S. Army erected Fort Dearborn amidst a sprinkling of settlers' cabins. Another generation passed before, in the shadow of a fort, the settlement of Chicago began in earnest.

In 1830, a century of spectacular growth was under way. Starting with just 50 persons, the new city (incorporated in 1833) boasted 4,000 residents by 1837. As the Erie Canal stimulated regional trade, Chicago became a boom town. A building lot that sold for $100 in 1830 brought $15,000 by 1835. The population soared—growing by 50 percent or more between 1840 and 1900. So great was the demand for housing that the city emerged as a center for innovative architectural techniques, a tradition it has maintained. "Balloon frame" housing—assembled quickly with machined lumber rather than heavy timbers—was an early Chicago strategy to provide homes for waves of new arrivals.

The key to the economic success of the city was its position in the growing urban trade network. Chicago was linked to the East by the Great Lakes and the Erie Canal; to the South by river and canal to the Mississippi River; and, by mid-century, to the West by the railroad. On November 20, 1848, a locomotive carried the first load of wheat into the city. Although it was a trip of only 10 miles, the significance was clear: With the railroad, Chicago became the center for the entire Midwest, a break-of-bulk point for goods shipped in all directions.

By 1855, 96 trains a day entered and left the city. In the 1850s, the McCormick Reaper Company made Chicago a center for farm machinery. The famed stockyards developed during the Civil War and, with the making of steel rails, Chicago also took its place as a manufacturing center. In short, "Chicago had become Chicago" (Mayer and Wade, 1969:24).

In the following decades, Chicago's wealth and influence continued to grow. Railroad lines converged on the city from all directions, and water traffic expanded as lumber, grain, and livestock trade increased dramatically. Factories proliferated, forming new industrial districts. Many industrialists became rich beyond imagination: Cyrus McCormick

---

[1]Much of the history of Chicago that follows is based on Harvey M. Mayer and Richard C. Wade, *Chicago: Growth of a Metropolis* (Chicago: University of Chicago Press, 1969).

Chicago's skyline offers a striking array of architectural styles that enhance its visual appeal. Within the city itself, as in all cities, a population also rich in diversity often grapples with problems of housing and crime that affect quality of life and satisfaction with urban living.

with his reaper and other agricultural inventions; Henry B. Clarke in hardware; and Archibald Clybourne, Gustavus Swift, and Philip Armour in beef and meat packing. By 1885, Armour employed some 10,000 workers in his meatpacking business. Prosperity seemed to be everywhere:

> The old boundaries could no longer contain the burgeoning commerce and industry. . . . Lumber yards, factories, [grain] elevators, warehouses, docks, and depots lined the river and pushed north and south along the banks of both branches; commercial facilities steadily expanded at the city's center, forcing residential construction to move out to the edge of town. . . . urban displacement . . . had begun. (Mayer and Wade, 1969:54)

Industrial giants such as McCormick, Clybourne, Clarke, Swift, and Armour became the city's first elite. As the rich did elsewhere, these men displayed their new wealth with spectacular homes away from the city's center that contrasted sharply with the working people's squalid settlements near Packingtown and other industrial areas. Further enriching the lifestyle of the privileged residents was the opening of an opera house and art gallery in 1850 and, a decade later, of Marshall Field's, the nation's first modern department store.

The Burning and Rebuilding of Chicago

According to Chicago lore, on the night of October 8, 1871, near the corner of 12th and Halsted Streets, Mrs. O'Leary left her cottage to milk her cow in the small barn in the back. But the cantankerous old cow kicked over her lamp and started the fire that burned down the city of Chicago. Fanned by a stiff southwest wind, the fire swept northward along the lake, consuming 1,700 acres within 24 hours. As in London in 1666 and Atlanta in 1864, the destruction was virtually total. In a day, 100,000 Chicagoans were rendered homeless, and the heart of the city's business district lay in ashes.

However, the forces that had created Chicago—the quest for commercial and industrial success—were very much alive. The "second" Chicago began even while the ashes of the old city were still warm. Surveying the ruins, John Stephen Wright predicted: "Chicago will have more men, more money, more business within five years than she would have had without the fire." As if in response, the next day one enterprising citizen opened a fruit and cider stand amid the debris (Mayer and Wade, 1969:11).

The new Chicago became more of a "growth machine" than ever before. In 1884, the city opened the age of the urban skyscraper with the construction of a ten-story steel building. By 1890, Chicago's population passed the 1 million mark. Pushing its borders outward, the nation's second-largest city once again dominated the Midwest.

Jane Addams and Hull House

In 1889, Jane Addams—suffragist, activist, and the first woman to win a Nobel Peace Prize—founded Hull House in an old mansion at the corner of Halsted and Polk Streets amid Chicago's West Side slums. Her house was a refuge for displaced people to "aid in the solution of social problems engendered by the modern conditions of life in a great city" and to help her neighbors "build responsible self-sufficient lives for themselves and their families" (Addams, 1910).

Hull House was situated in an ethnically diverse section, astride Italian, Bohemian, Greek, Jewish, Polish, and Russian neighborhoods. To build pride and respect for ethnic heritage, she implemented the Hull House Labor Museum, which portrayed the labor of immigrant parents in their native countries and connected it to the jobs held by young adults in Chicago. Unlike most of her contemporaries, Addams recognized the unique problems of African Americans and became a pioneer in the fight against racial discrimination (Addams, 1930).

In *Democracy and Social Ethics* (1902), Addams discussed the social ethics of immigration quota laws. In *The Spirit of Youth and the City Streets* (1909), she voiced concern over the breakup of the sense of community caused by industrialization, which tended to segregate social classes as well as immigrants, and even the generations within the same social class. Gifted as a speaker and writer, she often addressed the issue of respecting diversity in others:

> Possibly another result of our contemptuous attitude toward immigrants who differ from us is our exaggerated acceptance of standardization. Everyone wants to be like his neighbors, which is doubtless an amiable quality, but leading to

one of the chief dangers of democracy—the tyranny of the herd mind. (1930:330)

Through it all, Hull House remained the center of her activism.

> Hull-House expanded to include many buildings. Eventually 70 people experienced collective living and more than 2,000 others crossed its doorway daily. It became a community center for all of Chicago; there was an art museum, a theater, a boys' club, a music school, a coffee house, meeting rooms for discussion clubs, a gymnasium, an employment bureau, a lunchroom, a library, apartments for working women and their children, a kindergarten, and much more. Scholars from the universities, leaders from Chicago society, and international leaders came to observe and learn. (Lundblad, 1995:662)

Addams's social activism included successfully lobbying the Illinois state legislature to pass strong child labor laws and laws protecting women. She conceived of and helped create the juvenile court system, set up school playgrounds, demanded enforcement of housing and sanitation laws, worked for woman's suffrage, advocated for the legal protection of immigrants, and much more. Among Hull House firsts were:

- the first public swimming pool in Chicago;
- the creation of four labor unions (Women Skirt Makers, Women Cloak Makers, Dorcas Federal Labor Union, Chicago Women's Trade Union League);
- the nation's first private venture capital fund for neighborhood business development;
- the first domestic violence court in Chicago in conjunction with the Chicago Metropolitan Battered Women's Network (Domestic Violence Court Advocacy Program);
- the first infant care facility in a Chicago high school;
- the first community-based foster care program of its kind in the country (Neighbor to Neighbor).

Equally important, Addams believed that dramatic changes could be made in U.S. society and, to that end, she provided a forum where people of all classes, races, and genders could speak together (Deegan, 1991). An especially important feature of Hull House was its role as a nurturing, fertile arena for women to engage in intellectually stimulating debates with men. With Hull House as a model, scores of settlement houses sprang up in slum neighborhoods in other cities. Everywhere, settlement houses served as a breeding ground for feminism and activism. At least half the women residents went on to life-long careers in some branch of social service.

Jane Addams was a close associate of George Herbert Mead, who gave lectures at Hull House. Her contributions to the founding of the science of sociology and to the first department of sociology at the University of Chicago are pivotal intellectual achievements. The noted educator John Dewey was also an associate and a good friend of Jane Addams; Dewey modeled his classes at the Laboratory School, University of Chicago, after the children's activities at Hull House. Clearly, Jane Addams was a major force not only on the Chicago urban scene, but at the national and international levels as well. Her achievements, contributions, and humanitarian efforts still shape our lives today.

Chicago in the Early Twentieth Century

> Chicago . . . offered a world of hope and opportunity to the beginner. It was so new, so raw; everything was in the making . . . the youth, the illusions, the untrained aspirations of millions of souls. . . . Chicago [at the turn of the century] meant eagerness, hope, desire. It was a city that put vitality into almost every wavering heart. It made the beginner dream.
>
> Theodore Dreiser

Chicago plunged into the new century with clear title as the metropolis of the Midwest. The city shot upward as a towering skyline took form. Immigrants from Europe swelled the city's population: Germans, Swedes, Irish, Poles, and Italians. For many, such as the Rudkis family (the Lithuanian immigrants described in Chapter 1), life in

Chicago's poorest neighborhoods was often brutal, unsanitary, and exceedingly crowded. An estimate at the turn of the century revealed that if all of Chicago "were as densely populated as its worst slums [900 people per acre], the whole of the Western Hemisphere could have been housed in Chicago" (Felter, as cited in Mayer and Wade, 1969:256).

Over time, however, the dreams of many working-class Chicagoans became a reality. More and more sons and daughters of immigrants moved outward from the old crowded neighborhoods into newer middle-class housing. This outward flow spilled into newly annexed developments on the city's edge.

But success did not come to all. African Americans had an especially hard time. Drawn to Chicago in ever-increasing numbers in the early 1900s, blacks settled primarily on the city's South Side. There, unlike many others, they experienced little prosperity, and few migrated outward. The black ghetto simply expanded to the north and west of the city. Periodically, too, racial violence erupted. On July 27, 1919, after a confrontation on a local beach, a black youth drowned, leading to five days of rioting in the South Side ghetto. Damage was extensive, and many blacks suffered death and injury at the hands of white mobs.

By the 1920s, when the sociologists of the University of Chicago began studying their city intensively, they found Chicago shaped by a complex social stratification system based on race, ethnicity, occupation, and income. Soon, organized crime asserted itself in the form of "gangsters," fed by the public's thirst for alcohol despite Prohibition. Nowhere did guns speak louder than in the smaller city of Cicero, adjacent to Chicago, where Johnny Torrio, Al Capone, and "the mob" had their headquarters. "It was said that the way to determine when one crossed the Chicago line into Cicero was simply to sniff. 'If you smell gunpowder, you're in Cicero'" (Asbury, 1940:260–61).

To consolidate his control of the city, Capone launched a campaign of terror on election day in April 1924. This represented urban political corruption at its peak of

LOOKING BACK

Al Capone's Cicero, 1924

Banks of heavily armed gangsters, commanded by Capone and campaigning for Mayor Klenha and the Democratic ticket, terrorized the city from dawn to dusk. A man was killed in Eddie Tanel's saloon. Two others were shot dead in Twenty-second Street. Another man's throat was slashed. A policeman was blackjacked. Citizens who attempted to vote Republican were slugged and driven from the polls. "Automobiles filled with gunmen paraded the streets," said the Illinois Crime Survey, "slugging and kidnaping election workers. Polling places were raided by armed thugs and ballots taken at the point of the gun from the hands of voters waiting to drop them in the box. Voters and workers were kidnapped, taken to Chicago and held prisoners until the polls closed." Late in the afternoon honest citizens appealed to Chicago for help, and seventy policemen were sworn in as deputy sheriffs by County Judge Edmund K. Jarecki and rushed to Cicero by automobile. A police squad commanded by Detective Sergeant William Cusick came upon Al Capone, his brother Frank, Dave Hedlin, and Charley Fischetti, with pistols in their hands, standing in front of a polling place at Cicero Avenue and Twenty-second Street. Frank Capone shot at Patrolman McGlynn, but missed, and McGlynn killed him. Hedlin was wounded. Fischetti was chased into a field and captured after a gun battle in which no one was hurt. Al Capone fled down Cicero Avenue, encountered another group of policemen, and with a gun blazing in each hand fought them off until darkness came to his aid and he escaped. . . .

Mayor Klenha and his ticket were, not unexpectedly, elected by tremendous majorities, and Al Capone was master of Cicero. Almost overnight the city became one of the toughest in the United States. . . . The one-time peaceful streets of downtown Cicero were filled with arrogant, roistering, swaggering gangsters, and crowded with saloons and gambling-houses. One hundred and sixty of these places ran full blast day and night, with sidewalk barkers urging passers-by to step in. . . . Torrio and Capone owned many of the gambling-houses and had shares in others. In every independent resort was posted an agent of the syndicate; his job was to protect the dive and see that Torrio and Capone received their split, which ranged from twenty-five to fifty percent of the gross receipts.

Source: Herbert Asbury, *The Chicago Underworld* (New York: Ace, 1940), pp. 260–61.

power, and the mob's victory gave gangsters control of much of the city, as the Looking Back box explains. Still, some people fought back and, by 1931, Capone was convicted of income tax evasion, and he spent the rest of his life in prison.

Then came the Depression, which cut deeply into Chicago's economic life. Unemployment soared, construction stalled, and even the city's second World's Fair in 1933 couldn't conceal the widespread social injury. Homeless Chicagoans sleeping in public parks or milling about street corners became commonplace. Only with World War II did the economy finally recover.

The Postwar Period

Post–World War II growth took place largely beyond Chicago's city limits. A familiar pattern changed the social character of Chicago as the more affluent population moved out, leaving behind the growing ranks of minorities and the poor. By 1960, with people demanding more services as the economic base continued to contract, some began speaking of the "death of the city." Chicago fought back under the leadership of a new mayor, Richard J. Daley, whose long and controversial record lasted from his election in 1955 until his death in 1976.

The Chicago Machine

An old saying about Chicago holds that "the Jews own it, the Irish run it, and the blacks live in it" (Rokove, 1975:32). This is partly incorrect—the greatest wealth in the city is controlled by white Anglo-Saxon Protestants—but the Irish have controlled the politics of the city for most of its history, although they now face a growing political challenge from blacks and Hispanics, who constituted 63 percent of the city's population in 2000 (Census Bureau, 2000c).

The Chicago political machine of the Democratic Party came to power in the 1930s, later than in many other cities, and did not reach its greatest strength until Richard J. Daley became the undisputed city boss. Political life in Chicago under Daley carried the tone of the immigrant political machines of the late nineteenth century. Its leaders, from block captains to the mayor himself, tried to meet the needs of their constituents and, in return, they expected people's votes.

Daley focused on maintaining the quality of the central business district—the Loop. Centered along State Street, the Loop is the economic heart of the city, of vital concern to the city's powerful business interests. In addition, the city revitalized the lakefront to make Chicago attractive and exciting both to visitors and to Chicagoans themselves. The record of improvements was uneven, however. While all residents of the city benefited to some degree from better lighting, street cleaning, and snow removal, poorer neighborhoods got the short end of the stick. A political opponent of Mayor Daley observed:

> Get off the subway anywhere in the central business area and you won't find a broken city sidewalk. Get off the subway almost anywhere else, and you will. Between the central business area and the outskirts lie large, almost uninterrupted grey areas of urban dry rot. This is where most Chicagoans live. (Leon Despres, cited in Rokove, 1975:78–79)

Chicago also boasts three of the five tallest buildings in the nation—including the Sears Tower, one of the tallest in the world—yet commitment to improving housing for the poor has been lacking until recently, a topic highlighted in the next chapter. Especially for African Americans, segregation remains all too evident, prompting a greater political voice from the black community (now 37 percent of the population). Hispanics, too, are a growing political force (26 percent of the city's people).

Since Daley's death in 1976, the Irish-dominated machine has held on in Chicago, although with considerably less power. Soon after Daley's death, Jane Byrne became the city's first woman mayor, followed by Harold Washington, Chicago's first black mayor, elected in 1983 following a divisive racial campaign. Presently, Richard Daley, son of the late mayor, is Chicago's leader.

Ordered Segmentation

Race and ethnicity are thus fundamental parts of the social organization of Chicago, as Gerald Suttles (1968) discovered through a participant-observer study of the Addams area on Chicago's West Side. Most observers considered this area, once prime turf for the Capone mob, little more than a disorganized slum. Suttles's most important finding was that while some housing was surely dilapidated and many people were poor, the area was far from "disorganized." Rather, Suttles found a marked social order he termed "ordered segmentation" based on race and ethnicity.

How did it work? Back then, four categories—African, Italian, Mexican, and Puerto Rican Americans—made up the bulk of the area's population. Each had its own distinctive way of life, claimed its own "territory," and had its own ideas about all the others who lived nearby. Suttles found the Italians very closely knit and trusting of one another. African Americans, in contrast, seemed alienated from each other, typically distrustful, and very poor. The Mexican Americans and Puerto Ricans fell somewhere in between. They were somewhat better off than the blacks economically and had more of a sense of community.

Contacts across racial and ethnic lines were rare. Most people kept their distance from others who, according to local stereotypes, were different and best avoided. The positive irony here is that such divisiveness allowed most people to establish community ties with those whom they did trust. By avoiding African Americans, Italians, and Mexican Americans, in other words, Puerto Ricans could form a sense of identity and community among themselves, thereby providing some defense against a hostile outside world. Suttles concluded:

> For all its shortcomings . . . the moral order they have developed includes most, if not all, of their neighbors. Within limits, the residents possess a way of gaining associates, avoiding enemies, and establishing each others' intentions. In view of the difficulties encountered, the [ordered segmentation] of the Addams Area has provided a decent world within which people can live. (1968:234)

Chicago Today

Across Chicago today, remarkable changes are under way—physically, economically, and among its residents. Its trademark skyline will soon include more rooms with a view than ever before, as high-rise residences sprout up throughout the downtown area and nearby neighborhoods. The opening of eight high-rise condominium buildings in 2000, with prices ranging from $120,000 to $400,000 for a one-bedroom unit, heralded a pace of building activity outstripping other U.S. city centers. Several other major condo development projects are underway, office space remains in high demand, and new theater venues and restaurants in the Loop have brought vitality to the downtown (Bruno,

2001:16; Roeder, 2002:57). The city's recently reopened 3,000-foot-long Navy Pier—a mix of year-round entertainment, shops, restaurants, exhibition facilities, and attractions, including a 525-seat Shakespeare Theater, a 440-seat IMAX theater, a 150-foot Ferris wheel, and a stained glass window museum—attracts hundreds of thousands of visitors annually.

City officials expect Chicago's downtown population to jump 32 percent, to 152,295 by 2010, from 113,341 in 1998—a big shift from the city's decades-long trend of suburban flight. The in-migration results from an improved city economy, a decline in crime, the downtown's growing range of retail and entertainment services, and other quality-of-life amenities, some as simple as the aesthetic improvement of Michigan Avenue with the placement of large flowerpots on the mid-road dividers (Balu, 1999).

Another significant change is in Chicago's population composition. Since 1980, the city's black and white populations have both been declining, as new immigrants introduce fresh dimensions of social diversity. As recently as the 1970s, most immigrants were Europeans; today, however, the European-born population of Chicago has fallen to less than 8 percent. In their place are now Hispanics, whose numbers tripled since 1970 to more than 753,000 by 2000, and Asians, who total about 126,000 (U.S. Census Bureau, 2002b).

In the Chicago of today, neighborhoods that once contained Germans, Poles, and Czechs bustle with African, Filipino, Korean, Mexican, Puerto Rican, and Vietnamese Americans, and many other ethnic groups. Within each category, of course, there is greater diversity still. Some new immigrants come to Chicago with wealth, extensive schooling, and bilingual fluency. Others, by contrast, are poor. Like immigrants throughout history, they come with little, seeking something more. As one might expect, those with the greatest social advantages tend to spread most widely throughout the city; most of Chicago's new immigrants from India, for example, are professionals and are widely dispersed. On the other hand, those with the fewest social advantages are re-creating

In the 1990s, Chicago experienced both a renaissance of its older commercial streets and a building boom along Michigan Avenue at the edge of Lake Michigan. Navy Pier—with its mix of amusements, exhibitions, restaurants, shops, theaters, and touring boats—is a year-round attraction for hundreds of thousands of residents and visitors each year.

the racial and ethnic enclaves that have existed in Chicago throughout its history, evident in the clusters of signs marking Mexican, Korean, and Chinese neighborhoods.

Most of the new racial and ethnic communities in Chicago are still too small to have a marked impact on the political scene. Yet, in the heyday of the Irish-dominated political machine, probably few could have imagined that the city would ever elect a black mayor. But as new performers step to the stage in the twenty-first century, the leaders of this large and complex city will need to have big shoulders indeed.

SUMMARY

Cities are marked by social diversity. Throughout history, one characteristic of the city has been its ability to generate more opportunity

for its people than rural living can. Seeking this opportunity, billions have streamed into cities. Certainly this was the wheel driving the Great Immigration to North American cities that occurred between 1880 and 1920. By and large, people found much of what they were hoping for. As time passed, many immigrants and many more of their descendants moved from poverty into relative affluence.

But this was not true for all. North American cities also became home to an impoverished class. Historically, the worst off have been the city's newest arrivals: northern Europeans until 1830, southern and eastern Europeans until 1920, "new minorities," including African, Asian, Hispanic, and Native Americans since then.

Women with few privileges have typically worked out of necessity. Middle-class women, though, have moved in and out of the labor force over time. Today, most women work for pay, a fact that shapes the city by fostering various support services to meet the needs of dual-career families and single parents. Moreover, as women become better represented in decision-making positions, we can expect further change in how cities use space.

Finally, our case study of the Windy City, Chicago, illustrates all these themes. From its beginnings as the Midwest's regional center to its emergence as this nation's "second city," Chicago (like any other North American city we might have studied) exhibits a clear-cut stratification system based on differing amounts of wealth, prestige, and power. At the top were such industrialists as the Armours and the McCormicks. At the bottom were, first, poor European immigrants; somewhat later, African Americans; and, most recently, immigrants from Latin America and Asia.

Earlier in this century, Chicago's power reins were shared by organized crime (particularly in the 1920s) and the great Democratic Party machine that arose in the Depression and reached its culmination in the 21-year administration (1955–1976) of boss Richard J. Daley. Like machines elsewhere, this one benefited some people and largely ignored others.

Among the latter were various racial and ethnic minorities, such as those who lived in the Addams area on Chicago's West Side. It was here that Jane Addams founded Hull House and centered her highly productive career of social activism. In his later study of this district, Gerald Suttles noted the persistence of racial, ethnic, and territorial divisions, an organization pattern he termed "ordered segmentation." As European immigrants organized themselves within urban neighborhoods in decades past, so do many of the "new immigrants" today.

CONCLUSION

The larger insight from Suttles's work is that prejudice always works to distinguish some "ingroup" from some "outgroup." Looking around them, people conclude that "they" simply don't look, think, or act the way "we" do. Kenneth Clark (1980) has suggested that such prejudice and the resulting discrimination are at the heart of the disadvantages faced by African Americans, a visible minority based on skin color. Much the same applies to people with a different language, who are also set apart as different and become easy targets for discrimination. Thus, some of the success experienced by white ethnics is due to their ability, over time, to "pass," that is, to assimilate into the dominant urban culture. The same opportunity is not afforded others with more clearly identifiable differences.

This pattern reminds us that cities do not exist in a cultural vacuum, for the values, norms, and stratification that shape the broader society also shape cities. Thus the unequal distribution of wealth and power that characterizes North America, as well as structures of prejudice and discrimination, play out most clearly in our cities.

HOUSING, EDUCATION, CRIME
Confronting Urban Problems

I am an optimist about the possibilities and a pessimist about the probabilities.

Lewis Mumford

We did not all come over in the same ship, but we are all in the same boat.

Bernard Baruch

With four out of five North Americans living in cities, we are unquestionably an urban people. But most of us recognize that urban living involves not just opportunities and excitement, but also various problems. Indeed, troubles such as poor housing, poor education, and crime seem more intense in cities than elsewhere.

A close look at such problems reveals that most do not exist in isolation. On the contrary, many connections exist among such problems as poverty, poor housing and education, crime, and racial and ethnic tensions. Focusing on any one alone not only hinders understanding but also frustrates any efforts at solutions. Urban problems are part of a "package," partly a product of cities but also a product of the structure and values of society itself.

Urban living is the search for a high quality of life. Three aspects of good living are adequate shelter, a good education, and physical and emotional security. How well, then, do our cities provide housing for everyone, including the poor? How well do they educate our children? How well do they offer safety for all citizens? This chapter explores the issues of housing, education, and crime, three key issues that define the quality of our urban lives.

HOUSING: A PLACE TO LIVE

Chapter 10 explained that the lifestyles of the urban population are strikingly diverse, a fact that is clearly evident in people's choice of housing. Some urbanites prefer the life of a downtown apartment; others desire the liveliness of row houses in an ethnic neighborhood; still others are drawn to a spacious single-family suburban home. Of course, housing and neighborhood are not simply a matter of personal choice. Differences in wealth set the range of choices available. Also important are past and present economic forces that have created the city, and the cultural factors that set many of our personal priorities.

Adequate Housing: Who Has It?

To define housing as either "adequate" or "substandard" is, of course, somewhat arbitrary. It is also culturally variable, because even the worst housing in the United States is of far better quality than that which commonly exists in poor nations of the world (Chapter 13).

Still, we can all agree that housing characterized by structural defects, inadequate plumbing, heating, or sanitation, or lead paint easily ingested by children poses a threat to the health and safety of those who live there. Millions of people do live in such substandard housing, and most of them live in our cities. Since most North Americans never have any direct experience with such housing, we might well be shaken if we were to confront the daily reality of the worst-housed members of our society.

Like everything else of value, quality housing is distributed quite unequally in urban North America. Not surprisingly, the worst housing is concentrated in areas occupied by the poor and minorities who are subject to discrimination—in short, people who have the fewest social choices. Such people's options have been further reduced by changes in the housing market itself: a steady decline in the number of low-rent housing units and a commensurate increase in the number of higher-rent housing units. Beginning about 1980, the U.S. government reduced its funding for low-income housing, pushing the number of available units downward even as demand rose (Children's Defense Fund, 1991).

Years of neglect have led to a serious backlog of repairs among the 1.1 million assisted and 350,000 unassisted units insured by HUD. An Abt Associates study estimates that restoring systems in these buildings to their original working condition would have cost $4.2 billion in 1995, up from $2.2 billion in 1989. The price tag for repairing a typical two-bedroom unit would be $2,800 in newer assisted properties and $3,845 in older properties. An estimated fifth of these costs relate to repairs to systems essential to health and safety.

On top of losses due to neglect and demolition, increasing numbers of subsidized units may be lost as property owners convert their units to market-priced rentals. In 1998 alone, the nation lost 17,000 subsidized units as owners opted out of federal programs, bringing total losses since late 1996 to 30,000.

During the next five years, contracts on two-thirds of all Section 8 units—involving 14,000 properties and 1 million apartments—are set to expire. Forty-four states thus stand to lose more than half the affordable units subsidized through Section 8 (Joint Center for Housing Studies, 1999).

Small wonder, then, that some critics claim that the combination of declining stock of low-cost housing and the constant need for such housing is a key cause of today's homelessness.

Housing Problems: A Brief History

To better understand current housing problems, we need to look to their roots in the past. Many of the older cities' tenements are nineteenth-century structures that present some of the same problems today that they did back then.

Nineteenth-Century Housing Problems

Housing problems in North America are hardly new. In fact, in the great metropolises of the nineteenth century, housing conditions were far worse than they are today. In an examination of conditions in New York in 1870, James D. McCabe, Jr., recorded the following impressions:

If the people [housed in tenements] are sufferers, they at least live upon the surface of the earth. But what shall we say of those who pass their lives in the cellars of [these] wretched buildings . . . ?

[Most] have but one entrance and that furnishes the only means of ventilation . . . and . . . the filth of the streets comes washing down the walls into the room within. The air is always foul. The drains of the houses above pass within

a few feet of the floor, and as they are generally in bad condition the filth frequently comes oozing up and poisons the air with its foul odors. . . . The poor wretches who seek shelter here are half stupefied by it, and pass the night in this condition instead of in a healthful sleep. (1970:405, 406, 409)

Despite such horrors, for generations government leaders made little effort to regulate housing. For their part, private builders, concerned mainly with profits, did little on their own. Indeed, only the collapse of the U.S. economy in the 1930s forced the government to enact a housing program—part of President Franklin Roosevelt's "New Deal."

A New Deal

Under the Roosevelt administration, the federal government became more involved in everyday life than ever before. Officials argued, first, that inadequate housing was so widespread that it amounted to a serious social problem and, second, that only governmental intervention was likely to lead to a solution.

Under the New Deal, federal housing programs had four specific goals. First, government directed federal funds to encourage the construction of new housing. Second, since some 500,000 families had lost their homes due to inability to pay their mortgage debts, agencies offered assistance to homeowners faced with foreclosure by banks. Third, the Federal Housing Administration (FHA) guaranteed construction loans to increase the housing supply. Fourth, the Public Works Administration, begun in 1938, hired unemployed people to build low-rent public housing in 30 cities.

Taken together, these programs rapidly improved urban housing. According to the housing census of 1940, however, about 40 percent of urban housing in the United States still had at least some serious defect (such as a lack of running water or other inadequate plumbing).

Postwar Programs

All housing construction, public and private, slowed for the duration of World War II. Soon afterward, however, the United States faced a great housing shortage as military personnel returned home and families began having children. This shortage, along with the continued need to improve the overall quality of housing, led government to devise several new strategies.

One was a broadening of federal mortgage guarantees through the FHA and the Veterans Administration (VA). The latter agency, created under the Servicemen's Readjustment Act of 1944 (popularly known as the GI Bill of Rights), provided federally backed loans to military personnel and veterans. These programs greatly enhanced the home-buying ability of moderate-income families.

Another major initiative was passage of the Housing Act of 1949. This program provided a two-pronged attack on urban decline by launching major efforts at slum clearance and the construction of new housing.

The program, called *urban renewal*, rested on local governments' ability to seize a decaying area through the right of eminent domain and sell the property to a private developer who would rebuild it. Of course, developers sought *profitable* redevelopment, so the new construction was seldom affordable to the low-income residents who had previously occupied the neighborhood. Most often, urban renewal projects created new housing for the middle class. A classic example is Boston's once-thriving Italian West End. Declaring it in need of renewal in 1953—despite the fact that the outwardly aging buildings were, on the inside, extremely well-kept by residents—the city bought up the area between 1958 and 1960, evicted its residents, and let the developers have a go at renewal. The personal trauma of such relocation was often enormous. Said one evicted West Ender,

> I wish the world would end tonight. . . . I wish they'd tear the whole damn town down . . . damn scab town . . . I'm going to be lost without the West End. Where the hell can I go? (Gans, 1982:331)

What was built in the "new" West End were high-rise luxury apartments, beyond the reach of virtually all of the area's earlier residents. As this pattern was repeated throughout the 1960s, critics often charged that urban renewal meant "poor or Negro removal." Many of the displaced poor had no choice but to crowd into other low-grade housing that they could afford. The resultant overcrowding only hastened the decay of those buildings; thus, ironically, "slum clearance" actually created more slums.

Urban renewal often made the housing crisis worse in another way, since many redevelopers did not build as many housing units as had been destroyed. The predictable result was fewer homes and thus more competition and more overcrowding. Today there are about 2.3 million subsidized rental housing units in the United States but that is not enough to meet the need, (U.S. Bureau of the Census, 2002c).

Public Housing

Public housing has never been very successful in the United States. Our cultural orientation has long viewed private home ownership as the foundation of a virtuous life and a stable social order (Bellush and Hausknecht, 1967). Therefore, people tend to judge those living in publicly supported rental housing as somehow deficient. Add to this the fact that public housing is almost exclusively the preserve of poor minorities, and we see why such a stigma is attached to housing projects. Instantly they become ghettos, places to be avoided, out-of-the-way reservations designed to contain an unwanted segment of society.

Although sometimes conceived as incorporating exciting housing innovations, too many of these projects turned into unmitigated human disasters, plagued by crime, low income, overcrowding, and terrible sanitary conditions. Even poor people soon looked on them as residences of last resort. People in almost every major city can tell of such a high-rise housing project nightmare. One of the most infamous of cases is St. Louis's Pruitt-Igoe project, described in the Looking Back box.

Some later housing projects—notably Philadelphia's Society Hill—overcame the mistakes of these first programs. Still, the failures far outnumber the successes. Scott Greer suggests

LOOKING BACK

— St. Louis

Pruitt-Igoe: A Case of Minimal Charity

It sounded so promising in 1951—a public housing project designed to improve the lives of thousands in a badly run-down area of East St. Louis. Taking advantage of the 1949 Housing Act, local officials sought to break through the "collar of slums which [was] threatening to strangle [the] downtown business section" (_Architectural Forum_, 1951:129).

Three years later, residents fully occupied the 2,762 apartments in 33 innovative high-rise buildings. But by 1959, Pruitt-Igoe "had become a community scandal" (Rainwater, 1970:8). Crime, dirt, and accidents were rampant; the project became "a concrete shell where anarchy prevailed" (Green, 1977:179). Essentially a concentration of poor, welfare-dependent African American families (57 percent were female-headed households with children), Pruitt-Igoe's population declined as more and more residents could not bear to remain. The history of Pruitt-Igoe came to a dramatic close in 1972 when the St. Louis Housing Authority dynamited the buildings into oblivion.

that, in the light of the dismal results, we can justly call the program one of "minimal charity" (1965:16).

Exactly why life in public housing is often so bad is a matter of bitter disagreement. Urban critics such as Edward Banfield (1970, 1974) suggested that residents themselves are largely to blame, since many do not work, have children they cannot afford, and generally act in irresponsible ways. Architectural critics (as we'll discuss shortly) point to the design of such structures, condemning high-rise buildings as anonymous spaces vulnerable to crime and vandalism (Newman, 1972, 1996). Others, such as Ronald Utt (1996) and Lee Rainwater (1970), point to the pathologies of concentrated poverty—not the people themselves—as the fundamental cause of public housing's rather dismal record.

Different Approaches

In the climate of criticism and social reform that characterized the late 1960s, the federal government renewed efforts to ensure a "decent home for every American," the elusive goal first put forth in 1937 and reaffirmed in 1949.

The Housing Act of 1968 provided for the construction or rehabilitation of 26 million housing units, targeting 6 million of them for low- and moderate-income families. Even then, experts acknowledged, meeting this objective would not entirely end the housing crisis (Pynoos et al., 1973:7).

An important innovation of the 1968 legislation was its attempt to place home ownership within reach of more families through loan guarantees and direct subsidies. Ideally, this program provided an alternative to public housing and helped to improve neighborhoods by increasing the number of families who had a long-term stake in the area as homeowners. To succeed, the program depended on the cooperation of real estate and government personnel. Too often, however, this didn't materialize: The program provided unscrupulous real estate speculators and public officials with opportunities that would have delighted corrupt urban politicians of a bygone era.

The basic plan was laudable: Low-income families would pay only 20 percent of their income toward the home; the government would pick up the rest. This was a major step

_Ed_ Banfield — Blame the residents

Ronald Utt (Rutt) Lee Rainwater — pathologies of concentrated

Since the dynamiting of Pruitt-Igoe in 1972, a similar fate befell other high-rise public housing as city governments attempted to correct past mistakes (not considering social as well as physical factors) with low-rise replacements. This photo shows the implosion of one of three remaining 13-story buildings of the Scudder Homes complex in Newark, New Jersey in 1996.

toward extending to the poorest people the federal assistance already made available to middle-class families by the earlier FHA program (Green, 1977). However, while the government labored to protect the investments of developers and lending banks, it overlooked protecting the home buyers as well. Often, purchasers ended up with an overpriced house in need of extensive repairs that they could not afford to maintain. The result was foreclosure. But the banks then received full payment from the government, leaving the "owners" back on the street. In the end, the government owned more and more undesirable houses.

By the early 1970s the handwriting was on the wall and the program was cut back. By 1975 over $4 billion had been spent and the government was saddled with 100,000 bad houses. "With hindsight," Green concluded, "it can safely be said that private concerns [investors, developers, banks] were given too much rope, and with it, they hung the poor" (1977:181).

An alternative approach, begun in 1974 and still active, is the Section 8 Program, which provides rent subsidies to low-income tenants in private housing. This assistance program enables tenants to choose where to live instead of forcing them into a public housing project. The program offers subsidies to developers to build or rehabilitate rental housing. Developers then set aside a certain portion of the units for low-income families and, in a subsidy contract with the government, they receive 30 percent of the rent from the tenant and the rest from the government. Although Section 8 and other rental assistance programs have increased the stock of low-cost rental housing, the program is severely underfunded, thereby stranding families for years on waiting lists. For example, in New Orleans in 2002, the waiting list for Section 8 vouchers contained 19,000 names (Housing Authority of New Orleans, 2002).

Evaluation

Even this brief history makes clear that federally supervised urban housing programs fell well short of their lofty goals. Some specific problems are worth highlighting.

Boston's West End [handwritten note]

First, did the urban housing programs prior to the 1990s help the poor? Because of the deep involvement of private banking and construction industries in renewal programs, for many, profit overshadowed any sense of social responsibility to help the poor. Furthermore, the design of some redevelopment projects was intended for more affluent buyers, at prices out of the reach of those who originally lived there. Scott Greer charges that the original intention of urban housing programs of the 1930s—to improve the housing of the poor—was "slowly transformed into a large-scale program to redevelop the central city," usually with economic interests predominating (1965:32). Thus, Greer (1965) and Lowe (1967) concluded that, while urban renewal created "tall towers and green malls," these programs actually reduced the total amount of low-cost housing across urban North America.

All about profit [handwritten note in margin]

A second problem is that, given the tendency of investors and developers to pursue profit rather than assist the poor, local residents had little voice in the decision-making process. Herbert Gans studied the redevelopment of Boston's West End, claiming that local residents were unorganized and lacked understanding of the programs that seemed to "attack" them. Thus, for many, renewal was a bitter experience.

A typical fate befell the residents of Poletown, a mostly ethnic but racially integrated neighborhood in Detroit, whose 465 acres contained over 1,300 homes and apartments, 143 businesses, 16 churches, 2 schools, and a hospital. In 1981, anxious to keep a new General Motors plant and 6,000 jobs in the city, municipal leaders exercised their right of eminent domain to take over Poletown, razed it (at a cost exceeding $200 million), and sold the land to GM (for $8 million) to build its new plant. Residents, joined by consumer advocate Ralph Nader and Gray Panthers leader Maggie Kuhn, futilely tried to stop the forced uprooting and destruction of their homes, churches, and businesses. To this day, much bitterness remains among those dispossessed people.

Poletown – Detroit [handwritten note]

Third, Gans and other critics like Jane Jacobs argued that redevelopers didn't even try to see that many areas subject to redevelopment were actually healthy, safe neighborhoods. In effect, many development programs reflected the bias of middle-class planners against the lifestyle of low-rent areas. Somehow, such areas just weren't what the planners considered "normal."

> Reformers [who] have long observed city people loitering on busy corners, hanging around in candy stores and bars and drinking soda pop on stoops . . . have passed a [class-biased] judgment, the gist of which is: "This is deplorable! If these people had decent homes and a more private . . . outdoor place, they wouldn't be on the street!" [Such a judgment] makes no more sense than to drop in at a testimonial banquet in a hotel and conclude that if these people . . . could cook, they would give their parties at home. (Jane Jacobs, 1961:55)

At present, we find some promise for public housing, even as the U.S. government seeks to severely cut back funding. We will discuss the bright spots in both public and private housing shortly. First, though, we will discuss housing troubles in the private sector that also plague the cities.

Deterioration and Abandonment in the Inner City

Picture this: block after block of empty, dilapidated buildings, many burned, as if the area had collapsed under a full-scale bomb attack. Do such urban "ghost towns" really exist in the United States? Especially in the older, industrial inner cities of the Midwest and Northeast, the answer is, sadly, yes.

As the economic activity of cities spread outward after World War II with the decline of older industries and the globalization of trade, the older central cities fell on hard times. Without the resources necessary for repairs and improvements, many inner-city neighborhoods deteriorated sharply, in some cases falling victim to extensive vandalism and arson. In 1977, estimates placed the number of abandoned buildings in U.S. center cities at 2 million (W. Conway, 1977). Although some were later torn down and others rehabilitated, the number of additional abandoned buildings grew some 150,000 yearly well into the 1980s. In the 1990s, the numbers dropped considerably, thanks to the economic revitalization in many cities and the gentrification process. Still, in 2000, Philadelphia had nearly 28,000 abandoned buildings, while Baltimore had 15,000, Houston 8,000, Detroit 7,500, and Kansas City 5,000 (Bayles, 2000:21).

While no older city escaped this problem, devastation was unparalleled in New York's South Bronx, an inner-city area where mostly poor African Americans and Puerto Ricans replaced out-migrating whites. In the South Bronx some 30,000 buildings were abandoned, and many were burned, during the 1970s (Hanson, 1980). This averages out to some eight buildings a day over an entire decade!

Why would people simply walk away from otherwise usable buildings in cities where housing was in short supply? The answer is a complex vicious circle of decline. Faced with the mounting expenses of taxes, insurance, heating fuel, and repairs due to vandalism, not to mention the loss to the suburbs of middle-income renters, and often constrained by rent control caps, some building owners reduce or entirely eliminate routine maintenance and repairs in an effort to retain some profit. Angered tenants often withhold rent, which, in turn, encourages owners to withhold more services to obtain rents. If the building eventually represents more costs or trouble than rental income warrants, some owners simply default on their mortgages or cut off the utilities. In some cases buildings are deliberately "torched" in an effort to secure payment of insurance claims. As desperate ex-tenants scatter in search of other housing, vandals and looters seek whatever of value remains (including sinks, bathtubs, and plumbing). First the building, then the block, and then eventually the whole neighborhood succumbs to the process. In the end, just hollow buildings remain: giant headstones marking the grave of a now-dead urban neighborhood. The Urban Living box on page 347 tells of a major New York property management firm struggling to avoid this vicious circle of decline.

Other developments in the private sector are more encouraging. In recent years, housing in the South Bronx as well as throughout New York City and in other major cities has vastly improved. Although much more needs to be done, notable progress is clearly evident, as we shall now explain.

The Inner City Today: A Revival?

> When a city begins to grow and spread outward from the edges, the center which was once its glory . . . goes into a period of desolation, inhabited at night by the vague ruins of men. . . . Nearly every city I know has such a dying mother of violence and despair where at night the brightness of the street lamps is sucked away and policemen walk in pairs. And then one day perhaps the city returns and rips out the sore and builds a monument to its past.
>
> John Steinbeck, *Travels with Charley*

Although the success of public programs has surely been limited, efforts by private groups to rebuild certain inner-city areas have achieved significant results in the past few decades. Two trends deserve attention: urban homesteading and gentrification.

Urban Homesteading

In 1973, the city of Wilmington, Delaware (burdened with some 1,200 abandoned homes) revived the mid-nineteenth-century Homestead Act that gave away land and mules to pioneers if they built on vacant land in the West and lived on it for five years (W. Conway, 1977). The city offered buildings it acquired through default of tax payments for a token fee of a few hundred dollars to people agreeing to rehabilitate them and stay there a minimum of three years. The Housing and Community Development Act of 1974 enabled the federal government to assist in transferring urban

The South Bronx in the 1980s looked like a war zone and its violent crime rate made it feel like one. Arson and abandonment led to the loss of 30,000 buildings in the 1970s, leading to scenes such as this one where a boy flies a kite in a street bordered with fire-gutted buildings and debris-strewn lots. By the mid-1990s though, positive changes renewed this area.

dwellings to local governments for this program. Many cities soon initiated their own homesteading programs, often transferring houses to people at the top of long waiting lists who were willing to become "urban homesteaders"—pioneers in rebuilding an urban area.

In New York's ravaged South Bronx, local citizens' groups such as the People's Development Corporation stood up against seemingly impossible odds to return deteriorating inner-city buildings to life. With little capital to invest, such groups could rely only on their own physical efforts to be successful; their collateral was not future earnings or property but their own sweat, giving rise to the term "sweat equity." The Cityscape box on page 349 captures some of the 1970s spirit that inspired people to accept the challenge of building something out of almost nothing. Danny Soto and his friends were just a few of the thousands who reclaimed the South Bronx. Nonetheless, urban homesteading has had only limited success, because too many abandoned homes have deteriorated and

been vandalized beyond rehabilitation. Others stand amid so much ruin and desolation that they are not worth salvaging. Furthermore, both the cost of repairing the building to meet occupancy code standards and the difficulty of getting rehabilitation loans eliminates most urban poor from participating in urban homesteading.

Sometimes demand far outstrips supply, as on August 31, 1999, when over 2,000 people lined up in Washington, D.C., to participate in a housing lottery for 68 boarded-up buildings that were offered for $250 each and a pledge to renovate them to bring them up to housing code standards and live in them for five years. The mostly three- and four-bedroom houses and a few small apartment buildings had been vacant for more than a decade, with the exception of occasional visits by drug dealers, prostitutes, and the homeless. Now they are part of the city's housing renewal (Fleishman, 1999).

Another form of urban homesteading requiring sweat equity of incoming homeowners, but

URBAN LIVING

Landlords: Fighting the Bottom Line

In the risky business of low-income housing, David T. Diamond and Robert C. Rosenberg are counted among the landlords who have figured it out: their buildings are generally well kept and they make a profit. . . .

Together they own and operate about 3,000 apartments in buildings scattered throughout the Bronx. They have more than 100 employees, including 50 building superintendents, and a computer system that tracks both the company's response to code violations and the heat levels in its buildings. . . .

They also retain two "tenant relations specialists" who work out rent-payment plans, help fill out forms for government subsidies and even provide rides to doctors' offices.

The partners adhere to a credo of enlightened self-interest. For example, they offer to pay college application fees for tenants, figuring that education can lead to better jobs that will make paying the rent easier. They give out T-shirts that say "Junior Tenant Patrol," hoping to instill children with pride in their homes. They plant trees and shrubbery in their concrete courtyards.

But even the Rosenberg-Diamond model is showing cracks. It is getting harder and harder, they say, to make the numbers work. In 1996, for the first time in their 20-year partnership, the two men fell significantly behind in their taxes—as much as $1 million—and had to refinance some buildings to pay off those taxes to avoid the unpalatable choice between paying for fuel for tenants or paying taxes.

A ruthless arithmetic is at the root of the problem. The city estimates that the average cost of operating a rent-stabilized apartment in a building built before World War II is about $386 a month, not including mortgage payments or profit. But the state's shelter allotment for welfare, that inefficient yet indispensable element of the low-income housing equation, has remained stable for almost a decade, at $286 for a family of three. [Tenants pay the difference] but with low-income housing that can prove almost impossible.

"There are whole neighborhoods in the city where the household income is nowhere near enough to pay a $386 monthly rent," said Frank P. Braconi, executive director of the Citizens Housing and Planning Council. Since the precarious Rosenberg-Diamond empire relies heavily on government subsidies (more than two-thirds of their tenants receive welfare payments, vouchers or some other government assistance), significant cuts in those subsidies would jeopardize its continuance.

Meanwhile, a militant tenant organization, the Association of Community Organizations for Reform Now (ACORN), and the Rosenberg Diamond Development Corporation are presently embroiled in several multimillion dollar lawsuits and attacks against each other in the press over who is at fault for the conditions of the buildings.

Source: Dan Barry, "For Landlords, Hard Numbers and Obligations," *The New York Times*, October 10, 1996, p. D1; Greg Wilson, "Tenants, Landlord Duke It Out in Court," *New York Daily News*, November 17, 2000, p. 49; Greg Wilson, "Developer Hit with Bias Suit," *New York Daily News*, May 9, 2001, p. 1.

overcoming some of the obstacles just mentioned, is Habitat for Humanity. Habitat is a nonprofit organization that utilizes volunteer labor and some donated materials from area churches and organizations to build new housing for low-income families. Those screened to become homeowners pay interest-free, low mortgage charges and must work to build their

Habitat for Humanity is a nonprofit organization that builds new low-income family housing. It has built more than 125,000 homes around the world to date through church fundraising, volunteer labor, and donated materials, as here in Washington, D.C. How do urban homesteading projects, such as Habitat for Humanity and gentrification offer alternative solutions to problems of urban housing?

house along with the volunteers. Since its founding in 1976, Habitat has built over 45,000 houses across the United States, most in areas of massive urban blight, ultimately transforming many places into attractive, stable neighborhoods. The organization now has over 1,500 local affiliates in all 50 states, plus another 400 active affiliates in 83 countries, where it has built over 80,000 homes (Habitat for Humanity, 2003).

Gentrification

Unlike urban homesteading, which is limited to the reclamation of just a few buildings or blocks at a time, gentrification is a broader process. The word *gentrification*, coined by the wealthy "landed gentry" in the nineteenth century to describe the renovation of run-down London homes, today refers to the movement of more affluent North Americans back into older, often decaying areas in the city. Virtually every major city in Canada and the United States is experiencing this spreading urban

renaissance, following a path taken by Paris and London years earlier.

Today's gentry, like those of the past, are a rather select group of people. They are usually the cosmopolites or unmarried and childless groups discussed in Chapter 10. Or, to put it another way, they are frequently the "yuppies" we spoke of at the end of Chapter 3. More to the point, they are people with enough money to buy a brownstone in Manhattan, a Society Hill townhouse in Philadelphia, a brick cottage in the German Village of Columbus, Ohio, or a Victorian house in San Francisco's Haight-Ashbury district. However, sometimes working-class neighborhoods undergo gentrification while retaining their socioeconomic group identity, as in several of Baltimore's row-house districts.

Why, though, would middle-class people *choose* central-city neighborhoods when the trend for the last century has been to escape to the suburbs? The reasons vary, but certainly many find that the central city still has the greatest amount of variety and stimulation. Theater,

CITYSCAPE

Sweat Equity in the South Bronx

Talking rapidly and in bursts, Danny Soto Diaz hunkered down amid broken plaster and other products of demolition that littered the South Bronx tenement. . . . Street sounds—portable radios and playing children and laughing adults idle on a midweek afternoon—punctuated the tomblike quiet of the gutted building.

Danny Soto, a 22-year-old Puerto Rican, lives in the South Bronx, so he is certainly familiar with tenements. Yet this one—at 1186 Washington Avenue—is very special to him and unusual to anyone: It has been rehabilitated through the labor of a group of mostly poor young blacks and Puerto Ricans trying to improve their own neighborhood. This is the process of "sweat equity"—which simply means that people invest their own labor rather than money in a residence. And labor, in the strongest sense of the word, is what is involved. Writer Roger Williams explains:

"Toil" is almost a euphemism for the work involved—exhausting and sometimes dangerous demolition, performed in the extremes of climate and the accumulation of several decades' worth of structural abuse and neglect. . . .

The first requirement was to clean out and gut the rotting six-story structure; it was an exhausting and at times a loathsome task, performed by the group with no outside financial assistance. Rubble, rats, and feces were everywhere, and dead dogs were commonplace. The basement was the worst: ice-cold mud up to the knees, refuse that defies the imagination, fleas that accompanied the workers home. . . .

Sweat equity is not likely to become popular with people who have the money to buy a fashionable home, but it is one option for the poor who have the skills and strength to undertake such a monumental task. In some of the poorest neighborhoods of many cities, people like Danny Soto try to turn housing that is all but falling down into livable homes for themselves and other local residents. The benefits of sweat equity are very real—this one building became 28 apartments—but, just as important, a project of this kind brings neighborhood residents together with a sense of common purpose. Urban homesteading projects are still quite rare and hardly likely to eliminate the massive housing problem in the United States. Yet people like Danny Soto are optimistic that they can make a real change in at least a small piece of their city:

All around this area you see people sleeping in doorways, drinking all day, cleaning a car for three dollars when they can get it. Their fathers taught 'em nothing, and they don't know nothing. We want to create a village of ten thousand people surviving on their own, with their own firemen, police patrols, schools—people for maybe forty blocks living good, the way everybody else lives good in this country.

This particular building had been seized by New York City for default of taxes. Soto's group, the People's Development Corporation (PDC), bought the building from the city for one dollar. Once they completed the onerous task of cleaning out the building, the group restored the structure, including all the necessary plumbing, wiring, and carpentry. The work was time-consuming and difficult, but, Williams explains, the group had an evident sense of spirit driving them on:

Talking about a forthcoming celebration of the PDC's success at 1186 Washington Avenue, Danny Soto chuckled sardonically and said, "Man, wait till you see the politicians who show up for that party, trying to take credit for what we've done."

Source: Adapted from Roger M. Williams, "The New Urban Pioneers: Homesteading in the Slums," *Saturday Review,* July 23, 1977, pp. 9–14.

music, chic stores—all flourish in the greatest concentration downtown. Second, as we noted in Chapter 9, economic restructuring increased the number of administrative and professional jobs available in central cities. The well-paid "gentry" taking these jobs need a place to live, and central-city living eases the time and costs of getting to work. Third, as more women enter the work force (in 2000, 66 percent of women worked for pay) and as two-career couples become common (61 percent of all married couples in 2000), the time needed to maintain a single-family suburban house often makes it too burdensome (U.S. Bureau of the Census, 2002c). Fourth, suburban housing is expensive, and, while some central-city housing is extremely costly (brownstones in Manhattan often top $1 million), one can still find bargains, particularly in districts where the average income is low. Fifth, and finally, remember that much central-city housing built from about 1880 to 1910 has a level of craftsmanship and quality—with details like solid oak floors and stained-glass windows—rarely found in today's suburbs.

Indeed, the fact that deteriorating housing eventually may become a bargain for someone with cash and energy is what causes critics like Edward C. Banfield to look hopefully on inner-city decay. But, with the exception of local sweat-equity projects like those in the South Bronx, once again the poor get the short end of the bargain. Gentrification of deteriorating neighborhoods almost always displaces the previous poorer inhabitants by causing tax assessments and rents to rise (DiGiovanni, 1984; LeGates and Hartman, 1986:194–97; Zipp and Cook, 1999:1).

Political economy theorists see gentrification as a logical flow of investment capital. Beginning in the 1950s, investment capital moved out of the cities into the suburbs, where profit rates were higher. Later, with the emergence of a "rent gap" (profits above costs) in the inner city, capital returned to make greater profits there, as low-valued property rose in value (Smith and LeFaivre, 1984; Zipp and Cook, 1999). This return to the inner city certainly contradicts the predictions of an ever-outward migration of the affluent made by Ernest W. Burgess in the 1920s (Chapter 7). The Critical Thinking box however explains why these predictions still hold true in Canada.

The New Urbanism

Perhaps the best-known critique of public housing came from Jane Jacobs in *The Death and Life of Great American Cities* (1961), a still-influential book on urban form and function. Critical of conventional planners, Jacobs wrote:

> One of the unsuitable ideas behind projects is the very notion that they are projects, abstracted out of the ordinary city and set apart. To think of salvaging or improving projects, as projects, is to repeat this root mistake. The aim should be to get that project, that patch upon the city, rewoven back into the fabric—and in the process of doing so, strengthen the surrounding fabric also. (1961:392)

One of the most encouraging developments in restoring the vitality of older cities is a new approach in urban design called the "New Urbanism" that informs physical planning with sociological principles. Initially a response to the perceived lack of community in sprawling suburbs, the New Urbanism has caused a rethinking of the entire city. Today, in both central cities and suburbs, its goal is creating spaces that encourage people to socialize and watch out for each other.

Seaside, Florida, offers an example. Built in the mid–1980s in Florida's Panhandle, this planned community has codes mandating that houses have front porches close to the sidewalk so that residents sitting outside can converse easily with pedestrians. The town boasts corner stores that serve a function more important than providing provisions: The store's frequently slamming screen door announces friends coming to chat with one another over a cup of coffee.

Far more impressive is what architects and planners influenced by the New Urbanism are accomplishing in old, problem-infested neighborhoods.

Columbia Point/Harbor Point

In Boston, a government-funded housing project known as Columbia Point, built in

CRITICAL THINKING

Gentrification and the Burgess Concentric Zone Model

A look back at Figure 7–4 will remind you of Ernest Burgess's concentric zone theory, which argued that progressively wealthier residential areas would be located at an increasing distance from the CBD. How valid is that model today, with so much gentrification occurring to attract affluent singles and families?

According to two Canadian researchers who conducted a 20-year longitudinal study of 14 Canadian cities, the Burgess model is still a valid one. Here is their explanation as to why:

Our analysis shows that changes in urban development in the last several decades, such as urban renewal, gentrification, mass transit systems, as well as other demographic and social changes such as occupational composition and female labour force participation have not invalidated the association found between SES [socioeconomic status], family size and concentric zones. Though the original description by Burgess of the character of the zones should be re-examined in modern-day Canadian cities, the gradient pattern itself not only persists but may have intensified as far as socio-economic status and family size are concerned. This is especially evident for medium-sized cities on SES, but the intensification has occurred for all sizes for family size. The relationship with family size remains stronger than that with SES.

We speculate that there are two basic factors which explain the durability of these patterns. First, the norm of owning a single-family,

detached dwelling is so embedded in North American culture, that those who can afford the time and cost of transportation continue to opt for locations with more of this type of housing, which increase with distance from the center of cities. This is especially true for those who today have families with children. Smaller families and an increase in marriage dissolutions have not eroded this value. Instead, they have intensified the contrast between two sharply divergent styles of life: the one devoted to singlehood, childlessness, freedom from family commitment and often oriented to cosmopolitan participation in the amenities of the inner zones of refurbished cities; the other devoted to traditional family life, yet attempting to provide a full range of educational opportunities for children, often relying on dual or multiple wage earners to meet the rising scale of expenses, and living in the suburbs.

Second, though mass transit systems are not widely used in Canada except in Toronto and Montreal, the development of freeways and other roads within cities has been effective enough to enable extensive use of the automobile for the journey to work. In spite of the increase in the area and population size of the metropolitan areas in Canada, for most Canadians the journey to work has not increased proportionately. The majority can still commute comfortably in less than an hour. Therefore, for one with the economic resources, the motivation to move from the centre continues to be strong.

Source: T. R. Balakrishman and George K. Jarvis, "Is the Burgess Concentric Zonal Theory of Spatial Differentiation Still Applicable to Urban Canada?" *Canadian Review of Sociology & Anthropology* 28:4 (November 1996), 526–39. Used by permission of the publisher.

1953 on a small, swampy peninsula near the first suburbs of Dorchester and Roxbury, long stood as evidence of the insensitivity of urban planners. There architects laid out 28 bland, institutional-style buildings three and seven

stories high, a full mile from the closest subway stop. And the surrounding water and lack of roads isolated residents even more. With few stores in the area, shopping became a major effort, more expensive and more time-consuming than for other city residents nearer the mainstream of Boston life.

Eventually, the 1,502-unit development fell victim to the same problems that plagued public housing nationwide. By 1984, only 350 families wanted to stay on when, encouraged by the U.S. Office of Housing and Urban Development, the Boston Housing Authority leased the land for 99 years at $1 a year to a partnership of the remaining tenants and a private developer. Architects for the project decided to redesign Columbia Point, modeling it after some of Boston's active, thriving neighborhoods. Also influencing their design was the New Urbanism idea that cities are enriched by the creation of a "public realm" that highlights amenities such as waterfront views. Architects thus set down a new street pattern, canted at 45 degrees, so that all residents would have a view of both the harbor and the Boston skyline (Kamin, 1995).

Reopened in 1990, what is now called Harbor Point is a mixed-income complex, with two-thirds market-rate apartments and one-third low-income housing, but with no physical distinctions between the two types of apartment buildings. Moreover, architects designed a variety of building types: blue and gray townhouses with wood clapboard siding as well as red and brown brick apartment houses. They kept ten of old Columbia Point's flat-topped residential buildings, but peaked roofs, decoration, and a reddish stain made them indistinguishable from the new buildings. To free Harbor Point completely from the stigma of public housing, they added other visual subtleties such as rounded and pointed rooftop gables. Still other amenities were added:

Along the harbor, where thieves used to dump stolen cars, is a 6-acre landscaped park where a visitor hears not gunshots but screeching sea gulls and water coursing over rocks. Slicing through the center of the complex is a 1,000-foot by 199-foot grassy mall with old-fashioned street lamps, benches and tennis courts patterned after Boston's Commonwealth Avenue. . . .

Narrow by design, the streets are tightly framed on each side by apartment buildings

and townhouses in contrast to the open spaces and freely placed structures of tower-in-the-park urbanism. Front doors face the streets. Most apartment windows look directly at the streets. The arrangement eliminates unsupervised pockets of dead space where drug dealing and other illicit activities can occur. (Kamin, 1995)

Fully leased, Harbor Point is now among Boston's safest neighborhoods. Yet some wonder whether this safety is the result of a security fence and a guard station at the main vehicular entrance to keep away outsiders. In short, Harbor Point seems to work, but is it "rewoven back into the [city's] fabric," as Jacobs urged? Critics claim that it remains physically isolated from the rest of Boston.

Today . . . Harbor Point seems too much like a world apart, a residential complex that has adopted the forms of the city without the functions, like corner bars, that fill neighborhoods with life. Harbor Point, in short, has mixed incomes but not the mixed uses that make cities hum. Its architecture, while free of cloying post-modernism, still has the contrived variety of a planned community. (Kamin, 1995)

Hopefully, someday soon greater linkage will occur. Still, Harbor Point stands as a successful alternative to an urban nightmare and offers vivid testimony to the extraordinary transformations that the New Urbanism can achieve.

Water as an Amenity

Just as Harbor Point's architects redesigned its grid to enable all residents to enjoy the view of surrounding water, so too has the New Urbanism enabled many cities to rediscover the aesthetics and social use possibilities of public space at water's edge (Whyte, 1980). Baltimore's Inner Harbor and New York's South Street Seaport are thriving, rebuilt areas enjoyed by tourists and natives alike. Chicago, Cleveland, Cincinnati, Louisville, and many other cities have converted decaying piers and waterfront properties into park areas and mixed-use sites. San Antonio converted what was essentially a narrow and dirty drainage canal into the charming 2.5-mile cobblestone River Walk—with lush green lawns, flowering shrubs and trees, and a view of paddleboats—where one delights in many interesting shops, restaurants, and night clubs. Here and at many other renovated water's edge locales, cities have successfully merged social and commercial activities into a vibrant urban atmosphere.

Replacing High-Rises

As Harbor Point demonstrates, the New Urbanism is transforming public housing, as the "superblocks" of giant high-rises come down, replaced by modest townhouses and low-rises that don't "look like projects."

> Imagine leveling whole blocks of decaying, crime-ridden slums in one great sweep, and building in their stead modern apartments with plenty of light and fresh air and high-rise views. Think about replacing crowded streets and decrepit playgrounds with paths for pedestrians and bicycles, winding between wide lawns. (Adler and Malone, 1996:70)

Many cities are addressing the failure of high-rise public housing by blowing up the buildings. Scudder Homes, seven high-rises built in 1963 in Newark, New Jersey, to house 1,800 low-income families, are gone, replaced by 150 single-family townhouses. In place of the 1,206 units in that city's seven hulking 13-story Stella Wright homes are town houses for low- and moderate-income residents. In Atlanta, a developer demolished over 1,000 housing units in Techwood Homes—the first U.S. public housing project, completed in 1935—to build a mixed-income "village," with new stores, community facilities, schools, and apartments. Today this once predominantly black enclave has been transformed into Centennial Place, a residential complex of 900 units that is host to a variety of races, ethnicities, and income levels. In Chicago, the Housing Authority is in the process of demolishing the eight high-rise buildings of Cabrini-Green and redeveloping its 65 acres through construction of 2,000 units of new, low-rise housing units, a new Town Center, a 145,000-square-foot shopping center, new schools, an

East Chicago District police headquarters, and a library. Half the housing units will be sold at market prices, with another 20 percent reserved as "affordable" units for less-affluent working families. The remaining 30 percent of the units will be occupied by tenants now living at Cabrini, thereby creating a mixed-income site similar to Harbor Point and totally unlike the all-low-income site Cabrini-Green has been until now. The designs of all three developments—in Newark, Atlanta, and Chicago—use grid patterns to link them to the surrounding neighborhoods rather than setting them apart, minding Jacobs's recommendation that housing projects be rewoven into the urban fabric (Adler and Malone, 1997; Fegelman, 1997).

These rebuilding programs seek to achieve two key goals of the New Urbanism. First, don't isolate the poor by themselves, but create a mixed-income housing complex to integrate all strata of society. Second, create an environment that is physically attractive and facilitates walking and social interaction, fostering a sense of control and community among residents.

Limitations

As promising as the New Urbanism may be, three major problems prevent its broader impact. First, in every case noted, there are now fewer low-income housing units than there were before. As with post–World War II urban renewal, displacement of the poor has occurred in these redevelopment projects as well. Of course, one might argue that at least some poor people are better off living in safer and more vibrant communities, but what of the rest of the displaced poor?

Second, weaving a housing project into the surrounding area is enormously difficult in the midst of extensive, nightmarish ghettos. If little more than empty lots or bombed-out buildings are nearby, for example, reorganizing a public housing project as an inward-facing enclave may be the only strategy, at least in the short run.

Finally, even at its best, the New Urbanism cannot, by itself, address the extensive poverty that makes public housing such a problem in the first place. For instance, in San Francisco, the Robert Pitts Plaza development project replaced a notorious, dangerous high-rise called Yerba Buena. The new 203-apartment, neo-Victorian complex in no way looks like a public housing development. Its architecture blended in with neighboring apartment buildings and included projecting cornices and pastel shades of blue—a far cry from the high-rise "boxes" so common in public housing. Completed in 1991, it contained other amenities such as an internal rectangular courtyard with lush sod, bushes, and neat lines of trees, and a colorful playset for children in a sand playground.

Three years later, though, broken glass lay everywhere. Gone were the sod and sprinkler heads; gone too were the bushes and plants, ripped out by vandals. Profane graffiti covered concrete seating ledges. Burglar bars shielded ground-floor windows following a rash of burglaries suspected to have been committed by residents. Wire mesh covered many other windows, suggesting an escalating sense of fear. The problem is poverty, and all that goes with it:

> Standing in the courtyard, the on-site manager of the complex, Ken Babb, explained the mess by saying that the tenants—less than a quarter of whom work—did not have an ownership mentality. . . . (Kamin, 1995)

A Comparison

The lesson here is that new architecture and even new planning strategies such as the New Urbanism can't, by themselves, turn the city around. Robert Pitts Plaza reveals that simply replacing high-rise buildings with low-rise buildings, even if wonderfully designed, is not enough. Without role models, development of community pride, regular maintenance, social services, and, most of all, *jobs*, old habits and behaviors will persist. In contrast, Harbor Point is a good example of at least the beginnings of connecting low-income housing to its surroundings—through a return to traditional urban forms that promote interaction *and* a mix of income groups to eliminate public

housing's isolation. In short, any successful approach to improving urban life must take account of not only local planning considerations but also broader structural concerns that include social stratification and the region's economy.

EDUCATION: THE URBAN CHALLENGE

Schools in urban settings face a variety of challenges, often more daunting than those school districts face elsewhere. These difficulties include larger proportions of immigrant children with limited English proficiency, greater concentrations of low-income families, and a weaker tax revenue base, all of which place a heavy burden on the schools to educate, fully and effectively, the students they serve.

Immigration remains primarily an urban phenomenon, although it affects suburban and rural schools and communities as well. In the 1990s, for example, nearly half of all immigrants chose to live in just a dozen metropolitan areas (New York; Los Angeles; Miami; Chicago; Washington; D.C.; Orange County, California; Houston; San Jose; Boston; Oakland; San Francisco; Fort Lauderdale; and San Diego), according to the U.S. Immigration and Naturalization Service (2002:73). Urban schools in these and other cities, therefore, must accommodate a large influx of immigrant pupils, and it is not unusual for half of a school's population to lack proficiency in English (Schnailberg, 1999). This creates the need for hiring a greater number of bilingual or English-as-a-Second-Language (ESL) teachers, in addition to teachers of regular subjects. The schools must also deal with other cultural adjustment issues, such as clothing, food, religious observances, role behavior, and parents whose own language and educational deficiencies may limit support for at-home study.

Whether immigrant or native-born, many students come from home environments where poverty, family instability, or poor health may limit educational success. Other

Schenectady, NY
Magnet
Howe is one of four magnet schools in Schenectady, New York, one of the nation's oldest cities. With over 300 enrollees in grades K–5, its global curriculum and emphasis on cultural diversity combines basic New York State curriculum standards with a wde variety of multicultural learning activities through a nurturing and challenging educational environment.

dangers or obstacles that can work against educators' goals are conflicting values about the importance of education in the student's home or on the street; the lack of positive, academically successful role models; and the presence of gangs, street crime, drugs, and violence. In 1999, 18 percent of students aged 12 to 18 reported street gang presence at school (U.S. Department of Education, 2002). Further undermining academic achievement in many city schools is the lack of funding. Unlike affluent communities, cities lack the tax base to provide adequate per-student expenditures, even with additional state aid. As a result, students in urban schools are more likely to enter older, dilapidated buildings, where they face overcrowded classrooms with limited supplies, poor discipline, insufficient libraries and labs, and often a shortage of qualified teachers.

A deepening dissatisfaction with traditional public schools has engendered several innovations to give parents other options for educating their children, thus providing competition to force all schools to do a better job.

Three of the most popular programs to improve urban education are magnet schools, a school voucher system, and charter schools.

Magnet Schools

Magnet schools (schools offering special programs to attract students from many districts to achieve integration) began as an alternative to mandatory busing, but their success in raising students' scholastic achievement gained them even more popularity. They offer special facilities and programs to promote educational excellence in a particular area, such as computer science, foreign languages, science and mathematics, or the arts. Parents can choose the school best suited to a particular student's talents and interests, enabling these advanced programs to attract talented students from beyond traditional neighborhood boundaries. This permits magnet schools to overcome residential segregation patterns to create a more diversified student population.

About 20 percent of U.S. students living in or around cities attend one of the nation's more than 5,000 magnet schools (Toch, 1991). However, about 21 percent are partial-site magnet schools (a mixture of traditional and special programs), resulting in desegregated buildings that have racially segregated classrooms (West, 1994). The drawbacks to magnet schools' becoming more widespread are (1) they are expensive to operate; (2) they have limited appeal; and (3) critics charge they are "elitist" in luring the best students and teachers, thereby relegating the majority of students to the "mediocrity" of ordinary city schools (Toch, 1991).

School Vouchers

Another choice option in some school districts is to give parents a voucher equal to the state's share of the cost of educating a child (usually about 90 percent of the average private school's tuition). Parents can then use this voucher to place their child in a public or private school of their choice. The program is limited at present because there are not enough private-school spaces to meet demand; usually a lottery determines who goes to choice schools in such cases. Among the cities utilizing a school voucher plan are Cleveland, Indianapolis, Milwaukee, and Minneapolis. Critics (including teachers' unions) charge that this approach siphons off much-needed public education funding, thus undermining the nation's commitment to public education, and does little to improve central-city schools where the need is greatest (Martinez et al., 1995).

Because many of the private schools are church-affiliated, voucher opponents charge that this system violates the First Amendment provision concerning the separation of church and state. State supreme court and federal appeals court decisions in 1998–1999 gave mixed signals on this issue. Arizona, Ohio, and Wisconsin supreme courts ruled that voucher programs did not violate the state or federal constitution by including religious schools. In contrast, the supreme courts of Vermont and Maine, as well as a federal appellate court in a separate Maine case, ruled

against religious schools on constitutional grounds. After years of conflicting lower court opinions about Cleveland parents using vouchers at private schools, the U.S. Supreme Court ruled in 2002 that they could do so. Experts believe this ruling may be as significant as the 1954 *Brown v. Topeka* decision on school desegregation, as it gives the green light nationwide to this program (Brokaw, 2002).

Charter Schools

Charter schools are a recent alternative to traditional public schools and, in cities where a voucher plan exists, a major beneficiary of such payments. Charters are private schools that operate with less state regulation so that teachers and administrators can try out new teaching strategies. Unlike public schools, however, they are held accountable for achieving educational results. If a school fails to meet the terms of its charter with the local school board or state, the charter can be revoked and the school closed. In essence, then, a charter school receives greater autonomy to operate in return for greater accountability for student performance. Over 1,400 charter schools now exist in 36 states, the District of Columbia, and Puerto Rico (U.S. Department of Education, 2002).

Perhaps more important than numbers are the types of learning environments being cultivated within these schools. According to *The State of Charter Schools: Fourth Year Report* (U.S. Department of Education, 2000), small school size appears to be a principal reason for the high demand for charter schools. The median enrollment of charter schools in the study was 137, compared with a median enrollment of 475 students in the regular public schools in the same states. Smaller classes afford teachers the space to be more creative with curriculum and the time to provide more individualized instruction. Some charter schools have been founded with a particular type of student in mind. Whether for the arts-oriented or the at-risk, these schools provide assistance to students who are otherwise underserved by the public school system.

URBAN LIVING

The New Urban Schools

On a typical morning, just north of Milwaukee, at the Marva Collins Preparatory School of Wisconsin, 180 students—kindergarten through the fifth grade—neatly dressed in their uniforms, enter an old building and climb three flights of stairs to their school on the top floor. A few miles to the east, next to a busy freeway and across from a clinic for the homeless, the 360 students at Messmer High School file in. In the hallways of this Roman Catholic institution hang portraits of Dr. Martin Luther King, Jr., Abraham Lincoln, and Jesus. Closer to the heart of the city, the 600 students in grades K–5 at the Elm Creative Arts School learn through an arts-driven curriculum. Today, while many are away performing at a concert downtown, a group of fifth graders—divided into small teams—is sprawled out on a classroom floor piecing together colorful math games while big-band music plays on the class stereo.

Welcome to public education, Milwaukee-style. These three schools, scattered throughout the city and featuring vastly different educational settings and philosophies, have one thing in common: public tax dollars.

One is a charter school adopted by the City Council; one is a private, religious school; and one is a magnet school operated by the school district. All three are part of a growing roster of alternatives available in a city that is ground zero for the school choice movement nationwide.

The definition of public schooling in the United States has changed dramatically in recent years, and nowhere is it changing faster than in Milwaukee. The city's long tradition of forward-looking views on government and politics has provided fertile soil for experiments and innovations in its public schools.

Here, in one place, are schools based on ideas that not too long ago were unheard-of in a U.S. school district: students attending religious schools with public money, a private school that has essentially been hired by the district to become a public school for a year, and a city government that has bypassed the local school board to create its own charter schools.

Yet Annette Williams, a Democratic state representative and author of the state's 1989 voucher legislation, has concerns. Williams, an African American, says she originally intended the voucher program to help mainly black-run schools and low-income students. But today, she contends, vouchers and charter schools mainly benefit white churches, white-run private schools, and white students. "Affluent folks are going to take it all on as their own," she says. "Yuppies who have choices are going to be the beneficiaries now."

Others fear in Milwaukee the emergence of a dual private and charter school system, one black, one white, and a community whose loyalty to schools is divided along racial and socioeconomic lines. Only time will tell whether or not the alternative school programs are an improvement over traditional efforts or simply another form of racial segregation in the schools.

Source: Adapted from Kerry A. White, "Ahead of the Curve." Reprinted with permission from *Education Week* Vol. 18, No. 18, January 13, 1999.

Supporters of charter schools hope that local educators, ministers, parents, community members, school boards, and other sponsors will provide new models of schooling and exert competitive pressures on public schools that will improve the current system of public education. Others fear, however, that charter schools, at best, may be little more than escape valves that relieve pressure for genuine reform of the whole system and, at worst, may add to centrifugal forces that threaten to pull public education apart.

In fact, some charter schools are no better than their public school counterparts. Critics say that many have weak curricula and teaching, substandard buildings, and a surprising prevalence of financial abuses. Basic classroom supplies are often lacking, labs and libraries are rare, and staff turnover is high among the low-paid, inexperienced teachers. Also, the segregation of many charter schools along ethnic, racial, and religious lines has created church–state conflicts in conjunction with the voucher controversy (Toch, 1998).

It is too soon, though, to assess the success of magnet schools, vouchers, or the charter school reform movement. Only time will tell whether or not they are an improvement. The Urban Living box on page 357 gives a further insight into these innovations.

CRIME: PERCEPTION AND REALITY

The problems of poor housing and poor education affect only part of the urban population. But, surveys suggest, almost everyone expresses concern about the extent of crime. Often, people living in outlying areas point to fears about personal safety as the primary reason they chose not to live in the city. And many city people conclude that a higher risk of crime is just part of the price one pays for the advantages of urban living. But are such perceptions correct? Is crime worse in the city than elsewhere? Is there more crime in bigger cities than in smaller ones? Are visitors to the city more likely than residents to fall victim to crime?

Urban crime gets extensive media attention and influences public perception. Yet the public's fear about crime overlooks the important fact that the U.S. crime rate has actually dropped each year since 1991. From 1993 to 2000, violent crimes (murder, rape/sexual assault, robbery, assault, personal theft) dropped by 44 percent, as did property crimes (burglary, motor vehicle theft, property theft, arson). As a result, overall criminal victimization rates are at their lowest levels in two decades (U.S. Bureau of Justice Statistics, 2002).

Crime in Canada also dropped throughout the 1990s, then rose in 2001 to its highest level in over five years. In contrast, property crimes continued to fall to their lowest level in decades. Before that increase occurred, a 1999 national poll showed only 15 percent of Canadians afraid when walking alone in their neighborhoods after dark and only 20 percent worried when home alone at night (Statistics Canada, 2002).

Public Perception of Crime

The American public has grown less pessimistic about the severity of the nation's crime problem, reflecting the actual decline in the crime rate in recent years. However, broad concern remains, as 36 percent of those questioned in an ABC News/*Washington Post* poll called the crime problem "very bad," while another 44 percent called it "bad," for a total of 80 percent (ABC News, 2000). In another ABC News poll, in 2002, 57 percent of adults said that concerns about crime influence the way they live their lives—a 9 percent increase from a similar poll four years earlier (ABC News, 2002). And the poor worry most of all: 71 percent of people earning over $50,000 but just 48 percent of those earning less than $20,000 felt very safe in their neighborhoods. When controlled for race only, 54 percent of blacks and 61 percent of whites said they felt safe in their neighborhoods (U.S. Bureau of Justice Statistics, 2002).

In light of the facts, why do so many of us think we are living in a high-crime period? Part of the answer lies in more extensive news reporting of violent crime. A study by the Center for Media and Public Affairs (1999) revealed that, in the 1998–1999 television season, nearly 1,800 acts of serious violence were reported over a two-week period, 80 percent of them on broadcast television and 20 percent on cable programs. In addition, the frequent "promos" of upcoming violent crime stories, the popularity of "reality-based" cop shows, and tabloid sensationalism spread the image of crime well beyond the news programs themselves.

Another frightening fact is that, despite a decline in the murder rate, an increasing share of killings are stranger-on-stranger homicides, such as the 1997 murder of Bill Cosby's son, Ennis. Also, drug-related shootings sometimes result in stray bullets killing innocent people, sometimes in their homes or blocks away from the source. Moreover, alarmingly, there is a steady involvement of children in deadly violence. As one analyst explains,

> Crime now seems more "senseless" because deadly acts are carried out by people too young to realize the implications of their decisions. Altercations that twenty years ago would have ended in a fistfight and a bloody nose now terminate with a corpse riddled by twenty-two-caliber bullets fired from an automatic machine pistol. (Douglas Massey, 1995:1204)

The homicide victimization rate for youths aged 14 to 17 increased almost 150 percent from 1985 to 1993. Since 1993, victimization rates for teens and young adults have declined, but they still remain considerably higher than the levels of the mid-1980s (U.S. Bureau of Justice Statistics, 2002).

Attitudes about crime, then, are a mix of facts and fears. To gain a more accurate sense of crime in the city, we need to look at additional statistics.

Crime and City Size

Most violent crimes take place in cities, often growing out of street, school, or social club altercations. Indeed, the negative attitudes of non–city dwellers and their reluctance to enter cities stems in large measure from their fear of becoming an urban crime statistic. But are cities really more dangerous? Table 12–1 compares crime in various types of communities.

Note, first, that violent crime may have dropped throughout the 1990s, but some rates are higher than in 1980. Moreover, comparing community types, we see that violent crime rates are higher in large metropolitan areas (including central cities and suburbs) than they are in smaller cities and, especially, in rural areas. Such data would seem to support the conclusion that large cities are dangerous places.

Louis Wirth, whose theory of urbanism was central to Chapter 5, might claim that the size, density, and social heterogeneity of cities are to blame. Perhaps. But if this were true, we would expect the largest metropolitan areas to have the highest crime rates, which is not the case. As Table 12–2 shows, the highest crime rates occur in smaller, third-tier cities (under 500,000) and in second-tier cities (500,000 to 999,999 population).

TABLE 12–1   Crime Rates per 1,000 Residents by Type of Community, 1980 and 2000

	Property Crime		Violent Crime		Total Crime	
	1980	2000	1980	2000	1980	2000
U.S. Total	53	36	5.8	5.1	59	41
Metropolitan Areas	61	39	7.0	5.6	68	44
Other Cities	50	41	3.5	4.0	54	45
Rural Areas	21	17	1.8	2.1	23	19

Source: Federal Bureau of Investigation, *Crime in the United States—2000.* Accessed at www.fbi.gov/ucr/cius_00/00crime213.pdf.

These data point to the conclusion that, although cities have higher crime rates than other types of communities, city size by itself does not explain crime rate. How else can we explain the fact that New York, the nation's largest city, has less crime per capita than 132 other U.S. cities (Morgan Quitno, 2002)?

Before going further, however, a warning is in order. Crime statistics are notoriously imperfect. For example, many crimes are not discovered, or reported to police, or recorded carefully. All the statistics in Tables 12–1 and 12–2 reflect official police records. Many criminologists argue that a more accurate portrait of crime comes from the Census Bureau's semiannual random population survey. By questioning people (rather than police), the victimization survey uncovers many unreported crimes missed in the crime index and crime rate calculations. While such studies confirm the decline in crime over time, they suggest that the actual number of crimes may well be twice the level of the official statistics.

Further, criminologists agree that, as with other problems, the amount of crime varies throughout the urban area. The greatest concentration of offenses occurs in inner-city districts with poverty-stricken minority populations. In 2000, for example, the poorest U.S. households with incomes under

TABLE 12–2   City Size and Crime Rate, 2000

Population Size	Crime Rate
1,000,000 or higher	5.5
500,000–999,999	7.1
250,000–499,999	7.3
100,000–249,999	5.6
50,000–99,999	4.5
25,000–49,999	4.2
10,000–24,999	3.8
Under 10,000	4.2
Suburban Areas	3.3
Suburban Counties	3.0
Rural Counties	1.9

Source: Federal Bureau of Investigation, 2002.

$7,500, were more likely to suffer a theft and three times more likely to be robbed than more affluent households with incomes over $75,000 (U.S. Bureau of Justice Statistics, 2002). Urbanists at the University of Chicago first identified this pattern back in the 1940s, and it holds true for both the inner city and the suburbs (Shaw and McKay, 1969; Stahura et al., 1979).

The Race Issue

In the United States, discussions of crime almost always raise the issue of race, because many people link crime to nonwhite minorities. In truth, however, two-thirds of the arrests police make for serious crimes involve white people. Even so, relative to population size, African Americans are more likely to be arrested than whites are.

Keep in mind, too, that crime is largely intraracial. This means that about 84 percent of single-offender violent crimes committed by blacks are against black victims, just as 73 percent of such crimes committed by whites involve white victims (U.S. Bureau of Justice Statistics, 2002).

Moreover, the crime problem is worst in overwhelmingly black urban ghettos, where homicide is at a crisis level. Between 1985 and 1997, the percentage of murder victims who were black males doubled (Bureau of Justice Statistics, 2002). Nationwide, the leading cause of death by far for black males between the ages of 15 and 24 is homicide (U.S. Bureau of the Census, 2002a:81). Black adults aged 18 to 24 are six times more likely to be murdered than white young adults. In 2000, blacks killed 2,723 blacks—only 137 fewer killings than of whites by whites, who outnumber blacks by more than six to one (U.S. Bureau of Justice Statistics, 2002; FBI, 2002).

Explaining High-Crime Areas

Why are some communities terrorized by crime? We know that the highest crime rates occur in the poorest sections of cities. But precisely why? Social scientists offer a variety of theories to explain concentrations of urban crime. Four of the main causative explanations involve (1) cultural patterns; (2) lower intelligence; (3) persistent racial inequality and prolonged poverty; and (4) residential segregation. As we shall see, each position has both advocates and critics.

Cultural Patterns

Edward Banfield (1970, 1974) claimed that crime flourishes in urban areas steeped in a lower-class culture, where people share a "present-time orientation," have low aspirations, and are generally morally irresponsible. Under such conditions, he contended, people victimize anyone who seems an easy mark, including one another.

Moreover, parents pass these cultural patterns on to their children, which explains the persistence of crime in some neighborhoods for decades. Rather than learning values and skills that ease their way toward success, children too often learn apathy, resignation, and fatalism; indifference toward schooling; a desire for immediate gratification; and a distrust of authority. In such an environment, crime simply thrives. Add to this the fact that high-crime neighborhoods tend to have high levels of single parenting; this means that children have less supervision, especially from fathers.

Critics, such as Charles Valentine (1968), responded that such cultural patterns should be viewed as the *consequences*, not the causes, of poverty. Among people who have few opportunities to work, are forced to live in crowded, run-down housing, and must contend with the worst schools a city has to offer, we should not be surprised that crime rates are high. Only structural changes that alleviate societal inequality are likely to bring about changes in the vicious circle of poverty and crime.

Lower Intelligence

In perhaps the most controversial effort to explain concentrations of crime and other social problems, Richard Herrnstein and Charles Murray asserted that criminality is concentrated in areas where average intelligence is low. In their book *The Bell Curve*, they suggested that crime—like poverty, welfare dependency, and illegitimacy—is strongly related to low IQ (1994:338–39). It is because the more talented people have long since left the inner cities, these researchers continued, that the plight of those who are left is worse than ever. And, given the cause, there is little that even a compassionate public can do about it.

Critics attacked this book on many fronts, suggesting that intelligence tests are unfair to begin with, or that it is far from clear what intelligence really is (Willie and Taylor, 1995; Fischer et al., 1996). More specifically, numerous studies show that low-income people test lower on IQ tests and that scores typically improve along with achievement of a higher socioeconomic status (Sowell, 1977:57).

Persistent Racial Inequality and Poverty

There is far broader support for the idea that the primary problem with crime lies in social structure, including our definitions of crime itself. A Marxist view, offered by Manuel Castells (1979, 1982), contends that capitalism's unceasing orientation toward profit defines "crime" and "criminals" largely in terms that protect the interests of the rich. People in capitalist societies do not believe that causing people to suffer a life of poverty is criminal, but rather that taking another's *property* is—especially if the victim is somebody "important." In a society in which most wealth and power lie in the hands of the few, high rates of criminality among the more deprived are simply to be expected because of how those in power define crime and enforce the law.

Non-Marxists also maintain that racial and economic inequalities breed high crime rates (Blau and Blau, 1982; Blau and Golden, 1986; Sampson, 1986). After studying the 125 largest U.S. metropolitan areas, Judith Blau and Peter Blau suggested that, insofar as a city concentrates people of highly unequal incomes, those with less than others see themselves as unjustly deprived. Therefore, even in the absence of *absolute poverty,* a city with significant *relative poverty* would still breed resentment and crime. In other words, Blau and Blau argue, African Americans and other poor people engage in more crime as offenders—and suffer more as victims—only because they are heavily represented among the economically deprived.

In contrast to the assertion by Banfield and also by Herrnstein and Murray that poor people are *themselves* to blame for criminality, this approach sees the poor as victims of injustices within society itself. The Blaus sum up:

> Thus, aggressive acts of violence seem to result not so much from lack of advantages as from being taken advantage of, not so much from absolute deprivation but from relative deprivation. In a society founded on the principle "that all men are created equal" economic inequalities rooted in ascribed positions [such as being born black or impoverished] violate the spirit of democracy and are likely to create alienation, despair, and conflict. (1982:126)

More practically speaking, people systematically prevented by lack of training or by prejudice from getting a good job may reasonably try to survive by turning to crime. It is, as Betty Lou Valentine (1980) argued, almost inevitable that such people turn to some form of "hustling." Living in a crime-riddled city probably places pressures on the individual to commit crimes, and also increases the likelihood that one *will be perceived as criminal* regardless of actual behavior. The Urban Living box on page 363 offers a glimpse into this interplay of joblessness, poverty, and crime.

Residential Segregation

A fourth factor noted by social scientists to explain the high rate of African American crime is that residential segregation—from slavery times to the present—makes the black situation unique. Douglas Massey and Nancy Denton coined the term *hypersegregation* to describe this extensive segregation existing on many

geographic dimensions simultaneously (1989: 373). Since then they have identified 20 hypersegregated metropolitan areas that contain nearly 40 percent of the total U.S. African American population (Massey and Denton, 1993).

In an important study, researchers Ruth Peterson and Lauren Krivo (1993) examined the relationship between black segregation and black homicide in 125 metropolitan areas. They found that black–white segregation far exceeded other variables such as income inequality and poverty, as well as several others, in explaining intercity variations in the black murder rate. In addition, they found that segregation had no bearing on homicide within families but clearly had an effect on acquaintance killings and homicides involving strangers. That is, the impact of segregation on the homicide rate manifested itself in public space, not in the home.

As Massey puts it, "Any social process that concentrates poverty also concentrates crime and violence to create an ecological niche characterized by a high risk of physical injury, violent death, and criminal victimization" (1995:1207). Rejecting the notion that black urban crime is simply a product of individual failings, he views such crime as "an inevitable outgrowth of social conditions created by the coincidence of racial segregation and high rates of black poverty." Believing that only federal policy initiatives could bring an end to the legacy of American apartheid, Massey is pessimistic—he predicts that many urban black communities will continue to deteriorate, with all of us paying a heavy economic and social price for a shameful "retreat from American democratic ideals" (1995:1231–32).

A modest decline in racial segregation occurred during the 1980s in many U.S. metropolitan areas. Analysis of 2000 census data shows very slow change since 1980 in residential segregation of African Americans (see Table 12–3). In some smaller and newer metropolitan areas, their segregation from whites declined markedly, but in the larger places where most African Americans live, segregation has remained high. Segregation of Hispanics and Asians has not changed in the last two decades (Lewis Mumford Center, 2002a).

URBAN LIVING

Poverty, Drugs, and Crime

West Adams Street is in the Austin District of Chicago, location of the Cabrini-Green housing project. This is just one story of thousands, a tragic commonality in our inner cities.

Nigel McKinney lived and died on West Adams. He was 11 when he was shot down in early October, perhaps involved in drug dealing, perhaps not. In this landscape, the culture of drugs is so pervasive, it becomes hard to tell if anyone is really untouched. . . .

Baby-faced drug dealers and teenage killers aren't unique to West Adams; nor is the neighborhood's distrust of police; both are a numbing reality in poor, minority communities.

But on West Adams these traits have a particular intensity, revealing in stark terms the dynamics that can turn members of the Vice Lords street gang into community leaders and police officers into the enemy, even if they're African-Americans.

It's an easy place for a child to lose his way, lose his life, or begin compiling a long police record. Though Nigel's murder has long since faded from the news, it remains a source of tension in Austin and has become an emblem of why the typical rules just don't apply here. . . .

Though there are undoubtedly some families on West Adams who live quietly and are disdainful of the drug trade, many families have someone who has dealt drugs, used drugs, or benefited from their sale.

"A lot of parents will not admit their kids are involved . . . because they are benefiting from the money that the children are bringing in," said Thomas J. Stewart, principal of Piccolo Middle School. "You are going to throw your own son out of the house? Nine (times) out of 10, a mother will not do it."

Those who don't turn a blind eye try to justify the illicit drug lifestyle by saying there are few, if any, other options. Drugs, they say, put food on the table, clothes on their children's backs, a new television in the living room, and a functioning car on the street. . . .

Police have recorded nearly 100 crimes this year on the [two-block] stretch of West Adams, from assaults and burglaries to car thefts and drug arrests.

In late October, police arrested two 11-year-old boys who lived in the neighborhood, but not on West Adams, for allegedly bringing three silencers, 12 bullets, and 56 packets of crack cocaine to class with them at Nash Elementary School, just a few blocks north of West Adams. One of the boys told police he stole the loot from an uncle. . . .

Nigel's brother has been a bona fide gang member since the age of 12. Now 15, Derris has been arrested for alleged drug dealing. He lives on his own and is recovering from three gunshot wounds he sustained in August while playing basketball in a West Side park.

Asked to explain why he was shot, the short, slim youth with a tough demeanor said simply that the gunman, a rival gang member, was "jealous."

Source: Jerry Thomas and Andrew Martin, "Notorious Block's Deadly Legacy," *Chicago Tribune*, web-pasted November 23, 1996.

Effects of Crime on Everyday Life

The toll of crime extends far beyond its immediate victims. For one thing, nothing pulls down property values like a high crime rate (Taylor, 1991). Owners lose equity in their investment, face high homeowners' insurance premiums, and lose neighbors or renters who otherwise would provide stability and community role models. If large numbers of people move out and cannot be replaced, owners may well abandon buildings they cannot sell, eroding the city's tax base. The vicious circle grinds on and on.

TABLE 12–3 Most Segregated Metropolitan Areas, Black and White, 2000

Metropolitan Area	Index of Dissimilarity
1. Detroit, Michigan	85
2. Milwaukee, Wisconsin	82
3. New York, New York	82
4. Chicago, Illinois	81
5. Newark, New Jersey	80
6. Cleveland, Ohio	77
7. Nassau-Suffolk, New York	74
8. Cincinnati, Ohio	75
9. St. Louis, Missouri	74
10. Miami, Florida	74

Source: Lewis Mumford Center for Comparative Urban and Regional Research, 2001a.

The fear of crime also reduces our use of public space. As William H. Whyte (1980) observed, "Streets are the rivers of life of a city. We come to partake of them, not to escape them." Certainly, in areas where people feel safe, extensive use of streets, parks, plazas, and other public places provides enjoyment for people at all hours of the day and night. Such urban areas contain the social dynamics and all the variety and excitement the city can offer. However, crime (and merely the fear of crime) restricts the use of public spaces. Another vicious circle is thus set in motion, since empty streets, plazas, and subway stations are unprotected and become ever more dangerous. In some communities, "take back the streets" campaigns have had some success, but the bitter reality remains that urbanites' enjoyment of public space is more limited than it once was, especially after sunset, in too many areas.

What Is the Solution?

Can high crime rates in urban places be reduced? Is there a way to make our cities safe so that people can walk through a park in the daytime (let alone at night!) without fear? Here, again, a number of proposals are noteworthy.

Urban planner Oscar Newman (1972, 1996) maintained that building design plays an important part in controlling crime. High-rise apartment blocks, Newman explains, serve to encourage crime because they isolate inhabitants from each other, creating many unwatched places where crime can easily occur. Newman argues that crime can be reduced if

> designers can position windows, and entries, and prescribe paths of movement and areas of activity so as to provide inhabitants with continuous natural surveillance of the street. (1972:15)

Where designs create what Newman calls "defensible space," people can protect their own communities naturally as they go about their daily lives rather than relying on security guards and police for protection.

To support his argument, Newman compiled crime data from various low-income public housing projects, first in New York, then in other cities in a subsequent study. Some of his key findings are as follows:

1. The average crime rate is higher in taller buildings (over six stories) than in lower ones. Tall buildings with many (over 1,000) living units are worst of all and appear to encourage isolation, stigmatization, apathy, neglect and withdrawal, the latter two first on the part of the residents, then by housing management, and finally by the municipal agencies that service the project: police, education, parks and recreation, refuse collection, and social services (1996:28).

2. In larger, taller buildings, crime occurs mostly in public areas (for example, elevators, halls, and lobbies), which are the places residents cannot easily monitor. Crime in such spaces is far less frequent in low-rise buildings, where residents can more easily supervise their surroundings.

3. In a comparison of two low-income projects in New York—low-rise Brownsville and high-rise Van Dyke—that had comparable residents but different architecture, Newman found rates of crime and vandalism to be significantly higher in the "less defensible" Van Dyke project.

We can conclude, then, that improving the physical design of buildings is a partial solution to the urban crime problem. But, regardless of architectural design, residents of a building must be motivated to notice and respond to potentially criminal situations. There is evidence, for example, that the belief that police will not promptly respond to reported crimes keeps some residents—even in "defensible" buildings—from becoming personally involved in crime prevention (Merry, 1981).

Another crime-fighting strategy, advocated by Curtis Sliwa of the Guardian Angels, a volunteer crime patrol group, is street patrols by local citizens. Patrols, as well as Neighborhood Crime Watch organizations, sensitize community members to the problem as they involve everyone in watching for suspicious behavior. Studies have found that both do reduce neighborhood crime (Belkin, 1983; Weillisz, 1983).

Another approach, suggested by urban critic Roger Starr (1985), is that cities adopt a "get tough, no nonsense, this has gone far enough!" approach. Specifically, he proposes that (1) cities target vulnerable areas—subways, for example—and make special efforts to control crime there; (2) cities create citizens' boards (with racially and ethnically mixed membership) to fight for more jails, more police, and to pressure legislators to reform the laws that let many criminals slip through with little or no punishment; (3) cities adopt a policy of tougher punishment, increasing the severity of the jail sentences for each subsequent offense; and (4) cities ask parents and educators to commit themselves to instilling in children and students a sense of social responsibility so that fewer young people will be drawn into crime.

Proposals such as these have already yielded important positive effects. Still, one wonders whether any of them can produce real, long-term results. Frequently, communities mobilize against, say, drug dealing and succeed in getting the dealers, pushers, and addicts off the streets. But once the vigilance weakens, drug traffic reappears, suggesting a need for broader changes.

At present, New York City is boasting a remarkable drop in crime. A few years ago, city

A recent form of community policing measures to reduce crime in many North American cities has been the utilization of police officers on bike patrols, such as this multiethnic trio in Los Angeles. Using bicycles provides greater mobility and coverage of territory than covering a beat on foot, yet allows closer observation and interaction than in a car.

officials enacted stronger community and strategic policing measures, as well as a "get tough" approach. Violent crime dropped almost in half, and the city became a model for other cities. Homicides, for example, dropped from 2,245 in 1990 to 580 in 2002, compared to 648 in Chicago, a city about one-third its size. This is a truly remarkable achievement. But will the improvement hold? As some critics see it, "get tough" approaches do little to solve the root causes of crime; rather, they deal only with the consequences.

Ultimately, achieving long-term reductions in crime probably depends on increasing economic opportunity in poor communities. Doing so may involve providing greater mobility for inner-city residents so they are able to reach jobs on the metropolitan periphery, or providing job training and economic incentives through government to encourage businesses to locate in economically depressed areas. In addition, of course, community efforts at policing the streets, greater involvement by churches and local community groups, and efforts at upgrading neighbor-hoods (such as Habitat for Humanity) all will help.

SUMMARY

Poor housing, substandard education, and crime are three significant problems plaguing our cities. Certainly, there are others, includ-ing environmental pollution, inadequate public transportation, and governmental cor-ruption. This chapter highlighted housing, education, and crime because they seem to be the issues of greatest concern to the public as a whole.

All urban problems are closely linked to the state of a city's economy and, especially, to the extent of urban poverty. Thus, we can see that urban problems are complex, inter-related issues (consider the links between poverty, crime, and drug abuse) with roots that extend beyond a particular city to society as a whole.

In the 1930s, as part of Franklin Roo-sevelt's New Deal, the federal government first enacted public housing policies. Finan-cial assistance to homeowners and builders, together with public works programs, quickly improved urban housing. Even so, by 1940, some 40 percent of U.S. urban housing still lacked amenities such as adequate indoor plumbing. The Housing Act of 1949 launched urban renewal programs and initiated the construction of more public housing. How-ever, private developers never provided any-where near as many low-income housing units as were torn down, resulting in the displace-ment of the poor. Moreover, high-rise public housing stigmatized and isolated the poor and created unsafe neighborhoods. Rent sub-sidies were a better idea, giving families choic-es other than public housing.

Rising taxes and increased maintenance costs, coupled with rent levels limited by local policy and the inability of tenants to pay, even-tually resulted in hundreds of thousands of landlords abandoning buildings. More recently,

urban homesteading, gentrification, and the New Urbanism are improving the urban scene. Each approach, however, has limita-tions and none can solve all the cities' housing problems.

Beset by problems of old buildings in need of repair, limited funding, a growing minority student population with limited English profi-ciency, a shortage of qualified teachers, and inadequate teaching resources, the nation's urban schools face serious challenges in their efforts to provide a quality education. A deep-ening dissatisfaction with the failure of urban schools to do their job has led to alternative approaches. Magnet schools, vouchers, and charter schools become more popular each year, but they also have their critics. Charges of elitism, violation of church–state separa-tion, and the siphoning off of much-needed funds for urban public schools are controver-sies that surround these innovations.

Rates of serious crime are going down (al-though still rising among juveniles). Media coverage and the increase of stranger-on-stranger violence has raised public worries about crime. The greatest concentration of crime is in poor inner-city neighborhoods. Various explanations of the existence of high-crime areas highlight cultural patterns, al-leged intellectual deficiencies, persistent racial inequality and poverty, and residential segregation.

Crime victimizes everyone by eroding prop-erty values, increasing insurance premiums, and generating a climate of fear. Crime also reduces use of parks, streets, and mass transit, denying urbanites free use of their city.

Trying to build "defensible spaces" is a partial solution to the crime problem, as are "get tough" policies that target vulnerable areas for extra police protection. Yet neither approach can ultimately solve the problem of crime. Strengthening families in order to provide good adult role models for young people, as well as generating jobs for adults and building a sense of community through churches and other local organizations, are also needed.

CONCLUSION

While there is ample reason for pessimism and concern, recent decades have witnessed positive signs of improvement in urban life. For example, New York City has dramatically curtailed violent crime. Many other cities have also reduced crime, but whether such a trend will persist remains to be seen. Similarly, time will tell whether or not the recent innovations in housing and education improve the quality of life and life chances for all segments of the cities' population.

As cities convert the failed high-rise projects to more livable, mixed-income housing complexes that no longer isolate and stigmatize the poor, they are being guided by important lessons learned at mid-century. But what is happening to cities in developing countries? Are they learning from Western mistakes or is their situation even worse? In the next chapter we will discuss Latin American, African, Middle Eastern, and Asian cities to learn the answers.

CHAPTER 13

CITIES IN THE DEVELOPING WORLD

When most of us think of large cities, we usually imagine towering New York City or sprawling Los Angeles. However, São Paolo, Brazil, with a population exceeding 9.8 million, is the largest city in the Western Hemisphere. Mexico City follows close behind with a population of 8.6 million. The 9.9 million inhabitants of Mumbai (Bombay) easily surpass New York City's 8 million, while the 8.9 million people in Shanghai are more than twice the population of Los Angeles (3.7 million).

These major cities, and many others throughout Africa, Asia, Latin America, and the Middle East, have an urban history unlike that of Canada and the United States. That past partly explains their present situation. All of these regions had indigenous cities that fell under the control of colonizers, but eventually gained their political independence. Today, these areas are in the midst of rapid and far-reaching urban transformation and are growing at a startling rate, as vast numbers of people pour into their cities. Furthermore, the economic well-being of these cities (as well as of those in Canada and the United States) is linked to the changing global economy, which is dominated by the more-developed countries (MDCs). So, for the most part, the past, present, and future of cities in less-developed countries (LDCs) are interrelated with the fortunes of the MDCs.

Although Mexico City is somewhat atypical in the magnitude of its annual growth rate, it symbolizes in many ways the current state of poor cities around the globe. Pouring in are tens of thousands of people who must compete for extremely limited resources. Not surprisingly, those meager resources have not been shared equally. Nowhere in sub-Saharan Africa is there a city approaching the size of Cairo (the continent's megacity), but large cities are numerous throughout Africa. Kinshasa, Congo (formerly Zaire) boasts 4.7 million inhabitants, while Capetown, South Africa, is home to 2.4 million people, Durban has 2.1 million, Johannesburg has about 1.5 million, and Pretoria has about 1.1 million residents. Most of the other sub-Saharan nations have at least one city with 1 million or more residents.

Moreover, *primate cities* (principal cities that are extremely large in comparison with other cities in the country)—appearing only in the last half of the twentieth century—dominate virtually all African countries as they do in Latin America. In many cases, a single city is home to more than half a country's urban population.

This chapter explores the development of cities throughout the developing world, with an eye to what they have in common, how they vary, and how they compare with Canadian and U.S. cities. This is a formidable task. Africa and Asia are vast continents of striking geographic and cultural contrasts. Africa has over 1,000 spoken languages and Asia has four major cultural traditions (in China, India, Japan, and Southeast Asia). Latin America, although it mostly shares a Spanish heritage, nonetheless varies significantly from one country to another in its population composition, resources, and economic development. The Middle East is a region where countries (and their cities) vary considerably in economic development, political structure, and quality of life. Still, many common elements exist in the global urbanization we are witnessing.

HISTORICAL CONTEXT

At a basic level, cities seem to be relatively large, dense agglomerations of socially heterogeneous people characterized by a complex division of labor and a multifaceted set of interactions and experiences. Beyond this, cities are shaped by their cultural and historical context. Each of the developing world cities discussed in this chapter is working out its own version of the urban story; nevertheless, a few common themes emerge when we compare how their histories impact on their present condition.

Latin American Cities

Most of the cities we think of as Latin American—Rio de Janeiro, Brazil; Buenos Aires, Argentina; Bogotá, Colombia; Santiago, Chile;

Lima, Peru; La Paz, Bolivia—did not exist before the sixteenth century. They, and many others, are the products of colonization by Spanish and Portuguese conquerors. Before the founding of such cities, however, other urban centers existed. The most outstanding examples were the capitals of the Mayan and Aztec civilizations in Central America and Mexico and the Inca Empire on the western coast of South America.

Pre-Columbian Cities

Teotihuacan, the Mayan capital located in central Mexico, was primarily a religious center. Teotihuacan reached the peak of its development between 450 and 650 C.E., when its population was about 200,000. For reasons still unclear, its streets fell silent in about 750 C.E.

The Inca Empire in Peru reached its peak of development somewhat later, between 1430 and 1525. Containing a population of over 6 million and stretching from present-day Ecuador into northern Argentina with a land area of over a million square miles, its center was the city of Cuzco, home of "the Inca," the absolute ruler of the civilization.

During the same period in Mexico, another mighty yet completely independent empire thrived. In 1325 the Mexica, one of several tribes now known as the Aztecs, settled in the Texcoco Lake basin and, on an island, established the city of Tenochtitlan, 30 miles southwest of the old city of Teotihuacan. The site was remarkably favorable—easily defensible in war and providing trade access to the surrounding region. Within 100 years, bolstered by conquests and commercial prosperity, the city controlled a population of between 5 and 6 million. The Looking Back box describes its awe-inspiring splendor.

Tragically for Tenochtitlan, the Aztec king, Montezuma, respectfully but cautiously welcomed Cortés and his officers. He invited the Spaniards into the city, housed them in a great palace, and gave them gifts of gold—in retrospect, a serious mistake. As Miguel Leon Portilla, who was present, later wrote: The Spaniards "picked up the gold and fingered it like monkeys: they seemed transported with

joy, as if their hearts were illuminated and made new . . . they hungered like pigs for that gold" (quoted in Cottrell et al., 1979:46). This experience foreshadowed what was about to happen in all of Latin America. Cortés and other European explorers did not come to live in peaceful coexistence with the indigenous populations. They came to conquer and become rich. They were about to destroy pre-Columbian civilization.

European Domination

In April 1521, Cortés and his forces encircled Tenochtitlan and cut off its food and water for three months. In August, overcoming the last resistance, he entered the city victorious. To ensure that the remnants of the proud Aztec Empire never rose again, Cortés utterly demolished Tenochtitlan and, on its rubble, erected a city focused around a completely European culture. He called it *Ciudad Imperial de Mexico*—Mexico City. To complete his domination, the surviving Mexicans were made to serve their conquerors.

In the conquest of the Inca Empire in Peru about a decade later, Francisco Pizarro followed the same pattern. He conquered and destroyed the Inca cities and replaced them with Spanish cities. Although a pre-Columbian urban civilization did not exist in Brazil, the Portuguese invaders established cities up and down that country's coast (Morse and Hardoy, 1992).

Exploitation

All over Latin America, new colonial cities were constructed as administrative centers for local domination and export-oriented trade. Inland settlements such as Mexico City were linked with port cities such as Vera Cruz. Where no important port existed, the Europeans built one; Lima (Peru), Valparaiso (Chile), Buenos Aires (Argentina), and Rio de Janeiro (Brazil) are examples. However, the "trade" of these cities was a one-way operation, with precious gold, silver, tobacco, and coffee shipped to Spain and Portugal. Served in this way, these relatively poor and weak nations in Europe hoped to become rich and powerful.

LOOKING BACK

The Magnificent City of Tenochtitlan

The Aztec rulers built Tenochtitlan into a city of incredible magnificence. While London was still a backwater of Europe and New York was nonexistent, Tenochtitlan was probably, after Rome, the world's greatest city. Here are two brief descriptive accounts:

Half city and half floating garden, its profile etched by dozens of temples dominated by the Pyramid dedicated to the worship of Huitzilopochtli and Tlaloc, [Tenochtitlan] rose majestically above the lake and green groves of trees. The setting was imposing: snow-covered peaks, cultivated slopes, and the densely populated fertile valley. (Hardoy, 1975:12)

An island-metropolis, Tenochtitlan was set like a radiant jewel amid the clear, calm turquoise of saline Lake Texcoco, linked to mainland suburbs by three great paved causeways. Elegant palaces and pyramid temples, interspersed with broad plazas and exotic gardens, gleamed spotless white in the brilliant crystalline air more than 7,000 feet above sealevel. (Cottrell et al., 1979:37)

In 1519, the Spaniard Hernan Cortés and his men gazed with disbelief on this city. Cortés later described it as "the most beautiful city in the world," and one of his soldiers, Bernal Diaz, described the Spanish reaction this way:

We were amazed. . . . [I]t was like the enchantments they tell of in the legend of Amadis, on account of the great towers and [temples] and buildings rising from the water, and all built of masonry. And some of our soldiers even asked whether the things that we saw were not a dream. . . . I do not know how to describe it, seeing things as we did that had never been heard of or seen before, not even dreamed about. Some . . . among us who had been in many parts of the world, in Constantinople, all over Italy, and in Rome, said that so large a market and so full of people and so well-regulated and arranged, they had never beheld before. . . . (1956:218–19)

Commerce was the lifeblood of the city:

Everything consumed by the Aztec capital was imported daily by bearers who traveled the highways linking the city and the lake's edge, or was unloaded from canoes. Tenochtitlan and Tlatelolco procured goods from the provinces by means of tribute imposed after successful military campaigns or the threat of military occupation. Their artisans, among them specialists in luxury articles, found sure buyers for their work in the city and among the local merchants who controlled regional trade. Tenochtitlan based a large part of its economic strength, which was unrivaled in Mesoamerica after the mid-fifteenth century, upon commerce and tribute. (Hardoy, 1975:12)

The strategic location of most of these cities in relation to the hinterland also allowed colonists to dominate the native population. Ensconced in fortifications on the coast, the Europeans could defend themselves from internal attack and receive supplies from the sea. Such battlements also protected them from an external enemy—pirates—who lusted after the wealth these cities harbored.

Military might alone, however, did not ensure European dominance of the new cities and their hinterland. One of the most tragic aftermaths of the conquest was the literal decimation of the indigenous population. Anthropologists and historians estimate the loss of native human life in Central America in the sixteenth century at roughly 95 percent (Cottrell et al., 1979:48). This means that, in scarcely a single century, the Indian

FIGURE 13–1 Map of Major Central American Cities

FIGURE 13–2   Map of Major South American Cities

population plummeted from more than 25 million to perhaps 1 million. There were many reasons for this frightening loss of life, chief among them the brutal wars with the colonists and the toll taken by European diseases, such as measles and smallpox, against which native Latin Americans had no biological defense.

Cultural Impact

Imposing European culture on Latin America had other long-lasting effects. Decreeing a set of principles called the "Laws of the Indies," the Spanish constructed all their new cities along very similar patterns, resulting in the breakdown of local cultural patterns. Although local geography and earlier customs brought some variations, most colonial cities were constructed around a grid plan with a central plaza—the *plaza mayor*. At one end of the plaza was an imposing Catholic church. On the other three sides were government offices, residences of the wealthy, and some businesses. Such a design established the dominant institutions of European culture—the church, the state, the power of the elite, and commerce—at the very heart of the city.

Around the city center, in a second district, were the residences of the city's middle class: artisans, government clerks, and small merchants. Further out still, in a third zone, were the much more dilapidated residences of the city's poor. Finally, on the outskirts, were large parcels of land originally called *encomiendas*, given in trust to the local elite by the Spanish government. After independence in the nineteenth century, many of these large parcels of land became part of the equally exclusive *hacienda* system: large farms or ranches run by elites and worked by serfs.

Although physically similar to European cities, these preindustrial colonial cities were even more exclusive, favoring only a small and extremely powerful elite of European descent. Under normal circumstances, native Latin Americans could never become members of the elite. Although remnants of pre-Columbian culture remained—particularly in rural communities—the dominance of colonial cities in Latin America ensured the dominance of European culture in most areas of life (Skidmore and Smith, 2000:20–21).

Independence and Urban Growth

By the early 1800s, the willingness and ability of the European colonists to maintain Latin American outposts was waning. They had long ago taken most of the easily extracted raw materials. Then, too, local insurgents, such as Simón Bolivar, were mounting more frequent challenges to colonial governance. Soon after a series of wars of independence (1816–1825), most Latin American nations gained their freedom.

With colonial restrictions removed, many Latin American cities began to prosper through trade with cities in England, France, and the United States. At the same time, populations began to increase. For example, between 1797 and 1914, the population of Buenos Aires jumped from 30,000 to 1.5 million, and between 1800 and 1900, Rio de Janeiro's population climbed from 43,000 to 800,000 (Boyer and Davies, 1973:33). Similar patterns appeared in Mexico City, Montevideo, Caracas, Santiago, Lima, and Havana. Indeed, by the early twentieth century, these few cities had grown so much that they dominated all other cities in their respective countries, becoming what urbanists call *primate cities*, as the Critical Thinking box on page 376 explains.

Not all of the growth of primate cities resulted from rural migrants seeking greater economic opportunity in the city; some was attributable to foreign immigration. Between 1860 and 1930, Latin America absorbed millions upon millions of Jews, Russians, Poles, Italians, Swiss, and Germans. Because of their generally higher level of education and greater familiarity with business, these immigrants soon came to control much of the medium-scale commerce of Latin America's primate cities, dominating such areas as construction, small industry, workshops, artisan and craft activities (Hardoy, 1975:49–50). As a result, immigrants occupied many middle-class jobs at the expense of the impoverished indigenous population that also was streaming into the cities.

"Law of the Indies"

Throughout Latin America the Spanish influence manifests itself in both architecture and urban design. One common feature is a large church or cathedral, as well as a government palace, adjacent to or dominating a central plaza in the heart of the old city area. Illustrating this pattern is Murillo Plaza in La Paz, Bolivia.

African Cities

African urbanization is uneven, with most contemporary African cities located on or near the continent's coastlines. The greater urbanization on Africa's north coast is a historical legacy of trade, both with Europe and with the Islamic countries of the Middle East. To reach Europe, Africans transported their goods from the interior, crossing the forbidding Sahara Desert, then loading them onto ships that plied the Mediterranean or sailed Europe's west coast. Established during the seventeenth and eighteenth-century European colonization to facilitate exports (including slaves), cities on Africa's west and east coasts soon became the most technologically and economically developed settlements on the continent.

Early African Cities

Though unknown to most westerners, complex civilizations, complete with highly developed urban centers, existed in Africa as early

Africa

as 3000 B.C.E. One such civilization, Kush, with its core cities of Meroë, Musawarat, and Naga, was centered about 100 miles north of the modern city of Khartoum. According to unearthed archaeological evidence, these Kushite cities, originally imitators of the pharaonic cities of Egypt, were highly sophisticated. By 590 B.C.E., Meroë traded extensively with Saharan and Mediterranean peoples in slaves, gold, ivory, iron, and copper (Wenke, 1999). In fact, Meroë's trade in copper was so extensive that great slag heaps from the manufacturing process are still evident in the city's ruins.

Other early African cities, particularly those in the sub-Saharan region, served as capitals of indigenous African empires, as craft or manufacturing centers, or as break-of-bulk points on major trade routes. Gao, in present-day Mali, was built in the seventh century C.E. as the capital of the Songhai Empire. More impressive was Kumbi, capital of the Empire of Ghana around 1000 C.E. Backed by a large army equipped with iron weapons, Kumbi had an estimated population of 30,000, supported

CRITICAL THINKING

The Evolution of Primate Cities

A primate city is one that grows in population and influence far beyond other cities in a nation or region. In many poor countries, the largest city may have several times the combined population of the next-largest two or three cities. Primate cities thus resemble, to use Alejandro Portes's metaphor, "gigantic heads of dwarfish bodies" (1977:68), absorbing an enormous portion of the available labor, trade, and population.

The extent of the dominance of a primate city in its own country can be shown by a *primacy ratio*, computed by dividing the primate city's population by the population of the second-largest city in the country. In the table below are some examples.

Selected Developing World Cities in 2002*		Selected Developed World Cities in 2002*	
Bangkok	10.9	London	7.2
Lima	9.9	Paris	7.1
Santiago	9.3	Vienna	6.7
Managua	8.4	Copenhagen	3.8
Beirut	5.5	Prague	3.1
Mexico City	5.2	Berlin	2.0
Havana	4.9	New York	2.0
Nairobi	4.6	Rome	2.0
Jakarta	3.4	Moscow	1.8
Tokyo	2.4		
Cairo	2.1		

*All ratios computed from populations reported in "Nations of the World," 2003 *Britannica Book of the Year* (Chicago: Encyclopaedia Britannica, 2003).

Note that, with the exception of four cities, the primacy ratios for the largest Western cities (New York, Moscow, Rome) are relatively low. This suggests that primacy is linked to more than a good location and established trade patterns. Recent research suggests that primate cities develop more frequently (1) in small countries—Copenhagen and Vienna are clear examples; (2) in countries that, for historical reasons, have only one or a few cities with anything approaching modern facilities—certainly true of poor countries around the world; and (3) in countries that were once or still are under foreign control either politically or economically—colonial cities, for example (Berry, 1961; Linsky, 1965).

Some urbanists argue that primate cities are helpful to a region's urban development. They speed up the evolution of a modern urban facility, which, in time, makes possible the "trickling down" of advanced urban technology and economic vitality to smaller cities. These urbanists point to this process in the more-developed countries. Historically, for example, London was England's primate city. With the advent of industrialization, however, large numbers of modern middle-level cities emerged in England: Birmingham, Manchester, Leeds, and Sheffield.

Other theorists are much less optimistic. They argue that cities in highly industrialized nations are not comparable with those in poor regions. Rich countries, like the United States and England, were, at the time of the emergence of their middle-level cities, much more economically advanced and politically stable than most poor countries today. In the latter, because the rest of the country is so poor, people flock to the primate city as the only chance to better their lives. This hampers the development of a series of middle-level cities and ensures, if growth goes unchecked, that the primate city itself will become overwhelmed with migrants. Thus, the only way to prevent overgrowth is to strictly limit further population growth in the primate city and to build middle-level cities that will drain off some of the population (Kasarda and Crenshaw, 1991).

by a rural population numbering in the hundreds of thousands. Trade in gold and ivory—as well as in salt, kola nuts, slaves, and iron weapons—provided the empire's economic base (Wenke, 1999).

As Wenke suggests, trade was crucial to these cities. In the eighth century C.E., shortly after the establishment of Islam as a major religion, cities based on trade with Arab countries and the East began to appear throughout Africa—cities such as Mogadishu in Somalia and Mombasa in Kenya. As exchange became more lucrative, the Muslim traders conquered the North African cities in the name of transforming them into major shipping centers to Europe. Their trade networks linked these cities to dozens of inland, sub-Saharan cities to the south. One such city was Kano, founded in 999 C.E. Another was the legendary Timbuktu, founded in 1100 and the intellectual capital of western Sudan, with its stone palaces, many-windowed homes, city university, and bustling marketplace.

All these early African cities were typical preindustrial cities with a walled enclosure, narrow and winding streets, and daily life organized around religion, crafts, and the crown. Residence was often determined by craft—for example, metalsmiths might cluster together—or by tribal or religious affiliation. There was nothing resembling the modern Western pattern of a CBD surrounded by residential rings determined by income. Rich and poor, commercial and residential uses all intermingled.

European Domination

The isolation of African cities did not continue forever, however. Although this period of empire building, trade, and urbanization (from approximately 500 B.C.E. to 1500 C.E.) was modern Africa's formative period, in which the dynamics of growth and change produced uniquely African cultures and civilizations, all became progressively submerged in the coming centuries. Looking for an easy passage to the East, the Portuguese arrived in the late 1400s. Other European colonists—the French, British, Danish, and Dutch—were not far behind (Davidson, 1998).

The First Wave The initial opening of Africa by Europeans stimulated one of history's most wretched practices: slavery. Although the use of slaves has a long history—ancient Egyptians, Greeks, and Romans, for example, regularly subjugated those they conquered—the slave trade between 1500 and 1850 is second to none in barbarity. The Spanish and Portuguese secured African slaves (often with the help of other black Africans) and exported these human beings to Latin America to replace the decimated Indian population. For their part, English and U.S. traders joined in shipping vast numbers of slaves to the New World to do the backbreaking work of building a new country. Other European countries participated as well. All enlisted the aid of a cadre of professional slave traders—Europeans, Muslims, Africans—to bring the "black gold" to market at Daka in Senegal, Elmina on the coast of Ghana, Zanzibar in Tanzania, and other slave-trade towns established up and down the continent's coasts.

The first European invasion also upset many of the delicate economic, political, and interpersonal linkages of precolonial Africa. The Portuguese demolished the east coast cities and destroyed the trade alliances that linked these cities to the Persian Gulf, India, and the Far East. In other parts of Africa, Europeans destroyed many of the political allegiances that had kept African tribes and empires in balance with one another. Added to this was the incalculable confusion and suffering brought about by the slave trade, which forcibly separated husband from wife, brother from sister, mother from child. In the wake of such practices, much of African society was brought close to collapse.

— 1862 — 1915

The Second Wave The character of urban Africa changed radically in the nineteenth century when Europeans arrived in force. No longer looking for a passage east, and with the slave trade waning, the rapidly industrializing colonizers now eyed Africa with much the same plundering eye that Cortés and Pizarro had cast upon Latin America more than three centuries before. After all, Africa is a source of almost incalculable raw materials. And so they

— known for m.s. walls

Taroudannt, Morocco, is a city of 30,000 that traces its origins to the eleventh century. Its sixteenth century, 23-foot fortified walls are in excellent condition and still define three-fourths of the city's borders. Walled cities once existed on all continents except Antarctica as a defensive measure and those that remain offer vivid testimony to how cities once defined their boundaries.

swarmed like locusts over the continent, trying to claim as much land and other wealth as they could.

Between 1862 and 1915, Europeans established city after city. Where no previous cities existed, they built them. Where indigenous urban centers were in place, they "Europeanized" them. Among those established or transformed during this period—some easily betraying their colonial origin by their European names—were Dar es Salaam (1862); Accra (1876); Leopoldville (1881)—now Kinshasa; Brazzaville (1883); Johannesburg (1886); Salisbury (1890)—now Harare; Kampala (1890); Nairobi (1899); Stanleyville (*c.* 1900)—now Kisangani; Jos (1903); Elisabethville (1910)—now Lubumbashi; and Albertville (1915)—now Kalima.

Unlike Latin America, where the "Laws of the Indies" produced a continent of similar cities, the presence of many European nations in Africa resulted in a variety of different policies for urban areas. The British, for example, subscribed to a policy of indirect rule, content to let local African rulers maintain their positions as long as they bowed to the colonial government. The French, on the other hand, insisted on the eventual assimilation of Africans into the French way of life. To promote this they dismantled indigenous governments, taught only French in public schools, and encouraged the local population in total identification with French culture.

In still other instances, where prominent African settlements had existed prior to the coming of the colonizers, dual cities appeared. In cities like Kano, Ibadan, and Kampala, the Europeans paired the African city with a new city of their own next to it. The contrast was striking: An African city constructed of mud bricks and organized around its religious life and craft associations would coexist with a European city built of stone and organized around a growing CBD.

In all cities, however, a policy of racial segregation prevailed—a form of *apartheid* (the

FIGURE 13–3 Map of Major African Cities

practice as it came to be known in South Africa) by which Europeans dominated the local people. Obviously, such a system imposed tremendous economic, political, and social hardships on Africans while enriching the Europeans. Racism was at its worst in southern Africa—particularly in the then Union (now Republic) of South Africa and in Namibia—

Esfahan, Iran
Masjed e Jame
mosque

The Islamic world is one rich in art, architecture, culture, history, and tradition. Religion is the centerpiece of that world and its ornate mosques dominate each cityscape, much as Christian cathedrals dominate older cities in Europe. A Muslim example is the Masjed-e-Jame mosque, in Esfahan, a city of 1.3 million people in central Iran.

where only recently have black majorities gained power. In more northerly parts of the continent, different colonizers and different urban traditions allowed the races some contact, and thus mitigated the racism somewhat. Thus, although racial tensions remain in West, East, and North Africa, conflict has been greatest in the south in the Republic of South Africa, Namibia, and Zimbabwe, where rigid racial segregation and stratification ended only a few years ago.

Middle Eastern Cities

Chapter 2 highlighted early Middle Eastern cities. In this region the world's first-known city —Jericho—developed nearly 10,000 years ago. It was followed by other early cities such as Catal Hüyük and Eridu and, beginning in the fourth millennium B.C.E., by the domination of the Persian and Egyptian empires. As these empires faded—a process hastened by the invasions of Philip of Macedon, Alexander the Great, and the Romans in the last four centuries

before the birth of Christ—they left behind established sites on which more modern cities would flourish.

A second period of city building occurred after Alexander's conquest in 334 B.C.E. Seeking to bolster his empire through trade, Alexander established a string of colonies from present-day Syria all across the coast of northern Africa. As Romans followed Greeks, additional cities, typically military outposts, were added, including Tangier, Algiers, Tunis, and Carthage. After 300 C.E., the declining fortunes of Rome, plus soil erosion and overgrazing, led to the eclipse of some of these coastal cities. Many ruins remain to this day, stark reminders of long-faded cultures.

Islamic Cities

The prophet Muhammad died in 632, unleashing a religious movement that swept over the entire Middle East, into Europe via Spain and the Balkan states, across some of sub-Saharan Africa, and, eventually, as far east as Pakistan, India, Indonesia, and the southern

Philippine Islands. As it spread, Islam generated an impressive array of cities. Even as European cities contracted during the Middle Ages, Islamic cities along the coast of North Africa were entering their greatest period. The Muslims' status as among history's greatest "middlemen" helped assure the success of these cities, as traders utilized the Middle East's geographic location to become the link between Europe and the Far East and, in the case of North Africa, between Europe and the sub-Saharan region.

But the inland cities were probably Islam's greatest triumph. For centuries, as nomads and overland traders, the people of the Middle East had learned how to live and prosper across vast distances of inhospitable terrain. As trading centers, they established Mecca, Riyadh, Baghdad, Tehran, and Kabul, among others.

All the Islamic cities had a similar form, as described in the Cityscape box. By and large, the Muslim city reflected the power of the city's royal and religious elites, and many find these the most beautiful of all the world's cities. The following passage, excerpted from Robert Bryon's writings on his travels in the Middle East in the 1930s, describes Isfahan in Iran:

Robert Byron

The beauty of Isfahan steals on the mind unawares. You drive about, under avenues of white tree trunks and canopies of shining twigs; past domes of turquoise and spring yellow in a sky of liquid violet-blue; along the river patched with twisting shoals, catching that blue in its muddy silver, and lined with feathery groves where the sap calls; across bridges of pale toffee brick, tier on tier of arches breaking into piled pavilions, overlooked by lilac mountains, by the Kuh-I-Sufi shaped like Punch's hump and by other ranges receding to a line of snowy surf; and before you know how, Isfahan has become indelible, has insinuated its image into that gallery of places which everyone privately treasures. (1950:174)

But this image is misleading, for enduring internal conflict often characterized Islamic cities. Given the division of the city into multiple residential quarters—sixteenth-century Damascus contained no fewer than 70 quarters in the city itself and 30 more in the suburb of al-Salihiyyah—ingroup solidarity often led to surging outgroup hostility, particularly when central religious values were at stake:

So intense was neighborhood communal solidarity that at times faction fights broke out between quarters. . . . [It was] a society where economic grievances could seldom be articulated without group violence. Political communication with the ruling . . . caste was limited. Food shortages or abusive taxation provoked street demonstrations, assaults on officials, pillage of shops and the closure of markets. . . . [Youth gangs, associated with different quarters] preyed upon the quarters, running protection rackets, pillaging, and murdering. (Costello, 1977:15–16)

Islamic cities reached their zenith during the Middle Ages. Thereafter, like their Persian, Egyptian, Greek, and Roman predecessors, they began to slide into decline. Again, the land near the cities became overgrazed and the topsoil depleted, leading to evaporation of precious water supplies and increasing dust and erosion. This, in turn, triggered a loss of timber, a crucial raw material any preindustrial society consumes for heat, artifacts, houses, ships, and tools (Costello, 1977:18).

City populations plummeted. For instance, in the sixteenth century Baghdad dropped to a population of less than 100,000, one-tenth of its former size. In Syria, Egypt, Iran, and Saudi Arabia, cities were reduced to shadows of what they had been. Even in the largest cities such as Alexandria and Aleppo (in Syria), trade slowed to a trickle.

European Domination

Not until the nineteenth century, under European influence, did urban growth begin once more. Europeans saw in the Middle East waiting markets for their goods, a potential source of raw materials and, in some areas such as Suez, strategic locations for military affairs.

But the Europeans never viewed the Middle East as the valuable prize that Latin America and Africa were. Thus, they made limited efforts at colonization. Britain administered

FIGURE 13–4   Map of Major Middle Eastern Cities

Egypt as a protectorate from 1882 to 1914, but otherwise was content to trade. But trade with outsiders was sufficient to weaken the centuries-long Islamic pattern. Despite efforts by many Muslims to bar nonbelievers and their way of life (including books, telephones, and automobiles), their world was changing.

As European influence spread across the region, new urban patterns emerged. For example, the French textile industry in Egypt after 1830 sparked urban growth throughout the rest of that century. From Cairo to Beirut to Tehran, suburban districts swelled beyond the quarters of the old cities, and new, wider roads were routinely clogged with motor vehicles (Roberts, 1979).

The real change, however, went deeper than the physical level. Foreign traders ventured into rural areas to make better deals for agricultural products, thereby passing up the ancient

CITYSCAPE

The Islamic City

In the typical Islamic city, environmental and cultural elements dominant in the Middle East combined to produce a unique urban place. The surrounding wall, for example, served a dual function, first as a defense against marauders, and equally important, as a barrier to dust-laden winds coming from a variety of directions depending on the time of day or season of the year. When bush shrubs were planted along the wall, the effect on wind and dust was that of an almost total barrier, and with strategic planting of vegetation within the settlement, wind and dust could be kept aloft and away from inhabited areas across the whole extent of the settlement.

The bustle and intensity of activity on the main thoroughfares were a notable feature of the Islamic town. The animated nature of its commercial sections and the awareness of a rich texture of human contact and activity were, and in some cases still are, the very life force of Islamic urbanism. In sharp contrast to the harsh desolation and silence of the desert, the *sugs* or bazaars provided access to a multitude of goods and services. . . .

Turning away from the main thoroughfares, a further contrast was encountered as the traveler ventured into the residential quarters on either side. Here the streets were much narrower, with walls often within touching distance on either side. The intimacy and semi-private atmosphere of these streets were borne in on the visitor as the shade provided by the dense building pattern created cool conditions in which to linger. The noise of the main streets was quickly cut to a distant murmur as the traveler moved further into the quarter. . . .

On gaining entry to a private house, yet another contrast was unveiled as the anonymous faces of the outsides of houses presented to the street were transformed by the wealth of detailed internal decoration, apparent in even quite modest homes. Houses were usually built on the courtyard principle with rooms opening onto a central space, often embellished with a fountain. This space provided the chief communal living area for the family. In keeping with the modesty of Islamic tradition, rooms of one part of the house were used only by women and the overall layout catered for the entertaining of guests without their need to encounter all members of the household.

The courtyard principle provided the ultimate achievable protection of private open space from the extremes of temperature, dust and wind outside the settlement. In an almost cell-like structure the town was set within its walls as a first line of protection from the environment. The residential quarters, often within their own walls, were then located close together in a pattern which afforded mutual protection of each building by all the others. The building density did nothing to compromise the privacy of individual houses orientated inwards as they were, so that a third and final line of protection between courtyard and residential street was afforded by the house itself. . . .

Moving finally towards the centre of the town, the traveler was confronted with the mosque. These were originally built not so much as houses of God but as a means by which to exclude unbelievers from regular prayer ceremonies. The addition of minarets, though partly only ornamental, was made to project the muezzin's call to prayer, with other mosques built once the call was out of earshot in an expanding city.

The more recent urban settlements in the Middle East often lack the high degree of unity and atmosphere found in the still-existing, specific features of the older Islamic towns. The flavor of these old urban communities, in complete contrast to the desolation all around them, was at once intimate, intricate and intense. Thus, cities such as Baghdad, Cairo, Fez, or Tehran—situated in one of the harshest environments in the world—could provide comfortable living conditions for populations running into the hundreds of thousands.

Source: From *An Urban Profile of the Middle East* by M. Hugh Roberts. © 1979 by M. Hugh Roberts. Used with permission of W. H. Freeman and Company/Worth Publishers.

bazaars. Foreign investors opened businesses and factories in Middle Eastern cities and began undercutting the prices of the traditional guilds. In sum, new competition altered the face of the entire region's economy. Where local sheikhs had administered land communally and restricted the open-market sale of goods, now people began to sell land, goods, and skills to the highest bidder. The ultimate cost was a weakening of traditional authority and an erosion of long-established communities. Before long, Middle Eastern cities had begun to alter their earlier self-sufficient subsistence economies, becoming export-oriented and dependent on the economies and needs of Europe and North America. Of course, this process only accelerated with the discovery of the new "black gold" of the region: oil.

Asian Cities

The richness and complexity of Asian culture forces us to be highly selective. Indeed, of all global regions, Asia provides the greatest challenge because it encompasses almost 30 percent of the earth's land area and is a region of many sharp contrasts: Japan is a highly industrialized, rich nation, with one of the world's lowest birth rates. China is very poor, with a highly centralized urban policy to manage the largest urban population of any country in the world. Southeast Asia stands out as having no real tradition of indigenous cities at all; yet, despite this history, major cities now are growing at a startling rate. Despite some gains, India is still struggling to address urban problems as serious as those anywhere in the world. We begin there.

India

Chapter 2 revealed that the Indus Valley region of India and Pakistan had thriving cities such as Moenjo-Daro and Harrappa as early as 2500 B.C.E. And in antiquity, the fabled opulence and beauty of ancient India and China held nearly mythical fascination for westerners. These myths enticed that most famous of world travelers, Marco Polo, to set out from Venice in 1271 to find an easy route to the East.

The next Looking Back box offers some of his impressions of India.

Early Contact   The tales of Marco Polo only further fired the European imagination. Yet his stories also chronicled the enormous difficulties of reaching India and China via an overland route. So the Europeans had no recourse but to take to the sea. Beginning in the early 1400s, the Portuguese moved down the west coast of Africa, establishing outposts as they went. By 1460, they reached Sierra Leone, and by 1488, the Cape of Good Hope. Eleven years later, after moving up the east coast of Africa, Vasco da Gama made the leap across the Indian Ocean and arrived in India. By 1534, the Portuguese had outposts at Goa and Diu along India's west coast. The passage, however, was hardly easy, for between India and Europe lay more than 10,000 miles of ocean. Consequently, when the riches of the New World were discovered in the early 1500s, Portugal turned its attention to the considerably closer continent of South America.

European Domination   A century later, the British began the colonization of India in earnest. In 1639, they established George Town (later to become Madras) at the mouth of the Cooums River on India's southeast coast. By 1661, the British gained control of Bombay Island from the Portuguese and, in 1690, they established the city of Calcutta. As in Latin America and Africa, such cities had a dual purpose: as centers of political control and as bases for economic exploitation.

Where cities already existed, as in the case of Delhi, the British simply constructed a second settlement next to it, in this case New Delhi. John Brush described this pattern of separation, which is identical to the dual-city African settlements described earlier:

> . . . every city or town with pre-British origins which has grown at all during the last century shows a striking contrast between the indigenous part and the Anglicized part. . . . [The] typical urban center contains a congested old section, adjacent to which may be found *carefully planned* and often spacious sections dating from the British period. (1961:58–59)

LOOKING BACK

Marco Polo's India: The Cities of Malabar and Guzzarat

After three years of difficult travel, Polo and his two brothers finally found themselves deep in Asia at the capital of the great Kublai Khan in Peking. The Khan took a liking to the Polos, gave them every comfort, and over the next 20 years they toured extensively in China. Finally, they convinced the Khan, who had grown very attached to them, to allow them to go home. En route they visited two thriving cities on the western coast of India. Note the quality of Polo's description: He sees the Indian cities primarily in terms of wealth and objects. Although he described the culture of India as well as its treasures, it was such passages that fueled European interest in opening these areas to trade.

Malabar

Malabar is an extensive kingdom of the Greater India, situated toward the west, concerning which I must not omit to relate some particulars. The people are governed by their own king, who is independent of every other state, and they have their proper language. . . .

In this kingdom there is vast abundance of pepper, ginger, cinnamon, and Indian nuts. The finest and most beautiful cottons are manufactured that can be found in any part of the world. The ships from Manji bring copper as ballast. Besides this they bring gold brocades, silks, gauzes, gold and silver bullion, together with many kinds of drugs not produced in Malabar, and these they barter for the commodities of the province. There are merchants on the spot who ship the former for Aden, from whence they are transported to Alexandria. . . .

Guzzarat

The kingdom of Guzzarat, which is bounded on the western side by the Indian Sea, is governed by its own king, and has its peculiar language. The north star appears from hence to have six fathoms of altitude.

Here there is great abundance of ginger, pepper, and indigo. Cotton is produced in large quantities from a tree that is about six yards in height, and bears during twenty years; but the cotton taken from trees of that age is not adapted for spinning, but only for quilting. Such, on the contrary, as is taken from trees of twelve years old, is suitable for muslins and other manufactures of extraordinary fineness.

Great numbers of skins of goats, buffaloes, wild oxen, rhinoceroses, and other beasts are dressed here, and vessels are loaded with them, and bound to different parts of Arabia. Coverlets for beds are made of red and blue leather, extremely delicate and soft, and stitched with gold and silver thread; upon these the Majometans are accustomed to repose. Cushions also, ornamented with gold wire in the form of birds and beasts, are the manufacture of this place; and in some instances their value is so high as six marks of silver. Embroidery is here performed with more delicacy than in any other part of the world.

Source: Manuel Komroff, ed., *The Travels of Marco Polo* (Norwalk, CT: Heritage, 1964), pp. 408–11.

The older area (the original city) typically has a form much like that of the Islamic cities described in the last section. Crowded into a central market or bazaar, numerous small retail shops offer a vast range of goods, including foods, cloth, hardware, and jewelry. Surrounding the marketplace is a residential area strictly divided into quarters. These quarters divide Muslims from Hindus and separate Hindus according to their caste position:

FIGURE 13–5 Map of Major Asian Cities

Brahmins and other high castes are usually in the best-built residential areas in or near the center of the old cities. Muslims are clearly separate from Hindus and are themselves divided into quasi-castes and economic classes. The laboring castes and the menial outcastes of lowest socioeconomic status occupy the poorest houses and tend to be located in the outskirts rather than the center. (Brush, 1961:60)

The British part of the city, on the other hand, is very Western in form, with broad streets, often arranged in a grid pattern. At the center is a trading and manufacturing area, with a railroad leading outward.

China

Like India, China is a land of ancient cities. Beijing (Peking), as profiled in Chapter 8, has long stood as a magnificent center of Chinese culture. Today, some of traditional China remains, although much has been changed, as our historical account will explain.

Foreign Domination   From the mid-nineteenth century until the end of World War II, China was subjected to foreign control, first by Europeans and then by the Japanese. Invaders occupied the cities, particularly the so-called treaty ports opened to them by the Treaty of Nanking, which ended the Opium Wars in 1843. From Shanghai to Canton, Europeans remade parts of Chinese cities. Hotels, parks, tennis courts, and residential areas emerged, all catering to non-Chinese. To oversee European control of the area's economy, each city had a European-style CBD, complete with banks, corporate headquarters, and docks equipped to handle Western ships. As always, the Europeans imagined themselves on a "civilizing" mission. Said J. H. Wilson in 1887:

> Progress has planted her foot firmly on the banks of [Shanghai's Wusung River] and from her safe and abiding place in the foreign city is sure, slowly but inevitably, to invade and overcome the whole vast empire.

Despite such arrogant pronouncements, European-style "progress" apparently had little need of the Chinese themselves. Placed at the entrances to Shanghai's foreign-built park, one sign summed up the matter: "No Dogs or Chinese Allowed." Similarly, Shanghai's European merchants routinely recruited unsuspecting Chinese laborers for work on ships bound for far-off ports. Thus did the idea of being "shanghaied" come into our language.

Communist Anti-Urbanism   Not surprisingly, the Chinese people resented such treatment. Thus, when the People's Republic was established in 1949, Mao Zedong and his followers made a concerted effort to eradicate all aspects of European influence and privilege from China's cities. Moreover, believing cities to be by their very nature destructive of revolutionary ideals, Mao encouraged China's citizens to remain in their rural villages and transform the country from there.

More extreme action was also taken. During the 1970s, the highly regimented and often brutal Maoist system forced perhaps 25 million urbanites from large cities into small towns and rural villages. Despite these efforts, however, China's urban population continued to grow. Although reliable data are hard to come by, only about 10 percent of the Chinese population was urban in 1950, while the urban share had increased to 33 percent by 2002 (*Britannica Book of the Year*, 2003:579; Davis, 1969, 1972).

Japan

The urban roots of the country extend back at least to the eighth century C.E., when ruling elites established a series of provincial capitals. A warrior caste (the *samurai*) protected these capitals, which were weakly linked to an emperor living in the capital city of Kyoto. Within this feudal structure, local elites kept the citizenry in subjugation over the next few centuries while they warred with each other for control of various regions.

At the end of the sixteenth century, a samurai named Ieyasu emerged victorious over the warring elements. The emperor named Ieyasu *shogun* (leader and protector of Japan), and Ieyasu established his capital at the city of Edo (now Tokyo). Ieyasu and his successors set

Edo = Tokyo

about reorganizing the administrative system of Japan, putting greater emphasis on cities. Hall (1984a:221) reports that by the eighteenth century Edo had a population of nearly 1.5 million, making it the largest city in the world (London at the time had a population of 900,000). Osaka and Kyoto had populations of over half a million (Yazaki, 1973:144).

Over the centuries the growth of Japanese cities produced, as it had in Europe and North America, a wealthy and powerful middle class. By the mid-1800s, these merchants controlled the purse strings of the country, and the power of the shogun declined considerably. When Commodore Perry of the United States and representatives of various European interests (British, French, Russian, Dutch) arrived in the 1850s, intent on opening Japan to Western trade, the shogun had little power to resist.

Amid cries for revolution, the shogun stepped down in 1868. The new 16-year-old emperor, Meiji, urged his country to end centuries of economic isolation and become a modern nation strong enough to resist attempts at colonization. The Japanese responded. In less than half a century, Japan became a world power economically, technologically, and militarily. As people flocked to the cities, a transformation occurred. The following passage from an 1881 guidebook to Tokyo expresses this change:

> A great change has taken place since 1868 in the outward appearance of many parts of the city which were formerly covered with the *ya-shiki* or mansions of the territorial nobility. Many of these have been pulled down to make room for new official buildings. At the same time the disappearance of the two-sworded men [*samurai*], the displacement of the *palanquin* [an enclosed carriage, carried by people] by the *jin-riki-sha*, the adoption of foreign dress . . . and the European style of wearing the hair, now almost universal, have robbed the streets of the picturesque aspect which was formerly so great an attraction to the foreign visitor. (Quoted in Maraini, 1977:84)

Industrialization proceeded throughout the twentieth century. Japan's lack of the natural resources needed to run its industrial machine, as well as its own imperialistic ambitions, led the country into foreign expansion and finally into the disaster of World War II.

Common Legacies

With the exception of some parts of the Middle East, Southeast Asia, and Japan, all of the regions covered in this chapter were colonized. Although the specifics of such colonial control varied (it lasted for a longer period in Latin America than in Africa; it destroyed indigenous culture more thoroughly in Latin America than in Asia), its legacy has been much the same.

Economic Legacies

Colonization left behind an urban system with an underdeveloped economy. As we have seen, in most instances it was a process established for the benefit of a ruling elite and the citizenry of the mother country. Most colonial cities specialized in exports and showed little interest in generating wealth or opportunities for the bulk of the local population or in developing industrial capabilities. Thus, they prospered only to a point and remained relatively small. For example, in 1780, a full two centuries after its founding, Buenos Aires was a city of only 25,000 with few roads and virtually no contact with other cities. Compare this with the postcolonial cities of the United States. Freed of their ties with England, they exploded in population and wealth as they forged links with each other and the westward frontier. However, when independence came for developing countries in the twentieth century, they found their cities well behind Western cities in competitive advantage and without the technical know-how or capability to catch up. Despite their efforts, most are still unable to provide enough jobs or wealth for their populations.

Even in areas of the developing world never colonized directly, economic underdevelopment remains the rule rather than the exception. In noncolonial Southeast Asia (Thailand, for example), urban industrial capacities lag far behind those of the West, primarily because there is no tradition of vital indigenous cities and also because of disadvantageous export-oriented trade agreements with Western countries. In the noncolonial Middle East, the situation is much the same. Although indigenous cities have long existed, the insular policies of Islam and foreign domination of trade in the last century produced cities unable to provide for the growing needs of their populations. (This situation may change as oil money continues to pour into the region.)

The only exceptions to this pattern are Singapore, Hong Kong, and Japan. Singapore, by means of its rigid politics, controls its population growth and maintains a steadily rising standard of living. Hong Kong, no longer a British colony, has accomplished the latter goal (though not for all of its people by any means) but not the former. Japan has done both, and this makes Japan unique among these countries. Yet Japan's history is markedly different: It has a tradition of vital indigenous cities, no colonization, a strong commitment to industrialization a century ago, a basically stable political system, and a social structure flexible enough to allow most of its people the chance to improve their standard of living.

Political Legacies

Colonization also left political instability in its wake in many areas of the developing world. The leadership vacuum created by departing elites left the rule of the country either to a foreign-trained native elite or simply "up for grabs" between competing factions. Foreign-trained elites (as in much of Latin America) have typically re-created the limited-opportunity social structure of colonial days—advantageous to the few, difficult for the many. Competing factions (in much of Africa) have typically generated continued violence and unrest in urban areas. All these conditions have further retarded economic growth. What business corporation wants to invest heavily in a city where a coup may cause the loss or nationalization of its entire investment? Ironically, when corporations do invest, often another negative reaction follows. Many regard this type of investment as a contemporary form of colonialism—an alliance between multinational corporations and government elites—

and see it as a continuing strategy to exploit the people (Bradshaw, 1985).

National Boundaries

A third consequence has to do with how little the national boundaries established by the European colonizers related to the territorial boundaries of indigenous populations. The Spanish and Portuguese carved up Latin America in terms of what they were able to conquer, without concern for any native group's natural homeland. As a result, many peoples previously separated by political, linguistic, and other cultural factors for centuries became citizens of a single, newly constructed country. In the same way, the new national boundaries arbitrarily separated some groups who, traditionally sharing a given territory, now found their lands split by the European conquerors. (European powers enforced a similar but much more severe carving-up process in Africa.) When political independence came, many nations had yet one more barrier to rapid entry into the modern world: a local citizenry divided against itself by an artificial historical boundary. Many analysts see this situation as contributing to the political instability in many African and Latin American nations today.

THE MODERN ERA

The crisis of developing world cities goes beyond economic dependency on other nations. All over the globe, poor countries are experiencing a demographic transition based on falling death rates, with predictable consequences for population size.

Latin American Cities

Most Latin American cities have not followed the pattern of rapid industrialization typical of Europe, Canada, and the United States. Despite a century and a half of independence, in terms of wealth and productive capacity Latin American cities lag far behind the cities of these other regions.

Why? First, from the outset, most Latin American cities were export-oriented. Their valued products or raw materials—gold, silver, cattle, coal, oil, grains, coffee, fruits, wool—were sent to other countries, not consumed by their own populations. The demand by other nations for these goods did not change after independence, and Latin American cities continued such one-way trading. The problem is that selling raw materials generates far less money than processing and marketing finished products. As a result, Latin American cities generated much less wealth than cities that engaged in processing and distributing goods to consumers.

Second, with raw material exports as their primary source of wealth, most Latin American cities never developed much of an industrial base. Modern cities without major industries not only develop fewer jobs for their populations, but also cannot compete on numerous levels (skilled labor, investment opportunities) with cities that have them. Consequently, export-oriented cities simply fall further behind their industrialized counterparts. This is the pattern that led Barbara Ward, as early as 1962, to write of the worsening gap between "the rich nations" and "the poor nations."

This disadvantageous situation is not simply the result of poor investment policies and lack of foresight on the part of Latin Americans. Many urbanists argue that rich nations and their corporations have contributed significantly to the problem (Geisse and Sabatini, 1988; Morse and Hardoy, 1992; Greenfield, 1994). Still seeking raw materials and cheap labor in Latin America, these countries and corporations have thrown their aid and political support to Latin American governments that favored export over local development. Many Latin American business and government elites have become rich "playing ball" in this way, but this pattern has done little for the overall development of their countries. Thus the old colonial pattern of external domination is preserved in another guise.

Some Latin American countries—particularly Argentina, Brazil, and Mexico—have benefited somewhat by gaining the industrial operations that have been closed down in deindustrializing rich nations such as the United States. The *maquiladoras* program—creating enterprise zones in which multinational corporations control production and marketing, employ cheap labor, and often receive subsidies from the host nations—has brought some industrialization into these nations' economies. However, the extensive use of women's and children's labor helps perpetuate a culture of paternalism. Further, automation, together with other modern technology and production techniques, results in these companies' not generating many skilled jobs. Industrial development, therefore, is not creating enough employment opportunities to keep pace with the rural migration to the cities, so shantytowns on the cities' perimeters grow despite industrial development (Fernandez-Kelly, 1991).

African Cities

During the colonial era, most African cities grew slowly, hampered like their Latin American counterparts by one-sided trade policies (exporting raw materials at low prices). Only a few cities—coastal ports or mining cities, for example—grew more swiftly, because of their location or because of their special wealth. The post–World War II era ushered in a major change. Four factors coincided, leading to the independence of virtually all African nations. First, the oppressive systems of racial segregation and political and economic inequality began to spawn nationalist opposition movements. Second, such movements encouraged the revival of each country's precolonial heritage, long suppressed by Europeans. Third, Africa became a confrontation site for world ideologies. Siding with the Africans in most cases were leftist or Communist countries, prominent among them the former Soviet Union, China, and, later, Cuba. Such countries often equipped local insurgents with arms to fight the colonizers. Finally, colonies were becoming very costly to maintain, both economically and politically, and Europeans were having second thoughts about the whole business.

In the 1960s, 32 former colonies in Africa gained their freedom. In 1960 alone—dubbed the "African Year"—more than 3 million square miles and 53 million of Africa's people saw an end to colonialism (Herskovits, 1962:303). This success only further fueled independence movements, with the result that the retreating colonizers became more and more eager to let go.

In some cases, the aftermath of rapid withdrawal was debilitating political disorder. For decades, Africans had had little experience with political rule, so freedom often unleashed tribal warfare and a succession of military coups. For example, after the hurried Belgian retreat from the Congo in 1960, that country endured five years of bloody civil war as factions warred for control. The civil war and horrendous slaughter in the mid-1990s between the Hutu and Tutsi tribes in the former English colony now known as Rwanda is partly attributable to the same legacy.

In global perspective, Africa is still the least urbanized continent, but it has the highest rate of increase in urbanization. Just 15 percent of the African population lived in cities in 1950, but by 2000, that proportion had more than doubled to 37 percent. Demographers estimate that the number of African urbanites will reach 53 percent by 2030 (U.N. Population Division, 2002).

This increase is due to in-migration from the hinterland as well as to natural population increase. Some nations—including Zambia, Zimbabwe, Gambia, Botswana, Kenya, Madagascar, Mauritania, Namibia, and Tanzania—have had success in bringing down fertility rates. Ethiopia, Nigeria, and the Congo, in contrast, have not. Nigeria is presently one of ten countries with over 100 million people, a level that Ethiopia and the Congo will reach within the next 50 years. Tragically, the AIDS epidemic is worst in sub-Saharan Africa, where about two-thirds of the world's HIV infections (about 28.5 million cases in 2002) currently exist. In some nations, including Botswana, Lesotho, Swaziland, and Zimbabwe, at least 30 percent of the population is HIV-infected (Goliber, 2002). Despite this tragic epidemic, the UN medium projection series predicts a sub-Saharan population growth from 650 million in 2000 to 1.8 billion in 2050 (U.N. Population Division, 2002).

Together these factors help explain why Africa is a continent in severe crisis. Aside from Africa's health crisis, much of its population is starving. As an indication, consider this: Of the 25 poorest countries in the world, 18 are in Africa. Ethiopia, in central Africa, is the world's most destitute nation—the average income per person per year is only about $100 (in U.S. dollars). Zambia, in south central Africa, is only the 25th poorest country in the world, but its average per capita income is only about $310. No statistic better captures the stunning reality of such poverty than the chilling fact that, across central Africa—from Mauritania in the west to Ethiopia and Somalia in the east—the average child dies before age ten (World Bank, 2002b).

Middle Eastern Cities

The main effects of economic development in the Middle East have been (1) to increase the prominence of coastal cities, downplaying the significance of inland urban areas, and (2) to spark a major migration to all cities. Urban migration, as we have seen in Latin America and Africa, has the effect of taxing the city's capacity to provide for its people. Turkey's urban population, for example, increased 138 percent—from 5.4 million to 10.6 million—between 1950 and 1965. By 2000, 50.2 million people, or 75 percent of Turkey's 66.7 million people, lived in cities—a sixfold increase since 1965. The urban population in Saudi Arabia increased just as fast from 1950 to 1970—from 509,000 to 2.8 million. By 2000, 17.4 million people, or 86 percent of the total population of 20.3 million in Saudi Arabia, were urbanites, an astounding increase of 625 percent since 1970 (U.N. Population Division, 2002).

Political conflicts in the region have only made the population problem worse. Until recently, the most prominent example has been the plight of the Palestinian Arab refugees, nearly a million of whom, after the creation of the state of Israel in 1948, set up temporary "homelands" in cities in Lebanon, Kuwait, Saudi Arabia, and Jordan. The Palestinian Authority has yet to build an infrastructure and a viable economy to overcome the destitution of these former refugees still mired in poverty or to attract Palestinians living in shantytowns in other Arab countries.

Another change has been that capitalist markets have created in the Middle East, as elsewhere, a relatively large middle class of affluent entrepreneurs. By and large, this middle class has settled in new and exclusive suburbs outside the old cities.

Finally, rapid urban growth has established a primate-city pattern for the entire region. Tehran, for instance, has outdistanced all other Iranian cities in size, market strength, and problems. In similar fashion, Baghdad, Kuwait City, Damascus, Beirut, Amman, and Cairo dominate their countries. As elsewhere in poor regions, the existence of such primate cities is seen by some urbanists as curbing the growth of other cities and creating virtually insoluble problems.

In short, contemporary Middle Eastern cities are in a period of intense social change. They are no longer the pure Islamic cities of the past millennium, nor are they likely to become fully westernized. Like the cities of Latin America and Africa, these cities are in the process of forging a new and complex urban tradition. The emphasis here is on the word *complex*. As Janet Abu-Lughod has argued: "If, at some previous point in time, it was possible to generalize about cities in the wide region encompassed by Arab-Islamic culture, it is clear that such generalizations are no longer realistic" (1984:116).

Abu-Lughod identifies no fewer than five different patterns of current urbanization in the Middle East. These she calls (1) "neocolonial," typified by cities in Tunisia and Morocco; (2) "state socialist," the urban pattern in Algeria, Iraq, and Syria; (3) "charity cases," exemplified by cities in countries such as Jordan, Egypt, and Lebanon that are supported by other countries; (4) "oil and sand," including cities in Libya, Saudi Arabia, and Kuwait; and (5) "fourth world," cities in countries that are astonishingly poor such as the Republic of

Yemen and the Sudan. Such a varied pattern, Abu-Lughod contends, follows from countries and cities of the Middle East being so deeply enmeshed in world economics and politics. In a sense, then, their urban development is not of their own making. Abu-Lughod concludes: "It is unlikely that this situation will change drastically in the near future" (1984:117).

Asian Cities

As previously mentioned, the complexity of Asian history and culture negates a generalist approach, and so in this section we focus on India, China, Southeast Asia, and Japan.

India

India's high rate of population increase (about 2 percent annually) leads demographers to project that its 2000 population of 1 billion may grow to more than 2 billion before the increase ends, and that within 40 years India will pass China to become the world's most populous nation. In Uttar Pradesh state (by itself, this region's population of 166 million would make it the sixth largest country in the world), the average woman has five children (U.N. Population Division, 2002).

India produces enough food to feed its people—if the food were distributed equally to everyone. But this is not the case. Thus, poverty pushes people off the land and cities pull them in with the promise of a higher standard of living. But many of the urban migrants end up in *bustees,* India's version of the shantytowns we have seen in other poor countries. Here living conditions are often appalling, with people crowded into huts, without heat, safe water, electricity, sewerage, or other normal amenities, and offering inadequate protection from the elements.

Calcutta Although Calcutta is favorably located for trade in northeastern India, its land slopes away eastward and westward from the Hooghly River to marshes and swamplands, thereby confining the metropolitan area to a strip three to five miles wide on either bank. Reclamation projects, however, have allowed

Like many Asian and Middle Eastern cities, <u>Delhi</u>, *India* a city of over 7 million people, suffers from growing pains, as India's growing population increasingly worsens traffic congestion. Streets are typically jammed with some cars, but mostly pedicabs and bicycles, throughout each day as traffic moves at a snail's pace through the many intersections.

some expansion. With the exception of the grid pattern in the central area where Europeans formerly lived, the narrow roads have a haphazard character. With Kazi Nazrul Islam Avenue as the only express highway and few river crossings, Calcutta's transportation system—like its utilities and municipal facilities—is heavily overburdened. Most of the city's heavily used roads are in poor repair. India's only subway system began in Calcutta in 1986, offering residents an alternative to the older trams and buses.

Calcutta remains the world's largest producer of <u>jute</u>, but the city also operates as a port, shipping coal, iron, manganese, mica, petroleum, and tea from its hinterland. However, with a river channel, Calcutta handles only a small share of India's imports and exports. Although it is set in one of the poorest and most overpopulated regions of India, Calcutta's artistic, cultural, and intellectual life thrives. Home to three major universities and known as the "cultural capital" of India, Calcutta is unmatched among Indian cities in the

volume of people who flock to its art exhibitions, book fairs, and concerts. But never very far away are hundreds of *bustees*, which contain fully one-third of the city's 11 million residents. Worse off still are the hundreds of thousands of Calcutta's people who are entirely homeless and sleep on the streets or wherever they can find temporary shelter. People dump all manner of human and other refuse into open sewers. Needless to say, disease is widespread.[1]

Bombay   *Black cotton soils*   Not only is Bombay, a port city on India's west coast, unable to care for its people now, but legions of newcomers continue to stream in from the countryside, where life is even worse. Such migration—the primate city pattern—depletes the rural areas of people and creates huge cities that are unworkable.

[1]For more information on Calcutta, go to this web site: http://ezinfo.ucs.indiana.edu/~mduttara/wb/caltoc.html

About two-thirds of Bombay's 15 million residents are concentrated on Mumbai (Bombay) Island, giving this city one of the highest population densities in the world. Bombay has another distinction, that of being India's most culturally and religiously diverse city. More than half its residents are Hindu, with the remainder divided among Muslims, Christians, Parsis, Buddhists, Jains, and Sikhs. To make matters more complex, Bombay's people speak three major languages: Marathi, Gujarati, and Hindi.

The surrounding Black Cotton Soils, India's greatest cotton-growing area, has made Bombay one of the largest cotton textile centers in the country. This industry employs almost half of Bombay's factory workers. Most of the rest are employed in the production of silk, artificial fibers, chemicals, and glassware and in the dyeing, bleaching, and printing industries. However, most rural migrants are illiterate and lack industrial skills. Unable to find factory work, they get by as best they can, typically living in deplorable conditions. Perhaps 40 percent of Bombay's people lack an adequate diet, and virtually everyone contends with an unsanitary environment.

Outlook   The long-run picture for India's cities may be somewhat brighter. Some real progress has been made in recent years against hunger. In addition, transportation, electricity, and schooling are more widely available than ever before. Some rural areas—notably the Punjab in the north—have become self-sufficient; and smaller cities (under 100,000 people) seem to be faring better than the major cities like Bombay, Delhi, Calcutta, and Madras. Real economic growth in the 1980s and 1990s permitted a small but significant rise in average living standards.

Production, trade, and investment reforms since 1991 have provided new opportunities for Indian businesspeople and for an estimated 100 to 200 million middle-class consumers. India is attracting foreign investment, which has boosted people's confidence about the future. Moreover, India's strong entrepreneurial class and the central government's recognition of the need for market-oriented approaches to economic development bode well for the future. Negative factors include the desperate poverty of hundreds of millions of Indians and the impact of the huge and expanding population on an already overburdened environment. Whether the positive trends and hopes can finally eradicate the urban horrors remains to be seen.

China

In the 1970s, China introduced major reforms aimed at curbing population growth and stimulating economic growth in order to help Chinese cities "catch up quick." Its controversial "one-child" policy, applying both incentives and pressures to prevent couples from having more than one child, led its leadership in 1995 to boast of great success in reducing its birth rate. Even so, China's population, almost 1.3 billion in 2000, may still increase to 1.5 billion by 2025. On the economic front, China allowed cities to introduce private enterprise in an attempt to create a flexible, market-driven economy but one that remained under one-party, centralized political control. Declaring that communism would still be the main orientation of China but that controlled private enterprise was no threat to the goals of the revolution, China's ruler, Deng Xiao-Ping, said in 1984 that his nation could be one country with two systems. As a result, China's gross domestic product has quadrupled since 1978. By 2000, China ranked as the second largest economy in the world after the United States, as measured on a purchasing power parity basis (CIA *World Factbook*, 2002).

Special Economic Zones   Perhaps Deng's most radical innovation was the establishment of so-called "Special Economic Zones." One example is the new city of Xiamen in southern China. Xiamen is so liberalized from the old policies that it seems almost capitalist. The city is a free-trade zone where China's manufacturers can wheel and deal with their Western counterparts without the restrictiveness that characterized the Mao regime. Chongqing, a city with a 5.8 million population, serves as another example. The Beijing government gave the city free rein to make deals with foreign companies and encouraged Chongqing's citizens to use their ingenuity to find ways to make the city more productive. Another city, Guangzhou, is alive with Deng's new spirit of free enterprise. With glittering window displays of cosmetics, fashions, and video appliances, major streets like Dongfanglu look more like Nathan Road in Hong Kong than like anything previously seen in China. On the side streets, private stalls selling clothes, stir-fried food, and household commodities line block after block. Along with Guangzhou's surging economic energies, however, have come some elements that worry hard-line Maoist conservatives. These "evil winds," as the Maoists call them, include open gambling, pool halls, prostitution, a thriving smuggling operation that deals in China's antiquities, and crime.

Deng's successors have continued these policies. Whether this attempt at reforming Chinese cities will be successful in pulling them up by their bootstraps in the next few years is very much open to question. Even if significant economic progress is made, will the price be too great? Will China's cities exchange one "evil" for another, gaining wealth at the expense of a citizenry divided against itself—rich against poor, law-abiding against law-breaking—the very divisions the Communist revolution was fought to eliminate? Only time will tell.

Hong Kong   In 1997, Hong Kong came once again under Chinese sovereignty, returned by Great Britain, which had forced China to cede the 380 square miles after the First Opium War (1840–1842). Located on the southeast coast of mainland China just 80 miles southeast of Canton, Hong Kong has 6.9 million residents, giving it a population density of over 16,000 people per square mile, double that of Los Angeles (U.N. Population Division, 2002). Indeed, so great is the space problem that the city's roofs are prized possessions, as illustrated by the City in Literature box.

Not surprisingly, overcrowding is omnipresent. Shantytowns, which have virtually disappeared from the People's Republic, house some 15 percent of the city's population, despite determined efforts to provide public housing. Other, particularly older, housing is bursting at the seams. Even the port itself has become a kind of slum, housing hundreds of thousands of the city's poor on Chinese-style boats called junks. In some areas one can literally walk across much of the harbor by simply stepping from one moored junk to another. On one level Hong Kong has been and continues to be very successful. It has become the most important trade port on the China coast other than Shanghai and has generated an industrial machine that is the envy of much of the world, replacing a number of other major manufacturing points. That industrialization, however, together with high population density, has resulted in serious pollution problems. For generations, Hong Kong filtered, but did not chemically treat, its sewage, which was pumped out into Victoria Harbor near the main container terminals. Years of industrial sewage as well as human waste turned the city's "fragrant harbor" both toxic and foul. However, in the late 1990s Hong Kong finally built a real sewerage treatment system in which waste water is collected from points around Hong Kong's urban center and chemically treated before being dumped back into the sea.

On another level, however, Hong Kong has problems well beyond density and pollution. Many of the city's migrants are extremely poor, and an adequate number of jobs to absorb them is not on the immediate horizon. Perhaps as a result, crime is rampant and growing. Robbery, often accompanied by violence, is commonplace; youth gangs terrorize many of the city's communities; and public and private corruption is rife. If one is not careful to shop in the government-controlled stores, one can easily be sold counterfeit or damaged goods. And an unwary shopper may find in his bag a cheaper item than the one he thought he had bought. Nonetheless, Hong Kong is one of the most successful urban areas in Asia and so far under Chinese Communist control is remaining what it was under British rule.

THE CITY IN LITERATURE

Hong Kong: Up on the Roof

The roof-tops were a civilisation for themselves, a breath-taking theatre of survival against the raging of the city. Within their barbed-wire compounds, sweat-shops turned out anoraks, religious services were held, mahjong was played, and fortunetellers burned joss and consulted huge brown volumes. Ahead . . . lay a formal garden made of smuggled earth. Below, three old women fattened chow puppies for the pot. There were schools for dancing, reading, ballet, recreation, and combat; there were schools in culture and the wonders of Mao, and this morning . . . an old man completed his long rigmarole of calisthenics before opening the tiny folding chair, where he performed his daily reading of the great man's Thoughts.

The wealthier poor, if they had no roof, built themselves giddy crow's-nests, two feet by eight, on home-made cantilevers driven into their drawing-room floors.

Source: John Le Carré, *The Honourable Schoolboy* (New York: Bantam, 1978), pp. 115–16.

Southeast Asia

Unlike India and China, Southeast Asia has little tradition of large indigenous cities. Most of its urban areas are the product of Chinese or European influence within the past few centuries. However, the principal cities of the region—Yangon, formerly Rangoon (in Myanmar, formerly Burma), Bangkok (in Thailand), Ho Chi Minh City (formerly Saigon, in Vietnam), Manila (in the Philippines), Jakarta (in Indonesia), and Singapore (Republic of Singapore)—essentially reflect the themes we have encountered throughout Asia. A few portraits will illustrate.

Singapore   Situated at the southern end of the Malay Peninsula, Singapore is the largest port in the region and the fourth largest in the world. Despite a dearth of natural resources, it prospers as a center of East–West trade. In 2000, Singapore had a population of 4 million, about 77 percent Chinese, 14 percent Malayan, and 8 percent Indian. Eighty-five percent of these people live in the city itself, on 28 square miles of land. Density (12,602 people per square mile) is thus a problem (U.N. Population Division, 2002). To reduce congestion and pollution, the government bans cars from the city center during working hours; only those few with an expensive entry permit may drive into the CBD in the daytime.

As population increased throughout the twentieth century, shantytowns (*kampongs*) and squatter settlements appeared on Singapore's periphery. To alleviate the situation, the government took a novel, if heavy-handed, approach: It ripped up old neighborhoods, constructed thousands of high-rise apartment buildings, and literally forced the city's population into them. Importantly, most residents own or are in the process of purchasing their apartments through a government-incentive program. The process has transformed an old Asian city into an ultramodern one. From a distance, today's Singapore appears Western, with a clearly recognizable downtown and apartment high-rises almost as far as the eye can see. The high-rises have absorbed over four-fifths of the city's population, and each group of well-maintained buildings boasts its own school, parking lot, community center, social facilities center, and lush landscaping. Singapore thrives with its open market-based economy, strong service and manufacturing sectors,

Hong Kong, as viewed from Victoria Peak, could easily be mistaken for a North American city from a distance. But even this highly successful city, now under Chinese communist rule after 150 years of English control, contains shantytowns. Some poor residents live in shacks on the city's outskirts while others live in the harbor in Chinese-style boats called "junks."

and excellent international trading links derived from its history as a break-of-bulk port. The manufacturing, financial, and business services sectors dominate economic growth. Exports are booming, led by the electronics sector, particularly U.S. demand for disk drives. Rising labor costs threaten Singapore's competitiveness, but productivity seems to be keeping up. In applied technology, per capita output, investment, and labor discipline, Singapore has key attributes of a developed country (*World Factbook*, 2002).

Significantly, Singapore's population growth is under control. Its growth rate of about 1.2 percent a year is much lower than in almost all other developing world cities. Its success in population control is the product of an all-out attack: Singapore's government made contraceptives and abortion readily available, decreased taxes for families with fewer children, increased educational and housing benefits for small families, and raised hospital costs to families for each additional child.

All of this progress comes at a price: Singapore has a highly autocratic government. For example, residents or businesses in a district marked for redevelopment have no choice but to accept government compensation and leave. Although past practices of suppressing political opposition have ended and the first popular election of a president occurred in 1993, rigid social regulations control people's lives. Violators receive harsh punishments, even for minor offenses—littering is punishable by a heavy fine, and the punishment for drawing graffiti is caning. Singapore thus is a tightly controlled society, but its citizens accept the regimentation and prosper.

Jakarta Indonesia, lying along the equator between the Asian mainland and Australia, consists of 17,000 islands, of which only 6,000 are inhabited. As the fourth most populous country in the world, Indonesia is the largest Muslim nation. Nearly 80 percent of the country's total population (growing from 79.5 million in 1950 to 212 million in 2000) resides on the three islands of Java, Madura, and Sumatra. As a primate city, Jakarta on the island of Java, with its 9.3 million residents, has a population density of 44,200 persons per square mile, but in Java as a whole the population density is 2,070 persons per square mile (U.N. Population Division, 2002). To reduce the strain on severely crowded areas of the archipelago, Indonesia initiated a voluntary transmigration program through which poor, landless families in overpopulated areas move to underdeveloped regions and begin a new life with a house, land, and technical assistance. The program is a modern version of the Homestead Act that settled much of the western United States. Since the program started in 1950, more than 12 million Indonesians have relocated, half of them without government sponsorship.

Until the usurpation of the title by Singapore in the nineteenth century, the Indonesian capital, Jakarta, was unquestionably the most important city in Southeast Asia. Today, it is a primate city par excellence, with a growing number of high-rise buildings and monumental traffic jams. People migrate to Jakarta for the same reasons they trek to all cities: They want a better life, and the city's booming economy is an attractive lure. Per capita income is close to $3,000, classifying Indonesia as a middle-income economy. In 1965, more than 60 percent of Indonesians lived in poverty. By 2000, that figure was about 27 percent. Indonesia has made significant improvements in education, health care, nutrition, and housing over the past quarter century. Another indicator of the potential for improving the quality of life in Jakarta and its hinterland is that, between 1985 and 2001, the total fertility rate dropped from 4.1 to 2.6, thereby bringing Indonesia's population more under control. Although Indonesia remains a poor country in most respects, its rising levels of education and literacy, combined with falling fertility, may help accelerate socioeconomic development and bring greater prosperity to Jakarta and its people (*World Factbook*, 2002).

Bangkok   Like Jakarta, Bangkok is relatively typical of Southeast Asia's cities and serves as the capital of Thailand, a country never colonized. Currently with a population of 5.6 million, the city has more people than all 118 other Thai municipal areas combined. It is also over 20 times as large as Nonthaburi, the country's second-largest city, making Bangkok the premier primate city of the world.

A few figures illustrate the overdominance that such primacy causes in Thai affairs. Bangkok contains over three-fourths of the nation's telephones and half its cars, consumes over four-fifths of its electricity, holds three-fourths of all commercial bank deposits, and generates two-thirds of its construction. All automobile roads, railroads, and airplane routes converge on the city (so much so that to go from one place to another you have to go through Bangkok, even if it is out of your way); most Thai universities are in Bangkok, as are all the country's television stations; the city has about 20 daily newspapers (a few other cities have one); and it is the seat of the federal government.

With such advantages, people are still drawn to the city by the millions, further strapping its meager resources. A massive "riverboat culture," much like that in Hong Kong, houses many of the city's poor. City officials identify 331 slum areas in the city's 18 districts, where over 433,000 people live. Population density in the metropolitan area averages 3,621 persons per square kilometer, ranging by social class from a low of 390 in the Nong Chok neighborhood to 43,335 in Pom Prap (Bangkok Ministry of Interior, 2002). Bangkok thus is a city of contrasts. Its population growth intensifies further its overcrowding, traffic jams, and pollution. Yet the city's cultural, economic, and educational opportunities attract many tourists, business leaders, and students.

Comparative Review   Southeast Asia remains one of the least urbanized areas of the world (see Chapter 1, Table 1–2), yet its urban growth rate is incredible. In the past 20 years Jakarta, Kuala Lumpur (Malaysia), and Hanoi (Vietnam) tripled their populations. In the same period Surabaja (Indonesia), Yangon, Manila, and Ho Chi Minh City doubled theirs. This pattern of overurbanization is not likely to stop, as natural population increase and inmigration continue for the foreseeable future.

#1 primate city in da world

Only Singapore seems an exception, both in population growth and in economic self-sufficiency. But this exceptional status is easily explained: Singapore is a city-state in a small area (248 square miles) and it draws population from a limited hinterland. In all other cases, primate cities cannot keep up with staggering growth nor meet obvious needs. Unlike Singapore, they draw population from the whole geographical spans of their countries. For example, people from all over Thailand (almost 200,000 square miles) flock to Bangkok. As a result, overurbanization is rampant, causing a scarcity of jobs and services.

This situation may be typical of Southeast Asia and the developing world generally, but Japan, where we turn next, provides a sharp contrast to the rest of Asia.

Japan

The economic success of contemporary Japanese cities is remarkable. In the 1950s Americans looked with disdain on Japanese products, viewing them as cheaply made and prone to breakage. Today, the same critics shun U.S. products in favor of Japanese watches, TVs, stereos, radios, cars, motorcycles, and cameras. Part of the reason for this change is that government–industry cooperation, a strong work ethic, mastery of high technology, and a comparatively small defense allocation (roughly 1 percent of GDP) helped Japan advance with extraordinary rapidity to the rank of second most powerful economy in the world. <u>Fosco Maraini</u> suggested that another reason for Japan's success lay in its unique combination of the spirit of free enterprise and a collective orientation:

> Industrial enterprise, whether in the small workshop or gigantic factory, is typical of Tokyo, something deeply engrained in the character of the *Edokko* the true Tokyoite. An *Edokko* likes to start in business on his own, adventurously, perhaps opening a small workshop in his backyard, helped at first by his immediate family and later taking on additional employees who become no less members of his "family." . . . Tokyo . . . has many thousands of [such] small firms with only a [few] employees, and such businesses continue

A new apartment high-rise building towers over old Thai houses by a lake in central Bangkok. Rapid growth fueled by foreign investment has changed the face of the once-sleepy Thai capital as the country emerges as one of Asia's most vibrant countries. This stark contrast of old and new is a common sight throughout the Asian continent.

to make an extremely important contribution to the national economy.

> The other, more familiar, side of Tokyo industry is the larger scale <u>*kaisha*</u>. The dictionary defines *kaisha* as a company, corporation, firm or concern, but it is really much more than that. It is a whole way of life. Whereas a Western company "engages" an employee, a kaisha "envelops" him. The individual gives his *kaisha* a life of devotion in exchange for life-long security. . . . The system derives from [a combination of] both the feudal *han* (clan) and from the family unit, the *ie* (house). . . . A good employer

is expected to have the responsible attitude of a good parent—a kind of "uncle" figure who advises his workers on their personal problems, helps them with their housing arrangements. . . . In return, the employee gives maximum loyalty and effort, takes the attitude of a good team player that does not wish to let his side down. (1977:157–59)

This economic growth, at the expense of urban services, does not, however, enable the Japanese to enjoy a standard of living comparable to that of other industrialized nations. Exorbitant land costs and expensive housing either force urbanites to live in small-sized dwellings with wall-to-wall lots without any traditional Japanese gardens, or else to commute long distances by subway or commuter rail lines. Almost half of those who live in the cities are not connected to a sewage system, and only 20 percent have central heating. The typical commuter, forced to live in a satellite town because of high city housing costs, travels 1½ hours each way to and from work. During rush hour, commuter lines operate at 250 percent of capacity, necessitating the employment of "pushers" to force additional passengers into overcrowded cars. Heavy automobile traffic clogs the city streets, including the express roads built above the streets because of space limitations (Sterngold, 1994).

The country is also coping with a severe pollution problem brought on by its rapid industrial development amidst a densely packed population. Air pollution from power plant emissions results in acid rain, and the acidification of lakes and reservoirs degrades water quality and threatens aquatic life. Moreover, Japan's appetite for fish and tropical timber is contributing to the depletion of these resources in Asia and elsewhere.

On the positive side, Japan has established an exemplary health care system, and life expectancy (80.8 years) is among the world's highest. The Japanese have made great gains in reducing crime, unemployment (only 4.7 percent in 2000), and slums, have set the strictest air pollution standards in the world and, perhaps most important, have controlled their population growth. Japan's success in

establishing a high-quality urban life also impresses Western visitors, who express amazement at the tidiness of urban facilities, the reliability of public transportation, and the quality of restaurants.

Thus, the cities and urban life of Japan stand in marked distinction to most of Asia. Their familiar neon lights and thriving central business districts place Japanese cities solidly in the frame of the industrial nation. Indeed, the first-time visitor to Japan, even a visitor from the United States or western Europe, is bedazzled: Tokyo's Ginza district alight at night makes New York's Great White Way and London's Piccadilly Circus seem tawdry in comparison. In Asia, only Hong Kong and Singapore provide partial parallels.

What makes Japan such an exception to the overurbanization–underdevelopment pattern so common elsewhere in the nonindustrial world? At least four factors seem crucial. First, Japan was never colonized. It was thus spared the social indignities and exploitation-oriented urban economy characteristic of so many other regions.

Second, without colonization, it was able to generate, maintain, and revitalize numerous urban centers (controlled by different warlords) over the centuries. Although Tokyo–Yokohama is a major primate city, it is only twice the size of the Osaka–Kobe–Kyoto complex, and other vital urban centers (Hiroshima and Nagasaki, for example) exist elsewhere in Japan. All have industrialized effectively, spreading wealth and opportunity throughout the country. This keeps "overload" on a single city to a minimum.

Third, as already mentioned, encouragement of and opportunity for individual and collective advancement within the Japanese social structure is common. Although not everyone is rich, through hard work most Japanese can better their lives economically and socially. This is not the case in urban areas and countries still regulated by caste (India, for example) or by rigid ethnic boundaries. Nor do elites so tightly control access to the higher reaches of the status system that the less fortunate can never hope to better their situation.

Finally, despite past major population increases, Japan's current demographic pattern is distinctly different from patterns in the rest of Asia. Its multi-year low birth rate and current 1.3 total fertility rate means that its total population is shrinking. Because of this, despite its current economic slump, Japan has been able to provide jobs for its citizens and keep the lid on the massive shortage and pollution problems that bedevil many other cities throughout the world.

Common Problems

We have now completed our examination of cities and urban life in those areas in which most of the world's urban population lives. Perhaps the first comparative lesson is that these cities vary enormously from the Western cities with which we are most familiar. The diversity of history, cultural traditions, religion, and politics account for these differences. Thus, Islamic cities of the Middle East are in many respects radically unlike cities of the United States. Equally important, the cities of the developing world—Latin America, Africa, the Middle East, and Asia—vary tremendously among themselves. No brief formula can ever grasp the diversities existing among La Paz, Kano, Calcutta, and Tokyo. However, these diverse cities do share some common concerns.

Spiraling Populations

Latin America—much more urbanized than Asia or Africa—had a population equal to that of North America as recently as 1950. By 2002, though, the total population in Latin America and the Caribbean had skyrocketed to 531 million, far more than the 319 million people in North America. The growth rate in Latin America dropped from 2.0 percent in 1994 to 1.7 percent in 2002. Still, this level of growth increase (which will increase the population to 815 million by 2050) is considerably higher than the annual percentage increases of Canada (0.3) and the United States (0.6). Throughout Latin America and the Caribbean, the total fertility rate or TFR (the average number of children a woman has during her lifetime) was 2.7 in 2002, versus 1.5 in Canada and 2.1 in the United States (Population Reference Bureau, 2002).

Should the AIDS epidemic now rampaging through Africa be stopped, population growth (now about 2.4 percent annually) will only increase that much faster, given its 2002 total fertility rate of 5.2, by far the highest in the world (PRB, 2002). In 1990, only six African cities had a population exceeding 1 million; but by 2020 some 30 cities will reach this level. Between Benin City and Accra, demographers anticipate a region containing 25 million inhabitants, with five cities of 1-million-plus people. Accommodating these burgeoning urban populations is a challenge that will require massive investment in infrastructure and social services, as well as wise, talented, and patient leaders (Diagne, 1995).

As for Asia—where three-fifths of the world's population live—demographers project that its 2002 population of 3.8 billion, at its present 2.6 TFR, will increase by 1.3 percent annually and reach 4.7 billion by 2025. The growth rate is higher in the Middle East (2.0 percent), where the present TFR of 3.9 will result in its population of 197 million in 2002 increasing to 298 million by 2025 (PRB, 2002). By 2030, the urban population will reach 72 percent in the Middle East, 54 percent in Asia, 84 percent in Latin America and the Caribbean, and 53 percent in Africa (United Nations, 2000b).

In the future, demographers fear, population totals in less-developed countries will soar further. In most of these nations, one-third or more of the population is under the age of 15, so they have not yet entered their childbearing years. At the present rate of increase, Latin America will contain more than twice as many people as the United States by 2025 (PRB, 2002). Another factor promoting a strong population increase in the LDCs is that scientific advances and technological improvements (vaccinations, better sewage systems, and the like) have brought death rates down sharply. Although this is good news in a basic sense, it also contributes to a bigger problem of overpopulation as time goes on.

As suggested in the discussion of primate cities, cities receive the great bulk of this population increase. This fact is easy to understand, since improvements in health care and sanitation are mostly available in cities. In fact, the world's cities are growing by 1 million people each week (Brockerhoff, 1996:4)! Primate cities—so preeminent in national affairs that other cities fail to draw significant migration —dominate many of the less-developed countries. This exacerbates the overpopulation that already exists in each primate city and simultaneously saps the strength of other cities and rural areas.

Quality of Life

As the cities in poor countries swell in size, they are less and less able to provide sufficient employment and even basic services in water, sanitation, waste removal, gas, electricity, and police and fire protection. In Latin America alone, where only one city exceeded a million people in 1930, 50 cities reached that level by 2000. Most of these cities include large numbers of poverty-stricken people. In 2002, the National Center for Policy Analysis estimated that, over the past two decades, the number of impoverished Latin Americans had increased by 3 percent. In the 1990s, impoverished Latin Americans increased from 200 to 211 million, or roughly 40 percent of the region's population. This poverty is increasingly visible. Almost all Latin American cities are surrounded by *cinturones de miseria*, large belts of extreme poverty often lacking the most basic comforts, infrastructure, and social services. Similarly, in Africa, Asia, and the Middle East, cities struggle with street congestion, overcrowding, an inadequate infrastructure, and pollution.

Many of the less-developed countries are extremely poor—so much so that they simply cannot generate the wealth they need to solve their cities' problems at this time. Chronic underemployment and unemployment characterize many cities—a legacy of historical dependency on one or two trade goods and the lack of a diversified industrial base. One way many nations attempt to improve this situation is by encouraging tourism. A mixed blessing, tourism brings the world's richest citizens into contact with its poorest, a contrast only the most myopic tourists fail to see.

Finally, political corruption, crime, and urban violence are everywhere on the rise. For example, in Lagos, Nigeria, one of Africa's most economically and technologically advanced cities, violent crime is a constant risk and many streets have become so dangerous that few people go out at night. Armed carjackings and kidnappings are common, even during daylight hours. The situation has become so bad that, since the late 1990s, various travel advisory organizations have warned travelers to take stringent safety precautions and, as much as possible, to avoid passing through the streets of Lagos. In the Caribbean, Latin America, Africa, and Asia, one can easily become a crime victim in almost any city.

Shantytowns

One of the major problems accompanying rapid urbanization has been the growth of city slums or squatter settlements and shantytowns on the periphery of the cities, as mentioned throughout this section (see the accompanying Urban Living box). They have many names: *bidonvilles* ("tin-can cities") in former French African colonies, *bustees* in India, *los villas miserias* ("cities of the miserable") throughout Latin America, and other names elsewhere. They also take many forms: mud and cardboard shacks outside Seoul, Korea; junks moored in Hong Kong harbor; shacks in Africa and Latin America made from castoff lumber and tin. Their varying names and forms, however, are incidental to one underlying truth: They are the locales of abject poverty, malnutrition, poor sanitation, and disease. A quiet determination, strong family ties, and steadfast hope are often their positive counterparts as the inhabitants cling to the edge of survival, but these shantytowns nonetheless constitute the worst side of urban life in the developing world.

SUMMARY: WORLD URBANIZATION IN PERSPECTIVE

In decades past, social scientists debated whether economic growth was preferable to the preservation of local urban traditions. People taking the preservationist position usually argued, quite convincingly, that "creeping

Bidonvilles

African shantytowns, like their Latin American counterparts, typically exist throughout the continent on the outskirts of cities. These *bidonvilles* have a different name from similar places elsewhere but they are still squatter settlements and pose the same health, economic, and psychological problems found in other slum settlements in the developing world.

Westernization" by way of industrialization and foreign-oriented trade was rapidly obliterating ancient urban traditions, valuable not only to their peoples but also to the world as examples of the alternative forms that the urban process could take.

Although the preservation argument has lost none of its appeal today, the simple fact is that most cities in the developing world are inundated with so many people that they cannot provide adequately for their populations without major advances in economic vitality and technological efficiency. Already—as we have seen perhaps most dramatically in Calcutta—millions upon millions of the world's urban dwellers are suffering tremendous deprivation. As Daniel Vining succinctly stated, "Some of the large cities in developing nations are so crowded and polluted that it appears they have reached the limit of the carrying capacity of their environment" (1985:42).

Once again, the city is literally transforming our world, as it has twice before. In Chapter 2 we spoke of the first and second urban revolutions—the first occurring when people moved into cities in large numbers for the first time, from approximately 8000 to 2000 B.C.E.; the second occurring during the capitalist and industrial revolutions, which began around 1700 C.E. and continued through the first half of the twentieth century. This second urban revolution was responsible for a demographic transition—an unprecedented growth in population, made possible by the city's ability to provide a higher level of income, technological efficiency, and health care than rural areas. Now, once again, the city is fostering a demographic transition, only this time with two differences: (1) The greatest population growth is not in capitalist or communist worlds but in developing countries, and (2) the magnitude of the change makes

URBAN LIVING

Shantytowns Throughout the World

Africa

From its name, Mandela Village might sound like a pleasant, relaxed South African neighbourhood. In reality, it is a dilapidated shantytown, originally built in 1990 from wood and corrugated iron sheeting salvaged from a former bus station in the surrounding township of Soweto. In the decade since then, South Africa has seen dramatic political changes, with the end of the segregationist apartheid regime and the installation of the first democratically elected government, a shift that brought high social expectations.

Some of the 7,000 residents of Mandela Village are beginning to lose hope that the end of apartheid actually will improve their daily lives. Their shacks are tiny, the pathways between them narrow and lined with open gutters. There is no electricity and the entire settlement has only five water taps. Perhaps because the community is well organized and run by activists of the ruling African National Congress (ANC), its representatives were able to persuade the municipal authorities to provide 90 portable toilets around its perimeter. Virtually all inhabitants are unemployed . . . [and] what little income residents have . . . comes from the pension cheques of the settlement's seniors, from petty trading, and from automobiles stolen in nearby Johannesburg and sold to a "chop shop" just across the road from Mandela Village. . . .

For the residents of Mandela Village and other urban areas, the greatest problem is the lack of secure, regular employment. Estimates of private sector job losses between 1994 and 1999 range around 500,000. The government judges that during the 1990s, an average of 50 per cent of the potential labour force was unable to secure a formal sector job, with employment in manufacturing stagnant overall and job cuts hitting mining and agriculture especially severely.

Ernest Harsch

Asia

Squatters in Kuala Lumpur [Malaysia] are distributed in groups by ethnic origin. Settlement patterns and types of dwelling reflect the type of community—Chinese, Malays, Indians—living in each area, although settlement types within the same ethnic group may vary from rural village-like patterns, particularly on the periphery of the city to compact and dense patterns in commercial and other central city areas.

---

the demographic transition of the 1700–1950 period look meager by comparison. This is the third urban revolution. No one ever expected the kind of growth we are seeing now.

Massive overurbanization is occurring in the less-developed parts of the globe. Werner Fornos (1996), president of the Population Institute, put it starkly:

> While populations in developing countries are doubling every 25 to 30 years, their large cities are doubling every 10 to 15 years. And the urban slums and shantytowns in these cities are doubling every 5 to 7 years. In 1950, only one city in the developing world had a population greater than 5 million; by the year 2000, there will be 46 such cities. By no later than the year 2025, the combined populations of Asia and Africa will be 6.5 billion, significantly more people than now live on the entire planet.

Alternatively, consider this: A generation or two ago, one correctly thought of more-developed countries as the locales of the

. . . In terms of living conditions in the *kampungs,* the most striking features were lack of basic amenities and environmental hazards. The connection of households to the main system of water supply was extremely rare. The majority of squatter households depended on water from wells and, in some cases, from standpipes along main roads. Connections to the main network of electricity distribution were also rare; only about 5 percent of dwellings were supplied, but an additional 8 percent had installed their own generators.

Modern waste disposal was similarly lacking. Night soil buckets and the use of abandoned mining pools or streams for drop toilets, in that order, were prevalent. Sewered toilets, septic tanks, and water-sealed systems were very rare or entirely absent. Most of the squatter settlements were subject to flooding and suffered from pollution, especially noise pollution from car traffic and railway noise. As to the physical conditions of the dwellings, roofing was almost entirely galvanized iron, except in one area where a tarp cover was used. Most houses, with the exception of one area, were painted.

Ardeshir A. Anjomani
and Faizah Binti

Latin America

They live anywhere they can [in Mexico City]: in abandoned boxcars, in shacks teetering on hillsides, in public parks, in roadside hovels.

. . . Lawmakers say at least 48,000 families—as many as 200,000 people—live illegally in 360 shantytowns built on property they don't own. . . .

Squatters often live without drainage, with frayed electric cables hooked illegally into the city's electricity grid, and with drinking water from buckets or leaky rubber hoses. A fire apparently sparked by illegal electric hookups swept through about 100 shacks in "The Last Hope" squatters' camp in an industrial area of downtown Mexico City on February 25 [1998]. No serious injuries were reported.

Most area residents didn't even know the tar paper shacks had been built between two factories until the squatters' burned possessions were shoveled into the street.

The problem isn't confined to the capital. Dozens of squatters in the Pacific resort city of Acapulco were killed in October when Hurricane Pauline sent a river roaring down the dry stream bed where local officials had let them settle—and charged them rent.

Mark Stevenson

Sources: Ernest Harsch, "South Africa Tackles Social Inequalities," *Africa Recovery,* United Nations, 2002; Ardeshir A. Anjomani and Faizah Binti, "Squatter Settlement in Kuala Lumpur: Evaluation and Alternatives," *Ekistics* 59 (1992), 159–65; Mark Stevenson, "Mexico City Launches Crackdown on Squatters' Settlements," *Los Angeles Times,* May 3, 1998, p. 11.

world's largest urban areas. No more: Rapid growth and urban migration already have moved numerous developing world cities into this category, as the first column of Table 13–1 shows. The shift to developing world dominance becomes even more pronounced when we consider the longer term (Table 13–1, right-hand columns). By the year 2015, the only Western city in the top ten will be New York. Next, look at the magnitude of the urban areas in the 2015 column: The smallest

one is larger than six of the top ten cities in the 2000 column. These will truly be megacities, unprecedented in human history.

THE FUTURE: THEORIES AND POSSIBLE SOLUTIONS

Given the apparent inability of less-developed countries to cope with their urban problems, can anything be done to reduce the ever-increasing difficulties and suffering that seem

TABLE 13–1   The World's Ten Largest Urban Areas, 2000 and 2015

2000		2015	
Urban Area	**Population**	**Urban Area**	**Population**
Tokyo, Japan	26,400,000	Tokyo, Japan	27,200,000
Mexico City, Mexico	18,100,000	Dhaka, Bangladesh	22,800,000
São Paulo, Brazil	18,000,000	Mumbai (Bombay), India	22,600,000
New York, USA	16,700,000	São Paulo, Brazil	21,200,000
Mumbai (Bombay), India	16,100,000	Delhi, India	20,900,000
Los Angeles, USA	13,200,000	Mexico City, Mexico	20,400,000
Calcutta, India	13,100,000	New York, USA	17,900,000
Shanghai, China	12,900,000	Jakarta, Indonesia	17,300,000
Dhaka, Bangladesh	12,500,000	Calcutta, India	16,700,000
Delhi, India	12,400,000	Karachi, Pakistan	16,200,000

Source: United Nations Population Division, *World Urbanization Prospects*, 2002.

to lie ahead? Everyone recognizes that there is an unparalleled problem in most nonindustrial cities, but extremely different opinions exist as to what is responsible. Hence there are radically different suggestions about what should be done to make the problem disappear.

Modernization Theory

One theory, which many social scientists favor, suggests that developing world cities and countries everywhere are going through an inevitable process of modernization and economic development. This process is quite similar to that undergone by European and North American cities in the past few centuries. These now-developed areas of the world once experienced the growth of primate cities and severe poverty; however, modern industrial technology was responsible for greater productivity than ever before. At the same time, as people throughout the population adopted modern attitudes—an openness to change, a willingness to work for the future, a high regard for technical skills and education, a tolerance for others—they began to increase substantially their standard of living. Wealth grew in all sectors of the population; other cities evolved,

reducing the primacy problem; and eventually population growth itself declined.

Modernization theorists such as Ernest Gellner (1983) and Walt W. Rostow (1978) have argued that although some intervention might be helpful in alleviating the most immediate and severe of the nonindustrial world's urban problems, time is the main factor. In time, the modernization process itself will solve the problem. Thus, modernization theory explains global inequality in terms of technological and cultural differences among societies. The difficulty with this position, critics respond, is that developing world cities and countries simply are not evolving in the same way as other areas of the world. For one thing, the more-developed countries had declining rural population growth patterns as their cities grew. The long-term production of wealth in cities thus was able to catch up with population growth. This has not been the case in most contemporary developing world cities. As more and more people continue to swell their ranks, the low level of technology and economic growth has been unable to cope with the overload. Worse, the overload cannot be dispersed. Conditions in the overpopulated countryside are worse, and there are no frontier countries left to absorb the overflow. As a result, no matter what has been done, conditions in many nonindustrial cities have only gotten worse.

A second criticism of modernization theory is that nonindustrial areas of the world are making economic progress only very slowly. Meanwhile, the West continues to raise its standard of living by leaps and bounds. In other words, nonindustrial nations continue to fall further behind, despite modest gains. Another criticism is that this perspective suggests that the causes of global poverty lie mostly in the poor societies themselves; the critics insist that equal attention should be given to the behavior of rich nations and the impact of international relations (Wiarda, 1987, 1999).

Dependency Theory

A second interpretation of the world urban crisis suggests that full modernization will never occur in most nonindustrial cities and nations because Western nations are continuing to extract the valued products of such cities and nations. Without the technology or diversified industrial base to generate their own wealth internally, nonindustrial areas of the world have had no choice but to cater to the wants of Western nations; hence, they are dependent. For example, foreign investors and multinational corporations siphon off a large proportion of the profits generated in developing world economies, leaving the countries themselves with an insufficient supply of capital, technology, and skilled personnel. Consequently, most nations in these regions continue to rely heavily on exports of a small number of such commodities as oil, sugar, rubber, and cocoa. This has two results: (1) These nations remain dependent for their foreign earnings on goods whose prices are notoriously unstable; and (2) the overall terms of trade have moved against their interests, for while the price of raw commodities fluctuates both upward and downward, the prices of the manufactured products for which they are exchanged move in only one direction—up. As a result, much of Latin America is dependent on crucial economic and political decisions that are being made far

beyond its borders in cities such as London, New York, Washington, Paris, Moscow, and Tokyo. Thus, dependency theory explains global inequality in terms of the exploitation of poor societies by rich ones.

Immanuel Wallerstein (1974, 1979, 1983, 1984) sees global stratification as the still-continuing result of European colonization begun 500 years ago. To him, the world economy benefits rich societies (by generating profits) and harms the rest of the world (by perpetuating poverty). Evans and Timberlake (1980) studied 50 countries around the world and found that dependency was strongly associated with greater levels of income inequality. That is, dependent countries, when compared with other countries, tended to have a wider gap between the very rich and the very poor and to have fewer people in the middle income brackets. More important, Evans and Timberlake argue that greater modernization will not decrease this inequality; rather, it will exacerbate it. The few rich will get richer while the many poor get poorer. The poor cannot rise higher on the income ladder because (1) there are so many of them and (2) access to the well-paid jobs is strictly controlled by the elite. In a more complex set of findings, Jaffee (1985) found that while export dependence did stimulate economic growth, the growth was smallest when foreign investors controlled the local economy.

Although dependency theory informs us that the global economy does not allow any nation to develop (or fail to develop) in isolation, critics complain that it is too simplistic in blaming capitalism as the single cause of global inequality. Ethiopia, for example, is a poor country that has had little contact with rich nations, while Singapore, Hong Kong, South Korea, and Japan have prospered in their trade with rich countries (Vogel, 1991; Firebaugh, 1992). Moreover, factors inside a country contribute to their economic plight. Iran's brand of fundamentalist Islam, for example, discourages economic ties with other countries, and its economy stagnates. Corrupt and/or reckless leaders (Ferdinand Marcos, the Philippines; François Duvalier, Haiti;

Manuel Noriega, Panama; Mobutu Sese Seko, Congo; Saddam Hussein, Iraq) have impoverished their countries. Critics fault dependency theory as a vague call to world socialism and, given the failures of socialist societies in meeting the needs of their own people, ask why we should expect such a system to rescue the entire world from poverty.

Interventionist Theory

Nonindustrial cities, under any political system, continue to face the grim prospects of continuing overpopulation. It is this phenomenon that a third group of urbanists suggests is the root cause of the nonindustrial urban crisis. Without control of this problem, the modernization-versus-dependency and capitalism-versus-communism debates are moot.

Government intervention is one way to begin to stem the tide. First, governments could attack urban overgrowth directly by limiting population increases. They could provide free contraceptives and birth-control information, set a higher minimum age for legal marriage (thereby decreasing the number of fertile years for a couple), provide benefits for families or communities that show lower birth rates, reward voluntary sterilization, or even force sterilization. China, Singapore, and, to a lesser extent, India exemplify this approach.

A second possibility is that governments could support smaller cities, hence helping to solve the primate-city problem. Of course, this is difficult to do because the primate city is seen by virtually everyone in these countries as the place where the action is and where the opportunities are greatest (usually not a misplaced evaluation). Because of this, governments must actively establish or benefit smaller cities by governmental investment or by giving major breaks—through taxes or incomes—to industry or workers. Indonesia's transmigration program is a step in this direction.

Third, if such benign measures fail, more authoritarian policies could be instituted. Residence permits might be required of city dwellers, with new arrivals immediately deported back to the countryside or imprisoned. This would, however, demand strict record-keeping and

unbribable officials. (Both Jakarta and China have failed in their attempts along these lines.) Couples having more than a specified number of children could be denied social services, housing loans, or jobs in government. A policy like this has worked in Singapore but has not had much success elsewhere.

Finally, systematic planning for the whole society could be undertaken. Cities do not exist in isolation, and planning the entire settlement continuum—from rural area to village to small city to metropolis—could have substantial benefits. Colombia devised one such plan in 1973. Envisioning both continued population growth and urbanization, the plan called for the development of cities of between 30,000 and 200,000 people, emigration of the unemployed to selected zones for resettlement, and provision of agricultural credit and health, education, and recreation services in the countryside. Unfortunately, a change in government ended this plan. The failure to institute such a plan with a real possibility of solving urban overpopulation problems illustrates the great difficulty of curbing the current urban crisis: Ideas are one thing, but implementing them in a complex cultural, economic, and political setting is quite another (Turner, 1976:960).

All of these measures have their costs and benefits, considered simply in their own right; however, if one complicates the issues raised by considering them in a specific setting, the waters get much murkier. Can free contraceptive information ever be a viable possibility in Catholic Latin America? Can economically strapped governments effectively subsidize smaller cities? Will people take happily to enforced sterilization or mandated moves to the countryside? Recent experiments in India and China suggest that such policies have their limitations.

The City Is Not the Problem: Jane Jacobs's Theory

Many people, looking at the overgrowth of developing world cities and the suffering that is rampant within them, believe, like those just cited above, that the solution to the world's urban problems is to get city growth under control. But this is to miss the forest for the trees, argues urban economist Jane Jacobs (1984). The city is not the problem, according to Jacobs. On the contrary, the city has been, and continues to be, the most important generator of wealth in human history. Poverty is surely a serious world problem, but why consider dismantling or crippling the very thing that has shown itself capable, historically, of decreasing poverty?

The problem, suggests Jacobs, is not the basic idea of modernization, either. Modernization can work (we have lots of evidence of this), but only under certain conditions. Rather, the problem is dependency—but not merely the type that dependency theorists talk about. Dependency cripples a city only when the city is dependent on other cities much more complex and sophisticated than itself. Thus, while it is undesirable that weak cities in LDCs be dependent for trade on strong cities in MDCs (as most dependency theorists suggest), the institution of a socialist system is no panacea either, especially if it results in weaker socialist cities being forced into unequal trade arrangements with stronger socialist cities. That, too, is dependency, simply of another sort.

The key, Jacobs insists, is the relationship between trade and the process of urban development. History shows us that cities develop fastest when they trade with other cities that are like them in terms of needs, jobs, and wealth. Such cities pull themselves up by their bootstraps, because what one city needs, the other invents. Here is how Jacobs describes the process:

> What this means is that the trade among vigorously developing cities is volatile, continually changing in content as cities create new kinds of exports for one another, and then in due course repeatedly replace many of them. So it was with the development of the backward cities of Europe. They were forever producing new exports for one another—bells, dyes, buckles, parchment, lace, carding combs, needles, painted cabinetwork, ceramics, brushes, cutlery, paper, sieves and riddles, sweetmeats, elixirs,

> files, pitchforks, sextants—replacing them . . . [and] becoming customers for still more innovations. . . . They [became] exceptionally good markets for innovations because they [could] afford them. . . . They were developing on one another's shoulders. (1984:144)

In other words, the great problem with developing world urban development now is that most cities in less-developed countries trade with cities that are much more complex and wealthy than themselves. They can only give to those cities raw materials or cheap labor or cheaply made goods. In return, they buy from those more sophisticated cities goods they cannot afford—like televisions, John Deere tractors, computers—and get themselves ever deeper into debt and dependency. To solve the problem, Jacobs suggests that such underdeveloped cities give up such trade arrangements, realize that the road to modernization cannot be instantaneous, and set about building themselves up, step by step, with vigorous trade with cities like themselves. If they do not do so, such cities will continue to languish in the shadow of the developed cities for the indefinite future.

If Jacobs's thesis is plausible, is the action she suggests likely? Are developing world cities likely to give up their dreams of being like their more materially developed cousins, especially if that means giving up the symbols of that development—the most modern and sophisticated technologies and machinery and fashions? Visitors to the developing world find one attitude characteristic of most of the peoples: their desire to be like the people of more affluent countries. They want modernization and they want it as soon as possible. The imported movies and TV programs have done their job only too well. The allure is too great, the neon of those "fancier" cities is too bright, the lifestyles of the rich and famous who live in those cities are too captivating. So it is likely that, right or wrong, Jacobs's pleas will fall on deaf ears, at least for the present.

However, we need to make one final observation. It is unlikely that developing world cities will eventually become just like their European or North American counterparts.

While some westernization is evident, they will never simply mirror cities elsewhere; rather, they will continue to absorb and transform Western urban characteristics according to their own cultural traditions. If this prediction is correct, we may expect that developing world cities of the future will remain a fusion of many cultural and historical forces.

CONCLUSION

Thus we come, at the end of this overview of global urbanization, to no single solution to the problems we have encountered. Scholars themselves are divided about the causes and the most efficient solutions.

One conclusion, however, seems certain. Whatever is done, most cities of the developing world are going to continue to grow at enormous rates for the foreseeable future. With this growth will come, inevitably, greater problems, including congestion, pollution, and major shortages of basic necessities. As each country copes with its crises, perhaps one, or a combination of two or more, of the solutions we have discussed will emerge as clearly superior, thereby lightening the load on other overburdened cities some decades hence.

It is no small task. Millions of poor people in less-developed countries are unable to advance greatly because, given the ever-increasing population, there simply will not be enough jobs, houses, or health services to go around. The evolution of developing world cities thus provides a marked contrast to that of European and North American cities. Perhaps the most remarkable aspect has been the speed at which their modern development has taken place—in decades compared with more than a century in Canada and the United States. So-called *overurbanization* in the developing world may well get a good deal worse before it gets better.

The evolving cities throughout the developing world each have their own complex cultural traditions and unique histories. Previously we discussed how Herbert Gans stressed the primacy of culture over space in detailing the variety of lifestyles *within* a city (Chapter 10), and how cultural values shape a city's physical and social form (Chapter 8). In this chapter we saw how cities throughout the developing world may share some common legacies and problems, but are also different in many ways from one place to another. The expanding global economy and telecommunications networks will link these cities more closely to one another than ever before, but they will also evolve through varied patterns of development, each nation's cities with its own distinct characteristics.

CHAPTER 14

PLANNING THE URBAN ENVIRONMENT

As we have seen, cities do not always work well. Occasionally a city may approach its potential as a "pinnacle of human civilization" (some historians say this about Hellenic Athens, for example), but, typically, cities struggle with various problems like those detailed in the last four chapters.

In this chapter we will introduce the work of individuals who responded to the shortcomings of cities with bold and provocative plans for improvement. Some tackled urban problems at the neighborhood level; others imagined radically transforming the entire city—or even society as a whole.

As anyone would expect, such plans have been controversial, frequently challenging cherished cultural beliefs or clashing with vested economic interests. However, only by giving these ideas serious consideration can we keep all the possibilities alive in the urban debate.

VISIONS

And when all the world came back
And the light crept up between the shutters
And you heard the sparrows in the gutters,
You had such a vision of the street
As the street hardly understands

> *T. S. Eliot, Preludes**

In the late 1800s, what a vision Ebenezer Howard had! Deeply influenced by Edward Bellamy's novel *Looking Backward* (a utopian vision of the year 2000 in which all the problems of the city have been solved), Howard dedicated his life to realizing Bellamy's goal in Britain. As Howard saw it, the industrial city was a virtual nightmare: People streamed to these overcrowded cities, leading only to misery and despair.

Howard conceded that the city had advantages—opportunity, entertainment, diversity—but he asked why cities should deny people the best of the country—a healthful environment, low densities, and a sense of freedom. Thus, Howard set out to solve this

dilemma by creating what he called the "Garden Cities of To-morrow." In 1898, he wrote:

> The two magnets must be made one. As man and woman by their varied gifts and faculties supplement each other, so should town and country. The town is the symbol of society—of mutual help and friendly co-operation, of fatherhood, motherhood, brotherhood, sisterhood, of wide relations. . . . The country is the symbol of God's love and care. . . . All that we are and all that we have comes from it. Our bodies are formed of it; to it they return. We are fed by it, clothed by it, and by it we are warmed and sheltered. . . . It is the source of all health, all wealth, all knowledge. . . . Town and country must be married, and out of this joyous union will spring a new hope, a new life, a new civilization. (1898; 1965:48)

Celebrating the "marriage of town and country," Howard worked out the details of his Garden Cities plan and hoped to convince others that realizing his plan was not only desirable but entirely possible. The specific outline of his vision is illustrated in Figure 14–1 and described in the Critical Thinking box on page 414.

Unfortunately, Howard's vision was, as T. S. Eliot's poem suggests, a vision that the street of his day could not understand. It struck conservatives as outlandish and liberals as too complex. Said the ultraliberal *Fabian News*:

> Mr. Howard proposes to pull [our cities] all down and substitute garden cities, each duly built according to pretty colored plans, nicely designed with a ruler and compass. . . . We have got to make the best of our existing cities, and proposals for building new ones are about as useful as would be arrangements for protection against visits from Mr. [H. G.] Wells' Martians [a reference to Wells's novel *The War of the Worlds*, which depicts a Martian invasion of earth]. (quoted in Osborn, 1965:11)

Undaunted, Howard pushed on. In 1903, in conjunction with a group of businessmen, he established his first garden city, Letchworth, about 35 miles from London. A second city, Welwyn (pronounced "well-en"), sprang up nearer London in 1919. On balance, both

*From T. S. Eliot, *Preludes*, published by Faber & Faber. Reprinted by permission of Faber & Faber.

were quite successful. Still, until the 1940s, they remained Britain's only attempts at "planned" towns.

The entire history of urban planning is in many ways evident in the story of Howard's new towns. As the *Fabian News* noted, to alter established cities would be a massive, expensive, and disruptive undertaking. Cities are not only bricks and mortar, they are people's lives, and rest on historical traditions, entrenched power relationships, and vested economic interests. No one should be surprised that plans for urban redesign have typically been greeted with suspicion. Moreover, given the consequences of *bad* city planning, this is not a task to be undertaken lightly.

CITY PLANNING IN WORLD HISTORY

Ebenezer Howard was hardly the first to undertake urban planning on a large scale. Moenjo-Daro, the Indus River Valley civilization of 2500 B.C.E. discussed in Chapter 2, had streets laid out in a grid pattern, broad thoroughfares, and individual houses designed for comfort and efficiency. Even more impressive were the Mexican cities of Teotihuacan around 700 C.E. and Tenochtitlan around 1500 C.E. Both capitals were large and richly symbolic. Expansive plazas, massive temples, and elaborate gardens were central features of these cities. Finally, recall the case study in Chapter 8, where we discussed the tightly controlled plan of Ming Dynasty Peking. Here we saw planned city within planned city, all connected to convey key themes of China's culture.

Western cities too show a long history of planning. The Greeks planned Hellenic Athens, just as the Romans planned much of the pomp and majesty of Imperial Rome. Even towns of the Middle Ages show some planning, especially in the walls built for protection as well as in the various "zones" set aside for specific activities. There were planned markets, squares, residential quarters, and, always, the medieval church at the city's center. Still later, during the Renaissance, there arose a veritable boom in urban planning, with careful efforts

to achieve efficient traffic circulation and also to provide fortification against invasion. It was at this time that planners designed the radial boulevards of Paris—roadways as beautiful as they are practical.

Why Plan?

Early city planners sought, first, to solve specific urban problems. They planned underground sewage lines for health reasons, walls for protection, parks for leisure hours, and thoroughfares to facilitate movement.

Second, we know that the motives of city planners in Rome, Teotihuacan, Tenochtitlan, and Beijing were also to glorify those in power. Thus, the Emperor Augustus and his successors, declared gods by the Roman Senate in the first few decades of the Christian era, were "immortalized" by buildings, parks, plazas, and innumerable statues. City planners had a good reason to glorify the ruling elite: These people, after all, employed them. City planning, in short, often proceeds "from the top down." To ask "Why plan?" then, we also need to keep in mind another question: "For whom are cities planned?"

A third focus of urban planning is often the glorification of important cultural values. Ming Peking was not only a monument to the all-powerful emperor, but a reminder to everyone of beliefs central to the Chinese way of life. Centuries later, during the Renaissance, the residency of the pope was reestablished in Rome. To showcase the Church as the wealthiest and most important institution in the Western world, Pope Julius decided to replace the old St. Peter's Basilica with the greatest cathedral and piazza in Christendom. The result was the large, grand Piazza of St. Peter. A long processional way leads the visitor to a massive circular area before the cathedral, which leads to the cathedral itself. The faithful find a powerful religious experience in this setting; everyone is awed by the size and magnificent design of St. Peter's. Both reactions were important to the piazza's designers.

Something different is symbolized in Figure 14–2, showing Sir Christopher Wren's

CRITICAL THINKING

Sir Ebenezer Howard's Garden Cities of To-Morrow

Howard's Garden City was to cover about 1,000 acres at the center of a 6,000-acre tract. Figure 14–1 shows the idealized layout of the whole municipal area.

Six magnificent boulevards—each 120 feet wide—traverse the city from centre to circumference, dividing it into six equal parts or wards. In the centre is a circular space containing about five and a half acres, laid out as a beautiful and well-watered garden; and, surrounding this garden, each . . . in its own ample grounds, are the larger public buildings—town hall, principal concert and lecture hall, theatre, library, museum, picture-gallery, and hospital.

The rest of the large space encircled by the "Crystal Palace" is a public park, containing 145 acres, which includes ample recreation grounds within very easy access of all the people. Running all round the Central Park (except where it is intersected by the boulevards) is a wide glass arcade called the "Crystal Palace," opening on to the park. Here manufactured goods are exposed for sale, and here most of that class of shopping which requires the joy of deliberation and selection is done. The space enclosed by the Crystal Palace is, however, a good deal larger than is required for those purposes, and a considerable part of it is used as a Winter Garden—the whole forming a permanent exhibition of a most attractive character, whilst its circular form brings it near to every dweller in the town—the furthest removed inhabitant being within 600 yards.

Passing out of the Crystal Palace on our way to the outer ring of the town, we cross Fifth Avenue—lined, as are all the roads of the town, with trees—fronting which, and looking on to the Crystal Palace, we find a ring of very excellently built houses, each standing in its own ample grounds; and, as we continue our walk, we observe that the houses are for the most part built either in concentric rings, facing the various avenues (as the circular roads are termed), or fronting the boulevards and roads which all converge to the centre of the town. . . . [T]he population of this little city may be . . . about 30,000 in the city itself, and about 2,000 in the agricultural estate. . . .

On the outer ring of the town are factories, warehouses, dairies, markets, coal yards, timber yards, etc., all fronting on the circle railway, which encompasses the whole town, and which has sidings connecting it with a main line of railway which passes through the estate. This arrangement enables goods to be loaded direct into trucks from the warehouses and workshops, and so sent by railway to distant markets, or to be taken direct from the trucks into the warehouses or factories; thus not only effecting a very great saving in regard to packing and cartage, and reducing to a minimum loss from breakage, but also, by reducing the traffic on the roads of the town,

plan for the rebuilding of London after the Great Fire of 1666 (see the Chapter 2 case study). Here, although the magnificent St. Paul's Cathedral (B) is a dominant focus, all roads lead not to the cathedral but to the city's stock exchange (A). The dominant feature of the plan (which ultimately was not adopted) was the financial and trade element of the city's life. London at the time was fast becoming the most powerful economic center in the world. City planning thus reflected this change.

Three concerns, then, appear again and again in the history of urban design. People plan their cities, or parts of them, (1) to solve specific problems, (2) to serve the interests of

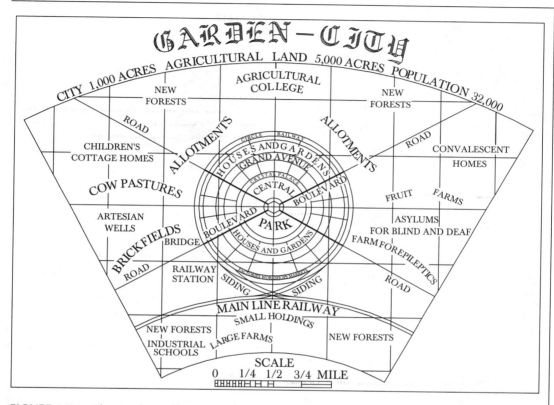

FIGURE 14–1   The Garden Belt and Rural Belt

Source: Ebenezer Howard, *Garden Cities of To-Morrow* (Cambridge, MA: MIT Press, 1965), p. 52.
Reprinted by permission of MIT Press.

lessening to a very marked extent the cost of their maintenance. The smoke fiend is kept well within bounds in Garden City; for all machinery is driven by electric energy, with the result that the cost of electricity for lighting and other purposes is greatly reduced.

Source: Ebenezer Howard, *Garden Cities of To-Morrow* (Cambridge, MA: MIT Press, 1965), pp. 50–56.

those with wealth and power, and (3) to reflect and intensify cultural ideals.

Planning in the Industrial Era: 1800–1900

Ebenezer Howard shared many concerns about the overcrowded industrial cities with the classical sociological theorists—Tönnies, Durkheim, Weber, Marx, Simmel, Park, and Wirth—whom we discussed in Chapter 5. Howard saw little hope for the industrial city, which he believed was a monument to greed and to the interests of the few rather than the many. Effective city planning, he believed, could never exist in cities of such size.

E

A. Stock Exchange
B. St. Paul's Cathedral
C. Tower of London
D. London Bridge
E. Old Walls

B

A

C
×

THAMES RIVER
D

FIGURE 14–2   Sir Christopher Wren's Plan for the Rebuilding of London, 1666
Source: Arthur B. Gallion and Simon Eisner, *The Urban Pattern,* 4th ed. (New York: Van Nostrand, 1980), p. 43.
Reprinted by permission of Van Nostrand Reinhold.

In many ways, he was right. Planning on a citywide scale did not exist in early cities. While quite a few industrial towns were built during the 1800s—Manchester and Birmingham in England and Paterson, New Jersey, in the United States (see Chapter 3) are good examples—by and large the underlying concern was limited to profit and efficiency.

Back in the early 1600s when the Dutch settled New Amsterdam at the tip of Manhattan Island, street development evolved more or less haphazardly, as in medieval European cities. But as the city expanded northward two centuries later, city leaders in 1807 adopted a rigid gridiron plan that they applied to the entire island regardless of topography. Profit and efficiency carried the day: "Straight-edged and right-angled houses," reported the city commission, when adopting the gridiron plan, "are the most cheap to build and the most convenient to live in" (Eisner, Gallion and Eisner, 1993:49).

In the new trade-dominated city, tradition counted for little. Buildings went up only to be torn down as commercial interests dictated. Builders adopted architectural styles, such as Greek facades, "for show," and not for their deeper symbolism of a revered historic tradition (Goldberger, 1979:xiv). With the major

(and wonderful) exception of Central Park, the profit motive fundamentally shaped all of New York. The Boston Commons park in midtown Boston is another notable exception.

The "City Beautiful" Movement

In the United States, some architects, planners, and civic leaders had other ideas. The first significant innovation in U.S. city planning grew out of the 1893 Chicago World's Fair, which showcased architect Daniel Burnham's "White City" (a vision opposing grimy, sooty industrial cities). Burnham proposed a city built around monumental civic centers, with careful zoning and active citizen participation groups. Inspiring a "City Beautiful" movement, Burnham's ideas had considerable influence among urban planners across the country. Chicago, Cleveland, Detroit, Los Angeles, Minneapolis, St. Louis, San Francisco, and Washington all initiated City Beautiful projects after the fair.

Yet the costs of this movement soon led even advocates to scale back their plans. Moreover, some private interests, especially businesses, resisted compromising their narrow objectives. Before long, the City Beautiful movement simply went away.

"TILL WE HAVE BUILT JERUSALEM": THE NEW TOWNS MOVEMENT

I will not cease from mental strife,
Nor shall my sword sleep in my hand,
Till we have built Jerusalem
In England's green and pleasant land

William Blake

This stanza from the great English poet and artist William Blake opens Sir Ebenezer Howard's book *Garden Cities of To-Morrow.* Howard's belief that his New Town movement would solve all of urban society's ills influenced many others both in and beyond his native England.

A Socialist–Feminist New Town

Howard greatly influenced Alice Constance Austin, an upper-class radical from Santa Barbara, California. Convinced that women were greatly oppressed, Austin proposed in the early 1900s a series of new towns based on communal living and kitchenless houses. Only a "Socialist City," she maintained, could relieve women "of the thankless and unending drudgery of an inconceivably stupid and inefficient system, by which her labors are confiscated. . . ." (1935:63).

With help from coinvestors, Austin founded her new town, Llano del Rio, in California. But, like Howard, she soon found that such a venture was fraught with difficulties. After a brief tenure, the Llano group folded in 1917. Although they later resettled in New Llano, Louisiana, Austin's Socialist City movement never attained further success (Hayden, 1978:286–87).

Later New Towns in Great Britain

The devastation of London during World War II created a desperate housing shortage and renewed interest in Ebenezer Howard's vision. In 1946, Britain passed the New Towns Act, providing for government sponsorship of new urban communities to draw population away from London and other cities. New communities—complete with industrial, housing, and commercial areas—were built at some distance from larger cities.

Another central goal of the New Towns Act was to limit London's increasing sprawl by surrounding the city with a "green belt"—an idea taken directly from Howard. The new towns were to be built beyond the green belt.

In all, Great Britain built 34 new towns, their success in large measure assured because of deep government involvement. The first group of new communities—called the Mark I towns—adhered closely to Howard's ideas and were modeled after Letchworth and Welwyn. Mostly single-family houses organized in neighborhoods, these communities of about 30,000 residents each were completely self-sufficient centers of industry, housing, education, and transportation facilities.

A second wave of new towns—the Mark II group—was begun in the 1950s and 1960s and deviated rather significantly from Howard's original plan. Typified by Cumbernault, outside Glasgow, Scotland, these towns reflected the government's concern that small cities of just 30,000 would do little in the long run to alleviate population problems in the larger cities. A second concern was that too many small towns would eat up too much of what Britain had too little of—land. Thus, the Mark II towns, with population projections of 80,000, began to sacrifice greenery for density and to emphasize central (rather than neighborhood) shopping and recreational facilities. The most recent new towns are larger still. One example, Milton Keynes, lies west of London with a population of about 207,000 living in its 120 square miles, and it is expected to grow to 232,000 by 2006.

Britain's new towns, Howard's "marriage of the city and country," proved eminently successful at providing decent housing and sufficient jobs. On other levels, however, the new towns fell short. With their small number (34) and limited size, they have not had much

This aerial view of a London suburb reveals a lifestyle unlike that found in typical North American suburbs. This is high-density and contains mostly multiple-family dwellings, not single-family homes. It reflects part of a comprehensive plan for roads, housing, schools, and stores in keeping with the new towns concept.

impact on the large populations of Britain's large cities. Moreover, most of these towns are socially rather cliquish, with the same ethnic and class prejudices encountered in most large cities. Some critics claim that homogeneity is a product of the planning process itself, with its emphasis on neighborhoods. As sociologists often note, ingroup solidarity (which neighborhood living facilitates) often creates a corresponding sense of outgroup hostility.

Another problem has been the inflexibility of many of the new-town plans. Rather than

recognizing that cities are dynamic entities that must adjust to changing human needs, many new towns have stuck rigidly to their original plans. The result often has been a sense of inefficiency and even oppression that, as we will see, crops up again and again in city planning efforts.

New Towns in Western Europe, Australia, and Brazil

To some degree, early British new towns were anti-city. They were small towns, their limited size suggesting a distinct dislike of large urban areas. They were also anti-growth, strictly limiting population in the belief that more was always less. Bigness was equated with disorder and the destruction of a delicate ecological balance between people and the environment. Several more recent new towns, however, take a very opposite view. In Holland, Spain, and France, new-town development attempts to stimulate the growth of an entire urban region. Creating jobs around a cluster of industries, communities attempt to draw population from the countryside, while also luring away people from nearby established cities. After 1965, for example, France developed several new towns near Paris —including Marne-la-Vallée, Saint-Quentin-en-Yvelines, Melun-Sénart, and Evry—in an effort to collect the population in the immediate area and lessen migration into Paris itself.

Sweden

The Scandinavian countries, particularly Sweden, look on new towns as a form of "suburb-control." Stockholm, like many European and North American cities, had a problem with suburban sprawl in the 1950s. In an effort to curb decentralization, the Swedish government planned a series of satellite cities linked to the central city and to each other by efficient transportation. The five cities, known as the Vallingby Complex, are distinct entities but look to the larger city for goods, many services, and jobs. Each city has approximately 10,000 people living in low-density housing within 300 yards of a subway-station/plaza complex.

As in Britain, the Swedes also built higher-density new towns. Instead of low-rise brick buildings that promote a sense of community and allow open space, the newer towns contain physically parallel rows of unattractive, look-alike, concrete-slab buildings of six to eight stories. These drab structures look much like sterile, low-income housing projects in the United States. Not surprisingly, these developments repel the middle class; only impoverished immigrants or low-income natives concentrate in them. Such places can also be found in France, Germany, and Italy, and there, as well as in Sweden, crime, drugs, and welfare dependency are common.

Australia

Australia presents us with a different new town, one designed to be the core of a new urban region and home to the national government. Located in the outback (isolated rural area), Canberra is some 180 miles from the seacoast metropolis of Sydney. Settled as early as 1912, Canberra was to be a new, inland city that would not only house the Australian government but would also develop the Australian hinterland (Robinson, 1975). This was no simple task. Canberra was far from Australia's normal trade routes and had no major resources (mineral deposits or cheap water power) to attract investors. Thus, government and planners were in complete control, which might well have pleased Ebenezer Howard.

The result is a physically beautiful city with a population now exceeding 353,000. Economically, however, the city has suffered because of its off-track location, unavoidable overreliance on a single activity (government services), and the implementation of relatively rigid plans that often put off businesspeople. For example, the government retains control of all land, so that businesses do not cluster near the center, but are scattered throughout the city—a pattern that many find inefficient.

Canberra's widely dispersed single-family dwellings have also hindered the development of a sense of community. Similarly, the city's dependence on one major employer—the government—essentially created an upper- and middle-class city. Because of the high cost of living, most low-income families simply cannot afford to live there.

Brazil

Brasilia, the inland capital of Brazil, presents a contrasting case. Conceived in the 1950s as a showcase for a modernizing Brazil, the city is about 600 miles from the coastal megalopolis of Rio de Janeiro. As with Canberra, Brasilia's location helped develop the nation's interior, with the intent of siphoning off population from the country's older cities.

An artificial lake surrounds much of the city and separates it from the suburban towns to the north. The cross-shaped plan of the central city, designed by the Brazilian architect Lúcio Costa, utilizes the North–South Axis, Brasilia's main transportation artery, and the East–West, or Monumental, Axis, lined by federal and civic buildings.

With just 12,000 people in 1957, Brasilia grew to more than 500,000 by 1970 and surpassed two million by 2000. Expanding faster than anticipated as people streamed into the city looking for construction jobs, Brasilia abandoned or modified many parts of the original plan. As elsewhere in poor nations, migrants unable to find adequate housing constructed their own out of anything they could find. Thus Brasilia evolved huge *favelas* or squatter shantytowns filled with working-class and poverty-stricken people and lacking waste removal, water, and electricity. Ironically, then, this "model" Brazilian city reflects all the problems that beset other Latin American cities.

All the new towns and cities considered so far were government sponsored, with limited involvement of private investors. The opposite was true in the United States. Except for one program in the 1930s, U.S. new towns are distinguished by their nearly complete dependency on the investments, plans, and ideals of private businesses.

New Towns in the United States

We begin with the exceptions to the rule. Only three government-built new towns exist, all with their origins in the Great Depression of the 1930s, when millions of Americans were out of work.

In 1935, President Franklin Delano Roosevelt signed the Emergency Relief Appropriation Act and the National Industrial Recovery Act. One of the provisions of these acts was a federally sponsored project called "Greenbelt Towns." As its name implies, the project was deeply influenced by Ebenezer Howard. Its stated objectives:

1. To give useful work to men on unemployment relief;
2. To demonstrate in practice the soundness of planning and operating towns according to certain garden city principles;
3. To provide low-rent housing in healthful surroundings, both physical and social, for families in the low-income bracket. (Stein, 1957:119)

The three towns constructed as part of the project were Greenbelt, Maryland (13 miles northeast of Washington, D.C.), Greendale, Wisconsin (7 miles from Milwaukee), and Green Hills, Ohio (5 miles north of Cincinnati). Planners had high hopes that these towns would help to solve big-city problems and create the jobs needed to help end the Depression.

But the hopes faded. Unlike new towns in Great Britain, these settlements never attracted their own industry. Built before the age of superhighways, they simply did not provide enough economic incentive for major industry to relocate there. Then, too, soon after the towns were started, World War II intervened, diverting funding to military objectives. And by the time the war was over, the Cold War was upon us, leading many to charge that government-sponsored towns smacked of "communism." By 1949, government began selling off

the new towns to private interests. The Greenbelt Towns became, and remain, more like suburbs of the large cities nearby than like the independent small cities they were envisioned to be.

Nevertheless, private developers have founded more than 100 new urban environments (Michelson, 1977). Among them are Baldwin Hills Village near Los Angeles (1941); Park Forest (1947) and Park Forest South (1968) near Chicago; Jonathan, Minnesota (1969); St. Charles, Maryland (1970); and Soul City, North Carolina (1972). But by far the most well-known U.S. new towns are Radburn, New Jersey (1928); Reston, Virginia (1962); and Columbia, Maryland (1963).

Radburn   Developed by architect and planner Clarence Stein (see his classic *Toward New Towns for America* published in 1957), Radburn—about 20 miles west of New York City—was a direct attempt to adapt Ebenezer Howard's garden city to the United States. Radburn is laid out using what Stein called "superblocks," each surrounded by a green space. Radburn also attempted to completely separate pedestrian and automobile traffic. Stein and cofounder Henry Wright planned access roads only for service purposes and built houses facing the inner green areas. In 1929 Geddes Smith described Radburn as follows:

> [It is a] town built to live in—today and tomorrow. A town "for the motor age." A town turned outside-in—without any backdoors. A town where roads and parks fit together like the fingers of your right and left hands. A town in which children need never dodge motor-trucks on their way to school. (as quoted in Stein, 1957:44)

Like so many new towns, however, Radburn ran into financial difficulties as the years passed and was never completed as originally planned. About 670 families live in Radburn today, creating a population of about 3,100 within the New Jersey borough of Fair Lawn. Reston and Columbia, on the other hand, both near Washington, D.C., overcame economic crises to achieve moderate success as separate entities.

Reston Twenty-five miles from downtown Washington, in suburban Virginia, Reston is the brainchild of developer Robert E. Simon, with a name made from his initials. He planned his "quality urban environment" around two town centers linking seven villages of approximately 10,000 residents each in a beautiful, contemporary design replete with trees, lakes, and pathways. He intended Reston to be economically self-sufficient and diverse, with mixed-income housing (high-rise luxury apartments side by side with single-family homes). Now owned by Westbrook Communities, Reston is home to 2,000 businesses and about 57,000 residents, about 9 percent of whom are black and 10 percent Asian. However, Reston has become mostly an affluent community, with a median family income exceeding $80,000. Its housing includes single-family homes, townhouses, condominiums, waterfront homes, homes on the golf courses, and homes that back up to woods and nature paths. The price of some homes is over $1 million. One of Reston's main focal points is Town Center, which includes high-rise offices, a Hyatt Regency hotel, boutiques, national retailers, and restaurants. Town Center has a covered outdoor ice-skating rink that doubles as a concert and events shelter during the rest of the year (Reston, 2002).

Columbia Columbia, Maryland, was also designed as a money-maker. James Rouse, the town's developer, intended "to create a social and physical environment which works for people and nourishes human growth and to allow private venture capital to make a profit in land development and sale" (as quoted in J. Bailey, 1973:16). To apply the best thinking available to the execution of his city, Rouse employed a host of specialists in the planning phase, including government employees, family counselors, recreationalists, sociologists, economists, educators, health specialists, psychologists, and transportation and communications experts.

Larger than Reston, with current population exceeding 88,000, Columbia does have low-to-moderate-income housing. A racially integrated community (one-fifth of its residents are African American), Columbia successfully scattered its several hundred subsidized units throughout the city. Covering over 14,000 acres with a planned population total of 110,000, the new town is composed of communities of 800 to 900 homes, each with its own elementary school, neighborhood center and convenience store, swimming pool and recreational facilities. The plan then groups four neighborhoods into villages (of which there are nine), each with a middle school, meeting hall, supermarket, and some other shops clustered around a small plaza. In the town center are office buildings, large department stores, and a larger shopping center. Enhancing the town in its variety of programs is Howard Community College. Columbia has 5,300 acres of permanent open space, including 144 tot lots (children's playgrounds), 227 pedestrian bridges, the 40-acre Symphony Woods, three lakes, 19 ponds, and natural open space areas interlaced with more than 78 miles of pathways for walking, biking, and jogging. There is also a vast network of plazas, picnic areas, public areas, tennis courts, and two par-course fitness trails.

Irvine Also begun in the 1960s, Southern California's Irvine is the largest planned community in North America, set on 47 square miles, and is headquarters for more than 100 major corporations. It is also home to a 15,000-acre campus of the University of California. An upper-middle-class city, with a city population exceeding 156,000, its average household income in 2000 was $62,469. Its racial–ethnic breakdown is 57 percent white, 1 percent African American, 30 percent Asian American, and 7 percent Hispanic (Irvine, 2002).

Celebration A new project is the Walt Disney town of Celebration in central Florida, near Walt Disney World Resort. Planned through the collaboration of nine of the nation's leading architects, this community is the most visible example of the New Urbanism (see Chapter 12). Celebration, say Disney officials, will be "sustainable and holistic," demonstrating that development can be responsive to environmental issues. It will be a normal community, not an exclusive, gated enclave.

Disney began the project by building the downtown—a lively mix of retail shops, restaurants, offices and apartments, town hall, post office, grocery store, and cinema—situated along a wide promenade circling the lake in the center of town. Most notable is the Art Deco–style movie complex and a cylindrical post office. In late 2002, more than 6,000 people called Celebration their home, with an eventual total population planned to reach approximately 12,000. Homes are designed in six varying architectural styles: Victorian, Classical, Colonial Revival, Coastal, Mediterranean, and French. Oversized porches and verandas encourage old-time neighborhood socializing, and the community is surrounded by a 4,700-acre protected greenbelt with miles of walking paths.

The tallest point in Celebration neighborhoods will not exceed three stories. There is a model school, kindergarten through twelfth grade, run by the county school system but with the best equipment that a $9 million cash boost from Disney can buy. There is a 60-acre "health campus"—a cross between a full-service gym and a hospital—where people can keep in shape downstairs to avoid the medical wards upstairs. Unlike the average "designer suburb," where all the houses carry a similar price tag, Celebration's $1 million estates will coexist with $170,000 terrace homes as well as with a sizable number of rental apartments, to form a social mix not seen in the United States since small towns went out of style.

Celebration is clearly an attempt to return to the pedestrian-friendly, compactly built town of the past, as compared with what the New Urbanists describe as the car-dominated suburban sprawl of freeways, malls, and widely dispersed single-family homes. Admired by many, Celebration also receives criticism from others who call it a retreat to a dreamworld of

the past that only appeals to a small segment of the population.

Failure Elsewhere   Encouraged by the partial success of Columbia and Reston, in 1970 the federal government instituted the New Communities Program, directing money toward building 13 more new towns. The program was a near disaster. It was reduced to a salvage operation by 1974 and completely shut down in 1983, when 12 of the 13 communities were unable to meet their financial obligations (Rodwin and Evans, 1981). Except for Irvine and Celebration, the new-town movement in the United States is now all but dead. Why has such an appealing idea fared so poorly? To find out, we need to critically review the major goals of the global new-town movement.

Have They Worked?: Criticisms of New Towns

Many new towns have been built worldwide since Ebenezer Howard sounded the clarion call in 1898. Yet just a few (particularly in Europe) have been successful; most have not. Why?

One major goal of most new towns was to spread population more broadly. Howard and his followers viewed big cities as destructive of human well-being. Congestion bred inefficiency and anonymity, they argued, and a city's economic dominance sapped vitality from the rest of the region.

Critics point out that new towns really haven't done much along these lines. Even in Britain, after decades of new-town development, barely 1 percent of the population lives in them. It is doubtful that governments could raise the tax money needed to build new towns on a much larger scale. And even if they could, there is little reason to think that a large share of any country's population would want to live in one. A better idea may be the improvement of already-existing center-city housing (Alonso, 1970).

New towns were also to be centers of employment and economic activity. But here

Celebration, Florida, is a planned community that is anticipated to have about 12,000 residents on 4,900 acres surrounded by a 4,700-acre protected greenbelt. Designed as a pedestrian-friendly place to live, work, and play, the new town has a lake adjacent to its traditional retail and business district, a 109-acre office park, miles of walking paths and nature trails, village parks and recreational areas, and an 18-hole public golf course.

Source: Used by permission from the Celebration Company © Disney Enterprises, Inc.

again, few of them attracted much industry or other business. The problem is largely economic: At a distance from major cities, new towns present businesses with added costs for materials and transportation. Thus, especially in North America, new towns have ended up with a strong suburban flavor—bedroom communities for people who, by and large, work elsewhere.

The collapse of the U.S. New Communities Program of 1970 reflected these issues. First, the costs of building new towns are enormous, and years go by before any profits are returned. Second, government never made more than a halfhearted commitment to such programs. New towns are the dream of a few—some city planners, a few public officials, architects, builders, mayors. But others think these efforts could be more effectively placed elsewhere—in inner-city development,

for example, or in the elimination of slum housing. The overall result is that the New Communities Program is dead in the United States, and there is little likelihood that any such program will take its place in the foreseeable future.

This is not to ignore the many contributions of the new-town idea. As sociologist Roland Warren writes of Columbia's developer, James Rouse: "One can but laud . . . the broad social concern and purpose shown by the developer . . . in undertaking a project of this economic magnitude and social audacity and with the degree of human concern that went into it from the onset" (1978:165). We might also direct such tribute to Ebenezer Howard, who aspired to so much in his new towns vision. Nevertheless, no one yet has built "Jerusalem." Moreover, as Albert J. Robinson (1975:141) says bluntly: "The new town is not the panacea for all urban problems." There are other visions to consider.

UTOPIA UNLIMITED: ARCHITECTURAL VISIONS

The possible will be attempted only because we
have postulated the impossible.

Goethe

An irony marks Ebenezer Howard's ambition—to change all of society through building cities that were very small. Some visionaries argue that solving the city's problems demands not outlying new towns, but completely new *central cities*—more efficient, more humane, and for *everybody*. Here we examine three large-scale "visions of the street." Each is the work of an architect; each is refreshingly different.

Le Corbusier: The Radiant City

Among the most important figures of modern architecture, Le Corbusier was also an influential urban planner. In his books *The City of Tomorrow* (1922) and *The Radiant City* (1933), Le Corbusier, like Howard, condemned modern cities and outlined a vision of a new urban society. But his solution was the very opposite of Howard's. Rejecting widespread decentralization, Le Corbusier saw obvious benefits to concentrating people in tall, architecturally magnificent buildings surrounded by huge open spaces. Such mammoth structures, Le Corbusier reasoned, allowed keeping 95 percent of available land free from any building at all. Le Corbusier's plan for a "Contemporary City" is shown in Figure 14–3.

A second innovation was doing away with the typical Western city's central concentration "by substituting virtually equal densities all over the city. This would reduce the pressure on central business districts, which would in effect disappear. Flows of people would become much more even across the whole city, instead of strong radical flows into and out of

the center which characterize cities today" (Hall, 1975:75).

Decentralization with density, concentrated living and open space, administrative efficiency and spontaneity, organization and individuality—many such oppositions are intentionally built into Le Corbusier's work. To him, the city should be a place where human paradoxes could be explored and exploited.

Although no such urban utopia was ever built, Le Corbusier's influence on city planning was great. One classic example is the Alton West estate in Roehampton in southwest London, built after World War II. A second example of a Le Corbusier–influenced project is Manhattan's Stuyvesant Town. Red brick buildings stand between wide walkways and lawns in this parklike setting constructed in 1947. Although Stuyvesant Town has been controversial because of its isolation from the surrounding neighborhood, architecture critic Paul Goldberger (1979) believes that its successes outweigh its problems. Still, Goldberger concedes that the satisfaction felt by residents may be as much a function of their comfortable income as it is of the project itself.

Le Corbusier expressed his vision to its fullest extent in his 1953 design of Chandigarh, India, which calls itself "the city beautiful." Structurally, Chandigarh is a very modern city, with a population of some 810,000. Each of the city's 49 sectors is a block about one square kilometer in size with markets, shopping centers, and schools to limit people's need to travel. Citywide transportation (buses, auto-rickshaws, and taxicabs) links the sectors. Chandigarh is best known for its outstanding modern and folk architecture. The State Library, Super Market, Sukhna Lake, Gulab Bag (rose garden), Shanti Kunj, the Art Museum, the High Court, Bidhan Sabha (secretariat), and the Punjab University—each is a wonderful example of modern architecture. One factor Le Corbusier was unable to control was population density; as India's sixth-most-densely populated city, with 7,903 people per square kilometer, its density is four times what Le Corbusier wished.

Frank Lloyd Wright: Broadacre City

Frank Lloyd Wright, the most famous of all U.S. architects, viewed Le Corbusier's urban vision as a nightmare. Such high-density living is to be avoided at all costs, Wright maintained, and he championed instead what he called "organic architecture"—the living union of architectural design with the natural environment. He reasoned that if homes could be constructed in an "organic" way, why couldn't the same be done for entire cities?

Like both Howard and Le Corbusier, Wright accepted the integral role of modern technology. Unlike them, however, he sought to vastly increase the space occupied by his utopian city to greatly lower its density. He thought a city might easily spread over 100 square miles or even more. With automobiles (or even airplanes), he contended, people could live on their own acres of land and still easily reach neighbors and shopping facilities.

Figure 14–4 depicts Wright's vision of Broadacre City. A central structure (the tall building in the background) is the local administrative center. At its foot, on the shores of the lake, lies a stadium. In the foreground, the circular building with the spires is a cultural center. Interspersed throughout the area are agricultural fields and dwelling complexes— an idea very much like Howard's. Roads link these areas, and overhead whirl the personal helicopters of Broadacre residents.

Broadacre City was a fusion of what Wright saw as the ideals of Jeffersonian democracy (fundamentally, extensive personal freedoms), the North American dream of plenty of land for personal use, and modern technology. He believed as well that people should pay no rent for land; rather, a "single tax" would support all urban costs. After that, people were on their own (Fishman, 1982).

Broadacre City never was more than a dream, of course. The plan met with massive criticism during Wright's lifetime (1867–1959). Critics dismissed Broadacre City as too expensive, too expansive, and far too radical. Although stung by the negative reaction, Wright never gave up on

FIGURE 14–3 Le Corbusier's Contemporary City

From *The Radiant City* by Le Corbusier translated by Derek Coltman. Translation copyright 1967 by Grossman Publishers, Inc. and Faber & Faber Ltd. Used by permission of Viking Penguin, a division of Penguin Putnam, Inc. © 2003 Artists Rights Society (ARS), New York/ADAGP, Paris/FIC.

his ideas. He rewrote his Broadacre treatise, *The Living City*, for the fourth time at age 90.

Paolo Soleri: The Arcology

One of Wright's students was a young Italian named Paolo Soleri. Like many genius students of other geniuses, Soleri both respected and rebelled against his master's teaching. He accepted Wright's central notion of organic architecture, but he rejected entirely his teacher's vision of Broadacre City.

Siding with Le Corbusier, Soleri advocated a dense concentration of people in an urban area. But his vision is even more extreme: a completely self-contained unit housing up to half a million people in a structure many times larger than the Empire State Building, occupying just the space of a few city blocks!

Soleri calls such cities "arcologies," or architectural ecologies—environmentally safe, architecturally beautiful, and totally efficient. His key idea is, at long last, to make the city "in the human image," concentrating and intensifying everything human. Because cities are vital elements of human evolution, dispersed concepts like Broadacre City do not apply.

FIGURE 14–4 Frank Lloyd Wright's Broadacre City reflected an ideal fusion of urban and rural, where agricultural fields and residential areas intermingled, with proximity to sports complexes and cultural centers. It was a place where everyone developed multiple abilities in farming, mechanics, and intellectual pursuits, and enjoyed great freedom of choice and movement.

Frank Lloyd Wright, Living City, drawing 5825.002, Air View MOMA#266. Height: 35 1/4, Width: 42 1/4, Media: sepia. The drawings of Frank Lloyd Wright are Copyright © 2000 The Frank Lloyd Wright Foundation, Scottsdale, AZ. © 2000 Artists Rights Society (ARS), New York.

Babel Soleri's Babel IIB, designed for a population of 520,000, contained underground industrial and commercial areas; the city center at ground level; a public area and a promenade on the first level; a neighborhood and a park (both outdoors) on the second level; gardens, a community area (for recreation), and a living–working area on the third level (about 1,500 feet high!); and housing at the very top. All service facilities—elevators, heating, and exhaust systems—are contained in the central core of the city.

Structures like these (Soleri designed dozens) are so audacious, even in the history of utopian urban planning, that few take them seriously. Critics dismiss the arcologies as gigantic beehives. Soleri counters by claiming they are "miniatures" compared with today's cities. They occupy a fraction of the land, free up the surrounding countryside for enjoyment, and allow that countryside a chance to return to nature. Imagine, he suggests, the population of Los Angeles, which now sprawls over 500 square miles, contained in 10 to 12 well-dispersed Babels. Everywhere else: no freeways, no smog, just beautiful Southern California. No doubt, however, such structures would be astronomically expensive, and no one came forward to finance constructing one.

Arcosanti Undaunted, Soleri proceeded on his own. Rising out of the desert at Cortez Junction in Arizona, about an hour's ride north of Phoenix, is Arcosanti, Soleri's "urban laboratory" prototype to demonstrate the viability of his

Arcosanti, Soleri's vision of the integration of architecture, ecology, and urban planning, is presently home to only 1 percent of its planned 7,000 inhabitants. This model shows Arcosanti in its planned final form. Intended to occupy less than 30 acres of the 4,060-acre preserve, it will serve as a research and study center for the social, economic, and ecological implications of its architectural framework.

vision fusing architecture, ecology, and urban planning. Arcosanti, shown in model form in the illustration, is planned to be completely self-sufficient and has been under construction since 1970. When complete, Arcosanti will house approximately 7,000 people, providing an urban infrastructure with workplaces, cultural centers, and service facilities, while allowing easy access to the surrounding natural environment. To Soleri, Arcosanti serves to (1) maximize the interaction and accessibility associated with an urban environment; (2) minimize the use of energy, raw materials, and land, as well as environmental pollution; and (3) allow ready access to the surrounding natural environment.

The city, including an array of large-scale solar greenhouses, will occupy only 30 acres of a 4,060-acre preserve and will serve as a research and study center for the social, economic, and

ecological implications of its architectural framework. More than 30 years after its inception, Arcosanti presently consists of eight various mixed-use buildings and public spaces, and construction is progressing at a very slow pace. Each year its 70 residents host 50,000 visitors in the Gallery, Café, and Bakery, produce nearly 15,000 windbells in the Foundry and Ceramic Studios, and conduct educational seminars for over 400 people (Arcosanti, 2002).

Utopia's Limitations: A Critique

Planned utopias, like those of Le Corbusier, Wright, and Soleri, share many of the limitations found in the New Town movement. First, as Arcosanti amply demonstrates, they are financially impractical. Second, each is a rigid vision developed by a single person who assumed that everyone would see the basic logic of his vision and support it (Fishman, 1982). To his credit, Paolo Soleri has been more flexible than other planners in this respect, changing his designs frequently after dialogue with others. Third, such plans seem sociologically naive. As Peter Hall (1975) notes, these utopians are all *architects* who believe that altering the physical world will automatically alter the social world as well. But, of course, beautiful designs do not necessarily do away with racial prejudice or poverty.

Yet, in the final analysis, society needs utopian thinkers. They are, by their work, natural consciousness raisers. They challenge our thinking about cities, point to obvious problems, and prod us to consider visionary solutions that we "on the street" barely understand.

MEANWHILE . . . DOWNTOWN: MORE FOCUSED URBAN PLANNING

The problem with utopian planners is that their schemes are simply too grandiose and impractical. A city is simply *too complex a phenomenon* to be controlled as though it were a programmable computer. Other planners argue that urban planning only works when it is focused on a limited segment of city life—say, a neighborhood or park. We may never be able to manage the city as a whole, but we can handle the urban scene one segment at a time.

Sidewalks, Neighborhoods, and Local Initiative

Since the 1960s, the trend has been away from comprehensive visions such as those of the utopian city planners. Robert Fishman explains this reaction as

the loss of confidence in the reality of a common good or purpose which can become the basis of city life. The planner's claim to be serving the interests of all . . . is now seen as either a foolish delusion or, worse, a hypocritical attempt to impose his own limited values on

everyone else. . . . [Comprehensive] planners saw the chaos and diversity of the great city as a kind of disease and the worst enemy of social harmony. Their critics have no desire to conform to an all-embracing harmony that leaves people unable to plan for themselves. They put their trust in diversity and see in urban disorder the last, best hope for individual freedom and self-realization. (1982:267)

Leading this reaction was Jane Jacobs, author of *The Death and Life of Great American Cities* (1961). To Jacobs, the greatest value of the city is its diversity; the city's "life" lies in its myriad interactions and the multiple uses of its streets, parks, sidewalks, and neighborhoods. Hence, anything that diminishes this quality (as does comprehensive planning, by definition) leads cities to their "death." Put otherwise, urban living is never *planned* in any broad sense. People of the city *invent* their lives, as they meet their own needs and solve their own problems.

Consider sidewalks. In any vital city, a sidewalk has uses far beyond easing the passage of pedestrians. Front steps facing the sidewalk are places for neighbors to sit and visit, just as corners are places to "hang out." Second, sidewalk street life serves as a means of public surveillance, through which people come to know each other and to identify strangers. Jacobs points out that, in areas where street life abounds, crime rates are low. Third, sidewalks are environments where children explore their neighborhood, test themselves, and grasp the rules of urban social life. Finally, street life brings a sense of community to a neighborhood. South Philadelphia, New York's Lower East Side, New Orleans's French Quarter, and San Francisco's Haight-Ashbury district all maintain a positive identity based on their street life.

In general, then, Jacobs supports local planning initiatives but loathes grandiose designs. What city planners should do, she says, is facilitate diversity and vitality and let local people do the rest. The best planning, then, is sometimes the least planning. The Critical Thinking box on page 429 outlines Jacobs's suggestions to a city planning board.

CRITICAL THINKING

Jane Jacobs: Planning for Vitality

Consider, for a moment, the kind of goals at which city planning must begin to aim, if the object is to plan for city vitality.

Planning for vitality must stimulate and catalyze the greatest possible range and quantity of diversity among uses and among people throughout each district of a big city; this is the underlying foundation of city economic strength, social vitality and magnetism. To do this, planners must diagnose, in specific places, what is lacking to generate diversity, and then aim at helping to supply the lacks as best they can be supplied.

Planning for vitality must promote continuous networks of local street neighborhoods, whose users and informal proprietors can count to the utmost in keeping the public spaces of the city safe, in handling strangers so they are an asset rather than a menace, in keeping casual public tabs on children in places that are public.

Planning for vitality must combat the destructive presence of border vacuums [vacant land at the edges], and it must help promote people's identification with city districts that are large enough, and are varied and rich enough in inner and outer contacts to deal with the tough, inescapable, practical problems of big-city life.

Planning for vitality must aim at unslumming the slums, by creating conditions aimed at persuading a high proportion of the indigenous residents, whoever they may be, to stay put by choice over time, so there will be a steadily growing diversity among people and a continuity of community both for old residents and for newcomers who assimilate into it.

Planning for vitality must convert the self-destruction of diversity and other cataclysmic uses of money into constructive forces, by hampering the opportunities for destructiveness on the one hand, and on the other hand by stimulating more city territory into possessing a good economic environment for other people's plans.

Planning for vitality must aim at clarifying the visual order of cities, and it must do so by both promoting and illuminating functional order, rather than by obstructing or denying it.

Source: Jane Jacobs, *The Death and Life of Great American Cities* (New York: Random House, 1961), pp. 408–9.

Open Spaces: Squares, Parks, and Architecture

Not everyone who shares the belief in more focused city planning, of course, goes as far as Jacobs. While agreeing that holistic city planning is undesirable, some argue that good planning can be more comprehensive than Jacobs allows.

August Heckscher spent two years studying cities such as Omaha, Dallas, Cincinnati, Buffalo, Rochester, and Milwaukee. To Heckscher, the vitality of a city is fundamentally a matter of how well it organizes its space:

Each city is a place of its own, its uniqueness determined in large measure by patterns created by the alternation of structure and void, of buildings and spaces between. The large green spaces, parks and parkways, river banks and waterfronts, give to a city a coherence that allows the urban dweller to have a feeling of the whole. . . . What is expressed in open spaces is the essential quality of urban life—its casualness and variety, its ability to crystallize community feeling. (1977:4)

Heckscher notes that the spatial organization of cities reflects deep cultural values. Grounded in the values of individualism, freedom, and material success, U.S. cities typically adopted a grid pattern. With a grid, vistas open up; people can look down whole streets, even out to the countryside, thus introducing regularity and suggesting control. Curved streets and irregular building patterns (as found in medieval towns), by contrast, are enclosing, limiting, unpredictable, not future-oriented.

Heckscher highlights the value of squares, parks, architecture, and artwork to urban life. These are especially important in cities—like those in North America—dominated by economic concerns. They prompt people to remember that there are "other things" to city life. Squares provide small, natural meeting places, as well as settings for more formal occasions such as political rallies and concerts. They provide a vital physical and psychological break in the city's structure. New Orleans's Jackson Square, located in the French Quarter, is one such vital square. Others include Fountain Square in Cincinnati, Union Square in San Francisco, City Hall Square in Toronto, Rittenhouse Square in Philadelphia, and Washington Square in New York.

Parks are equally important. Roy Rosenzweig (1992) speaks for many in celebrating New York's Central Park, 843 acres on the upper half of Manhattan Island, which preserves a bit of country in the city. Although perhaps not as well known as Central Park, a similar public space is found in virtually every major North American city where residents delight in recreation and informal activities of all kinds. Atlanta has Piedmont Park (185 acres), Chicago has Grant Park (305 acres), and San Diego has Balboa Park (1,158 acres). There is Schenley Park in Pittsburgh (456 acres), Stanley Park in Vancouver (1,000 acres), and Griffith Park in Los Angeles (4,063 acres), and Philadelphia boasts the largest city park in the world, Fairmount Park (4,079 acres).

Architecture, too, is a crucial source of a city's flavor and excitement. Buildings provoke human *feelings*. Frank Lloyd Wright's Guggenheim Museum in New York always demands a response, as do San Francisco's brightly painted Victorian houses. Walking through the world's great cathedrals—St. Paul's in London or Notre Dame in Paris, for example—creates a powerful reaction, much the same as gazing on the New York skyline from the Brooklyn Bridge. It is for this reason, no doubt, that many advocate protecting a city's architecture as the means of preserving a city's soul.

In a study of urban spaces, William H. Whyte found that many people simply thrive on the streets. Observing the Seagram Plaza in midtown Manhattan, he wrote that "On a good day, there would be a hundred and fifty people sitting, sunbathing, picnicking and schmoozing—idly gossiping, talking 'nothing talk'" (1980:14). Moreover, claims Whyte,

> [People] go to the lively places where there are many people. And they go there . . . not to escape the city but to partake of it. . . . The multiplier effect is tremendous. It is not just the number of people using these small urban places, but the larger number who pass by and enjoy them vicariously, or the even larger number who feel better about the city center for knowledge of them. For a city such places are priceless, whatever the cost. (1980:100–101)

Rouse Revisited: The Middle Ground

Later in his life, James Rouse, the creator of Columbia, Maryland, shifted his attention to mid-size projects of urban regeneration. Most of these have been spectacularly successful. These are neither comprehensive, all-encompassing visions like Columbia, nor small-scale, local efforts like those championed by Jane Jacobs. They are in-between—the middle ground. While such planning takes account of the needs of the whole city, it targets a small portion of the city's space. The most well-known of Rouse's mid-sized efforts are the Faneuil Hall complex in Boston, New York's South Street Seaport, Baltimore's Inner Harbor, and the Grand Avenue Mall in Milwaukee.

All of these projects reclaim portions of a dying center city. Rouse sought to reverse the deterioration of central cities in the 1950s and 1960s. He noted that "we have lived so long with grim, congested, worn out inner cities and sprawling, cluttered outer cities, that we have subconsciously come to accept them as inevitable and unavoidable. Deep down in our national heart is a lack of conviction that cities can be beautiful, humane, and truly responsive to the needs and yearnings of our people" (cited in Demarest, 1981:37–39).

So he set to work. Before Rouse began, the Faneuil Hall area of Boston had become as tawdry as one could imagine. The site of the city center in Revolutionary War days, the area abounded with old, dilapidated warehouses that abutted on the harbor. No one lived there and only a few businesses remained. With a generous spirit, one would have called the locale "down and out."

Today, it is transformed. The old warehouses have been outwardly maintained, but the inner cores have been thoroughly modernized. Faneuil Hall has been revamped in the same manner. Inside, food shops run its football-field length. On either side of the Hall are pedestrian areas with benches, outdoor eating areas, and places where street musicians play. The refurbished old warehouses on either side are now the place of business of high-quality shops. On any summer day, the place is teeming with people—locals, tourists, visitors from the suburbs. Looking at the project from the vantage point of one of the high-rises in the area or from the harbor, one sees how Rouse's vision works: The new buildings mimic or harmoniously blend with the old buildings of the area. Perhaps most important, the businesses in the project are profitable, and the success of the Faneuil Hall project has stimulated development throughout Boston's downtown. Much the same happy story applies to Baltimore's Inner Harbor and, on a smaller scale, to New York's South Street Seaport.

Critics charge that Rouse's successes pander to the wealthier elements of urban areas and do little for the poor. There is truth in this accusation. Still, Rouse's changes have helped turn around one stunning problem by replacing collapsing inner-city districts with thriving, vibrant urban places.

THE REALITIES OF URBAN PLANNING

Whatever the philosophical stance one ultimately takes about urban planning, shaping the city always forces us to contend with traditions, vested interests, and environmental conditions. Such realities operate both as barriers and as opportunities.

Economics and Politics

Radical alterations in the urban landscape have hardly ever gotten far off the ground. Even Ebenezer Howard could establish only two garden cities. Even with government support, the British new-town effort has been quite limited. In the United States, Stein's Radburn, New Jersey, fell victim to financial troubles, while Columbia and Reston went through dire straits for the same reason. Partially because of expense (and partially because of its audacity), Paolo Soleri's Arcosanti has barely taken form, and Frank Lloyd Wright's Broadacre City was never even started. The stark reality is that, in capitalist societies, urban planning rarely strays very far from the interests of business.

Local politics, too, swirls around city planning, as interest groups contend with each other to achieve their various goals. Sometimes the complexities of even projects that are small in scale lead to challenges that intimidate elected officials not wanting to alienate voters.

The Difference That Values Make

In the final analysis, urban planning is always a question of values: which and whose are the key issues. Throughout this chapter, we have seen that city planning has always reflected

Prefabricated concrete apartment buildings built throughout the old Soviet Union and Eastern European communist countries resulted in a sterile look of uniformity. This is the Nibelungen-Ring housing complex in Leipzig in eastern Germany, with other apartment buildings in traditional rows in the upper left. In most socialist cities, these gray buildings created a drab, somber look for the first-time visitor.

cultural values. In Catholic Rome we found planning that glorified the Church; in monarchic France we found planning that celebrated the king; in nineteenth- and twentieth-century New York, we found planning that augmented the pursuit of the almighty dollar.

Values also permeate, explicitly or implicitly, the work of urban planners. In a review of Jane Jacobs's *Death and Life of Great American Cities*, sociologist Herbert Gans (1962a: 170–75) points out that Jacobs is a typical product of her society. She complains that, too often, city planning has not been left up to the people. What could be more Western, more North American, Gans asks, than a complaint that we need more emphasis on the individual, and should make way for local initiative?

Of course, the values implicitly criticized by Jacobs appear in virtually all U.S. city planning. Even planners like Columbia's James Rouse, who have tried to improve people's lives in cities, do so with the expectation of being well paid for it. Said Rouse in an interview:

> The business mentality today is that the pursuit of profit is the purpose of life, and that people come second or third. I think that's deplorable. It's why development has such a bad name and why cities suffer from so much ugliness. What should be important is to produce something of benefit to mankind. If that happens, then the profit will be there. (Pawlyna, 1981:64)

Similarly, because most of us are deeply committed to the values of individuality and personal initiative, we are put off by the all-inclusive plans of Le Corbusier, Soleri, or Wright that seem to demand submission to the group. Indeed, perhaps the characteristic element of North American urban planning has been the lack of comprehensive planning. From the 1600s on, U.S. and Canadian cities have developed with very limited intervention by any governmental agency. In short, the United States has no overall plans or policies for its cities because its population does not want them. If private investors, like Jim Rouse, can't make our cities better, then most people seem content to live with the consequences. French and Hamilton sum up well:

> State intervention and control [in cities] in Western countries is aimed at, and can only hope to achieve, the amelioration of the inadequacies of the existing system because planning has to operate within the limits imposed by private ownership of land and buildings, private control of investment, and the greater freedom of choice and action possessed by the individual, even when such action may not be in the public interest. (1979:19; emphasis added)

In recent years a growing number of scholars and practitioners have become interested in private, market-based programs to address urban economic and social ills. As explained in *The Voluntary City: Choice, Community, and Civil Society* (2002), many areas of civic and commercial life do not necessarily require government involvement. Various authors of this edited volume offer numerous examples of the nongovernment sector effectively providing for roads and bridges, education, housing, social welfare, land-use planning, commercial law, even policing and criminal prosecutions. The private, self-governing enclaves and large-scale industrial communities with complex physical infrastructure and services (such as Chicago's Manufacturing District) are examples that challenge the orthodoxy that government alone can improve community life. So perhaps the private sector can play a greater role in urban planning and policy.

Some Canadian and U.S. cities already illustrate the vitality wrought by good government planning. Among them are Portland, San Francisco, Seattle, and Vancouver, cities frequently cited in public opinion polls as the "best" cities. Another city fulfilling all of these qualifications is Toronto, Ontario, whose planning successfully addresses the challenges of urban diversity and urban sprawl. We will examine Toronto as a model of good urban planning in our final case study.

❖ CASE STUDY ❖
Toronto, Ontario

Toronto is a Great Lakes port and, through the St. Lawrence Seaway, an ocean port as well. With 4.8 million people living in the region, Toronto is the most populous metropolitan area in Canada. Almost one in six Canadians live there and it continues to attract newcomers, as illustrated in an 8.5 percent population growth between 1997 and 2001 (Statistics Canada, 2002). The Toronto region has the nation's major concentration of industrial jobs and serves as the commercial and financial center of the country. The central area, downtown Toronto, is the predominant regional center, encompassing major government, financial, medical, and education services.

Although it contains a large industrial base, Toronto has not experienced the problems of crime and population loss that plague another nearby industrial city, Detroit. Toronto attracts a large number of immigrants from the developing world and has an increasing number of people requiring welfare assistance, but its school system and financial stability are stronger than those of many U.S. cities in a similar situation. Although Toronto faces suburban and edge city development as do other cities, its central city remains strong, the region's growth patterns are not wasteful of environmental resources, and the transportation systems are more efficient, with greater reliance on mass transit. What makes Toronto more successful in these areas than its sister cities elsewhere? The answer lies in a metropolitan approach to governance and policy-making that enables Toronto to address spatial development and quality-of-life issues in a more comprehensive manner and with greater resources at its disposal, as we will discuss shortly.

The Physical Setting

Situated on the northern shore of Lake Ontario, Toronto is almost entirely flat, except 3 to 4 miles inland where the land sharply rises about 40 feet at the shoreline elevation of the former glacial Lake Iroquois. Streets are in a grid design except for the diagonal roads along the shoreline. Railroad tracks and an expressway separate the lakefront from the downtown area. The central business areas are around Bloor, Queen, and Yonge streets, while the central financial district is south of the old city hall in the vicinity of King and Bay streets. The CN Tower (1,815 feet) dominates the city skyline—along with the Toronto-Dominion Centre, Commerce Court, and First Canadian Place—all of which are more than 50 stories high.

North of the central business district lies a fashionable shopping area. The Ontario Parliament Buildings and the University of Toronto rise south of Bloor Street in a section with tall shade trees and grassy areas known for its parklike atmosphere. One of the most attractive residential areas in Toronto is Rosedale, an older neighborhood of distinguished homes set on winding, tree-lined streets quite close to the downtown center, which itself contains many attractive streets of modest, well-designed houses.

History

Inhabited first by the Seneca and later by the Mississauga Indians, the area that was to become the city of Toronto was first established as a trading post in the seventeenth century because of its strategic location at the crossing of ancient Indian trails going west to the Mississippi and north to Lake Simcoe and the vast wilderness beyond. The French built three small forts there in the eighteenth century, which were subsequently destroyed after the English defeated the French in 1759. During and after the U.S. War for Independence, about 40,000 loyalists fled the United States and settled in this region.

In 1787, Lord Dorchester, the Canadian governor-in-chief, peacefully negotiated the purchase of 250,000 acres from three Indian chiefs for the future capital of Ontario. Its name was changed from Toronto to York in 1795, and the small settlement of about 700

residents was temporarily occupied by U.S. forces during the War of 1812. By 1834, the population had grown to 9,000 and its original name was restored.

The coming of the Grand Trunk and Great Western railways in the 1850s sparked rapid development. As a break-of-bulk port city, Toronto flourished, shipping agricultural products, minerals, and timber from the surrounding region. Industrialization further spurred growth, as the city and its environs soon produced more than half of Canada's manufactured goods. Through annexation of adjacent villages and towns, the city doubled in area by 1900, then doubled again by 1920. In 1930, the metropolitan area included the central city, four towns (Leaside, Mimico, New Toronto, and Weston), three villages (Forest Hill, Long Branch, and Swansea), and five townships (Etobicoke, East York, North York, Scarborough, and York).

Creation of a Metropolitan Government

The Great Depression of the 1930s caused severe financial problems for the city, and these still remained at the end of World War II in 1945. Already having difficulty finding funds to provide water and sewage systems to outlying areas, Toronto saw its municipal burden increase further with a rapid rise in population at that time. After investigating various options, the Ottawa Municipal Board in 1953 recommended that the 13 municipalities (named in the previous paragraph) create a federated form of government unique in North America. Passage that year of the Municipality of Metropolitan Toronto Act united the metropolitan area, and the 25-member Council of Metropolitan Toronto began its task of finding ways to deal with such common concerns as revenues, education, transportation, and urban growth. This combined form of government offered greater credit than each individual municipality had, thereby enhancing financing for various public projects. A significant feature of this metropolitan government system was that council members were appointed to it by virtue of their election as mayors, aldermen, or controllers of a particular municipality, which ensured good communication and a high level of coordination between the central body and the local municipalities.

The Metropolitan Council worked well. It authorized construction of new schools and renovation of older ones and also introduced a regional system of parks in an attempt to control future development. It greatly improved transportation by upgrading or building new roads and expressways and by constructing an excellent subway and a new airport terminal building. Toronto's transit system now consists of a grid network of streetcars, buses, three underground rapid transit lines, and a light rail transit system that together account for 70 percent of all trips to the central city. This transportation network is integrated with the multi-centered urban structures located along the rapid transit lines and brings workers from the surrounding regions to the downtown area.

In 1967, the Corporation of Metropolitan Toronto reorganized. It reduced its 13 municipalities to six and increased from 25 to 33 the number of seats on the Council. The Council also considerably extended its responsibilities in education and social services and added others, such as ambulance and library services, urban renewal, and waste disposal. The reorganized council subsequently succeeded in resolving many of the difficult sewage and water problems to create effective systems for both.

Essentially, Toronto functioned with a two-tiered government, with local government focus on neighborhood issues and metropolitan focus on issues facing the metropolitan region. Regional government has thus enabled Toronto to consolidate its resources and to develop a coordinated plan for the growth of both its urban and suburban schools. In a 1990 comparison of Toronto and Detroit, which are about 230 miles apart, *The Economist* reported that the Toronto region avoided many of the problems that plagued Detroit in the areas of crime, education, and social services because it could evenly control use of space

and distribution of resources throughout the metropolitan area. As a result, the Council has been credited with contributing substantially to shaping Toronto into "one of the most effectively planned metropolitan areas in North America" (United Nations, 1995).

> Major achievements have included a strong industrial base, a successful mass transit system providing 70 percent of trips to an enlarged central area, concentration of office employment near subway stations, and provision of housing for an additional 1 million residents, well-located with respect to public transport. In addition [the Municipality of Metropolitan Toronto] has upgraded the road system to provide improved access to industrial and commercial employment throughout the metropolitan area and provided an effective water supply and sewerage system (United Nations, 1995:256).

Two Phases of Urban Planning

In a provocative book, *City Form and Everyday Life: Toronto's Gentrification and Critical Social Practice* (1994), Jon Caulfield described two distinct planning phases—modern and postmodern—that Toronto experienced in its inner-city development. The first of these began in the 1950s and lasted until the early 1970s, and was characterized by an all-out pro-development attitude and adherence to the principles of modernist planning. This approach emphasized intense specialization of land use, massive infrastructure (particularly urban expressways), and the redevelopment of older areas (Filion, 1995).

In Toronto, city officials identified a number of districts within the city as blighted and obliterated them to make room for expressways, public housing projects, private high-rise apartment developments, or an expansion of downtown's commercial functions. With little regard for existing neighborhoods in these designated areas, the wrecking ball and bulldozer razed some of the city's architectural gems and destroyed communities in such places as Alexandra Park, Rusholme Road on the east side, St. Jamestown, and Regent Park.

These old neighborhoods were seen as an inconvenience between two modernist sectors: the suburbs and a rapidly redeveloping central business district (Caulfield, 1994:7).

Alexandra Park exemplifies the outcome of the modern planning approach found in many other North American cities as well. Once it was an area of mixed use, consisting of old residential houses and commercial activities that were linked with the rest of the city. Now it is an area reflecting simplification, segmentation, withdrawal, and a land use that is segregated from the day-to-day activities of the rest of the city. Most people living in Alexandra Park these days need public assistance, and the area has become an isolated, virtually impenetrable ghetto (Caulfield, 1994:11–13).

Toronto officials and local developers continued to raze prominent architectural landmarks and stable working-class neighborhoods, replacing them with modern, "efficient" structures, until local activist groups began to fight city hall's urban renewal plans. The reformers pointed to the decay of U.S. inner cities and argued that Toronto could avoid their mistakes if it remained "people-oriented" and emphasized neighborhood preservation. Their arguments were persuasive; they succeeded in preserving such areas as Rusholme Road on the west side, Old City Hall, Toronto Island, Church of the Holy Trinity, Union Station, and Trefann Court. This "cultural resistance," suggests Caulfield, played an important role in the introduction of the second phase of planning: postmodern inner-city development. Post-modern urbanism is a celebration of traditional urban form and of social and cultural heterogeneity (Caulfield, 1994:97).

From the late 1960s onward, the postmodernist movement—overlapping the modernist movement for a few years before emerging as the dominant force—found sufficient support in Toronto's Metropolitan Council to halt modernist redevelopment of most inner-city neighborhoods. Echoing the anti-modernist perspectives of Jane Jacobs and Lewis Mumford, planners began emphasizing the benefits of a diversified, small-grained urban texture and the importance of preserving older buildings. Ironically, the preservation and upgrading of the built environment led to the loss of its social diversity, as middle- and upper-income people—seeking easy downtown access and a more stimulating environment than was available in the suburbs—displaced the working-class and ethnic populations previously there (Sewell, 1993).

Toronto Today

In 1998, Toronto restructured its municipal government once more, merging its 2.4 million people in six local governments into one city. At the same time, the city's responsibilities, revenues, and property tax base were reformed, all without disruption of city services to residents and businesses. Although the new Toronto government centralized its administration, the city still maintains community councils to deal with purely neighborhood matters, and its various local civic and social services remain in local communities, with the six former city halls now functioning as "municipal civic centres" (Toronto, 2002).

As a result of its planning reforms and metropolitan governance, Toronto has emerged into a dynamic city with one of the world's safest urban environments. It is, as Jane Jacobs remarked, "a city that works." *Fortune* magazine in 1996 named it "the best global city for business." It is Canada's number one tourist destination, the financial center of Canada, and the fourth largest financial center in North America. The city has one of the highest percentages of fiber optic telecommunications cables installed, and more wireless phones per capita than anywhere else in North America. It also contains the continent's largest continuous underground pedestrian system, connecting 1,100 stores and restaurants, 48 office towers, six major hotels, and several entertainment centers (Toronto, 2002).

Toronto is also one of the world's most multicultural cities, as about half of all Canada's immigrants come to the Greater Toronto Area. Not surprisingly, then, half the city's population of 2.4 million are immigrants, a much higher proportion than anywhere else in the country. The 315,000 immigrants who settled in Toronto between 1990 and 1996 are equivalent to a city the size of Victoria or Halifax. With the exception of Oceania (the countries of the Pacific and South Pacific), every part of the world has sent at least 10,000 emigrants to Toronto in recent years. During the 1990s Asia supplied about 60 percent of all immigrants arriving in Toronto. The leading countries have been China, Hong Kong, the Philippines, Vietnam (East Asia); India and Sri Lanka (South Asia); and Guyana, Jamaica, Trinidad, and Tobago (West Indies). Italy and the United Kingdom remain the top two countries of origin for all immigrants living in Toronto but, if present migration patterns continue, that will change in a few years. The postwar suburbs of North York, Scarborough, and York have become the main immigrant settlement areas as the central city, as mentioned earlier, has proven an attractive locale for middle- and upper-income residents.

Toronto is also an important cultural center, with a rich fare of ballet, concerts, films, opera, and theater offerings. In fact, it is the third-largest English-language theater center after London and New York. It is home to the Toronto Symphony Orchestra, three major theaters, and many small experimental theaters, as well as the Art Gallery of Ontario, the Royal Ontario Museum, the Ontario Science Centre, and a zoo. Often called "Hollywood North," it ranks third in TV and film production. Its institutions of higher learning include the Ontario College of Art, Ryerson Polytechnical Institute, the University of Toronto, and York University. The Toronto Maple Leafs (ice hockey), the Argonauts (football), and the Blue Jays (baseball) are professional sports teams that add to the city's excitement and vitality. Like any vibrant city, Toronto also offers an appealing array of restaurants, boutiques, movie theaters, festivals, exhibits, and recreational and social activities (Toronto, 2002).

Toronto is not entirely free of problems. Increased traffic congestion, a shortage of affordable housing, and a need for more waste disposal sites are three of its main concerns. Following the consolidation of its six municipalities, the city set about developing and implementing a new Official Plan—a vision of how Toronto will change and grow in the new millennium—by setting priorities for social, environmental, and economic development (see the Cityscape box on page 438). The plan's aim is to (1) protect the best of what it has; (2) invest in areas that are aging and need revitalizing; (3) ensure that new development is consistent with the existing character of the area; and (4) convert former industrial lands into uses that fit into the surrounding neighborhoods and add to community vitality (Toronto, 2002). Facing its future, Toronto's leaders recognize that good, people-oriented planning is essential to its continued vitality as "a city that works."

CONCLUSION

Can we honestly say that one type of city planning has been spectacularly more effective than any other? Our review suggests a number of conclusions.

First, all the evidence suggests that changing a city's physical form does not automatically reshape social life. In new towns the world over—from Ebenezer Howard's Letchworth to James Rouse's Columbia to Lúcio Costa's Brasilia—new structures have become home to many old problems, including harmful prejudices, class antagonism, and environmental pollution. So we may conclude that changing the city physically, while sometimes necessary, is not sufficient to realize the idealistic environment envisioned by planners. The best planning blends good sociology with dramatic architecture.

Second, all of the planning experiments of the last century have fallen short of their goals. New towns have not solved the problems of large cities, nor have they been able

Toronto Plans Its Future

Below are introductory excerpts from an official master plan—developed, publicly discussed, and adopted in 2002—in which the city of Toronto designed its evolution over the next 30 years.

Building a successful Toronto means that we have to make sustainable choices about how we grow. We have to see connections and understand the consequences of our choices. We have to integrate environmental, social and economic perspectives in our decision making. We have to meet the needs of today without compromising the ability of future generations to meet their needs.

There is no such thing as an isolated or purely local decision. Each of us makes choices every day about where to live, work, play, shop and how to travel. They seem like small choices, but together and over time the consequences of these choices can affect everyone's quality of life. That's why planning matters. . . .

This Plan is about the basics of successful city-building. Holistic and integrated thinking is a fundamental requirement for planning a modern city like Toronto. Integrated thinking means

seeing, understanding and accounting for all the connections as we go about our decision making. Sometimes it means thinking differently about solutions. Always it means searching for outcomes that demonstrate integration, balance and interdependence and that earn social, environmental and economic rewards. . . .

Toronto cannot plan in isolation or expect to stand alone in dealing with the effects of urban growth. Our view of the quality of urban life tends to be based on the local conditions in our own neighbourhoods. These conditions are in turn affected by events happening in the larger region. The quality of the air, water, services and region-wide transport systems all affect the quality of life in our neighbourhood, where we work and where we play. The way in which growth and change are managed in Toronto must mesh with that of our neighbours because we are integrally linked in many ways. . . .

Building a successful city means making choices that improve our quality of life. As our City grows and matures, we can create a more beautiful environment, healthy and vibrant communities and greater prosperity. . . .

In order to remain economically competitive in today's global economy, a city must be more than functional. It has to work well, but it also must be beautiful, vibrant, safe, and inclusive.

to solve many of their own troubles. Utopian designs intrigue us, but offer few real solutions. Finally, small-scale efforts, such as those proposed by Jane Jacobs, August Heckscher, William H. Whyte, and James Rouse, are helpful but often leave untouched the larger problems of the city—such as racial prejudice and desperate poverty.

Third, we always must bear in mind that urban planning occurs within a framework of certain unbending realities. Economic and political considerations limit the scope of any plan. If it costs too much, it won't be done. If

sponsored by the rich, it probably won't be much help to the poor. What some people want, others are sure to resist. Urban planners, if they are to have any chance to work their craft, must become skillful politicians.

Surely, planning is vital to the future of our cities. But we must merge two often-contradictory forces—the planners' desire to shape the urban environment, and a free people's need to choose. We must also overcome the tendency to think in purely local terms and recognize instead the need for a regional, integrated view of metropolitan regions. Cities and suburbs do

Great cities do not happen by accident—they are designed and orchestrated so that individual private and public developments work together to create cohesive blocks, neighbourhoods and districts. Good urban design is not just an aesthetic overlay, but an essential ingredient of city-building. Good urban design is good business and good social policy.

Civic pride is infectious. The City and the private sector should work together as partners in creating a great city and achieving Toronto's architectural and urban design potential. The City can play its part by organizing, designing, maintaining and improving the streets, parks and public buildings. The private sector can do its part by building the structures and landscapes that define and support these public places. This Plan demands that both the public and private sectors commit to high quality architecture, landscape architecture and urban design.

Beautiful, comfortable, safe and accessible streets, parks, open spaces and public buildings are a key shared asset. These public spaces draw people together, creating strong social bonds at the neighbourhood, city and regional level. They convey our public image to the world and unite us as a city. They set the stage for our festivals, parades and civic life as well as for daily casual contact. Public space creates communities.

This Plan recognizes how important good design is in creating a great city. Great cities are judged by the look and quality of their squares, parks, streets and public spaces and the buildings which frame and define them. People flock to the world's great cities not just to enjoy the culture, but to wander the streets, to explore their parks and plazas, to enjoy the street life, to shop and to people watch. The same characteristics and qualities that make these cities great places to visit also make them great places to live. What do these places share in common? All are very urban, high density, mixed use, mixed income, transit and pedestrian oriented vibrant places.

Great cities not only have great buildings—but the buildings work together to create great streets, plazas, parks and public places. Great cities inspire and astonish. Whether it's a bustling shopping street lined by vibrant shop windows and sidewalk cafes, an intimate, residential, tree-lined street, or a public plaza in the central business district—everywhere you look there is evidence that the place has been designed. The buildings, both public and private, work together to create the "walls" for the city's great outdoor "rooms".

Source: Toronto Urban Development Services, *Toronto Official Plan* (May 2002). Accessed online at http://www. city.toronto.on.ca/.

not exist independently of one another; their fates are inextricably linked, for many of the issues and problems that affect quality of life transcend municipal boundaries. Further, to ensure the vitality of cities in the twenty-first century, planners and the public need to gain an understanding of both the problems and the possibilities of urban life. And, yes, even try to learn from some of the utopian thinkers of the past.

As cities struggle to define their futures, people must ask some hard questions of themselves and of their leaders. Why should we plan in the first place? What are the issues that planners can address better than the people themselves? Whom does any plan really benefit? Guiding the discussion that such questions provoke, we also suggest, must be a fundamental commitment to the health and welfare of all people who live in the city. With such a dedication—evident today in the urban life of Toronto's people—it is possible that, in time, we will generate a vision of the street that perhaps all citizens can understand.

REFERENCES

ABBOTT, CARL. 1995. "Portland: People, Places, and Politics." *Urban Affairs*, Winter.

ABC NEWS. 2000. "Crime Fears Linger." Accessed online at http://abcnews.go.com/sections/politics/DailyNews/poll000607.html on September 23, 2002.

————. 2002. "Poll: Crime Worries Running High." Accessed online at http://abcnews.go.com/sections/us/DailyNews/crime_poll010604.html on September 23, 2002.

ABRAHAMSON, MARK. 1996. *Urban Enclaves: Identity and Place in America*. New York: St. Martin's Press.

ABU-LUGHOD, JANET. 1980. *Rabat: Urban Apartheid in Morocco*. Princeton, NJ: Princeton University Press.

————. 1984. "Culture, 'Modes of Production,' and the Changing Nature of Cities in the Arab World." Pp. 94–119 in *The City in Cultural Context*, edited by John A. Agrow, John Mercer, and David E. Sopher. Boston: Allen and Unwin.

ADAMS, ROBERT McC. 1966. *The Evolution of Urban Society: Early Mesopotamia and Prehistoric Mexico*. Chicago: Aldine Publishing Company.

ADDAMS, JANE. 1902. *Democracy and Social Ethics*. New York: Macmillan.

————. 1909. *The Spirit of Youth and the City Streets*. New York: Macmillan.

————. 1910. *Twenty Years at Hull House*. New York: Macmillan.

————. 1930. *The Second Twenty Years at Hull House*. New York: Macmillan.

ADLER, JERRY, AND MAGGIE MALONE. 1996. "Toppling Towers." *Newsweek*, November 4, pp. 70–72.

AIELLO, J. R., J. S. VAUTIER, AND M. D. BERNSTEIN. 1983. "Crowding Stress: Impact of Social Support, Group Formation, and Control," paper presented at the 91st annual convention of the American Psychological Association, Anaheim, California.

ALONSO, WILLIAM. 1970. "What Are New Towns For?" *Urban Studies* 7:35–45.

————. 1971. "A Theory of the Urban Land Market." Pp. 154–59 in *Internal Structure of the City*, edited by Larry S. Bourne. New York: Oxford University Press.

————. 1975. "The Economics of Urban Size." Pp. 434–51 in *Regional Policy*, edited by John Friedmann and William Alonso. Cambridge, MA: MIT Press.

American Demographics. 1997. "Crime Fears." July, p. 7.

AMERICAN LUNG ASSOCIATION. 2000. *State of the Air 2000*. Accessed at http://www.lungusa.org/air2000/sota_table2.html on August 4, 2002.

ANDERSON, ELIJAH. 1990. *Streetwise: Race, Class, and Change in an Urban Community*. Chicago: University of Chicago Press.

ANJOMANI, ARDESHIR A., AND FAIZAH BINTI. 1992. "Squatter Settlement in Kuala Lumpur: Evaluation and Alternatives." *Ekistics* 59:159–65.

Architectural Forum. 1951. "Slum Surgery in St. Louis." April, pp. 128–36.

ARCOSANTI. 2002. www.arcosanti.org.

ARMSTRONG, REGINA BELZ. 1972. *The Office Industry*. Cambridge, MA: MIT Press.

ASBURY, HERBERT. 1940. *The Chicago Underworld*. New York: Ace.

ASSOCIATED PRESS. 1999. "Cities Seen 'Criminalizing' Homelessness." *Boston Globe*, January 6, p. A7.

AUSTIN, ALICE CONSTANCE. 1935. *The Next Step*. Los Angeles: Institute Press.

AWANOHARA, SUSUMU. 1990. "Scapegoats No More." *Far Eastern Economic Review* 150 (November 22): 16.

————. 1991a. "All in the Family." *Far Eastern Economic Review* 151 (March 14): 36–37.

————. 1991b. "Political Indian Summer." *Far Eastern Economic Review* 151 (May 25): 35.

BACKHAUS, TARA N., PETER B. BELDEN, AND THOMAS J. ESPENSHADE. 1994. "AIDS, Low Birth Rates, and Future Growth in Thailand." *Population Today* 22 (October): 4–5.

BAGLEY, CHRISTOPHER. 1989. "Urban Crowding and the Murder Rate in Bombay, India." *Perceptual and Motor Skills* 69 (August): 1241–42.

BAHR, H. 1973. *Skid Row: An Introduction to Disaffiliation*. New York: Oxford University Press.

BAILEY, JAMES, ed. 1973. *New Towns in America*. New York: Wiley.

BALDASSARE, MARK. 1979. *Residential Crowding in Urban America*. Berkeley: University of California Press.

BALDWIN, JAMES. 1980. "Symposium: Literature and the Urban Experience." *Humanities* 1 (July/August): 4.

BALTZELL, E. DIGBY. 1964. *The Protestant Establishment*. New York: Vintage.

————. 1979. *Philadelphia Gentleman: The Making of a National Upper Class*. Philadelphia: University of Pennsylvania Press.

———. 1980. *Puritan Boston and Quaker Philadelphia*. New York: Free Press.

BALU, REKHA. 1999. "Rising to the Occasion in Chicago: Developers Answer Call for Downtown Living Space." *Wall Street Journal*, June 16, p. B8.

BANFIELD, EDWARD C. 1970. *The Unheavenly City*. Boston: Little, Brown.

———. 1974. *The Unheavenly City Revisited*. Boston: Little, Brown.

BANHAM, RAYNER. 2001. *Los Angeles: The Architecture of Four Ecologies*. Berkeley: University of California Press. (Orig. edition 1973, Viking Penguin).

BARFF, R., AND K. AUSTEN. 1993. "It's Gotta Be da Shoes: Domestic Manufacturing, Internal Subcontracting, and the Production of Athletic Footwear." *Environment and Planning* A:25.

BARRINGER, HERBERT, ROBERT W. GARDNER, AND MICHAEL J. LEVIN. 1993. *Asians and Pacific Islanders in the United States*. New York: Russell Sage Foundation.

BARRON, JAMES. 1985. "Battling an Unwelcome Image as Least Wonderful U.S. Town." *New York Times*, January 10, p. A17.

BARRY, DAN. 1996. "For Landlords, Hard Numbers and Obligations." *New York Times*, October 10, p. D1.

BAUDER, H., AND E. PERLE. 1999. "Spatial and Skills Mismatch for Labor-Market Segments." *Environment and Planning* 31:959–77.

BAYLES, FRED. 2000. "Nightmare of Buildings That Stand Empty Haunts Cities." *USA Today*, March 20, p. 21A.

BEITO, DAVID T., PETER GORDON, AND ALEXANDER TABARROK, (eds.) 2002. *The Voluntary City: Choice, Community, and Civil Society*. Ann Arbor: University of Michigan Press.

BELKIN, LISA. 1983. "Jersey Town: A Feeling of Community." *New York Times*, September 14, p. B1.

BELL, RALPH. 1982. "Personal Crime and Delinquency Rates in Los Angeles." *Mid-American Review of Sociology* 7:87–104.

BELL, WENDELL, AND MARION BOAT. 1957. "Urban Neighborhoods and Informal Social Relations." *American Journal of Sociology* 62:391–98.

BELLAH, ROBERT N., RICHARD MADSEN, WILLIAM M. SULLIVAN, ANN SWIDLER, AND STEVEN M. TIPTON. 1985. *Habits of the Heart: Individualism and Commitment in American Life*. New York: Harper & Row.

BELLUSH, J., AND M. HAUSKNECHT, eds. 1967. *Urban Renewal: People, Politics, and Planning*. Garden City, NY: Doubleday.

BERGER, BENNETT. 1960. *Working Class Suburb*. Berkeley: University of California Press.

BERGER, PETER. 1977. "In Praise of New York." *Commentary* (October).

BERMAN, DAVID. 1997. "Shopping on the Edge." *Canadian Business*, October 31, pp. 72–79.

BERRY, BRIAN J. L. 1961. "City Size Distribution and Economic Development." *Economic Development and Cultural Change* 9:573–81.

———. 1985. "Islands of Renewal in Seas of Decay." Pp. 69–98 in *The New Urban Reality*, edited by Paul E. Peterson. Washington, DC: Brookings Institution.

BERRY, BRIAN J. L., AND JOHN D. KASARDA. 1977. *Contemporary Urban Ecology*. New York: Macmillan.

BERRY, BRIAN J. L., AND PHILIP H. REES. 1969. "The Factorial Ecology of Calcutta." *American Journal of Sociology* 74:445–91.

BLAKE, WILLIAM. 1808. "Milton." P. 388b. In *Familiar Quotations*, edited by John Bartlett. Boston: Little, Brown.

BLAKELY, EDWARD J., AND MARY GAIL SNYDER. 1997. *Fortress America: Gated Communities in the United States*. Washington, DC: Brookings Institution Press.

BLAU, JUDITH R., AND PETER M. BLAU. 1982. "Metropolitan Structure and Violent Crime." *American Sociological Review* 47:114–28.

BLAU, PETER M., AND REID M. GOLDEN. 1986. "Metropolitan Structure and Criminal Violence." *Sociological Quarterly* 27.

BLOOD, ROBERT O. 1969. "Kinship Interaction and Marital Solidarity." *Merrill Palmer Quarterly* 15:171–84.

BLUMENFELD, HANS. 1964. *The Modern Metropolis*. Cambridge, MA: MIT Press.

BONAVIA, DAVID. 1978. *Peking*. New York: Little, Brown.

BONNES, MIRILIA, MARINO BONAIUTO, AND ANNA PAOLA. 1991. "Crowding and Residential Satisfaction in the Urban Environment: A Contextual Approach." *Environment and Behavior* 23 (September): 531–52.

BOOKCHIN, MURRAY. 1996. *The Limits of the City*. 2nd rev. ed. Toronto: Black Rose Books.

BORJAS, GEORGE J. 2001. *Heaven's Gate: Immigration Policy and the American Economy*. Princeton, NJ: Princeton University Press.

BORUKHOV, ELI, YONA GINSBERG, and ELIA WERCZBERG. 1979. "The Social Ecology of Tel Aviv." *Urban Affairs Quarterly* 15: 183–205.

BOTT, ELIZABETH. 1957. *Family and Social Network*. London: Tavistock.

BOWRA, CECIL M. 1977. *Classical Greece*. New York: Little, Brown.

BOYCE, JOSEPH N. 1997. "All Politics Is Local." *Wall Street Journal*, May 7, p. A1.

BOYER, R. E., AND K. A. DAVIES. 1973. "Urbanization in Nineteenth Century Latin America: Statistics and Sources." *Statistical Abstract of Latin America*. July supplement.

BRADBURY, CATHERINE, ANTHONY DOWNS, AND KENNETH SMALL. 1982. *Urban Decline and the Future of American Cities*. Washington, DC: Brookings Institution.

BRADSHAW, YORK W. 1985. "Dependent Development in Black Africa." *American Sociological Review* 50:195–207.

BRIDENBAUGH, CARL. 1964. *Cities in the Wilderness*. New York: Capricorn Books.

Britannica Book of the Year. 2002. Chicago: Encyclopaedia Britannica.

BROCKERHOFF, MARTIN. 1996. " 'City Summit' to Address Global Urbanization." *Population Today* 24 (March): 4–5.

BROKAW, TOM. 2002. NBC News, June 27.

BROOKS, VAN WYCK. 1936. *The Flowering of New England*. New York: Modern Library.

BRUCE, J. M. 1970. "Intergenerational Occupational Mobility and Visiting with Kin and Friend." *Social Forces* 49:117–27.

BRUNO, PAT. 2001. "Dinner and a Show: New Theaters Draw Diners Downtown." *Chicago Sun-Times*, September 7, p. 16.

BRUSH, JOHN E. 1961. "The Morphology of Indian Cities." Pp. 57–70 in *India's Urban Future: Seminar on Urbanization in India*. Berkeley: University of California Press.

BRYON, ROBERT. 1950. *The Road to Oxiana*. London: Methuen.

BUCKLAND, ROBERT. 1968. *Share My Taxi*. London: Michael Joseph.

BUREAU OF ECONOMIC ANALYSIS. 1996. *Survey of Current Business*. Washington, DC: U.S. Government Printing Office.

BUREAU OF JUSTICE STATISTICS. 1999a. *Students' Reports of School Crime: 1989 and 1995*. Accessed at http://www.ojp.usdoj.gov/bjs/pub/ascii/srsc.txt on December 26, 1999.

———. 1999b. *Criminal Victimization 1998: Changes 1997–98 with Trends 1993–98*. Accessed at http://www.ojp.usdoj.gov/bis/pub/ascii/cv98.txt on December 26, 1999.

BURGESS, ERNEST W. 1984. "The Growth of the City." Pp. 47–62 in *The City*, edited by Robert E. Park and Ernest W. Burgess. Chicago: University of Chicago Press.

BURN, A. R. 1970. *Greece and Rome*. Glenview, IL: Scott, Foresman.

BUTTERWORTH, DOUGLAS, AND JOHN K. CHANCE. 1981. *Latin American Urbanization*. New York: Cambridge University Press.

CAHNMAN, WERNER, AND RUDOLF HEBERLE. 1971. *Ferdinand Tönnies, On Sociology: Pure, Applied and Empirical*. Chicago: University of Chicago Press.

CALDWELL, WILLIAM A., ed. 1973. *How to Save Urban America*. New York: Signet.

CALHOUN, JOHN B. 1962. "Population Density and Social Pathology." *Scientific American* 206:139–48.

CALLOW, J. A., AND ALEXANDER B. CALLOW, JR., ed. 1969. *American Urban History*. 2nd ed. New York: Oxford University Press, 1977.

CANADIAN COUNCIL ON SOCIAL DEVELOPMENT. 2000. *Urban Poverty in Canada: A Statistical Profile*. Accessed at http://www.ccsd.ca/pubs/2000/up/ on October 13, 2002.

CANTOR, GEORGE. 1998. "Searching for New Living Arrangements: Redefining Neighborhoods." *Detroit News*, April 26, p. 1.

CARLTON, ERIC. 1977. *Ideology and Social Order*. London: Routledge and Kegan Paul.

CASA ALIANZA. 2002. *Street Children in Guatemala City*. Accessed at http://www.casa-alianza.org/EN/about/offices/guatemala/children.html on October 13, 2002.

CASTELLS, MANUEL. 1979. *The Urban Question*. Cambridge, MA: MIT Press.

———. 1982. *City, Class, and Power*. New York: Palgrave Macmillan.

———. 1985. *The City and the Grass Roots*. Berkeley: University of California Press.

———. 1991. *The Informational City*. Malden, MA: Blackwell.

CAULFIELD, JON. 1994. *City Form and Everyday Life: Toronto's Gentrification and Critical Social Practice*. Toronto: University of Toronto Press.

CENTER FOR MEDIA AND PUBLIC AFFAIRS. 1999. *Merchandizing Mayhem: Violence in Popular Culture*. Accessed online at http://www.cmpa.com/archive/viol98.htm on September 23, 2002.

CENTRAL INTELLIGENCE AGENCY. 2002. *World Fact Book*. Accessed at http://www.odci.gov/cia/publications/factbook/index.html on September 9, 2002.

CHANDLER, MITTIE O. 1988. *Urban Homesteading: Programs and Policies*. Westport, CT: Greenwood Press.

CHANDLER, TERTIUS. 1987. *4000 Years of Urban Growth*. Lewiston, NJ: Edwin Mellen Press.

CHANG, KWANG-CHIH. 1977. *Archaeology of Ancient China*. New Haven, CT: Yale University Press.

CHAVEZ, ERNEST L., ET AL. 1989. "Mexican American and White American School Dropouts' Drug Use, Health Status, and Involvement in Violence." *Public Health Reports* (November–December), pp. 594–604.

CHILDE, V. GORDON. 1950. "The Urban Revolution." *Town Planning Review* 21:3–17.

CHILDREN'S DEFENSE FUND. 1991. *The Nation's Investment in Children: An Analysis of the President's FY 1992 Budget Proposals*. Washington, DC: Children's Defense Fund.

CHRISTALLER, WALTER. 1966. *Central Places in Southern Germany*. Englewood Cliffs, NJ: Prentice Hall.

CHUA-EOAN, HOWARD G. 1990. "Strangers in Paradise." *Time*, April 9, pp. 32–35.

CIARDI, JOHN. 1959. *How Does a Poem Mean?* Boston: Houghton Mifflin.

CLARK, KENNETH. 1980. "The Role of Race." *New York Times Magazine*, October 5, pp. 25–33, 90–91.

CLARK, WILLIAM A.V. 1990. *The California Cauldron*. Guilford, CT: Guilford Press.

COHEN, MARK NATHAN. 1977. *The Food Crisis in Prehistory*. New Haven, CT: Yale University Press.

COHEN, WARREN, AND MIKE THARP. 1999. "Fed-up Cities Turn to Evicting the Homeless." *U.S. News & World Report*, January 11, pp. 28–30.

COMMUNITY SERVICE SOCIETY OF NEW YORK. 2002. *Poverty in New York City, 2001*. Accessed at www.cssny.org/reports on January 8, 2003.

CONGDON, PETER. 1995. "Socioeconomic Structure and Health in London." *Urban Studies* 32 (April): 523–49.

CONNOR, TIM. 2001. *Still Waiting for Nike to Do It*. San Francisco: Global Exchange.

CONWAY, DONALD J., ed. 1977. *Human Response to Tall Buildings*. Stroudsburg, PA: Dowden, Hutchinson, and Ross.

CONWAY, WILTRAM G. 1977. "People Fire in the Ghetto Ashes." *Saturday Review*, July 23, pp. 15–16.

COSTELLO, VINCENT F. 1977. *Urbanization in the Middle East*. New York: Cambridge University Press.

COTTRELL, JOHN, AND THE EDITORS OF TIME-LIFE. 1979. *The Great Cities: Mexico City*. Amsterdam: Time-Life.

COX, HARVEY. 1965. *The Secular City*. New York: Macmillan.

CRAIGSLIST. 2003. *New York City: Estate for Sale*. Accessed at http:newyork.craigslist.org on January 9, 2003.

CUMMINGS, KIM C. 2000. "Regenerating Social Capital in Urban Neighborhoods: A Case Study." *Journal of Applied Sociology* 17:56–68.

DANA, RICHARD HENRY. 1947. *Two Years Before the Mast*. New York: Heritage; originally published 1862.

The Dark Side of the American Dream. 1998. At www.sierraclub. org/sprawl/report98/report.asp. Accessed on January 9, 2003.

DASGUPTA, SATHI. 1992. "Conjugal Roles and Social Network in Indian Immigrant Families." *Journal of Comparative Family Studies* 23:465–80.

DAVIDSON, BASIL. 1998. *Africa in History: Themes and Patterns.* rev. ed. Carmichael, CA: Touchstone Books.

DAVIS, KINGSLEY. 1969, 1972. *World Urbanization, 1950–1970.* Vols. 1, 2. Berkeley, CA: Institute of International Studies.

DEAR, MICHAEL J. 2000. *The Postmodern Urban Condition.* Malden, MA: Blackwell.

DEEGAN, MARY JO. 1991. *Women in Sociology: A Bio- Bibliographical Sourcebook.* Westport, CT: Greenwood Press.

DEL PINAL, JORGE, AND AUDREY SINGER. 1997. "Generations of Diversity: Latinos in the United States." *Population Bulletin,* (October).

DEMAREST, MICHAEL. 1981. "He Digs Downtown." *Time,* August 24, pp. 36–43.

DENT, DAVID J. 1992. "The New Black Suburbs." *New York Times Magazine,* June 14.

DIAGNE, PAPA SYR. 1995. "Our Demographic Future: Predictions for the Next 50 years." *Population Today* (December): 3.

DIAZ, BERNAL. 1956. *The Discovery and Conquest of Mexico.* New York: Farrar, Straus, and Cudahy.

DICKENS, CHARLES. 1841. *The Old Curiosity Shop.* London: Chapman and Hall.

———. 1848. *Dombey and Son.* London: Chapman and Hall.

———. 1853. *Bleak House.* London: Chapman and Hall.

———. 1955, orig. 1854. *Hard Times.* London: Chapman and Hall.

———. 1860. *Great Expectations.* London: Chapman and Hall.

DICKERSON, MARLA. 1999. "Improvement Zones Spur Revival—and Division." *Los Angeles Times,* January 20, p. 1.

DIGIOVANNI, FRANK F. 1984. "An Examination of Selected Consequences of Revitalization in Six U.S. Cities." *Urban Studies* 21:245–59.

DIIULIO, JOHN J., JR. 1995. "Comment on Douglas S. Massey's 'Getting Away with Murder.' " *University of Pennsylvania Law Review* 143 (May): 1275–84.

DINER, HASIA R. 1983. *Erin's Daughters in America: Irish Immigrant Women in the Nineteenth Century.* Baltimore: Johns Hopkins University Press.

DOBRINER, WILLIAM. 1963. *Class in Suburbia.* Englewood Cliffs, NJ: Prentice-Hall.

DOCTOROW, E. L. 1975. *Ragtime.* New York: Bantam.

DOS PASSOS, JOHN. 1969. "San Francisco Looks West." Pp. 484–89 in *City Life,* edited by Oscar Shoenfeld and Helen MacLean. New York: Grossman; essay originally published 1944.

DOWNS, ANTHONY. 1981. *Neighborhoods and Urban Development.* Washington, DC: Brookings Institution.

———. 1985. "The Future of Industrial Cities." Pp. 281–94 in *The New Urban Reality,* edited by Paul E. Peterson. Washington, DC: Brookings Institution.

DREISER, THEODORE. 1925. *An American Tragedy.* New York: Boni and Liveright.

DUNCAN, BEVERLY. 1956. "Factors in Work–Residence Separation: Wages and Salary Workers." *American Journal of Sociology* 21:48–56.

DUNCAN, SUSANA. 1977. "Mental Maps of New York." *New York,* December 19, pp. 51–62.

DUNLAP, DAVID W. 1999. "Filling in the Blanks at Battery Park City." *New York Times,* February 7, p. RE2.

DURBIN, STEPHANIE. 1996. "Spotlight: Turkey." *Population Today* 24 (March): 7.

DURKHEIM, EMILE. 1964. *The Division of Labor in Society.* New York: Free Press; originally published 1893.

The Economist. 2002. "Cranes on the Skyline, Crashes on the Horizon?" August 17, p. 47.

EGAN, TIMOTHY. 1996. "Portland's Hard Line on Managing Growth." *New York Times,* December 30, p. A1.

EISNER, SIMON, ARTHUR GALLION, and STANLEY EISNER. 1993. *The Urban Pattern.* 6th ed. New York: Wiley.

ELIOT, T. S. 1964. "Preludes." *Collected Poems 1909–1962.* New York: Faber & Faber, Ltd.

ENGEL, MARIAN. 1981. *Lunatic Villas.* Toronto: McClelland and Stewart-Bantam.

ENGELS, FRIEDRICH. 1958. *The Condition of the Working Class in England,* trans. by W. O. Henderson and W. H. Chaloner. New York: Macmillan.

ENVIRONMENTAL WORKING GROUP. 2002. *Particle Civics.* Accessed at http://www.ewg.org/reports/particlecivics/ on August 4, 2002.

EVANS, PETER B., AND MICHAEL TIMBERLAKE. 1980. "Dependence, Inequality, and the Growth of the Tertiary." *American Sociological Review* 45:531–52.

FARAH, DOUGLAS. 1996. "From Mean Streets of Bogotá, Rebirth." *Washington Post,* July 5, p. A17.

FARLEY, REYNOLDS. 1976. "Components of Suburban Population Growth." Pp. 3–33 in *The Changing Face of the Suburbs,* edited by B. Schwartz. Chicago: University of Chicago Press.

———. 1997. "Modest Declines in U.S. Residential Segregation Observed." *Population Today* 25 (February): 1–2.

FARLEY, REYNOLDS, AND WILLIAM H. FREY. 1994. *Regional and Metropolitan Growth and Decline in the United States.* New York: Russell Sage Foundation.

FARLEY, REYNOLDS, ET AL. 1993. "Continued Racial Residential Segregation in Detroit: 'Chocolate City, Vanilla Suburbs' Revisited." *Journal of Housing Research* 4(1):1–38.

FEDERAL BUREAU OF INVESTIGATION. 2002. *Crime in the United States—2000.* Accessed at http://www.fbi.gov/ucr/ cius_00/00crime2_3.pdf on September 21, 2002.

FEDERAL RESERVE SYSTEM. 2000. *Federal Reserve Bulletin.* Washington, DC: U. S. Government Printing Office.

FEGELMAN, ANDREW. 1997. "15 High-Rises in Cabrini Left Out of Big Plan." *Chicago Tribune,* February 21. Accessed at www.chicagotribune.com.

FERNANDEZ-KELLY, M. 1991. "Labor Force Recomposition and Industrial Restructuring in Electronics." Paper presented at symposium: "Crossing National Borders: Invasion or Involvement." December 6, Columbia University.

FILION, PIERRE. 1995. "City Form and Everyday Life: Toronto's Gentrification and Critical Social Practice." *Journal of the American Planning Association* 61 (Spring): 281–82.

FIREBAUGH, GLENN. 1992. "Growth Effects of Foreign and Domestic Investment." *American Journal of Sociology* 98 (July): 105–30.

FIRESTONE, DAVID. 1996. "New York Costs for Its Programs Seen as Surging." *New York Times*, August 1, p. A1.

FISCHER, CLAUDE S. 1971. "A Research Note on Urbanism and Tolerance." *American Journal of Sociology* 76:847–56.

———. 1973. "Urban Malaise." *Social Problems* 52:221–35.

———. 1975. "Toward a Subcultural Theory of Urbanism." *American Journal of Sociology* 80:1319–41.

———. 1984. *The Urban Experience.* 2nd ed. Orlando: Harcourt Brace Jovanovich.

FISCHER, CLAUDE, R. M. JACKSON, C. A. STUEVE, K. GERSON, AND L. M. JONES. 1977. *Networks and Places.* New York: Free Press.

FISCHER, CLAUDE S., ET AL. 1996. *Inequality by Design: Cracking the Bell Curve Myth.* Princeton: Princeton University Press.

FISHMAN, ROBERT. 1982. *Urban Utopias in the Twentieth Century.* Cambridge, MA: MIT Press.

FLEISHMAN, SANDRA. 1999. "Abandoned Housing Is Now Hot Property." *Washington Post*, September 1, p. B01.

FLEM, LLOYD H., AND CARL SCHIERMEYER. 1997. "Rail Transit: The People's Choice." *Railway Age* 198 (September): 71–80.

FLORIAN, ELLEN. 1999. "Oh, No, It's Spreading." *Newsweek*, July 19, pp. 24–25.

FORBES, KATHRYN. 1943. *Mama's Bank Account.* New York: Harcourt, Brace.

FORNOS, WERNER. 1996. "Gaining People, Losing Ground." Speech at William Paterson University, Wayne, NJ, October 23.

FOX, RICHARD. 1977. *Urban Anthropology.* Englewood Cliffs, NJ: Prentice-Hall.

FRANCK, KAREN. 1981. "In Cities, Fast Friends Come Slowly." *Psychology Today*, (April), pp. 32–33.

FREEDMAN, JONATHAN. 1978. *Happy People.* New York: Ballantine.

FREEMAN, JO. 1975. *The Politics of Women's Liberation.* New York: David McKay.

FRENCH, R. A., AND F. E. IAN HAMILTON. 1979. "Is There a Socialist City?" Pp. 1–22 in *The Socialist City*, edited by R. A. French and F. E. Ian Hamilton. New York: Wiley.

FREUDENBERG, WILLIAM R. 1992. "Addictive Economics: Extractive Industries and Vulnerable Localities in a Changing World Economy." *Rural Sociology* 57 (3):305–22.

FREY, WILLIAM H. 1998. "Black Migration to the South Reaches Record Highs in 1990s." *Population Today*, (February): 1–2.

FREY, WILLIAM H., AND WILLIAM P. O'HARE. 1993. "Viva Los Suburbinos!" *American Demographics*, April, p. 32.

FRIED, MORTON H. 1967. *The Evolution of Political Society.* New York: Random House.

FUGUITT, GLENN V. 1984. "The Nonmetropolitan Population Turnaround." *Annual Review of Sociology* 21:259–80.

FUNK, WILFRED. 1978. *Word Origins.* New York: Bell.

GALINDO, LETTICIA D. 1993. "The Language of Gangs, Drugs, and Prison Life Among Chicanas." *Latino Studies Journal* 4 (September): 23.

GALSTER, GEORGE. 1990. "Racial Discrimination in Housing Markets during the 1980s: A Review of the Audit Evidence." *Journal of Planning Education and Research* 9(3):165–75.

———. 1996. *Reality and Research: Social Science and U.S. Urban Policy since 1960.* New York: Urban Institute Press.

GANS, HERBERT. 1962a. "City Planning and Urban Realities." *Commentary* 33:170–75.

———. 1962b. *The Urban Villagers.* New York: Free Press.

———. 1968. "Urbanism and Suburbanism as Ways of Life: A Re-evaluation of Definitions." Pp. 34–52 in *People and Plans.* New York: Basic Books.

———. 1982. *The Urban Villagers: Group and Class in the Life of Italian Americans.* New York: Free Press.

GARBER, JUDITH A., AND ROBY TURNER, eds. 1993. *Gender in Urban Research.* Thousand Oaks, CA: Sage.

GARCIA-HALLCOM, FRANCINE. 1997. *An Urban Ethnography of Latino Street.* www.csun.edu/~hcchs006/gang.html.

GARREAU, JOEL. 1991. *Edge City.* New York: Doubleday.

GEISSE, G., AND F. SABATINI. 1988. "Latin American Cities and Their Poor." Pp. 322–27 in *The Metropolitan Era*, edited by M. Dogan and J. Kasarda. Newbury Park, CA: Sage.

GELLNER, ERNEST. 1983. *Nations and Nationalism.* Malden, MA: Blackwell.

GEORGANO, G. N. 1973. *A History of the London Taxicab.* New York: Drake.

GERMANI, GINO, ed. 1973. *Modernization, Urbanization, and the Urban Crisis.* Boston: Little, Brown.

GIBBON, EDWARD. 1932. *The Decline and Fall of the Roman Empire.* New York: Modern Library; originally published in London, 1879.

GIBSON, OTIS. 1877. *The Chinese in America.* Cincinnati: Hitchcock and Walden.

GIOVANNINI, JOSEPH. 1983. "I Love New York and L.A., Too." *New York Times Magazine*, September 11, pp. 145, 147–49.

GIRARDET, HERBERT. 1994. "Keeping Up with Capital Growth." *Geographical Magazine* 66 (June): 12–15.

GLAAB, CHARLES N. 1963. *The American City: A Documentary History.* Homewood, IL: Dorsey Press.

GLAAB, CHARLES N., AND A. THEODORE BROWN. 1967. *A History of Urban America.* New York: Macmillan.

GLAZER, NATHAN, AND DANIEL P. MOYNIHAN. 1970. *Beyond the Melting Pot.* 2nd ed. Cambridge, MA: MIT Press.

GOFFMAN, ERVING. 1971. *Relations in Public.* New York: Basic Books.

GOLDBERGER, PAUL. 1979. *The City Observed: New York.* New York: Vintage.

GOLIBER, THOMAS J. 2002. "The Status of the HIV/Aids Epidemic in Sub-Saharan Africa." *Population Bulletin* (July).

GORDON, R., K. GORDON, AND M. GUNTHER. 1960. *The Split Level Trap.* New York: Bernard Geis.

GOTTDIENER, MARK. 1994. *The New Urban Sociology.* New York: McGraw-Hill.

———. 2001. *The Theming of America.* 2nd ed. Boulder, CO: Westview Press.

GOTTDIENER, MARK, AND JOE FEAGIN. 1988. "The Paradigm Shift in Urban Sociology." *Urban Affairs Quarterly* 24:163–87.

GOTTMANN, JEAN. 1961. *Megalopolis.* New York: Twentieth Century Fund.

GOULDNER, ALVIN. 1971. *Enter Plato.* New York: Harper & Row.

GRAY, ROBERT. 1978. *A History of London.* London: Hutchinson.

GREEN, CONSTANCE. 1957. *American Cities.* Welwyn Garden City, England: Broadwater Press.

GREEN, ROBERT L. 1977. *The Urban Challenge: Poverty and Race.* Chicago: Follett.

GREENE, WILLIAM CHASE. 1923. *The Achievement of Greece.* Cambridge, MA: Harvard University Press.

GREENFIELD, GERALD M. 1994. *Latin American Urbanization.* Westport, CT: Greenwood Publishing Group.

GREENGARD, SAMUEL, AND CHARLENE M. SOLOMON. 1994. "A City Rebuilds Its Symbol—and Rejuvenates Itself." *Personnel Journal* 73 (February): 64–65.

GREER, SCOTT. 1962. *The Emerging City.* New York: Free Press.

———. 1965. *Urban Renewal and American Cities.* Indianapolis: Bobbs-Merrill.

GUGLER, JOSEF. 1996. *The Urban Transformation of the Developing World: Regional Trajectories.* New York: Oxford University Press.

HABITAT FOR HUMANITY. 2002. *Habitat for Humanity Fact Sheet.* Accessed at http://www.habitat.org/how/factsheet.html on April 4, 2003.

HACKLER, TIM. 1979. "The Big City Has No Corners on Mental Illness." *New York Times Magazine,* December 19, p. A1.

HALE, ROBERT, AND D. MARK AUSTIN. 1997. "An Exploratory Factor Model of Social Area Analysis." *Sociological Spectrum* 17:115–25.

HALL, EDWARD. 1966. *The Hidden Dimension.* Garden City, NY: Doubleday. Chap. 13.

HALL, PETER. 1975. *Urban and Regional Planning.* London: Pelican.

———. 1984a. *The World Cities.* 3rd ed. New York: Palgrave Macmillan.

———. 1984b. "Geography." Pp. 21–36 in *Cities of the Mind,* edited by Lloyd Rodwin and Robert M. Hollister. New York: Plenum.

HAMBLIN, DORA JANE. 1973. *The First Cities.* New York: Time-Life.

HAMILTON, EDITH. 1993. *The Greek Way.* New York: Norton.

HANFF, HELENE. 1973. *The Duchess of Bloomsbury Street.* New York: Avon.

———. 1978. *Apple of My Eye.* Garden City, NY: Doubleday.

HANSON, FRANK. 1980. "Arson: Its Effects and Control." *Fire Surveyor* 9:32–36.

HARDOY, JORGE E. 1975. "Two Thousand Years of Latin American Urbanization." Pp. 3–56 in *Urbanization in Latin America,* edited by Jorge E. Hardoy. Garden City, NY: Anchor.

HARDOY, JORGE E., DIANA MITLIN, AND DAVID SATTERTHWAITE. 1992. *Environmental Problems in Third World Cities.* Washington, DC: Island Press.

HARRIS, CHAUNCEY D., AND EDWARD L. ULLMAN. 1945. "The Nature of Cities." *Annals* 242:7–17.

HARRIS, MARY G. 1994. "Cholas, Mexican-American Girls and Gangs." *Sex Roles: A Journal of Research* 30 (February): 289–301.

HARSCH, ERNEST. "South Africa Tackles Social Inequalities." *Africa Recovery,* United Nations, 2002.

HARVEY, DAVID. 1992. *Social Justice and the City.* Malden, MA: Blackwell; original ed. Baltimore: Johns Hopkins University Press, 1973.

HAUB, CARL V. 1996. "Spotlight: India." *Population Today* 24 (May): 7.

HAWKES, J. 1973. *The First Great Civilizations.* New York: Knopf.

HAWLEY, AMOS. 1971. *Urban Society.* New York: Ronald Press.

HAWLEY, AMOS, AND OTIS DUDLEY DUNCAN. 1957. "Social Area Analysis: A Critical Appraisal." *Land Economics* 33:337–44.

HAYDEN, DELORES. 1978. "Two Utopian Feminists and Their Campaigns for Kitchenless Houses." *Signs: Journal of Women in Culture and Society* 4:274–90.

HAYWARD, STEVEN. "The Scourge of New Jobs." *New York Times,* June 12, 1999, p. A15.

HECKSCHER, AUGUST, WITH PHYLLIS ROBINSON. 1977. *Open Spaces: The Life of American Cities.* New York: Harper & Row.

HEILBRONER, ROBERT L., AND WILLIAM S. MILBERG. 2001. *The Making of Economic Society.* 11th ed. Englewood Cliffs, NJ: Prentice Hall.

HEILBRUN, JAMES. 1974. *Urban Economics and Public Policy.* New York: St. Martin's Press.

HELPER, ROSE. 1969. *Racial Policies and Practices of Real Estate Brokers.* Minneapolis: University of Minnesota Press.

HENG, LIANG, AND JUDITH SHAPIRO. 1984. *Son of the Revolution.* New York: Vintage.

HERBERT, WRAY. 1996. "Rock and Roller Coasters: Hit Cleveland's New Museum and Cedar Point's Rides for Thrills, Then Chill Out on Lake Erie's Isles." *U.S. News & World Report* 120 (April 15): 71–74.

HERRNSTEIN, RICHARD J., AND CHARLES MURRAY. 1994. *The Bell Curve: The Reshaping of American Life by Differences in Intelligence.* New York: Free Press.

HERSKOVITS, MELVILLE J. 1962. *The Human Factor in Changing Africa.* New York: Knopf.

HEVESI, DENNIS. 1999. "Lofty Prices Send Loft Pioneers in Search of New Frontiers." *New York Times,* February 21, pp. RE 1, 6.

———. 2001. "East New York: A Neighborhood Reborn." *New York Times,* June 10, pp. RE1, 10.

HIGGS, ROBERT. 1980. *Competition and Conflict: Blacks in the American Economy, 1865–1914.* Chicago: University of Chicago Press.

HOCH, CHARLES, AND ROBERT A. SLAYTON. 1989. *New Homeless and Old: Community and the Skid Row Hotel.* Philadelphia: Temple University Press.

HOHENBERG, PAUL M., AND LYNN HOLLEN LEES. 1985. *The Making of Urban Europe, 1000–1950*. Cambridge, MA: Harvard University Press.

HOLUSHA, JOHN. 1985. "Midwest Cities Find New Economic Life on Old Waterfronts." *New York Times*, September 30, pp. A1, B12.

———. 2002. "Strong Demand for Store Space in Manhattan." *New York Times*, July 28, pp. RE1, 6.

HOPKINS, ELLEN. 1985. "The Dispossessed." *New York*, May 13, pp. 48–61.

HOUSING AUTHORITY OF NEW ORLEANS (HANO). 2002. Accessed at http://www.hano.org/S8WL%20Update.htm on September 22, 2002.

HOUSTON. 2002. Accessed at http://www.ci.houston.tx.us/abouthouston/houstonfacts.html on August 6, 2002.

HOWARD, EBENEZER. 1965. *Garden Cities of To-Morrow*. Cambridge, MA: MIT Press.

HOWE, IRVING. 1976. *World of Our Fathers*. New York: Harcourt, Brace, Jovanovich.

HOWELL, JOSEPH T. 1973. *Hard Living on Clay Street*. Garden City, NY: Anchor.

HOYT, HOMER. 1939. *The Structure and Growth of Residential Neighborhoods in American Cities*. Washington, DC: Federal Housing Administration.

HUMAN RIGHTS WATCH. 2002. "Street Children." Accessed at http://www.hrw.org/children/street.htm on October 13, 2002.

HUNG, KWING, AND SHARON BOWLES. 1995. "Public Perceptions of Crime." *Juristat* 15 (January): 1.

HWANG, SEAN-SHONG, ET AL. "The Effects of Race and Socioeconomic Status on Racial Segregation in Texas, 1970–1980." *Social Forces* 63:732–47.

INSTITUTE FOR CHILDREN AND POVERTY. 1993a. "What Does Homelessness Have to Do with Foster Care?" 2 (August): pp. 1–2.

———. 1993b. *Access to Success* (January).

———. 1994. *Job Readiness: Crossing the Threshold from Homelessness to Employment*. ICP Report 5 (March).

———. 1998. *The Cycle of Family Homelessness: A Social Policy Reader*.

International Social Development Review. 1969. "Growth of the World's Urban and Rural Population: 1920–2000."

IRVINE. 2002. Accessed at http://www.ci.irvine.ca.us/about/default.asp on October 19, 2002.

IRWIN, JOHN. 1977. *Scenes*. Beverly Hills, CA: Sage.

JACKSON, K. 1973. "The Crabgrass Frontier: 150 Years of Suburban Growth in America." Pp. 196–221 in *The Urban Experience: Themes in American History*, edited by R. Mohl and J. Richardson. Belmont, CA: Wadsworth.

JACKSON, KENNETH T. 1996. "Why America Has Gone Suburban." *New York Times*, June 5, p. A15.

JACOBS, ANDREW. 1995. "West Side Waterfront: 'Gold Mine' to Repair Piers for Public Use." *New York Times*, December 24, p. A7.

JACOBS, JANE. 1961. *The Death and Life of Great American Cities*. New York: Random House.

———. 1984. *Cities and the Wealth of Nations*. New York: Random House.

JAFFEE, DAVID. 1985. "Export Dependence and Economic Growth." *Social Forces* 64:102–18.

JARGOWSKY, PAUL A. 1996. "Take the Money and Run: Economic Segregation in U.S. Metropolitan Areas." *American Sociological Review* 61 (December): 984–98.

JASTROW, MARIE. 1979. *A Time to Remember*. New York: Norton.

JOHNSON, KIRK. 1996. "Giuliani Offers Plan to Nurture the City's New Industries." *New York Times*, May 1, p. A1.

JOHNSON, KIRK, AND THOMAS J. LUECK. 1996. "Region's Economy in Fundamental Shift." *New York Times*, February 19, p. A1.

JOHNSTON, R. J. 1976. "Residential Area Characteristics." Pp. 193–235 in *Social Areas in Cities*. Vol. I, *Spatial Processes and Form*, edited by D. T. Herbert and R. J. Johnston. New York: Wiley.

JOINT CENTER FOR HOUSING STUDIES. 1999. *The State of the Nation's Housing: 1999*. Accessed at http://www.gsd.harvard.edu/jcenter/ on December 26, 1999.

JONES, DEL. 1999. "Employers Battle Urban Sprawl Issues." *USA Today*, June 14, p. 1B.

JUBILEE LINE EXTENSION. 1997. "Archaeological Excavation at London Bridge." www.jle.lul.co.uk/arch/index.htm.

KADUSHIN, CHARLES. 1983. "Mental Health and the Interpersonal Environment." *American Sociological Review* 48:188–98.

KALISH, SUSAN. 1995. "Spotlight: China." *Population Today* 23 (September): 7.

KAMIN, BLAIR. 1995. "Unifying Cities." *Chicago Tribune*, June 19, p. B1.

KAMM, HENRY. 1974. "The Last Days of Empire." *New York Times Sunday Magazine*, August 18, p. 58.

KANE, HARNETT T. 1949. *Queen New Orleans*. New York: Bonanza.

KARP, DAVID A., GREGORY P. STONE, AND WILLIAM C. YOELS. 1991. *Being Urban: A Sociology of City Life*. New York: Praeger.

KASARDA, JOHN D. 1990. "The Job Skills Mismatch." *New Perspectives Quarterly* 7 (Fall), 34–37.

———. 1993. "Inner-City Concentrated Poverty and Neighborhood Distress: 1970 to 1990." *Housing Policy Debate* 4(3): 253–302.

KASARDA, JOHN D., AND EDWARD CRENSHAW. 1991. "Third World Urbanization: Dimensions, Theories, and Determinants." *Annual Review of Sociology* 17:467–501.

KAZIN, ALFRED. 1951. *A Walker in the City*. New York: Harcourt.

KEATS, JOHN. 1956. *The Crack in the Picture Window*. New York: Ballantine Books.

KELLER, SUZANNE. 1968. *The Urban Neighborhood*. New York: Random House.

KEMP, BARRY J. 1977–1978. "The Early Development of Towns in Egypt." *Antiquity* 51–52:185–200.

KEMPER, ROBERT V. 1977. *Migration and Adaptation*. Beverly Hills, CA: Sage.

KENNEDY, RANDY. 2002. "Study Finds Airport-Related Business in New York Hit Hard by 9/11." *New York Times*, October 25, p. B3.

KENYON, KATHLEEN. 1957. *Digging Up Jericho*. London: Ernest Benn.

————. 1970. *Archeology in the Holy Land.* New York: Praeger.

KIM, ILL SOO. 1981. *New Urban Immigrants: The Korean Community in New York.* Princeton: Princeton University Press.

KING, S. 1974. "Suburban Downtowns: The Shopping Centers." Pp. 101–104 in *Suburbia in Transition,* edited by L. Masotti and J. Hadden. New York: New York Times Books.

KOEGEL, PAUL, ET AL. 1996. "The Causes of Homelessless." *Homelessness in America.* Washington, DC: National Coalition for the Homeless.

KOMROFF, MANUEL, ED. 1964. *The Travels of Marco Polo.* Norwalk, CT: Heritage.

KORNBERG, W. 1975. "A Pre-Columbian Metropolis." *Mosaic* (September–October): 26–33.

KORZENIEWICZ, MIGUEL. 1994. "Commodity Chains and Marketing Strategies: Nike and the Global Athletic Footwear Industry." In *Community Chains and Global Capitalism,* edited by Gary Gereffi and Miguel Korzeniewicz. Westport, CT: Greenwood Press.

KOWINSKI, WILLIAM S. 2002. *The Malling of America.* Philadelphia: Xlibris Corporation.

KRAFT, SCOTT. 1995. "Down and Out in the City of Light." *Los Angeles Times,* July 19, p. 1.

KRUMHOLZ, NORMAN. 1978. "Cleveland: Problems of Declining Cities." In *Personality, Politics, and Planning,* edited by Anthony J. Catanese and W. Paul Farmer. Beverly Hills, CA: Sage.

KULHAVY, RAYMOND, W., AND WILLIAM A. STOCK. 1996. "How Cognitive Maps Are Learned and Remembered." *The Annals of the Association of American Geographers* 86 (March): 123–45.

KUNSTLER, JAMES. 1996. "Home from Nowhere." *Atlantic* (September): 43–66.

KWONG, PETER. 1987. *The New Chinatown.* New York: Hill and Wang.

LA GORY, MARK, RUSSELL WARD, AND THOMAS JURAVICH. 1980. "The Age Segregation Process." *Urban Affairs Quarterly* 16:59–80.

LAMBERG-KARLOVSKY, C. C., AND MARTHA LAMBERG-KARLOVSKY. 1973. "An Early City in Iran." Pp. 28–37 in *Cities: Their Origin, Growth and Human Impact.* San Francisco: W. H. Freeman.

LANDESCO, JOHN. 1929. *Organized Crime in Chicago.* Chicago: University of Chicago Press.

LANGDON, PHILIP. 1992. "How Portland Does It." *Atlantic,* (November).

LANGER, WILLIAM L. 1973. "The Black Death." Pp. 106–111 in *Cities: Their Origin, Growth and Human Impact.* San Francisco: W. H. Freeman.

LAO, SHE. 1979. *Rickshaw.* Honolulu: University of Hawaii.

LAURENTI, LUIGI. 1960. *Property Values and Race: Studies in Cities.* Berkeley: University of California Press.

LE CARRÉ, JOHN. 1978. *The Honourable Schoolboy.* New York: Bantam.

LE CORBUSIER. 1967. *The Radiant City.* New York: Grossman-Orion. Originally published 1933.

LEE, BARRETT A., AND PETER B. WOOD. 1991. "Is Neighborhood Racial Segregation Place Specific?" *Demography* 28:37.

LEE, SHARON M. 1998. "Asian Americans: Diverse and Growing." *Population Bulletin,* June.

LEFEBVRE, HENRI. 1970. *La Revolution Urbaine.* Paris: Gallimard.

————. 1991. *The Production of Space.* Malden, MA: Blackwell.

LEGACY, JAMES. 2000. Review of *Hoodwinking the Nation. Knowledge, Technology & Policy* 12 (Winter 2000): 94–95.

LEGATES, RICHARD, AND CHESTER HARTMAN. 1986. "The Anatomy of Displacement in the U.S." In *Gentrification of the City,* edited by N. Smith and P. Williams. Boston: Allen & Unwin.

LEPORE, STEPHEN J., AND GARY W. EVANS. 1991. "Social Hassles and Psychological Health in the Context of Chronic Crowding." *Journal of Health and Social Behavior* 32 (December): 357–67.

LEWIS MUMFORD CENTER FOR COMPARATIVE URBAN AND REGIONAL RESEARCH. 2001a. "Ethnic Diversity Grows, Neighborhood Integration Lags Behind." Albany: State University of New York. Accessed at http://mumford1.dyndns.org/cen2000/WholePop/WPreport/Mumford Report.pdf on September 28, 2002.

————. 2001b. *From Many Shores: Asians in Census 2000.* Accessed at http://mumford1.dyndns.org/cen2000/Asian Pop/AsianReport/AsianDownload.pdf on September 29, 2002.

————. 2001c. *The New Ethnic Enclaves in America's Suburbs.* Accessed at http://mumford1.dyndns.org/cen2000/suburban/SuburbanReport/SubReport.pdf on September 29, 2002.

————. 2002a. *Metropolitan Racial and Ethnic Change—Census 2000.* Accessed at http://www.albany.edu/mumford/census/ on September 21, 2002.

————. 2002b. *Hispanic Populations and their Residential Patterns in the Metropolis.* Accessed at http:// mumford1.dyndns.org/cen2000/HispanicPop/HspReportNew/MumfordReport.pdf on September 30, 2002.

LEWIS, OSCAR. 1960. *Tepotzlan: Village in Mexico.* New York: Holt, Rinehart and Winston.

————. 1961. *The Children of Sanchez.* New York: Random House.

————. 1966. *La Vida.* New York: Random House.

LEWIS, ROGER K. 1999. "Saving Tyson's Corner: Plans, But Little Progress." *Washington Post,* March 20, p. G3.

LIEBERSON, STANLEY. 1963. *Ethnic Patterns in American Cities.* New York: Free Press.

LIEBERSON, STANLEY, AND MARY WATERS. 1988. *From Many Strands: Ethnic and Racial Groups in Contemporary America.* New York: Russell Sage Foundation.

LIEBOW, ELIOT. 1967. *Tally's Corner.* Boston: Little, Brown.

LINSKY, ARNOLD, S. 1965. "Some Generalizations Concerning Primate Cities." *Annals of the Association of American Geographers* SS:506–15.

LIPTON, S. GREGORY. 1977. "Evidence of Central City Revival." *Journal of the American Institute of Planners* 43:136–47.

LLOYD, PETER C. 1986. "The Yoruba: An Urban People?" Pp. 107–23 in *Urban Anthropology,* edited by A. Southall. New York: Oxford University Press.

LOEWE, MICHAEL. 1964. *Imperial China.* New York: Praeger.

LOFLAND, LYN. 1985. *A World of Strangers: Order and Action in Urban Public Spaces.* Prospect Heights, IL: Waveland Press.

LOGAN, JOHN, AND HARVEY MOLOTCH. 1987. *Urban Fortunes: The Political Economy of Place.* Berkeley: University of California Press.

LOGAN, JOHN, AND LINDA STEARNS. 1981. "Suburban Racial Segregation as a Nonecological Process." *Social Forces* 60:61–73.

LOMNITZ, LARISSA. 1997. "The Social and Economic Organization of a Mexican Shanty-Town." Pp. 204–17 in *Cities in the Developing World,* edited by Josef Gugler. New York: Oxford University Press.

LONDON, BRUCE, AND WILLIAM G. FLANAGAN. 1976. "Comparative Urban Ecology: A Summary of the Field." Pp. 41–66 in *The City in Comparative Perspective,* edited by John Walton and Louis H. Masoni. Beverly Hills, CA: Sage.

LOWE, JEANNE R. 1967. *Cities in a Race with Time.* New York: Random House.

LU, ZIFEN. 1984. "Garden City Grows." *China Daily,* October 17, p. 1.

LUECK, THOMAS J. 1994. "Public Needs, Private Answers." *New York Times,* November 20, p. A1.

———. 1995. "Taking Heart in New York City." *New York Times,* October 8, p. A5.

LUNDBLAD, KAREN SHAFER. 1995. "Jane Addams and Social Reform: A Role Model for the 1990s." *Social Work* 40 (September): 661–69.

LYNCH, KEVIN. 1960. *The Image of the City.* Cambridge, MA: MIT Press.

———. 1984. "Reconsidering the Image of the City." Pp. 151–61 in *Cities of the Mind,* edited by Lloyd Rodwin and Robert M. Hollister. New York: Plenum.

MACFARQUHAR, RODERICK. 1972. *The Forbidden City.* New York: Newsweek.

MACIONIS, JOHN J. 1978. "The Search for Community in Modern Society." *Qualitative Sociology* 1 (May): 130–43.

———. 1997. *Sociology.* 6th ed. Upper Saddle River, NJ: Prentice Hall.

———. 1999. *Sociology.* 7th ed. Upper Saddle River, NJ: Prentice Hall.

MACIVER, ROBERT. 1962. "The Great Emptiness," in *Man Alone: Alienation in Modern Society,* edited by Eric and Mary Josephson. New York: Dell Laurel.

MACMANUS, SUSAN, AND CHARLES BULLOCK. 1995. "Electing Women to Public Office." In *Gender in Urban Research,* edited by Judith A. Garber and Robyne S. Turner. Thousand Oaks, CA: Sage.

MANUEL, MARION. 1997. "A City Without Limits," *Atlanta Journal/Atlanta Constitution,* November 3, p. 1.

MARAINI, FOSCO. 1977. *Tokyo.* Amsterdam: Time-Life.

MARDOCK, LORI. 1998. *Predicting Housing Abandonment in Central: Creating an Early Warning System.* Accessed at http://tcfreenet.org/org/npcr/reports/npcr1089.html on September 14, 1999.

MARIN, PETER. 1987. "Helping and Hating the Homeless." *Harper's* 274 (January): 40–41.

MARQUAND, JOHN P. 1943. *So Little Time.* Boston: Little, Brown.

MARSHALL, LEON S. 1969. "The English and American Industrial City of the Nineteenth Century." Pp. 148–55 in *American Urban History,* edited by Alexander B. Callow, Jr. New York: Oxford University Press.

MARTIN, HUGO. 1999. "The Road Ahead: Focus on Traffic." *Los Angeles Times,* June 24, p. 1.

MARTINES, LAURO. 1979. *Power and Imagination: City-States in Renaissance Italy.* New York: Knopf.

MARTINEZ, VALERIE J., R. KENNETH GODWIN, FRANK R. KEMERER, AND LAURA PERNA. 1995. "The Consequences of School Choice: Who Leaves and Who Stays in the Inner City." *Social Science Quarterly* 76 (September): 485–501.

MARX, KARL. 1859. "A Contribution to the Critique of Political Economy." Excerpted in *Marx and Engels: Basic Writings on Politics and Philosophy,* edited by Lewis S. Feuer. Garden City, NY: Anchor Books.

MARX, KARL, AND FRIEDRICH ENGELS. 1846. *The German Ideology.* New York: International Publishers, 1976.

MASSEY, DOREEN. 1994. *Space, Place, and Gender.* Minneapolis: University of Minnesota Press.

MASSEY, DOUGLAS S. 1984. "Processes of Hispanic and Black Spatial Segregation." *American Journal of Sociology* 89:836–73.

———. 1985. "Ethnic Residential Segregation: A Theoretical Synthesis and Empirical Review." *Sociology and Social Research* 69:315–50.

———. 1990. "American Apartheid: Segregation and the Making of the Underclass." *American Journal of Sociology* 96:329–54.

———. 1995. "Getting Away With Murder: Segregation and Violent Crime in Urban America." *University of Pennsylvania Law Review* 143 (May): 1203–32.

———. 1999. "America's Apartheid and the Urban Underclass," pp. 125–39 in Fred L. Pincus and Howard J. Ehrlich (eds.), *Race and Ethnic Conflict: Conflicting Views on Prejudice, Discrimination, and Ethnoviolence.* Philadelphia: University of Pennsylvania Press.

MASSEY, DOUGLAS S., AND BROOKS BITTERMAN. 1985. "Explaining the Paradox of Puerto Rican Segregation." *Social Forces* 64:306–31.

MASSEY, DOUGLAS S., AND NANCY A. DENTON. 1989. "Hypersegregation in U.S. Metropolitan Areas: Black and Hispanic Segregation Along Five Dimensions." *Demography* 26:373–91.

———. 1993. *American Apartheid: Segregation and the Making of the Underclass.* Cambridge, MA: Harvard University Press.

MATHEWS, JAY. 1992. "Rethinking Homeless Myths." *Newsweek,* April 6, p. 29.

MATOS, EDUARDO M. 1990. *Teotihuacan, The City of Gods.* New York: Rizzoli.

MATSUOKA, JON K. 1990. "Differential Acculturation Among Vietnamese Refugees." *Social Work* 35 (July): 341–45.

MAYER, HAROLD M., AND RICHARD C. WADE. 1969. *Chicago: Growth of a Metropolis.* Chicago: University of Chicago Press.

MAZEY, MARY ELLEN, AND DAVID R. LEE. 1983. *Her Space, Her Place: A Geography of Women.* Washington, DC: Association of American Geographers.

McCabe, James D., Jr. 1970. *Lights and Shadows of New York Life.* New York: Farrar, Straus and Giroux; originally published 1872.

McCarthy, Kevin F., and Georges Vernex. 1997. *Immigration in a Changing Economy: California's Experience.* Santa Monica, CA: Rand Corporation.

McKenzie, Evan. 1993. "Trouble in Privatopia." *The Progressive* 57 (October): 30–36.

———. 1994. *Privatopia: Homeowner Resocialization and the Rise of Residential Private Government.* New Haven: Yale University Press.

McLarin, Kimberly J. 1995. "Poverty Rate Is the Highest in 16 Years, a Report Says." *New York Times,* July 14, p. A3.

McLaughlin, Jeff. 1999. "Where Do We Grow from Here?" *Boston Globe,* June 20, p. 1.

McMahon, Edward T. 1997. "Stopping Sprawl by Getting Smarter." *Planning Commissioners Journal* 26 (Spring): 4.

Meredith, Robyn. 1996a. "What's Doing in Detroit." *New York Times,* May 26, p. 13.

———. 1996b. "G.M. Buys a Landmark of Detroit for Its Home." *New York Times,* May 17, p. 12.

Merry, Sally E. 1981. "Defensible Space Undefended: Social Factors in Crime Control Through Environmental Design." *Urban Affairs Quarterly* 16:397–422.

Merton, Robert K. 1968. *Social Theory and Social Structure.* New York: Free Press.

Miami. 2002. Accessed at http://www.ci.miami.fl.us on August 6, 2002.

Michelson, William. 1976. *Man and His Environment.* New York: Oxford University Press.

———. 1977. "Planning and Amelioration of Urban Problems." Pp. 562–640 in *Contemporary Topics in Urban Sociology,* edited by Kent P. Schwirian et al. Morristown, NJ: General Learning Press.

Milgram, Stanley. 1970. "The Experience of Living in Cities." *Science* 167:1461–68.

———. 1972. "A Psychological Map of New York City." *American Scientist* 60:194–200.

Miller, D.W. 2000. "The New Urban Studies," *Chronicle of Higher Education,* August 18, pp. A15–16.

Miller, David. 2002. *The Regional Governance of Metropolitan America.* Boulder, CO: Westview Press.

Millon, Rene. 1970. "Teotihuacan: Completion of Map of Giant Ancient in the Valley of Mexico." *Science* 170:1077–82.

———. 1973. "Teotihuacan." Pp. 82–92 in *Cities: Their Origin, Growth and Human Impact.* San Francisco: W. H. Freeman.

Min, Pyong Gap, and Andrew Kolodny. 1994. "The Middleman Minority Characteristics of Korean Immigrants in the United States." *Korean Journal of Population and Development* 23:179–202.

Miner, Horace. 1953. *The Primitive City of Timbuctuo.* Princeton, NJ: Memoirs of the American Philosophical Society 32.

Molotch, Harvey. 1976. "The City as a Growth Machine." *American Journal of Sociology* 82:309–33.

Montreal. 2002. Accessed at http://www.frommers.com/destinations/montreal/0018010001.html on August 6, 2002.

Moore, Joan. 1994. "The Chola Life Course: Chicana Heroin Users and the Barrio Gang." *The International Journal of the Addictions* 29:1115–26.

Moorhouse, Geoffrey. 1979. *San Francisco.* Amsterdam: Time-Life.

Moreno, Sylvia. 1997. "Cabbies Threaten Strike in Alexandria." *Washington Post,* December 31, p. B4.

Morgan Quitno. 2002. "Most Dangerous Rank Order of 327 Cities." http://www.morganquitno.com/cit02dang.htm.

Morganthau, Tom, and John McCormick. 1991. "Are Cities Obsolete?" *Newsweek,* September 9, pp. 43–44.

Morris, Charles. 1980. *The Cost of Good Intentions.* New York: W. W. Norton.

Morris, Jan. 1976. "Entering L.A.: Historical Monument." *Rolling Stone,* July 1, pp. 28–32, 77–84.

Morse, Richard J., and Jorge E. Hardoy, eds. 1992. *Rethinking the Latin American City.* Washington, DC: Woodrow Wilson Center.

Mosley, Michael E. 1975. "Chan Chan." *Science* 187: 219–25.

Muller, Peter O. 1981. *Contemporary Suburban America.* Englewood Cliffs, NJ: Prentice Hall.

Mumford, Lewis. 1961. *The City in History.* New York: Harcourt, Brace and World.

Murphy, Rhodes. 1984. "City as a Mirror of Society." Pp. 186–204 in *The City in Cultural Context,* edited by John A. Agnew, John Mercer, and David E. Sophen. Boston: Allen and Unwin.

Muschamp, Herbert. 2002. "Don't Rebuild. Imagine." *New York Times Magazine,* September 8, pp. 46–60, 63.

Myerhoff, Barbara. 1980. *Number Our Days.* New York: Touchstone Books.

Nash, Gary B. 1979. *The Urban Crucible.* Cambridge, MA: Harvard University Press.

National Center for Policy Analysis. 1997. *Study Finds Immigration Benefits.* Accessed at http://www.ncpa.org/pd/immigrat/july97a.html on October 26, 2002.

National Coalition for the Homeless. 2002. *Who Is Homeless?* Accessed at www.nationalhomeless.org/who.html on January 24, 2003.

National Law Center on Homelessness and Poverty. 2002. *Working Together to Accelerate New York's Recovery.* Accessed at http://www.nlchp.org/FA_HAPIA/ on September 30, 2002.

Newman, Oscar. 1972. *Defensible Space.* New York: Macmillan.

———. 1996. *Creating Defensible Space.* Washington, DC: U.S. Department of Housing and Urban Development.

Newsweek. 1957. April 1, p. 42.

New York City Chamber of Commerce. 2002. Accessed at http://www.nycp.org/impactstudy/Update_02_11_02.pdf on October 25, 2002.

Noble, Jeanne. 1996. "Spotlight on Indonesia." *Population Today* 24 (June–July): 7.

O'Brien, David J., and Mary J. Roach. 1984. "Recent Developments in Urban Sociology." *Journal of Urban History* 10:145–70.

O'Hare, William P. 1996. "A New Look at Poverty in America." *Population Bulletin* 51 (September).

O'Hare, William, and William Frey. 1992. "Booming, Suburban, and Black." *American Demographics* (September): 32–36.

O'Meara, Molly. 1999. "How Mid-Sized Cities Can Avoid Strangulation." *Public Management* 81 (May): 8–15.

Orfield, Gary. 1988. "Ghettoization and Its Alternatives." In *The New Urban Reality,* edited by Paul E. Peterson. Washington, DC: Brookings Institution.

Orfield, Myron W., and David Rusk. 1998. *Metropolitics: A Regional Agenda for Stability and Community.* Washington, DC: Brookings Institution.

Osborn, Frederick J. 1965. Pp. 9–28, "Preface" to Ebenezer Howard, *Garden Cities of To-Morrow.* Cambridge, MA: MIT Press.

Oser, Alan S. 1994. "When Housing Comes, Can Stores Be Far Behind?" *New York Times,* October 9, p. A7.

Padilla, Elena. 1958. *Up from Puerto Rico.* New York: Columbia University Press.

Pahl, R. E. 1989. "Is the Emperor Naked? Some Questions on the Adequacy of Sociological Theory in Urban and Regional Research." *International Journal of Urban and Regional Research* 13:709.

Palen, J. John. 1995. *The Suburbs.* New York: McGraw-Hill.

Park, Robert E. 1950. *Race and Culture.* Glencoe, IL: Free Press.

———. 1967. "The City: Suggestions for the Investigation of Human Behavior in the Urban Environment." Pp.1–46 in *The City,* edited by Robert E. Park and Eugene W. Burgess. Chicago: University of Chicago Press, originally published 1916.

Parrillo, Vincent N. 1996. *Diversity in America.* Thousand Oaks, CA: Pine Forge Press.

———. 2002. *Contemporary Social Problems.* 5th ed. Boston: Allyn and Bacon.

———. 2003. *Strangers to These Shores.* 7th ed. Boston: Allyn and Bacon.

Pasternak, Judy. 1998. " 'Edge City' Is Attempting to Build a Center." *Los Angeles Times,* January 1, p. 5.

Pawlyna, Andrea. 1981. "James Rouse, a Pioneer of the Suburban Shopping Center, Now Sets His Sights on Saving Cities." *People,* July 6, pp. 63–71.

Pedersen, Paul O. 1967. *Modeller for Befolkningsstrucktur og Befolkningsudvikling I Storbymorader Specielt med Henblik pa Storkobenhavn.* Copenhagen, Denmark: Stat Urban Planning Institute.

Pederson, Daniel, Vern E. Smith, and Jerry Adler. 1999. "Sprawling, Sprawling. . . ." *Newsweek,* July 19, pp. 23–27.

Perez-Pena, Richard. 1996. "New York's Foreign-Born Population Increases." *New York Times,* March 9, p. A25.

Perrin, Noel. 1980. "Rural Area: Permit Required." *Country Journal,* (April): 34–35.

Peters Atlas of the World. 1990. New York: Harper & Row.

Peterson, Ruth D., and Lauren J. Krivo. 1993. "Racial Segregation and Black Urban Homicide." *Social Forces* 71.

Petry, Ann. 1998, orig. 1946. *The Street.* Boston: Houghton Mifflin.

Piel, Gerard. 1997. "The Urbanization of Poverty Worldwide." *Challenge,* January/February.

Pirenne, Henri. 1952. *Medieval Cities.* Princeton, NJ: Princeton University Press; originally published 1925.

Pittman, John, and Howard Andrews. 1986. "The Use of Zip Coded Population Data in Social Area Studies of Service Utilization." *Evaluation and Program Planning* 9:309–17.

Ploeger, Nancy. 2002. "Six Months Later. New York: Manhattan Chamber of Commerce.

Pollard, Kelvin M., and William P. O'Hare. 1999. "America's Racial and Ethnic Minorities." *Population Bulletin,* September.

Population Reference Bureau. 1996. "Percentage of African Men in Polygamous Marriages, Late 1980s–early 1990s." *Population Today,* (June/July): 6.

———. 1998. "AIDS, Population Growth Shape Sub-Saharan Africa's Future." *Population Today,* (January): 1–2.

———. 2002. *World Population Data Sheet.* Washington, DC.

Porter, Roy. 1994. "Curtains for the Capital." *New Statesman & Society* 7 (November 11): 30–31.

Portes, Alejandro. 1977. "Urban Latin America: The Political Condition from Above and Below." Pp. 59–70 in *Third World Urbanization,* edited by Janet Abu-Lughod and Richard Hay, Jr. Chicago: Maaroufa.

Portes, Alejandro, Carlos Dore-Cabral, and Patricia Landolts, eds. 1997. *The Urban Caribbean: Transition to the Global Economy.* Baltimore: Johns Hopkins University Press.

Pristin, Terry. 1999. "Harlem's Pathmark Anchors: A Commercial Revival on 125th Street." *New York Times,* November 13, p. B1.

Prokesch, Steven E. 1985. "U.S. Companies Weed Out Many Operations." *New York Times,* September 30, pp. A1, D5.

Public Purpose. 1999. Accessed at http://publicpurpose.com/dm-nyc.htm on December 11, 1999.

Purdum, Todd S. 1999. "Suburban 'Sprawl' Takes Its Place on the Political Landscape." *New York Times,* February 6, pp. A1, A12.

Purdy, Matthew. 1994. "Left to Die, the South Bronx Rises from Decades of Decay." *New York Times,* November 13, p. A1.

Pynoos, Jon, Robert Schafer, and Chester W. Hartman, eds. 1973. *Housing Urban America.* Chicago: Aldine.

Raban, Jonathan. 1974. *Soft City.* London: Hamish Hamilton.

Rainwater, Lee. 1970. *Behind Ghetto Walls.* Chicago: Aldine.

Reich, Robert B. 1991. *The Work of Nations: Preparing Ourselves for 21st Century Capitalism.* New York: Alfred A. Knopf.

Reid, T. R. 1985. "Mall-Adjusted Americans Fuel Amazing Money Machines." *Washington Post,* August 30, pp. A1, A12.

Reitzes, Donald C. 1983. "Urban Images: A Social Psychological Approach." *Sociological Inquiry* 53:314–32.

Reston. 2002. http://fairfaxtimes.com/ffxguide/community.html#reston. Accessed January 24, 2003.

Riesman, David. 1958. "The Suburban Sadness." Pp. 375–408 in *The Suburban Community,* edited by William Dobriner. New York: G. P. Putnam's Sons.

Riis, Jacob. 1890, 1957. *How the Other Half Lives.* New York: Hill and Wang.

Robberson, Tod. 1995. "Mexico City's Street Children." *International Herald Tribune,* May 25. Text available at www.tc.umn.edu/nlhome/m027/bonzi/kids/latin/mexico.htm.

ROBERTS, M. HUGH. 1979. *An Urban Profile of the Middle East.* New York: St. Martin's Press.

ROBINSON, ALBERT J. 1975. *Economics and New Towns.* New York: Praeger.

RODRIGUEZ, CLARA E. 1996. "The Puerto Rican Community in the South Bronx: View from Within and Without." In *Sociology,* 5th ed., by Beth B. Hess, Elizabeth W. Markson, and Peter J. Stein. Boston: Allyn and Bacon.

RODWIN, LLOYD, AND HUGH EVANS. 1981. "The New Communities Program and Why It Failed," pp. 115–36 in *Cities and City Planning,* edited by Lloyd Rodwin. New York: Plenum.

ROEBUCKS, JANET. 1974. *The Shaping of Urban Society.* New York: Scribner's.

ROEDER, DAVID. 2002. "Outlook Good for Downtown Condos." *Chicago Sun-Times,* February 15, p. 57.

ROKOVE, MILTON L. 1975. *Don't Make No Waves, Don't Back No Losers.* Bloomington: Indiana University Press.

ROSENTHAL, J. 1974. "The Rapid Growth of Suburban Employment." Pp. 95–100 in *Suburbia in Transition,* edited by L. Masotti and J. Hadden. New York: New York Times Books.

ROSENZWEIG, ROY. 1992. *The Park and the People: A History of Central Park.* Ithaca, NY: Cornell University Press.

ROSTOW, WALT W. 1978. *The World Economy: History and Prospect.* Austin: University of Texas Press.

ROTHCHILD, JOHN. 1995. "A Mouse in the House." *Time,* December 4, pp. 62–63.

ROUSSEAU, FRANCOIS, AND LIONEL STANDING. 1995. "Zero Effect of Crowding on Arousal and Performance: On 'Proving' the Null Hypothesis." *Perceptual and Motor Skills* 81 (August): 72–74.

RUBIN, LILLIAN. 1994. *Families on the Fault Line.* New York: HarperCollins.

RUSK, DAVID. 1995. *Cities Without Suburbs.* Washington, DC: Woodrow Wilson Center Press.

RUSTEMLI, AHMET. 1992. "Crowding Effects of Density and Interpersonal Distance." *The Journal of Social Psychology* 132 (February): 51–58.

RYAN, JOHN A., A.I. ABDELRHMAN, JOHN F. FRENCH, and GLORIA RODRIGUEZ. 1999. "Social Indicators of Substance Abuse Prevention: A Need-Based Assessment." *Social Indicators Research* 46:23–60.

RYAN, MARY. 1979. *Womanhood in America: From Colonial Times to the Present.* 2nd ed. New York: Franklin Watts.

SACCO, VINCENT F. 1995. "Fear and Person Safety." *Juristat* 15 (March): 9.

SACCO, VINCENT F., AND HOLLY JOHNSON. 1990. "Patterns of Criminal Victimization in Canada." *General Social Survey Analysis Series.* Ottawa: Statistics Canada.

SACHS, SUSAN. 1999. "As New York City Immigration Thrives, Diversity Broadens." *New York Times,* November 8.

SAGAN, CARL. 1977. *The Dragons of Eden.* New York: Ballantine.

ST. CLAIRE, CLYDE, AND ROBERT CLYMER. 2000. "Racial Residential Segregation by Socioeconomic Status." *Social Science Quarterly* 81:701–15.

SALT LAKE CITY. 2002. Accessed at http://www.ci.slc.ut.us/ on August 6, 2002.

SALZAR, CARLA. 1997. "Rescued Film Crew Tells Tale of Lost City." *Boston Globe,* November 9, p. A4.

SAMPSON, ROBERT J. 1986. "Effects of Inequality, Heterogeneity, and Urbanization on Intergroup Victimization." *Social Science Quarterly* 67:751.

SANDBURG, CARL. 1944. *Chicago Poems.* New York: Harcourt Brace Jovanovich.

SASSEN, SASKIA. 1991. *The Global City: New York, Tokyo, and London.* Princeton: Princeton University Press.

———. 1994. *Cities in a World Economy.* Thousand Oaks, CA: Pine Forge Press.

SCHEID, ADREAN. 1995. "The Precarious Situation of Nicaragua's Street Children." *Mesoamerica.* Text available at www.tc.umn.edu/nlhome/m027/bonzi/kids/latin/nicaragu.htm.

SCHEIDER, WILLIAM. 1992. "The Suburban Century Begins." *Atlantic* (July).

SCHEIN, VIRGINIA E. 1995. *Working from the Margins: Voices of Mothers in Poverty.* Ithaca, NY: Cornell University Press.

SCHLESINGER, ARTHUR. 1969. "The City in American Civilization." Pp. 25–41 in *American Urban History,* edited by Alexander B. Callow, Jr. New York: Oxford University Press.

SCHMIDT, JULIE. 1999. "Nike's Image Problem: After Global Outcry, Company Makes Some Strides to Improve." *USA Today,* October 4, p. 1B.

SCHMITT, ERIC. 2001. "Most Cities in U.S. Expanded Rapidly Over Last Decade." *New York Times,* May 7, pp. A1, A12.

SCHNAILBERG, LYNN. 1999. "Immigrants: Providing a Lesson in How to Adapt." *Education Week on the Web,* January 17, accessed at www.edweek.org/ew/1999/20immig.h18 on September 11, 1999.

SCHWIRIAN, KENT P., F. MARTIN HANKINS, AND CAROL A. VENTRESCA. 1990. "The Residential Decentralization of Social Status Groups in American Metropolitan Communities, 1950–1980." *Social Forces* 68(4):1143–63.

SCOTT, ALLEN J. 1980. *The Urban Land Nexus and the State.* London: Pion.

———. 1988. *Metropolis.* Berkeley: University of California Press.

SENNETT, RICHARD. 1969. *Classic Essays on the Culture of Cities.* Englewood Cliffs, NJ: Prentice-Hall.

SEWELL, JOHN. 1993. *The Shape of the City: Toronto Struggles with Modern Planning.* Toronto: University of Toronto Press.

SHAW, CLIFFORD R., AND HENRY MCKAY. 1969. *Juvenile Delinquency and Urban Areas.* Rev. ed. Chicago: University of Chicago Press; originally published 1942.

SHEVKY, ESHREF, AND WENDELL BELL. 1955. *Social Area Analysis.* Stanford, CA: Stanford University Press.

SHEVKY, ESHREF, AND MARILYN WILLIAMS. 1949. *The Social Areas of Los Angeles.* Berkeley: University of California Press.

SIDEL, RUTH. 1974. *Families of Fengsheng: Urban Life in China.* Baltimore: Penguin.

SIERRA CLUB. 1999. "What Is Sprawl?" At www.sierraclub.org/transportation/sprawl/Sprawl_report/mat.html, accessed on August 10, 1999.

SIMMEL, GEORG. 1964. "The Metropolis and Mental Life." Pp. 409–24 in *The Sociology of Georg Simmel,* edited by K. Wolff. New York: Free Press; originally published 1905.

SIMON, JULIAN L. 1999. *Hoodwinking the Nation.* New Brunswick, NJ: Transaction Publishers.

SINCLAIR, UPTON. 1947. *The Jungle.* New York: Viking.

SJOBERG, GIDEON. 1965. *The Preindustrial City.* New York: Free Press.

———. 1973. "The Origin and Evolution of Cities." Pp. 19–27 in *Cities: Their Origin, Growth, and Human Impact.* San Francisco: W. H. Freeman.

SKIDMORE, THOMAS E., AND PETER H. SMITH. 2000. Modern Latin America. 5th ed. New York: Oxford University Press.

SMITH, NEIL, AND MICHELE LEFAIVRE. 1984. "A Class Analysis of Gentrification." In *Gentrification, Displacement, and Neighborhood Revitalization,* edited by J. John Palen and Bruce London. Albany: SUNY Press.

SNIPP, C. MATTHEW, AND GARY D. SANDEFUR. 1988. "Earnings of American Indians and Alaskan Natives: The Effects of Residence and Migration." *Social Forces* 66:994–1008.

SORKIN, MICHAEL, ed. 1992. *Variations on a Theme Park: The New American City and the End of Public Space.* New York: The Noonday Press, Farrar, Strauss, and Giroux.

SOWELL, THOMAS. 1977. "New Light on Black I.Q." *New York Times Magazine,* March 27, p. 57.

SOYA, EDWARD W. 2000. "Postmetropolis: ck I.Q." *New York Times Magazine,* March 27, p. 57.

SPAIN, DAPHNE. 1992. *Gendered Spaces.* Chapel Hill: University of North Carolina Press.

SPECTORSKY, A. C. 1957. *The Exurbanites.* New York: Berkley.

SPENGLER, OSWALD. 1928. *The Decline of the West.* New York: Knopf. Excerpted in *Classic Essays on the Culture of Cities,* edited by Richard Sennett. Englewood Cliffs, NJ: Prentice Hall, 1969.

SROLE, LEO. 1972. "Urbanization and Mental Health: Some Reformulations." *American Scientist* 60:576–83.

STACK, CAROL. 1974. *All Our Kin.* New York: Harper & Row.

STAHURA, JOHN C., RONALD HUFF, AND BRENT L. SMITH. 1979. "Crime in the Suburbs." *Urban Affairs Quarterly* 15:291–316.

STARK, ANDREW. 2002. *Conflict of Interest in American Public Life.* Cambridge, MA: Harvard University Press.

STARR, ROGER. 1985. "Crime." *New York Times Magazine,* January 17, pp. 19–25, 58–60.

STATISTICS CANADA. 2002. Accessed at www.statcan.ca on October 19, 2002.

STAVRIANOS, L. S. 1983. *Global History: The Human Heritage.* 3rd ed. Englewood Cliffs, NJ: Prentice Hall.

STEFFENS, LINCOLN. 1904. *The Shame of the Cities.* New York: McClure, Phillips.

STEIN, CLARENCE. 1957. *Toward New Towns for America.* Cambridge, MA: MIT Press.

STEINBECK, JOHN. 1962. *Travels with Charley: In Search of America.* New York: Franklin Watts.

STENGEL, RICHARD. 1986. "Down and Out and Dispossessed." *Time,* November 24, 27–28.

STEPHENSON, R. BRUCE. 1997. "A Vision of Green: Lewis Mumford's Legacy in Portland, Oregon." *Journal of the American Planning Association* 65 (Summer): 259–69.

STEPHENSON, SUSIE. 1999. "DINKS Dine Out." *Restaurants & Institutions,* April 1, pp. 78–81.

STERNGOLD, JAMES. 1994. "Life in a Box: Japanese Question Fruits of Success." *New York Times,* January 2, pp. A1 and A6.

STEVENSON, MARK. 1998. "Mexico City Launches Crackdown on Squatters' Settlements." *Los Angeles Times,* May 3, p. 11.

STILL, BAYRD. 1974. *Urban America.* Boston: Little, Brown.

———. 1994. *Mirror for Gotham: New York as Seen by Contemporaries from Dutch Days to the Present.* New York: Fordham University Press.

STOKES, MYRON, AND DAVID ZEMAN. 1995. "The Shame of the City." *Newsweek,* September 4, p. 26.

STREET, D., AND ASSOCIATES. 1978. *Handbook of Contemporary Urban Life.* San Francisco: Jossey-Bass.

STRONG, JOSIAH. 1885. *Our Country: Its Possible Future and Its Present Crisis.* New York: Baker and Taylor.

SUISMAN, DOUGLAS R. 1990. *Los Angeles Boulevard: 8 X-Rays of the Body Politic.* Princeton, NJ: Princeton Architectural Press.

SUNSITE. 2002. *Population in Metropolitan Bangkok.* http://sunsite.au.ac.th/thailand/bangkok/pop_index.html.

SUTTLES, GERALD. 1968. *The Social Order of the Slum.* Chicago: University of Chicago Press.

———. 1972. *The Social Construction of Communities.* Chicago: University of Chicago Press.

———. 1984. "The Cumulative Texture of Local Urban Culture." *American Journal of Sociology* 90:283–304.

SWEETSER, FRANK. 1965. "Factor Structure as Ecological Structure in Helsinki and Boston." *Acta Sociologica* 26:205–25.

TAEUBER, KARL, AND ALMA TAEUBER. 1965. *Negroes in Cities.* Chicago: Aldine.

TAYLOR, R. 1991. "Urban Communities and Crime." Pp. 106–34 in *Urban Life in Transition,* edited by M. Gottdiener and C. G. Pickvance. Newbury Park, CA: Sage.

TAYLOR, ROBERT L. 1985. *The Travels of Jaimie McPheeters.* New York: Arbor House.

TEAFORD, JON C. 1990. *The Rough Road to Renaissance.* Baltimore: Johns Hopkins University Press.

TERRILL, ROSS. 1975. *Five Cities of China.* Boston: Atlantic–Little, Brown.

THEROUX, PAUL. 1976. *The Family Arsenal.* Boston: Houghton Mifflin.

THILL, JEAN-CLAUDE, AND DANIEL Z. SUI. 1993. "Mental Maps and Fuzziness in Space Preferences." *The Professional Geographer* 45 (August): 264–76.

THOMAS, JERRY, AND ANDREW MARTIN. "Notorious Block's Deadly Legacy." *Chicago Tribune,* web posted November 23, 1996.

THOMAS, JIM. 1983. "Toward a Critical Ethnography." *Urban Life* 11:477–90.

THOMPSON, WILLIAM C., JR. 2002. *One Year Later: The Fiscal Impact of 9/11 on New York City.* New York: Office of the Comptroller of the City of New York.

TIMMER, DOUG A., D. STANLEY EITZEN, AND KATHRYN D. TALLEY. 1994. *Paths to Homelessness: Extreme Poverty and the Housing Crisis.* Boulder, CO: Westview Press.

TOBIN, G. 1976. "Suburbanization and the Development of Motor Transportation: Transportation Technology and the Suburbanization Process." Pp. 95–111 in *The Changing Face of the Suburbs,* edited by B. Schwartz. Chicago: University of Chicago Press.

TOCH, THOMAS. 1991. "Schools That Work." *U.S. News & World Report*, May 27, pp. 58–66.

———. 1998. "The New Education Bazaar." *U.S. News & World Report*, April 27, pp. 34–46.

TOCQUEVILLE, ALEXIS DE. 1955. *The Old Regime and the French Revolution*. New York: Anchor Books; originally published 1856.

TODARO, M. P. 1999. *Economic Development*. 7th ed. New York: Longman.

TÖNNIES, FERDINAND. 1963. *Community and Society*. New York: Harper & Row; *Gemeinschaft und Gesellschaft*, originally published 1887.

TORONTO. 2002. Accessed at www.city.toronto.on.ca/ on October 19, 2002.

TRI-MET. 2002. http://www.tri-met.org/factsandphotos/index.htm.

TRIMET. 2003. *Max System Overview*. At www.trimet.org/history/maxpage.htm. Accessed on January 9, 2003.

TURNER, CRAIG. 1997. "Has Canadian Land's End Hit Its Limit?" *Los Angeles Times*, November 22, 1997, p. A1.

TURNER, FREDERICH C. 1976. "The Rush to Cities in Latin America." *Science* 192:955–62.

TURNER, WALLACE, 1985. "Portland, Oregon, Has a New Mayor and a New Style." *New York Times*, February 8, p. A16.

ULLMAN, EDWARD L. 1941. "A Theory of Location for Cities." *American Journal of Sociology* 46:853–64.

———. 1962. "Presidential Address: The Nature of Cities Reconsidered." *Regional Science Association: Papers and Proceedings* 9:7–23.

UNITED NATIONS DEVELOPMENT PROGRAMME. 1995. *Human Development Report 1995*. New York: Oxford University Press.

UNITED NATIONS DEVELOPMENT PROGRAMME. 1996. *Human Development Report 1996*:256. New York: Oxford University Press.

UNITED NATIONS POPULATION DIVISION. 2002. Accessed online at http://esa.un.org/unpp/ on September 8, 2002.

UNITED NATIONS POPULATION INFORMATION NETWORK. February 28, 2001. *World Population Prospects: The 2000 Revision*. Accessed at www.un.org/popin/data.html on January 2, 2003.

United Nations Sourcebook. 1999.

UNITED NATIONS WORLD URBANIZATION PROSPECTS. Accessed at http://promarket.com/wpopdir.htm on September 15, 1999.

U.S. BUREAU OF THE CENSUS. 2001. *Poverty in the United States, 2000*. Washington, DC: U.S. Government Printing Office.

U.S. BUREAU OF THE CENSUS. 2002a. *Statistical Abstract of the United States 2001*. Washington, DC: U.S. Government Printing Office.

———. 2002b. *Profile of Selected Social Characteristics: 2000*, Summary File 3.

———. 2002c. Accessed at www.census.gov/hhes/www/ahs.html on January 24, 2003.

U.S. BUREAU OF JUSTICE STATISTICS. 2002. www.ojp.usdoj.gov/bjs.

U.S. CONFERENCE OF MAYORS. 2002. *A Status Report on Hunger and Homeless in America's Cities*. Accessed at www.usmayors.org on September 30, 2002.

U.S. DEPARTMENT OF EDUCATION. 2000. *The State of Charter Schools: Fourth-Year Report*. Washington, DC: U.S. Government Printing Office.

———. 2002. *The Condition of Education*. Washington, DC: U.S. Government Printing Office.

U.S. FEDERAL DEPOSIT INSURANCE CORPORATION. 1998. *Statistics on Banking*. Washington, DC: U.S. Government Printing Office.

U.S. IMMIGRATION AND NATURALIZATION SERVICE. 2002. *2000 Statistical Yearbook*:73. Washington, DC: U.S. Government Printing Office.

UTT, RONALD D. 1996. *Time for a Bipartisan Reform of Public Housing*. Heritage Foundation. Accessed at http://www.heritage.org/library/categories/regulation/bg1081.html on September 14, 1999.

VALENTINE, BETTY LOU. 1980. *Hustling and Other Hard Work*. New York: Free Press.

VALENTINE, CHARLES A. 1968. *Culture and Poverty: Critique and Counterproposals*. Chicago: University of Chicago Press.

VAN ARSDOL, MAURICE D., SANTO F. CAMILLERI, AND CALVIN F. SCHMID. 1958a. "The Generality of Urban Social Area Indexes." *American Sociological Review* 33:277–84.

———. 1958b. "An Application of the Shevky Social Area Indexes to a Model of Urban Society." *Social Forces* 37:26–32.

———. 1961. "An Investigation of the Utility of Urban Typology." *Pacific Sociological Review* 4:26–32.

VANDERPOOL, TIM. 1999. "But Isn't This My Yard?" *Christian Science Monitor*, August 18, p. 2.

VERBRUGGE, LOIS M., AND RALPH B. TAYLOR. 1980. "Consequences of Population Density and Size." *Urban Affairs Quarterly* 16:135–60.

VIDICH, ARTHUR, AND JOSEPH BENSMAN. 1968. *Small Town in Mass Society*. Princeton: Princeton University Press.

VIDICH, CHARLES. 1976. *The New York Cab Driver and His Fare*. Cambridge, MA: Schenkman.

VIGIL, JAMES DIEGO. 1991. "Car Charros: Cruising and Low Riding in the Barrios of East Los Angeles." *Latino Studies Journal* 2 (May): 71–72.

VINING, DANIEL J. 1985. "Growth of Core Regions in the Third World." *Scientific American* 282:42–49.

VOGEL, EZRA F. 1991. *The Four Little Dragons: The Spread of Industrialization in East Asia*. Cambridge, MA: Harvard University Press.

WADE, ROBERT C. 1958. "Urban Life in Western America, 1790–1830" *American Historical Review*, October, pp. 14–30.

WALDINGER, ROGER. 1996. *Still the Promised City? African-Americans and New Immigrants in New York*. Cambridge, MA: Harvard University Press.

WALLERSTEIN, IMMANUEL. 1974; 1997. *Modern World-System I: Capitalist Agriculture and the Origins of the European World-Economy in the Sixteenth Century*. New York: Academic Press.

———. 1979. *The Capitalist World-Economy*. New York: Cambridge University Press.

————. 1983. "Crises: The World Economy, the Movements, and the Ideologies." Pp. 21–36 in *Crises in the World-System*, edited by Albert Bergesen. Beverly Hills, CA: Sage.

————. 1984. *The Politics of the World Economy: The States, the Movements, and the Civilization.* Cambridge: Cambridge University Press.

WALTON, JOHN. 1981. "The New Urban Sociology." *International Social Science Journal* 33.

————. 1993. "Urban Sociology: The Contributions and Limits of Political Economy." *Annual Review of Sociology* 19:301–20.

WARD, BARBARA. 1962. *The Rich Nations and the Poor Nations.* New York: Norton.

WARNER, SAM BASS, JR. 1962. *Streetcar Suburbs.* Cambridge, MA: Harvard University Press/MIT Press.

WARREN, ROLAND L. 1978. "Some Observations on the Columbia Experience." Pp. 158–68 in *Psychology of the Planned Community*, edited by Donald C. Klein. New York: Human Sciences.

WASHINGTON, DC. 2002. Accessed at http://www.washington.org/index on August 6, 2002.

WATTEL, H. 1958. "Levittown: A Suburban Community." Pp. 287–313 in *The Suburban Community*, edited by W. Dobriner. New York: G. P. Putnam's Sons.

WAYNE, GARY. 2002. *The Universal CityWalk.* Accessed at http://www.seeing-stars.com/Shop/CityWalk.shtml on October 27, 2002.

WEBER, ADNA. 1899. *The Growth of Cities.* New York: Columbia University Press.

WEBER, BRUCE. 1995. "Town Square of Midtown: Drug Dealers' Turf Is Now an Office Oasis." *New York Times*, August 25, p. A1.

WEBER, MAX. 1966. *The City.* New York: Free Press.

WEIBEL-ORLANDO, JOAN. 1991. *Indian Country, L.A.: Maintaining Ethnic Community in a Complex Society.* Urbana: University of Illinois Press.

WEILLISZ, CHRISTOPHER. 1983. "Bronx Neighborhood: 'One Big Family.'" *New York Times*, September 14, p. B1.

WEISNER. THOMAS S. 1981. "Cities, Stress, and Children." Pp. 783–803 in *Handbook of Cross-Cultural Human Development*, edited by Ruth H. Moore, Robert I. Monroe, and Beatrice B. Whiting. New York: Garland.

WENKE, ROBERT J. 1999. *Patterns in Prehistory.* 4th ed. New York: Oxford University Press.

WEST, KIMBERLY C. 1994. "A Desegregation Tool That Backfired: Magnet Schools and Classroom Segregation." *Yale Law Journal* 103 (June): 2567–92.

WHITE, KERRY A. 1999. "Ahead of the Curve." *Education Week on the Web*, January 13.

WHITE, MORTON, AND LUCIA WHITE. 1964. *The Intellectual Versus the City.* New York: Mentor.

WHITMAN, DAVID. 1995. "Welfare: The Myth of Reform." *U.S. News & World Report*, January 16, pp. 30–39.

WHITMAN, WALT. 1959. *Leaves of Grass.* New York: Viking Press. Originally published 1855.

WHYTE, WILLIAM FOOTE. 1981 (orig. 1943). *Street Corner Society.* 3rd ed. Chicago: University of Chicago Press.

WHYTE, WILLIAM H. 1956. *The Organization Man.* Garden City, NY: Anchor Books.

————. 1974. "The Best Street Life in the World." *New York*, July 14, pp. 26–33.

————. 1980. *The Social Life of Small Urban Spaces.* Washington, DC: Conservation Foundation.

WIARDA, HOWARD J. 1987. "Ethnocentrism and Third World Developments." *Society* 24:55–64.

————. 1999. "Toward Consensus in Building Latin American Politics: Developmentalism, Dependency, and 'The Latin American Tradition.'" *Studies in Comparative International Development* 34: 50–69.

WILDER, THORNTON. 1939. *Our Town.* New York: Coward-McCann.

WILFORD, JOHN NOBLE. 1985. "A Legendary 'Lost City' in Andes Gives Hint of Mysterious Culture." *New York Times*, February 1, pp. A1, A11.

WILLIAMS, ROGER M. 1977. "The New Urban Pioneers: Homesteading in the Slums." *Saturday Review*, July 23, pp. 9–14.

————. 1978. "The Assault on Fortress Suburbia." *Saturday Review*, February 18, pp. 17–24.

WILLIE, CHARLES, AND HOWARD TAYLOR. 1995. "The Bell Curve Debate." Panel discussion at Eastern Sociological Society annual meeting, Philadelphia, March.

WILSON, GREG. 2000. "Out in the Court." *New York Daily News*, November 17, p. 49.

————. 2001. "Developer Hit with Bias Suit." *New York Daily News*, May 9, p.1.

WILSON, THOMAS C. 1986. "Community Population Size and Heterogeneity." *American Journal of Sociology* 94:1154–69.

————. 1991. "Urbanism, Migration, and Tolerance: A Reassessment." *American Sociological Review* 56:117–23.

WILSON, WILLIAM J. 1987. *The Truly Disadvantaged.* Chicago: University of Chicago Press.

WIMBERLEY, HOWARD. 1973. "Conjugal-Role Relationships and Social Networks in Japan and England." *Journal of Marriage and the Family* 35:125–30.

WIRTH, LOUIS. 1938. "Urbanism as a Way of Life." *American Journal of Sociology* 44:1–24.

————. 1964. *On Cities and Social Life.* Chicago: University of Chicago Press.

WOLFE, LINDA. 1983. "Friendship in the City." *New York*, July 18, pp. 20–28.

WOLFE, TOM. 1969. *The Pump House Gang.* New York: Bantam.

————. 1998. *A Man in Full.* New York: Farrar, Straus, Giroux.

WOLFINGER, NICHOLAS H. 1995. "Passing Moments: Some Social Dynamics of Pedestrian Interaction." *Journal of Contemporary Ethnography* 24:323–40.

WORLD BANK. 2002a. Accessed online at http://devdata.worldbank.org/data-inquiry on September 8, 2002.

————. 2002b. "Urban Upgrading in Latin America and the Caribbean," en breve. Accessed online at http://lnweb18.worldbank.org/External/lac/lac.nsf/en+breve/ on October 13, 2002.

WRIGHT, ARTHUR F. 1977. "The Cosmology of the Chinese City." Pp. 33–74 in *The City in Later Imperial China*, edited by G. William Skinner. Stanford, CA: Stanford University Press.

WURDOCK, CLARENCE J. 1981. "Neighborhood Radical Transition: A Study of the Role of White Flight." *Urban Affairs Quarterly* 17:75–89.

YAZAKI, TAKEO. 1973. "The History of Urbanization in Japan." Pp. 139–62 in *Urban Anthropology*, edited by Aidan Southall. New York: Oxford University Press.

YOSHIHASHI, PAULINE, AND SARAH LUBMAN. 1992. "Intra- and Inter-Ethnic Group Conflicts: The Case of Korean Small Business in the United States." *Wall Street Journal*, June 16, p. A1.

ZANGWILL, ISRAEL. 1919. *The Melting Pot.* New York: Macmillan.

ZIER, JULIE A. 1994. "TV Violence Study Released." *Broadcasting & Cable*, August 8, p. 56.

ZIPP, YVONNE, AND CHRISTOPHER D. COOK. 1999. "Genuine Urban Renewal, At Last in This Golden Economy, Even Bastions of Blight Start to Sparkle." *Christian Science Monitor*, August 19, p. 1.

ZUCCHINO, DAVID. 1994. "Today's Violent Crime Is Old Story with a Twist." *Philadelphia Inquirer*, October 30, pp. A1, A22.

ZUKIN, SHARON. 1993. *Landscapes of Power: From Detroit to Disney World.* Berkeley: University of California Press.

———. 1995. *The Cultures of Cities.* Malden, MA: Blackwell.

PHOTO CREDITS

INDEX